THE ROUTLEDGE HISTORY OF MADNESS AND MENTAL HEALTH

The Routledge History of Madness and Mental Health explores the history and historiography of madness from the ancient and medieval worlds to the present day. Global in scope, it includes case studies from Africa, Asia, and South America as well as Europe and North America, drawing together the latest scholarship and source material in this growing field and allowing for fresh comparisons to be made across time and space.

Thematically organised and written by leading academics, chapters discuss broad topics such as the representation of madness in literature and the visual arts, the material culture of madness, the perpetual difficulty of creating a classification system for madness and mental health, madness within life histories, the increased globalisation of knowledge and treatment practices, and the persistence of spiritual and supernatural conceptualisations of experiences associated with madness. This volume also examines the challenges involved in analysing primary sources in this area and how key themes such as class, gender, and race have influenced the treatment and diagnosis of madness throughout history.

Chronologically and geographically wide-ranging, and providing a fascinating overview of the current state of the field, this is essential reading for all students of the history of madness, mental health, psychiatry, and medicine.

Greg Eghigian is Associate Professor of Modern History at Penn State University. His most recent book is *The Corrigible and the Incorrigible: Science, Medicine, and the Convict in Twentieth-Century Germany* (2015). He is presently writing a book on the history of the UFO phenomenon.

THE ROUTLEDGE HISTORIES

The Routledge Histories is a series of landmark books surveying some of the most important topics and themes in history today. Edited and written by an international team of world-renowned experts, they are the works against which all future books on their subjects will be judged.

A full list of titles in this series is available at: https://www.routledge.com/Routledge-Histories/book-series/RHISTS

THE ROUTLEDGE HISTORY OF MADNESS AND MENTAL HEALTH

Edited by Greg Eghigian

LONDON AND NEW YORK

First published 2017 by Routledge

2 Park Square, Milton Park, Abingdon, Oxfordshire OX14 4RN
52 Vanderbilt Avenue, New York, NY 10017

Routledge is an imprint of the Taylor & Francis Group, an informa business

First issued in paperback 2019

British Library Cataloguing in Publication Data
A catalogue record for this book is available from the British Library

Library of Congress Cataloging in Publication Data
Names: Eghigian, Greg, 1961– editor of compilation.
Title: The Routledge history of madness and mental
health / edited by Greg Eghigian.
Other titles: History of madness and mental health
Description: Milton Park, Abingdon, Oxon ;
New York, NY : Routledge, 2017. |
Includes bibliographical references and index.
Identifiers: LCCN 2016050178| ISBN 9781138781603
(hardback : alkaline paper) | ISBN 9781315202211 (ebook)
Subjects: LCSH: Mental illness—History.
| Mental health—History. | Psychiatry—History.
Classification: LCC RC438 .R68 2017 | DDC 616.89—dc23
LC record available at https://lccn.loc.gov/2016050178

ISBN: 978-1-138-78160-3 (hbk)
ISBN: 978-0-367-86996-0 (pbk)

Typeset in Baskerville
by Swales & Willis Ltd, Exeter, Devon, UK

CONTENTS

CONTENTS

CONTENTS

FIGURES

CONTRIBUTORS

Greg Eghigian is Associate Professor of Modern History at Penn State University. His most recent book is *The Corrigible and the Incorrigible: Science, Medicine, and the Convict in Twentieth-Century Germany* (2015). He is presently writing a book on the history of the UFO phenomenon.

Jesse Ballenger is author of *Self, Senility and Alzheimer's Disease in Modern America: A History* (Johns Hopkins University Press, 2006) and co-editor of *Concepts of Alzheimer Disease: Biological, Clinical and Cultural Perspectives* (Johns Hopkins University Press, 2000) and *Treating Dementia: Do We Have a Pill for It?* (Johns Hopkins University Press, 2009). He is an associate teaching professor in the Health Administration Department at Drexel University, where he teaches bioethics and health care history.

German E. Berrios is Emeritus Chair of the Epistemology of Psychiatry and Life Fellow at Robinson College, University of Cambridge, UK.

Waltraud Ernst is Professor in the History of Medicine, 1700–2000 at Oxford Brookes University in the UK. She specialises in the history of madness and mental health in South Asia. Her publications include *Colonialism and Transnational Psychiatry* (Anthem, 2013) and *Mad Tales from the Raj* (Anthem, 1991, 2010) and a number of edited books, such as *Work, Psychiatry and Society* (University of Manchester Press, 2016), *Transnational Psychiatries* (Cambridge Scholars Publishing, 2010), *Plural Medicine, Tradition and Modernity* (Routledge, 2002) and *Race, Science and Medicine* (Routledge, 1999).

Rhodri Hayward is a Reader in the History of the Human Sciences at Queen Mary, University of London and a co-founder of the Queen Mary Centre for the History of the Emotions. He has published on the history of dreams, Pentecostalism, demonology, cybernetics, and the relations between psychiatry and primary care. His current research examines the rise and political implications of psychiatric epidemiology in modern Britain. His book *Resisting History: Popular Religion and the Invention of the Unconscious* was published by Manchester University Press in 2007 and *The Transformation of the Psyche in British Primary Care* by Bloomsbury in 2014.

Laura Hirshbein is a historian and psychiatrist at the University of Michigan. Her published works include *American Melancholy: Constructions of Depression in the Twentieth Century* (Rutgers University Press, 2009) and *Smoking Privileges: Psychiatry, the Mentally Ill, and the Tobacco Industry in America* (Rutgers University Press, 2015).

Peregrine Horden is Professor of Medieval History at Royal Holloway, University of London. He has published extensively on medieval medicine, hospitals, and charity, as well as on the history of disease and the Mediterranean environment.

Andreas Killen teaches the history of modern Germany and of the human sciences at the City College of New York and the CUNY Graduate Center. He is the author of, among other works, *Berlin Electropolis* (Berkeley 2005), and is finishing a book titled *Homo Cinematicus: Science and Cinema in Germany 1895–1945* (University of Pennsylvania Press, forthcoming in 2017).

Benoît Majerus is a historian at the University of Luxembourg. His published works include *Parmi les fous: Une histoire sociale de la psychiatrie au 20e siècle* and "Making Sense of the 'Chemical Revolution.' Patients' Voices on the Introduction of Neuroleptics in the 1950s," *Medical History*, 60 (2016): 54–66.

Ivana S. Marková is a Reader and Honorary Consultant in Psychiatry at the Hull York Medical School, University of Hull, UK. She has an MPhil in History and Philosophy of Science from Cambridge University. Her research is focused on the epistemology of psychiatry and descriptive psychopathology.

Elizabeth Mellyn is an Associate Professor of History at the University of New Hampshire, where she teaches a range of courses in early modern European history. Her book *Mad Tuscans and their Families: A History of Mental Disorder in Early Modern Italy* was recently published by University of Pennsylvania Press. She is currently at work on a history of Santa Dorotea, Florence's first hospital devoted to the care of the severely mentally ill.

Manuella Meyer is a historian at the University of Richmond. Her published works include *Reasoning Against Madness: Psychiatry and the State in Rio de Janeiro, 1830–1944* (Rochester University Press Medical History Series, forthcoming in 2017). She has published research articles in *Bulletin of the History of Medicine* and *Atlantic Studies*, as well as a number book reviews.

Richard Noll, a clinical psychologist, is Associate Professor of Psychology at DeSales University in Center Valley, Pennsylvania. He is the author of *American Madness: The Rise and Fall of Dementia Praecox* (Harvard University Press, 2011), which won the 'BMA Medical Book Award – Highly Commended in Psychiatry' from the British Medical Association.

Toine Pieters is a historian and pharmacologist at the University of Utrecht. He has published extensively on the history of drugs, psychopharmacology, genetics, and digital humanities. He is project leader and research coordinator of multiple projects in the fields of history of pharmacy, history of animal experimentation, and digital humanities with a focus on semantic text mining and linked data.

Geoffrey Reaume teaches Mad People's History in the Critical Disability Studies graduate program at York University, Toronto, Canada. He is the author of *Remembrance of Patients Past: Patient Life at the Toronto Hospital for the Insane, 1870–1940* (Oxford University Press, 2000) and is co-founder of the Psychiatric Survivor Archives of Toronto.

Jonathan Sadowsky is the Theodore J. Castele Professor of Medical History at Case Western Reserve University. His interests include colonial psychiatry in Africa, the history of somatic treatments in psychiatry, and the history of psychoanalysis. He is the author of *Imperial Bedlam: Institutions of Madness and Colonialism in Southwest Nigeria* (University of California Press, 1999) and *Electroconvulsive Therapy in America: The Anatomy of A Medical Controversy* (Routledge, 2016).

Andrew Scull is Distinguished Professor of Sociology and Science Studies at the University of California, San Diego. He is past president of the Society for the Social History of Medicine and has received fellowships from, among others, the Guggenheim Foundation, the American Council of Learned Societies, and the Shelby Cullom Davis Center for Historical Studies. His articles have appeared in leading journals in History, Sociology, Psychiatry, Medicine, and Law, and he is the author of many books, most recently *Madness in Civilization: A Cultural History of Insanity from the Bible to Freud, and From the Madhouse to Modern Medicine* (Thames and Hudson, 2015; and Princeton University Press, 2015), which is being translated into more than a dozen languages.

Sonu Shamdasani is Vice-Dean (International) of the Faculty of Arts and Humanities, and Co-Director of the Health Humanities Centre, University College London. He works on the history of psychology and psychiatry from the ninteenth to the mid-twentieth centuries and is the author and editor of numerous books.

Akihito Suzuki has published on social history of psychiatry in England and Japan. His publications includes *Madness at Home* (University of California Press, 2006). He is now preparing a book on mental illnesses in early twentieth-century Tokyo based on an extensive archive of a private psychiatric hospital.

Sally Swartz is an Associate Professor and member of the University of Cape Town's Psychology Department training faculty in the clinical psychology program. Her research is in the fields of colonial psychiatric history and psychoanalytic psychotherapy in South Africa, and her monograph *Homeless Wanderers: Movement and Mental Illness in the Cape Colony in the Nineteenth Century* (University of Cape Town Press) was published in 2015.

Chiara Thumiger is a classicist and historian of ancient medicine. She is currently a Wellcome Research Fellow in Medical Humanities at the University of Warwick, where she is researching the ancient mental disease phrenitis and cooperates with the research group 'Medicine of the Mind, Philosophy of the Body' at the Humboldt Universität zu Berlin. She has worked on ancient medical ideas about mental health, history of psychology and psychiatry, classical theatre, and ancient views about animals. Her published works include the monographs *Hidden Paths* (BICS, 2007), the edited volumes *Eros in Ancient Greece* (Oxford University Press, 2013, with E. Sanders et al.) and *Homo Patiens. Approaches to the Patient in the Ancient World* (Brill, 2015, with G. Petridou). Her monograph on classical medical views on mental health and the life and health of the mind in early Greek medical thought is forthcoming (Cambridge University Press, 2017).

Claire Trenery completed her Ph.D. on representations of madness in twelfth-century English miracle collections at Royal Holloway, University of London, in 2016. She has published articles on childhood madness in the Middle Ages and on medieval conceptions of demonic possession.

Madalina Vartejanu-Joubert is Associate Profesor of Ancient Near East History and Hebrew Bible at the National Institute for Oriental Languages and Civilisations (INALCO) in Paris. Her approach belongs to the French school of anthropological study of Antiquity and her main interest resides in the anthropology of knowledge in ancient Judaism. She published and edited, among others, *Folie et société dans l'Israël antique* (L'Harmattan, 2004), *Herméneutique et bricolage. Territoires et frontières de la tradition dans le judaïsme* (as editor, Peter Lang, 2008), *Le Proche-Orient ancien à la lumière des sciences sociales*, Special issue of *Yod* (2013).

Ilya Vinitsky is Professor of Russian Literature at Princeton University. His main fields of expertise are Russian Romanticism and Realism, the history of emotions, and nineteenth-century intellectual and spiritual history. His most recent book is *Vasily Zhukovsky's Romanticism and the Emotional History of Russia* (Northwestern University Press, 2015). He is a co-editor *of Madness and the Mad in Russian Culture* (with Angela Brintlinger), published by the University of Toronto Press in 2007 (new paperback edition, 2015). Prior to arriving at Princeton in 2016, he taught a variety of classes at the University of Pennsylvania, including an undergraduate course on madness in Russian cultural history.

INTRODUCTION TO THE HISTORY OF MADNESS AND MENTAL HEALTH

Greg Eghigian

In 2013, the American Psychiatric Association (APA) released the fifth edition of its *Diagnostic and Statistical Manual of Mental Disorders*, otherwise known as the *DSM-5*. In preparation for the new manual, the APA Task Force and Work Group responsible for drafting it reviewed scholarly literature, conducted field trial tests, and solicited the opinions of numerous specialists in the field of mental health.[1] Both before and after the volume's publication, the task force drew the ire of some observers from both within and outside the psychiatric community. Among other things, critics complained that key decisions were made surreptitiously "behind closed doors," that the pharmaceutical industry had too great an influence on the process and final product, that lobbying interests were driving diagnostic changes, and that new criteria were redefining things like mundane grief as forms of mental illness. All in all, many contended, the APA was responsible for irresponsibly medicalizing normality.[2]

These changes and debates going on in the United States were not without relevance for those outside its borders. For the ways in which American clinicians, researchers, institutions, and clients think about and treat mental disorders have also been exported abroad. In the process, they have not only altered indigenous beliefs about madness throughout the world; they have also contributed to the rise of new cases of disorders globally.[3]

According to a 2001 report of the World Health Organization (WHO), one in four people in the world are stricken with a mental or neurological disorder at some point in their lives; two-thirds of whom, however, never seek help. There are a number of reasons for this. Unlike many other forms of disease and disability, and despite some shifts in public attitudes, those exhibiting signs of mental illness often face stigmatization and discrimination. And while some states have actively taken up the task of addressing the problem, the WHO estimated at the time that over 40 percent of the countries in the world had no mental health policy, and around 25 percent no mental health legislation.[4]

The kinds of somatic and psychological distress behind what was formerly referred to in English as "madness" and now is associated with "mental illness" are unquestionably, and to a considerable degree, universal. Recent studies indicate that not only human beings, but also animals ranging from chimpanzees to birds to perhaps even honeybees, can show signs of anxiety, depression, and genetic mutation akin to their human counterparts.[5] Healing responses to these afflictions, too, appear to have a

1

long evolutionary history.[6] That said, because psychiatric symptoms so directly affect the self-conception, behavior, affects, and consciousness of humans, psychological disorders have consistently raised challenges to governing social norms and values.[7] Madness has always been entangled in the transformation and interactions of changing human aspirations and moralities.

Madness, then, has a history – or perhaps better put, it has histories. As societies and their institutions and values have changed, so too have the ways in which madness has been experienced, understood, and treated. Mental disorders, therefore, present moving targets for the historian that more often than not defy facile generalizations. Moreover, the record of the healers and healing disciplines that have attempted to treat afflicted individuals is one of only qualified success in ameliorating symptoms. Even those historians who consider the neurobiological psychiatry of today to represent a watershed appear to concede that the story of psychiatry is difficult to relate in terms of an unbroken, linear chain of cumulative knowledge.[8]

This has not always been the case. When the history of madness and psychiatry was first established during the first half of the twentieth century, it was written mostly by clinical practitioners. They tended to produce celebratory narratives about the rise of modern psychiatry, concentrating exclusively on the conceptual development of the discipline. Their approach consisted largely in praising those historical figures who "anticipated" contemporary knowledge, while accusing those who did not of ignorance or bias.[9]

Study of the history of mental disorders began to find a place outside medical circles by the 1960s, however, after sociologists of social deviance took up the subject for analysis. Figures like George Rosen in the United States and Michel Foucault in France began seeing the ways in which the mad had historically been understood and treated as contingent upon changing social and cultural conventions.[10] The American historian Gerald Grob brought his sensitivity to the plight of the socially disenfranchised to explore key trends in the history of American asylums and mental health policy.[11] In time, social historians were increasingly drawn to the subject, a trend inspired in great measure by the works of British historian Roy Porter. In books and articles he began publishing in the late 1980s, Porter attempted to recover the voices of those who had been deemed mad, while also emphasizing the need for careful archival research about local actors, their social positions, and their interactions.[12]

By the end of the century, the history of madness had evolved into a vibrant subfield of history, with contributions from scholars presenting an expanding range of interests. In 1994, a volume edited by Porter and Mark Micale offered something of a snapshot of the state of research at the time, revealing that investigators were widening their geographical scope as well as reassessing the historiography.[13] Scanning over a list of some of the English-language monographs published between 1985 and 2001 shows that scholars were increasingly pushing the history of mental illness toward themes of broadly interdisciplinary interest; professionalization,[14] imperialism,[15] gender and sexuality,[16] literature and the novel,[17] imagery and representation,[18] criminal justice,[19] and trauma,[20] to name just a few, were all brought into focus.

Despite its expanding agenda, however, it was apparent that historical scholarship on madness remained – and, to some extent, still remains – skewed temporally, geographically, and topically. After initially being drawn to the study of the mad-doctors and reformers of the eighteenth century, research shifted its focus to developments in the nineteenth and twentieth centuries. To be sure, histories of madness in the ancient, medieval, and early modern worlds have continued to be written, but these studies have been outnumbered by those centering on the modern period (a pattern one sees, of course, in history more generally). At the same, studies of western and central Europe, Great Britain, and the United States dominated the field until more recently, when a growing number of scholars began exploring the history of mental health in south and east Asia, Africa, South America, the Arab world, and eastern Europe.[21]

Perhaps most noteworthy, however, has been historians' interest in moving beyond the once common focus on asylums, psychoanalysis, or psychiatric professionalization to cast their gaze on prominent, yet previously neglected, features and figures. Psychopharmacology,[22] families,[23] nurses and mental health workers,[24] outpatient treatment,[25] and madness as a form of disability[26] are just a few of the major topics that have begun moving to center stage. A survey of publications and conference announcements from the scholarly blog *h-madness* from mid-2014 to mid-2016 alone provides a glimpse into some of the topics that are now emerging: the development of child, adolescent, and geriatric psychiatries; the perspectives of patients and the mad themselves; the globalization of psychiatric diagnoses and methods; the history of specific diagnostic categories such as schizophrenia, mania, depression, hysteria, psychopathy, dementia, and autism; historical studies of expert reports, self-harm, prison psychiatry, "brainwashing," deinstitutionalization, and psychiatric epidemiology; the development of treatment techniques like hypnosis, lobotomy, work, and talk therapies; and the history of emotions.[27]

Neuroscience, psychopharmacology, genetics, cultural history, gender studies, the social study of race, colonial and post-colonial studies, science and technology studies, literary studies, cultural anthropology, critical psychology, and bioethics have all now left their mark on how mental disorders and their treatment have come to be understood as historical artifacts. It seems, therefore, a good time to take stock again and consider the state of the field. This book represents such an attempt. It seeks to provide researchers and those interested in the history of madness with a snapshot of the discipline – an opportunity to see how leading scholars go about their work, the kind of evidence they use, the conclusions they are reaching, and their assessments of the historiography of madness today.

As editor, it has been my intention from the beginning to ensure that the book was as representative as possible of the field as it now stands. I could only be partly successful in realizing this goal, however. Invariably there have been any number of impediments, chief among them limitations of space and the contingencies that come with recruiting so many contributors to one volume. As a result, there are areas that remain relatively overlooked, while the focus is weighted toward developments since the eighteenth century. That said, an attempt has been made to fashion a volume that reflects the temporal, geographical, and topical interests of active researchers, gives voice to diverse approaches and assessments, and includes perspectives from scholars throughout the world and at different stages in their careers. As should be the case with any edited volume, the purpose here is as much to inspire future research as it is to address lingering historical questions.

In most edited volumes, the convention is to introduce and summarize the individual chapters within. Rather than recapitulate the arguments of each author, however,

I think it more useful to take the opportunity of the introduction to flag a number of prominent themes and trends that emerge from reading across the different contributions presented here.

To start with, numerous authors remind us of *the limitations of historical sources, the importance of avoiding anachronism, and the pitfalls of retrospective diagnosis.* Both Madalina Vartejanu-Joubert and Manuella Meyer emphasize in their chapters that madness has always presented ambiguities to both those personally stricken by it and to those observing it. Indeed, in countless instances, questions were – and still are – often raised as to whether an individual's behavior was, in fact, attributable to the presence of a mental disorder.

Richard Noll perhaps puts it best: "madness is a moving target." For historians interested in avoiding an all-too-comforting presentism and the privileging of European and American psychiatry's perspective on things, the term "madness" does provide a way to capture the diverse global experiences associated with it. "Madness implies no necessary historical or geographical or epistemic center," Noll adds. Sonu Shamdasani says much the same about the history of psychotherapy as well: it has no one origin, no one clear genealogy. Thus, many historians of madness appear to be in agreement with German Berrios and Ivana Marková in accepting that the concepts at work in psychiatry as well as the other healing arts dealing with mental health "obtain their meaning from the historical periods in which they are allowed to be active." As they point out, it will most often "not be possible to arrange the versions of madness thereby generated in a 'progressive' series."

That said, however, madness has been seen consistently as something that presents society with a message, something that carries with it some meaning or set of meanings that must be decoded. But how are we to make sense of these historical meanings? The kind of coding and decoding encountered in the ancient Hebrew tradition, Vartejanu-Joubert points out in her conclusion, does not map neatly onto clinical or anthropological models and frameworks. Rather, its literature is rooted in religious, political, and legal traditions (a point Meyer also makes about colonial Latin American sources). Thumiger, too, emphasizes that madness in ancient Greece and Rome was just as often framed in terms of moral as medical semantics, making it very hard for us now to assume a one-to-one correspondence with our psychiatric concepts and categories today. And before presuming that such non-materialistic ways of considering states of mental disorder have been confined solely to pre-modern societies, Rhodri Hayward's chapter shows that supernatural interpretations continued to flourish in the nineteenth and twentieth centuries.

Take melancholia, for instance. As Chiara Thumiger points out, it is mentioned only a handful of times in ancient Greek texts, and its implications are inconsistent. Only later authors would come to see it as something on which to build an entire category of disorders. In her chapter, Laura Hirshbein reinforces this point, suggesting that those who see in earlier descriptions of melancholia a clinical picture of contemporary "depression" often do so out of an eminently understandable, yet nevertheless anachronistic, interest in confirming the validity of the clinical depression diagnosis today.

This problem is especially acute when it comes to cross-cultural studies of mental illness. As Sally Swartz points out, "histories of colonial encounters in Africa rehearse racial difference while often obscuring cultural variation; and the 'otherness' of encounters across racial difference is too easily mapped onto meanings of 'otherness' signified by states of insanity." Local context is essential, both Swartz and Waltraud Ernst rightly emphasize, when considering how diagnoses and treatments have been historically applied.

A second set of insights concern the ways in which *madness has been associated with social deviance*. Across time and place, one can see that a certain kind of strangeness has frequently been attributed to the experiences and behavior of those deemed mad. This oddness, of course, has always been perceived through the lenses of prevailing cultural assumptions. Racial, gender, and class/caste distinctions, for instance, have played a significant role in this regard. Meyer, for example, points out that recent research in Bolivia, Mexico, and Argentina makes it clear that officials and physicians there consistently treated indigenous populations, the poor, and women as threats to both modernizing initiatives and prevailing cultural hierarchies, leading to the fact that the madness label was attributed to them disproportionately. Things played out similarly in Africa. Swartz tells us that nineteenth-century European colonizers widely believed Africans to be inherently "strange" and "primitive" and, as a result, they considered their indigenous subjects beyond help and unworthy of European standards of care. A similar principle of racial segregation, Ernst reveals, also governed Indian asylums before the country's independence in 1947.

Frequently transgressing an array of social norms, those suffering from mental illness have often found themselves unwelcome and shunned. As Thumiger tells us, "there are grounds to believe that persecution, marginalisation, and stigma often followed the mad" already in ancient times. Their presumed loss of self-governance – a criterion applied since ancient times – meant that the mad have consistently prompted a decisive response from key social institutions: the household, the law, religious orders, and medicine.

And yet, a number of authors here remind us that the history of madness is also marked by compassion, tolerance, inclusiveness, and even respect toward the mad. This appears to have been especially the case in the medieval Islamic world and in colonial Latin America. Andrew Scull informs us that medieval Arab asylums for the mad combined both restrictive and nurturing techniques in handling those in their charge. And any thought that Foucault was right in his claim of there having been a "great confinement" of the mad in the seventeenth and eighteenth centuries seems now to have been definitively put to bed. If societies have been interested in socially controlling those considered insane, then it is clear that this has only recently been done to any significant extent – and even then, only unevenly – through confinement. On the eve of the French Revolution, Scull reveals, a famous and influential institution like the Salpêtrière in France housed relatively few insane patients. If we turn our gaze toward East Asia, as Akihito Suzuki has us do, we discover that the practice of institutionalizing the mentally ill only first took place there in the late nineteenth century.

In more recent times, however, we appear to be witnessing a new trend, one in which the stigma attached to madness has been substantially undermined, not only by sufferers, but by powerful market interests. The growth in the mass marketing of psychoactive drugs in Europe and the United States during the second half of the twentieth century, Toine Pieters informs us, highlights a somewhat surprising development. The normalization of individuals formerly marginalized as social deviants came to be seen as a business opportunity for some, namely big pharmaceutical companies and psychotherapists. Suppliers of drugs and services thus have had a professional stake in seeing madness normalized (and, perhaps as well, in seeing "normal" experiences like grief pathologized). The cost of normalization – in this instance, at least – appears to have been the commercialization of mental disorders.

Yet another theme that emerges here is that madness has served as *a powerful symbol in cultural life*. In their chapter, Claire Trenery and Peregrine Horden show that madness was used widely in literature and the visual arts to represent death, anarchy, weakness (especially in royalty), but that it also offered characters the possibility of spiritual renewal. Elizabeth Mellyn, too, notes that early modern authors of various kinds turned to madness as a metaphor to describe humanity and to capture the wretchedness of the human condition along with the vanity of earthly ambition.

Modernity only continued this pattern of seeing mental disorder as somehow representative of something more than a disease. Ilya Vinitsky, in his contribution, points us to the many physicians who, by the early nineteenth century, came to share the view of artists and writers that madness was a profound enigma. As such, they believed its story could best be told in highly personal and more inventively expressive ways than medicine conventionally offered. Indeed, as Vinitsky puts it, "In cultural interpretation, madness is not a state but a story." With so many outside observers historically dismissing the person and utterances of those deemed to be lunatics, "literature and art," he elegantly argues, "turn the mad to us and force us to look into their eyes. In other words, writers and artists give voice and image to the ones who are silenced and invisible." Suzuki, in his chapter, makes it clear that literature in modern Japan has also served a similar function there, namely giving form to the voices of mentally disordered individuals.

That said, it equally must be granted that more often than not these very same artists engaged in the same familiar process of projection, seeing in madness something that revealed more about themselves than about the mad whom they invoked. It is therefore not terribly surprising to see that mental illness and those it afflicts are not the only ones who have provided inspiration for popular culture and social criticism. Psychiatrists, psychotherapists, nurses, and mental health workers, too, have been the stuff of popular films and television dramas (think, for instance, of the 2005–8 Israeli drama *BeTipul*, which was adapted for television in over a dozen other countries). Even treatments have found a place in popular culture. As Pieters notes, by the 1960s an unexpected alliance of psychiatrists, pharmaceutical companies, and countercultural gurus collectively touted the transformative powers of psychoactive drugs and, in the process, helped mint the notion of "the chemically transformable mind."

The growing interest in the historical use of medications for mental illness exposes another dimension that is garnering increased attention among historians: *the material culture of madness and its treatment*. This interest has revealed itself in a number of different ways. One way has been to acknowledge the long history of materialist explanations for madness. As Thumiger demonstrates, already in ancient Greece, medicine emphasized somatic, rather than metaphysical, dimensions in explaining and treating the insane. Physicians at the time offered a variety of arguments about the etiology of mental disease; environment, habits, and internal organs were flagged as possible culprits, understood to be more or less in conflict, more or less in harmony, or simply running parallel alongside one another.

6

Now emerging among historians, however, is an appreciation that psychiatric practice has had its own material infrastructure – an aspect of its work previously overlooked. The enthusiasm over fMRI procedure today perhaps makes us more acutely aware of the presence of technologies in the care of the mentally ill, but their existence is hardly new. In his chapter, Andreas Killen shows how new technologies of visual media – lithography, photography, cinematography – "have been used to produce knowledge of disease pictures, to awaken understanding and sympathy for patients and for their physicians and caretakers, as well as to communicate knowledge of reforms and warnings about particular kinds of health risk." As he highlights, attention to the visual material culture surrounding psychiatry forces us to take more carefully into account the performative facets of psychiatric authority. Moreover, the increasingly mechanical and chemical nature of this materiality during the modern period has seemed to provide psychiatry with an aura of objectivity – a status the profession generally has sought since practitioners first linked the discipline's future to laboratory science in the nineteenth century.

In his chapter, Benoît Majerus takes up the subject of material culture head on, reminding us that the mundane, yet ubiquitous, objects that literally have surrounded institutionalized patients structured their lives. And, in fact, that was their very purpose. Alienists and psychiatrists in the nineteenth and twentieth centuries were quite deliberate in the design and use of the objects and environments – gates, windows, doors, floors, furnishings, grounds, and so on – that they integrated into the milieu of patients. For a field of medical care that historically has had relatively few instruments in its arsenal, these objects simultaneously served therapeutic, sedative, and disciplinary functions. Their symbolic value proved equally important, however. As Majerus points out, for example, the constant presence of beds – products closely associated with recuperating from illness – in asylums reinforced the message on an everyday basis that insanity was a disease and the resident a patient.

In a very direct fashion, the growing reliance of psychiatry on tools, synthetic drugs, and instruments reflects the powerful draw materialist explanations of mental illness have had on the field. Without question, Western medicine and science has for centuries wrestled with understanding human beings through the poles of a presumed mind–body dualism. And even if we now recognize, as Jonathan Sadowsky does in his chapter, that the distinction is a rather clumsy and artificial construct for understanding our status as living things, it nevertheless has had a profound effect on the way people have come to make sense of madness and the mad.

The consequences of accepting this construct as ontological reality, Sadowsky explains in his intriguing, revisionist analysis of somatic therapies, invariably has led observers of all kinds to draw mistaken conclusions about the veracity and ethical nature of both psychiatry and psychotherapy. For example, opponents of somatic treatments often work from the assumption that those treatments are less humane and more abusive than talk therapies. But while any given somatic treatment might be shown to be abusive, harmful, or dehumanizing, it is not so simply by virtue of being a somatic treatment. As cases of malpractice involving psychotherapists attest, "talk" interventions can be equally harmful. As Sadowsky sums up, "coerciveness of a treatment varies by context, rather than being a property inherent in the treatment itself."

By the same merit, it needs to be acknowledged that the perennial hopes of materialists to successfully reduce mental disorders to a biological fundament continue to be disappointed. Assessing the state of contemporary psychiatric genetics, Pieters here puts it this way:

> the addictive promise of the psychoactive magic bullet with a controllable and specific effect on the chemistry of the brain has not and will not materialize due to the complex and contextualized nature of mental disorders. Even molecular biologists have had to admit that they cannot find a single genetic cause for depression, anxiety or schizophrenia. The one-gene-one-disease ('O-GOD') champions of the 1990s met their Waterloo in mental illness and have turned to epigenetics to develop new forms of neurogenetic and neuropharmacological modeling.

The murky etiology of mental disorders has contributed to another feature of the history of psychiatry that a number of authors here discuss, namely the seemingly endless *search for a reliable classification system for mental illnesses*. As Thumiger points out, the tradition of building a taxonomy of madness began in the ancient world with Celsus. Berrios and Marková reveal, however, that until the eighteenth century European physicians did not rely on any one classification system and, in fact, drew no distinction between symptom and disease. The "mental symptom" as such had to wait until the first half of the nineteenth century to be constructed – under the influence of developments in semiotics, philosophy, and natural science – and used as a model for alienists. It was from this point forward that psychiatric professionals defined the condition of "mental disease" as a cluster of mental symptoms. This, in turn, meant that the same mental symptom could in fact "participate in the formation of more than one disease," making diagnostics in the field especially tricky.

Berrios and Marková also show that institutional factors have played a prominent role in the classification of mental disorders. The growth of European and American asylum populations in the nineteenth century, among other things, placed a premium on the taking of case notes, thus helping to spur the interest in taxonomies. At the same time, as patients stayed ever longer in asylum care, "the possibility of longitudinal observation contributed to the introduction into psychopathology of the dimension of time, and the possibility that mental disorders could also be studied along a temporal axis."

Numerous authors here make similar points to the effect that any number of social factors have played a prominent, though often unacknowledged, role in shaping the nosologies on which modern psychiatry has depended. In his chapter, Jesse Ballenger notes how clinicians could differ in their classification of symptoms and a disease – such as dementia in the case of Alzheimer's disease – not simply due to existing or incomplete evidence. They could also be influenced by institutional pressures or by professional competition for recognition. Killen demonstrates that illustrations and, then later, photographs and film, were used to provide teaching tools for alienists and psychiatrists to refine their classifications and diagnoses, but the presence of these technologies was rarely theorized.

The power of taxonomies has also been considerable. Take psychosis, as Noll does. Long used as a noun in medical circles, changes in classification precipitated by the *Diagnostic and Statistical Manual of Mental Disorders-III* (1980) meant that by the mid-1990s, the World Health Organization joined the American Psychiatric Association in dumping the term in favor of its adjectival form ("psychotic"). Disorder and disorder identities can come and go, it appears, often very quickly. And as new disorders and diagnoses have arisen, treatments and treatment specialists have appeared on the scene to address them. Part of the longevity of psychotherapy as a profession, Shamdasani points out, "has resided in its effectiveness in ever formulating and catering for new disorders."

The relationship between patients and psychiatric taxonomies has been a complicated one, however. Systems have drawn criticism from a number of different directions. For example, as Swartz points out, twentieth-century ethnopsychiatrists expressed reservations about the ways in which the universalist claims of clinical psychiatry and psychology elided local contexts. And yet, both Majerus and Geoffrey Reaume point out that there has also been a demand side to the diagnostic categories circulating within and outside modern psychiatry. Majerus shows that, as medications began to be tailored to distinct diagnoses, patients demanded specific medications based on these distinctions. At the same time, Reaume concurs with Porter in noting that while there has been a long history of patients rejecting clinical categories, many narratives penned by those suffering from mental illness demonstrate a convergence of their personal stories and prevailing psychiatric "lore and language." Many clearly have found validation and solace in psychiatry's diagnostic terminology.

If the etiology of mental disorders has remained elusive, it is also the case that *the boundaries between psychotherapeutic and somatic treatments have been historically quite porous*, a fact confirmed by multiple contributors to this book. Ancient authors such as Celsus, for instance, tied their talk interventions with instructions about diet and milieu designed to alter the body and its organs. The medieval tradition continued this syncretism, Trenery and Horden note, with most healers at the time considering physiological, psychological, and metaphysical causes not to be mutually exclusive in precipitating episodes of madness. Mellyn then shows that this trend carried on into the early modern period. It is especially remarkable to see how incantations, pleas, prayers to holy figures, and visits to shrines – all of which had been part of the ancient, pagan world – continued unabated throughout predominantly Catholic parts of early modern and even modern Europe. As Mellyn describes it, the varieties of explanations and treatments found in early modern Europe presented consumers with a highly "competitive market" of services, and consumers gladly took the opportunity to turn to any number of healers to find relief.

Looking more closely at the modern period, Sadowsky calls the conventional distinction between "somatic" or "biological" treatments and "talk" therapies a "philosophical mistake." It is, in his estimation, a distinction that fails to acknowledge how ostensibly physical treatments have always aimed to alter spiritual or mental well being as well as how psychotherapies have necessarily relied on having physical effects on clients. To be sure, clinicians, insurers, courts, policymakers, and those suffering from mental illness along with their families, continue to struggle over the question of whether mental disorders are principally biological or social in nature. But history demonstrates, in Sadowsky's words, that "most societies [in practice] have treated madness eclectically."

In his chapter on the history of psychotherapy Shamdasani makes a similar point, namely that already in the nineteenth century proponents of "psycho-therapeutics" justified its use by noting the ways in which thought and imagination could stimulate the body's organs and glands and promote both mental as well as physical health. He points to the French physician Hippolyte Bernheim, for example, who claimed that hypnotic suggestion was "effective in cases of paralyses, contractures, insomnia, muscular pain, hemiplegia, paraplegia, rheumatism, anaesthesia, gastric disorders, neuralgia and sciatica." Hypnosis, it turns out, played a pivotal role in the history of talk therapies, for as Shamdasani shows us, the spread of psychotherapy in the nineteenth century took place less through the adoption of the so-called "moral treatment" than via the popularity of the hypnotic movement and the growing interest in theories of suggestion. While Freud and his disciples would later place greater emphasis on interpretation, suggestion remained an alluring theme throughout the history of psychotherapy, providing the field with a compelling way to adapt itself to changes accompanying the twentieth century, whether it be through mass marketing and consumerism or counter-cultural social criticism.

While contributors to this book show that psychotherapy and other forms of persuasive talk were hardly the invention of the twentieth century, so too do a number of authors here make clear that *there has been a longstanding interest among professionals and the public not only in treating mental disorder, but also in achieving and maintaining spiritual and mental wellbeing.* As Thumiger and Mellyn both reveal, healers dating back to the ancients regularly offered consumers advice on fostering a stable and harmonious inner life. And this has not been confined to Europe. In her chapter, Ernst tell us that the "three main South Asian traditions – Ayurveda, Unani, and Siddha – consider health as a state of complete well-being, both physical and mental, rather than as an absence of a particular illness." Thus, one could write the history of madness not as a chronicle of efforts aimed at understanding and treating disorders, but as a story of humanity's attempt to find and promote the good life.

It is in this context that we encounter the ubiquitous notion that mental illness is due to some kind of moral flaw – often, immoderate habits – on the part of the sufferer, but one that education, self-reflection, and ethical training can potentially address. Prescriptions for the maintenance of mental health were repeatedly talked about in terms of prevention, and ancient, medieval, early modern, and modern healers consistently emphasized that prophylactic measures were an integral part of treatment of mental disorders. To a considerable degree, this has been due to the fact that these same healers have been well aware of the limitations on the efficacy of their treatments when it comes to cases of madness.

The rise of synthetic, mood-enhancing drugs during the last part of the twentieth century, a process discussed here by Hirshbein and Pieters, testifies to an intensification of the clinical focus on the goal of promoting mental health rather simply treating acute symptoms. Contemporary psychiatry's interest in catering to the demands of outpatient clients who increasingly sought to elevate their moods or make themselves more productive, Pieters insists, is what fueled the extraordinary growth in the consumption of psychoactive drugs from 1950 onwards. Lest we think the only financial beneficiaries were pharmaceutical companies, however, Shamdasani reminds us that the boom in psychotherapies at this same time also represented a response to this demand. "Psychotherapy," he tells us, "had become not only a palliative for psychological disorders, but a form of life enhancement."

One of the most prominent topics authors in the book take up is *the global spread of knowledge and treatment practices*. In her chapter, for instance, Meyer emphasizes that the growth of mental health in Latin American countries during the nineteenth and early twentieth centuries emerged out of broader national modernization projects. These social reform projects – deliberately undertaken around the same time on both sides of the Atlantic – were cast in terms of public health initiatives and employed "the language and methods of sanitarianism and hygienic improvement in which disease and poor health were attributed to a combination of environmental hazards, the population's ignorance of basic hygiene and unhealthy behaviors and practices."

At the same time, new research on developments in Asia reveals that western European paradigms and models were exported there – often forcibly through the institutions of colonization – over the course of the nineteenth and twentieth centuries. As Suzuki points out, for instance, the institutionalization of the mentally ill was foreign to Japan, China, and Korea until around 1900, after which "the representations of madness were quickly transformed and dominated by the images of the closed world of psychiatric hospitals." In Japan, at least, this was deliberate, with universities sending off their finest students to study under the tutelage of prominent European psychiatrists, such as the German Emil Kraepelin. But as Suzuki points out, even this had little impact on asylum-building, something that only took off in Japan during the second half of the twentieth century – ironically enough, at the same moment when deinstitutionalization was becoming the new trend in Europe and the United States. Thus, as Ernst points out about developments in modern south Asia, it needs to be kept in mind that local Asian practices were re-localized at the same time they were being globalized, "informed by attention to commercial interests and the politics of medical competition and national(ist) agendas that have driven the popularity of particular approaches."

This bears being underscored. If there is evidence of increasing universalization and standardization of psychiatric ideas and practices throughout the world since the late nineteenth century, historians are quick to point out that this pattern has hardly squelched vernacular understandings of madness. Both Ernst and Swartz warn that we should not be too eager to write off indigenous views of mental disorders in places like Africa and India. Any number of limiting factors often ensured that imperialist ambitions to medicalize native populations failed. For example, while Africans were historically subject to northern and western standards of "civilized" rationality and normality, Swartz stresses that "psychiatric interventions in Africa were too small scale to constitute any form of social engineering or interference in locally constructed sets of cultural practices." Moreover, nineteenth-century colonial clinicians were severely hampered by their lack of knowledge about black patients' biographies, local contexts, and indigenous languages. And the bifurcation of facilities and care provided in African and south Asian colonial settings – with settlers receiving better treatment and living conditions than the indigenous population – itself helped undercut efforts at exporting the supposedly more advanced, progressive treatment regimens common on the Continent well into the twentieth century.

Perhaps nothing better testifies to the limitations on any imperialist ambitions on the part of modern, materialist-minded psychiatrists than *the persistence of spiritual, supernatural understandings of experiences associated with madness.* Hayward's chapter makes this point explicitly. A great many prominent, Western psychiatrists and neurologists in the nineteenth and twentieth centuries made it their common goal to purge spiritual understandings of madness from clinical research and treatment. Despite this, however, religion was never fully excised nor segregated from modern psychiatry. In Europe and the United States, Christian notions of a universal human nature capable of reform, and of an obligation to care for the infirm, informed late eighteenth- and early nineteenth-century moral treatments. Nineteenth-century psychiatry was forced to explain and accommodate phenomena such as clairvoyance and spirit communication. Pastoral counseling adopted psychological principles and practices and, in turn – through figures like Carl Rogers – returned the favor by influencing secular psychotherapies of the twentieth century. New religions like scientology and the Process Church rooted themselves in psychotherapeutic traditions, while New Age encounter movements such as EST incorporated similar techniques as it created its own quasi-religious following. And as welfare states established themselves from the 1940s onwards, religious organizations and institutions continued to play key roles in mental health care.

The persistence of demotic attitudes and practices toward madness is a reminder of another key aspect of the latter's history, namely that *those with mental illnesses historically have had numerous caretakers, allies, and spokespersons beyond physicians and professional counselors.* In their chapters, Mellyn, Meyer, and Suzuki all highlight the fact that from the early modern – and well into the modern – period, households and families took the lead in attempting to arrange care for their loved ones. As Mellyn puts it, "the family continued to be the custodial and therapeutic institution of first resort." In assuming this role, however, it is clear that, instead of operating independently of officials and professionals, guardians tended to work collaboratively with local authorities and often relied on self-help books for guidance.

Nurses and mental health workers of various kinds also have played a pivotal role in tending to institutionalized patients. Their histories, however, have only recently started to be written. In this book, Majerus takes the opportunity to point out how the work and interaction of modern hospital staff with patients was distinctive from that of doctors: staff interactions with their charges were not only more direct and lengthier, but – similar to patients – their daily routines were thoroughly structured by the material objects and strict regimen of the mental health facility.

A number of authors also direct our attention to an important change in caretaking that took place primarily in the twentieth century: organized activism. Reaume, in noting the more recent rise in advocacy writing among patients, former patients, and those self-identifying as mentally ill, quite rightly argues that this side of mental health care has been mostly neglected by historians. Yet it is clear that the self-help and political organization of the mentally ill and their families is an aspect that needs to be integrated into the broader history of madness in the modern world.[28] This is particularly the case, as Hirshbein emphasizes in her chapter on moods and emotions, when it comes to disorders and problems often associated with socially disadvantaged populations, such as women. Indeed, in his contribution, Ballenger details how increasing attention to the plight of the elderly suffering from senile dementia helped spur the growth of political activist groups acting on their behalf, such as the American Association of Retired Persons. Organizations like these, in turn, have had a measurable impact on clinical research and practices. That said, it must be conceded that feedback loops such as these have not been confined to the late twentieth century. For as Shamdasani emphasizes, these kinds of looping effects between healers and patients were a fundamental part of the rise of psychotherapy, with subjects routinely being schooled by popular culture and word-of-mouth about therapies before and during their encounters with professionals. In turn, the latter found themselves having to adapt to rising consumer expectations.

With the growing recognition of the need to attend to the perspectives of those deemed or self-identifying as mentally ill, *historians are turning their attention to the ways in which madness is experienced over the life course of individuals.* Reaume points out that recent decades have witnessed a veritable renaissance in publications written by those afflicted, with a plethora of biographies, autobiographies, memoirs, and accounts of advocacy work. They reveal that attitudes among those with mental illnesses toward symptoms, treatments, and the healing professions can vary considerably. Moreover, these narratives also confirm that the madness experience must also be placed within the life history of the individuals affected. In fact, Majerus insists we extend this line of thinking still further to include the material objects surrounding the mentally ill. Instead of seeing them as static elements in a backdrop, he argues, we need to acknowledge that these objects have functions and meanings that change and shift over time. Objects, too, have biographies.

Psychiatry's own engagement with the life history of patients has a history as well. Suzuki, for instance, shows that the biographical dimensions of madness were largely foreign to traditional Japanese attitudes about mad persons until relatively recently. It took a deliberate turn on the part of psychiatrists and prominent writers toward western thought about individuality to first thematize life history there when considering the plight of the insane. Ballenger, too, chronicles how life course increasingly came to play a role in modern mental health care. In the United States at least, changes in law and in the organization of welfare institutions around the turn of the twentieth century forced the disabled elderly into mental facilities – a trend that only first reversed itself beginning in the late 1950s and 1960s. Psychiatry's confrontation during the first half of the century with a growing number of patients suffering from what appeared to be senile dementia, as Ballenger puts it, brought "age-associated dementias into mainstream American psychiatry." This spurred not only new psychosocial theories and treatments about the disease, but also research into the broader social experience of aging in post-World War II America as well as new attitudes toward retirement as a phase of life.

It is the nature of historical research today to underscore the local differences and peculiarities in how madness has been represented, interpreted, and managed. The chapters here offer ample evidence that broadly universal arguments about mental disorders and those suffering from them must confront a history that demands their qualification. Nevertheless, these chapters remind us that madness is a part of the human condition, a dimension of human experience. Ballenger, for example, shows that engaging the problem of senile dementia historically has raised all sorts of questions about the aging process and about our notions of cognitive problems. Hirshbein reminds us that an interest in emotions has been ever-present in western society, despite the efforts of many intellectuals to relegate them to an inferior status. And Noll in his chapter makes a compelling case for appreciating how the symptoms

13

associated with psychosis are part of an array of experiences that are quite integral to human existence and, thus, not easily captured and segregated under the rubric of mental illness. The history of madness is, therefore, not a story about some supposed "them." It is a set of stories very much about ourselves.

Notes

1 APA, "Timeline," www.dsm5.org/about/Pages/Timeline.aspx, accessed 18 January 2016.
2 Martyn D. Pickersgill, "Debating DSM-5: Diagnosis and the Sociology and Critique," *Journal of Medical Ethics*, 40 (2014): 521–525.
3 Ethan Watters, *Crazy Like Us: The Globalization of the American Psyche* (New York: Free Press, 2010).
4 World Health Organization, "Mental Disorders Affect One in Four People," 2001. www.who.int/whr/2001/media_centre/press_release/en/, accessed 18 January 2016.
5 Shreya Dasgupta, "Many Animals Can Become Mentally Ill," *BBC Earth*, 9 September 2015, www.bbc.com/earth/story/20150909-many-animals-can-become-mentally-ill, accessed 26 February 2016.
6 Horacio Fabrega Jr, "Sickness and Healing and the Evolutionary Foundations of Mind and Minding," *Mens Sana Monographs*, 9 (2011): 159–182.
7 Horacio Fabrega Jr., "Why Psychiatric Conditions Are Special: An Evolutionary and Cross-Cultural Perspective," *Perspectives in Biology and Medicine*, 49 (2006): 586–601.
8 Edward Shorter, *What Psychiatry Left Out of the DSM-5: Historical Mental Disorders Today* (New York: Routledge, 2015).
9 Edwin R. Wallace IV, "Philosophy and Methodology of History, with Special Emphasis on Medicine and Psychiatry; and an Appendix on 'Historiography' as the History of History" in *History of Psychiatry and Medical Psychology*, ed. Edwin R. Wallace IV and John Gach, (New York: Springer, 2008), 3–115.
10 George Rosen, *Madness in Society: Chapters in the Historical Sociology of Mental Illness* (Chicago: University of Chicago Press, 1968); Michel Foucault, *Histoire de la folie à l'âge classique* (Paris: Plon, 1961).
11 Among his earliest works, see *Mental Illness and American Society, 1875–1940* (Princeton: Princeton University Press, 1983); *Mental Institutions in America: Social Policy to 1875* (New York: Free Press, 1973); and *The State and the Mentally Ill: A History of Worcester State Hospital in Massachusetts, 1830–1920* (Chapel Hill: University of North Carolina Press, 1966).
12 See, for example, his books *A Social History of Madness: The World Through the Eyes of the Insane* (New York: Weidenfeld and Nicolson, 1988) and *Mind-forg'd Manacles: A History of Madness in England From the Restoration to the Regency* (London: Athlone, 1987).
13 Mark S. Micale and Roy Porter, eds, *Discovering the History of Psychiatry* (New York: Oxford University Press, 1994).
14 Jan Goldstein, *Console and Classify: The French Psychiatric Profession in the Nineteenth Century* (New York: Cambridge University Press, 1987).
15 Jonathan Sadowsky, *Imperial Bedlam: Institutions of Madness in Colonial Southwest Nigeria* (Berkeley: University of California Press, 1999).
16 Ann Goldberg, *Sex, Religion, and the Making of Modern Madness: The Eberbach Asylum and German Society, 1815–1849* (New York: Oxford University Press, 1999); Mark S. Micale, *Approaching Hysteria: Disease and its Interpretations* (Princeton: Princeton University Press, 1995); Elaine Showalter, *The Female Malady: Women, Madness, and English Culture, 1830–1980* (New York: Pantheon, 1985).
17 Helen Small, *Love's Madness: Medicine, the Novel, and Female Insanity, 1800–1865* (Oxford: Clarendon, 1996).
18 Lynn Gamwell and Nancy Tomes, *Madness in America: Cultural and Medical Perceptions of Mental Illness Before 1914* (Ithaca: Cornell University Press, 1995); Sander L. Gilman, *Disease and Representation: Images of Illness From Madness to AIDS* (Ithaca: Cornell University Press, 1988).

19 Joel Eigen, *Witnessing Insanity: Madness and Mad-Doctors in the English Court* (New Haven: Yale University Press, 1995); Ruth Harris, *Murders and Madness: Medicine, Law, and Society in the Fin de Siècle* (Oxford: Clarendon, 1989).
20 Mark S. Micale and Paul Frederick Lerner, eds, *Traumatic Pasts: History, Psychiatry, and Trauma in the Modern Age, 1870–1930* (Cambridge: Cambridge University Press, 2001).
21 See, for instance, Debjani Das, *Houses of Madness: Insanity and Asylums of Bengal in Nineteenth-Century India* (New Delhi: Oxford University Press, 2016); Theodore Jun Yoo, *It's Madness: The Politics of Mental Health in Colonial Korea* (Oakland: University of California Press, 2016); Mat Savelli and Sarah Marks, eds, *Psychiatry in Communist Europe* (New York: Palgrave Macmillan, 2015); Howard Chiang, ed., *Psychiatry and Chinese History* (New York: Routledge, 2014); Junko Kitanak, *Depression in Japan: Psychiatric Cures for a Society in Distress* (Princeton and Oxford: Princeton University Press, 2012); Waltraud Ernst, *Mad Tales from the Raj: Colonial Psychiatry in South Asia, 1800–1858* (London: Anthem, 2010); Jonathan Ablard, *Madness in Buenos Aires: Patients, Psychiatrists and the Argentine State, 1880–1983* (Athens: Ohio University Press, 2008); Richard C. Keller, *Colonial Madness: Psychiatry in French North Africa* (Chicago: University of Chicago Press, 2008); Lynette A. Jackson, *Surfacing Up: Psychiatry and Social Order in Colonial Zimbabwe, 1908–1968* (Ithaca: Cornell University Press, 2005); Mariano Plotkin, ed., *Argentina on the Couch: Psychiatry, State, and Society, 1880 to the Present* (Albuquerque: University of New Mexico Press, 2003); Vivien W. Ng, *Madness in Late Imperial China: From Illness to Deviance* (Norman: University of Oklahoma Press, 1990); and Michael W. Dols, *Majnun: The Madman in Medieval Islamic Society* (Oxford: Clarendon, 1992).
22 David Healy, *The Creation of Psychopharmacology* (Cambridge: Harvard University Press, 2002).
23 Akihito Suzuki, *Madness at Home: The Psychiatrist, the Patient, and the Family in England, 1820–1860* (Berkeley and Los Angeles: University of California Press, 2006).
24 Susan Benedict and Linda Shields, eds, *Nurses and Midwives in Nazi Germany: The "Euthanasia" Programs* (New York and London: Routledge, 2014); Louise Hide, *Gender and Class in English Asylums, 1890–1914* (New York: Palgrave, 2014).
25 Ian Dowbiggin, *The Quest for Mental Health: A Tale of Science, Medicine, Scandal, Sorrow, and Mass Society* (New York: Cambridge University Press, 2011).
26 Sander L. Gilman, "Madness as Disability," *History of Psychiatry*, 25 (2014): 441–449.
27 *h-madness*, https://historypsychiatry.com, accessed 14 May 2016.
28 See Nancy Tomes, "The Patient as a Policy Factor: A Historical Case Study of the Consumer/Survivor Movement in Mental Health," *Health Affairs* 25 (2006): 720–729.

Part I

MADNESS IN THE ANCIENT
AND MEDIEVAL WORLDS

REPRESENTATIONS OF MADMEN AND MADNESS IN JEWISH SOURCES FROM THE PRE-EXILIC TO THE ROMAN-BYZANTINE PERIOD[1]

Madalina Vartejanu-Joubert

Madness is one of the topics inextricably related to an *etic* approach since its meaning depends on the criteria used by its observers and the definition these latter give to it. Consequently a certain consensus is established as a point of departure about what the signs of madness are, so that it becomes possible to acknowledge and examine it in distant past temporal contexts. This consensus is not as relative as one might be tempted to believe, and it focuses either on lexical labels (the use of certain words for "mad person" or "madness") or on textual descriptions (certain behaviors are considered to be characteristic of madness). The words and behaviors usually indicate the divorce of the individual from reality in a given context, one determined by one's alteration of cognition. The symptoms of this transformation of the self as well as its social consequences can vary; this involves a permanent to-and-fro movement between the observer and the subject of study as expressed in a historical source, a circulation giving rise to a dialectics destined to adjust the starting-point presuppositions about the topic. The historical and cultural specificity of madness lies in the interstices of this process.

The Jewish representation of madness in ancient times can be found in textual sources that are very different in nature, ranging from the discourse of legal documents to prophetic oracles and philosophical reflections.

Madness in the Hebrew Bible

Let us start by considering the lexical aspect. The word for "mad person" in Biblical Hebrew as well as in Modern Hebrew is *mešugga'* and the one for "madness" is *šigga'on*. We should first take into consideration the fact that the Hebrew of the Mishna and the Talmud uses a different type of vocabulary (see below). *BDB*[2], *KBL*[3] and *HAL*[4] translate the root *šg'* by "madness/mad person", depending on the use of the nominal or verbal forms. In *BDB*, *pu'al* means "mad", *hitpa'el* "show madness", and the noun, *šigga'on* "madness" (or *be-šigga'on* "madly"). Koehler-Baumgartner keeps the same translation in English and gives two German equivalents: *rasend/Raserei*, *Verrücktheit*. As far as etymology is concerned, *HAL* posits the improbability of the hypothesis that *shafel* is a derivation of *g'h*. On the contrary, one could find correspondents in three other Semitic languages. Thus, in Akkadian, *šegu* means "to be mad, to be like a bear with a sore head"; in Arabic, *šaga'a* signifies "to squeal like a pig"; in Ethiopian, *zange'a* means "to be mad" (*HAL*).

The lexical approach should be completed by a narratological one which could pave the way for a historical perspective. This approach I propose does not pertain to psychiatric history but to cultural anthropology. I do not mean to establish a modern psychiatric diagnosis, but I will first and foremost try to identify the elements of that model of intelligibility the fool rebels against. This does not mean we should discredit the psychiatric model, and of course we should a priori admit the epidemiological reality of certain mental diseases. Nevertheless, I believe that modern transpositions should be treated with caution, especially because of the lack of information we have about them. The Bible is not a medical treatise; it cannot be compared, from this point of view, with Hippocratic treatises or Akkadian medical texts. We don't have at our disposal a term allowing a systematic medical reflection, as the concept of "symptom" is in the case of medical texts. The Bible offers us a number of descriptions, favoring the narrative genre. "Madness" therefore appears in the Bible in the gist of various situations, events, characters and their discourse. The key for perusing these texts resides in the construction of their plot through the hypotheses and endings of various narrative situations, through repetitions and the choice of vocabulary. We may consider, with Victor Turner,[5] that not only stories but also the social processes own a narrative structure or a proto-narrative one: transgression of the status quo, crisis, and reparation. Thus, the root *šg'* stands for the point of departure for the present study, a focal point around which other terms and notions in close connection to it can be gradually amassed. This is the case, for instance, with expressions like *timhon levav*, with roots like *hll* or with phenomena such as "blindness." Since the lexical field of madness cannot be defined with complete accuracy, especially with regard to the concept of "stupidity," I have chosen a number of texts that allow us to partially grasp the specificity of madness in early Judaism.

We can distinguish among three categories: royal madness (Saul, David, Jehu); prophetic madness (Hosea, Jeremiah, etc.) and a special category that we could call "Deuteronomic" madness, after the name of the book from the Bible to which it corresponds.[6] Undoubtedly, these categories are not completely separate: for instance, royal madness and prophetic madness intersect with one another several times and through this very fluctuation they denote an essential way of approaching Biblical madness. Taken together, the texts under analysis cover a long period of time: they include the pre-exilic period (1 Samuel 8–31, Hosea, 2 Kings 16, Deuteronomy 28); the dawns of exile (Jeremiah); the exilic and post-exilic (Zachariah); and the Hellenistic period (Daniel 4). The precise dates of these passages are still open to debate, and we believe that the arguments to date are inconclusive.

Royal madness

Saul

Saul, the founder of the institution of monarchy, represents the emblematic figure for madness in the Hebrew Bible. Chapters 8–31 from the first book of Samuel recount the story of the foundation of monarchy while simultaneously drawing the portrait of a king whose decline is attributed to cognitive troubles. The very complex text aims to dismantle the all-inclusive, "totalitarian" character of his misfortune. From a literary point of view, this is expressed by the repetitive representation of Saul's failures: each chapter of his biography highlights in its own way an anomaly, a misunderstanding, a bad judgement. The symptoms of his madness are multiple and eclectic and it is their very disruptive nature which gives rise to a sense of their global effects on Saul: madness reaches to the depth of his soul and body.

Saul enters the stage in Chapter 9, following the story of his appointment as king which continues in Chapter 10 and, in other versions, in Chapter 11 as well. The description of his rise to power is related to the description of his decline and fall. God's prophecy and spirit (*ruah*) intervene both jointly and separately in these two episodes. But can Saul be called a possessed person? The relations of madness to the act of being possessed are most problematic in all cultures; since the phenomenology is usually identical, other criteria should be used in order to distinguish between madness and possession notions. Chapters 9–10 from the first book of Samuel present the germs of the story or, put differently, the origin of evil. All this makes up an etiology which, from a literary point of view, describes Saul's *failed initiation* to kingship and, from an anthropological perspective, associates the origin of evil to a *founding event* in the sense that initiation represents the rebirth of an individual. Chapter 11 also focuses on Saul's access to royal power. The ordeal that the hero must pass through involves the battlefield; he must pass the test of his military aptitudes and of his capacity to ensure the victory of his people (that of being a *Nikephoros* type of leader). Apparently nothing comes to stain Saul's victory over Nahash the Ammonite, a success leading to his renewed appointment for a royal position. The only problematic element to be considered is represented by the spirit of God (*ruah YHWH*) cast over him, one which angers Saul. Just as in the case of the prophecy from the previous chapters, the *ruah* causing Saul's anger has a double connotation or, better said, it has bipolar consequences: the consequences are formative in Chapter 11 but later prove to be profoundly disturbing, in Chapters 16, 18 and 19.

A turning point in Saul's biography starts with Chapter 13. What was previously a latent, simple potentiality of his personality now becomes explicit speech and gesture. In order to describe this misfortune, the intellectual level overlaps with the institutional level. The first accusation against Saul refers to a transgression that involves a double connotation; by carrying out the act of sacrifice without waiting for Samuel's arrival, Saul disobeys the divine commandment and becomes the subject of an implacable judgment:

> Thou hast done foolishly (*niskalta*): thou hast not kept the commandment of the Lord thy God, which he commanded thee [. . .] But now thy kingdom shall not continue.
>
> (1 Samuel 13,13–14)

In the next chapter Saul tries to establish a norm that proves once again to be an inappropriate act and judgment. On the eve of combat, he imposes fasting on his army but in transgressing the norm his son Jonathan starts to *see clearly*: the honey he eats makes his eyes shine (*how mine eyes have been enlightened*) (1 Samuel 14,29). Honey makes up a meal filled with symbols: it helps Isaiah *refuse the evil and choose the good* (Isaiah 7,15), while for Ezekiel the Torah scroll tastes like honey (Ezekiel 3,3).

Following a mythological point of view, this episode uses metaphors and symbols to once again reveal Saul's failure to rise up to his position. The terms by which Jonathan describes the vows taken by his father are extremely harsh: *my father brought misfortune into the land – 'akar 'et ha-'aretz* (1 Samuel 14,29).[7] Chapter 15 exposes for the third time Saul's faulty positioning in respect to the norm when the king fails to accomplish the *herem* demanded by God. The disobedience incarnated by his character stands for the human being's failure to adapt to institutional demands. Royalty implies the enactment of new rules and demands of the person total individual commitment to the divine will.

Starting with Chapter 16 the king is confronted with his rival and the rest of the story is constructed around the antithesis between Saul and David. The point of view completely changes and the scarce description of incongruous gestures leaves room for an introspective tone at the beck and call of emotions. Saul's madness is now transformed from an "act of insanity" to the more consuming act of "suffering". The story of David's ascent is *inextricably* tied to the story of Saul's downfall. The narrative structure of Chapter 16 straightforwardly announces this by placing two founding events in sequence: on the one hand, there is David's unction and appointment by the spirit of God (1 Samuel 16,13); on the other hand, the departure of the spirit of God and Saul's torments by the evil spirit (16,14). The link between cause and effect is not textually expressed, nor is the temporal context specified; the text puts forth its message by the simple use of juxtaposition. We can once again detect here the presence of an etiological approach which restrains itself from designating the cause and merely suggests it by simple and efficient literary means.

All stories involving madness one way or another imply the question of a divorce from reality. The imaginary of the mad person, his world of thoughts and images, appears false to the eyes of the community. In this sense, Saul had already shown his lack of comprehension, but he was previously out of joint with reality from an ethical and religious point of view: he couldn't understand God's commandments. By opposing David, Saul goes one step forward; he no longer simply manifests his *hybris*, but he wrongly interprets the facts of ordinary life. Chapters 16–26 draw up the picture of these incongruous facts and gestures.

The philistine menace represents another revelatory aspect of Saul's personality; he does not resign to a passive stance but takes up the only path to freedom he still has at his disposal, the woman-medium living in Ein Dor. However, this proves to be a misleading way that only increases the burden of Saul's dismay. While David rejoices in success after success, especially in the military arena, Saul lies dispirited in the house of the necromancer. In this whirlwind, the final act of Saul's epic life story takes place on Mount Gilboa, his violent death bearing the traces of his self-destruction.

The story of Saul's madness ends with his death. No part of his life escapes the spread of misfortune, everything is minutely included: *prophetic madness* (the delirium of the trance); *transgressive madness* (disobedience of the divine order); *derealization* (skewed perceptions of reality); and *self-destruction* (suicide). From his "rebirth" as a king up to his death, Saul's biography comprises sequences of episodes undergirding his non-conformity. Similar to what medical anthropology has pointed out with regard to the contemporary status of the ill, the subject's voice in this case is rarely expressed directly; both the causes and symptoms of his disease are described by means of external voices, those of the narrator or of other characters. For much of the story, Saul does not consider himself a patient: with the exception of attacks from the evil spirit, it is only in Chapter 26 that he admits "I acted as a mad person." Madness is a disease unlike the others: its symptoms refer to the relation established with reality, the soundness of perceptions and judgments. These symptoms are a permanent subject of debate; the assessment of the relation established with reality first and foremost belongs to the area of social caution. If in the case of the other diseases the decision about their existence is taken "jointly" by the patient and his circle of acquaintances, in the case of madness, it is only the Other that determines whether one suffers or not from this illness.

Jehu

We usually understand the emergence of madness in the world as the affliction of an individual or occasionally a group. Nevertheless, the situation of Jehu represents another modality in which madness manifests itself: this is the case of events which are unjustifiable or incomprehensible within the framework of an organized history, they are nonsensical. The very advent of Jehu's reign is an expression of such a madness, one which rules supreme in the world in moments of distraction. Jehu is a usurper with behavior tinged with madness, but whose reign reflects the divine will to punish his predecessors' withdrawal from the house of Ahab. The author-editor of the Book of Kings approaches this episode by foregrounding the most dreaded punishment by means of which God "hides his face" and thereby decreases the extent of the world's intelligibility. Is the "news" of madness "good" or "bad," and for whom?

The emissary announcing Jehu of his being anointed by God seems disconcerting – the prophet's madness prevents him from understanding the piece of news. Or, in the ancient Near East, the messenger shares the nature of his message as being either good or bad.[8] If the messenger is mad or at least perceived as such, his message is disconcerting and double-edged: we can interpret it either way, just as we can take it seriously or not. This ambiguity is well illustrated by two different reactions: that of Jehu and that of his officers; the former gives the impression he is indifferent, the latter show themselves concerned:

> Then Jehu came forth to the servants of his lord: and one said unto him, Is all well? wherefore came this mad fellow (mešugga) to thee? And he said unto them, Ye know the man, and his communication ('atem yeda'tem 'et-ha-'iš ve-'et-siho). And they said, It is false; tell us now. And he said, Thus and thus spake he to me, saying, Thus saith the Lord, I have anointed thee king over Israel. Then they hasted, and took every man his garment, and put it under him on the top of the stairs, and blew with trumpets, saying, Jehu is king.
>
> (2 Kings 9,11–13)

This is how the first act ends. The second act, about the effective exercise of power, is constructed after the same pattern; the recognition of the messenger by the sentry, the form of greeting, the actual rendering of the message:

And there stood a watchman (*ha-tzopheh*) on the tower in Jezreel, and he spied the company of Jehu as he came, and said, I see a company. And Joram said, Take a horseman, and send to meet them, and let him say, Is it peace (*ha-šalom*)?

(2 Kings 9,17)

The three chevaliers successively sent to encounter and stop Jehu do not manage to successfully end their mission and all three of them rally his army. On the occasion of this latter failure, the sentry gets to perceive an important clue – the appearance of the "messenger":

the driving (*minhag*) is like the driving of Jehu the son of Nimshi; for he driveth madly (*be-šiga'on ynhag*)!

(2 Kings 9,20)

This translation corresponds to a first level of reading and understanding. The image of the leader of the group discernible after the image of his "driving" still gives rise to a number of questions. How does Jehu lead his team? The writers of the Septuagint have translated *be-šigga'on* by *en parallagè*, a term whose primary meaning is that of "change", "instability." This is probably the image from the scene retained by translators. However, Iamblichus also uses this term with the sense of "madness" and, for Hippocrates, *parallaxis*, a word pertaining to the same family, means "mental aberrations" (*Liddel-Scott, ad loc*). As to the Targum version of the Bible, it completely ignores this aspect and translates by *bnyh mdbr*, "calm driving."

I believe it would be an error to see in this a simple stampede episode. The Hebrew text wants to say much more: it plays on the ambivalence of the root *nhg* and of its derivative *minhag*. The verb *nahag* means "to drive the herd" (Genesis 31,18; Exodus 3,1), "to drive the herds" (1 Chronicles 20,1), even "to drive one's heart" with wisdom (Qohelet 2,3). 2 Kings 9,20 is the only context in which the verb is used in the sense "to drive the cart." In its turn, the word *minhag* is a biblical *hapax*, but in Mishnaic Hebrew it designates one's "custom," one's "manner of behavior." By using this vocabulary, the biblical author almost gives voice to a prophetic speech and foretells a bad omen: *the way of behaving is that of Jehu who drove [his people] as a mad person.* His attitude must have already been notorious since it was recognized and identified from the look-out situated far away. Just as the prophet who anoints Jehu, the appearance of Jehu informs us of his madness as well as other things, namely pointing to the turbulent reign to come.

Jehu shares with the emissary-prophet the disconcerting ambiguity of madness. Their messages cannot be decoded because madness keeps its secret well-hidden. If, on reception of a message, the major question focuses on its content – "Is the piece of news good or bad?" – when this gets transposed to the case of our biblical story, the question becomes: "Is the anointment of Jehu a good or a bad piece of news?" By having as emissaries of the messages two persons known to be mad, what kind of an answer does the author try to transmit to us? Does he want to tell us that history comprises events whose sense we are sometimes unable to figure out? Does he want to imply that the divine project is deployed via episodes which it might not be possible to justify in the eyes of humans? It is highly plausible that Jehu's reign raises such an issue to the biblical historian because it is difficult for such a scholar to explain usurpations in general and Jehu's abuses in particular.

Nebuchadnezzar

The third example of royal madness in the Bible is represented by the portrait of Nebuchadnezzar in the Book of Daniel. The metaphorical language therein is different from that employed in the cycle of Saul and the story of Jehu: it takes its sources from the Hebrew and Babylonian traditions, presenting everything from the perspective of the world predominant in the Hellenistic era, the time when the Book of Daniel was completed.[9]

From verse 4,16 we learn that:

> Let his heart be changed from man's, and let a beast's heart be given unto him; and let seven times pass over him (*liv'veh min-'enoša' yešannon u-levav heyvah ytyehiv leh*).

The heart in the Bible – *lev/levav* in Hebrew, *levav* in Aramaic – designates the seat of *reason* and *will*, sometimes even of *emotions*. In this way, by losing his "heart of man," Nebuchadnezzar loses his faculties of judgment and discernment. Nevertheless the author is not content with simply depriving him of his "heart" thanks to an expression like *hasar lev* – lit. "lack of heart,"[10] a familiar term in the *Proverbs*. He does not allow emptiness to take possession of Nebuchadnezzar, but assigns "a heart of a beast" to the king, thereby giving a concrete form to madness. What follows in the economy of the story is the description of royal behavior in the grip of this new heart:

> That they shall drive thee from men, and thy dwelling shall be with the beasts of the field, and they shall make thee to eat grass as oxen, and they shall wet thee with the dew of heaven, and seven times shall pass over thee, till thou know that the most High ruleth in the kingdom of men, and giveth it to whomsoever he will.
>
> (4,25)

> The same hour was the thing fulfilled upon Nebuchadnezzar: and he was driven from men, and did eat grass as oxen, and his body was wet with the dew of heaven, till his hairs were grown like eagles' feathers, and his nails like birds' claws.
>
> (4,33)

Man is transformed into a beast. The medical lingo has already catalogued this type of behavior under the name of *lycanthropy*. The stakes are far higher, though. The content of Nebuchadnezzar's madness is not chosen at random, but responds to criteria of anthropological conception circumscribed to a specific era and civilization. In fact, following the author, Nebuchadnezzar's madness is "Jewish" and not "Babylonian", and so is the topic at hand. Yet the inspiration for the "literary motif" representing this madness can be found in the life of the Babylonian king Nabonidus, one whose politics and religious preferences have baffled a number of his contemporaries. One

25

document from the priests of Marduk known as the *Nabonidus Verse Account* does not hesitate from proffering *the king is mad* (IV,5), since the king had forsaken his capital, Babylon, ten years before and had taken refuge in Arabia (at Têmâ, according to *The Chronicle of Nabonidus*). This made impossible the celebration of the New Year which demanded the presence of the king. *The Chronicle* records this annual absence of the king, by noting: "The king is at Têmâ; the New Year festival was not held." Another discovery in Qumran shows the manner in which Nabonidus's biography has propagated itself in time and space, becoming a genuine legend. This is *The Prayer of Nabonidus* (4Q242) which recounts how Nabonidus went into solitary confinement because of his disease (*bšhn' by'š'*), how he asked for God's help because he couldn't find a cure, and how the latter aided him by sending out a Jewish *gzyr*.[11]

The Nebuchadnezzar from the Book of Daniel is at the crossroads of these images. His character is built on the basis of a Babylonian literary canon and proves to be extremely prolific: that is how a rich exegesis based on the Book of Daniel will emerge.

If the first transfer of images above is carried out by drawing upon a mass of historical memories and literary motifs, the second transfer of Nebuchadnezzar towards Antiochus IV Epiphanes is suggested by allusions. The structure of the Book of Daniel in its entirety and the choice of layout for each chapter are the means used in order to give rise to this new image. The presumed author of the Book of Daniel has primarily achieved these aims by the juxtaposition of the part dedicated to Nebuchadnezzar – Daniel A – with that dedicated to views announcing the end of the Greek kingdom – Daniel B.

The historical thread linking Nebuchadnezzar to Antiochus IV is their shared discriminatory attitude towards the Jewish religion. The former literally destroys his place of worship, the Temple of Jerusalem, the latter dedicates it to another divinity. Their actions have similar consequences; the destruction of a religious practice and, by that, of a whole identity. The "destructive" component is associated in these two cases to the "deification of the king" component, one that Jews interpreted as an instance of "self-deification." Here we once again witness a game of images in which the Other (Babylonian) is perceived according to one's own (Jewish) categories. In fact the transfer in this case goes in the opposite direction, from Antiochus to Nebuchadnezzar, with the former genuinely worshipped in contrast to the latter. It is in the Book of Daniel that the Babylonian king is drawn in this light and is the subject of such a satire. In the Babylonian royal ideology, the king is the "messenger" of gods and he benefits from their protection but, unlike the case of Egypt, he is not a god himself.[12] Following the Jewish approach, the common point between Nebuchadnezzar of Daniel, revised after the traits of Nabonidus, and Antiochus IV, the unnamed but hinted-at king from the same book, is not only represented by their having "destroyed" the Temple. This gesture is completely incomprehensible from the point of view of Jewish monotheism; hence they can only explain it as madness. As we have already noted, Daniel relies a lot on allusions and *implicit* references: just as the name of Antiochus is never mentioned in the book, the term "mad" is never employed in section Daniel B. The term is employed, however, by other early authors such as Polybius and Diodorus who transmit to us, by also relying on irony, the change of *Epiphanes* into *Epimanes* – "the Mad." There is thus a similarity between the meaning conveyed by the complex literary conceits of Daniel and by Greek sources.

The madness of prophets

Anthropologists draw our attention to how each society distinguishes between the mad person and the religious pundit.[13] By this, they mean to avoid the confusion that Westerners usually have in this respect given the resemblance in their behavior. In point of biblical data, we need to follow the reverse path. Verses 2 Kings 9,11; Jeremiah 29,26 and Hosea 9,7 clearly show that the designation "mad" – *mešugga'* – applies to the prophet – *navi'* – and this goes beyond the simple framework of derision. What are the elements that have paved the way for such similarities? If in Jeremiah the verse allows us to understand madness as an accusation inside a prophetic conflict, and if in Hosea this comes up as a punishment for the behavior of an entire people, in 2 Kings the relative synonymy presented above is omnipresent: the prophet is called "mad" on simply being seen, even before he has delivered his speech. This situation strangely resembles that of the Akkadian *muhhum* present in Mari's tablets. The *Ritual of Ištar*, for instance, draws our attention to the fact that when in a "state of equilibrium," the *muhhum* cannot exercise his function (*Archives Epistolaires de Mari*[14] I/1, no. 222: *Ritual of Ištar* ii 21ss). These crises of "prophetic madness" also display a number of particular characteristics which do not belong to the class of the *muhhi*, such being the case of Šelebum (*Archives Epistolaires de Mari* I/1, no. 232) and of Ahatum, the daughter of Dagan-Malik (*Archives Epistolaires de Mari* I/1, no. 214). The same association between *muhhum* (ass. *mahhu*) and the mad person, *zabbu*, can be found in Assyrian texts.[15]

Under the circumstances, the question to address no longer concerns avoiding a linguistic trap and, by that, a socio-anthropological blunder, but it revolves around the attempt to understand the motivations for such a "confusion" of terms with which the sources themselves operate.

Nevertheless, biblical scholars have not shied away from putting forth all sorts of hypotheses in this respect. Taking cues from the explanations offered by other disciplines such as anthropology, sociology and even ethno-psychiatry, biblical scholars early on associated "the madness of prophets" to the notions of trance, possession and ecstasy. Peter Michaelsen has made an inventory of all these different approaches,[16] one which can be used for an analysis and systemization of the various explanatory devices found around the notions of ecstasy and possession. A similar endeavor was carried out by Robert R. Wilson in the introduction to his article, "Prophecy and Ecstasy: A Reexamination",[17] in which he explicitly presents the epistemological bases of this conceptual transfer: "A person who is in a state of trance can put forth a behavior that superficially resembles the symptoms of a disease" (p. 328). Thus by virtue of the fact that the symptomatology of the trance – be it a trance of possession or a trance of ecstasy – resembles, in the eyes of many observers, the symptomatology of madness, biblical scholars consider they are right to assert the truth of reverse reasoning: given this, the term "mad" has been interpreted as referring to the state of trance.

Certain biblical descriptions invite associations with the "initiation disease" of the shaman. Ethnographers have described the shaman's first contact with the "world of spirits" as a traumatic event, a series of troubles later associated with various psychical diseases.[18] These comprise exuberant gesticulations, the appearance of scum around one's lips, deformations in one's tone of voice, catalepsy, and body shaking.[19] Scholars have often tried to find out if the shaman is a "cured mad person," a normal being who adopts an extravagant type of behavior, a representative of the elite whose charisma is made up of exceptional attitudes, and to see if this pathological behavior attracts collective adherence. In a number of circumstances, the prophets express the suffering they underwent on the occasion of the encounter with divinity. At the moment of delivering their oracles or concluding a "symbolic act," their bodies often fall prey to strange sensations. See, for example, Isaiah 21,3–4, and Jeremiah 4,19; 20,7–9; 23,9.

A second revelatory element is represented by the expression "the hand of YHWH."[20] We can find it in several biblical contexts, always associated with prophetic activities. Thus, in 1 Kings 18,46 Eli sports an extraordinary level of physical resistance, by running continuously for a very long distance. The case of Elisha is completely different: we no longer witness an out-of-the-ordinary physical prowess, but a divine oracle. Thus, "the hand of YHWH" becomes a consequence of music, and the oracle, the consequence of "the hand of YHWH" (2 Kings 3,15). The same effect of the transmission of a divine oracle takes place in Isaiah (8,11) and in Jeremiah (15,17). Overall, the prophet Ezekiel is the one most often grasped by "the hand of YHWH." The effects coming out of this situation are multiple: the gift of vision (Ezekiel 1,2–4; 8,1–2), oracle (3,22), transport and ubiquity (3,14; 8,1–3; 37,1). Ezekiel lives through a mitigated experience. On the one hand, his story transmits a sense of pain and suffering: *ve-'elekh mar be-hamat ruhi* (3,14). On the other hand, and in contrast to the former situation, "the hand of YHWH" soothes and cures him of the disease (33,22).

There are numerous prophetic acts to consider and it would take an entire separate study to attempt their exhaustive analysis, especially since this is a new topic. Georg Fohrer has already offered a literary study, and Samuel Amsler has revisited the question from the perspective of the theory of communication.[21] Following these latter scholars, these prophetic acts represent a *means of communication aimed to unblock the dialogue between God and his people, if this is possible* (p. 217). I will argue that, contrary to this position, the examples I analyze in what follows suggest the presence of a gap in communication by means of the facts and gestures they put forth. The cases in which these prophetic acts are explicitly problematic for the audience and in which they clearly identify an anomaly are not that numerous: they can be primarily found in Ezekiel 24; Isaiah 20; and Jeremiah 20, therefore it is not difficult for us to investigate their possible connections to madness. Ezekiel's experiences have been most intriguing for researchers, and the assessment of his personality has resulted in several possible medical interpretations,[22] and his acts have often stunned the audience. In Chapter 24, for instance, he is ordered not to wear mourning clothes for his daughter, but to adopt the everyday garb and attitude. This inevitably gives rise to the following question:

> And the people said unto me, Wilt thou not tell us what these things are to us, that thou doest so?
>
> (Ezekiel 24,19)

His message here is hermetic. Do the people at least know that this is an omen? This is a difficult question, one with a complex answer. The interest we have vested in him and the authority we eventually recognize in him results from the fact that we expect the prophet to explain the sense of his behavior. But the fact that the oracle pronounced as an answer asserts: "Thus Ezekiel is unto you a sign (mophet)" (24,24), gives the impression that the audience has not grasped the symbolical scope of his gesture. The prophet is an *omen*, a presage: the Bible states this several times: Ezekiel 4,3; 12,6; 12,11; Isaiah 8,18; 20,3. His gestures of divine inspiration are often bizarre, they leave room for doubts and run counter to social conventions. In a traditional society, the failure to perform the mourning rituals, or any type of ritual, is considered abnormal. The nudity sported by Isaiah for three years equally belongs to the same category of socially intolerable actions and gestures (Isaiah 20,4). In a different context, another prophet, Jeremiah, describes to us the attitude of rejection and mockery to which he fell prey (Jeremiah 20,7–8).

The prophet is not just the messenger of divine orders contained in his oracles; his own life is a parable. This parable sometimes borrows tortuous paths that are hard to express; from time to time it puts forth a bizarre plot. We have already mentioned, in this sense, the surprise that arose for the previously examined gestures of prophets Ezekiel, Isaiah, and Jeremiah. This sense of surprise does not result from a judgment of value identical with the strangeness of their actions. On the other hand, the condition of "being strange," which a prophet must assume, is a difficult one, placing him in a tight spot on two levels: that of his relations with the environment in which he lives; and that of his interior, private sense of an extraordinary experience. In order to accomplish his mission, the prophet has to deviate. He must transgress social conventions and let the community reject him. This vocabulary of rupture chosen by God in order to communicate with his people is a source of surprise. That is so because it gives rise to a blockage in the act of transmitting and understanding the divine message. And the prophet, the very person destined to ensure a bridge of communication between the human and the divine, is paradoxically constrained to fail, the grammar of his behavior not being accessible. God's vocabulary proves to be strange and unknown for human beings and we find a confirmation of this in Isaiah:

> For the Lord shall rise up as in mount Perazim, he shall be wroth as in the valley of Gibeon, that he may do his work, his strange work (*zar ma'asehu*); and bring to pass his act, his strange act (*nokhriah 'avodato*).
>
> (Isaiah 28,21)

The two adjectives characterizing God's oeuvre, *zar* and *nokhriah*, first of all mean "strange," and it is with this meaning that they appear in most biblical contexts. "Strange" and "stranger" are two joint notions so it is not surprising that they are expressed by one and the same root. Isaiah pinpoints here a fundamental tenet of biblical theology: God is different from humans, his oeuvre and language are distinct, his signs can be unintelligible.

How is it possible, then, that he who is "different from man" can make the latter understand truths which are by nature "strange?" For this, God must necessarily render himself intelligible to man and he can only do this by using language. On the other hand, however, if the language used by God is exclusively human, how can it be possible that He reveals Himself in His alterity? It follows that some "divine" substance, something which is different, unexpected, strange lies at the core of the divine discourse and can have a signification to be understood by men. Here, the "strange" behavior irrupts in the world under the guise of madness, a "deviant" behavior of God meant to make of his messenger an "omen." Human beings do not recognize this

29

sign. Should they be held accountable for this? The fault of human beings might well be that they trust appearances, they do not worry about a possible hidden meaning of things, and they do not value alterity. Or the mad person proves to be "different" and bizarre given his "difference" and following all sorts of reasons springing from the contingent context.

Deuteronomy: blindness, madness and loss of identity

The only two mentions of the root *šg'* from the Pentateuch appear in Deuteronomy 28. They are part of a collection of maledictions which are doubly part of an apodosis whose main feature is madness – *šigga'on*:

> But it shall come to pass, if thou wilt not hearken unto the voice of the LORD thy God, to observe to do all his commandments and his statutes which I command thee this day; that all these curses shall come upon thee, and overtake thee (28,15). [. . .]The LORD shall smite thee with madness (*šigga'on*), and blindness, and astonishment of heart (28,28). [. . .] So that thou shalt be mad for the sight of thine eyes which thou shalt see. (*ve-hayita mešugga'*)
>
> (28,34)

Built upon the model of the political treatises of the Near East, Chapter 28 from Deuteronomy draws up an alliance by means of a series of maledictions. The transgression of the terms of this alliance will be sanctioned without delay by the advent of misfortunes which run the gambit from body afflictions represented by various types of diseases to national consequences including defeat and deportation.

Let us first note the disposition of the three forms of punishment, *madness* (*šigga'on*), *blindness* (*'ivvaron*), and *confusion* (*timhon levav*) (Deuteronomy 28,28) by closely considering the burdens of skin lesions (28,27) and then focus on servitude and the absence of any possibility of being saved (28,29). The first sequence refers to physical afflictions, the second mixes troubles of the spirit with blindness, while the third sequence identifies social dysfunctionalities: "medical" and "social" aspects are melted in a single whole. In its second occurrence (28,34) the triad madness–skin disease–submission to the enemy returns in reverse order:

> Thou shalt be only oppressed and crushed (*'ašuq ve-ratzutz*) always so that thou shalt be mad (*mešugga'*) for the sight of thine eyes which thou shalt see. The Lord shall smite thee in the knees, and in the legs, with a sore botch (*šehin ra'*) that cannot be healed, from the sole of thy foot unto the top of thy head.
>
> (28,33–35)

This is not simply the case of a reversed order; this is primarily an essential change in the relation between sight and madness. Blindness and madness no longer stand on the same level, they are no longer seen as equivalent to a certain degree, but their relation is one of causality: the landscape one has in front of one's eyes and the sight of desolation – these are the elements that render a human being mad. What henceforth leads to madness is the atrocity of becoming aware of one's situation rather than darkness, which used to previously be the metaphor for anomie and for the loss of vital reflexes.

Deuteronomy thus brings forth a double perspective on madness: an absent perception of reality, signified by the loss of sight, but also the "too whole" real, an unforgiving truth that the human being cannot integrate and which he instinctively represses by taking refuge in madness. It might be interesting to link this to the nature of punishments provoking the state of desolation. As we have previously noted, these divine sanctions target the dismantling of one's identity: diseases and enemies do nothing else than destroy Israel in its physical and "national" constitution. In this case, "what the eyes will see" is a "void," a non-sense: the individual passes through the unbearable experience of perceiving his dissolution and falls into an unescapable madness.

The history of madness in early Jewish culture comprises a major hiatus in what concerns the treatment of Hellenistic sources such as the manuscripts of Qumran, pseudo-epigraphs, and Philo. Some fragments from Qumran prolong the act of biblical reflection: one of them underlines the prophetic and healing gift of David,[23] another cites Deuteronomy 28,28 in a liturgical text, *Words of the Luminaries*; yet another, the *Prayer of Nabonidus*, mentions the disease of the Babylonian king and the sage Danel.[24] A global approach should take into consideration the books of wisdom from Qumran and the pseudo-epigraphs in general.

The very lengthy oeuvre of Philo has not made the object of a study targeting madness, the interest of researchers having especially fallen on the philosophy of the intellect and of the cognitive faculties extant in the approach of this Jewish thinker, an approach strongly imbued with Greek culture. Nevertheless, we can retain certain elements from Philo's understanding of madness and observe its thematic continuity with the Bible since we can find it in the political field and in the field of divine knowledge.[25] On the one hand, Philo develops the critique of a mad leader (Gaius, for example) and, on the other hand, he develops the critique of the revolt of the masses which he also qualifies as madness because this attitude destroys the greatest public good, namely order (*Vita Mosis* [On the Life of Moses] ii 161).[26] In another register, the rebellion of those mad takes up the contours of *hybris* in the episode from the Tower of Babel, which is also qualified as a case of madness: "this was a tower that the eager people of the times built out of dementia as well as out of a mad desire for greatness, for reaching the sky (ὑπ' ἀνοίας ἅμα καὶ μεγαλαυχίας οὐρανοῦ ψαῦσαι). Every alienation of mind, then, is grievous (πῶς γὰρ οὐ φρενοβλάβεια δεινή)" (*De confusione linguarum* [On the Confusion of Tongues] 5). Madness is also considered to be a form of voluntary evil (*De confusione linguarum* 21)[27] or a crime, as in the case of Cain whose forehead sign can be explained by the fact that "madness is an immortal evil" (*Quaestiones et Solutiones in Genesin* [Questions and Answers in Genesis] 178).[28] Finally, mystical ecstasy is interpreted as a madness of divine inspiration since this was the way in which Philo understood the expression associated with Abraham in Genesis 15.12 ("about sunset there fell on him an ecstasy") this way:

> He refers to our mind under the symbol "sun". [. . .] So long as the mind surrounds us with its illumination, pouring fourth as it were a noon time beam into the whole soul, we remain in ourselves and are not possessed. But when it comes to its setting there falls upon us in all likelihood an ecstasy, a divine possession, a madness (καὶ ἡ ἔνθεος ἐπιπίπτει κατοκωχή τε καὶ μανία).
> (*Quis Rerum Divinarum Haeres Sit* [Who is the Heir of Divine Things] 263–265)[29]

In spite of bibliographic mishaps, one can notice that the Judeo-Hellenistic textual corpus shows a thematic continuity with the Bible in its treatment of madness, in particular to the use of the themes of monarchy and power, prophecy, and sin. Only at the end of the Roman period and especially during the Byzantine era can one note a change of perspective. The following section tackles this very change.

Late antiquity: Halacha and Aggada

The vocabulary of mental incompetence in the Halacha

During the Roman period,[30] the Jewish representation of madness undergoes some partial evolution. Apart from the fact that the lexicon of madness changes and the Biblical vocabulary, albeit not disappearing, is completely marginalized, we should first note another novelty that appears at this time, namely the legal character of texts which stands out against the narrative genre or speculative character of the texts of the Bible or of Philo. The nature of sources decisively influences the nature of the information put forth, and this occurs in one of two ways. On the one hand, the corpus constituted by the Mishna and the Gemara, as *halachic* texts, understands madness from a legal perspective and focuses on the question of individual responsibility and accountability for one's actions. On the other hand, the manner of construction of these texts, their rationality and architecture, asks for a specific grid of perusal. In fact, the omnipresence of case law, the abundant and apparently non-referential questioning, the elliptic style and the definitions based on criteria that might appear unrepresentative, all these are the traits of rabbinical texts and especially of the Talmud, all of them demanding high effort for analysis. In order to propose a valid interpretation of such texts, one needs to undertake two endeavors: to dig inside the text beyond its literal meaning and practice a certain form of comparison which permits one to situate these documents in their historical context, at the crossroads of the Roman, Babylonian and Persian cultures. Let us also note a major methodological difficulty in front of us, namely the lack of critical editions for most of the treatises of the Babylonian Talmud, which represents our main source.

I will therefore not start from the vocabulary in these texts but from the situations they describe, especially those which foreground the legal category of accountability for one's actions or its opposite, irresponsibility. In this sense, the rabbinical law several times mentions the conditions for the validity of a ritual (i.e. to offer sacrifice), a commandment (i.e. to read the weekly portion of the Torah), or a legal act (i.e. the document for divorce), by indicating the categories of people who are excluded or exempted from this. We therefore learn that, in most cases, those who make the object of these limitations are the *šoteh*, the *hereš* and the *qatan*. If each of these terms should be understood differently, there is something that unites these three categories of people, namely their lack of intelligence – *daat, deia, mahševa*. On the contrary, the individual capable of accomplishing the ritual duties and of drawing up all the documents with legal value must be *piqeah*, "sound, sensed, in full possession of mental capacities." The rabbinical thought establishes cognition and sound mental faculties as the decisive criteria for defining law.[31]

If the *qatan* generally designates the "minor child," the one who is not yet 12 years old for a girl and 13 years old for a boy, the designations of *hereš* and especially *šoteh* are more complex and uncertain.

In ordinary language, the term *hereš* means "deaf," but in the legal vocabulary it seems to refer to the "deaf-and-dumb," the one who lacks both the use of hearing and sight. Even the Talmud feels the need to specify this distinction (Hagiga 2ab, Meguilla 19b, Hullin 2a) by asserting that each time the law mentions this triad, the term *hereš* must be understood as referring to the deaf-and-dumb. In anthropological terms, this is a novelty in comparison to biblical texts which considered that the organ of judgment was represented by sight and not hearing, as we have already shown. Consequently, for them, blindness not deafness represented the metaphor for and the equivalent of madness. I believe that this major conceptual change can be explained by the partial adoption of another view of man, the one that is expressed by Aristotle's thinking; according to this new view, the ear is in direct relation to the level of a person's intelligence. The person who is deaf by birth and, by that, incapable of articulating sounds does not possess the capacity to use language and symbols, therefore his human status is diminished.[32] It is hard to ascertain if this conception of the human being which is new to Judaism simply represents an elite type of appropriation or does not actually constitute the opinion commonly shared by the Jewish people.

As to the *šoteh*, this term is understood in the entire Jewish tradition as identifying the mad person. A rabbinical text dating from the eighth or the ninth century, *The Alphabet of Ben Sira* 28, indiscriminately uses both *mešugga'* and *šoteh* to refer to the biblical episode of King Jehu. A few centuries later, in his commentary of the Talmud, Rashi feels the need to specify the meaning of the Talmud terms he uses and once again gives *mešugga'* and *šigga'on* as equivalents. Their synonymy seems to be a fait accompli. The root *šaga'* is absent from the literature of the Tannaim and Amoraim and the lexical change to the benefit of the root *šatah* stands out and deserves attention. The distinction between foolishness and madness does not seem to be excessively lexicalized, leaving room for a monotonous image of the states of mental incapacity. Apart from the pressure exercised by Aramaic and Aramaisms, the above-presented idea can represent one of the explanations for this change of vocabulary.

Despite the importance that the Talmud vests in differentiating between the gesture that matters and the gesture that does not matter, between the accomplished and non-accomplished ritual, there is just one single passage which takes up the task of offering a definition of this so-called *šoteh* category of incompetent people, as seen from the point of view of the Halacha. This passage is Hagiga 2a-4a, it is a central text in the sense that it will serve as basis for all future debates regarding diagnosis and verdicts, attributes vested only in the *beit din*, the rabbinical court. At a first glance, the criteria that it poses do not appear pertinent or sufficient for defining and recognizing the mental incompetence that results in severe if not complete legal and ritual incapacity. Thus, a good understanding of this passage involves becoming aware of the non-said, the elliptic style of the rabbis, an endeavor which will allow us to trace the text's broad cultural hypotheses. The rabbis are less interested in defining the *šoteh* than in recognizing it – since they repeatedly assert such a person's lack of intelligence, *daat/deia*, or capacity for thought, *mahševa*. To that end, they at first enumerate three major criteria for recognizing the *šoteh* within a Hebrew phrase attributed to the sages of the first two centuries before the common era – *baraitha*.

> The rabbis taught: What is called an insane/fool (*šoteh*)? He who goes out alone in the night, and who sleeps in a cemetery, and who tears the clothes he wears.

(Hagiga 3b)

These criteria are not specific enough and consequently they are not sufficient enough with which to operate. Both the Babylonian and Palestinian Amoraim were brought to explain and interpret these assertions. The first point to elucidate involves understanding if the three above-noted signs from the *baraitha* should be counted together or whether one of them is enough. Following the specific rhetoric of the Talmud, the editor of this passage involves the reader in the complex paths of the demonstration. We therefore learn that tradition has conserved two divergent opinions: that of the Babylonian Amora of the fourth century – Rav Huna – and that of the Palestinian Amora of the third century – Rabbi Yohanan: according to Rav Huna, the decision must be based on observing the unity of the three acts, while for Rabbi Yohanan one single act of the three is enough. How can one decide which interpretation to follow? The editor proceeds with his demonstration by alternating realist and nominalist positions. He starts by the realist position: if the three acts are drawn up out of madness (*derekh štut*), then one of them is enough to qualify someone as mad/*šoteh*; if the same acts are not drawn up out of madness (*derekh štut*), then even if all of them are accomplished, this does not qualify one as mad. Permanently challenged by legal realism which takes up the position of devil's advocate, the rabbinical doctrine almost always finishes by taking up the nominalist stance. That is also the case here because realism is counterbalanced by the enunciation of the following principle: if the three acts are vouched for, this must always be understood as the result of madness (*derekh štut*). Nominalism prevails in the end, but the theoretical debate highlights a delicate epistemological aspect in the understanding of madness: the signs are commonplace, hence relative, since they are likely to give rise to ambivalences. The rabbis of the Talmud are completely aware of this human fragility as far as knowledge goes. They therefore establish some safeguards in their own way meaning multiplication of formal barriers instead of deepening enquiry about reality. In this way, in order to establish the principle of the association of the three signs and its value as uncontestable proof of legal irresponsibility, they draw an analogy between the biblical law about the animal attacking the other animals and the rabbinical halacha concerned with designating who qualifies as mad. It is interesting to learn at first to what type of madness each one of the three signs corresponds:

> The one who sleeps in cemetery, means that he wants the spirit of impurity (*ruah tumah*) to lean upon him; the one who walks alone in the night means that the *gandripos* seized him; the one who tears his clothes means that he is lost in his thoughts (therefore he does not realize what he is doing).

(Hagiga 3b)

Ruah tumah designates the inspiration which does not come from sacred sources, but is idolatrous (v. Sanhedrin 65b), in opposition to the prophetic inspiration induced by one possessing the spirit of a saint or the spirit of God. The word *gandripos* is a corrupted calque of the Greek terms *kynanthropos* or *lycanthropos*, and it designates the

34

human being who thinks he is a wolf or a dog and passes his nights around tombstones.[33] This second sign can be easily related to the first one. In spite of possible biblical ante-cedents of the figure of the lycanthrope (Nebuchadnezzar), it seems more plausible to detect here another borrowing from the Roman-Greek culture. Finally, the third sign, the tearing of clothes, is accounted for by a degree of concentration of thought that makes decency forgotten. Each case of equivalence indicates a form of self-loss (idolatry and possession, lycanthropy and, following *coincidentia oppositorum*, excessive concentra-tion of thought), but when taken separately, no such case can constitute a legal proof. It is only the combination of the three that can stand as proof given formal analogic rea-sons and rabbinical rhetoric. In fact, the Halacha often requires the multiplication of proofs, usually by threes, in order to settle upon a decision. The same type of procedure is applied in this case too, on the basis of the biblical passage concerning the harms and damages caused by animals:

> When he does all these things, he is like an ox goring another ox, a camel, and an ass, after which he is considered vicious as to all creatures (*muad la-kol*).[34]

In the same manner the three inappropriate acts which are different in nature and indicate each, on its own, a particular form of madness lead to the conclusion that the individual in question must be seen as acting out of madness in all circum-stances and declared *šoteh*, i.e. legally irresponsible and exempt from executing any commandment.

The above excerpt from the Hagiga concludes on a humorous note. The opinion of Rav Huna prevailing over that of Rabbi Yohanan, the act of ignoring the first sign of madness may lead to catastrophe, an anxiety expressed by the Talmud in an imaginary way:

> Said R. Papa:[35] If R. Huna had heard the following boraitha, which states, "Who is a fool? When he destroys all things that are given to him", he would have retracted his decree.
>
> (Hagiga 4a)

Beyond the attempt to offer a semiological definition, what we retain from the above passage is the distinction it carries out between self-madness (*derekh štut*) and the legal category of the mad person (*šoteh*). What ensues from here is the central idea according to which legal irresponsibility cannot be confounded with cognitive distur-bance even if it is induced by it. The implementation of this precept during the very period of the writing of the texts is still unknown to us, but the post-Talmud Halachic literature takes possession of it in order to establish its own decisions especially in what concerns marriage and divorce. As to the Talmud, it multiplies the number of prohibitions concerning the *šoteh* but it simultaneously specifies the situations for which one is not constrained to accomplish the commandments. There is no exhaus-tive study of such Talmudic prohibitions placed and analyzed in the context of Late Antiquity, yet, we have the more or less complete lists of these in the articles linking Jewish tradition with modern medicine. Not being in a position to establish a rela-tion of causality between actions and their consequences, the *šoteh* is exempt from punishment in case of harm done to others or an animal. He does not have any more consciousness about what belongs to him and thus he cannot get involved in commercial transactions; moreover, the *beit din* can administer his goods so he can upkeep his wife and children to the best of his abilities by offering *tsedakah* on his behalf since, by that, he can benefit from his positive decline. Furthermore, the *šoteh* is not entitled to carry out commandments in the name of the community, by blowing the shofar, for instance. He is not entitled to conclude a marriage or a *halitza*, but he can conclude a Leviratic marriage.

With the rabbinical court as the only instance entitled to give a diagnosis, the Talmudic precepts have been persistently updated. We have at our disposal responsa concerning the *šoteh* and theoretical considerations due to important thinkers such as Maimonides or, in the twentieth century, Rabbi Moshe Feinstein. This area nevertheless remains largely unexplored and the analyses to date are partial, with the exception of two works. One is the recent study by Ephraim Shoham-Steiner[36] focusing on the issue of marginality in the Jewish society of the European Middle Ages and dedicating one chapter to the *šoteh*. The other text is the study of Samuel Wolfman[37] on the issue of divorce, in which he reviews the set of rabbinic regulations as to incompetence preventing one to marry, the obligation to divorce one's wife and the legal status of a wife who becomes insane.

The literature on this issue also comprises a category of articles and studies which treat together medieval, modern, or contemporary responsa and transpose their vocabulary into that of present-day medicine. Below is an example extracted from Rael Strous, "Halachic Sensitivity to the Psychotic Individual: the *Shoteh*."[38] For starters, here the three categories of mad people are homogeneous neither from a chronological nor a textual point of view: some of them are Talmudic in origin, others appeared later. What is even more interesting, the author relates each one of these categories to the contemporary classification of diseases:

1. *šoteh* gamur[39] (completely insane): perhaps best illustrated by the chronic schizophrenic patient, whose prognosis remains poor and whose baseline functioning is seldom regained.

2. *šoteh* who exhibits 'itim halim 'itim *šoteh*[40] (who cycles in and out of psychosis): for example, the manic depressive, or bipolar, patient, for whom the prognosis is generally good and who may be considered sane and competent when not cycling in the psychotic state.

3. *šoteh* le-davar ehad (who is insane in only one domain, remaining sane and coherent in all others): as seen in the contemporary delusional disorder, in which there is a fixed manifestation of non-bizarre delusions involving situations that may occur in real life, such as being followed, poisoned, infected, deceived, diseased, etc. This individual, despite remaining psychotic in a specific area, may be adjudged competent to engage in certain other domains of responsibility and obligation which would otherwise remain off limits to other *šotim*.

The above-identified correspondence is not the only one, other such forms of equivalence are possible and practised following the model of the Halacha which is not unique nor does it have universal value. The Jewish tradition remains an important fact that many contemporary practitioners integrate in their reflections and protocols. A number of institutions and publications have as their goal reconciling the Torah with science, including the journals *Assia* and *Torah u-Mada*, Tzomet Institute, and Shaarei Tzedek Hospital.

The vocabulary of mental incompetence in the Aggada

The rabbinical vocabulary signaling mental incompetence and cognitive retardation is not resumed in the case of the *šoteh*. This one appears as a technical term, an integral part of the legal jargon. On the other hand, the texts of the Aggada and Midrash use terms such as *teruph da'at*, *miša'amum*, *tipeš*, *nirdaph al yadei ruah ra'ah*, *tunba'*. We also note the poor lexicalization of the distinction between "madness" and "stupidity" denoted by the term *miša'amum* or by the expression *teruph da'at*. Otherwise, Aggada passages put forth an understanding of madness and man closer to those that were previously included in the Bible. I will provide in what follows a number of examples in support of these assertions.

The biblical topos of madness as punishment clearly stands out from a Talmudic excerpt interpreting Deuteronomy16.19: *For a gift doth blind the eyes of the wise and pervert the words of the righteous*:

> Our Rabbis taught: *For a gift doth blind the eyes of the wise* (Dt 16.19) and much more so those of the foolish (*tipšin*); *And pervert the words of the righteous* (*tzaddikim*), and much more so those of the wicked (*reša'im*).
>
> Are then fools and wicked men (*tipšim ve-reša'im*) capable of acting as judges (*bnei dina*)? — But it is this that is meant: *'For a gift doth blind the eyes of the wise,'* even a great Sage who takes bribes will not depart from the world without [the affliction of] a dullness of the mind (*smiut ha-lev*), *'And pervert the words of the righteous,'* even one who is righteous in every respect and takes bribes will not depart from this world without [the affliction of] confusion of mind (*teruph da'at*).
>
> (Ketubot 105ab)

The faithfulness to biblical anthropology is wonderfully highlighted in this case. Created by using chiasmus, just like Deuteronomy 28,28–34, this midrash considers blindness and madness and designates the heart as the siege of understanding, close to the case of many biblical verses.

Another rabbinic tradition, attributed to Mar Samuel, evokes a close kinship with the mental universe of Deuteronomy:

> Scabs (*'arbubita*) of the head lead to blindness (*'avira*); scabs (*'arbubita*) of garments cause madness (*ša'amumita*); scabs (*'arbubita*) of the body cause boils and ulcers.
>
> (Nedarim 81a)

Not only the visual metaphor but also the epidermic metaphor is associated with madness. As we have already seen, Deuteronomy 28,28 borrows from Babylonian cosmology and anthropology, which can also be the situation at hand here if we take into consideration the attribution of this tradition to the Babylonian Amora of the third century, Mar Samuel.[41]

In a sense close to that of irresponsibility we find the term *tunba'*, coming from the root *tanav*, "to be rigid," usually translated by *stupor*. The goals of such a person cannot be taken into consideration: they are not trustworthy, as the person is not really his or her normal self. To give an example, such is the case of the woman that does not feel the pain of her menses, while the "work" inside her body has not ceased or it is expected not to have ceased (Nidda 37b). Or, in the Halacha, it is important to respect the duration of a woman's impurity, one which takes into consideration not only her visible loss of blood, but also the imminent one whose foreshadowing sign is pain.

In another context, the state of unconsciousness is invoked so as to protect the patient from herself and in order to render concrete the principle of the preeminence of life. Thus, when a patient refuses to eat despite the physician's advice, the opinion of the latter prevails since, seized by *tunba'*, the patient does not have the capacity to interpret the signals of her body and to translate them in rational and responsible ways (Yoma 83a). This form of incapacity seems temporary and related to corporeal insensibility to pain, one leading to disqualification.

Following the traditional way of Midrash Aggada, the rabbinic literature also proposes a philosophical meditation on madness. In its ancient version, this reflection can be found in the collection *Midrash Tehillim* (or *Midrash Shoher Tov*) on Psalm 34, but it also appears in the *Alpha Beta de Ben Sira* 9, from the Gaonic era, and in the medieval work *Yalkut Shimoni* in 1 Sam 21, comment 131, dating from the thirteenth century. These midrashim link a verse of Qohelet – "He made everything beautiful in its proper time" – with an episode from the life of David in which he must escape Saul and feign madness. Wondering about the order and rationality of Creation, the anonymous commentator explains the raison d'être of madness as protection in front of the enemy. It is by taking up the traits of a derisory and ridiculous person that David can save himself from the philistine king of Gath.

Conclusion

The history of madness in the early Hebrew tradition belongs to the field of political, religious, and legal anthropology. Based upon the available literature, it cannot be studied from the perspective of medical anthropology or the history of medicine. That is the case because the problematic of the disease and of the cure only comes up secondarily, always circumscribed by the act of reflecting upon the issue of political or religious leadership or that of the social competence of the individual.

We can therefore notice a rupture happening around the first century of our era, indicating the passage from an understanding of man kindred to that revealed in Assyrian-Babylonian texts to one borrowing from Aristotle and, more broadly, Greek thought. The cognitive faculties, especially the act of thinking, are associated with the eye in the former instance and with the hearing in the latter case, therefore with one's speech depending upon the use of the mouth and the ears. The human being endowed with reason is a clairvoyant, in the former instance, and a person able to articulate sounds and thereby make sense, in the latter instance. Nourished by the continuous interpretation of texts, the Jewish tradition has modulated over the course of centuries textual ideas, in contemporary times going as far as negotiating the coexistence of Jewish law and modern science.

Notes

1 I express my deep gratitude to my colleagues Dana Mihailescu (University of Bucharest) who translated the text from French into English, and Agnes Woog (INALCO, Paris) for her reading and suggestions. Except when otherwise mentioned, the biblical quotations are from the King James Version and the Talmudic ones from the traditional Vilna edition.

2 F. Brown, S.R. Driver, C.A. Briggs, *A Hebrew and English Lexicon of the Old Testament* (Oxford: Clarendon Press, 1891–1905).

3 L. Koehler, W. Baumgartner, *Lexicon in Veteris Testamenti Libros* (Leiden: Brill, 1948ff).

4 L. Koehler, W. Baumgartner, J.J. Stamm, M.E.J. Richardson, *The Hebrew and Aramaic Lexicon of the Old Testament* (Leiden: Brill, 1994ff).

5 Victor Turner, *Schism and Continuity in an African Society: A Study of Ndembu Village Life* (Manchester: Manchester University Press, 1957) and W.J.T. Mitchell, "Social Dramas and Stories about Them" in *On Narrative* (Chicago: University of Chicago Press, 1981), 137–164.

6 For a comprehensive study on madness in the Hebrew Bible, see Madalina Vartejanu-Joubert, *Folie et société dans l'Israël antique* (Paris: L'Harmattan, 2004).

7 The same verb can be found in Joshua 6,18 in relation to another key term, *herem*: the Israelites are not authorized to take hold of the loot delivered to the *herem* as they would *attract misfortune on their country*.

8 This concept of "revelatory appearance" also manifests itself in the case of the bearer of bad news. See 2 Samuel 4,10.

9 According to Henze, we cannot speak of a single original but only of several variants of the same flux of traditions. See Mathias Henze, *The Madness of King Nebuchadnezzar. The Ancient Near Eastern Origins and Early History of Interpretation of Daniel 4* (Leiden, Boston, New York: Brill, 1999).

10 See, for example, Proverbs 6,32; 7,7; 9,4; 9,16, etc. This expression which appears twelve times in the Proverbs and once in the Qohelet is generally translated by "nonsense" or "lacking sense."

11 For the *Pamphlet* see S. Smith, *Babylonian Historical Texts: relating to the capture and downfall of Babylon* (London: Methuen & Co., 1924), 27–97 (*BHT*), or James B. Pritchard, ed., *Ancient Near Eastern Texts Related to the Old Testament* (Princeton: Princeton University Press, 1950), 312–315; Sylvie Lackenbacher, "Un pamphlet contre Nabonide, dernier roi de Babylone," *Dialogues d'Histoire Ancienne*, 18 (1992): 13–28. For the *Prayer* see J.T. Milik, "Prière de Nabonide et autres récits d'un cycle de Daniel. Fragments araméens de Q 4 (Pl. I)," *Revue Biblique*, 63 (1956): 407–415; Emile Puech, "La Prière de Nabonide (4Q242)" in *Targumic and Cognate Studies. Essays in Honour of Martin McNamara*, ed. Kevin J. Cathcart, M. Macher, (Sheffield: Sheffield Academic Press, 1996), 208–227. For *Nabonide's Chronicle* see S. Smith, *BHT*, ch. IV, 98–123.

12 In the works of Greek authors, his image was that of a great builder, a fact which impressed the Greek spirit to such a degree that they attributed to Nebuchadnezzar the achievements of Belus, the founding king of Babylon. Or the Greeks assimilated Belus to the image of a god. See Ronald H. Sack, "Nebuchadnezzar and Nabonidus in Folklore and History," *Mesopotamia*, 17 (1982): 67–131.

13 See, among others, I.M. Lewis, *Ecstatic Religion. An Anthropological Study of Spirit Possession and Shamanism* (Harmondsworth: Penguin, 1971); Erica Bourguignon, *Religion, Altered States of Consciousness and Social Change* (Columbus: Ohio State University Press, 1973) and *Psychological Anthropology* (Westport: Greenwood, 1994); Roberte Hamayon, "Du chaman au chamanisme," *L'Ethnographie*, 78 (1982): 13–48; Jean-Pierre Olivier de Sardan, "Possession, affliction et folie. Les ruses de la thérapisation," *L'Homme*, 34, 3 (1994): 7–27.

14 J.-M. Durand, *Archives épistolaires de Mari*, Partie I/1, coll. Archives Royales de Mari, vol. XXVI/1 (Paris: Editions du CNRS, 1988).

15 See Simo Parpola, *Assyrian Prophecies* (Helsinki: Helsinki University Press, 1997), XLV–XLIX; Martti Nissinen, *References to Prophecy in Neo-Assyrian Sources* (Helsinki: Neo-Assyrian Text Corpus Project, 1998), 55–56; Pierre Villard, "Les prophètes à l'époque néo-assyrienne" in *Prophètes et rois. Bible et Proche Orient*, ed. André Lemaire (Paris: Les éditions du Cerf, 2001), 55–84.

16 Peter Michaelsen, "Ecstasy and Possession in Ancient Israel. A Review of Some Recent Contributions," *Scandinavian Journal of the Old Testament*, 2 (1989): 28–54.

17 Robert R. Wilson, "Prophecy and Ecstasy: A Reexamination," *Journal of Biblical Literature*, 98 (1979): 320–337.

18 See the critical study by Philippe Mitrani, "Aperçu critique des approches psychiatriques du chamanisme," *L'Ethnographie*, 78 (1982): 241–257.

19 See Roberte Hamayon, "Des chamans au chamanisme," *L'Ethnographie*, 78 (1982): 13–48.

20 See the detailed analysis of J.J.M. Roberts, "The Hand of Yahweh," *Vetus Testamentum*, 21 (1971): 244–251.

21 Samuel Amsler, *Les actes des prophètes* (Geneva: Labor et Fides, 1985). A complete list of the passages of interest can be found on pp. 91–92.

22 Georg Fohrer, *Die Hauptprobleme des Buches Ezekiel* (Berlin: A. Töpelmann, 1952); Edwin Broome, "Ezekiel's Abnormal Personality," *Journal of Biblical Literature*, 65 (1946): 277–292; Bernhard Lang, *Ezekiel. Der Prophet und das Buch* (Darmstadt: Wissenschaftliche Buchgesellschaft, 1981), 57–76; David J. Halperin, *Seeking Ezekiel. Text and Psychology* (University Park: Pennsylvania State University, 1993).

23 Vartejanu-Joubert, *Op. cit.*, pp. 131–137.

24 Ibid., p. 157.

25 V. Ray Barraclough, "Philo's Politics: Roman Rule and Hellenistic Judaism" in *Aufstieg und Niedergang der römischen Welt. Geschichte und Kultur Rom sim Spiegel der neueren Forschung*, II.21.1, ed. H Temporini and W. Haase (Berlin and New York: Walter de Gruyter, 1984), 417–553; Richard Goulet, *La philosophie de Moïse: essai de reconstitution d'un commentaire pré-philonien du Pentateuque* (Paris: Vrin, 1987).

26 "the lower orders will never, no, nor will mad men (μανέντες) even, reject the customs and habits of their superiors" Cf. ii.164, 169. *De vita Mosis*, ed. L. Cohn, Philonis Alexandrini opera quae supersunt, vol. 4. Berlin: Reimer, 1902 (repr. De Gruyter, 1962), pp. 119–268. Philo Volume VI, Loeb Classical Library 289, tr. F.H. Colson, 1935. Cf. *De Praemiis et Poenis* [On Rewards and Punishments] 75–76.

27 τίς οὖν ἡ τῶν ἑκουσίων κακῶν συμφωνία, πάλιν ἐν μέρει σκοπῶμεν· τριμεροῦς ἡμῶν τῆς ψυχῆς ὑπαρχούσης τὸ μὲν νοῦς καὶ λόγος, τὸ δὲ θυμός, τὸ δὲ ἐπιθυμία κεκληρῶσθαι λέγεται. κηραίνει δὲ καθ᾽ αὑτό τε ἕκαστον ἰδίᾳ καὶ πρὸς ἄλληλα πάντα κοινῇ, ἐπειδὰν ὁ μὲν νοῦς ὅσα ἀφροσύναι καὶ δειλίαι ἀκολασίαι τε καὶ ἀδικίαι σπείρουσι θερίσῃ, ὁ δὲ θυμὸς τὰς ἐκμανεῖς καὶ παραφόρους λύττας καὶ ὅσα ἄλλα ὠδίνει κακὰ τέκῃ, ἡ δὲ ἐπιθυμία τοὺς ὑπὸ νηπιότητος ἀεὶ κούφους ἔρωτας καὶ τοῖς ἐπιτυχοῦσι σώμασί τε καὶ πράγμασι προσιπταμένους ἐπιπέμψῃ πανταχόσε· : *De confusione linguarum*, ed. P. Wendland, Philonis Alexandrini opera quae supersunt, vol. 2., Berlin: Reimer, 1897 (repr. De Gruyter, 1962), pp. 229–267; Philo Volume IV, Loeb Classical Library 261, tr. F.H. Colson, G.H. Whitaker, 1932.

28 This book has been transmitted only in Armenian. See for the English translation Philo Supplement I, Loeb Classical Library 380, tr. Ralph Marcus, 1953.

29 *Quis Rerum Divinarum Haeres Sit*, ed. P. Wendland, Philonis Alexandrini opera quae supersunt, vol. 3, Berlin: Reimer, 1898 (repr. De Gruyter, 1962), pp. 1–71. Philo Volume IV, Loeb Classical Library 261, tr. F.H. Colson, G.H. Whitaker, 1932.

30 Josephus Flavius is not interested in medicine, yet a chapter dedicated to psychiatry and psychology can be found in Samuel Kottek, *Medicine and Hygiene in the Works of Flavius Josephus* (Leiden: Brill, 1994).

31 Michna Arakhin, Arakhin 2a: *ein ba-hem daat*; Yevamot 99b, Gittin 23a, Arakhin 5b, Menahot 93a: *lav bnei deia/dea*; Hullin 13a: *aph al pi še-nitkavnu le-kakh einan baki iutan mipnei še-yeš lahen maaseh ve-ein lahen mahševa*.

32 Aristotle, *The History of Animals*, Book IV.9; *Metaphysics Book IX.4*; Little Physical Treaties, *On Sense and the Sensible* I.1.

33 Marcus Jastrow, *A Dictionary of the Targumim, the Talmud Babli and Yerushalmi, and the Midrashic Literature* (London and New York: Luzac and Putnam,1903), s.v. *Qanthropos, gandropos, gandripos*: lycanthrope; corrupt of *kunanthropos* or of *lukanthropos*.
34 Cf Baba Qama 37a.
35 Babylonian Amora of the fifth generation, from the fourth century.
36 Ephraim Shoham-Steiner, *On the Margins of a Minority: Leprosy, Madness, and Disability Among the Jews of Medieval Europe* (Detroit: Wayne State University Press, 2014).
37 See, for instance, Samuel Wolfman, "Mental Disease in Divorce Law in the Responsa Literature and in Rabbinical Court Rulings in Israel," *Jewish Law Association Annual*, XVI (2007): 229–249.
38 *ASSIA – Jewish Medical Ethics*, IV, 1 (February 2001): 30–34.
39 Rabbi Moses Isserles notes on the *Shulhan Aruch*, section *Even ha-Ezer* 44 (section devoted to the marriage and divorce questions, Poland, sixteenth century).
40 Ketubbot 20a; Yevamot 113b; Nedarim 36a; Gittin 5a, 23a; Rosh ha-Shana 28a; Talmud of Jerusalem (TJ), Ketubbot 1:25b; Gittin 2:44a.
41 Rashi : *ša'amumita* = *šigga'on*; Ran: he who does not wash his clothes is a prey to *šia'mum* and *timhon levav*.

2

ANCIENT GREEK AND ROMAN TRADITIONS

Chiara Thumiger

"Madness" in the Graeco-Roman world

The experience and conceptualization of madness in Graeco-Roman antiquity are tied up with the medium of literary expressions in a particularly strong way. More than the case with other historical objects, they are exclusively accessible through the written sources we have and the ideas and representations they put forth. This necessarily imposes key distinctions and qualifications: in terms of the social setting and context the modern reader is facing when considering a certain text, its aims, audiences and tradition; the literary genre to which the chosen sources belong; and, finally, the agenda at work in understanding madness. In the case of the latter, I am referring to whether madness is invoked in opposition to health or as marker of a moral flaw or – if in a metaphorical sense – as a paradigm of human ineptitude; as a marker of excellence and divine election; and, finally, as a form of possession by strong emotions, which might even be cast as a positive sign (such as erotic passion, warlike fury, and religious intensity, which are all repeatedly presented as forms of madness by ancient sources). If these complications are true for most, if not all, the historical contexts one wishes to consider, then for the ancient world it is necessary to frame the more structured discussions of medicine, biological science and philosophical ethics specifically within the cultural media in which they were produced and transmitted and *vis-à-vis* their respective audiences, since the borders between disciplines and traditional discourses are, at least at the beginnings of this history, shifting and marred by borrowings and contaminations.

In this chapter I shall focus in particular on the ideas on mental disorder that were brought forth by physicians and philosophers dealing with questions of medicine, rather than look at the poetic, or religious discourses on madness; I shall, however, open this historical reconstruction with a survey of the cultural representations of madness and "the mad" in Greek culture that constitute the background against which scientific thought developed its understanding of mental health and its disturbance.[1]

The Greeks and the irrational

In a famous and most influential work, *The Greeks and the Irrational* (1951), the classical scholar E.R. Dodds first placed "the irrational" at full title into the scholarly study of Greek culture, both as social datum and as personal experience. A reevaluation and even an open fascination with a darker, passionate, excessive Greek antiquity – a corrective to the neoclassical ideal of a Greek world dominated by "noble simplicity and calm grandeur"[2] – had been visible in twentieth-century culture since the beginning of the century, notably the "Dionysiac" Greece celebrated by Nietzsche (*The Birth of Tragedy*, 1898). It was Dodds' work, however, that introduced this element as a legitimate object of academic study for the first time in an anthropological perspective, positing it as an irreducible component of the complexity of ancient Greek culture. The Greeks' interest in the failure of mental abilities and in the loss of one's mental control has since been explored in a variety of perspectives. It is very visible, and now widely recognized that this culture was especially intrigued and attracted by madness as problem and multifarious human experience.

First, there is madness as literary theme or motif.[3] Theatrical texts make this especially evident: the surviving tragedies are so populated with mad characters and plots driven by madness that the element might well be considered a defining feature of the genre. From the famous grand madmen such as Orestes (Aeschylus *Oresteia*, Euripides' *Orestes*) and Ajax (Sophocles' *Ajax*), to more finely disturbed and pathological figures such as Pentheus (Euripides' *Bacchae*) and Heracles (Euripides' *Heracles*), to characters dominated by passion to the point of uncontrolled derangement such as Phaedra with her erotic passion (Euripides' *Hippolytus*) and Medea's thirst for bloody revenge (Euripides' *Medea*), tragedy as a genre, with all its diversity and complexity and the view of human life it conveys, appears to place the human mind as the locus of decision as well as fragility and vulnerability, where external forces and interpersonal conflicts most readily hit. This presentation is offered by the tragedians in a way that is neither simplistic nor monolithic. Although an exogenous model for mental suffering appears to be dominant, and it is certainly always present as traditional background, the nature of mental distress and the metaphysical explanations available for it is problematized from very early on. Take the exemplary case, Orestes, who becomes mad after having killed his own mother Clytemnestra in order to avenge the murder of his father Agamemnon, in turn, whom she has killed. His madness is presented traditionally as a state of possession by the Furies, the goddesses who defend the rights of the mother and punish the murder of blood kins by haunting the matricide. From Aeschylus' trilogy of the *Oresteia* to Euripides' play *Orestes* the discussion about the nature of the man's hallucinations runs through the work of the three tragedians. Are the young man's visions the Furies who have come to take revenge? Or are they mere *doxai*, "images," "perceptions" – the product of an illness? Or again, is it the very consciousness, the *synēsis* of Orestes, haunting him after the murder?[4] The fifth-century dramatists reflect at length on these questions, with clear awareness of all ethical, psychological, medical, and even political implications of a verdict of insanity.

In a completely different literary tradition, erotic love is typically associated with madness and possession. The lyric verses "I love and I don't love,/I am mad and I am not" (*ereō te dēute kouk ereō/kai mainomai kou maivomai*, Anacreon fr. 428) are only one example of a widespread *topos* readily assuming the equation of love and irrational possession. The association will remain a stock element in the history of Greek literature and beyond. So much so, that one of the most influential love poems in our tradition, fr. 31 Voigt of the sixth century BC poetess Sappho, identifies love with a proper form of psycho-physical suffering. The result is a picture of mental distress of strong bodily concreteness, a scene that many scholars have read as a kind of pathography:[5]

my heart jumps in my breast.
At mere sight of you
my voice falters, my tongue
is broken.
Straightway, a delicate fire runs in
my limbs; my eyes
are blinded and my ears
thunder.
Sweat pours out: a trembling hunts
me down. I grow
paler than grass and lack little
of dying.
(Sappho, fr. 31, vv. 5–16)

Far from being simply a decorative element or a feature of specific literary genres, madness is also powerfully present in Greek culture on a different metaphorical level. Exclusive religious experiences, such as those of an initiatory kind prescribe and celebrate states of loss of consciousness as part of the accomplished ritual. The very concept of *ek-stasis*, "being out of oneself" is symmetrical to the state of *en-thousiasmos*, "being in-god," and both are part of what ritual can offer.[6] Initiation is thus effectively a form of madness, and so is the prophetic trance which the priestess of Apollo at Delphi, the Pythia, experiences as she is possessed by the god. These forms of madness – as with erotic passion, albeit in different ways – can be seen as metaphorical forms in which mental alteration equals an intensified state and even signify election and extraordinariness. Nonetheless, they are also ways in which the ancient cultures thought of mental disturbance. The strength of such general beliefs receives its most famous elaboration in Plato's philosophical discussion of the four forms of the divine *mania*, the madness that is not an illness or a curse but a gift from the gods: "and we made four divisions of the divine madness, ascribing them to four gods, saying that prophecy was inspired by Apollo, the mystic madness by Dionysus, the poetic by the Muses, and the madness of love, inspired by Aphrodite and Eros, we said was the best" (*Phaedr.* 265b2–6).[7] As part of his philosophical project Plato recognizes eros, prophecy, poetry and initiation as different forms of a madness that are seen as positive signs, drawing on an idea strongly present in Greek imagination.

Legal and social aspects

In short, if we look at the testimony of high literature – lyric, tragedy, Platonic philosophy – we could easily get the impression of a view of mental disturbance deeply embedded in metaphysical discourses, be it ideological, religious, or ethical. It is easy, when approaching the ancient world, to be led by the grandeur of these poetics into believing an image of society and culture idealized and dangerously divorced from the real life of the time, as challenging and partial our access to it might remain. The sources I have mentioned so far all seem to present as view of the mad as dignified by contact with the divine through suffering and error (in tragedy), inspired by intense emotions (in lyric poetry), or even endowed with extraordinary powers (in the platonic account of the *Phaedrus*).

Other voices, however, must be sought which might give us a glimpse into what must have been the actual views about the mentally ill, their treatment within the family, in society at large, and not least of all from a legal point of view. Of course, there is no ancient parallel to modern policies (and politics) of confinement or to measures such as the interdiction of the mentally ill. The very ideas of hospitals and care systems, moreover, are alien to ancient society until the late antique period. Nonetheless, we can extract some information about social perceptions of the mentally ill that resemble modern experiences. In fact, there are grounds to believe that persecution, marginalization, and stigma often followed the mad.[8] The comedian Aristophanes in his play *Birds* (524–5) puts in a character's mouth the sentence, "now they throw stones at you *as one does to mad people.*"[9] Plato in his *Laws* (*Leges* 934c7) reports the recommendation to keep the mad at home, hidden from larger society. Again, at *Phaedrus* 244b6–7 the philosopher writes that "also among the ancients there were some who . . . *did not* regard mania as something bad or shameful," which implies that the opposite was the rule. These are scant pieces of evidence, and the socio-historical reality behind such expressions is of course impossible to pin down. We can, however, reasonably expect that isolation and disrupted relations should have been a visible part of the experience of insanity in the ancient world, in the classical period as much as they are nowadays. At the very least, they should offer us a caveat against idealizing the ancient past as a place in which mental distress could be more easily accommodated and the sufferers from mental conditions granted any status of privilege.

For reasons of space, I will not be able to explore the socio-historical developments that took place in the Graeco-Roman ancient world as a background to ideas about mental health. It has been necessary to offer an introduction of Greek madness, however, its specificity and its mythology in subsequent Western culture, before moving on to explore the medical accounts elaborated throughout antiquity.

Ancient medical ideas

In fact, the one I have traced so far in very broad lines is the "best known" story when it comes to madness in the ancient world, the one modern audiences think of most readily: insanity as exogenous possession, inserted into a metaphysical plane (religious or ethical) and framed as a personal conflict, corresponding to a disease of the soul, or possibly marking the extraordinariness of an individual or his or her destiny and experience. There is, however, another completely different story that is less known and yet constitutes a part of our cultural heritage immensely more influential than the features we have mentioned at the start. This is a story that from the very beginning strived to distance itself from the discourses of metaphysics and the themes – and language – of poetry and drama to concentrate on human beings as natural phenomena and on the stuff, humours, organs, and processes that are the main actors on human health. Throughout its varied and multifaceted history, ancient medicine sketched out a materialistic view of the human mind–body unit, where madness is characterised from the very start as an illness or a pathological sign that is one of many possible bodily ailments, has bodily origin and cure, and appears to be firmly endogenous in nature.[10]

This fundamental outlook will remain typical in the work of medical authors even at a later time, when the influence of philosophy will elaborate a new, more humanistic and moralizing view of mental health and disorder. In the early stages of its history, this ethical and spiritual side is entirely eschewed from the picture of mental health, with such radical coherence as to invite us to think of an intention, if not necessarily conscious, to define a professional and intellectual position: the "territory" of the doctor must be defined in opposition to, or at least in isolation from the dominant metaphysical ideologies of the time.

Fifth and early fourth-century medical authors: the authors of the Hippocratic Corpus

These early stages are dominated by the testimony of Hippocratic medicine.[11] There was, of course, in Greece a long and rich medical tradition prior to the original texts included in the so-called "Hippocratic Corpus"[12] – that is, those we can consider as dating to the age of Hippocrates and its immediate followers. Several references in the fragmentary sources on natural philosophy prior to Socrates and Plato show clearly the existence of a longer tradition.[13] The Hippocratic texts are the first and richest body of ancient medical ideas preserved, although within the same timeframe there are other important authors who continued the tradition of medical thinking developed by the Hippocratics, such as Diocles and Praxagoras (fourth century BC; their work survives in fragments), and developments in natural philosophy with explicit medical interest (the ps.Aristotelian *Problemata*).

The intellectual and professional horizon of the Hippocratic doctors was strongly characterized by a secular, materialistic, and methodologically rigorous attitude. The state of health or disease of the body was entirely accounted for in terms of physiology (the interaction of humoral balances, organ functioning, and processes such as breathing or nutrition), environmental influence and regimen (the diet one follows, the exercises, sleep and wake, sexual life, and so forth). No mention whatsoever is made of metaphysical aspects: indeed, in a famous passage of one of the classics of Hippocratic medicine, the discussion of epilepsy in *Sacred Disease*, the superstitious beliefs of many observers of mental affections are ridiculed and stigmatized.[14]

In the materialistic framework of this complex body of medical ideas we can organize the discussions on mental life as follows: 1) "theories of mind"; 2) nosology (or lack thereof); and 3) observation of the manifestations of mental life and disorder in actual patients or in pathological portraits (mostly in the reports of the *Epidemics*).[15] The latter constitutes by far the most substantial contribution of the Hippocratic texts to discussions of mental health, in stark contrast to what contemporary discussions of psychiatry tend to foreground, namely, etiological explanatory frameworks and the construction of taxonomies.

1. In our texts we find various "theories of mind," models that seek to account for mental life and health. The most famous one is encephalocentrism, the localization of mental faculties and activities in the brain. Its clearest formulation is offered by *Sacred Disease* (14, Jouanna 25,12 – 26,9 = L. 6.386,15 – 387,3), where the brain is described as the seat of cognitive judgment, perception and emotional life as well as character:[16]

> It ought to be generally known that the source of our pleasure, merriment, laughter and amusement, as of our grief, pain, anxiety and tears, is none other than the brain. It is specially the organ which enables us to think, see

and hear, and to distinguish the ugly and the beautiful, the bad and the good, pleasant and unpleasant, whether we judge according to convention or, at other times, according to the perceptions of expediency. It is the same thing which makes us mad or delirious, inspires us with dread and fear, whether by night or by day, brings sleeplessness, inopportune mistakes, aimless anxieties, absent-mindedness, and acts that are contrary to habit.

The second model, one that has a long tradition in Greek thought, posits air (*pneuma*) as playing a key role in intelligence:[17] we inhale air through breathing and perhaps through channels or kinds of "pores" in our bodies, and it is air that carries information to the organs of cognition. It is important to underscore that these "models" are not conceived in competition with nor even as alternatives to one another. The clearest account of the epistemological function of air/*pneuma* works in fact as a complement to encephalocentrism in *Sacred Disease* (16, Jouanna 29,4–11 = L.6.390,10–15):[18]

> for this reason I think that the brain is the most powerful organ of the human body, for when it is healthy it is an *interpreter* to us of the phenomena caused by the air, as it is the air that gives it intelligence. Eyes, ears, tongue, hands and feet act in accordance with the discernment of the brain; in fact the whole body participates in intelligence in proportion to its participation in air.

Another "theory of mind" that is traditional in medical texts as well as outside them and will play a central role in subsequent philosophical biology is haematocentrism, the idea that the blood is the centre of mental life[19] and the locus of its disturbance. So *Breaths*, 14 (Jouanna 121,9–13 = L. 6.110,16–20):

> Now I hold that no constituent of the body in anyone contributes more to intelligence than does blood. So long as the blood remains in its normal condition, intelligence too remains normal; but when the blood alters, the intelligence also changes.

There are then various versions of what one may call "enterocentrism," placing the internal organs located in the upper torso or in the belly as centers of emotions and cognitions: the *kardia* (only at a later stage to be firmly identified with the heart); the *phrenes* (whose location, at the start, is also fluctuating between the lungs, diaphragm and the upper cavity of the torso); and liver.[20]

Despite the key role cardiocentrism will play in Aristotelian biology, there is no trace in our texts of its having a status comparable to what the brain has in *Sacred Disease*. Rather, its mention is in line with general references to organs seated in the chest in association with mental health.[21] Finally, there is the *psyche*,[22] the soul identified traditionally in Greek culture with life, vitality, spirit, and sometimes ethical-psychological identity. We should acknowledge that *psyche* is not a central word in the vast majority of these medical texts, and it was mostly used with a non-psychological meaning (in the sense of being non-"personal," not as a seat of individuality, nor the "soul" of the individual person, including mental/emotional dispositions). There is, however, one exception that offers us the most articulate example of theory of mind in our texts: the unique account of the *psyche* as composed of fire and water, which comes to us through a sole testimony, *Regimen* 1.35 (Joly-Byl 150,29–156, 18 = L. 6.512,20–522,16). Fire and water and their varying proportions are major causes of alteration in mental capacities and experiences – cognition, emotions, and the processing of sensorial information. According to this passage, there are six possible "constitutions" of the *psyche* depending on six different blends of fire and water in it.[23] To these correspond different types of "mind," with varying cognitive capacities, sensorial performances, emotional responses, and even something that resembles a view of "character."

These various theories of mind, although they intermittently provide explanatory frameworks, do not play a key role in the accounts of mental pathology within the Hippocratic texts. They remain, so to speak, a parallel theoretical discourse, to which descriptions of mental pathology and the cases of insane patients hardly need to refer to in their discussions. This is the first important contrast with later medicine and modern expectations.

2. The second element involves nosology and taxonomy. In early medical texts there are no diseases that could be firmly categorized as psychiatric, let alone a possibility of establishing a psychiatric taxonomy. The "sacred disease," later identified with epilepsy, affects the mind, but is firmly categorized as a bodily dysfunction. *Phrenitis*[24] has a clear mental symptomatology, but also bears the indicator of high fever, heavily stressed as being a fundamental part of it and nowhere discussed as being especially "mental" in nature. *Mania*[25] is not conceived as a disease, but rather an ensemble of signs or a state of distress that can accompany various ailments. *Melancholia* is mentioned only a handful of times, and its psychological implications are not consistently formulated.[26] Although these will become the backbone of mental nosology for later authors returning to the Hippocratic authority in their discussions, their status as psychiatric objects in early medicine is problematic.

3. The third important aspect touches on the clinical discussions offered by the case histories within the *Epidemics* and the pathological descriptions in nosological treatises (*Affections*; *Internal Affections*; *Diseases I, II, III, IV*; *Diseases of Women*) that obviously present to us mental disturbances. Although defying diagnosis of a specific disease, let alone a psychiatric one, these texts offer a largely coherent representation of mental disorder, that we can summarize as follows:

- mental disturbance is entirely embodied and mostly assessed and described in visible terms. This means that madness is *seen*, it has an impact on the face of the patient, his movements, postures and gestures, and it can affect eating behaviours, sleep, and sexuality;
- mental disturbance impairs sensations and perceptions, a sphere to which these physicians paid great attention;
- mental disturbance affects the emotional responses and reasoning abilities of the patient, and its expressions in behavior were sometimes deemed as extraordinary.

This last aspect remains in these texts the least representative, however. It is the embodied, integrated image that is clearly dominant. Consider the following example, a patient in *Epidemics* 7 (*Epid.* 7.11, Jouanna 58,21–61,24 = L. 5.382,13–386,22), the wife of Hermoptolemus:

The wife of Hermoptolemus, in the winter, had fever and headache. Whenever she drunk she sat upright because of difficulty swallowing. She said that her heart had been damaged. Tongue livid from the outset. The cause seemed to be a chill after a bath. She was sleepless, night and day.

After the first days, when asked, she no longer said that her head hurt, but that her whole body hurt. Thirst, sometimes insatiable, sometimes moderate.

On the fifth and sixth day and up to the ninth, almost constantly delirious. Later, she babbled to herself half-intelligible things in the midst of coma. She would reach out with her hand from time to time towards the plaster wall, and to the cold pack on her head. She would put her hands on her chest and sometimes throw off the cover. There was a bloodshot area in the right eye and lacrimation. The urine of the sort that is always bad in children. The stool from the outset yellowish, later very watery and the same colour.

On the eleventh day the heat seemed more moderate, and she was without thirst sometimes to the extent that if one did not give something to her she would not ask. Sleep, after the initial period, was generally in the day, but towards night she was sleepless and towards night her suffering was worse.

On the ninth day her intestines were upset, passing watery excrement, and on the tenth. Through the subsequent days the movements were generally frequent and similar. She had bursts of temper in the previous days, and childish weeping, crying out, frights, and glancing about, whenever she roused from coma.

On the fourteenth day it was a task to restrain her as she leaped out and shouted suddenly and intensely, as though from a blow or a dreadful pain or fright, whenever anyone took hold of her and held her down briefly. Then again she lapsed into coma and she was quiet and persisted in drowsiness, seeing nothing, and sometimes not hearing. And she alternated often between uproar and quiet virtually that whole day.

Towards the following night she passed a bloody movement, like mucus, and again muddy, and later very greenish and dark.

On the fifteenth day sharp tossing. The frights and the shouts became gentle, but she persisted in her wildness, her anger and tantrums if what she wanted was not done for her quickly. She recognized everyone and all objects straightaway after the first days. The eye condition settled down. But the mania, inappropriate behavior, crying out, and the alternations I described, persisted until the coma. She heard irregularly: some things very clearly, even if one said them quietly, but for some it was necessary to talk louder. Her feet were throughout as warm as the rest of her body until the final days, but on the sixteenth day less so.

On the seventeenth day she was more comfortable than on the other days, but towards night she drew herself together as though a chill was coming on, and her fever increased. There was much thirst. Everything else continued the same.

But trembling developed in her hands and she kept tossing her head. The area under her eyes, and the looks of her eyes were bad.

Her thirst was powerful. When she had drunk she would ask for more, snatch it and drink violently. They could not take it away from her. Her tongue was dry, quite red, and her whole mouth and lips ulcerated, parched.

She kept moving both hands to her mouth and chewing them, trembling, and if anyone gave her something to chew or sip, she drunk and sipped it violently, madly. The area around her eyes was bad.

On the three or four days before the end shivers came on her at times so that she would draw her body together, cover up, and breathe hard. Cramps in her legs, cold feet. The thirst as before, and mental affection similar. Bowel movement either nothing or small and thin with brief straining. On the last day, the twenty-third, her eye was large in the morning and her vision short. She was quiet at times, without huddling under covers and coma.

Towards evening there was movement of the right eye, as though seeing or seeking something, from the outer corner towards the nose. She showed recognition and answered what was asked. Her voice lisping after much talking, and broken and hoarse from the shouting.

This patient is clearly affected by mental distress as well as other various bodily complaints: she "said that her heart had been damaged" and "that her whole body hurt"; she is constantly delirious; she babbles to herself; she has "bursts of temper . . . and childish weeping, crying out, frights"; there is talk of "wildness, her anger and tantrums," "mania," "inappropriate behaviour." The large share of her mental suffering, however, is conveyed through the careful reports of her irregular sleep, her pathological cravings and refusal of drinks, her compulsive postures and hand gestures, tossing around, gazing around madly, and sensorial disruptions.

This case, one of the longest and richest of the collection, is at the same time perfectly representative of these texts and their emphasis on the seen body, as opposed to an invisible, spiritual locus of alteration and distress. This approach is characteristic of the medical thought of the time. Not only that, but its bodily determinism when it comes to the explanation of mental facts will persist throughout the tradition of Greek medicine. Nonetheless, important innovations are visible in the medical texts of the post-Hellenistic era,[27] although the Hippocratic texts will remain hugely influential in the subsequent medical tradition. Thus, it is important to stress the conspicuous absence of key aspects which later authors will read back into these early texts to the service of their own doctrine: psychiatric nosology, on the one hand, and ethical-psychological approaches to mental disorder on the other.

The first psychiatric taxonomy of antiquity: Cornelius Celsus

An important watershed in the available ancient testimony about views of mental disorder comes to us from a text which is medical in nature, but (possibly) does not come from the hand of a physician: a chapter in the encyclopedic work *De Medicina* (which dates at around the beginning of our era), itself a part of a much larger encyclopedia which would have included different branches of human knowledge.[28] Although we do not know if the author, the Roman writer Cornelius Celsus, was a physician or not, it is evident from his discussion of medical issues that he had a competent and perceptive understanding of the medicine of his time and the tradition preceding it. When it comes to the topic of mental illness, he offers the reader a detailed survey of medical opinions on causes and triggers of mental suffering as well as therapies.

Most importantly, he preserved for us a classification of types of mental disorder that must have been widespread, if not unanimously accepted, at the time. It is the first example of psychiatric taxonomy in the Western tradition: the ideas found in this text represent a canonical distribution which will remain a fundamental part of nosological discussions in the years to come. The relevant section, *De Medicina* III, 18 opens by stating that there are "three types of madness" (*tria genera insaniae*), which can be classified in terms of duration: an acute, quick one (*furor*, which corresponds to the Greek *phrenitis*, as Celsus says explicitly[29]), a longer one, without fever (*mania*), and a "*longissimum*" kind, *maestitudo*, which corresponds to what had become a melancholic "profile" in ancient culture. In many ways the discussion in Celsus constitutes a showcase for all subsequent nosologies: the distinction between acute and chronic, for example, which is only present *in nuce* in the Hippocratic authors; the element of fever, which differentiates *mania* from *phrenitis*; the partition into three types, something that will remain a central feature in subsequent discussions; the centrality of *phrenitis*, which here as elsewhere appears to be the very emblem of mental suffering, presented first in the discussion and receiving by far the longest description.

One additional element stands out in Celsus's report and signals a shift from earlier presentations: the great care the Roman author pays to the manifestations of disease in different patients, recognizing individual variations,[30] and the importance of what we may call the psychological element, that personal level of mental health that Hippocratic medicine entirely shunned. Especially in the lengthy section devoted to therapeutics – a fact in itself and the length of which shows a different approach from the Hippocratics, who mention no cure or care whatsoever to be given to the mentally ill *qua* mentally ill – a psychotherapeutic approach surfaces in Celsus alongside the usual care for the physiology of the body and dietetic aspects that should befit the needs of each. Different kinds of manners and attitudes are regarded as effective, mild and tender as well as firm and occasionally restrictive, depending on the patient's character and illness. Music, light and darkness, and entertainment are advised, and even fictional consolatory situations are conjured:

> But in dealing with the spirits of all patients suffering from this type of insanity, it is necessary to proceed according to the nature of each case. Some need to have empty fears relieved, as was done for a wealthy man in dread of starvation, to whom pretend legacies were from time to time announced. Others need to have their violence restrained as is done in the case of those who are controlled even by flogging. In some also untimely laughter has to be put a stop to by reproof and threats; in others, melancholy thoughts are to be dissipated, for which purpose music, cymbals, and noises are of use.[31]

Moreover, forms of occupational therapy and cognitive exercises are prescribed, and social activities are recognized as beneficial for the mind:

> More often, however, the patient is to be agreed with rather than opposed, and his mind slowly and imperceptibly is to be turned from the irrational talk to something better. At times also his interest should be awakened; as may be done in the case of men fond of literature, to whom a book may be read, correctly when they are pleased by it, or incorrectly if that very thing annoys

them; for by making corrections they begin to divert their mind. Moreover, they should be pressed to recite anything they can remember. Some who did not want to eat were induced to do so, by being placed on couches between other diners.[32]

All these prescriptions appear alongside the traditional physiological instructions about diet, environmental considerations, and pharmacological remedies. The easy integration of psychotherapeutical discourses with physiological measures is arguably a sign of the profound influence of philosophical ideas on medical discourses about the soul and its health. At the same time, it exposes a reality of clinical attention to mental disturbance that sometimes surfaces in practice: for instance, discussing restraint, Celsus specifies that "one should not trust a patient that has been physically restrained and wants to be set free, even though he speaks in a reasonable and sorry manner, because this is a typical trick of the insane" (*neque credendum est, si uinctus aliqui, dum leuari uinculis cupit, quamuis prudenter et miserabiliter loquitur, quoniam is dolus insanientis est*).

The philosophers and mental wellbeing

The discussion in Celsus remains a unique source for this inquiry. Other, sparse testimonies from non-medical authors, however, are useful to map the philosophical territory in which a psychotherapeutic approach to mental illness developed and was later integrated into medicine, especially by Galen.

From early on, in fact, the philosophers responded with interest to the models elaborated by medicine in their reflections on human wellbeing and the opportunity to preserve and foster its flourishing.[33] In this way, a complementary approach to that of the Hippocratics, which will converge into a more composite medical project only later, is visible in various forms from the classical age. Already Democritus spoke of a "madness of the many" and of the folly of mortals as ethical flaw as well as a medical condition (Democritus' philosophical take on the care of the individual[34]). Plato, in his *Phaedrus* (265a 9–10), spoke of a "madness that comes from human diseases" (μανία ὑπὸ νοσημάτων ἀνθρωπίνων), for him different from the divinely inspired *mania* that is at the center of his discussion in the dialogue. Especially in his *Timaeus* (86 b 1–7), a work that is heavily influenced by medicine, Plato furthers the exploration positing a distinction between "diseases of the body" (τὰ περὶ τὸ σῶμα νοσήματα) and "diseases of the soul" (τὰ περὶ ψυχήν) in their association to the state of the body (διὰ σώματων ἕξιν). Notwithstanding the mention of the body, these are framed as forms of ethical flaw, with a language that shifts continuously between the ethical, evaluative level and the somatic component of the disease. These "diseases of the soul" have their origin in a form of ἄνοια, folly, which can be expressed as "madness" (μανία) or "ignorance" (ἀμαθία, 86 b 4[35]). The discussion of these combines together an impaired bodily physiology and a failure in the education of the individuals that determines the various "diseases of the soul," which are described as "unhappiness, affliction, temerity, cowardice, forgetfulness and intellectual idleness" – psychological aspects of character, that education can help improve.

Another important ethical-philosophical contribution comes from a section of the Aristotelian *Nichomachean Ethics,* where Aristotle discusses a category of human beings, the *acratic*, "powerless" or "impotent" (ἀκρατής), who are conspicuously placed at a crossroad between physiological impairment and moral corruption (*EN* 7, 1148b15–1149a20). Aristotle states clearly that moral flaws and disease forms can be the cause of the same human weaknesses and deviations: taste for immoderate pleasures can intervene "in some cases because of defects, in others because of character/habit (δι' ἔθη), in some others because of a depravation of nature (διὰ μοχθηρὰς φύσεις)."[36]

Finally, to give a third example from the Greek philosophical tradition prior to Celsus, we should mention the section in the pseudo-Aristotelic *Problemata Medica* 30.1, with its extraordinary and influential description of *melancholia*. This passage traces a portrayal of a pathological category that is a complex interlacement of physiological detail, dietetic habits, and pathological ailments, on the one hand, with aspects of character, emotional responses, and intelligence traits, on the other – so much so as to open the section with the ethical question, "why is it that all men who have become extraordinary in philosophy, politics, poetry, or the arts are obviously melancholic?"

Despite the loss of most of Hellenistic medicine, the ethical discourses, of which we have seen some key examples and which will be much furthered by Hellenistic philosophy,[37] allow us to see how philosophy progressively appropriated the idioms and discourses of medicine, elaborating on an idea of "disease of the soul" and "madness of all mankind" in order to fashion its own brand of philosophical medicine. Far from being a mere metaphor, the medical presentation of ethical-spiritual flourishing (and flaws) corroborates the stance for the social and existential relevance of philosophy in human life. Conversely, philosophical language and agendas are absorbed by the medical profession. Thus, when Celsus introduces the therapy of *phrenitis* with the fully rounded psychology I have described, this novelty can be related to the influence of philosophical discourses.

Galen

The best example of the synthesis between philosophy and medicine in the discussion of mental soundness is offered by Galen of Pergamon, perhaps the most famous physician of antiquity. Originally from Asia Minor, but active in Rome for a long time between the first and the second century AD, Galen often appears to have had limited interest in the category of the psychiatric per se[38] and more generally in nosology. As a consequence, we should not look for extensive discussions of individual disease entities in his works or psychiatric theories strictly defined. On the other hand, he had much to say about the ethical aspects of mental health, and the combination he offers of ethical reflections and materialistic physiology of mental health are a key chapter in the history of Western psychology.

We can recognize, in fact, a tension in Galen between two approaches to the life and health of the mind. On the one hand, we find an entirely materialistic and deterministic approach (biological, as we would say). In his work *The Capacities of the Soul Depend on the Mixtures of the Body* (*QAM*), Galen sets out to affirm clearly the statement of the title, reinforcing its therapeutic usefulness:[39] "I have found this doctrine true on all accounts and useful to those who wish to improve their souls." This physiological discussion of the bodily foundation of human morals in this treatise goes so far as to include a corollary: there are mental (i.e. ethical) flaws that are beyond redemption or cure, as they are caused by severe damage in one's bodily conditions. And so, even though there might be no individual responsibility for these body-determined flaws, such individuals should nonetheless be eliminated for the sake of their own, and everyone else's good:

> and we kill the irremediably bad for three good reasons: lest they do any harm, if they should live; so that they might instill fear in those similar to them, that they would be punished for the evil doings they will commit, and thirdly; and as a third reason, it is better for them to die, since they are so corrupt in their soul that they cannot be educated even by the Muses, nor can they receive any improvement from Socrates or Pythagoras
>
> (*QAM*, 11. 814-6, my translation)

Elsewhere, in pathological discussions, Galen discusses the physiological changes that are responsible for certain mental disorders along similar lines: for instance, with reference to melancholy in *On the Affected Parts* (iii, 9–10), where Galen explores the possible localization of this illness in the head or in the stomach, with mental consequences of different kinds; and with *phrenitis*, a disease which Galen also categorizes as an alteration of the body (in this case, in the context of a high fever) with mental consequences.

A second story, and remarkable in its contrast with the first, is offered in Galen by the elaborated ethical reflection about mental well-being and human flourishing with which the physician engaged alongside his work as a scientist and a physician. At first sight, the works produced by this effort resemble for a modern reader the style and purpose of self-help manuals or psychological treatises. In these texts Galen engages a personal level of experience, both his patients' and interlocutors' and his own. He offers advice on how to counteract one's moral weaknesses and presents precisely that possibility for mental and ethical self-improvement that he rules out in *QAM*, often in a confidential, exhortative tone. I refer in particular to the treatise *The Diagnosis and Treatment of the Affections and Errors Peculiar to Each Person's Soul* (*Aff.Dign.Pecc.*) and to the epistle *Avoiding Distress* (*Ind.*).[40] In these texts the physician discusses sources of mental suffering such as excessive anger or grave losses (material and affective), equating them with pathologies and sketching out a form of philosophical and psychological therapy that allows one to bear material losses without letting mood and happiness be affected and not falling prey to the irrational drive of anger. In *Aff.Dign. Pecc.* 3 he even proposes to those who want to "free themselves from the affections of the soul" to elect a "supervisor," a trustworthy, loyal, but also critical friend who would observe the person and offer honest feedback on one's flaws and behavior: a therapeutic, authoritative figure, but also a psychological aid and an ethical master all in one.

In this second group of writings Galen advocates an ethical training that improves the state of one's soul and offers the possibility (to an extent, at least) of healing pathological states in one's mind-soul, combatting the flaws that corrupt human life. For example, in *Avoiding Distress* he recounts how he was able to overcome his own loss of a huge patrimony of books and precious medical materials in a fire via philosophical means, practicing a form of distancing from material possessions:

I believe all things to be of little importance – so hardly could I take tools, drugs, books, fame and riches as worth troubling oneself for . . . And one who regards all things as unimportant, what concern could he have because of their presence, or deriving from them? It follows then that a person who believes to have been deprived of great things should always be in pain because of that and worry over it, while the one who believes he has been deprived of unimportant things should continue to dismiss them as before.

(*De Indolentia* 65–66, my translation)[11]

There is a contradiction between this psycho-therapeutic and philosophical project and the deterministic harshness of the verdict Galen hands down in *QAM*, where mental flows are attributed to a bodily hardware in large part inherited and incurable. This contradiction remains unresolved. In Galen's work, however, we can first of all observe the integration of evaluative and philosophical aspects into an idea of mental health. Second, the possibility, and even the necessity, of a philosophical, cognitive training for the cultivation of the health of the soul is affirmed. Both aspects mark a radical change from the approach the Hippocratic physicians adopted when dealing with patients suffering from mental disturbances.

Later nosology and encyclopedias

Notwithstanding his prolific activity, Galen did not pay much attention to nosological taxonomies nor to discussions of diseases or syndromes per se. In the first centuries of our era, however, a nosological genre began to affirm itself in the Greco-Roman world, represented by treatises "on chronic and acute diseases" of which many examples survived and by encyclopedic compilations. These texts itemize diseases in lists, discussing for each the etiology, symptoms, and therapy. The so-called Anonymus Parisinus, an anonymous treatise *On Acute and Chronic Diseases* (possibly first–second century AD); Areateus' *On the Causes and Symptoms of Acute and Chronic Diseases* and *Therapies of Acute and Chronic Diseases* (second century AD); Soranus' (lost) *Acute and Chronic Diseases* (first–second century AD); Caelius Aurelianus' *On Acute Diseases and on Chronic Diseases* (fifth century AD); Aetius of Amida *Libri Medicinales* (sixth century AD) and Paul of Aegina's *On Medicine* (seventh century AD).[12] While we cannot dwell on each of these authors and on their works, it is important, however, to notice that mental diseases in these texts are clearly categorized: mania, melancholia, *phrenitis* receive each a section with etiology, symptomatology, and therapy; other diseases are conceptualized as having an important mental component, like *hydrophobia*, a syndrome characterized by fear of water, fever, derangement and death following the bite of a dog. A proof of the increased awareness of the pathological category is offered by Caelius Aurelianus, who discusses hydrophobia in his *Acute Diseases* 3, 98–106, 9–11, and devotes a chapter to the following question: "whether hydrophobia is *a disease of the mind (animae) or of the body (corporis).*" Regardless of the answer he offers, the fact itself of posing the question signals a level of discussion that was unknown to earlier phases of Greek medicine. Ethical, cognitive, and psychological aspects are integrated both in the symptomatological account of these conditions and in their therapy. Aspects of character and individual dispositions are now an important part of the picture. Evaluation and judgment on the part of the physician is inserted into the clinical discussion. A striking example for all is Caelius Aurelianus's discussion of the *Malthacoe* and *Tribades*, "pathic"/"passive homosexuals" and "female homosexuals" respectively (*Chronic Diseases* 4, 9). Their affection appears to be clearly mental in nature and an unnatural condition (*non . . . ex natura*). Caelius explicitly labels it as the expression of "vices of a corrupt mind" (*vitia corruptae mentis*), while individuals suffering from it are understood in terms of shamefulness (*obscenis usibus*) and insatiability (*nulla satietatis spes*). They comprise a moral and characterological class before being a category of patients.

Long and composite as it is – stretching over a thousand years of medical history – the ancient Graeco-Roman tradition on mental health and disorder can be said to show some clear trends of its own, at least when it comes to its influence on later visions. While its beginning is characterized by a deep continuity between mind and body and of a radically somatic interpretation of mental illness, categorized as a bodily disease and approached physiologically (this is evident in our classical sources, Hippocrates, and contemporaneous writers), a spiritualist element begins to influence medical ideas about the mind starting from the reflections of the philosophers (especially Plato and Aristotle, and the Hellenistic Schools). Thus, in the early centuries of our era, a combination of physiological principles of mental illness and of philosophical, eudemonistic values becomes evident. At the same time, a general interest in nosology begins to emerge in the sphere of mental health as in other branches of medicine. The great portrayals of the main mental syndromes are progressively codified and some taxonomic fixity imposed on a material that had been much more magmatic and undefined before. In the course of this codification an order much firmer than had been the case is read retrospectively in earlier authors (most of all, in Hippocrates). In this way, from a pathological point of view, an outlook on mental health made of organized, discrete entities is handed over to late-ancient and medieval thinkers. Parallel with this, the psychiatric discussion becomes coloured with a strong sense of ethical evaluation, increasingly promoting a normative ideal of mental soundness as spiritual accomplishment, a view into which Christian ideas of salvation and personal amelioration will naturally converge. These two aspects may be seen as the fundamental core of the ancient legacy to the formation of modern psychology and psychiatry.

Chronology

"Hippocrates"	Fifth–early fourth century BCE
Democritus	Fifth century BCE
Plato	Fifth–fourth century BCE
Aristoteles	Fourth century BCE
Hellenistic Medicine	Fourth–first century BCE
Celsus	Turn of the first century CE
Galen	First–second century CE
Anonymus Parisinus	Possibly first–second century CE
Aretaeus	First–second century CE
Rufus	First century CE
Soranus	First–second century CE
Caelius Aurelianus	Fifth century CE
Aetius	Sixth century CE
Paul of Aegina	Seventh century CE

Notes

1 For a general cultural-historical discussion, Agnes Garr Vaughan (*Madness in Greek thought and custom.* Baltimore: J.H. Furst Company, 1919) and Ainsworth O'Brien Moore (*Madness in ancient literature*, Diss. Princeton University 1924) still have useful information, although outdated in their methodological foundations; Patricia Clarke (*The Balance of the Mind*, Diss. Washington, 1993), on the contrary, is very perceptive and the fullest account available, although unfortunately only available as an unpublished dissertation; see Bennett Simon (*Mind and Madness in Ancient Greece: the Classical Roots of Modern Psychiatry.* Ithaca: Cornell University Press, 1978) for a psychoanalytical approach, and the studies in William V. Harris (ed.) *Mental Disorders in the Classical World* (Leiden: Brill, 2013).

2 The famous Winkelmannian formula: "eine edle Einfalt und eine stille Grosse."

3 On which see Josef Mattes, *Der Wahnsinn im griechischen Mythos und in der Dichtung bis zum Drama des fünften Jahrhunderts.* Heidelberg: Bibl. d. klass. Altertumswiss. N.F. 2:36, 1970); Ruth Padel, *In and Out of the Mind. Greek Images of the Tragic Self* (Princeton: Princeton University Press, 1992) and *Whom Gods Destroy. Elements of Greek and Tragic Madness* (Princeton: Princeton University Press, 1995); Debra Hershkowitz, *The Madness of Epic: Reading Insanity From Homer to Statius* (Oxford: Oxford University Press, 1998); Allen Thiher, *Revels in Madness: Insanity in Medicine and Literature* (Ann Arbor: University of Michigan Press, 2004); Peter Toohey, *Melancholy, Love, and Time: Boundaries of the Self in Ancient Literature* (Ann Arbor: University of Michigan Press, 2004), dealing with different periods and with varying approaches.

4 Aeschylus, *Libation Bearers* 1051–2, "What images upset you, most beloved of all men? Come, do not be overcome by fear." | "These of my suffering are no mere images to me." Or again, at Eur. *Or.* 395–6, the deranged Orestes is addressed: "what are you suffering? Which disease is destroying you?" | "Awareness, because I know I have done something terrible."

5 Vincenzo Di Benedetto, "Intorno al linguaggio erotico di Saffo," *Hermes* 113 (1985): 145–56; Franco Ferrari, "Saffo: nevrosi e poesia," *SIFC* 19 (2001): 3–31.

6 See Armand Delatte, "Les conceptions de l'enthousiasme chez les philosophes présocratiques," *L'Ant. Class.* 3 (1934): 5–79; Wesley D. Smith, "The So-Called *Possession* in Pre-Christian Greece," *Transactions of the American Philological Association* 96 (1965): 403–4 for an important challenge to received ideas on ancient possession; Giulio Guidorizzi, *Ai confini dell'anima. I Greci e la follia* (Milano: Raffaele Cortina, 2010) for an informative miscellaneous narrative about ancient experiences of possession; Yulia Ustinova (*Caves and the Ancient Greek Mind. Descending Underground in the Search for Ultimate Truth*, Oxford/New York: Oxford University Press, 2009); and "Consciousness alteration practices in the West From Prehistory to Late Antiquity" in *Altering Consciousness: Multidisciplinary Perspectives*, ed. by E. Cardeña, M. Winkelman, (Praeger: Santa Barbara, 2011).

7 Transl. by Harold N. Fowler (Plato, *Phaedrus.* Cambridge, MA: Harvard University Press; London: William Heinemann Ltd, 1925).

8 See Vaughan, *Madness*, 37–45 for a survey on the topic, see also 39 for the mad being made objects of laughter, quoting Plat. *Euthyphr.* 3b9–c2, "when I say something . . . they laugh at me as if I were mad" (ἐμοῦ γάρ τοι, ὅταν τι λέγω . . . καταγελῶσιν ὡς μαινομένου); Padel, *Whom Gods Destroy*, 100–2 for an anthropological perspective on stones and the practice of stoning the ill and insane in Greek antiquity, and (1995) 154–5 on the association of shame, derived from social stigma, and madness; Christian Laes, "Learning from Silence: Disabled Children in Roman Antiquity," *Arctos* 42 (2008) 112–16 on attitudes of mockery and aggression towards disability in the ancient world more generally.

9 Little is known about the legal status of the insane: Vaughan, *Madness* 59–72 surveys the main sources; Sarah Francis, "From private disabilities to public illnesses: placing the mentally incapacitated in Roman society," in *Medical Conceptions of Mental Illness From Celsus to Caelius Aurelianus*, ed. by Chiara Thumiger and Peter N. Singer (Leiden: Brill, 2017).

10 For an introduction to key themes in ancient psychopathology, still valid today, see Israel Edward Drabkin, "Remarks on ancient psychopathology," *Isis* 46 (1955) 223–34; Jackie Pigeaud, *Folie et cures de la folie chez les medicins de l'antiquité gréco-romaine. La manie* (Paris: Les Belles Lettres, 1987).

11 For a full account of mental health and disorder in Hippocratic medicine see Chiara Thumiger, *A History of the Mind and Mental Health in Classical Greek Medical Thought* (Cambridge: Cambridge University Press, forthcoming).

12 That of "Hippocratic Corpus" is the traditional label under which a heterogeneous ensemble of texts has been preserved, several of which are much later than the time of Hippocrates (fifth century) or of his immediate disciples (fourth to early fourth century). Indeed, several of these texts belong to a much later period, Hellenistic (late fourth to second century BC) or as late as of the first centuries of the common era. I refer to texts as "Hippocratic" as those that are safely taken to be from the classical age – see Jacques Jouanna, *Greek Medicine From Hippocrates to Galen* (Leiden: Brill, 2012) 373–416; Elizabeth M. Craik, *The "Hippocratic Corpus." Content and Context* (London: Routledge, 2015) for chronological discussions.

13 Key figures in this sense are Alcmaeon, Democritus, and Diogenes of Apollonia; see Vivian Nutton, *Ancient Medicine* (Oxford: Oxford University Press, 2004), 37–52 on "pre-Hippocratic" medicine.

14 *Morb.Sacr.* 1 (Jouanna 7,3–8,13 = L. 6.358.19-362.6). One should not take this as a non-religious irreverence towards the traditional deities, but as a belief in a higher form of piety towards the "real gods," who are not appeased through rituals nor act contrary to nature.

15 *Epidemics* can be divided in three groups, I–III (end of the fifth century BC), II, IV and VI (late fifth to early fourth century BC), and V and VII (mid-fourth century BC).

16 Other texts with an encephalocentric positioning are *Places in Man* and *Nature of Man* (see Paola Manuli, "La *techne* medica nella tradizione encefalocentrica e cardio emocentrica," in *Corpus Hippocraticum,* ed. by Robert Joly (Mons: Éditions Universitaires de *Mons,* 1977): 182–95.

17 Diogenes of Apollonia also states that air is endowed with intelligence (DK 64, B4-5) and that its distribution in the body accounts for the variations in intelligence, sense perception and pleasure (DK 64 A19, *De Sens.* 45).

18 See Philip Van der Eijk, *Medicine and Philosophy in Classical Antiquity* (Cambridge: Cambridge University Press, 2005), Chapter 4; 129 n. 22; Jacques Jouanna (ed. and transl.), *Sacred Disease (Morb.Sacr.) La maladie sacrée* (Paris: Les Belles Lettres, 2003) lix–lx.

19 On the history on hemo-cardiocentrism in ancient medicine and philosophy, see Manuli "La *techne* medica," 190–4; van der Eijk, *Medicine and Philosophy,* 132 ff; 206–37 on blood, cognition and senses in Aristotle.

20 See Volker Langholf, *Medical Theories in Hippocrates. Early texts and the Epidemics* (Berlin: Walter de Gruyter, 1990) 42–3 for more on these; Richard B. Onians, *The Origins of European Thought: About the Body, the Mind, the Soul, the World, Time and Fate* (Cambridge: Cambridge University Press, 1951) 84–9 on the liver and the belly; on imagery and poetry, Padel, *In and Out of the Mind,* 12–48; Beate Gundert "Soma and psyche in Hippocratic Medicine," in *Psyche and Soma: Physicians and Metaphysicians on the Mind-Body Problem from Antiquity to Enlightenment,* ed. by John P. Wright, Paul Potter (Oxford: Oxford University Press, 2000) 13–36, 28; Rossana Stefanelli, *La temperatura dell'anima: parole omeriche per l'interiorità* (Padova: Unipress, 2010) esp. 97–137 for a recent discussion.

21 See *Morb.* 2.5 (Jouanna 136,7–15 = L. 7.12,16-24.), *Virg.* 2 (Lami 22,13–17 = L. 8.466,15–20) for some references in this sense.

22 Even a representative bibliography on ψυχή is a hopeless task; see however, for religious and cultural representations, the classic Erwin Rohde, *Psyche* (1925); Onians, *The Origins of European Thought;* Robert Renehan, "The meaning of ΣΩΜΑ in Homer: a study in methodology," *CSCA* 12 (1981): 269–81 on ψυχή and σῶμα; Jan Bremmer, *The Early Greek Concept of the Soul* (Princeton: Princeton University Press, 1983); on poetic representations Clarke (1999), *Flesh and Spirit;* Shirley D. Sullivan, *Aeschylus' Use of Psychological Terminology: Traditional and New* (Montreal: McGill-Queen's University Press, 1997); *Euripides' Use of Psychological Terminology* (Montreal: McGill-Queen's University Press, 2000); *Psychological and Ethical Ideas: What Early Greeks Say* (Leiden: Brill, 1995); *Sophocles' Use of Psychological Terminology: Old and New* (Ottawa: Carleton University Press, 1999); Padel, *Whom Gods Destroy, passim;* Michael Frede, "On Aristotle's conception of the soul," in *Essays on Aristotle's De Anima,* ed. by Martha C. Nussbaum and Amélie Rorty (Oxford: Oxford University

Press, 1992) 93–107 on philosophical views (Plato and Aristotle); Stefanelli *La temperature dell'anima*, 139–85; Hynek Bartoš, *Philosophy and Dietetics in the Hippocratic on Regimen. A Delicate Balance of Health* (Leiden: Brill, 2015) 165–229.

23 For the tradition of the constituents of the soul, see Raymond Klibansky, Erwin Panofsky, and Fritz Saxl, *Saturn und Melancholie* (Frankfurt: Suhrkamp, 1990) 39–54; Gabor Betegh "Eschatology and Cosmology: Models and problems," in *La costruzione del discorso filosofico nell'età dei Presocratici = The Construction of Philosophical Dscourse in the Age of the Presocratics*, ed. by M.M. Sassi (Pisa: Edizioni della Normale, 2006): 29–50 on what he calls the "portion" model in the tradition about the soul; Jacques Jouanna, "Rhetoric and Medicine in the Hippocratic Corpus: A Contribution to the History of Rhetoric in the Fifth Century," in *Greek Medicine From Hippocrates to Galen* (Leiden: Brill 2012) 39–54 for a discussion from Empedocles to *Regimen*.

24 On this important ancient disease with mental implications, see Jackie Pigeaud, "Caelius Aurélien, 'Maladies Aiguës 1, 1 De *phrenitide*': quelques problèmes philologiques (remarques en vue d'une édition)," in *Tradición e innovación de la medicina latina de la antigüedad y de la Alta Edad Media*, ed. by M.E. Vázquez Buján (Santiago de Compostela: Universidad de Santiago de Compostela, 1994) 29–44; Byl and Szafran (1996); McDonald (2009, 2014).

25 On ancient *mania* the bibliography is vast, characteristically spanning from religious and cultural perceptions to medical notions. See Pigeaud, *Folie* and Chiara Thumiger ("The Early Greek Medical Vocabulary of Insanity," *Mental Diseases in Classical Antiquity*, ed. by William V. Harris (Leiden: Brill, 2013) 61–95 on medicine; the classic Eric R. Dodds, *The Greeks and the Irrational* (Berkeley: University of California Press, 1951); Guidorizzi, *Ai confine dell'anima*; Yulia Ustinova, *Caves and the Ancient Greek Mind. Descending Underground in the Search for Ultimate Truth* (Oxford/New York: Oxford University Press, 2009) for broader perspectives.

26 See Jacques Jouanna, "At the Roots of Melancholy: Is Greek Medicine Melancholic?" in *Greek Medicine from Hippocrates to Galen* (Leiden: Brill, 2012) 229–58; Thumiger, "Early Greek Medical Vocabulary," 63–70. On the history of melancholia, see also Walter Müri, "Melancholie und schwarze Galle," in *Antike Medizin*, ed. by Hellmut Flashar (Darmstadt: Wissenschaftliche Buchgesellschaft, 1971); Hellmut Flashar, *Melancholie und Melancholiker in den medizinischen Theorien der Antike* (Berlin, Walter de Gruyter, 1966); Klibansky, Panofsky and Saxl, *Saturn und Melancholie*.

27 Very little survives of Hellenistic medicine, unfortunately, and particularly nothing of relevance to the reconstruction of ideas about mental disorder.

28 See Jackie Pigeaud, "La reflexion de Celse sur la Folie," in *La médecine de Celse: aspects historiques, scientifiques et littéraires*, ed. by Guy Sabbah and Philippe Mudry (Saint-Étienne: *Mémoires XIII*, 1994), 256–79; Heinrich von Staden, "Aulus Cornelius Celsus on Kinds of *insania*: Classifications, Causes, Therapies, and Sources," in *Mental Illness in Ancient Medicine. From Celsus to Caelius Aurelianus*, ed. by C. Thumiger and P. Singer (Leiden: Brill, forthcoming).

29 Celsus's quote of the Greek word is imprecise: our texts have φρένησιν as translation of *furor* (Marx 122, 15), rather than φρενίτιδα, as we would expect; the disease *phrenitis* is however in point here (on the word change see von Staden, forthcoming).

30 For instance, at Marx 122, 24–27, "there are various types of [phrenitis]: and so of the phrenitics some are sad, some are cheerful; some are more easily restrained and speak in a deranged way; other jump up and act with violence" (*eius autem plura genera sunt: siquidem ex phreneticis alii tristes sunt; alii hilares; alii facilius continentur et intra uerba desipiunt; alii consurgunt et uiolenter quaedam manu faciunt*).

31 *Aduersus autem omnium sic insanientium animos gerere se pro cuiusque natura necessarium est. Quorundam enim uani metus leuandi sunt, sicut in homine praediuite famem timente incidit, cui subinde falsae hereditates nuntiabantur. Quorundam audacia coercenda est, sicut in is fit, in quibus continendis plagae quoque adhibentur. Quorundam etiam intempestiuus risus obiurgatione et minis finiendus: quorundam discutiendae tristes cogitationes; ad quod symphoniae et cymbala strepitusque proficiunt*, Marx 124, 10–17).

32 *Saepius tamen adsentiendum quam repugnandum et paulatim et non euidenter ab iis, quae stulte dicentur, ad meliora mens eius adducenda. Interdum etiam elicienda ipsius intentio; ut fit in hominibus studiosis litterarum, quibus liber legitur aut recte, si delectantur, aut perperam, si id ipsum eos*

59

offendit: emendando enim conuertere animum incipiunt. Quin etiam recitare, si qua meminerunt, cogendi sunt. Ad cibum quoque quosdam non desiderantes reduxerunt i, qui inter epulantes eos conlocarunt, Marx 124, 17–24).

33 Jackie Pigeaud, *La maladie de l'âme. Étude sur la relation de l'âme et du corps dans la tradition medico-philosophique Antique* (Paris: Les Belles Lettres, 2006) addresses precisely this interface; Marke Ahonen, *Mental Disorders in Ancient Philosophy* (Berlin and New York: Springer, 2014); Chris Gill, "Peace of Mind and Being Yourself: Panaetius to Plutarch," in *Aufstieg und Niedergang der römischen Welt* II.36.7, ed. by Wolfgang Haase and Hildegard Temporini (Berlin: Walter De Gruyter, 1994) 4599–640; 1996; *Naturalistic Psychology in Galen and Stoicism* (Oxford: Oxford University Press, 2010); "Philosophical Therapy as Preventive Psychological Medicine," in *Mental Disorders in the Classical World*, ed. by William V. Harris (Leiden: Brill, 2013) 339–60).

34 See Brooke Holmes, *The Symptom and the Subject* (Princeton: Princeton University Press, 2010) 216–27 on Democritus and the links between ethical-eudaimonistic themes and physiological representations of the body; the convergence of ethics and epistemology in Democritus discussed by Charles H. Kahn, "Democritus and the origins of moral psychology," *AJPh.* 106 (1985): 1–31 and James Warren "Democritus on social and psychological harm," in *Democritus: Science, The Arts, and the Care of the Soul*, ed. by Aldo Brancacci and Pierre-Marie Morel (Leiden: Brill, 2003).

35 T.M. Robinson, "The Defining Features of Mind-Body Dualism in the Writings of Plato," in *Psyche and Soma: Physicians and Metaphysicians on the Mind-Body Problem from Antiquity to Enlightenment* (Oxford: Oxford University Press (2000) 37–55; Chris Gill, "The body's fault? Plato's *Timaeus* on psychic illness," in *Reason and Necessity*, ed. by Matthew R. Wright (London: Duckworth, 2000) 59–84; Maria Michela Sassi, "Mental Illness, moral error, and responsibility in late Plato," in Harris, *Mental Disorders in the Classical World* (Leiden: Brill, 2013): 413–26.

36 On this passage see extensively van der Eijk (2013) 323–6; Sassi, "Mental Illness," 423; Ahonen, *Mental Disorders*.

37 See Ahonen, *Mental Disorders*, 103–38, 179–216 for a survey.

38 Nutton, *Ancient Medicine*. On Galen and psychology see Stanley W. Jackson, "Galen – On Mental Disorders," *Journal of the History of the Behavioral Sciences* 5 (1969): 356–84; Rudolf E. Siegel, *Galen on Psychology, Psychopathology, and Function and Diseases of the Nervous System: An Analysis of His Doctrines and observations on Bloodflow, Respiration, Tumours, and Internal Diseases* (Basel: S. Karger, 1968); Pigeaud, "La psychopathologie de Galien"; Luis García Ballester, "Diseases of the soul in Galen: the impossibility of a Galenic psychotherapy," CM 9 (1974) 35–43; Michael Dols, *Majnun. The Madman in Medieval Islamic Society* (Oxford: Oxford University Press, 1992), Gill, *Naturalistic Psychology*), Peter Singer, *Galen: Psychological Writings. Avoiding Distress, Character Traits, The Diagnosis and Treatment of the Affections and Errors Peculiar to Each Person's Soul, The Capacities of the Soul Depend on the Mixtures of the Body* (Cambridge: Cambridge University Press, 2013); "Galen and the Philosophers: Philosophical Engagement, Shadowy Contemporaries, Aristotelian Transformations," in *Philosophical Themes in Galen*, ed. by Peter Adamson, Rotraud Hansberger and James Wilberding, *Bulletin of the Institute of Classical Studies Supplement* 114 (2014) 7–38; James Hankinson, "Partitioning the Soul. Galen on the Anatomy of the Psychic Functions and Mental Illness," in *Partitioning the Soul. Debates from Plato to Leibniz*, ed. by Klaus Corcilius and Dominik Perler (Berlin/ Boston: Walter de Gruyter, 2014) 85–106.

39 On this text, see Singer, *Galen: Psychological Writings* 335–73.

40 See Singer, *Galen: Psychological Writings* on these texts for an introduction and translation.

41 See Veronique Boudon-Millot and Jacques Jouanna in collaboration with Antoine Pietrobelli, *Galien. Ne pas se chagriner* (Paris: Les Belles Lettres, 2010) for the text and commentary; Vivian Nutton, "Avoiding Distress," in Singer, *Galen: Psychological Writings.* 45–76 for an introduction to this text.

42 On these later authors and their ideas on mental disorders, see the essays in *Medical Conceptions of Mental Illness from Celsus to Caelius Aurelianus*, ed. by Chiara Thumiger and Peter N. Singer (Leiden: Brill, forthcoming).

Texts used

Caelius *Aurelianus. On Acute Diseases and on Chronic Diseases.* Transl. by I.E. *Drabkin.* Chicago (1950).

Caelius *Aurelianus. On Acute Diseases and on Chronic Diseases* (Celerum passionum libri III, Tardarum passionum libri V). J. Kollesch et D. Nickel (eds.) *CML* VI 1, Berlin 1990/1993.

[Hippocrates] *Epidemics* V, VII (*Epid.* V, VII). J. Jouanna (ed. and trans.) *Epidémies V et VII.* Paris (2000).

[Hippocrates] *Sacred Disease* (*Morb.Sacr.*). J. Jouanna (ed. and trans.) *La maladie sacrée.* Paris (2003).

Galen, *The Capacities of the Soul Depend on the Mixtures of the Body* (*Quod Animi Mores Temperamenta Sequantur, QAM*). I. Müller (ed.) *CMG,* II (1891).

Galen, *Avoiding Distress* (*De Indolentia, Ind.*). V. Boudon-Millot, and *J. Jouanna* (eds.), in collaboration with Pietrobelli (A.) *Galien. Ne pas se chagriner.* Paris (2010).

Galen, *The Diagnosis and Treatment of the Affections and Errors Peculiar to Each Person's Soul* (*De affectuum et peccatorum dignotione libri, Aff.Pecc.Dig.*) J. Marquardt (ed.) Leipzig (1884).

Pormann, P. (ed.) Rufus of Ephesus: On Melancholy. Tübingen: Mohr Siebeck (2008).

The Extant Works of Aretaeus the Cappadocian. Transl. by F. Adams, Boston (1856).

3

MADNESS IN THE MIDDLE AGES

Claire Trenery and Peregrine Horden

Introduction

Different people held different views as to what the disease . . . was. Some said it was a kind of great frenzy. Others claimed he was possessed by a demon. Now there were some indications of both these afflictions, but nonetheless I always heard that never once in the whole course of his illness did he want to injure anyone except himself. This is not what one hears about the frenzied or the possessed.[1]

The sufferer here was the great Flemish painter Hugo van der Goes (1433/40–1482). He entered a religious house near Brussels in 1477 and his case was reported, decades later, by one of the brethren, Gaspar Ofhuys. Hugo had recently completed the major commission of the 'Portinari altarpiece' for a hospital church in Florence. He included in the picture a symbolically charged array of flowers, all related to religious healing, and among them a sprig of black columbines in a jar – *melan* being the Greek for black, *anacolie* being columbine in French – as if he was praying for release from melancholy.[2] That may have been a premonitory sign of the condition that came to a head a few years after Hugo entered the religious house. On a visit to Cologne he succumbed to 'a strange disease of his cognitive [or imaginative] faculties' (as Ofhuys puts it). He repeated that he was eternally damned and tried to kill himself. When those travelling with him returned to Brussels, they summoned the prior. He thought that Hugo had the same affliction as Saul, an unclean spirit, and he therefore applied the remedy of David (who played his harp). He arranged some music therapy before Hugo rejoined the brethren, among whom no instrumental music was allowed. It did not work.

Ofhuys worries away at Hugo's diagnosis, deploying a respectable degree of medical learning (for which, doubtless, he had been made monastic infirmarer). While God alone knew the truth, he thought there were two possibilities. The first was that the condition was natural, arising from melancholic foods; from strong wine; or from an emotional excess, of anxiety, fear or sadness. Hugo accepted too many commissions, which made him anxious, and drank too much with his patrons. Some thought indeed that his anxiety had been so great as to rupture the particular delicate vein in his head that nourishes imagination and fantasy. A second possibility was divine providence. Hugo had been puffed up by the grandeur of his guests and by the exalted status within the order that his skill as a painter brought him. God sent him this affliction as a humiliation and penance, not to kill him, but to save him from torment in eternity.

For neither Ofhuys nor his readers would any of those possibilities – physiological (diet), psychological (morbid imaginings), possession by a spirit or demon, divine providence – have been seen as mutually exclusive. Illness was conceived by the medical authorities of his time as genuinely psychosomatic, in terms of a two-way traffic between soul and body. Demons made their way the more easily into a physically disordered person. God used body and soul as means of chastisement and correction.

Very few 'mad' people other than saints and rulers are known to us as named individuals with biographies from the Middle Ages. That is why even so abridged and heavily moralizing a text as Ofhuys's chronicle is precious. It is, incidentally, the only documented medieval European case of music therapy practised rather than just recommended. More broadly, it shows the hesitations over definition and diagnosis that were probably a feature of so many encounters with those whose utterances and behaviour confounded normality. It also brings out the inseparability of religious and medical responses, and the extent to which a naturalistic diagnosis of madness was always possible, even within a milieu such as a monastery that was well accustomed to the demonic.

The historiography of medieval madness, which it is the aim of this chapter to exemplify and survey, has taken some time to come to terms with cases such as Hugo's – even though the painter's art and character have long attracted specialist attention, and even though scholarly and wide-ranging monographs on medieval 'folly' or 'madness' have been appearing for decades. The older studies of the 1970s, followed by a further clutch around 1990, brought together law, theology, religious practice, medicine, vernacular literature, and various other kinds of evidence. They have not been superseded. Some were perhaps too much in thrall to Foucault, some engaged in too much retrospective diagnosis, some were too anecdotal or relied on questionable secondary material. Their greatest problem, however, was the lack of a context in medical, religious and social history to enable them to knit together the data provided by each kind of evidence into any overarching narrative. We still do not know how to do that. As the field has grown, so it has, not surprisingly, fragmented. Synthesis lies even further beyond the horizon than it did in 1990.[3]

The way into this complex field that we have chosen is through the broad intellectual setting: ideas about insanity that were most widely diffused and that help us to understand at least some of the commonest reactions to cases of madness. We shall move though medical and religious considerations before turning to legal provision for the insane in the community and the question of hospitalization. We shall then look to literary representations before ending (as we began) with some well-known mad individuals. As a postscript, we add a brief section that looks eastwards.

The aetiology of madness

Madness, unreason, and the Christian mind

Aristotle held that what separated the soul of man from the souls of animals was man's possession of reason and intellect.[4] This idea resonated with later Christian writers who were interested in the role that man's reason played in his relationship with God. One of the best-known biblical cases of madness – that of Nebuchadnezzar – encapsulates this relationship between reason and madness, man and beast, and divine favour and punishment (Daniel 4:1–37).[5] Understanding the role of the mind was vital for theorists contemplating Christian spirituality and practice, and discussions of the mind and the soul feature prominently in Christian philosophy. E. Ruth Harvey has examined the relationship between philosophical and medical teachings on the nature of the body and mind.[6] She argues that

> because of the ambiguous nature of the bodily spirits, which both partook of the physical constitution of the body, and provided the link by which the mind communicated with the bodily organs, the doctors were led to the treatment of disordered reason almost as though it were a purely physical function; whereas the philosophers insisted that reason as such fell outside medical control.[7]

A study of medieval madness requires an analysis of contemporary understanding of body, mind, and 'bodily spirits'. Not only does such understanding elucidate medical theories of madness; it is a necessary primer to considerations of Canon Law. Harvey demonstrates, moreover, that the essence of subsequent debates penetrated beyond the spheres of philosophy and medicine into literature and folklore.[8] The concept of the 'bodily spirits' – Harvey's 'inward wits' – influenced and permeated perceptions of, and approaches towards, madness. Their origins in philosophy and medicine emerged from considerations of the mind, connecting philosophical teachings on the mind with madness. Christian theology of the mind has been studied extensively by historians, though it is rarely connected with madness, largely because ancient and medieval philosophers themselves seldom focused on madness specifically.[9] It is thus worth briefly examining the origins of medieval philosophies of the mind before moving on to investigate theories concerning madness itself.[10]

The medieval concept of 'bodily spirits' can be traced back to the Stoic school of the fourth century BC, which was influenced by Aristotle. An answer was needed to the question of how the material body was made physically animate under the control of the immaterial soul. The explanation offered by Stoic philosophers was that the soul operated through the agency of *pneuma* (*spiritus* in Latin), or bodily spirits. These animating spirits could be witnessed by the physician in the air that was breathed in and out of the body. *Pneuma* was material, but its form was finer than that of other elements, allowing it to express the soul's intentions through the physicality of the body. The Stoics placed the source of *pneuma* in the heart (the hydraulic model), but Hippocratic thought located it in the brain, and connected it with the three faculties of imagination, reason, and memory.

The hydraulic model of the mind and its influence in Anglo-Saxon England is the subject of Leslie Lockett's book *Anglo-Saxon Psychologies*, in which she examines both metaphorical and literal applications of cardiocentric psychologies in Anglo-Saxon vernacular and Latin writings.[11] Lockett traces the development in Ancient Greek epic, Aristotelian philosophy, and Biblical narrative of the localisation of reason and emotion in the organs of the chest and abdomen.[12] She draws attention to the fundamental discussion of the relationship between body, mind, and soul, and the strong connection between all three in the hydraulic model, which denied the total incorporeality of the soul because of its physical association with specific areas of the body.[13]

The increased circulation of Patristic texts from the eighth to ninth centuries onwards brought to prominence the Augustinian model of the soul, as an incorporeal entity, without physical location, and possessing the faculties of reason.[14] This raised crucial questions regarding the moral implications of madness in the soul and the ability of mad individuals to engage with the Christian community. Thomas Aquinas, whose philosophical writings were widely circulated in the later Middle Ages, contemplated the participation of the mad, as members of a Christian society, in Christian worship. There were circumstances – such as the imminent likelihood of fatality – in which the mad, especially those who had not been mad since birth and had previously consented to baptism, could be baptized. Mad men and women, Aquinas argued, were members of the Christian community because, unlike irrational animals, they possessed rational souls, but had lost the use of their reason through *bodily* impairments.[15] Likewise, the Sacrament could be given to those who had lost their reason but had formerly shown devotion towards the host.[16] It seems that the inability to express devotion through one's rational faculty did not mean that the incorporeal soul could not benefit from the Sacrament.

Nonetheless, whilst the human soul was incorporeal, it was certainly not incorruptible, and could be led astray either by the passions of the physical body, or through the temptation of demons. From as early as the fourth century, one particular condition of the brain's faculties was associated with spiritual impairment. *Acedia* was related to melancholy; the two conditions were differentiated by the presence of delusions in melancholic patients.[17] *Acedia* was initially thought to be exclusive to anchorites (those who had chosen a solitary religious existence in the harsh landscape of the Egyptian desert), but later it was a diagnosable state of mind affecting mostly monks and nuns. Stanley Jackson suggests that the 'condition was characterized by exhaustion, listlessness, sadness or dejection, restlessness, aversion to the cell and the ascetic life, and yearning for family and former life.'[18] *Acedia* was sometimes associated with the sin of sloth, and the necessary treatment for this was confession, but it could also be attributed to excess phlegm or black bile in the rational faculty and could supposedly be eased with relaxation and music.[19] Undesirable behaviour could be connected with a problem in the brain and, crucially, could require both physical and spiritual treatment.

Medical approaches

Historical considerations of medieval madness as a medical condition are generally found within larger studies of medieval medicine or within broad overviews of madness. In-depth studies of individual conditions – such as Mary Wack's work on lovesickness and Amy Hollywood's analysis of *melancholia* – have striven to place specific medical conditions within their social contexts.[20] Luke Demaitre's volume on *Medieval Medicine* examines conditions in a head-to-toe format, based on that commonly adopted by medieval medical writers themselves.[21] Demaitre dedicates a chapter to conditions of the head, which, in the medieval medical manuals known as *practica*, included discussions of 'the hair, the skull and brain, mental function, and motor control'.[22] However, as Demaitre himself concedes, such medieval conditions cannot be easily divided into the modern categories of psychological and neurological complaints.[23] To understand medieval conceptions of madness, we have to consider what influenced medical ideas.

There is some evidence for the dissemination of learned medical theories in the Christian west prior to the eleventh and twelfth centuries, but the rise of university-based medical learning in the High Middle Ages brought with it a plethora of theological and practical medical manuscripts.[24] Monica Green is compiling a list of Latin medical manuscripts in circulation in the twelfth century, and notes 375 codices, totalling at least 145 distinct texts, in her 2009 article.[25] Some works of the great medical writers of antiquity – Hippocrates and Galen – had been translated into Latin as early as the sixth century, but scholarly interest in their theories was renewed in the eleventh century in and around the medical schools of Salerno.[26] As Salerno's reputation grew, its medical texts were widely circulated amongst European universities and monasteries, with the humoral model forming the basis for discussions of health and sickness. The body's functions were believed to be reliant on four humours and their associated qualities: blood (hot and wet); yellow bile or choler (hot and dry); black bile (cold and dry); and phlegm (cold and wet). These humours needed to be regulated (for example, by diet) in order to maintain a natural state of health. Imbalances in the humours led to what modern practitioners would classify as physical and mental health conditions. Treatment for these conditions consisted of various methods to restore humoral balance.

One of the most famous and widely circulated medical encyclopaedias of the later Middle Ages was the *Canon of Medicine* by the Persian physician known in the West as Avicenna. Originally compiled in the early eleventh century, the *Canon* was translated into Latin in the twelfth century and became a standard medical text for most university physicians. According to Avicenna, the substance of the brain was cold and moist.[27] Following humoral principles, its stability could be damaged by an excess of heat or dryness. The location of this damage determined the nature of the brain condition and its symptoms. The simplest model of the brain divided its material substance into three parts. The imaginative faculty, located at the front of the brain, processed the information received by the senses, hence its proximity to the sense-receptors of the face. This information was passed on to the central brain faculty, rationality, which formed it into concepts and judgments. Memories were stored at the back of the brain, as images literally imprinted on the wet matter.[28] Mental illnesses were caused by humoral or anatomical abnormalities in one or more of these three areas. For example, amnesia indicated a problem in the memory faculty, such as the rising of hot vapours to the back of the head, which interfered with the storing of images.[29]

Madness, or *amentia/insania* in Latin, was not often discussed as a distinct condition in medical manuals. Instead, it could be symptomatic of other conditions, or it was used as a generic term for illnesses of the imaginative and rational faculties that affected the cognitive functions of the brain. The three main conditions that were associated with madness in medical texts were frenzy (*frenesis*), mania (*mania*), and melancholy (*melancholia*). Precise symptoms and healing techniques varied slightly from writer-to-writer but those found in the *Pantegni* – a theoretical and practical medical manual translated from Arabic into Latin in the late eleventh century and widely circulated in western Christendom from the thirteenth century – are indicative of commonly held beliefs. Frenzy was caused by a hot brain abscess, most often comprised of yellow bile, which upset the natural coolness of the brain.[30] Primarily affecting the imaginative faculty at the front of the head, the face and head would usually become warm to the touch. Sleep was disturbed and the patient could awaken in the night, screaming. In this state of unrest, the patient was prone to bouts of inexplicable laughter or crying and breathlessness.[31] Treatment relied upon the medieval principle that opposites cure; thus the coolness of the brain could be restored by lowering the temperature of the head. One technique was to shave the head and drench it in water or oil. If the patient's general health allowed for it, the artery to the head could be phlebotomized in order to draw hot blood away from the brain.[32] There has, to date, been no full-length historical study of medieval frenzy – although Danielle Jacquart has explored the Greek and Arabic traditions – and more research would greatly benefit our understanding.[33]

Both mania and melancholy were chronic conditions. Mania was characterized by frantic behaviour.[34] It was associated with stupor of the mind, a condition also connected with frenzy.[35] Gariopontus, an eleventh-century Salernitan physician, noted that the symptoms of madness could be similar in both conditions, but explained that maniacs lacked the fever from which frenetics suffered.[36] Physicians observed that, because the symptoms of mania often seemed inexplicable, the condition could be associated with demonic or divine activity.[37] One theory put forward by medical writers themselves was that mania was the result of an excessive diet, and thus purgatives that would induce vomiting or sweating were used to restore humoral balance.[38]

Melancholy could also result from humoral imbalance. Excess black bile in the form of a vapour could rise from the stomach to the brain, affecting a patient's understanding in the rational faculty. Melancholic patients were often sad and suspicious, and their inability to rationalize the world around them left many in a worrying predicament.[39] Hallucinations and delusions were common, with some patients barking like dogs and others crowing like roosters.[40] Various herbal remedies could be applied with the intention of restoring humoral balance to the patient through purging.[41] In his assessment of medieval understandings of melancholy, Jackson stresses that whilst both relaxation and, at the other end of the spectrum, binding were used for melancholic patients, these did not always constitute cures in themselves; entertainment provided a distraction and lightened the mood, whereas binding prevented a patient from hurting himself and others whilst treatment was ongoing.[42] Fernando Salmón argues that medical treatments for madness relied very much on the physician's interaction with the needs of the patient; thus, for a melancholic who believed she was headless, a lead helmet was provided to give some psychological comfort.[43]

Evidently, such conditions as frenzy, mania, and melancholia were difficult – and sometimes dangerous – to treat. It is difficult to know how successful the cures outlined above would have been and whether or not physicians actually applied them. Constantine was careful to make sure that the herbal remedies he recommended to treat melancholy were fairly simple for the physician to prepare, which perhaps indicates an expectation on his part that such treatments would be attempted.[44] Modern scholarship has suggested that, as early as the twelfth century, learned medical ideas were disseminated outside the university and university-based physicians, specifically to monastic communities who almost certainly had access to medical *practica* in their libraries.[45] Evidence of medical terminology can be found in hagiographies and miracles collections of the later Middle Ages, which proposed medical diagnoses for sick pilgrims who travelled to saints' shrines hoping for miraculous cures. The miraculous cures of many mad pilgrims were recorded at shrines, and these records did sometimes refer to medical ideas, though with notably less frequency than was the case for other conditions.[46] Leigh Ann Craig has suggested that a 'constructed diagnostic uncertainty' was applied by miracle compilers specifically to avoid clarifying the cause of madness.[47] Multiple theories coexisted regarding the nature of madness, and to advocate a humoral diagnosis may have resulted in the exclusion of other theories that were equally regarded and well-established. The synchronicity of various models of madness in the Middle Ages is further exposed below by a study of practical provisions for the mad, and of literary and artistic portrayals of madness.

Demonic possession

As the case of Hugo van der Goes demonstrates, states of unreason, and even medical conditions, like frenzy, could be connected with demonic interference. Catherine Rider has shown that many medieval physicians themselves were willing to admit the possibility of a demonic aetiology for madness.[48] The often spectacular descriptions of demonic possession from the Middle Ages have attracted historians to this phenomenon, which was associated by contemporaries, like Aquinas, with impairments of imagination and reason.[49] Nonetheless, it is important to treat such accounts of demonic possession with caution. Was possession the same as madness, and in what ways were demons believed to influence physical and cognitive function?

Following Augustine, earlier writers stipulated that, whilst demons had no ability to enter the soul of a human, they could enter the body and manipulate the mind, either by confusing the imagination with erroneous images, or by impairing reason so that the victim was unable to comprehend the information received by his/her senses.[50] As interest in the human spirits grew from the twelfth century onwards, so too did attention to the movements of demonic spirits in the natural world. Nancy Caciola has examined the discernment of spirits (the process by which demonic spirits were differentiated from divine spirits) and its development in the later Middle Ages.[51]

In hagiographic records (saints' Lives and collections of the miracles performed by saints at medieval shrines), distinctions were not always made between demonic possession and madness.[52] As was the case with madness, signs of demonic possession included wild gestures, violence, twisted facial expressions, and shouting.[53] Signs more typical of demoniacs were abnormal powers, convulsions, blaspheming, abhorrence of sacred objects, and aggression.[54] Madness, especially violent madness, could be associated with demonic interference. The language of possession – that victims were 'seized' or 'tormented' by demons – illustrates the violence with which this affliction was connected.[55] From the thirteenth century, 'madness was becoming naturalised', and the language of demonic possession became less prominent.[56] Nonetheless, despite the waning use of demonic terminology in official records, there is still evidence of widespread belief in demonic influence over the mind: canonization dossiers recorded that those cured of madness had *believed* that they were possessed.[57] It is important, when considering medieval perceptions of madness, to acknowledge that 'the medieval period witnessed great diversity of belief in the sphere of the natural and the supernatural'.[58] Demonic and humoral explanations for madness were not mutually exclusive, and the precise aetiology of cognitive malfunction was often difficult to discern.

Provision for the mad

Medieval law

For the best-preserved legal records from medieval Europe, historians have turned to England, and some headway has been made with understanding the legal position of the mad there. Naturally, a discussion of madness and the law is limited by the source material available, which notably focuses on the everyday legal standing of the landed insane and on the legal treatment of the criminally insane. Mad men and women who had no possessions and who had not committed a crime were far less likely to enter the legal record. In England, the survival of legal material from the post-Conquest period is far more plentiful than from its Anglo-Saxon predecessor. Nonetheless, Nigel Walker proposes that the Anglo-Saxon state offered leniency and protection for mad offenders, provided that it could be proved that a felony had not been committed during a lucid interval.[59] Stefan Jurasinski challenges this thesis by drawing attention to the absence of leniency in cases of mad suicide, and by suggesting that, whilst the mad were to be pitied, they were often deemed responsible for their actions, which, though beyond their present control, may have resulted from past sin or illicit demonic activity.[60] Alexander Murray looks in detail at the legal status of medieval suicide, concluding that, in cases of suicide by the mad, verdicts were far from consistent. Technically, a suicide committed without the conscious knowledge of the perpetrator was not a felony, but it was very difficult to establish the mental state of the dead perpetrator. Nonetheless, establishing the nature of a suicide, criminal or otherwise, was vitally important, because a criminal suicide could not bequeath possessions to his/her heirs and could not receive a Christian burial. It is for this reason that mad suicides feature in the legal record, and yet Murray has demonstrated startling contradictions in the application of verdicts and punishments.[61]

Sara Butler considers the potential "leniency" of the insanity defence in medieval England.[62] In her sample of 192 criminal cases, taken from eyre rolls and coroners' rolls from thirteenth- and fourteenth-century England, Butler finds only 15 attributed to demonic activity (mostly suicide cases), whereas the vast majority of cases described violent madness (frenzy or fury).[63] Medieval juries recognized these forms of madness as an 'illness', and rarely mentioned sin or any fault on the part of the sufferer as a contributing factor to this illness.[64] Alexandra Pfau has found that a similar state of affairs existed in medieval France, where officials were wary of prosecuting mad offenders, who were barred, because of their lack of understanding, from bringing cases to court and from acting as legal witnesses.[65] Wendy Turner has also investigated the 'legal diagnosis' of madness.[66] She argues that cognitive capability could be gauged by a memory test (where the subject was asked questions about his/her family, community, and daily activities). Juries would also consider whether or not a person's 'emotional' reaction was appropriate to the situation in which they found themselves. Laughing whilst committing or recounting a violent crime, for example, was, understandably, deemed inappropriate.[67]

69

Turner has also reflected upon the social implications of the legal provisions for madness in High Medieval England, looking predominantly at the care and custody of the landed insane.[68] The mad were predominantly cared for by their families or communities, and the wardship of a mad landowner was given to a guardian. Care was taken to preserve the landowner's interests by ensuring that the guardian was not a direct heir, but this did not mean that the system was immune to exploitation by profit-seeking guardians who could take the revenues from their ward's lands. Kate Parkin, in her investigation of 47 cases of idiocy (a term usually applied to those who had been mad since birth) in the Inquisitions *Post Mortem* between 1399 and 1447, found that the provisions for mad landowners were based more on custom than on written law codes.[69] Furthermore, families would sometimes attempt to hide an heir's idiocy in the hope that they could avoid jurisdictional interference and simply restore the line of inheritance when the idiot died.[70] In Parkin's words, legal provision for the mad was a 'flexible process'.[71]

Canon Law, the Papacy, and Christian morality

Colin Picket's synopsis of madness in Canon (Church) Law, although written for the priest and not for the historian, is a fair starting point for understanding the complexities of ecclesiastical provisions for madness (demonic possession is excluded from his study).[72] Naturally, stipulations did not remain static throughout the Middle Ages and Picket provides a historical overview prior to his canonical commentary.[73] For the purposes of this chapter, it will suffice to summarize the areas of Canon Law in which some consideration of madness was necessary. The question of whether the mad could receive the Sacraments was much debated. Such reception was largely dependent on the past faith of the mad person. For example, a mad person could be baptized so long as others bore witness to his/her previous devotion.[74] Similarly, while a mad person could not enter into a contract of marriage, a marriage contract that had been made when both parties were sane remained valid if either party became mad.[75] Consent was crucial to the partaking of the Sacraments; whilst the mad were not capable of giving consent, previous consent, if proven, was sufficient. There was, however, a concern that those who had been mad since birth had never possessed the ability to consent to baptism. There was some disagreement over this issue but the consensus seems to have been to place the life-long mad in the same category as infants; they could be cleansed of original sin but, as they did not possess the reason to commit further sins, penance was redundant.[76] Following the same line, mad criminals were to be given a lesser penance upon recovery of their senses; some atonement had to be made for their crimes but it was acknowledged that, without the capacity to reason, their actions had likely lacked criminal intent.[77]

Despite the biblical connections between sin and madness (Nebuchadnezzar), it does not seem that Church authorities specifically categorized madness as resulting from sin. Jerome Kroll and Bernard Bachrach call into question the medieval association between sin and madness, arguing that the attention that modern historians have given to this explanation of illness is a result of modern society's desire to paint the medieval period as comparatively backward in terms of psychological knowledge and care.[78] In their study of pre-Crusade saints' lives and chronicles, in which they define mental illness broadly to include madness, epilepsy, possession, and drunkenness,

Kroll and Bachrach find that a relatively small percentage of mental illness cases were attributed directly to sin.[79] Those that were often stemmed from a desire on the part of the author to discredit the sufferer, for example, for his/her rejection of the power of a saint.[80] Madness could thus be used by Christian writers to make a moral point, but the condition was not perceived in a universally negative light.[81]

Sabina Flanagan has more recently explored the Church's stance on heresy in relation to madness. Canon II of the Fourth Lateran Council (1215), which dealt with Amalric of Bena, a French theologian whose theories were deemed heretical, specifically stated that Amalric's writings were not so much heretical as mad, and Flanagan concludes that, in the eyes of the Church, madness seemed a lesser transgression than heresy, and could even be used as a defence against a charge of heresy.[82] In her subsequent examination of the relationship between madness, heresy, and the Devil, Flanagan points out that multiple theories existed on this subject at the turn of the thirteenth century (as they would in the time of Hugo van der Goes), and that many contemporary observers found it difficult to distinguish between humoral madness, demonic madness, and madness as a cover for heresy.[83] There was, however, a suspicion that madness could be feigned, which led to a tightening of regulations concerning it and heresy.[84]

Hospitals

How much space did those labelled mad or foolish from birth find in institutions? A good many of the diverse foundations in medieval Europe that we can group under the heading of 'hospital' specifically excluded the insane, along with pregnant women or the acutely ill. Care of these was beyond their resources. It might also corrupt the liturgical and sacramental life that, throughout the Middle Ages, lay at the heart of such institutions.

Only towards the end of the period did hospitalization of the insane become more widely acceptable. But even in the late fifteenth century the facilities for the mentally ill in the most medicalized and best-endowed European hospitals remained rudimentary. At Santa Maria Nuova in Florence, a harbinger of the modern hospital in its medical staffing if ever there was one, the insane were simply chained up in a cell and purged or given the occasional sedative. 'We have set apart another place for those who have lost their minds through illness, where they are kept in chains.'[85] This brief notice, in a version of the hospital statutes prepared in order to impress Henry VII of England, follows pages of detail about how the other, physically sick patients are to be received and treated. It suggests a regime little different from the fetters and chains found in the more famous mad hospital of 'Bedlam' during a visitation earlier in the fifteenth century.[86]

An older historiography would place the turning point to even this basic level of management in fourteenth to fifteenth-century Spain.[87] It locates the stimulus to change in the arrival of Islamic hospitals (later than elsewhere around the Mediterranean and Middle East as we shall see below), which had long evinced a much stronger tradition of functioning as asylums for the mad and placing them under medical supervision. Yet there is some evidence of mad people in hospital-like institutions from well before any Islamic evidence could be invoked to explain the acceptability of this type of care.[88]

Literature and art

Literary criticism of medieval representations of madness is richly endowed, and takes a broad approach to the term 'madness'.[89] Stephen Harper has highlighted the dangers of 'applying the theological conventions of madness to all medieval literature works both to homogenize and to oversimplify the picture of madness in the Middle Ages'.[90] Like the historian, the literary scholar must bear in mind that few medieval writers conformed unerringly to the models of madness outlined above. The literary renderings of madness discussed here are not patterns to which every text can be made to conform; instead they are influential tropes that illustrate aspects of madness that have been identified by critics and could be interrogated further.

Penelope Doob classifies three popular literary portrayals of madness as 'the Mad Sinner', 'the Unholy Wild Man', and the 'Holy Wild Man'. All three, she argues, were influenced by the popular biblical figure of Nebuchadnezzar whose madness inspired many later literary depictions.[91] Nebuchadnezzar's sin and ultimate redemption informed constructions of madness as both a punishment and a spiritual therapy, which in turn illustrated God's agency in the world. Harper extends Doob's thesis by arguing that alongside traditional precedents, medieval writers were also influenced by the contemporary setting of their text, thus allowing spiritual and humoral explanations of madness to co-exist.[92]

In her study of madness in French literature, Sylvia Huot explores literary madness as a form of 'otherness', which triggered various responses, including 'fascination, fear, laughter, pity, and revulsion'.[93] Huot uses this starting point to unravel the role of the literary madman/madwoman, who could both be employed as a figure of comedy and as a vehicle of tragedy.[94] She also discusses the function of 'madness' as a literary metaphor for 'death'.[95] The mad character 'dies' a symbolic death and a new identity is constructed for him/her, which allows the narrative to take a different trajectory (consider Tristan, Lancelot, Yvain).[96] This was a common trope in Arthurian literature. Madness could be used as a form of redemption for the mad character who, after alienating himself/herself from society, was able to find spiritual renewal.[97] Renée Curtis has explored the role of feigned madness in this process.[98] Madness, even when feigned, resulted in rejection from human society, and thus could act as a moral punishment and a means by which the character could reconnect with God.[99]

The dual concept of madness as both a moral punishment reducing the sufferer to the status of a beast, and, at the same time, a form of spiritual redemption is further expressed in medieval art. Doob highlights the popularity of Nebuchadnezzar, who represented both facets, and whose image was widely repeated.[100] Caciola argues that artistic depictions of demonic madness also followed 'scriptural precedent' by portraying the wildness of demoniacs (loose hair, torn clothes) and the physical occupation of a demon, which was often shown entering or leaving a victim through his/her mouth.[101] Aside from the physical presence of a demon, Sander Gilman has explored how else the mad and the possessed were physically identified in literature and art. Like Huot, Gilman argues that the mad were typified by 'otherness' and thus required some form of physical marking to distinguish them. This distinction could be shown in a wild appearance (lack of clothes, hairiness), the carrying of a staff, or a hunched stance.[102] In the later Middle Ages, the isolation of the mad, and the tempestuousness of their minds, was shown in the Ship of Fools, an image that endured into the Early Modern period and typified the anarchy of madness.[103]

Notorious madmen and madwomen

Aside from the great figures of literature (and Hugo van der Goes), it is difficult to engage individually with mad people of the Middle Ages. Nonetheless, a few distinguished individuals are well-documented and provide important case studies.

Margery Kempe, 1373–1458

Since the rediscovery of the *Book of Margery Kempe* in 1934, historians have been particularly interested in using this text to explore medieval connections between madness, divine inspiration, and mysticism.[104] Although narrated in the third person, the *Book* is widely held to be the first autobiography written in the English language. It relates Margery's spiritual journey beginning with an episode of madness.[105] Kempe described her madness as an attack from demons, causing her to make slanderous accusations against her family, renounce her faith, tear at her own skin, and contemplate suicide. The rest of the *Book* focuses on her spiritual journey and her conversations with Jesus and God.[106]

King Charles VI of France, r. 1380–1422, and King Henry VI of England, r. 1422–61

The lives of mad monarchs stand out prominently in the historical record because of the impact that the madness of a king could have on an entire kingdom. This is a phenomenon that has been investigated by Vivian Green, who also questions whether the label of madness was bestowed on weak rulers to discredit them rather than on those who would otherwise have been recognized as mad.[107] Were the symptoms of madness recognized by contemporaries in their kings the same as those recognized in mad commoners?

R. C. Famiglietti has probed this thesis in relation to King Charles VI of France. He argues that both contemporaries and historians have adopted the viewpoint that Charles' politically-sound decisions were made during lucid intervals whereas flawed judgements indicate that the King was hindered by madness.[108] Bernard Guenée has explored extensively the contemporary evidence relating to Charles's 'madness', with a consideration of what contemporaries may have thought of their king, in light of the discretion that contemporary writers may have felt compelled to show when describing the scandalous madness of a king.[109]

Charles's grandson, King Henry VI, was King of England from 1422 until he was deposed in 1461. He was briefly restored to the throne in 1470, but the crown was assumed by Edward IV in 1471 and Henry died soon after. Cory James Rushton has argued that Henry's earlier bout of madness (1453–4) was 'a key component' in the collapse of his regime and that of the Lancastrian dynasty.[110] The Duke of York was appointed Lord Protector but later harboured ambitions for the throne: the future Edward IV was his son. Both Rushton and Turner have explored the issue of the wardship of Henry VI, as a mad king.[111] Turner draws attention to the difficulty of circumventing the leadership of a mentally incompetent king whose physical body remained representative of the body politic and thus could not be replaced.[112] A lack of personal self-governance in the figure of the king had huge repercussions for the political and symbolic governance and identity of the state.

Beyond the Christian West: Byzantium and Islam

For a final and unusually vivid example of a mad ruler, we could look back in time to the later sixth century and away from Europe to the eastern Mediterranean. When the late Roman (or Byzantine) emperor Justin II (r. 565–78) lost his reason, he made animal-like noises or rushed about his palace by turns hiding under the bed or trying to throw himself from a window. His attendants had to chase and restrain him, frightening him into submission. But they also tried to restore him to reason by pleasant diversions. They pulled him about (like a child) on a throne mounted on a little wagon and they played music to him on an organ (music therapy akin to that used with Saul – and with Hugo van der Goes). Our source for these amusements is the very hostile chronicler John bishop of Ephesus.[113] He saw in Justin's madness a divine punishment, achieved through demonic possession – a punishment for the emperor's persecution of those whom John upheld as orthodox Christians. The doctrinal details of that do not matter here. What is noteworthy, however, is the naturalistic treatment that John ascribed to Justin's attendants. It was not medical, but it was a form of psychotherapy. John was quite explicitly reporting city gossip rather than eyewitness accounts, yet it is of interest that the gossip was couched in such terms and not, say, attempted exorcism or prayer and penance.

Byzantium is worth including in any survey of medieval madness for two reasons: there is vivid evidence and some excellent scholarship that should be more widely appreciated; and it offers instructive similarities and contrasts with western Europe. Here, despite John's demonic aetiology of the emperor's insanity, is a world as capable as any other medieval culture of separating out, at least to some extent, possession from naturally occurring insanity.[114] Byzantium displays a medical tradition that maintained Galenic categories and treatments for mental illness broadly without interruption. There is some evidence of care in monasteries or at shrines for both the chronically possessed and those with such afflictions as an 'illness coming from the cranium'. But specific hospitals for the insane are not evidenced in the quite detailed prescriptions of founders or the descriptions by contemporaries that survive in plenty from the Byzantine millennium.[115]

So far so European. What marks Byzantium more strongly out from the West is the 'holy fool'. In Byzantium, the mad and the possessed might be killed or restrained, kicked or cast out. Yet, ironically, some of our best anecdotal evidence for the daily life of the insane on the streets of Byzantine cities comes from the biographies written of those who feigned madness. They had become 'fools for the sake of Christ': *saloi*, a special Greek term for this form of piety quite distinct from the vocabulary of insanity. They were following the exhortation of St Paul (I Corinthians 4: 10), to avoid attention from admirers of sanctity and still more as a critique of the corrupt norms of the society around them. Byzantine culture is quite distinct from those of medieval Europe in its high estimation of such forms of sanctity.[116] The few contemporary exceptions that can be mustered (as they have been by Sergey Ivanov) prove the rule that, as we have already seen, this type of feigned insanity was not widely valued in the West.[117]

To a brief Byzantine parallel, we should add medieval Islam:

> In general, insanity has been presented as a significant aspect of Islamic social history. Insanity as a medical concept was closely related to the development of Islamic sciences and institutions; religious healing [of the insane] was intimately associated with the growth of Muslim saints; and the madman as holy fool was vivid expression of the evolution of Muslim religiosity. Moreover, in the general areas of healing, perceiving, and protecting the insane, there is a remarkable continuity with the pre-Islamic Christian culture of the Middle East. The persistence of the Galenic medical tradition in both theory and practice is obvious. Less evident but equally important is the continuity in religious healing and magic, sacred and profane perceptions of madness, and the legal status of the madman.

Those are the conclusions of Michael Dols's posthumously published synoptic study of madness in the medieval Islamic Middle East.[118] They have not been bettered, though some might now question the extent to which he mixes medieval evidence with that of nineteenth-century travellers and modern ethnographers to support his vision of continuity. His monumental traversing of documentary evidence, narratives, law, medicine (both Galenic and the Medicine of the Prophet), theology and religious writings, and imaginative literature suggests, as he put it, 'social tolerance of the mentally afflicted'. Far more than in the Byzantine or western European worlds, moreover, the insane, while never free of the threat of severe restraint and maltreatment, might look for help and healing beyond the family to a variety of healers, saints and mystics, 'old wives', magicians, exorcists and doctors. Most strikingly, largely because of that Galenic inheritance, taken over into Arabic from the Greek and Syriac, those who were founding hospitals in the major cities were also patrons of Galenic learning, with its naturalistic and indeed largely somatic conception of mental illness. Their hospitals reflected the fact. From the tenth century onwards, an insane patient might be hospitalized and receive a treatment that relied as much on carefully modulated diet and the psychotherapy of pleasant surroundings, soothing sounds (including musical performances), and beguiling scents as on restraint or beatings.

Conclusions

All conclusions in this fraught area of the history of medieval madness, ripe for further study, must be incomplete or provisional. We have stressed, first, the importance of the background connections posited between mind, body and soul for any understanding of medieval conceptions of insanity; second, the close interplay of the religious and the medical, often more specifically the demonic and the natural, in accounts of causation; and finally the variety of overlapping treatments that might be available, from physical restraint to medication and psychological diversion, not to mention brutality or neglect. These themes run through much of the historiography we have discussed, but the overall picture remains, as we warned at the outset, fragmentary and incomplete. Synthesis of medical, legal, theological and social perspectives on the subject, and the placing of the result of that synthesis in the wider context of beliefs and practices about reason, health and the soul both remain to be accomplished.

Notes

1 Trans. Faith Wallis, *Medieval Medicine: A Reader* (Toronto: University of Toronto Press, 2010), 353. For what follows see Peter Murray Jones, 'Music Therapy in the Later Middle Ages: The Case of Hugo van der Goes', in *Music as Medicine: The History of Music Therapy Since Antiquity*, ed. Peregrine Horden (Aldershot and Burlington, VT: Ashgate, 2000), 120–44.
2 Wallis, 351–2, 356.
3 Leigh Ann Craig, 'The History of Madness and Mental Illness in the Middle Ages: Directions and Questions,' *History Compass* 12 (2014), 729–44, is a brief but bibliographically rich survey. Among older studies still the most valuable are: George Rosen, *Madness in Society* (London: Routledge, 1968), H. H. Beek, *Waanzin in de Middeleeuwen: Beeld van de Gestoorde en bemoeienis met de Zieke* (Nijkerk: Callenbach; Haarlem: de Toorts, 1969), Basil Clarke, *Mental Disorder in Earlier Britain* (Cardiff: University of Wales Press, 1975), Judith S. Neaman, *Suggestion of the Devil: The Origins of Madness* (New York: Doubleday Anchor Books, 1975), S. Kemp and K. Williams, *Medieval Psychology* (New York: Greenwood Press, 1990), Muriel Laharie, *La folie au moyen âge XI*-XIII*e* siècles* (Paris: Le Léopard d'Or, 1991), Jean-Marie Fritz, *Le discours du fou au moyen âge, XIIe-XIIIe siècles: Etude comparé des discours littéraire, medical, juridique et théologique de la folie* (Paris: Presses Universitaires de France, 1992).
4 E. Ruth Harvey, *The Inward Wits: Psychological Theory in the Middle Ages and the Renaissance, Warburg Institute Surveys* 6 (London: Warburg Institute, 1975), 33.
5 For an exploration of medieval representations of Nebuchadnezzar, Penelope B. R. Doob, *Nebuchadnezzar's Children: Conventions of Madness in Middle English Literature* (New Haven: Yale University Press, 1974).
6 Harvey, *The Inward Wits*, 33.
7 Ibid., 7–8.
8 Ibid., 2.
9 For example, Gerard O'Daly, *Augustine's Philosophy of Mind* (London: Duckworth, 1987) and Anthony Kenny, *Aquinas on Mind* (New York: Routledge, 1993).
10 Harvey, *The Inward Wits*, 4–6.
11 Leslie Lockett, *Anglo-Saxon Psychologies in the Vernacular and Latin Traditions* (Toronto: University of Toronto Press, 2011).
12 Ibid., 110–78.
13 Ibid., 17–53.
14 Ibid., 427.
15 Thomas Aquinas, *Summa Theologica*, trans. Roberto Busa (Rome: Leoninum, 1906), Tertia Pars, Quaestio 68, www.corpusthomisticum.org/sth4066.html (accessed 13 March 2016).
16 Ibid., Tertia Pars, Quaestio 80, www.corpusthomisticum.org/sth4080.html (accessed 13 March 2016).
17 Stanley W. Jackson, *Melancholia and Depression from Hippocratic to Modern Times* (New Haven: Yale University Press, 1986), 74, but see also Andrew T. Crislip, 'The Sin of Sloth or the Illness of Demons? The Demon of Acedia in Early Christian Monasticism,' *Harvard Theological Review* 98.2 (2005): 143–69.
18 Ibid., 66.
19 Ibid., 66–71.
20 Mary Francis Wack, *Lovesickness in the Middle Ages: The* Viaticum *and its Commentaries* (Philadelphia: University of Pennsylvania Press, 1990); Amy Hollywood, 'Acute Melancholia,' *Harvard Theological Review* 99.4 (2006): 361–80.
21 Luke Demaitre, *Medieval Medicine: The Art of Healing, from Head to Toe* (Santa Barbara: Praeger, 2013).
22 Jackson, *Melancholia and Depression*, 113.
23 Ibid., 127–8.
24 For Paul of Aegina's (625–690 CE) theories concerning madness, Jackson, *Melancholia and Depression*, 54–6. For archaeological and written evidence of Anglo-Saxon medical practice, Christina Lee, 'Body and Soul: Disease and Impairment,' in *The Material Culture of*

Daily Living in the Anglo-Saxon World, ed. Maren Clegg Hyer and Gale R. Owen-Crocker (Exeter: University of Exeter Press, 2011), 293–309.

25 Monica Green, 'Salerno on the Thames: The Genesis of Anglo-Norman Medical Literature,' in *Language and Culture in Medieval Britain: The French of England, c. 1100–c.1500*, ed. Jocelyn Wogan-Browne (Woodbridge: Boydell, 2009), 222.

26 Hastings Rashdall, *The Universities of Europe in the Middle Ages: Salerno, Bologna, Paris*, first edn 1895 (Cambridge: Cambridge University Press, 2010), 78.

27 Avicenna, *Canon medicinae (latine): a Gerardo Cremonensi translatus* (Venice: Bonetus Locatellus, 1490), 257.

28 Demaitre, *Medieval Medicine*, 129.

29 Ibid., 130.

30 For an examination of medial theories regarding frenzy, D. Jacquart, 'Les avatars de la Phrénitis chez Avicenne et Rhazès,' in *Maladie et maladies: histoire et conceptualisation. Mélanges en l'honneur de Mirko Grmek*, ed. Danielle Gourevitch (Geneva: Droz, 1992), 181–92.

31 Constantine the African, 'Liber Pantegni,' in *Opera Omnia*, ed. Isaac Israeli (Lyons: Trot, 1515), I-CXLIV [in the second set of foliation], fo. xlj^v.

32 Ibid., fo. xcviij^r.

33 Jacquart, 'Les avatars de la phrénitis.'

34 Constantine the African, 'Liber Pantegni,' fo. xcic^v.

35 Ibid., and fo. xli^v.

36 Gariopontus, *Passionarius Galeni* (Lyon: Trot, 1526), fo. v^v.

37 Ibid.

38 Constantine the African, fo., xcix^v.

39 Ibid., fo. xlij^v.

40 Ibid., fo. xlij^r.

41 Ibid., fo. xcix^v.

42 Jackson, *Melancholia and Depression*, 63–4.

43 Fernando Salmón, 'From Patient to Text? Narratives of Pain and Madness in Medieval Scholasticism,' in *Between Text and Patient: The Medical Enterprise in Medieval and Early Modern Europe*, ed. Florence Eliza Glaze and Brian K. Nance (Florence: Sismel, 2011), 390–1.

44 Constantine the African, 'Liber Pantegni,' fo. xcix^v.

45 Rachel Koopmans, *Wonderful to Relate: Miracle Stories and Miracle Collecting in High Medieval England* (Philadelphia: University of Pennsylvania Press, 2010).

46 Claire Trenery, 'Miracles for the Mad: Representations of Insanity in English Miracle Narratives From the Long Twelfth Century' (PhD diss., Royal Holloway University of London, 2016).

47 Leigh Ann Craig, 'The Spirit of Madness: Uncertainty, Diagnosis, and the Restoration of Sanity in the Miracles of Henry VI,' *Journal of Medieval Religious Cultures* 30.1 (2013): 61.

48 Catherine Rider, 'Demons and Mental Disorder in Late Medieval Medicine,' in *Mental (Dis)Order in Later Medieval Europe*, ed. Sari Katajala-Peltomaa and Susanna Niiranen (Leiden: Brill, 2014), 47.

49 Laharie, *La folie au moyen âge*, 25–6.

50 Nancy Caciola, *Discerning Spirits: Divine and Demonic Possession in the Middle Ages* (Ithaca: Cornell University Press, 2003), 191.

51 The growing interest in the discernment of spirits is explored in Caciola, *Discerning Spirits*.

52 Alain Boureau, *Satan the Heretic: The Birth of Demonology in the Medieval West*, trans. Teresa Lavender Fagan (Chicago and London: University of Chicago Press, 2006), 122–3.

53 F. Chave-Mahir, 'Les cris du démoniaque. Exorciser les possédés dans les récits hagiographiques des XIIe et XIIIe siècles,' in *Haro! Noël! Oyé! Pratiques du cri au Moyen Age*, ed. by D. Lett and N. Offenstadt (Paris: Publications de la Sorbonne, 2003), 131.

54 Sari Katajala-Peltomaa, 'Demonic Possession as Physical and Mental Disturbance in the Later Medieval Canonisation Processes,' in Katajala-Peltomaa and Niiranen, *Mental (Dis) Order*, 109.

55 D. Barthélemy, 'La guérison des possédées dans *Les Miracles de Saint Benoît*,' in *Abbon: Un abbé de l'an Mil* (Turnhout: Brepols, 2008), 343.

56 Boureau, *Satan the Heretic*, 123.

57 Ibid., 124.

58 Robert Bartlett, *The Natural and the Supernatural in the Middle Ages* (Cambridge: Cambridge University Press, 2008), 109.

59 Nigel Walker, *Crime and Insanity in England*, vol. 1 (Edinburgh: Edinburgh University Press, 1968), 15–34.

60 S. A. Jurasinki, 'Madness and Responsibility in Anglo-Saxon England,' in *Peace and Protection in the Middle Ages*, ed. T. B. Lambert and D. Rollason (Durham: Centre for Medieval and Renaissance Studies, 2009), 99–120.

61 Alexander Murray, *Suicide in the Middle Ages: The Violent Against Themselves* (Oxford: Oxford University Press, 1998), 162–5.

62 Sara M. Butler, 'Representing the Middle Ages: The Insanity Defence in Medieval England,' in *The Treatment of Disabled Persons in Medieval Europe: Examining Disability in the Historical, Legal, Literary, Medical and Religious Discourses of the Middle Ages*, ed. Wendy J. Turner and Tory Vandeventer Pearman (Lewiston: Edwin Mellen, 2010), 117–31.

63 Ibid., 122–5.

64 Ibid., 128.

65 Alexandra Pfau, 'Protecting or Restraining? Madness as a Disability in Late Medieval France,' in *Disability in the Middle Ages: Reconsiderations and Reverberations*, ed. Joshua Eyler (Farnham: Ashgate, 1988), 97.

66 Wendy J. Turner, 'Silent Testimony: Emotional Displays and Lapses in Memory as Indicators of Mental Instability in Medieval English Investigations,' in *Madness in Medieval Law and Custom*, ed. Wendy J. Turner (Leiden: Brill, 2010), 81–95.

67 Ibid., 84 and 81.

68 Wendy J. Turner, *Care and Custody of the Mentally Ill, Incompetent, and Disabled in Medieval England* (Turnhout: Brepols, 2013).

69 Kate Parkin, 'Tales of Idiots, Signifying Something: Evidence of Process in the Inquisitions Post Mortem,' in *The Fifteenth-Century Inquisitions Post Mortem: A Companion*, ed. Michael Hicks (Woodbridge: Boydell, 2012), 80.

70 Ibid., 79.

71 Ibid., 95.

72 Colin R. Pickett, *Mental Affliction and Church Law: An Historical Synopsis of Roman and Ecclesiastical Law and a Canonical Commentary* (Ottawa: University of Ottawa Press, 1952).

73 Ibid., 11–100.

74 Ibid., 30.

75 Ibid., 41.

76 Ibid., 50.

77 Ibid., 43–5.

78 Jerome Kroll and Bernard Bachrach, 'Sin and Mental Illness in the Middle Ages,' *Psychological Medicine* 14 (1984): 507.

79 Ibid., 509.

80 Ibid., 511.

81 Jerome Kroll and Bernard Backrach, 'Sin and the Etiology of Disease in Pre-Crusade Europe,' *The Journal of the History of Medicine and Allied Sciences* 41 (1986): 407.

82 Sabina Flanagan, 'Heresy, Madness and Possession in the High Middles Ages,' in *Heresy in Transition: Transforming Ideas of Heresy in Medieval and Early Modern Europe*, ed. I. Hunter, J. C. Laursen, and C. J. Nederman (Aldershot: Ashgate, 2005), 31 and 41.

83 Ibid., 35 and 41.

84 Ibid., 41.

85 Katherine Park and John Henderson, '"The First Hospital among Christians": The Ospedale di Santa Maria Nuova in Early Sixteenth-Century Florence,' *Medical History*, 35 (1991): 183. For context see further Henderson, *The Renaissance Hospital* (New Haven and London: Yale University Press, 2006), esp. 312–13.

86 Jonathan Andrews, Asa Briggs, Roy Porter, Penny Tucker and Keir Waddington, *The History of Bethlem* (London and New York: Routledge, 1997), 116.
87 For what follows see Peregrine Horden, 'The Late Antique Origins of the Lunatic Asylum?', in *Transformations of Late Antiquity: Essays for Peter Brown*, ed. P. Rousseau and M. Papoutsakis (Farnham and Burlington, VT: Ashgate, 2009), 259–78, esp. 276–7.
88 Horden, 'Origins,' 260–61.
89 Harper discusses various approaches to 'madness' and 'folly' and the boundaries of terminology in French and English scholarship. Stephen Harper, *Insanity, Individuals, and Society in Late-Medieval English Literature: The Subject of Madness, Studies in Medieval Literature* 26 (Lewiston: Edwin Mellen, 2003), 11–4.
90 Ibid., 19.
91 Doob, *Nebuchadnezzar's Children*, 54–5.
92 Harper, *Insanity, Individuals, and Society*, 20–1.
93 Sylvia Huot, *Madness in Medieval French Literature: Identities Found and Lost* (Oxford: Oxford University Press, 2003), 1 and 9.
94 Ibid., 2.
95 Ibid., 136–209.
96 Ibid., 180.
97 Corinne Saunders, '"The thoughtful maladie": Madness and Vision in Medieval Writing,' in *Madness and Creativity in Literature and Culture*, ed. Corinne Saunders and Jane Macnaughton (Houndmills: Palgrave Macmillan, 2005), 74.
98 Renée L. Curtis, 'Tristan *forsené*: the Episode of the Hero's Madness in the *Prose Tristan*,' in *The Changing Face of Arthurian Romance: Essays on Arthurian Romance in Memory of Cedric E. Pickford*, ed. Alison Adams, Armel H. Diverres, Karen Stern and Kenneth Varty (Woodbridge: Boyell, 1986), 10–22.
99 Ibid., 11.
100 Doob, *Nebuchadnezzar's Children*, 76.
101 Caciola, *Discerning Spirits*, 36–40.
102 Sander L. Gilman, *Seeing the Insane* (Lincoln: University of Nebraska Press, 1996), 2–21.
103 Ibid., 44–7.
104 Richard Lawes, 'The Madness of Margery Kempe,' in *Medieval Mystical Tradition: England, Ireland and Wales*, ed. E. A. Jones (Cambridge: D.S. Brewer, 1999), 147.
105 Alison Torn, '"Margery Kempe: Madwoman or Mystic – A Narrative Approach to the Representation of Madness and Mysticism in Medieval England,' in *Narrative and Fiction: An Interdisciplinary Approach*, ed. David Robinson, Pamela Fisher, Noel Gilzean, Tracey Lee, Sarah Jane Robinson, and Pete Woodcock (Huddersfield: University of Huddersfield, 2008), 79–80.
106 For a modern English translation, Anthony Bale, trans. *The Book of Margery Kempe* (Oxford: Oxford University Press, 2015). For the section on madness, 11–13.
107 Vivian Green, *The Madness of Kings: Personal Trauma and the Fate of Nations* (Stroud: Sutton, 1993), xiii.
108 R. C. Famiglietti, *Royal Intrigue: Crisis at the Court of Charles VI, 1392–1420* (New York: AMS Press, 1986), 1.
109 Bernard Guenée, *La folie de Charles VI: roi bien aimé* (Paris: Perrin, 2004), 23–34.
110 Cory James Rushton, 'The King's Stupor: Dealing with Royal Paralysis in Late Medieval England,' in *Madness in Medieval Law and Custom*, ed. Turner, 150.
111 Wendy J. Turner, 'A Cure for the King Means the Health of the Country: The Mental and Physical Health of Henry VI,' in *Madness in Medieval Law and Custom*, ed. Turner, 177–95.
112 Ibid., 177–8.
113 John of Ephesus, *Ecclesiastical History*, pt 3, bk 3, chs 2–3, ed. E. W. Brooks (Paris and Louvain: Corpus Scriptorum Christianorum Orientalium, 1935), vol. 105, 149–53 (Syriac); trans. R. Payne Smith (Oxford: Oxford University Press, 1860), 166–70. For full details of the text and editions see http://syri.ac/johnofephesus#EH (accessed 13 March 2016).
114 Margaret Trenchard-Smith, 'Insanity, Exculpation and Disempowerment in Byzantine Law,' in *Madness in Medieval Law and Custom*, ed. Turner, 39–55, at 44.

115 The main monographs, neither wholly reliable in their interpretations: Timothy S. Miller, *The Birth of the Hospital in the Byzantine Empire*, 2nd edn (Baltimore and London: Johns Hopkins University Press, 1997); Demetrios J. Constantelos, *Byzantine Philanthropy and Social Welfare*, 2nd edn (New Rochelle, NY: Caratzas, 1991).
116 Horden, 'Responses to Possession and Insanity in the Earlier Byzantine World', *Social History of Medicine*, 6 (1993): 177–194.
117 Sergey A. Ivanov, *Holy Fools in Byzantium and Beyond* (Oxford: Oxford University Press, 2006).
118 Michael W. Dols, *Majnūn: The Madman in Medieval Islamic Society* (Oxford: Clarendon Press, 1992), 475.

Part II

PROFESSIONS, INSTITUTIONS, AND TOOLS

4

HEALERS AND HEALING IN THE EARLY MODERN HEALTH CARE MARKET

Elizabeth Mellyn

From roughly 1500 to 1700, Europe teemed with representations of madness. Ships of fools, melancholy artists, brooding scholars, obsessive lovers, mad prophets, and the divinely or demonically possessed leapt from the pages of literary, philosophical, and theological works in greater numbers than ever before.[1] Intended to entertain as much as to caution and instruct, the mad and their madnesses were highly moral reminders of the wretchedness of the human condition, the vanity of earthly life, and the glory of the kingdom of God.

Authors no less illustrious than Martin Luther (1483–1546) went so far as to insist that the world itself was mad. Tommaso Garzoni (1549–89), a Lateran canon and prolific satirist, similarly envisioned the world as a gigantic hospital in which folly lorded over humanity. For him, the world was an "image of madness itself;" men and women, enfeebled by Adam's Fall, stumbled their way through it, only to succumb at some point in their lives to mental anguish in one form or another. But, if madness did indeed visit all men and women, the early modern period looked most favorably on melancholy. In the late fifteenth century, Marsilio Ficino (1433–99), a famous medically trained Florentine Neo-Platonist, dusted off and popularized the ancient idea that eminent philosophers, politicians, poets, and artists all tended to suffer from it.[2]

This sixteenth-century melancholy vogue once captivated scholarly imaginations. Beginning in the 1950s and 1960s, historians of art, literature, and philosophy trained their sights on Europe's fascination with madness generally and melancholy in particular as a way of understanding the monumental changes taking place in early modern European high culture. But mentally disordered men and women did not proliferate only in the European imagination.

Scholars have more recently sought sources that evoke something of the lived, rather than solely the imagined, experience of early modern mental disorder. To that end, they have mined Europe's rich legal archives, sifted through doctors' case books and pored over the records of Europe's early mental hospitals to catch ordinary men and women in the act of solving the practical problems mental disorder brought to their households and communities.[3] Sixteenth- and seventeenth-century legal records, for example, show mentally disturbed men and women appearing in Europe's civil and criminal courts more frequently than they had in the Middle Ages.[4] More and more, families were working with and sometimes against magistrates to make long-term custodial arrangements for their unhinged, incompetent, or criminally insane kin and judicial apparatuses were adapting to accommodate them.[5] At the same time, miracle books throughout Europe relate hundreds of stories of people going on pilgrimage to ask saints to free their mournful or frenzied relatives from the grips of madness.[6] Scholars have also found that mental disorder paced the gilded halls of early modern Europe's palaces. It hung so heavily on some crowned heads that one scholar has dubbed the sixteenth century the "age of the melancholy prince."[7] In contrast to the Middle Ages, madness in early modern European culture and experience was a darkness most visible.

Despite this heightened visibility, the archival record paints a general picture of evolutionary rather than revolutionary change. In many respects, the institutional and therapeutic strategies employed to address madness during the Middle Ages remained strikingly similar throughout the early modern period. Although European courts and magistracies increasingly intervened in the way families managed their mentally disturbed kin and mental hospitals began to appear in European cities, the family continued to be the custodial and therapeutic institution of first resort. The daily management of mental and physical health was very much "a domestic affair;" most care of the mentally disordered began and ended within the walls of the household.[8]

Medieval medical culture was also long-lived. In the high Middle Ages, the central organizing framework for understanding health and illness was the doctrine of the humors, a two millennia-old idea first forged by ancient Greeks and then transmitted to Europe in the eleventh and twelfth centuries via Arabic intermediaries.[9] Not the discovery of the New World and its exotic pharmacopeia nor the development of iatrochemistry, a chemically-based alternative to Greek medicine, displaced the humoral model. It remained instead the regnant paradigm for understanding health and illness, mental disorder included, until the eighteenth century.[10]

The humoral tradition was part of a durable worldview that saw man as a microcosm of the universe and recognized the powerful impact natural and supernatural forces had on the human body and mind. Religious upheaval in the sixteenth century transformed nearly every aspect of European life, and yet this worldview prevailed. The humoral body was thought to be at the mercy of its immediate natural and more remote cosmic environments. And so medieval and early modern men and women were just as likely to attribute mental disorder to an unfavorable alignment of stars, the phases of the moon, God or a demon as they were to a bodily illness.

Moreover, both medieval and early modern families who sought treatment outside of the household for their mentally disturbed relatives entered a pluralistic and competitive market for health care peddled by a range of healers from different social classes. In that market, efficacy rather than status or occupation determined a practitioner's success and promiscuity characterized the consumer's choices. To address all possible causes of mental derangement, be they celestial, terrestrial, or demonic, medieval and early modern men and women were likely to enlist the help of as many kinds of healers as they could afford, from priests and exorcists to occult healers and empirics to university- or guild-trained physicians.[11]

Although continuity is the dominant theme in the history of attitudes to and treatment of mental disorder from the Middle Ages through the early modern period, the significant historical changes taking place between the fifteenth and seventeenth centuries did affect how the problem was approached and addressed. First, unlike their medieval counterparts, early modern Europeans had access to a massive market in popular, vernacular medical self-help literature thanks to the print revolution of the sixteenth century.[12] Thus, an ever larger part of the lay public became conversant with the principles of academic medicine albeit in a popularized, nontechnical form. Second, they also had access to an increasingly large and complex market for health care, populated by a greater number and range of healers.[13] Third, in some regions, the religious reformations of the sixteenth century had a profound impact on how Europeans deployed spiritual physic. Inspired by Martin Luther, evangelical reformers considered petitions to Christian saints and their relics to be idolatrous thereby stripping them of their putative healing powers. They also repudiated medieval rituals like exorcism that smacked of priestcraft or magic. In regions that became Protestant, spiritual therapies intended to treat mind and body relied on individual and collective prayer and hymn-singing; in Catholic regions, saints' shrines continued to be important sites for healing sick bodies and addled minds and priests continued to exorcise malevolent supernatural entities.

At home with madness

It was once customary to tell histories of medieval and early modern madness from the perspective of the intellectuals who tried to define it and the professionals who claimed the ability to treat it. The learned output of physicians and natural philosophers provides excellent sources for observing how academic culture understood madness at its extremes, from the intellectually disabled, to the raving maniac, to the despairing melancholic. To be sure, extreme cases of madness are fascinating. Take for example the strange, sporadic mass outbreaks of dancing mania often referred to as St. Vitus's dance that erupted in England, the Netherlands, and throughout the Holy Roman Empire in the fourteenth through to the sixteenth centuries. In the words of one fifteenth-century German witness, during this "amazing epidemic," some of the frenzied dancers "jumped until their ribs or loins broke, and they died."[14] Some contemporaries called it "falling sickness," others St. John's disease. What it actually was remains a mystery. But, it is important to remember that in isolation, normative sources and sensational cases both silence how ordinary men and women experienced and grappled with mental disorder in their households on a day-to-day basis and conceal the complexity of the culture of health care in which they lived.

Medieval and early modern madness was very much a domestic affair, since real institutional alternatives to household care only began to emerge in the eighteenth century. The earliest hospitals were largely charitable institutions that administered acute care exclusively to the sick poor unless a wealthy family made them a material offer they could not sensibly refuse.[15] Hospitals that treated the severely mentally disordered or were specifically designed for that purpose did appear in Europe as early as the fourteenth and fifteenth centuries. Still, the number of families who used their services was negligible until the eighteenth and nineteenth centuries.[16] Monasteries and convents also tended to shun severely mentally disturbed men and women, seeing them as threats to the material and spiritual integrity of their communities.[17] Some of the criminally insane ended up in Europe's prisons. Yet, like hospitals and monasteries, they were ill-equipped to support or treat them. If responsibility was not successfully foisted back on their families, the criminally insane were often released back onto the streets only to end up in prison once again.[18]

Physical and mental health care also started in the household.[19] The principles on which that care was based were grounded in large part on humoral doctrine. This way of thinking envisioned a body composed of fluids or humors whose good temperament (*eukrasía*) promoted health and whose bad temperament (*dyskrasía*) caused disease. Health and illness were not distinct conditions, but existed along a spectrum as relative states of greater or lesser equilibrium. Since the body was thought constantly to teeter between health and illness, the management of one's temperament was an important part of one's daily routine. While the management of health involved maintaining humoral balance, the treatment of disease sought to restore it. In both cases, the approach was the same; namely, the regulation of the six non-naturals, those factors affecting the body and mind that were not part of the body itself: the environment and climate; diet; the evacuation and retention of bodily substances; exercise and rest; sleep and waking; and the passions of the soul.

The last non-natural, the passions of the soul, attests to the intimate connection thought to have existed between body and mind.[20] In the humoral system, the imbalance or corruption of bodily humors caused abnormal thought, feeling, and behavior, but mental disturbances were also thought to harm the body.[21] Intense emotions were blamed for all manner of physical ailments, from respiratory diseases to rheumatism; the inner turmoil created by broken hearts and unforeseen terror was considered powerful enough to kill.[22] The English astrological physician and rector of Great Linford, Richard Napier (1559–1634), for example, had a patient who "died of a consumption taken by grief of her husband's debts."[23] The common view that fear of the plague might make a person more susceptible to it may have induced cities like Pistoia to promulgate ordinances during the height of the 1348 epidemic to ban all bell ringers at the cathedral church from ringing bells during funerals so that the tolling would not produce anxiety in the sick.[24] Similarly, in the first half of the sixteenth century, the Bohemian physician Johannus Berka of Choceň advised those who owned expensive clothes to wear them during outbreaks of plague because of the salubrious pleasure they evoked.[25] Care of the body could not be separated from care of the mind in the humoral system; rather they were interconnected aspects of overall health.

The intimate connection between mind and body is also evident in a case the famous professor of medicine at Padua, Giovanbattista da Monte (1498–1552), consulted on in collaboration with two other physicians. The three doctors were called to offer their opinions on the grave condition of a Jewish merchant who had "gone out of his senses." The merchant's friends said that commercial activities in the recent past had frequently taken him from Italy to northern Europe where he was exposed to extremes of heat and cold. When he returned to Italy after one of these trips, he succumbed to severe mental disturbance: "his eyes moved without his control, [he had] an expression of rage, he wished to strike those around him, [and] he rolled himself from his bed."[44] All three decided that the merchant had fallen afoul of melancholy and his lifestyle was to blame:

his temperament, age, and the time of year all contributed to the generation of these symptoms. [The patient] went on a very long journey, during which his head suffered great heat, and then after the heat, cold. He worked a great deal without stopping; he ate rich, heat-producing foods as is the custom in Poland and northern Europe. He consumed more rich food in a day than we eat in a year. He drank strong wine, and ate all manner of substance that produced dryness and heat.[26]

One of the doctors prescribed adjusting his diet, proper sleep and therapeutic baths to temper the melancholy that environmental factors and bad habits had generated in his brain.[27] Da Monte, by contrast, believed the merchant was likely past the point where balance could be restored through the six non-naturals. He suggested bleeding instead – another procedure aimed at restoring balance, but through surgery. In the end, treatment proved futile. Da Monte reported that the merchant died in the days following his attack. The consultation as a whole suggests that the merchant need not have died had he lived differently, namely, had he paid attention to how the external environment, the demands of his occupation, and his eating and drinking habits affected his body and mind.

This case implies that although prevention and treatment were complementary parts of health care, prevention was thought to rest mainly in the hands of ordinary men and women while therapy belonged to the expertise of trained physicians. This division of labor was made possible by the dissemination of various types of medical self-help literature often written in or translated into the vernacular by academic physicians for lay audiences beginning in the mid-thirteenth century.[28] One of the most prominent examples of this important genre is Aldobrandino of Siena's *Régime du corps* composed around 1257 in French for Beatrice of Savoy (1205–67) at her request.[29]

In this highly popular text, Aldobrandino adapted the knowledge he had garnered from his academic medical education to accommodate a non-scholarly audience.[30] Based on the Greco-Arabic humoral tradition, the *Régime* outlined the basic guidelines for preserving health through the six non-naturals, instructed readers on the care of important body parts and organ systems, including the head and the brain, and disclosed the qualities of food and drink so readers could select the diet best suited to their temperament and avoid foods that imperiled it.[31] To distinguish the professional work of the trained physician from the daily hygienic practices men and women carried out at home, Aldobrandino introduced the *Régime* by saying that its purpose was not therapeutic, but prophylactic. It taught its audience not how to cure disease, but how to prevent it.[32] Aldobrandino's regimen of health and the many others like it that circulated throughout medieval Europe made hygiene, diet, and lifestyle choices all a part of daily mental and physical health care. Moreover, they placed the burden of preventive care largely on the shoulders of ordinary men and women.

The introduction of print and the rise of print culture in the sixteenth century served both to put an unprecedented number of relatively inexpensive vernacular health care books in the hands of laypeople and to accelerate the demand for them.[33] By the mid-sixteenth century, regimens of health, herbals, recipe books, collections of medical aphorisms, plague treatises, lapidaries, and electuaries were finding their way into the hands of a larger, more diverse lay audience hungry for information on how to stay healthy, how to get pregnant, how to fight infertility and cure impotence, how to age gracefully and live longer, and, of course, how to stay cheerful and avoid melancholy.[34] Books for a more sophisticated vernacular audience like Timothy Bright's *Treatise of Melancholie* (1586), André du Laurens' *Discour de la Conservation de la Veue des Maladies Melancholiques des Catarrhes et de las Viellesse* (1594), Jacques Fernand's *De la Maladie d'Amour ou Melancholique Erotique* (1610) and Robert Burton's bestseller, *Anatomy of Melancholy* (1612) also proliferated and enjoyed broad appeal.[35]

The most successful self-help book by far was a collection of recipes called the *Secrets of Alessio of Piedmont* (*Secreti del reverendo donno Alessio piemontese*), first printed in 1555. The *Secreti* would appear in seventy editions in almost every European language, including Latin by the end of the sixteenth century, and over a hundred by the close of the seventeenth. Among recipes to prolong youth, to soothe hemorrhoids, to cure coughs and sore throats, to increase breast milk in nursing women, to reduce swelling in knees, legs, and feet, to improve bad breath, to dye skin and hair, and to ameliorate an array of other bodily infelicities was a recipe to restore a madman (*pazzo*) to health. The recipe called for an elaborate prescription of laxatives as well as cautery and oils to be applied to the head to draw noxious humors out of the body from both ends. It concluded with a prophylactic diet that served to quell a number of potentially unhealthy passions of the soul.[36] The many recipes for scented pastes, perfumes, waters, powders, and oils that people used to purify or sweeten air, their furnishings, clothing, and bodies were similarly designed to generate mental and bodily equilibrium.[37]

Madness in the market for health care

Richard Napier's casebooks show that early modern men and women blamed a diverse array of supernatural and natural causes for mental disorder. Among the supernatural causes were witches, demons, malign spirits, the planets, and the phases of the moon while natural causes included environmental, dietetic, and emotional factors. Emotional causes were often mundane. People during this period struggled, as we all do, to cope with the wear and tear of daily life. Sometimes they were not equal to the task; sadness turned to suicidal despair and anger to blind rage.

Over the course of his career, 2039 people sought Napier's help curing mental disorders. In the words of the physician and demonologist William Drage the distressing experiences that taxed them the most were: "Sadness, fears, and scares, jealousy, discontents betwixt man and wife (the most lacerating of all grief), . . . loss of love, and disappointment in a marriage, destiny of friends and loss of estates," or, as Michael MacDonald succinctly put it: "love and marriage, death and money."[38] Lovers' quarrels, unrequited love, and betrayal caused 141 of Napier's patients terrible emotional distress. One hundred and thirty-four patients fell into pathological despair at the death of beloved relatives and neighbors. The acute stress surrounding childbirth sent 81 patients to seek Napier's help. Among them was a man so traumatized by his wife's pain that he went mad. And, contrary to an earlier strand in historiographical thinking that claimed mothers and fathers developed no affective bonds to their infants and toddlers because of high mortality rates, parents, especially mothers, experienced profound anguish when their young children died.[39]

Diverse causes of mental disturbance called for diverse methods of healing. On this point, the early modern health care market did not disappoint. When domestic strategies for treating mental disorders failed, early modern men and women, mostly though not exclusively in urban areas, had at their disposal a motley group of healers, selling a broad range of products and services. Consumers might purchase care from university- or guild-trained physicians and surgeons some of whom worked closely with local apothecaries. Physicians were likely to charge the heftiest fees, but their services were not necessarily out of reach for people of more modest means. From the thirteenth century, particularly in Italy, cities employed salaried physicians to care for the sick poor often at hospitals. In the fourteenth and fifteenth centuries, religious corporations, confraternities, and guilds also began to keep physicians on retainer to treat their members.[40]

A cheaper and more popular alternative to learned physicians were empirics, a large group that included alchemical, astrological, or occult healers, remedy sellers, tooth drawers, snake charmers, and charlatans. Contrary to what modern readers might think, consumers of health care did not see members of this group as outliers on the margins of mainstream medicine. Recent scholarship has found that they offered care to a huge portion of the European population, arguably larger than that of learned physicians.[41] Often the only thing that distinguished empirics from learned practitioners was the prestige that guild matriculation or a medical degree conferred. Sick men and women eagerly sought empirics' help and considered their treatments no less efficacious for their lack of academic credentials.

Suits brought against empirics by doctors' guilds and municipal or university medical boards suggest that medical elites were at times threatened by empirics' practice. Try as they might, however, they were never able to ban empirics from the scene. Perhaps to introduce a measure of quality control, some cities instituted regulations against certain types of medical practice. In Bologna, lower-rank healers were not permitted to administer oral medications.[42] Some cities also required empirics to apply for licenses. In order to obtain one, they had to demonstrate that their methods and remedies more or less conformed to humoral medicine. While charlatans were often showmen, prancing on portable stages in colorful costumes accompanied by prostitutes, comic dwarves and dancing monkeys, their proprietary nostrums tended to follow humoral doctrine.[43]

The numerous collections of patient consultations or *consilia* that survive from the Middle Ages and early modern period in manuscript and print demonstrate that most learned physicians treated their mentally disturbed patients with a combination of the six non-naturals, therapeutic baths, powerful emetics, and venesection.[44] In these sources the six non-naturals are as much about social and cultural therapy as they are about creating healthy environments and sensible diets, in other words, establishing harmony between the inner and outer worlds. A representative *consilium* written by the famous Sienese doctor, Ugo Benzi (1376–1439), prescribed for a melancholy young man "exercise in the morning on an empty stomach . . . by walking through pleasant places near the banks of rivers in good company."[45] Under no circumstances, Benzi cautioned, should the young man over-exert himself or tax his brain. Rather, he should exchange solitude and study for conversation with friends. Other pleasing and productive activities like gardening or home repair would help too. In this case, the two non-naturals best equipped to rid the youth of sadness were exercise and attention to the passions of the soul, or, put another way, activity and socialization. Combined with divine help, blood-letting and purgation, Benzi believed health was within reach.

When confronted with a young man who imagined himself to be a priest, Italian physician Bartolomeo Montagnana (c. 1380–1452) diagnosed the "pitiable" youth with melancholy.[46] Whereas Benzi had to cure his patient of idiopathic sadness, Montagnana had to cure his of gastrointestinal distress, insomnia, delusions and instantaneous and obsessive bouts of fear. The youth even acted out his fantasy of priestly life by praying, preaching, and delivering sermons to imaginary congregants. Like Benzi, Montagnana prescribed the six non-naturals. To offset the cold and dry environment melancholy had created inside the young man, Montagnana advised him to keep his room moderately warm and humid. As for diet, his bread should not contain bran, nor should it be more than two days old. For meat he should consume young chicken, lamb, veal, or goat. He should avoid salty, bitter, and acidic food, which might make digestion difficult. He should drink only clear, sweet, white wine diluted with water. In order to rid him of his delusions (corruptas imaginationes), Montagnana similarly prescribed conversation, but also music and light entertainment. The young man should hear songs sung and different types of musical instruments played around him. He should be told amusing tales especially those involving the carryings-on of women.[47] So as not to stir up his delusions, the youth should eschew the company of all monks, but particularly those wearing black robes.[48]

Benzi and Montagnana's cures for melancholy could have been written by any number of European physicians so common were these therapies. Three generations later, for example, the consilia of the famous Dutch doctor, Jason Pratensis (1486–1558), similarly prescribed dilute white wine and the flesh of young animals to cure melancholy. Music, he believed, was also an important part of therapy: "The elegant joining of sounds restores the soul," he wrote, ". . . and calms the tempest of the mind and arrests the hurricanes of its affections."[49]

Physicians from the fifteenth through seventeenth centuries consistently sought to soothe mentally disturbed men and women by prescribing easily digestible diets, good sleep hygiene, soothing surroundings, productive but light activity, and cheerful company. Baths, bloodletting, and medicinal purges were also in their therapeutic arsenal, but it was medicinal purges that consumers seemed most keen to buy. They judged the efficacy of purges on how successful they were at expelling excess or corrupt humors from the body; the more dramatic the evacuation the better.[50] A drug capable of causing multiple evacuations was considered best of all. A contemporary witness marveled after a sixteenth-century Bolognese actress took a drug that made her "sweat, urinate, and have a bowel movement," and then return to the theatre that same evening.[51]

To meet their patients' demands for purges, physicians prescribed and apothecaries and empirics sold all manner of oils, balms, unguents, electuaries, earths, powders, tinctures, plasters, pastilles, and quintessences. Since any imbalance of the humors could set the mind adrift, powerful purgatives were thought to stem the onset of mental disorder or set the mind aright after the scales had tipped toward any of the infinite species of psychological disturbances that men and women might suffer.

Richard Napier used several powerful purges to treat melancholy. He prescribed an ancient concoction called *hiera logadii* that contained "aloes, colocynth, and black hellebore," as well as the Arabic compound known as *confectio hamech*, which combined myrobalans, rhubarb, and senna.[52] All of these drugs had powerful laxative properties, intended to have an explosive effect on a patient's bowels. The discovery of the New World only added to Europe's already rich trade in purgatives. Tobacco, for example, became a popular emetic that Napier also prescribed. Robert Burton both touted its benefits and cautioned against its dangers when overused in his massive *Anatomy of Melancholy*.[53] How exotic, complex, and costly a drug was depended on how much a patient could pay. Napier, for example, adjusted the complexity of a drug and the number and quality of its ingredients in accord with his patients' means. Often, the less well-to-do denounced the cost and exclusiveness of medicine.[54]

The emergence of Paracelsan chemical medicine also added to Europe's rich pharmacopeia. The Swiss-born physician Paracelsus (1493–1541) refuted the Greek idea that diseases were caused by humoral imbalances and could be cured by means of opposites. Paracelsus, by contrast, argued that diseases originated from outside the body and were caused by poisons that had to be countered with powerful chemical agents.[55]

In *On the Diseases that Rob Man of Reason*, Paracelsus attributed madness to poisons, witchcraft, astral influence, sinful imagination, and disordered humors though he increasingly came to doubt that humors existed. Treatments ranged from bloodletting to powerful drugs, including quintessences of silver, iron, mercury, lead, gold, pearls, silver, coral, antimony, sulfur, and sapphires. Opiates ranked high on his list of drugs effective at combating a variety of mental disorders.[56] With some notable exceptions, few Italian physicians or empirics embraced Paracelsan medicine.[57] Chemical medicine fared better across the Alps, yet many physicians believed its remedies were dangerously strong. André du Laurens, a French physician and author of a treatise on melancholy, advised against using antimony because of its toxicity. Napier recorded a case in which mercury treatment poisoned a patient and drove him mad.[58] On the whole, Paracelsianism supplemented, but never displaced humoral medicine.

Many physicians and empirics sought cosmological as well as corporeal causes of mental disturbances. This astrological approach to medicine conformed to medieval and early modern cosmology in which the planets orbiting Earth and the fixed stars beyond them constantly exerted forces for good or ill on all of terrestrial nature. With the right knowledge and practice, these forces could be harnessed to heal or better temper the body and mind. According to Marsilio Ficino, the planet Jupiter—a particularly favorable one—impressed with its power, "silver, jacinth, topaz, coral, crystal, beryl, spodium, sapphire, green and aery colors, wine, sugar, and white honey."[59] Men and women could use these objects "to attract" Jupiter's influence.

Planets corresponded to bodily processes and psychological states as well. Jupiter, for example, had power over the bodily forces of "attraction, retention, digestion, and expulsion," meaning it played an important role in health.[60] Furthermore, one could attract the power of planets by adopting their psychological characteristics. Jupiter's influences could be drawn down by entertaining "thoughts and feelings which are especially jovial, that is, steadfast, composed, religious, [and] law-abiding."[61] By the same token, certain ways of thinking and acting could also expose bodies and minds to less benign planetary powers. Ficino warned that "withdrawal from human affairs, by leisure, solitude, constancy, by theology, the more esoteric philosophy, superstition, magic, agriculture, and by sorrow," attracted the dark influence of Saturn, the planet thought to induce melancholy.[62] The importance of the celestial realm is also evident in Napier's medical practice. Like many learned physicians, he consulted the zodiac and checked the planets' positions before prescribing venesection or preparing and administering drugs.[63] He also cast his patients' horoscopes to determine which forces were at play in their lives when they were experiencing their symptoms.[64]

Astral causes of mental illness demanded astral remedies. Napier used astral talismans in his medical practice to cure all manner of physical and mental ailments. These talismans included sigils, metal emblems bearing astrological figures that were cast at astrologically auspicious moments. The type of metal used to make the talisman be it brass, tin, silver or gold helped determine when it should be struck since each metal had its corresponding planet. Sometimes the talismans were strung on taffeta or silk and worn around a patient's neck at a propitious time. They could also be used to stamp astrological symbols on a patient's pills before he or she took them. Many of Napier's mentally disturbed clients received these talismans both to harmonize their relationship with the universe and to protect them from further cosmological imbalance.[65]

Gems and precious or semi-precious stones were also thought to be imbued with celestial powers and therefore capable of passing astral energies on to the body and mind of the wearer, bearer, or imbiber. To avoid the negative effects of excessive drinking, the physician Adam Huber of Riesenbach (d. 1613) advised people to carry a ring inlaid with a large amethyst which was believed to hinder harmful vapors rising up through the body and endangering the brain.[66] Along the same lines, Lorenzo de' Medici, Philip II of Spain, and Popes Leo X and Clement VII were only a few of Europe's notables treated with potions containing ground rubies, diamonds, and emeralds as they approached the end of their lives.[67]

Skirting the line between medicine and magic, however, was a delicate matter and generated much controversy. Ficino defended his stance by reminding his readers that the great Dominican theologian, Thomas Aquinas, acknowledged the intimate connection between terrestrial and celestial realms: "something is impressed on our body by celestial bodies . . . just as herbs and stones have certain wondrous powers from the heavens beyond their elemental nature."[68] In Ficino's mind, there was nothing wrong with tapping into the natural powers of the cosmos. Done properly it did not contradict or conflict with Christian belief and practice. Ficino also warned his readers never to "attempt anything forbidden by holy religion."[69] One should rather bear in mind that God imbued the stars and planets with the powers they possessed.

Some of the remedies that Napier borrowed from folk healers smack of more than natural magic. For example, he gave his patients prayers, charms, and incantations written on pieces of paper in macaronic Latin. One such paper charm designed to protect against evil spirits, bewitchment, and madness called for a prayer and the names of God and the archangels to be set down on a "little paper close written and tied with taffeta with a lead of mugwort or St. John's wort," and worn around the patient's neck.[70] Perhaps to lend at least the odor of orthodoxy to the amulets or charms he dispensed, Napier told his patients that they were ineffective on their own and had to be activated by prayer.[71]

Spiritual physic

For early modern men and women, the fear that hostile supernatural entities, including evil spirits, witches, demons, or the devil himself, might exploit mental disturbances was a real and terrifying possibility. Satan and his minions were thought to play on the anguish of those suffering melancholy, leading them to despair of their salvation and, in the worst cases, to take their own lives. For this reason, numerous medieval and early modern writers called melancholy the "Devil's bath."[72] Immoral behavior too was thought to upset physical and mental equilibrium and potentially leave the body open to demonic infiltration. In this context, madness was closely linked to sin and damnation. When men and women suffered afflictions that imperiled their immortal souls, they turned to spiritual physic, one of the most important approaches to healing in the medieval and early modern market for health care.

Where natural physic sought to restore balance to the body through the six non-naturals, spiritual physic sought to restore balance to the soul through what the Italian Minorite friar and exorcist Girolamo Menghi (1529–1609) called "soul remedies," namely, auricular confession, communion, pilgrimage, the laying on of hands, saints' relics, and exorcism.[73] Exorcism, the most famous and dramatic form of spiritual physic, was also the remedy of last resort. Men and women went to exorcists only after they had exhausted all other natural and spiritual remedies; spiritual physicians also resorted to exorcism only after all conventional sacramental alternatives had failed.[74] The most common spiritual remedies were prayer, hearing mass, the application of holy water, confession and receiving the Eucharist.

Before and after the religious reformations of the sixteenth century, clerics tried to allay the psychological anxieties of the laity through pastoral care. To the mentally disturbed, they offered comfort by encouraging them to repent their sins and seek God's mercy.[75] The medieval Catholic Church had institutionalized soul remedies like confession and penance at the Fourth Lateran Council of 1215. From this point, penance played an increasingly important psychological role in helping the laity in their struggles to be happy and healthy in a world rife with hardship, misfortune, and evil. Examples showing the success of pastoral remedies abound. Three sixteenth-century Bavarian men, one "vexed by many insects," another "terrified at night in his bed," and the third, "a terrified old man," for example, were "much relieved" after having mass read, going to confession, and taking communion. Similarly, a woman who suffered terrible anxiety after a financial transaction went sour slept well after making confession and receiving the Eucharist.[76]

Pilgrimage to a distant saints' shrine or prayer to a local saint were also popular forms of spiritual physic. Extant miracle books show that men and women regularly sought the help of saints to free them or their relatives from the grips of madness.[77] Some saints and their shrines even specialized in curing mental disorders. Mentally disturbed men and women from all over Europe, for example, were brought to the shrine of St. Dymphna at Geel in the Netherlands or to the Bavarian shrines of the Beata Alta at Pürten and St. Anastasia at Benediktbeuern to name a few.[78]

Men and women sought the healing power of saints both to cure extreme forms of mental disorder and to alleviate workaday anxieties. Acute fears of the dark, the perils of the night, traumatic experiences, and bad dreams sent men and women to shrines asking the saints to release them from mental anguish. A suicide attempt brought a distraught woman to the Marian shrine at Altötting after she lost both her husband and eight-year-old son in the space of three weeks.[79] Women, in fact, regularly went to shrines to relieve the many anxieties attendant on fertility and childbirth. One expectant mother, for example, went to Benediktbeuern, fearing she was the victim of enchantment; another fearing that witches had stolen her breast milk.[80] In each case, so the record goes, the pilgrim was miraculously cured.

Whether they sought natural or spiritual physic, men and women looking for care were met with a shared language to describe both healing strategies. Medieval and early modern clerical writers, for example, likened the disordered soul to the imbalanced body and bad habits (*mali mores*) to bad humors (*mali humores*). The regulation of diet could be compared to abstinence from sin, exercise could represent the performance of penance and physical purgation was similar to confession.[81] The archbishop of Florence, Antonino (1389–1459), for example, compared physical and spiritual healing strategies. "Penance," he wrote, "is a purging of ill humors, that is, an evacuation of vices . . . confession is like a rhubarb of decoction, which causes vomiting." [82] Almost two centuries later, the Dutch writer, Aegidius Albertinus (1560–1620) echoed Antonino's sentiment, saying that like the drug theriac, a common antidote for poison, penance was an antidote for the poison of sin.[83] The connections between natural and spiritual physic were both linguistic and substantive. Just as men and women could use the six non-naturals to prevent illness, they could also use preventive "soul remedies" like the sacraments to achieve the same end. Both bodily and spiritual hygiene then were necessary and complementary parts of maintaining physical and mental health.

If physicians were charged with reining in the humors, spiritual physic was the domain of the clergy. Many clerical voices asserted their primacy in this realm, arguing that spiritual physic was an independent branch of medicine. Menghi, for example, clearly distinguished between bodily physicians (*medici corporali*) and spiritual physicians (*medici spirituali*). The latter, he stated, treated the soul; the former, the body.[84]

For the most part, physicians of the body left the job of casting out demons or cleansing souls to their spiritual counterparts. After all, they sought the natural origins of mental disorders and treated them with natural remedies. When learned medicine failed to cure a sixteen-year old girl whose madness caused her to vomit up nails and brass pins and a ball of wax and hair, the Florentine physician Antonio Benivieni (1443–1502) suggested that she seek the expertise of spiritual doctors (*spiritualibus medicis*), likely referring to exorcists.[85] And yet, for many physicians, from the famous Florentine Niccolò Falcucci (d. 1411/12) in the late fourteenth century to the renowned Italian Girolamo Mercuriale (1530–1606) in the late sixteenth, regulation of the six non-naturals played a critical role in battling hostile supernatural entities, on the principle that demons had to work through natural means to infiltrate human bodies. According to Falcucci, the problem was not so much the demon, but the noxious internal environments such entities created. Demonic possession amounted to the pernicious manipulation of the humors to destroy bodies and minds. Physicians, Falcucci argued, were equally capable of manipulating these humors.[86]

Regardless of who was administering spiritual physic, the emergence of print culture and the religious reformations of the sixteenth century transformed the types of spiritual physic available to Europeans. Some forms of spiritual consolation became more accessible to a lay readership, for example. Just as the printing press put a range of vernacular self-help healing manuals in the hands of ordinary men and women, it also made the popular vernacular books of spiritual consolation, especially those dedicated to the "art of dying" (*ars moriendi*), available on an unprecedented scale. Evangelical reformers and defenders of Catholicism alike produced influential vernacular works, including sermons, catechisms, and lay penitentials. In his penitential, the German theologian and polemicist, Martin Eisengrein (1535–78), cautioned laymen and women against concealing their sins lest they suffer anxiety, produce noxious humors, and retain bodily waste.[87] Not to confess was to create an internal environment ripe for mental disturbance, sin, and the penetration of the devil. Men and women who did not regularly cleanse and purge their souls through spiritual physic risked falling prey to madness or a demon who might induce it.[88]

Pilgrimage and exorcism remained tried and true methods of attaining release from mental disturbances or casting out malevolent supernatural entities in Catholic Europe throughout the early modern period. Regions that adopted one of the proliferating forms of evangelicalism, however, disavowed the worship of saints, repudiated exorcism, and stripped the clergy of its purported supernatural powers. In the minds of Protestant divines, the age of miracles was over. Acts of devotion performed at saints' shrines and the supernatural rituals of the medieval church were both pointless and idolatrous. As a result evangelical spiritual physic whether there was demonic involvement or not, focused all the more on prayer, fasting, and congregational singing.[89] When the devil violently took possession of a girl from Platten in 1559, for example, he was driven out by congregational prayer and hymn-singing by nearly a thousand people. As he fled her body he was reported to have said: "All who refuse to go to church, preferring to stay at home to read, rejecting the sacrament, and wallowing in gluttony, drunkenness, and usury—are all mine, body and soul."[90]

The pluralism of the market for health care in early modern Europe transcended confessional divides. To meet their clients' demands, some spiritual physicians continued to mingle spiritual, natural, and magical remedies in their practices even at the risk of condemnation. Of the 2039 mentally disturbed patients Richard Napier treated, for example, nearly 300 complained of some kind of religious anxiety, from spiritual indifference to crippling fear of damnation; 91 worried that they would not be saved and 43 agonized over the sins they had committed.[91] Napier prescribed a range of spiritual, magical, and natural remedies from comforting speeches, formal prayer, religious exercises, and exorcism to amulets and sigils to dietary regimens, vomits, and purges.[92] Other spiritual physicians would have flatly rejected Napier's eclecticism. Catholics like Menghi, the Spanish jurist and demonologist, Martin del Rio (1551–1608) and the German Jesuit Peter Thyraeus (1546–1601) drew a sharp distinction between ecclesiastical physicians and folk healers who practised natural magic.[93] Moreover, after having eliminated exorcism from the Church of England's liturgy in the late sixteenth century, English Protestant reformers would have balked at Napier's willingness to exorcise his patients.

Napier's therapeutic eclecticism reflects that of the early modern market for health care. To cope with the anxiety-provoking vicissitudes of daily life as well as to cure the darkest or most violent mental disorders, men and women regularly sought the help of academic physicians, empirics, surgeons, apothecaries, priests, exorcists, and saints. From this motley range of healers they purchased natural, spiritual, and magical remedies. Resources permitting, they were likely to enlist the help of all of these healers and remedies as their particular situation demanded.

Notes

1 The scholarship on representations of melancholy in eary modern European culture is enormous. The work that inspired generations of scholars remains, Raymond Klibansky, Erwin Panofsky, and Fritz Saxl, *Saturn and Melancholy: Studies in the History of Natural Philosophy, Religion, and Art* (New York: Basic Books, 1964). See also, Walter J. Kaiser, *Praisers of Folly: Erasmus, Rabelais, Shakespeare* (Cambridge: Harvard University Press, 1963); Winfried Schleiner, *Melancholy, Genius, and Utopia in the Renaissance* (Wiesbaden: In Kommission bei Otto Harrassowitz, 1991); Noel L. Brann, *The Debate Over the Origin of Genius During the Italian Renaissance* (Leiden: Brill, 2002). For melancholy in Italian literature, see Ernesto Grassi and Maristella Lorch, *Folly and Insanity in Renaissance Literature* (Binghamton, NY: Medieval & Renaissance Texts & Studies, 1986). For melancholy in English literature, see Lawrence Babb's still classic, *The Elizabethan Malady: A Study of Melancholia in English Literature From 1580 to 1642* (East Lansing, MA: Michigan State University Press, 1951); Douglas Trevor, *The Poetics of Melancholy in Early Modern England* (Cambridge: Cambridge University Press, 2004); Adam Kitzes, *The Politics of Melancholy from Spenser to Milton* (New York: Routledge, 2006). For melancholy in Spanish literature, see Teresa Scott Soufas, *Melancholy and the Secular Mind in Spanish Golden Age Literature* (Columbia: University of Missouri Press, 1990). For melancholy in French literature, see Jacqueline Cerquiglini-Toulet, *La couleur de la mélancolie: La fréquentation des livres au XIVe siècle, 1300–1415* (Paris: Hatier, 1993).
2 Marsilio Ficino wrote about melancholy genius in *De vita*, trans. Carol V. Kaske and John R. Clark (Binghamton, NY: Medieval & Renaissance Texts & Studies, 1989).
3 This new orientation emerged in the 1980s and 1990s with a number of pathbreaking works, including Michael MacDonald, *Mystical Bedlam: Madness, Anxiety, and Healing in Seventeenth-Century England* (Cambridge: Cambridge University Press, 1981); Roy Porter, *Mind Forg'd Manacles: A History of Madness in England from the Restoration to the Regency* (Cambridge, MA: Harvard University Press, 1987); Graziella Magherini and Vittorio Biotti, *L'isola delle Stinche et i percorsi della follia a Firenze nei secoli XIV–XVIII* (Florence: Ponte alle Grazie, 1992). For more recent examples, see R.A. Houston, *Madness and Society in Eighteenth-Century Scotland* (Oxford: Oxford University Press, 2000); Vittorio Biotti, ed., *"È matto e tristo, pazzo e fastidioso": I saperi sulla follia, magistrati, medici, e inquisitori a Firenze e negli stati italiani del '600* (Florence: Nicomp, 2002); Graziella Magherini and Vittorio Biotti, 'Madness in Florence in the 14th–18th Centuries,' *International Journal of Law and Psychiatry* 21, no. 4 (1998): 355–68; Monica Calabritto, "A Case of Melancholic Humors and Dilucida Intervalla," *Intellectual History Review* 18:1 (2008): 139–54; Wendy J. Turner, *Madness in Medieval Law and Custom* (Leiden: Brill, 2010); Wendy Turner and Tory Vandeventer Pearman, eds., *The Treatment of Disabled Persons in Medieval Europe: Examining Disability in the Historical, Legal, Literary, Medical, and Religious Discourses of the Middle Ages* (Lampeter: Edwin Mellen Press, 2011); Elizabeth W. Mellyn, *Mad Tuscans and Their Families: A History of Mental Disorder in Early Modern Italy* (Philadelphia: University of Pennsylvania Press, 2014).
4 For an early study based on legal records, see Richard Neugebauer, "Mental Illness and Government Policy in Sixteenth- and Seventeenth-Century England" (Ph.D. diss., Columbia University, 1976).
5 Caroline M. Fisher, "The State as Surrogate Father: State Guardianship in Renaissance Florence, 1368–1532" (Ph.D. diss., Brandeis University, 2003); Idem., "Guardianship and the Rise of the Florentine State, 1368–93," in *Famiglie e poteri in Italia tra medioevo ed età moderna*, ed. Anna Bellavitis and Isabelle Chabot (Rome: École française de Rome, 2009): 265–67.
6 Midelfort, *A History of Madness*, ch. 6; David Lederer, *Madness, Religion, and the State in Early Modern Europe: A Bavarian Beacon* (Cambridge: Cambridge University Press, 2006).
7 H.C. Erik Midelfort, *Mad Princes of Renaissance Germany* (Charlottesville: University Press of Virginia, 1994). See also, Bethany Aram, *Juana the Mad: Sovereignty and Dynasty in Renaissance Europe* (Baltimore: Johns Hopkins University Press, 2005); Maria A. Gomez, Santiago Juan-Navarro, Phyllis Zatlin, eds., *Juana of Castile: History and Myth of the Mad Queen* (Bucknell University Press, 2008).
8 Sandra Cavallo and Tessa Storey, *Healthy Living in Late Renaissance Italy* (Oxford: Oxford University Press, 2013), 271; Sandra Cavallo, "Secrets to Healthy Living: The Revival of the

Preventative Paradigm in Late Renaissance Italy," in *Secrets and Knowledge in Medicine and Science, 1500–1800*, ed. Elaine Leong and Alisha Rankin (Burlington, 2001): 191–212 at 192. See also, Marilyn Nicoud, *Les régimes de santé au moyen âge* (Rome École Française de Rome, 2007); Donatella Lippi, *Díaita: The Rules of Health in the Manuscripts of the Biblioteca Medicea Laurenziana* (Florence: Mandragora, 2010). These studies owe a great deal to Heikki Mikkeli's *Hygiene in the Early Modern Medical Tradition* (Helsinki: Finnish Academy of Science and Letters, 1999).

9 For accounts of this transmission process, see Nancy Siraisi, *Medieval & Early Renaissance Medicine: An Introduction to Knowledge and Practice* (Chicago: University of Chicago Press, 1990) and Lawrence Conrad, et al., *The Western Medical Tradition: 800 BC–1800 AD* (Cambridge: Cambridge University Press, 1995).

10 Barbara Duden, *The Woman Beneath the Skin: A Doctor's Patients in Eighteenth-Century Germany* (Cambridge: Harvard University Press, 1991). For a detailed discussion of challenges to classical medical authority, see Roger K. French, *Medicine Before Science: The Rational and Learned Physician from the Middle Ages to the Enlightenment* (Cambridge: Cambridge University Press, 2003).

11 See Katharine Park, *Doctors and Medicine in Early Renaissance Florence* (Princeton: Princeton University Press, 1985); Idem., "Medicine and Society in Medieval Europe, 500–1500," in *Medicine in Society: Historical Essays*, ed. Andrew Wear (Cambridge: Cambridge University Press, 1992): 59–90; idem, "Medicine and Magic: The Healing Arts," in *Gender and Society in Renaissance Europe*, ed. Judith C. Brown and Robert C. Davis (London: Longman, 1998): 129–49.

12 See William Eamon, *Science and the Secrets of Nature: Books of Secrets in Medieval and Early Modern Culture* (Princeton: Princeton University Press, 1994). See also his recent article, "How to Read a Book of Secrets," in Leong and Rankin, *Secrets and Knowledge in Medicine and Science*: 23–46.

13 For the most comprehensive portrait of this marketplace, see Gianna Pomata, *Contracting a Cure: Patients, Healers, and the Law in Early Modern Bologna* (Baltimore: Johns Hopkins University Press, 1998); David Gentilcore, *Healers and Healing in Early Modern Italy* (Manchester: Manchester University Press, 1998); Idem., *Medical Charlatanism in Early Modern Italy* (Oxford: Oxford University Press, 2006); William Eamon, *The Professor of Secrets: Mystery, Medicine, and Alchemy in Renaissance Italy* (Washington, DC: National Geographic, 2010); Jonathan Barry and Peter Elmer have also created an online database to collect biographies of all medical practitioners active in England, Wales and Ireland *c.* 1500–1715, Wellcome Trust and the Centre for Medical History, University of Exeter, http://practitioners. exeter.ac.uk/, accessed November 21, 2015. See also, Andrew Wear, Robert K. French, and I.M. Lonie, *The Medical Renaissance of the Sixteenth Century* (Cambridge: Cambridge University Press, 1985; Andrew Wear, *Knowledge and Practice in English Medicine, 1550–1680* (Cambridge: Cambridge University Press, 2000); Laurence Brockliss and Colin Jones, *The Medical World of Early Modern France* (Oxford: Clarendon Press, 1997. Brockliss and Jones exclude the history of mental disorder in their study. Where they do address it they adopt the tantalizing, but inaccurate account of Michel Foucault in *Histoire de la folie à l'âge classique: Folie et déraison*. Paris: Plon, 1961), translated as *Madness and Civilization: A History of Insanity in the Age of Reason*. New York: Vintage Books, 1973). For reassessments of Foucault, see W.F. Bynum, Roy Porter, and Michael Shepherd, eds., *The Anatomy of Madness: Essays in the History of Psychiatry* (London: Tavistock Publications, 1985–8); Arthur Still and Irving Velody, eds., *Rewriting the History of Madness: Studies in Foucault's "Histoire de la folie"* (London: Routledge, 1992); and Colin Jones and Roy Porter, eds., *Reassessing Foucault: Power, Medicine, and the Body* (London: Routledge, 1994).

14 Midelfort, *A History of Madness*, 32–33. Midelfort argues that these types of peculiar practices complicate the history of madness for modern readers who want to interpret them through the lens of modern diagnostic categories rather than the cultural matrix of which they were a part.

15 John Henderson, *The Renaissance Hospital: Healing the Body and Healing the Soul* (New Haven: Yale University Press, 2006). See also, Gisela Drossbach, *Hospitäler in Mittelalter und Früher Neuzeit. Frankreich, Deutschland und Italien* (Munich: De Gruyter, 2007); Andrew Cunningham

and Ole Peter Grell, eds., *Health Care and Poor Relief in Protestant Europe, 1500–1700* (London: Routledge, 1997); Nicholas Orme and Margaret Webster, *The English Hospital 1070–1570* (New Haven: Yale University Press, 1995); Colin Jones, *The Charitable Imperative: Hospitals and Nursing in Ancien Régime and Revolutionary France* (London: Routledge, 1989); Lindsay Granshaw and Roy Porter, eds., *The Hospital in History* (London: Routledge, 1989); Daniela Lombardi, *Povertà Maschile, Povertà Femminile: L'Ospedale dei Mendicanti nella Firenze dei Medici* (Bologna : Il Mulino, 1988).

16 See Andrew Scull's essay in this volume. See also, Lisa Roscioni, *Il governo della follia: Ospedali, medici e pazzi nell'età moderna* (Milan: Bruno Mondadori, 2003) and MacDonald, *Mystical Bedlam*, 5.

17 Physcians believed that certain lifestyles imperiled mental health because of the way they affected a person's natural equilibrium. The habits of monks and nuns, they claimed, were particularly insalubrious. Long bouts of solicitude, the practice of extreme asceticism, and constant fear of God's judgment tended to induce melancholy among Europe's cloistered set. That said, records indicate that monasteries and convents refused to admit men and women with *severe* mental disorders where the safety of the individual or members of the community were at stake. See Sharon T. Strocchia, "The Melancholic Nun in Late Renaissance Italy," in *Diseases of the Imagination and Imaginary Diseases in the Early Modern Period*, ed. Yasmin Haskell (Turnhout: Brepols, 2011), 139–58 and Mellyn, *Mad Tuscans*, 155–56. Marsilio Ficino, *De triplici vita*, trans. Carol V. Kaske and John R. Clark (Binghamton, NY: Medieval & Renaissance Texts & Studies, 1989). Similarly, Marsilio Ficino directed his famous manual of healthy living to scholars whose excessive cogitations in solitude, he claimed, dried out their brains thereby inducing melancholy.

18 See Guy Geltner, *The Medieval Prison: A Social History* (Princeton: Princeton University Press, 2008) and John K. Brackett, *Criminal Justice and Crime in Late Renaissance Florence, 1537–1609* (Cambridge: Cambridge University Press, 1992).

19 New scholarship on domestic medicine is incredibly rich. For a comprehensive current bibliography, see Leong and Rankin, *Secrets and Knowledge in Medicine and Science*. See also Alisha Rankin, "Duchess, Heal Thyself: Elizabeth of Rochlitz and the Patient's Perspective in Early Modern Germany," *Bulletin of the History of Medicine* 82, no. 1 (2008): 109–44; and Sharon T. Strocchia, "The Nun Apothecaries of Renaissance Florence: Marketing Medicines in the Convent," *Renaissance Studies* 25, no. 5 (2011): 627–47.

20 Cavallo and Storey, *Healthy Living*, ch. 6.

21 MacDonald, *Mystical Bedlam*, 181.

22 Cavallo and Storey, *Healthy Living*, 189.

23 MacDonald, *Mystical Bedlam*, 182.

24 See A. Chiappelli, "Gli Ordinamenti Sanitari del Comune di Pistoia contro la Pestilenza del 1348," *ASI*, series 4, 20 (1887): 8–22. See also, MacDonald, *Mystical Bedlam*, 182.

25 David Tomíček, "Mental Health in Bohemian Medical Writings of the 14th–16th Centuries," in Albrecht Classen, ed., *Mental Health, Spirituality, and Religion in the Middle Ages and Early Modern Age* (Berlin: de Gruyter, 2014): 464–79 at 472.

26 Giovanbattista da Monte, *Consultationum Medicarum Opus* (Basel: Henricus Petri, 1565), 49. I cite this example in *Mad Tuscans*, 140–41.

27 Da Monte, *Consultationum Medicarum*, 52.

28 For a superb study of the spread of regimens of heath in medieval Europe, see Marilyn Nicoud, *Les Régimes de Santé au Moyen Âge: Naissance et Diffusion d'une Écriture Médicale, XIIIe-XVe Siècle* (Rome, 2007). See also the article by Pedo Gils Sotres "The Regimens of Health," in *Western Medical Thought from Antiquity to the Middle Ages*, ed. Mirko D. Grmek (Cambridge, 1998): 291–318 and Donatella Lippi, *Díaita*.

29 Later examples are the Florentine doctor Taddeo Alderotti's regimen of health written in Italian for his friend Corso Donati (*c.* 1260–1308. Taddeo then translated the work into Latin. According to Sandra Cavallo and Tessa Storey, the *Opera utilissima di Arnaldo da Villanova di conservare la sanità* is actually a translation of a regimen written by Maino de Maineri (d. 1341) and the *Tractato circa la conservatione de la sanitate*, attributed to Ugo Benzi (d. 1439), was really the translation of a Latin regimen by the doctor of the Sforza dukes, Benedetto Reguardati (1398–1469). See, Cavallo and Storey, *Healthy Living*, 17–18. In the

fifteenth century, Michele Savonarola, court physician to the Este translated a number of his Latin practical medical works into non-academic versions directed to a broader lay readership. On transitions between Latin and vernacular in the works of Alderotti see, Sonia Gentili, *L'Uomo Aristotelico alle Origini della Letteratura Italiana* (Rome, 2005), ch. 1. For the translation efforts of Savonarola, see Gabriella Zuccolin, "Nascere in Latino ed in Volgare. Tra la Practica ed il De regimine," in Michele Savonarola, *Medicina e cultura di corte*, 137–210.

30 Aldobrandino's text quickly spread throughout Europe. Seventy-four complete or abridged manuscripts in French survive, forming the basis for subsequent translations into Catalan and Flemish. It spread also to Italy where at least fifty Italian translations are extant. Some of these translations also formed the basis for medical manuals prepared for specific households. For the transmission history of Aldobrandino's *Régime*, see Sebastiano Bisson, Lada Hordynsky-Caillat, and Odile Redon, "Le Témoin Gênant: Une Version Latine du *Régime du corps* d'Aldebrandin de Sienne." *Médiévales* 42 (2002): 117–130, 119; Rosella Baldini, "Zucchero Bencivenni, *La santé del corpo*. Volgarizzamento del Régime du corps di Aldobrandino da Siena (a. 1310) nella copia coeva di Lapo di Neri Corsini (Laur. Pl. LXXIII 47)." *Studi di lessicografia italiana* 15 (1998): 21–300, 25; Marilyn Nicoud, *Les Régimes de Santé au Moyen Âge: Naissance et Diffusion d'une Écriture Médicale, XIIIe-XVe Siècle* (Rome, 2007), 953–88; Lippi, *Díaita*, 80-81.

31 Louis Landouzy and Roger Pépin, *Le "Régime du Corps" de Maitre Aldobrandin de Sienne: Texte Français du XIIIe Siècle* (Paris, 1911).

32 I have dealt with this text in an article arguing against the existence of a sharp division between academic and non-academic medicine during the Middle Ages. See Elizabeth Mellyn, "Passing on Secrets: Interactions between Latin and Vernacular Medicine in Medieval Europe," *I Tatti Studies: Essays in the Renaissance* 16 (November, 2013). For a similar view, see Sandra Cavallo, "Secrets to Healthy Living: The Revival of the Preventative Paradigm in Late Renaissance Italy," in *Secrets and Knowledge in Medicine and Science, 1500–1800*, ed. Elaine Leong and Alisha Rankin (Burlington, 2001): 191–212. For a different perspective, see William Eamon, "On the Skins of Goats and Sheep: (Un)masking the Secrets of Nature in Early Modern Popular Culture," in *Visual Cultures of Secrecy in Early Modern Europe*, eds. Timothy McCall, Sean Roberts, and Giancarlo Fiorenza (Kirksville, 2013): 54–75.

33 Cavallo and Storey, *Healthy Living*, ch. 1; Mary Fissell, "Popular Medical Writing," in Joad Raymond, ed., *Cheap Print in Britain and Ireland* (Oxford: Oxford University Press, 2011); Idem., "The Marketplace of Print," in Mark S. R. Jenner and Patrick Wallis, eds., *Medicine and the Market in England and Its Colonies, c. 1450–c. 1850* (Basingstoke, UK: Palgrave Macmillan, 2007): 108–32; Idem., "Readers, Texts, and Contexts: Vernacular Medical Works in Early Modern England," in Roy Porter, ed., *The Popularization of Medicine 1650–1850* (London: Routledge, 1992): 72–96.

34 Eamon, *Science and the Secrets of Nature*. See also Angus Gowland, *The Worlds of Renaissance Melancholy: Robert Burton in Context* (Cambridge: Cambridge University Press, 2006); and David Lederer, *Madness, Religion, and the State*, 37.

35 Midelfort, *A History of Madness*, 163.

36 Girolamo Ruscelli, *De' secreti del reverendo donno Alessio Piemontese* (Venice, 1562), 78.

37 Cavallo and Storey, *Healthy Living*.

38 MacDonald, *Mystical Bedlam*, 73 and 75.

39 Ibid., ch. 3.

40 For a discussion of salaried physicians, see Vivian Nutton, "Continuity or Rediscovery? The City Physician in Classical Antiquity and Mediaeval Italy," in *The Town and State Physicians in Europe from the Middle Ages to the Enlightenment*, ed. Andrew W. Russell (Wolfenbüttel: Herzog Aug. Bibliothek, 1981): 9–46.

41 For two evocative studies, see Gentilcore, *Medical Charlatanism* and Eamon, *The Professor of Secrets*.

42 Pomata, *Contracting a Cure*, 139.

43 Gentilcore, *Medical Charlatanism*, ch. 4.

44 Jole Agrimi and Chiara Crisciani, *Les Consilia Médicaux* (Turnhout: Brepols, 1994).

45 Ugo Benzi, *Consilia* (Venice: Octavianus Scotus, 1518), fol. 12v.

46 Bartolomeo Montagnana, *Consilia* (Venice, 1514): fol. 71rv.

47 Ibid.
48 Ibid.
49 This example is cited in Midelfort, *A History of Madness*, 153–54.
50 Pomata, *Contracting a Cure*, 131–35; MacDonald, *Mystical Bedlam*, 192.
51 Pomata, 131.
52 MacDonald, *Mystical Bedlam*, 187.
53 Ibid., 187–88.
54 Ibid., 192.
55 Eamon, *The Professor of Secrets*, 195. See also, Thomas Willard, "Paracelsus of Mental Health," in Albrecht Classen, ed., *Mental Health, Spirituality, and Religion in the Middle Ages and Early Modern Age* (Berlin: de Gruyter, 2014): 524–56.
56 Midelfort, *A History of Madness*, 110–32;
57 Gentilcore, *Medical Charlatanism*, 227–33.
58 MacDonald, *Mystical Bedlam*, 192.
59 Ficino, *De vita*, 249.
60 Ibid., 269.
61 Ibid., 249.
62 Ibid., 253.
63 MacDonald, *Mystical Bedlam*, 194.
64 Ibid., 27.
65 Ibid., 214.
66 Tomíček, "Mental Health in Bohemian Medical Writings of the 14th–16th Centuries," 475.
67 Liliana Lepardi, "Magic Healing and Embodied Sensory Faculties in Camillo Leonardi's *Speculum Lapidum*," in Albrecht Classen, ed., *Mental Health, Spirituality, and Religion in the Middle Ages and Early Modern Age* (Berlin: de Gruyter, 2014): 480–506 at 494.
68 Ficino, *De vita*, 281.
69 Ibid.
70 MacDonald, *Mystical Bedlam*, 214.
71 Ibid., 213–14.
72 Ibid., 223 and Lederer, *Madness, Religion, and the State*, 66.
73 Lederer, *Madness, Religion, and the State*, 6, 11.
74 Ibid., 196.
75 MacDonald, *Mystical Bedlam*, 176.
76 Lederer, *Madness, Religion, and the State*, 194.
77 Lederer, *Madness, Religion, and the State* and Midelfort, *A History of Madness*, ch. 6.
78 Lederer, *Madness, Religion, and the State*, 119 and Midelfort, *A History of Madness*, 283.
79 Midelfort, *A History of Madness* 297.
80 Lederer, *Madness, Religion, and the State*, 190.
81 Joseph Ziegler, *Medicine and Religion c. 1300: The Case of Arnau de Vilanova* (Oxford: Clarendon Press, 1998), 184–90.
82 Cited in Pomata, *Contracting a Cure*, 134.
83 Lederer, *Madness, Religion, and the State*, 67.
84 Ibid., 6.
85 Antonio Beniveni, *De abditis nonnullis ac mirandis morborum et sanationum causis*, ed. Giorgio Weber (Florence: Olschki, 1994), 67.
86 Niccolò Falcucci, *Sermones medicinales* (Venice: Bernardinus Staginus, 1490/91), fol. 72r.
87 Lederer, *Madness, Religion, and the State*, 65.
88 Ibid., 66.
89 Midelfort, *A History of Madness*, 200; 385–86.
90 Ibid., 72.
91 MacDonald, *Mystical Bedlam*, 220.
92 Ibid., 222–23.
93 Lederer, *Madness, Religion, and the State*, 13.

5

THE ASYLUM, HOSPITAL, AND CLINIC

Andrew Scull

The asylum, an institutional space devoted exclusively to the management of the mad, has in some respects a much longer history than is commonly realized. Hospitals for the sick and infirm had been established in the Byzantine empire in the fifth century CE, quite soon after the collapse of the Roman empire in the West. Usually charitable enterprises, hospitals spread into the Near East as Christian foundations well before the rise of Islam. In the years after the Prophet's death in 632, however, Arabs rapidly expanded the Islamic world, till by 750 it stretched from northern India all across north Africa and encompassed most of Spain. Under Islamic rule, hospitals proliferated from the late eighth century onwards, till by the late twelfth century, no large Islamic town was without its hospital. Like Christianity, Islam proclaimed the obligations of the rich to the poor, and Muslims could certainly not be seen to be less charitable than their Christian counterparts. Among those for whom these hospitals made specific provision were the insane, and given the special needs of those who had lost their senses, and the difficulty of coping with them in an institution also attempting to cope with physical illness, it was not uncommon to have the mad removed to a separate establishment.[1]

Evidence about what transpired in these asylums is fugitive and fragmentary. Travellers' reports frequently mention barred windows and chains, and speak of patients being beaten, something advocated even by the great Arab physician Avicenna (Ibn Sina, 980–1037), who saw it as a way to knock some sense into the wildly irrational. Much, though by no means all, of what we think of as Arab medicine was the creation of non-Muslims – Christians and Jews – and it borrowed liberally from the pagan medicine of Greece and Rome, the texts of the Hippocratics and of Galen. Unsurprisingly, then, besides the repressive measures employed to create some semblance of order, the inmates were also treated, as Galen had recommended, with cooling baths and diets designed to cool and moisten their bodies, therapies that aimed to counteract the heating and drying effects of the burnt black or yellow bile that was presumed to cause their madness. Herbal remedies were also widely employed (including lavender, thyme, pear or pomegranate juice, chamomile and black hellebore), and Avicenna suggested that milk and ointments applied to the head might be of some use.

Perhaps the largest asylum in the Arab world was the Mansuri Hospital in Cairo, founded in 1284. Its floor plan survives, showing separate cells for male and female patients. Given the great reluctance of Muslim men to expose their womenfolk in this fashion, this suggests that some female patients proved too difficult to manage

101

in a domestic setting. Yet even the Mansuri asylum provided for at most a few dozen lunatics at a time. Arab asylums elsewhere accommodated fewer still, and almost certainly were expected to house only the most frantic and unmanageable lunatics. For the most part, as was virtually always the case in Western Europe in this period, the mad were dealt with informally and remained very largely the responsibility of their relations.[2]

In its centuries under Islamic rule, Spain had seen the establishment of a number of hospitals, with the Granada hospital perhaps the most notable of these. In the aftermath of the Christian *Reconquista*, essentially complete by 1492, a whole series of asylums following Arab precedent are known to have existed – seven by the fifteenth century, including Valencia, Zaragoza, Seville, Valladolid, Palma de Mallorca, Toledo, and Barcelona. Graeco-Roman medicine had begun to be re-imported into Western Europe from the Arab world in the Middle Ages, partly in the aftermath of the Christianization of Spain and partly as the Crusades brought Europeans into contact with both Arab learning and with hospitals and asylums. The printing press greatly accelerated the cultural impact of Arab medicine, and then of the Greek and Roman medical texts that had largely been lost in the West, except for the survival of isolated manuscripts scattered in a handful of monasteries.[3]

Hospitals now began to appear in Western Europe, facilitated by the revival of trade and economic activity. They were often monastic foundations. As the shared root of "hospital" and "hospitality" reveals, they were not specifically medical enterprises, housing the sick, but also pilgrims, the orphaned, the halt, the lame and the blind. Still, some of these monastic hospitals gradually acquired a reputation for handling the mentally ill. Perhaps the most famous of these was Bethlehem; Londoners later abbreviated this to "Bethlem" and often pronounced it "Bedlam." The first asylum in the English-speaking world, Bedlam took its name from the monastic order that had founded the Priory of St. Mary of Bethlehem in Bishopsgate, London in 1247. In its early years, Bethlehem took in the usual heterogeneous population of unfortunates that found themselves in medieval hospitals, but by the time of a census taken in 1403, we know that of the nine people then resident, six were *menti capti*, deprived of their wits.[4]

Soon enough, its corrupted name "Bedlam" had become synonymous with madness itself, a process greatly accelerated by the appearance of mad scenes in Elizabethan and Jacobean drama. Not just Shakespeare, but Middleton, Fletcher, Dekker, Shirley, Ben Jonson, and Marston, among others, introduced Bedlam to a wider audience. The asylum itself remained quite small. In 1632, for example, if was reported to contain twenty-seven patients, and in 1642 forty-four. In this respect, it resembled its counterparts elsewhere in Europe. The entrepreneurial Dutch, for example, seeking to house a small number of violent and troublesome madmen, took to using lotteries to raise the necessary funds. The Amsterdam Dollhuis, founded on a small basis by private charity in 1562, was enlarged and rebuilt with the money thus raised, opening in 1617, and the city's example was soon followed by Leiden and Harlem. In the aftermath of the restoration of Charles II to the English throne in 1660, the burghers of London took the hint, and Bethlem was rebuilt on a grander scale in 1676 to a design by Robert Hooke, in Moorfields just outside the city wall. It was an unfortunate choice, since the uncompacted fill that had filled up the old moat proved unstable, and by the second half of the eighteenth century, the asylum's fabric had begun to crumble, as roof and walls separated, and rain began to inflict further damage on the structure (not to mention making the patients' lives miserable).

Undeniably, these charity asylums gradually grew larger in the seventeenth and eighteenth centuries, and new establishments added to their number: St. Luke's and then a number of provincial charity asylums in Britain; religious foundations in France and elsewhere. As England became a steadily more prosperous commercial society in these years, still another type of asylum began to emerge: the private, prof-it-making madhouse that emerged in a market free from all regulation, taking some of the more troublesome mad folk off the hands of wealthy families who sought relief from the troubles and scandal that a mad relative in their midst imposed, and soon expanding their services to take the most troublesome paupers who had lost their wits.[5] France, too, began to see some private madhouses founded in the eighteenth century, euphemistically called *maisons de sante*, where the high-born whose antics disturbed their relations could be shut up, in every sense of the term.

Michel Foucault has spoken of the long eighteenth century as witnessing the "Great Confinement" of the insane.[6] His conceit is to conflate the mad with a far larger population of the dissolute, the idle, and the morally disreputable like prosti-tutes, petty criminals, beggars, and the physically incapacitated who began to be swept up into the so-called *hopitaux generaux*, beginning with the founding of the first such establishment in Paris in 1656, and to pronounce the whole heterogeneous mass the exemplars of Unreason. Now it is perfectly true that the Salpetriere, the first of these, housed in an old gunpowder factory that gave it its name, housed perhaps a hundred lunatics when it opened, but these were, and their descendants remained, but a small fraction of the whole (they amounted to perhaps 1000 out of a total pop-ulation of 10,000 at the time of the French Revolution). The hopitaux generaux were not asylums in the conventional sense, and indeed their mad inmates, so far from being those who gave these institutions their identity, were simply an afterthought. Consider, for example, the description of who lurked in the Salpetriere provided by the French surgeon Jacques Tenon in 1788, the year before the Revolution and a hundred and thirty years after its foundation:

> The Salpêtrière is the largest hospital in Paris and possibly in Europe: this hospital is both a house for women and a prison. It received pregnant women and girls, wet nurses and their nurslings; male children from the age of seven or eight months to four and five years of age; young girls of all ages; aged married men and women; raving lunatics, imbeciles, epileptics, paralytics, blind persons, cripples, people suffering from ringworm, incur-ables of all sorts, children afflicted with scrofula, and so on and so forth. At the centre of this hospital is a house of detention for women, comprising four different prisons: *le comun*, for the most dissolute girls; *la correction*, for those who are not considered hopelessly depraved; *la prison*, reserved for persons held by order of the king; and *la grande force*, for women branded by order of the courts.[7]

Even confining our attention to the French case, the exaggerations and distortions of speaking of an eighteenth-century great confinement of the mad are manifest, the more so when we move beyond the French capital and consider the state of affairs in the provinces. In Montpellier, for example, a city of some 30,000 souls and home to France's second most prominent medical school, barely twenty mad folk were locked up when the Revolution broke out. In Dijon, the numbers were smaller still: a mere nine mad women were confined at the Bon Pasteur.[8] In a wider European perspective, the idea that the eighteenth century saw any systematic incarceration of lunatics in madhouses and asylums becomes even less sustainable. The flourishing trade in lunacy in England, for example, gave birth to a whole series of gothic novels portraying the horrors of the madhouse and the danger of sane women, in particular, being shut up improperly alongside the mad. But the reality was less lurid. By 1800, all these establishments together confined a grand total of no more than 2,500 lunatics.

The massive incarceration of the mad was instead a nineteenth-century phenomenon, and one that came to characterize the whole of Europe and North America besides. The English, who had locked up fewer than 3000 in asylums in 1800 confined 100,000 a century later. A similarly startling increase in the numbers housed in asylums could be seen in France, in Germany, in the Netherlands, in the Austrian empire, in Italy, in Ireland, and in Russia, not to mention the United States, Canada, and Mexico. Sending the insane to an asylum came to be seen as one of the hallmarks of a civilized society. Indeed, Sir James Paget, physician to Queen Victoria, was moved to call the asylum "the most blessed manifestation of true civilization the world can present."[9]

Such language reflects the utopian expectations that attended what David Rothman has called "the discovery of the asylum" in the nineteenth century. The new asylum was born of an extraordinary optimism about what a properly organized madhouse could accomplish. A powerful combination of moral architecture – that is, buildings designed as therapeutic instruments – and a moral treatment that mobilized the remnants of reason even the maddest patient still possessed, and encouraged the lunatic gradually to extend their powers of self-control till these allowed the suppression of unruly thoughts and behavior: these taken together, argued the enthusiasts for making the asylum the place of first resort in cases of madness, would restore a very large fraction of the insane to the ranks of the normal.

If eighteenth-century madhouses had acquired the reputation of being human zoos where the sane came to taunt and tease the inmates – recall William Hogarth's canonical image of the naked Tom Rakewell's confinement in Bedlam, being stared at by tittering society ladies amused by the sights of the crazed – or else as "moral lazar houses" where the deranged were hidden and hope and humanity abandoned, their nineteenth-century counterparts were everywhere held up to be vastly different. These asylums, their proponents insisted, had been transmuted into the "moral machinery" through which minds could be strengthened and reason restored. Like the Invisible Hand now held to regulate civil society, "the system is at once both beautiful and self-operating. [The] presence [of keepers] is required to regulate the machine, but its motions are spontaneous . . ." serving all-but-imperceptibly to secure "the tranquilization of the unhealthy mind."[10]

Moral treatment, the key to the reformed asylum, seems to have emerged in quite similar guises in England, France, and Italy,[11] and thence to have underpinned the movement to build whole networks of asylums at state expense. Interesting enough, in its most famous and influential English and French guises, it was initially the work of laymen: William Tuke, a Quaker tea and coffee merchant who had founded the

York Retreat in 1796, and developed the approach in a collaboration with the lay couple who administered the asylum, George and Katherine Jepson;[12] and Jean-Baptiste Pussin and his wife (who was nicknamed "the Governess") at the Bicêtre and the Salpêtrière respectively.[13] But very quickly the central tenets of moral treatment were absorbed and transformed by medical men, and used as the basis for their claims to be uniquely qualified to run the new asylums. What had begun in Tuke's hands as a critique of the failures of asylum medicine became instead central to the ideology of the medical superintendents who by the middle of the nineteenth century had achieved a medical monopoly of the treatment of the mad. In the nineteenth century, that is, the birth of the asylum simultaneously marked the emergence of a newly self-confident and organized group of specialists in mental medicine. The alienists' claims to expertise and to the capture of this new jurisdiction rested firmly on their management of the reformed asylums.[14]

Across Europe and North America, a veritable mania for building asylums at state expense marked the middle decades of the nineteenth century. France passed a law making the construction of provincial asylums compulsory in 1838, a belated response to an earlier report from Pinel's protégé and successor, J.E.D. Esquirol, documenting what he claimed were the horrors of treatment of the insane in prisons, jails, and the community. In England, permissive legislation passed in 1807, the County Asylums Act, allowed taxes to be collected and spent for the construction of reformed asylums, and two acts of 1845 made asylum construction compulsory, and introduced a national inspectorate, the Lunacy Commission, to oversee and police the new establishments, as well as the existing charity asylums and profit-making madhouses. In the United States, the doctrine of the separation of powers was held to preclude federal involvement, so alongside a handful of private asylums, it took state-by-state initiatives to create a national network of asylums.[15] That the process was accomplished in only a decade and a half was substantially due to the indefatigable efforts of the Yankee moral entrepreneur, who, not satisfied by dragooning state legislators north, south and west to do her bidding, also took time to browbeat British politicians into imposing tax-supported asylums on a hitherto resistant Scotland.[16] Political fragmentation in Italy and Germany led to more halting progress there, but eventually, they too embraced the mantra that for the most serious forms of mental disorder the asylum was the best and perhaps the only solution.

But the extravagant claims that lunacy reformers had made for the asylum rapidly proved an illusion. Cure rates were of the order of a third of patients treated, and the upshot was a steady increase in the fraction of patients who became long-stay patients, coupled with a steady rise in the size of the average asylum. The York Retreat, which served as a model for Anglo-American reformers, initially provided for no more than thirty patients. The so-called corporate asylums that brought moral treatment to America and served as the model for the first state hospitals there, were scarcely much larger.[17] By the 1860s, asylums containing upwards of 1000 patients were not uncommon. By the early twentieth century, there were asylums like Milledgeville in Georgia, United States, with a population well in excess of 10,000. At Epsom outside London, more than 12,000 patients were crowded on a single site. It was the hordes of the hopeless, the legions of chronic patients who constituted the public image of the asylum. The optimism that had marked the early part of the century was replaced by an equally profound pessimism. And the asylum's reputation once more sank till it was viewed as "the Bluebeard's cupboard of the neighbourhood."[18]

Over the past two decades, scholars have sought to complicate the picture of the late nineteenth-century asylum as little more than a warehouse for the unwanted. They have stressed the ways families used the asylum for their own purposes, to secure some temporary relief from the burdens of caring for a mentally ill family member. And they have pointed out that even in this era, there remained a not insignificant movement of patients out of the asylum and back into the community.[19] The public image of the asylum as a cemetery for the still-breathing is clearly somewhat at odds with the reality of the continued movement of not-inconsiderable numbers of patients from the asylum back into the community.[20]

Still, modern scholarship notwithstanding, the silting up of asylums with chronic patients is what dominated late nineteenth-century perceptions of the asylum. The effects were felt on many levels. Psychiatry as a profession had to account for its manifold failures as a therapeutic enterprise, a particularly acute problem given the utopian expectations that had accompanied the birth of the asylum, and to which the profession had contributed. Those who had choice in the matter, and that was not of course the poor and those with limited resources, redoubled their efforts to avoid the stigma and the sense of hopelessness that enveloped the asylum. And public authorities grew steadily less willing to expend what they perceived to be extravagant sums of money on a population whose prospects of reclamation seemed poor at best.

Psychiatrists increasingly argued that the inmate throngs who were the wards of the asylum were degenerates, evolutionary throwbacks whose biological defects were engraved upon their bodies and brains, visible in their physiognomy and incapable of being cured. Indeed, the risk of releasing these defectives into the community was that, lacking the restraints of the more sensible and civilized, they would recklessly multiply their kind, overwhelming the healthy stock that constituted the bulk of the population. It was an account which simultaneously explained away the profession's failures and provided a new rationale for building and maintaining asylums, as places to quarantine the biologically unfit and prevent a further increase in the numbers of defectives. It brought into being a new emphasis on eugenics – the purported science of encouraging the better sort to breed and precluding the defective classes from doing so, either through preventive detention in asylums, or via involuntary sterilization. The Nazis would later take the logic of this position a step further and order the extermination of these "useless eaters" as their propaganda proclaimed mental patients to be.

Mental illness has always carried with it enormous stigma. The language of biological degeneration and inferiority served only to strengthen those age-old prejudices, and the extraordinarily negative perceptions of the late nineteenth-century asylum encouraged the well-to-do to seek any possible alternative – treatment at spa towns in Germany and France; resort to an array of sanatoria and homes for the nervous; and quack remedies of all sorts. In the United States, for example, the Kellogg brothers took over a failing sanatorium in Battle Creek, Michigan, run by the Seventh Day Adventist Church and turned it into a lucrative business patronized by presidents and captains of industry, Hollywood stars and legions of the great and good, all of whom came to be de-toxified and to have their mental batteries recharged.

But whatever protection the theory of degeneration offered to those running asylums, it could not completely insulate psychiatry from the the perception of failure. American psychiatry came under sustained attack in the 1870s and 1880s from a group of rival specialists who had emerged from the carnage of the American Civil War. The asylum physicians, sneered the New York neurologist Edward Spitzka, were "experts at everything but the diagnosis, treatment and pathology of insanity" and he harshly condemned the "grated windows, crib-beds, bleak walls, gruff attendants, narcotics and insane surroundings of an asylum."[21] Invited to address America's assembled psychiatrists at the fiftieth anniversary of the formation of the professional association of asylum physicians, the Philadelphia neurologist was equally savage in his criticisms. Speaking for an hour, he denounced asylums and their doctors in no uncertain terms. He accused them of presiding over an assembly of "living corpses, . . . pathetic patients who have lost even the memory of hope, [and] sit in rows, too dull to know despair, silent, gruesome machines which sleep and eat, eat and sleep." "Asylum life," he concluded, "is deadly to the insane."[22] The leading English alienist, Henry Maudsley, who had gratefully cut his ties with the asylum system for an office-based practice, concurred: "I cannot help feeling, from my experience, that one effect of asylums is to make permanent lunatics."[23] Historians have generally agreed. In Gerald Grob's words,

> After 1860, . . . the continuous rise in the number of chronic patients had all but obliterated the therapeutic goals of many hospitals . . . virtually every hospital in the nation was confronted with a problem whose magnitude was clearly increasing rather than diminishing . . . Overcrowded conditions and the accumulation of chronic patients were increasingly the norm, as the transformation of mental hospitals into strictly welfare institutions as far as their funding and reputation were concerned [solidified] their custodial character.[24]

In France, the crisis of psychiatric legitimacy had surfaced as early as the 1860s and 1870s. Anti-psychiatric sentiments surfaced in the popular press. Many in the medical profession seemed poised to join the chorus of disapproval. The eminent neurologist Jean-Martin Charcot was beginning to experiment with the hypnotic treatment of hysterical patients, but while the scantily dressed women who drew crowds to his weekly demonstrations entertained *tout* Paris, they did little for the reputation of alienists and their institutions. And eventually, on Charcot's death, his hysterical circus would collapse, amidst recriminations, accusations that his demonstrations had been faked, and an abandonment of his whole approach.[25] Though the fears expressed by Jules Falret, a prominent asylum doctor, proved over-blown, the professional uncertainty his remarks revealed was real enough. "The law of 1838 and the asylums for the insane are being attacked on all sides,"[26] he complained, and in this he was not wrong. But in the final analysis, it turned out that the public had grown used to the mass confinement of the mad and showed little disposition to destroy the institutions that had cost so much to build, so psychiatry's position, while weak and marginal, was never truly threatened.

For the most part, the fate and standing of psychiatry remained very much bound up with that of the asylum. Psychiatrists were trapped in the asylum almost as securely

107

as their patients. Training for neophytes took place on an apprenticeship basis, as doctors were recruited to serve as lowly assistant physicians, a situation made possible in part by the overcrowded state of the medical profession in the closing decades of the nineteenth century. In essence, the profession had virtually no presence in universities in most countries. There was, to be sure, a lectureship in mental diseases at the University of Edinburgh in Scotland, but not even this sort of presence south of the border. In the United States, the first professorship of any note would not be filled until the end of the first decade of the twentieth century, and there would not be a second chair until the Rockefeller Foundation started extensively funding psychiatry in the 1930s. There were textbooks, to be sure, which provided some semblance of formal knowledge, but there was little in the way of sustained research and a general sense of intellectual stasis. Weir Mitchell's critique of psychiatry's failings was all too accurate. In unguarded moments, asylum doctors confessed as much. Bedford Pierce, superintendent of the York Retreat, the asylum that had been so influential in launching the drive to build these places in Britain and the United States, confessed to the "humiliating reflection . . . that it is not possible as yet to make a scientific classification of mental disorders."[27] And speaking as the newly installed president of the American Medico-Psychological Association, Charles Hill succinctly confessed that "our therapeutics are simply a pile of rubbish."[28]

By the end of the nineteenth century, asylums were being relabelled as mental hospitals, a piece of reform by word magic that did little to disguise an increasingly grim reality. Throughout the first half of the twentieth century, hospital censuses continued to grow, and at least until the outbreak of the Second World War, the profession's centre of gravity continued to rest firmly within the walls of the institutions. To be sure, Freud's psychoanalysis had suggested one pathway for the profession out of asylumdom, and the experiences of the First World War added a further stimulus to out-patient practice, as doctors who had been forced to deal with shell-shock patients in the field tried to translate the model of extra-institutional practice to civilian life. Child and marriage guidance clinics provided a small number of practitioners with an alternative site for their work, as did the newly emerging juvenile courts,[29] but these employed but a small minority of the profession, which otherwise continued to concentrate its attentions on a burgeoning population of compulsorily certified patients locked up in mental hospitals.

Only in Germany and Austria did a different pattern emerge during the course of the nineteenth century. From the mid-nineteenth century onwards, German psychiatry sought to emulate the linking together of clinical practice, the laboratory and academic research that was bringing the rest of German medicine into international prominence. Still politically fragmented until 1870, the congeries of principalities and kingdoms that made up Germany had chosen to compete for visibility and prestige through underwriting science and knowledge-production. University-based clinics and institutes brought together teaching and research in novel ways, and it was this approach that German psychiatry adopted as its own. Germany had its barracks-asylums, to be sure, but in addition it developed a series of smaller clinics attached to universities, where interesting patients could be studied, and laboratory research pursued.[30] As time went on, German psychiatrists developed research programmes examining the brain and spinal cord, creating new techniques for fixing and staining cells for microscopic examination, searching for the physical roots of madness. There were a handful of successes: Alois Alzheimer's identification of the neuro-fibillary tangles associated with the disease to which he gave his name; and the subsequent discovery by Noguchi and Moore of the syphilitic spirochete in the brains of patients suffering from general paralysis of the insane. For the overwhelming bulk of the insane, however, the hypothesized brain lesions remained elusive, as they still do today.

Asylums in this model served largely as a source of pathological material for the dissecting table. German psychiatry evinced little interest in treating patients seen, as elsewhere, as biological degenerates, and by the 1930s, many of the leading lights of the profession were collaborating eagerly with the Nazi regime, first sterilizing the mad, and then murdering them *en masse* as part of the drive to eliminate "useless eaters." Asylums were temporarily emptied, but not by some grand therapeutic breakthrough.

Elsewhere, there were few attempts to emulate the German model of research-oriented clinics. One exception was the Phipps Clinic at Johns Hopkins, established with funding from a Pittsburgh steel millionaire. Hopkins as a whole had sought to emulate the basic features of the German knowledge factories, and Adolf Meyer, the Swiss immigrant it appointed as its first professor of psychiatry, spoke airily of psycho-biology, and tried to turn the Phipps into a research enterprise that would solve some of the mysteries of madness.[31] While Meyer went on to train many psychiatrists who occupied chairs across the country as new academic departments were created, his programme produced no therapeutic breakthroughs and little by way of significant new research.[32]

Henry Maudsley, the most prominent British alienist of the late Victorian and Edwardian age (he hated the term psychiatrist), had grown distant from his professional colleagues, and left the fortune he had accumulated from his private practice to fund a hospital he intended as an alternative and a reproach to the asylum system he had left behind. The Maudsley Hospital and its associated Institute of Psychiatry sought to combine care of selected patients with academic research and professional training, and eventually, after the Second World War, came to be led by one of Meyer's protégés, Aubrey Lewis. But like the Phipps, it was better at producing psychiatrists than at unlocking the keys to madness.

Mental hospitals relentlessly grew in the first half of the twentieth century. In the United States, for example, they quadrupled in this period, while the general population simply doubled. On Long Island, the New York authorities built or expanded three barracks-asylums at Central Islip, Kings Park, and Pilgrim which together at their peak contained nearly 35,000 patients. Desperate to do something to stem the tide and to reinforce their own sense of professional competence, asylum superintendents had at their disposal large numbers of patients who were legally without rights by virtue of their status, hidden from public view, and seen by most as incapable of making rational choices about their own treatment. Many psychiatrists fell prey to the temptation to experiment on these captive bodies. In Austria, Hungary, Germany, Portugal, Britain and the United States, an orgy of experimentation ensued. Malarial therapy, deep sleep therapy, surgical excision of focal sepsis, insulin coma therapy, metrazol-induced seizures, electroshock therapy, and lobotomies – all these desperate remedies and more have attracted considerable scholarly attention in recent decades.[33]

Imperial powers had exported the asylum model to deal with mad white colonists even in the nineteenth century.[34] Despite the deteriorating public image of these places, their centrality to the provision of mental health services in the first half of the twentieth century saw versions of them exported to the colonies and to other parts of the non-Western world like China. These asylums, too, have begun to attract their historians. Asylum psychiatry in these settings was transformed in some interesting directions, for while Western-trained psychiatrists looked with condescension on indigenous beliefs and practices, imperial psychiatry in such settings almost universally experienced enormous difficulty in transforming popular local customs.[35] Very occasionally, there was resistance to the expansion of the asylum model in societies where Western influence was limited. Japan, for example, continued to rely largely on home confinement until the mid-twentieth century, and as a late adopter, has proved equally reluctant to move away from a reliance on the mental hospital.[36]

Though mental hospital censuses continued to grow in the 1930s and 1940s, conditions in the asylums were deteriorating even further. The Great Depression both meant more patients, some driven by want, and also decreased budgets. Total war, when it came, worsened an already deteriorating set of conditions, and in addition created shortages of both psychiatrists and staff. The Nazis were busy "solving" the problem of their institutionalized population by resorting to mass murder. Occupied Vichy, France took a different tack, savagely cutting mental hospital budgets to the point where patients starved – death rates tripled in the war years, with an estimated 45,000 patients in French mental hospitals dying of starvation and disease – an outcome some historians have called "soft extermination."[37] Elsewhere conditions did not deteriorate quite so far, though they were shocking enough in all conscience. In the immediate aftermath of the war, for example, conscientious objectors who had been forced to serve as mental hospital attendants published memoirs and photographs of scenes that resembled Dante's *Inferno*, while journalists just back from viewing the horrors of the Final Solution spoke of the conditions they found in their own country's state mental hospitals as making them "American Death Camps."[38]

This generation of critics sought reform of the mental hospitals, not their demise. The 1950s and 1960s, however, saw the publication of a set of sociological studies of the mental hospital that increasingly argued that the defects of these places were a structural feature of these "total institutions," as the Canadian-American sociologist Erving Goffman dubbed them, and thus their flaws were ineradicable.[39] "The abandonment of the state hospitals," said Ivan Belknap, summarizing an emerging consensus, "might be one of the greatest humanitarian reforms and the greatest financial economy ever achieved."[40] Renegade psychiatrists like Thomas Szasz, often labelled anti-psychiatrists, chimed in, equating mental hospitals with concentration camps.[41] And the then-British Minister of Health, Enoch Powell, gave a widely reported speech denouncing mental hospitals as a failed experiment, announcing his government's plan to close them all, and offering to be the first to set the torch to their funeral pyre.[42] The legitimacy of what had been the dominant response to serious mental illness for more than a century reached its nadir.

Powell proved to be a prophet. In Britain, mental hospital populations had reached their peak in 1954. In the United States, the inflection point came a year later, and in both countries the mental hospital census then declined year on year, quite slowly and almost imperceptibly at first, but by the second half of the 1960s, at an accelerating pace. Certainly, the systematic destruction of any sense that the mental hospital provided a therapeutic function, or even valuable sheltered care, was of considerable ideological importance, smoothing the way towards the abandonment of segregative modes of controlling madness. But scholars from a variety of perspectives have demonstrated that neither these shifts in sentiment, nor the other factor most often invoked to explain the demise of the mental hospital, the psychopharmacological revolution that began with the introduction of phenothiazine under the trade names Thorazine (in the United States) and Largactil (in Europe) were the primary factors behind the emptying out of the Victorian bins. Instead, many have argued, what took place was a conscious shift in social policy, much of it driven by fiscal concerns.[13]

Whatever the precise weightings one places on the various factors that contributed to deinstitutionalization and the virtual abandonment of the chronically mentally ill that has been a feature of social policy all across the industrialized world, the fate of the mental hospital is beyond doubt. A handful still linger, but in a much shrunken state. Most have shut their doors. On occasion, they have been reincarnated as luxury hotels, as on the island of San Clemente in the Venice lagoon, or as upscale housing for the *nouveaux riches*, in both cases taking care to disguise their stigmatizing history. But in most cases, they have just mouldered away: dust to dust, ashes to ashes as the Bible would have it. Mental hospitals have become a fast-vanishing relic of the past, their distinctive moral architecture preserved only through the lenses of some creative photographers who have devoted themselves to recording the last moments of museums of madness that will soon have vanished from our collective consciousness.[14]

Notes

1 See Lawrence Conrad, *Companion Encyclopedia of the History of Medicine* vol. 1, eds W.F. Bynum, and R.S. Porter, (London: Routledge, 1993), 676–727; Michael W. Dols, "Insanity and Its Treatment in Islamic Society," *Medical History* 31 (1987): 1–14; idem, "The Origins of the Islamic Hospital: Myth and Reality," *Bulletin of the History of Medicine* 61 (1987): 367–90; Timothy S. Miller, *The Birth of the Hospital in the Byzantine Empire* (Baltimore: Johns Hopkins University Press, 1985); Manfred Ullman, *Islamic Medicine* (Edinburgh: Edinburgh University Press, 1978).

2 Michael W, Dols, *Majnun: The Madman in Medieval Islamic Society* (Oxford: Clarendon Press, 1992).

3 W. Montgomery Watt, *The Influence of Islam on Medieval Europe* (Edinburgh: Edinburgh University Press, 1972).

4 For an excellent history of the asylum, which survives in the twenty-first century, see Jonathan Andrews, Asa Briggs, Roy Porter, Penny Tucker, and Keir Waddington, *The History of Bethlem* (London: Routledge, 1997).

5 The best general perspective on the trade in lunacy remains William Parry-Jones' book of that title (London: Routledge, 1972). See also Roy Porter, *Mind Forg'd Manacles* (London: Athlone, 1987); and Leonard Smith, *Lunatic Hospitals in Georgian England* (London: Routledge, 2014).

6 Michel Foucault, *Madness and Civilization*, translated by Richard Howard (New York: Pantheon, 1965), Ch. 2; also in the complete English translation of the French text, *The History of Madness*, translated by Jean Khalfa and Jonathan Murphy (London: Routledge, 2006), Ch. 2.

7 Jacques Tenon, *Memoires sur les hôpitaux de Paris* (Paris: Pierres, 1778), 85.

8 Colin Jones, "The Treatment of the Insane in Eighteenth and Early Nineteenth Century Montpellier," *Medical History*, 24 (1980): 371–90. To be sure, Tenon lists a handful of private

madhouses in Paris on the Faubourg St. Antoine and in Montmatre, but taken together these barely housed 300 lunatics.

9 Sir G.E. Paget, *The Harveian Oration* (Cambridge: Deighton and Bell: 1866), 34–5.

10 The quotes are from the Scottish alienist William Alexander Francis Browne's book, *What Asylums Were, Are, and Ought to Be* (Edinburgh: Black, 1837), 203, 213, but similar sentiments were voiced elsewhere. In the United States in the 1830s and 1840s, there emerged what historians have dubbed "the cult of curability" where estimates of the feasibility of cure were bid up (and allegedly supported by asylum statistics) from 60, 70 to 80 percent and more, till the day when Dr. William Awl of Virginia announced he had cured 100 per cent of those he had treated. (He was promptly renamed "Dr Cure-Awl.")

11 George Mora, "Vincenzo Chiarugi (1759–1820) and His Psychiatric Reform in Florence in the 18th Century," *Journal of the History of Medicine and the Allied Sciences* 14 (1959), 424–33.

12 See Anne Digby, *Madness, Morality and Medicine: A Study of the York Retreat, 1790–1914* (Cambridge: Cambridge University Press, 1985).

13 Dora Weiner, *Comprendre et soigner. Philippe Pinel et la medicine de l'ésprit* (Paris: Fayard, 1999); Jan Goldstein, *Console and Classify: The French Psychiatric Profession in the Nineteenth Century* (Chicago: University of Chicago Press, 2001).

14 For analyses of these processes in France, see Goldstein, op. cit, and Ian Dowbiggin, *Inheriting Madness: Professionalization and Psychiatric Knowledge in Nineteenth Century France* (Berkeley: University of California Press, 1991); for Britain, see Andrew Scull, *The Most Solitary of Afflictions: Madness and Society in Britain, 1700–1900* (London: Yale University Press 1993); and idem, with Charlotte MacKenzie and Nicholas Hervey, *Masters of Bedlam: The Transformation of the Mad-Doctoring Trade* (Princeton: Princeton University Press, 1996). For Germany, Eric J. Engstrom's *Clinical Psychiatry in Imperial Germany* (Ithaca: Cornell University Press, 2003) is illuminating.

15 See Goldstein op. cit., Dowbiggin op. cit., Scull, op. cit., and Rothman, op. cit, as well as Gerald Grob, *Mental Institutions in America: Social Policy to 1873* (New York: Free Press, 1973).

16 See David Gollaher, *Voice for the Mad: A Life of Dorothea Dix* (New York: Free Press, 1995).

17 Andrew Scull, "The Discovery of the Asylum Revisited: Lunacy Reform in the New American Republic," in A. Scull (ed.) *Madhouses, Mad-Doctors and Madmen: The Social History of Psychiatry in the Victorian Era*, ed. Andrew Scull (Philadelphia: University of Pennsylvania Press, 1981), 144–65.

18 Anonymous, "Lunatic Asylums," *Quarterly Review* 101 (1857): 353.

19 See, for example, David Wright and Peter Bartlett, ed., *Outside the Walls of the Asylum: The History of Care in the Community* (London: Bloomsbury, 2001); and Akihito Suzuki, *Madness at Home: The Psychiatrist, the Patient, and the Family in England, 1820–1860* (Berkeley: University of California Press, 2006).

20 See, for example, Joseph Melling and Bill Forsythe, eds, *Insanity, Institutions and Society: A Social History of Madness in Comparative Perspective* (London: Routledge, 1999); David Wright, "Getting out of the Asylum: Understanding the Confinement of the Insane in the Nineteenth Century," *Social History of Medicine* 10 (1997): 137–55.

21 Edward C. Spitzka, "Reform in the Scientific Study of Psychiatry," *Journal of Nervous and Mental Disease* 5 (1878): 201–29. For a useful discussion of these developments, see Bonnie Blustein, "A Hollow Square of Psychological Science: American Neurologists and Psychiatrists in Conflict," in *Madhouses, Mad-Doctors and Madmen: The Social History of Psychiatry in the Victorian Era*, ed. Andrew Scull, (Philadelphia: University of Pennsylvania Press, 1981): 241–70.

22 Silas Weir Mitchell, "Address Before the Fiftieth Annual Meeting of the American Medico-Psychological Association," *Journal of Nervous and Mental Disease* 21 (1894): 413–37.

23 Henry Maudsley, *The Physiology and Pathology of Mind* (New York: Appleton, 1871): 432.

24 Gerald Grob, op. cit., 1973, 238, 306–8.

25 Andrew Scull, *Hysteria: The Disturbing History* (Oxford: Oxford University Press, 2011).

26 Jules Falret quoted in Ian Dowbiggin, "French Psychiatry, Hereditarianism, and Professional Legitimacy, 1840–1900," *Research in Law, Deviance, and Social Control* 7 (1985): 135–65.

27 York Retreat, *Annual Report*, 1904.

28 Charles G. Hill, "Presidential Address: How Can We Best Advance the Study of Psychiatry," *American Journal of Insanity* 64 (1907): 1–8.

29 Margo Horn, *Before It's Too Late: The Child Guidance Movement in the United States, 1922–1945* (Philadelphia: Temple University Press, 1989).

30 There were, in addition, private clinics to which the well-to-do flocked, seeking, like their counterparts in other countries, to avoid the stigma of being confined in an asylum. For a study of these enterprises and the tendency of their patients to seek physical diagnoses for what often seem psychosomatic problems, see Edward Shorter, "Private Clinics in Central Europe, 1850–1933," *Social History of Medicine* 3 (1990): 159–95.

31 Susan Lamb, *Adolf Meyer: Pathologist of the Mind* (Baltimore: Johns Hopkins University Press, 2014).

32 Andrew Scull and Jay Schulkin "Psychobiology, Psychiatry, and Psychoanalysis: The Intersecting Careers of Adolf Meyer, Phyllis Greenacre, and Curt Richter," *Medical History* 53 (2009): 5–36.

33 Representative examples include Joel Braslow, *Mental Ills, Bodily Cures* (Berkeley: University of California Press, 1997); Jack Pressman, *Last Resort: Psychosurgery and the Limits of Medicine* (Cambridge: Cambridge University Press, 1998); Andrew Scull, *Madhouse: A Tragic Tale of Megalomania and Modern Medicine* (New Haven and London: Yale University Press, 2006); Edward Shorter and David Healy, *Shock Therapy* (New Brunswick: Rutgers University Press, 2007); Mical Raz, *The Lobotomy Letters: The Making of American Psychosurgery* (Rochester: University of Rochester Press, 2013).

34 See, for example, Waltraud Ernst, *Mad Tales from the Raj: Colonial Psychiatry in South Asia, 1800–58* (London: Anthem Press, 2010); Dolly McKinnon and Catherine Colebourne, *'Madness' in Australia: Histories, Heritage, and the Asylum* (St. Lucia, Queensland: University of Queensland Press, 2003); Sloane Malone and Megan Vaughan, ed., *Psychiatry and Empire* (London: Palgrave, 2007).

35 See, for example, Jonathan Sadowsky, *Imperial Bedlam: Institutions of Madness in Colonial Southwest Nigeria* (Berkeley: University of California Press, 1999); Waltraud Ernst, *Colonialism and Transnational Psychiatry: The Development of an Indian Mental Hospital in British India, c. 1925–1940* (London: Anthem, 2013); Emily Baum, "Spit, Chains and Hospital Beds': A History of Madness in Republican Bejing, 1912–1938 (PhD Diss., University of California, San Diego, 2013); Claire Edington, "Getting Into and Getting Out of the Colonial Asylum: Families and Psychiatric Care in French Indochina," *Comparative Studies in Society and History* 25 (2013): 725–55; idem, "Beyond the Asylum: Colonial psychiatry in French Indochina, 1880–1940," (PhD Diss., Columbia University, 2013); Richard Keller, *Colonial Madness: Psychiatry in French North Africa* (Chicago: University of Chicago Press, 2007).

36 Akihito Suzuki, "The State, Family and the Insane in Japan, 1900–1945," in *The Confinement of the Insane: International Perspectives, 1800–1965*, ed. R. Porter and D. Wright (Cambridge: Cambridge University Press, 2003), 193–225.

37 F. Chapirreau, "La mortalité des maladies mentaux hospitalisés en France pendant la deuxieme guerre mondiale," *L'Encephale* 35 (2009): 121–28; Marc Masson and Jean-Michel Azorin, "La surmortalité des maladies mentaux a la lumière de l'Histoire," *L'Evolution Psychiatrique* 67 (2002): 465–79.

38 Frank Wright, ed., *Out of Sight, Out of Mind* (Philadelphia: National Mental Health Foundation, 1947); Alfred Maisel, "Bedlam 1946," *Life Magazine* 20 (6 May 1946): 102–116; Albert Deutsch, *The Shame of the States* (New York: Harcourt, Brace, 1948); Harold Orlans, "An American Death Camp," *Politics* 5 (1948): 162–68.

39 Alfred Stanton and Morris Schwartz, *The Mental Hospital* (New York: Basic Books, 1954); H. Warren Dunham and S. Kirson Weinberg, *The Culture of a State Mental Hospital* (Detroit: Wayne State University Press, 1960); Erving Goffman, *Asylums* (New York: Doubleday, 1961); Robert Perrucci, *Circle of Madness: On Being Insane and Institutionalized in America* (Englewood Cliffs: Prentice-Hall, 1974); Russell Barton, *Institutional Neurosis* (Bristol: Wright, 1965); John K. Wing and George W. Brown, *Institutionalism and Schizophrenia* (Cambridge: Cambridge University Press, 1970).

40 Ivan Belknap, *Human Problems of a State Mental Hospital* (New York: McGraw-Hill, 1956), xi, 212.

41 Thomas S. Szasz, *The Myth of Mental Illness* (New York: Harper and Row, 1961).
42 Enoch Powell, "Speech to the Annual Conference of National Association for Mental Health," *Report of the Annual Conference* (London: Mind, 1961).
43 Andrew Scull, *Decarceration: Community Treatment and the Deviant* (Englewood Cliffs: Prentice-Hall, 1977); Paul Lerman, *Deinstitutionalization and the Welfare State* (New Brunswick: Rutgers University Press, 1982); Stephen Rose, "Deciphering Deinstittuionalization: Complexities in Policy and Program Analysis," *Milbank Memorial Fund Quarterly* 57 (1979): 429–60; William Gronfein, "Psychotropic Drugs and the Origins of Deinstitutionalization," *Social Problems* 32 (1985): 437–54; Gerald Grob, *From Asylum to Community: Mental Health Care in Modern America* (Princeton: Princeton University Press, 1992).
44 Christopher Payne, *Asylum: Inside the Closed World of State Mental Hospitals* (Cambridge, Mass.: MIT Press, 2009).

6

THE EPISTEMOLOGY AND CLASSIFICATION OF 'MADNESS' SINCE THE EIGHTEENTH CENTURY

German E. Berrios and Ivana S. Marková

Introduction

The process of divesting 'madness' from both meaning and mysteriousness started sometime during the middle of the eighteenth century. Although still pursued, this attempt at disenchantment[1] is unlikely ever to be completed. Written into the deep consciousness of man, madness remains first and foremost a cultural object and it will never become a 'natural kind'.[2] This entry provides historical and epistemological information to understand this state of affairs. To begin with, some definitions are required.

Issues historiographical

Since at least the fourteenth century the multivocal term 'madness' has been used in the English-speaking lands to name: a) a variety of deviant and anomalous behaviours; and b) objects or situations considered to be extraordinary, eccentric or ridiculous. Terms such as *Folie, Wahnsinn, Locura, Pazzia, безумие*, and so on, are likely to have played the same role in other European vernaculars. It would be temping to claim that the semantic coverage of all these terms is fully coterminous. As attested by translators who often struggle to render them into a different language this may not be the case. That these words overlap only partially is also suggested by similar difficulties found when comparing (within the English language) the meaning of madness, insanity, mental alienation, craziness, lunacy, mental disease, mental disorder, and so on. Be that as it may, in accordance with the editor's brief, we shall use the term 'madness' and to achieve historiographical balance envisage it as a nomadic cultural object that in order to meet the epistemological and social needs of successive historical periods has per force undergone partial reconstruction. According to this view madness has survived as a recognizable cultural object on account of the fact that within each historical period similar social and semantic demands have acted as veritable shaping 'invariants'.[3] It is likely that during each historical period the concept of madness has been repeatedly reconstructed in successive historical convergences.[4]

The convergence model requires an account of symptom- and disorder-formation. In this regard, madness can be considered as the secular name for forms of deviant experience configured by cultural templates.[5] Some of these experiences may actually have originated in disorganized neural networks but many are likely to reflect intersubjective turbulence. In this case the 'invariant' would not be a putative 'brain dysfunction' but the cultural configurators themselves.[6] The persistence of a cultural configurator could explain the secular reappearance of certain forms of madness without needing to posit a biological invariant.

Defining terms

Epistemology

'Epistemology' is conventionally defined as the study of the conditions, truth-value, and legitimacy of knowledge. This definition tends also to be universalist (one episte-mology for all forms of knowledge) and to consider the natural sciences as the only truth-makers and methodological paradigms.[7] It is likely that psychiatry, due to its hybrid nature[8] does require a broader theory of knowledge. Hence, epistemology will be considered in this chapter not as a normative, but as a descriptive, enter-prise whose central function is the identification of the manners in which disciplines choose to legitimize the 'knowledge' they produce. This means that, instead of a gen-eral theory of epistemology, the hybrid disciplines need to opt for a regional form of contextualized epistemology that may take into account their structural peculiarities and problems. This contextualization[9] makes it obvious that the search for universals of knowledge is not a priority for the epistemology of psychiatry. Indeed, this chapter will make use of a version of historical epistemology according to which concepts obtain their meaning from the historical periods in which they are allowed to be active.[10] For example, to meet the specific demands of successive historical periods, 'madness' has undergone refurbishments. However, without making a number of (unwarranted) assumptions, it might not be possible to arrange the versions of mad-ness thereby generated in a 'progressive' series.

Classification

'Classification' refers both to the act and to the results of grouping objects into classes.[11] This grouping activity gives rise to lists, orderings, and classifications. Confusion has been caused by using 'classification' to name all three. Lists do not make assumptions as to any putative association between the items they contain nor about the nature of the universe they come from. For example, *DSM-5* and all known 'psychiatric' classifications are effectively lists similar in epistemological structure to a supermarket catalogue. Orderings do assume that the objects grouped may be related. For example, the *Scala Naturae* or 'great chain of being'[12] groups all objects in the universe (God at the top and minerals at the bottom) and assumes that the grouping rules were God-made.

Classifications proper assume that the objects classified are related, that the group-ing rules are intrinsic to the universe they come from, and that this universe is a closed one.[13] This makes classifications epistemologically more useful than lists of groupings in that they can generate knowledge that may be hidden from view. For example, the periodic table of elements[14] or Linné's classification of plants[15] are such because both the universe of elements and of plants are assumed to be complete and the objects thereby contained to hold internal relationships. It does not matter whether all of the objects in question are known, what matters is that it is assumed that all exist some-where. Thus real classifications do have predictive power and are worth constructing. It follows that the phrase 'psychiatric classification' is a misnomer.[16]

The eighteenth century

During each historical period, priests, medics, philosophers, linguists, literati, poli-ticians, social reformers, lawyers, magicians, and other social agents have always felt the need to give a view on 'madness'. The eigtheenth century was no exception, and madness can be found mentioned in its annals of knowledge and practice.[17] Although much of what was then said was a repetition of earlier centuries, on occasions things novel can be identified.

As far as madness is concerned, the seventeenth century tended to repeat Galenic views. *Mutatis mutandi*, this claim is valid both for English writers such as Sydenham, Willis, and Locke and also for Continental ones like Ferrand, de Lorme, Guy Patin or Vieussens. Although it is the case that Galen did not say a great deal about madness, his general view that madness was a temporal functional disturbance of the body was repeated for centuries both in the West[18] and the Islamic world.[19] Making due allowance for the sui generis definition of body entertained by Galen,[20] this claim was interpreted as madness being due to a bodily disorder (due to an imbalance of the four humours).

During the seventeenth century, writings on madness tend to fall into three groups: those by medics such as Willis, Locke, or clergymen such as Napier;[21] by sufferers, who tend to configure their experiences in terms of the templates of the day, whether medical or religious;[22] and by lay writers.[23]

Madness and the enlightenment

The new epistemological freedoms and prohibitions that accompanied the 'Scientific Revolution'[24] and new questions about man and his afflictions brought about by the secularization of eighteenth-century culture,[25] drastically affected the concept of 'madness'. Completed only during the nineteenth century, the changes thereby ini-tiated led to the current view of madness.[26] These changes led to the view that mad-ness: a) was a natural kind, b) was sited in a specific region of space (i.e. a specific organ such as stomach or brain); c) was a temporalized process (i.e. it could have a beginning and an end); and d) did not emerge directly from matter but it needed to be mediated by a 'function' (first physiology and then psychology were to act as such intermediaries during the nineteenth century). The first and second changes were implemented during the eighteenth century; the third had to wait until the nineteenth century.

The idea that diseases and plants shared common features (as entities and objects of classification) was introduced by Thomas Sydenham.[27] According to this proposal, diseases were ontological entities, which later on were to be called 'natural kinds'.[28] It also meant that, like plants, diseases inhabited a closed universe and could be clas-sified accordingly. This '*more botanico*' taxonomy (according to which diseases should be classified in the style of Botany) became standard during the eighteenth century as illustrated by the work of great 'classificators': Linné, Sagar, McBride, Vogel, Boissier de Sauvages, Cullen, etc., some of whom, such as Linné, were also medics and botanists.[29]

117

The epistemological distinction between disease and symptom, the latter conceived as a linguistic 'signifier' representing a 'signified' (a disease), was completed only by the turn of the ninteenth century. Thus, during the eighteenth-century classificators did not differentiate between complaints and full-blown diseases and proceeded to list them together.[30] Likewise, 'psychiatric' disorders were 'classified' by most together with the rest of bodily diseases.[31] During this period, most classificators used Linné's method and privileged features of either plants or diseases to construct their groups.[32] Although this method was challenged by Adanson, who proposed that to achieve a proper classification no feature should be privileged,[33] it reigned supreme until the twentieth century. However, after the Second World War, a delayed implementation of Adanson's proposal made possible by the availability of computers and of pattern recognition statistical techniques was to develop under the name of numerical taxonomy.[34]

During the 1770s, William Cullen introduced a new classificatory criterion, namely putative aetiology. This allowed him to create a new class of disease called Neuroses.[35] The grouping criterion for Cullen's Neuroses therefore was no longer a privileged set of features intrinsic to the objects to be classified but an external, speculative aetiology.[36] The Neuroses included *comata*, *adynamiæ*, *spasmi* and *Vesaniæ*. Disorders such as diabetes, asthma, whooping cough, abdominal colics, diarrhoea, and so on, all were classified as 'Neuroses'. There were four insanities (*Vesaniæ*): *Amentia*, *Melancholia*, *Mania*, and *Oneirodynia*, none of which corresponds to conditions that currently may bear the same name.

Other classificators also mixed symptoms and disorders. For example, under *Mentales*, Linné included Order I: *ideales* (delirium, paraphrosine, amentia, mania, daemonia, vesania and melancholia); Order II: *imaginarii* (syringmos, phantasma, vertigo, panophobia, hypochondriasis and sonnambulismus); and Order III: *pathetici* (citta, bulimia, polydipsia, satyriasis, erotomania, nostalgia, tarantismus, rabies, hydrophobia, cacositia, antipathia and anxietas).[37]

Under *Vesaniæ*, Boissier de Sauvages (1772) included: Order I: *Hallucinations*, (vertigo, suffusio, dyplopia, syrigmus, hypochondriasis, somnanbulismus); Order II: *Morositates* (Pica, Bulimia, Polydipsia, antipathia, nostalgia, panophobia, satyriasis, nymphomania, tarantismus, hydrophobia); Order III: *Deliria* (paraphrosine, amentia, melancholia, Mania, Dæmonomania); and Order IV: *Folies Anomales* (amnesia, agripnia).[38]

The space occupied by the Vesaniæs

In addition to the view that it was a natural kind, the eighteenth century began to develop the view that madness also occupied a region of bodily space. Important in this respect is the work of David Hartley, who is one of the first writers to apply Newtonianism to the mind.[39] According to the received view, Hartley tried to give an account of the mind in terms of mechanistic, non-vitalistic neurophysiology by explaining nerve functioning and conduction in terms of micro-vibrations (*vibratiuncles*). To account for complex mental functions, Hartley resorted to the Association of Ideas.

Hartley used 'madness' as both a generic term for all 'imperfections of the rational faculty' and as a specific diagnosis. There were eight 'imperfections': 1. Erroneousness of judgement in children and idiots; 2. Dotage in the elderly; 3. Drunkenness; 4. Delirium in acute distempers; 5. Recurrence of the same ideas in the course of study; 6. Violent passions; 7. Melancholy; and 8. Madness.

None of these clinical categories corresponds to any used in current psychiatry. These imperfections resulted from a failure of the 'rational faculty'. According to Hartley there was no demarcation line between soundness and unsoundness of mind. Hartley tried to explain the difference between the imperfections of the mind in terms of different patterns of vibration. He discussed 'Madness' both under Melancholy and also as a disease in its own right; indeed, given time and other (unknown) factors, Melancholy could become Madness. Madness could be brought about by bodily or mental causes. Mental causes could be hereditary (a sort of predisposition) and they become 'actual' only when 'some bodily distemper gives it full scope to exert itself'. Hartley's plea still resonates nowadays: 'An accurate history of the several kinds of madness from those physicians, who are much conversant with this distemper, is greatly wanted'.[10]

The nineteenth century

The temporalization of madness, the last important change undergone by the concept of madness only took place during the early nineteenth century. By the end of the previous century, and due to the *more botanico* approach, madness was considered to be a natural kind. Overlaying this ontological view, there was still a remnant of the old non-temporal concept of madness, that is, the belief that it was an eternal process. This is the reason why clinical recoveries needed explanation. To resolve this problem, the fascinating concept of 'lucid interval' was introduced into European psychiatry, and one can find it in use well into the 1840s. For example, Haslam (1809) defined it as: 'I should define a lucid interval to be a complete recovery of the patient's intellects, ascertained by repeated examinations of his conversation, and by constant observation of his conduct, for a time sufficient to enable the superintendant to form a correct judgment.'[11] The same concept was used by lawyers, for example, in the French Manual for Notaries the question appears under Article 357 (Démence): 'Que doit-on entendre par Intervalle Lucide?' (46); and later accompanied by a warning: 'L'intervalle lucide n'est point une tranquillité superficielle, une ombre de repos. Il faut que ce soit une intermission si clairement marquée.'[12]

In terms of classification, there was nothing exciting at the beginning of the nineteenth century. The four *espèces d'aliénation* introduced by Pinel (Manie ou délire général; mélancolie ou délire exclusif; démence ou abolition de la pensée et idiotisme, ou oblitération des facultés intellectuelles et affectives) were more or less official. None was new and all were already present in various eighteenth-century classifications, including Cullen's whose work Pinel had partially translated into French.[43] Pinel's categories lasted well into the 1840s, when they were challenged and eventually broken up into fragments, many of which became mental symptoms in their own right and then clustered together again to become the mental disorders we have nowadays. The nineteenth century was the century of personal classifications, and literally hundreds were published in the main European psychiatric cultures.[44]

Efforts were made by the end of the nineenth century to develop classifications that were accepted in all countries so that communication could be facilitated. The bellic vicissitudes of Europe, however, often got in the way, and even after the war had finished, resentment and distrust delayed reconciliation and hence common psychiatric endeavours. In regards to the psychoses (madness), toward the end of the century a determined effort was made by Roubinovitch to identify clinical equivalences between the two great psychiatric powers of Europe (France and Germany).[45]

Alienism, semiology, and psychopathology

Whilst during the first half of the nineteenth century there were no developments in regards to psychiatric listings, there were important epistemological changes which in due course were to act as the structures on which alienism (now psychiatry) has been based to our own day. Epistemological changes led to changes in praxis and these in turn fed back on the theory of alienism. During this period: a) two new concepts were constructed – mental symptom (as a unit of analysis) and mental disease (as a cluster of mental symptoms); b) a new language of description for mental afflictions (based on the epistemology of 'medical semiology') was put together (descriptive psychopathology); c) alienism was professionalized as a trade, science, praxis, and so on, via the development of learned societies, guilds, texts, journals, examinations and other rites of passage; d) new physical spaces to hold the mentally afflicted were required and this led to the construction of mental asylums; and e) alienism entered into dynamic and often conflictive interfaces with the law, the church, and civil society.[46]

The new concepts of mental symptom and disease

Complaints related to bodily and mental sufferings are likely to be as old as mankind. Until the eighteenth century these complaints were often accepted as diseases in their own right and listed with other diseases. In other words, no ontological or epistemological distinction was made between symptom and disease. This was particularly the case in the field of madness where the concept of 'mental symptom' had to wait until the early nineteenth century to be constructed.[47] Griesinger, for example, in 1845 was already calling mental symptoms 'Die Elementarstörungen der psychischen Krankheiten' and relating them to specific mental functions (e.g. hallucinations to perception; delusions to thinking; depression to affect, and so on).[48] In the second part of his book Griesinger used these 'elementary' or 'basic' psychological abnormalities to construct mental diseases.

The cultural forces that led to the construction of the concept of mental symptom are multiple. There was, first, the construction of the concept of symptom in general as part of the development of Séméïologie[49] or Séméiotique,[50] which in the event acted as a model for alienism. Both writers were influenced by the new linguistic theory of Dégerando according to which complaints (symptoms) were actual signs (signifiers) of disease. Secondly, there was the impact of Locke's philosophy and the Newtonian method, that is, an epistemological approach according to which objects and concepts could be explained and understood by analysing them out into their smallest components. This tradition had arrived in France via the philosophy of Condillac (who developed his own interpretation of Locke's views) and lasted well into the nineteenth century.[51]

Once the concept of mental symptom became available, 'mental disease' (condition, disorder, illness) was redefined as a cluster of mental symptoms. *Ab initio*, the view was held that the same mental symptoms could participate in the formation of more than one disease. What differentiated diseases from one another was the 'glue' that kept them together (i.e. different predispositions or aetiologies). This model of mental disease has not changed much since its construction. The only issue that concerns researchers is the nature of the said glue (is it neurobiological, genetic, statistical, social, symbolic, cultural?). The issue of whether mental symptoms were just exaggerations of 'normal' mental functions or indeed new phenomena was also discussed during the nineteenth century. Psychologists like Ribot, Janet and Dumas argued for the former whilst alienists tended to argue for the latter.

Another interesting debate concerned the issue of whether the form and the content of the symptom were more significant within given symptom-clusters. By the second half of the nineteenth century, the old notion of 'pathognomonic symptom'[52] had been resuscitated to resolve some of these disputes, i.e. it was felt that in some cases a particular form or content of a symptom was specific to a particular disease.

The construction of descriptive psychopathology

Descriptive psychopathology names an artificial language constructed at the beginning of the nineteenth century to: 1) describe mental symptoms and 2) comply with the medical, epistemological and legal requirements of case-note keeping at the time. Legislation concerning a medical presence in mental asylums started to be passed in most European countries towards the beginning of the nineteenth century.[53] These regulations were triggered by reports of excessive asylum deaths due to epidemics, parasitic infections, and overcrowding. Therefore, the primary duty of the asylum doctor was to look after the physical health of the inmates. However, once established in these institutions, medics found themselves legally enjoined to keep case notes as they did in general hospitals. It became obvious that a language of description was required and gradually a new lexicon was put together. Asylums made available for longitudinal observation groups of patients with similar complaints and this was crucial to the development of psychopathology. Although there had been small private madhouses for the rich since the eighteenth century, the number of inmates never reached the levels required to create adequate homogenous cohorts.[54]

Following medical fashion, the new language of madness was also called 'semiology'. The term *Psycho-pathologie* (hyphened) was coined in German by Feuchtersleben (1845) to name a different referent, namely, a general theoretical approach to the mind.[55] The English translators of this book, however, transliterated it as 'psychopathology' (without the hyphen).[56] The term did not take on until very late in the century, when it returned to its original vernacular as *Psychopathologie* (e.g. Emminghaus in 1878 and Störring in 1900),[57] and this time to name the language of mental signs and symptoms. Jaspers borrowed it from these writers.[58]

The possibility of longitudinal observation contributed to the introduction into psychopathology of the dimension of time, and the possibility that mental disorders could also be studied along a temporal axis. As a consequence, concepts such as 'acute' and 'chronic' madness[59] gained a new meaning, as did that of 'recovery'. Likewise, the notion that some types of mental disorders were related to certain periods of life was soon taken up by Kahlbaum (1863).[60]

Another epistemological issue that the language of psychopathology had to deal with was that of differentiating normal from abnormal behaviour and experience. The epistemology of medicine was of little help in this regard, for madness presented far fewer 'signs' or biological markers than the rest of medical diseases. Alienists resorted to a different epistemological discourse, the value laden one of the then nascent human or social sciences. Mental abnormality was therefore based on social deviance and the criteria used for the latter (i.e. what at the time was considered proper, ethical, and acceptable). The alienists started using these social criteria to make diagnoses and speculation on what might be wrong with the brain of these 'patients' followed. Thus, psychopathology was constructed from the start on a hybrid platform, and this has not changed to our own day. It seems clear now, as it was during the nineteenth century, that the diagnosis of madness could not be based on brain-related criteria alone.[61]

By the middle of the nineteenth century, psychopathology incorporated within its purview the space of human subjectivity. The epistemology of French alienism, since the time of Main de Biran,[62] had been compatible with a form of intro-spected subjectivity, and hence it was easier for its practitioners to trust the data of introspection during the mental state examination.[63] Since the great books by Emminghaus (1878), Morselli (1885), Störring (1900), Chaslin (1912) and Marie (1911–12), descriptive psychopathology has changed little.[64] Jaspers (1913) completed this process by writing an *Allgemeine Psychopathologie* more in a philosophical than a clinical style. This shortish first edition (never translated into English) owes a great deal to earlier psychopathologies and also to Kant and Dilthey.[65] Later editions included more clinical material added on by Jaspers himself, Kurt Schneider and others.[66]

The professionalization of alienism

In each European country, the professionalization of alienism took place at a different pace and used different resources. By the middle of the nineteenth century, England, Germany, France, Italy, and so on, had started their professional societies, textbooks, journals, training procedures and examinations. In spite of bellic interruptions, international exchanges continued to the point that by the 1890s alienism in the main European countries had become more or less homogeneous. Efforts to share a uniform psychopathological and nosographic lexicon were also made, but not always met with success.

The mental asylums

To discharge their new duties experts in madness (mad-doctors as they have been called) needed a physical, social, and legal space. Starting in the 1810s, waves of asylums were built in the main European countries, and soon enough asylum architecture became a variable in the endless debates on the best way to manage the insane.[67] The social order of the asylums included doctors, keepers (later nurses), supporting staff, and inmates. The latter were housed according to a variety of criteria: public or private; male or female; agitated or quiet, acute or chronic, rational or irrational, continent or incontinent, epileptic or non-epileptic, organic or functional, criminal or non-criminal, and so on. In the second wave of asylums, some of these categories gained architectonic representation.[68]

In addition to legislation and clinical criteria, the form and location of asylums were also influenced by finances and politics. For example, the law stated that all English counties should have an asylum, so to save money some built one asylum on their corresponding geographical boundary, and in this way they claimed to be compliant with the law. Countries with overseas empires had to adapt colonial architecture to local climate. In other cases, like Bentham's panopticon, asylum architecture seemed to follow a top-to-bottom principle. By the end of the nineteenth century, the old forbidding monolithic asylums were being replaced by the Villa system, which continued in fashion well into the twentieth century. By providing ever-growing cohorts of patients that could be observed longitudinally and then examined post-mortem, asylums brought about a minor epistemological revolution, which, interestingly enough, led to a strengthening of organic theories of madness.[69]

The interfaces of alienism

Alienists had to ply their trade in a complex social and political context. In some South European countries, many hospitals (and later mental asylums) were run by religious congregations. Not all alienists were Roman Catholic, and hence frictions took place. For example, issues concerning the need for regular prayer, for dressing very modestly, and some of the disciplines imposed by nuns on inmates clashed with the libertarian views held by the house alienists.

Similar frictions can be found in the interface between psychiatry and the law. For centuries, the latter had been clear in regards to tests for legal categories such as insanity and dementia.[70] Alienists tended to have a less black-and-white view of insanity, and hence the interface between alienism and the law courts was not always easy and, on occasions, major disagreement led to the intervention of a higher authority to settle disputes.[71]

The metamorphoses of madness

Madness as a 'neurosis'

The nineteenth century inherited the Cullean view that the *Vesaniæ* (insanities) were forms of Neuroses, that is, disorders of the sense and movement of the nervous system without fever or focal lesion; in other words, they were just bodily diseases. This view influenced the way in which the French School of Medicine was to conceptualize insanity[72] and also caused the breaking up of the class of neuroses when conditions such as Parkinson's disease, multiple sclerosis, and so on, originally classified as neuroses, were found to be related to focal lesions of the brain.[73] This led to the gradual formation of a new medical specialism, namely, neurology. This process continued, and by the end of century, Cullen's old class of 'neuroses' had become almost emptied of content. Left behind, as conditions without focal lesions, were the insanities, hypochondriasis, hysteria, anxiety disorders, obsessional-compulsive disease, neurotic depressions, and Raynaud's phenomenon. The insanities were then reconceptualized as 'psychoses',[74] and the remaining conditions were still called 'neuroses', but explained differently. Earlier on they were conceived of as resulting from 'nervous irritation'[75]; and by the end of the century as being the symbolic expression of a psychological conflict.[76]

Organic versus functional psychoses

The notion of psychosis as referring to a clinical group of psychiatric disorders was only constructed during the nineteenth century by the convergence of: a) the word 'psychosis' (already used to name the subjective component of an experience); b) the old concept of madness; and c) behaviours/mental states such as hallucinations, delusions, mental confusion, irrationality, thought disorder, and so on.[77] Once in currency,[78] the 'psychoses' underwent a process of contrasting (with the neuroses and the personality disorders) and of typing: functional vs organic, endogenous vs endogenous, acute vs chronic, and so on.

One of the earliest references to 'functional' psychoses can be found in Mendel,[79] who used it to name a group of disorders constituted by *delirium hallucinatorium*, mania, melancholia, circular psychosis, paranoia and acute dementia. In respect of not having a 'known anatomical lesion', Mendel believed that these conditions 'resembled the functional peripheral neuroses'. He also listed the 'organic psychoses': progressive paralysis of the insane, senile dementia, and arteriosclerotic and syphilitic psychoses; and 'psychoses which are called forth by focal diseases of the brain' (e.g. apoplectic attacks, brain tumours, traumata, etc.) and 'psychoses arising from central neuroses' (e.g. epileptic, hysteric and choreic psychoses).

Endogenous and exogenous psychosis

The pair 'endogenous-exogenous' was used by Candolle in 1819 to name two forms of tree-growing.[80] Exogenous growth is from inside out and endogenous growth from outside inwards. Möbius has been credited with introducing the term into psychiatry,[81] but examination of the primary source shows that he listed under *exogenen Nervenkrankheiten* those caused by metal intoxication (e.g. *Saturnismus*), toxic substances, infections, syphilis, alcoholism, brain infections, and so on.[82] Under *endogene Nervenkrankheiten*, Möbius listed neurasthenia, hysteria, epilepsy, migraine, Huntington's chorea, myotonica congenita, dystrophia progressiva, and Friedreich's Ataxia. Nowhere did he mention 'psychosis' nor did he quote Candolle.

Interestingly enough, both the examples provided by Möbius and his reference to *Entartung* (degeneration)[83] suggest that his view was that the 'endogenous nervous diseases' grew from the inside out and hence did not depend upon 'external' factors. Likewise, his examples of 'exogenous nervous diseases' suggest that he believed them to be caused by 'external' factors. Now, this usage happens to be the opposite to Candolle's definition. Whether Möbius misunderstood the French botanist or whether he decided to use his own definitions remains unclear.

The twentieth century

The nineteenth century brought to fruition the epistemological changes started in earlier centuries, namely, mental disorders: a) were to be considered as natural kinds sited in the brain; b) should be conceived as existing within a temporal-spatial frame-work; c) could be classified according to either external features or aetiology;[84] and d) were mediated by the brain even when they might be caused by external factors.[85]

In regards to classifications, the twentieth century adopted the views of Kraepelin,[86] whose views became successful following the untimely death of Karl Wernicke in 1905.[87] Although Wernicke's views continued receiving support, their institutional base was not as strong as Kraepelin's and never achieved clinical centrality.[88]

The narrow view of madness adopted by the nineteenth century became an easy target for the philosophical changes that began to develop in Europe toward the end of the nineteenth century: there was the long shadow cast by Hegel and then the work of Bradley, Lotze, Nietzsche, Dilthey, and the idealist interpretation of Kant's philosophy. All these forces combined brought about a reaction against positivism and empiricism and proposed instead a symbolic and hermeneutic epistemology with which to understand man and his madness. These changes were certainly accelerated by the tragedy of the First World War.

As a result of the above, the rather comfortable medical epistemology of psychiatry was successfully challenged by two Jacksonian developments:[89] the new French clinical psychology as represented by writers such as Janet, Ribot, and Dumas[90] and Freud and followers. Other challenges came from clinical phenomenology,[91] antipsychiatry, and some of the neighbours of psychiatry (neurology, clinical psychology, palliative medicine, general practice, psychosomatic medicine, and so on).

Hermeneutic challenge

Freudian ideas posed an important challenge to conventional psychiatry. Although Freud did not call into question the old linear causal models nor the relevance of the brain in many cases of madness, from an epistemological viewpoint his contribution is to be found in a new view on the meaning of the symptom itself. Until his time, the simple sign-signifier structure of symptoms remained predominant. According to this structure, the experiential content of the symptom was a faithful reflection of the functionality of the neural substratum. For Freud the experiential content in question was allegorical or symbolic and hence needed decoding. He proposed a set of structures that were involved in the codification process and also decoding routines which he considered as therapeutic. Since then, there have been within the psychoanalytical movement various proposals as to what the real structures might be and what the best way to achieve the correct interpretation.

Countries responded differently to psychoanalysis. In some, like the United States, it was to become the predominant approach both in public and private psychiatry. In none of the European countries was it received with the same enthusiasm, although parts of its discourse became incorporated in their psychiatric practice. Psychiatrists the world over became aware of the possibility that madness also lived in a psychological space and that its successful management required interpretation.

Phenomenology

The phenomenologies were a family of philosophies issuing out of the work of Brentano and Husserl. They developed during a time when psychiatry was already under pressure from psychoanalysis and hence presented themselves as a second challenge. In historical terms, they offered new ways of conceiving the ontology and epistemology of sufferers and their sufferings and in due course entered into interesting conceptual coalitions with psychoanalysis.[92]

To this day, however, it remains unclear whether the phenomenologies had a lasting effect on psychiatry. Psychiatry has always needed detailed descriptions of experience as a basis for the construction of a useful clinical psychopathology. Even before Jaspers, who has been credited with making the fusion between phenomenology and psychiatry possible, there was already a rich descriptive tradition on Western psychopathology as illustrated by the work of Emminghaus, Morselli, Störring, Chaslin, Séglas, and so on, whose influence can be detected in Jaspers's 1913 book.[93] Furthermore, such a descriptive psychology tradition can also be found in the work of Dilthey,[94] who was not a phenomenologist[95] and whose ideas have also an important presence in Jaspers's book.

Since then, later writers have suggested that phenomenology opens an intermediate space between neuropsychological narratives describing changes occurring in the brain and the molar level of diagnosis.[96] Based on the existence of putative organising structures (e.g. temporality, self, embodiment), this interesting suggestion, however, requires further clarification.

Antipsychiatry

'Antipsychiatry'[97] names heterogeneous views on the meaning and contents of 'psychiatry' as developed in the West after the 1950s by writers such as Basaglia, Szasz, Lidz, Goffman, Laing, Deleuze, Guattari, Foudraine, Breggin, Antonucci, Cooper, Scheff, Esterson, and by the Scientology movement. Their critique was addressed to: a) the existence and meaning of the discipline in toto; b) its objects (mental symptoms and diseases);[98] or c) its treatments and management routines. Libertarian, spiritualist, existentialist, psychodynamic, religious, and ethical views combined formed the philosophical basis for antipsychiatry.

Antipsychiatry held a mirror to psychiatry and its practices, and psychiatrists suddenly found that their limited conceptual repertoire did not equip them to deal with the accusations that: psychiatry was a pseudoscience; diagnostic labelling meaningless, illegal and offensive; mental hospitals total institutions (like prisons or nunneries) based on moral coercion and violation of individuality; 'mental illness' a myth, an illusory and wrongly conceived concept; the experience of madness was a rare path to self-fulfilment and realization; and biological treatments brutish, misguided and coercive.[99]

All these criticisms were partially right. In its desperation to be a science and a proper medical specialism, Psychiatry had neglected to develop a solid and regional epistemological justification for its existence and its activities. All it could do is bring out tired arguments borrowed from the epistemology of general medicine. Ignorant of its history,[100] psychiatry was unable to realize that taking on the care of madness had been a formidable task which required an original and varied response; and that considering madness as just another brain disease would not work. Neglecting the obvious fact that it is a hybrid discipline[101] has cost psychiatry dearly, for it has deprived it from a language with which to build an adequate defence of its existence.

Boundary disputes

The apparent success of the neuroscientific narrative opened psychiatry to total (e.g., psychiatry is just neurology) or partial takeover bids (dementia is really a neurological disease). In some countries, clinical psychology is offering alternatives to the management of schizophrenia, depression, obsessive-compulsive, and anxiety disorders etc., and making a bid for those conditions; in others, psychosomatic medicine is competing with psychiatry in the field of general hospital consultation-liaison work; yet in other countries, palliative medicine is considering chronic psychoses as a legitimate target; and general practitioners seem to be treating an increasing number of patients with psychiatric disorders. Whether psychiatry will be able to deal with these frontier challenges remains to be seen.

The twenty-first century

The first two decades of the twenty-first century have added next to nothing to the epistemological, nosological, and nosographic routines of psychiatry as these were put gradually together during the last two centuries. The neuroscientific narrative still predominates and the reigning 'classification' is one offered by the American Psychiatric Association via the latest version of their *Diagnostic and Statistical Manual of Mental Disorder.* Efforts are also being made to harmonize the next version of the classification of mental disorders embedded in ICD-11 with *DSM-5.*[102]

During the last decades efforts have also been made to study the conceptual structure of psychiatry.[103] The centripetal approach makes use of off-the-shelf philosophical techniques to analyse the internal problems of psychiatry; the centrifugal approach studies the internal and regional problems of psychiatry by means of historical and epistemological tools specific to its needs.[104] Analytical philosophy has become a popular choice to implement the centripetal approach.[105] True to its conceptual origins, this approach tends to be ahistorical and justificatory of the findings of neuroscience.[106] The centrifugal approach tends to be historical and act as an independent auditor of all the narratives of psychiatry, including the neuroscientific.[107]

Notes

1 The concept of enchantment refers to attitudes of awe, mysteriousness and mysticism in which nature and society were held in earlier times. Disenchantment refers to the gradual erosion of these attitudes brought about by cultural rationalism. Re-enchantment names the current view that the disenchantment of nature has become excessive and that a degree of respect for its mysterious nature ought to be regained. RG Collingwood, *The Philosophy of Enchantment* (Oxford: Oxford University Press, 2005); N Gane, *Max Weber and Post-Modern Theory: Rationalization versus Re-enchantment* (London, Palgrave and Macmillan, 2002); G Graham, *The Re-enchantment of the World* (Oxford: Oxford University Press, 2007); G Levine, *Darwin Loves You: Natural Selection and the Re-Enchantment of the World* (Princeton: Princeton University Press, 2006).
2 GE Berrios, 'Psychiatry and its Objects,' *Revista de Psiquiatria y Salud Mental* 4: (2011): 179–182.
3 The fact that throughout the centuries the meaning of madness seems to have remained stable suggests that the shaping invariants in question (biological, cultural, linguistic, and functional) have not changed a great deal. However, its semantic stability cannot be used

as evidence of its being a natural kind. Social and cultural invariants are equally sufficient to keep a concept stable and going throughout time.

4 A convergence is a historical mechanism whereby new concepts are constructed. They bring together a word (madness), a concept (a vector constituted by operating invariants, accounts, explanations, etc.), and behaviours, attitudes, experiences, and so on. The duration of a convergence is likely to be determined by its social, political, aesthetic, economic, etc., usefulness. GE Berrios, 'Convergences That Are no More,' *History of Psychiatry* 22 (2011): 133–136.

5 GE Berrios, 'Convergences That Are no More,' *History of Psychiatry* 22 (2011): 133–136; GE Berrios and IS Marková, 'Symptoms-Historical Perspective and Effect on Diagnosis' in *Psychosomatic Medicine*, ed. M Blumenfield and JJ Strain, (New York: Lippincott William Wilkins, 2006), 27–38.

6 GE Berrios, 'The Role of Cultural Configurators in the Formation of Mental Symptoms' in *Philosophical Issues in Psychiatry III*, ed. KS Kendler and J Parnas (Oxford: Oxford University Press, 2015), 107–115.

7 I Niiniluoto, M Sintonen, and J Wolenski, eds, *Handbook of Epistemology* (Dordrecht: Springer, 2004).

8 GE Berrios and IS Marková (2015) 'Towards a New Epistemology of Psychiatry' in *Re-Visioning Psychiatry*, ed. LJ Kirmayer, R Lemelson, and CA Cummings (Cambridge: Cambridge University Press, 2015), 41–64.

9 IA Reed, 'Epistemology Contextualized: Social-scientific Knowledge in a Post-positivist Era,' *Sociological Theory* 28 (2010): 20–39.

10 In other words, like all objects, concepts have biographies and hence their content changes according to the social needs they must periodically satisfy. H Lehmann and M Richter, eds, 'The Meaning of Historical Terms and Concepts,' *New Studies in Begriffsgeschichte* (Washington: German Historical Studies, 1996), occasional paper 15; J Kmita, *Problems in Historical Epistemology* (Dordrecht: D Reidel, 1988); J Renn, 'Historical Epistemology and the Advancement of Science,' Max-Plank-Institut für Wissenschaftsgeschichte, 1996, Pre-Print 26; T Sturm and U Feest, 'What (Good) Is Historical Epistemology,' *Erkenntnis* 75 (2011): 285–543.

11 Raoul de la Grasserie, *De la Classification objective et subjective des arts, de la littérature et des sciences* (Paris: Alcan, 1893); JS Wilkins and MC Ebach, *The Nature of Classification. Relationships and Kinds in the Natural Sciences* (London: Palgrave Macmillan, 2014).

12 A Lovejoy, *The Great Chain of Being. A Study of the History of an Idea* (Cambridge: Harvard University Press, 1936).

13 Wilkins and Ebach, *Nature of Classification*.

14 ER Scerri, *The Periodic Table. Its Story and Significance* (Oxford: Oxford University Press, 2007).

15 JL Larson, *Reason and Experience. The Representation of Natural Order in the Work of Carl von Linné* (Berkeley: University of California Press, 1971).

16 GE Berrios, 'Classification in Psychiatry: A Conceptual History,' *Australian and New Zealand Journal of Psychiatry*, 33 (1999): 145–160 and 'Baillarger's "Essay on a Classification of different genera of insanity,"' *History of Psychiatry*, 19 (2008): 358–373; RK Blashfield, *The Classification of Psychopathology* (New York: Plenum Press, 1984); W De Boor, *Psychiatrische Systematik. Ihre Entwicklung in Deutschland seit Kahlbaum* (Berlin: Springer, 1954).

17 P Laffey, 'Two Registers of Madness in Enlightenment Britain. Part 1,' *History of Psychiatry* 13 (2002): 367–380; 14 (2002): 63–81 and 'Two Registers of Madness in Enlightenment Britain. Part 2,' *History of Psychiatry* 14 (2003): 63–81; R Porter, *Mind-Forg'd Manacles: A History of Madness in England From the Restoration to the Regency* (London: Penguin, 1990).

18 RE Siegel, *Galen on Psychology, Psychopathology, and Functions and Diseases of the Nervous System* (Basel: Karger, 1973).

19 MW Dols, 'Galen and Mental Illness' in *Majnūn: The Madman in Medieval Islamic Society*, MW Dols and DE Immisch (Oxford: Clarendon Press, 1992).

20 Galen did not conceive of the body as a tridimensional entity susceptible to be conceptualized by anatomy and physiology. He saw it as a *koinotetes*, that is, as a whole, characterized by

common features whose three main states are fluidity, dryness and something in between. Now in this system the brain was regent or *hêgemonikon* and there is no evidence that madness was considered as related to it. J Rocca, *Galen on the Brain* (Leiden: Brill, 2003).

21 LC Charland, 'John Locke on Madness,' *History of Psychiatry* 25 (2014): 137–153; M MacDonald, *Mystical Bedlam* (Cambridge: Cambridge University Press, 1981); T Willis, *The Practice of Physick* (London: Dring, Harper and Leigh, 1684).

22 K Hodgkin, *Madness in Seventeenth-Century Autobiography* (London: Palgrave, MacMillan, 2007).

23 A Ingram and M Faubert, *Cultural Constructions of Madness in Eighteenth-Century Writings. Representing the Insane* (London: Palgrave Macmillan, 2005).

24 These changes included the new Baconian view of science – S Gaukroger, *Francis Bacon and the Transformation of Early-Modern Philosophy* (Cambridge: Cambridge University Press, 2004) – Newtonianism – JE Force and S Hutton S, ed., *Newton and Newtonianism* (New York: Kluwer, 2004) – Cartesian dualism through which the body (and hence brain) were released from theological and metaphysical control – WF Bynum, 'Varieties of Cartesian Experience in Early Nineteenth Century Neurophysiology' in *Philosophical Dimensions of Neuro-Medical Sciences*, ed. SF Spicker S F and HT Engelhardt, (Holland: Dordrecht, 1976), 15–33 – and Locke's empiricism. During the eighteenth century all these led to a veritable 'ferment of knowledge'. GS Rousseau and R Porter, ed., *The Ferment of Knowledge. Studies in the Historiography of Eighteenth Century Science* (Cambridge, Cambridge University Press, 1980).

25 R Porter, ed., *Eighteenth-Century Science, Vol 4. The Cambridge History of Science* (Cambridge: Cambridge University Press, 2003). The process of secularization led on the one hand to the development of 'natural theology' – J Gascoigne, 'Rise and Fall of British Newtonian Natural Theology,' *Science in Context*, 2 (1988): 219–256 – and on the other to the growth of the human or social sciences TM Porter and D Ross, *The Modern Social Sciences Vol 7. The Cambridge History of Science* (Cambridge: Cambridge University Press, 2003) – that attempted to answer the question 'what is man?'.

26 GE Berrios 'The Nineteenth-Century Nosology of Alienism: History and Epistemology' in *Philosophical Issues in Psychiatry II*, ed. Kendler and Parnas, 101–123 and 'Defining and Classifying Mental Illness' in *Psychiatry: Past, Present and Prospect*, ed. S Bloch, SA Green, and J Holmes, (Oxford, Oxford University Press, 2014), 180–195.

27 Sydenham stated: 'In the first place, it is necessary that all diseases be reduced to definite and certain species, and that, with the same care which we see exhibited by botanists in their phytologies.' T Sydenham, *The Works of Thomas Sydenham MD*, Translated from the Latin Edition of Dr Greenhill by RG Latham. Vol. 1 (London: Printed for the Sydenham Society, 1848), 13.

28 The conventional view of natural kinds conceives of them as ontological entities characterized by: '(1) properties that are necessary and sufficient for membership in the kind, (2) micro-structural properties, (3) intrinsic properties, (4) modally necessary properties, and (5) properties that are discoverable by science' (515) MA Khalidi, 'Kinds: Natural versus Human' in *Encyclopaedia of Philosophy and the Social Sciences*, ed. B Kaldis, (Los Angeles: Sage, 2013), 515. The view that mental disorders are natural kinds is widely supported (Murphy, 2006; Cooper, 2005). R Cooper, *Classifying Madness* (Berlin: Springer, 2005); D Murphy, *Psychiatry in the Scientific Image* (Cambridge, MA: MIT Press, 2006).

29 JM López Piñero and Meseguer JM Morales (1970) *Neurosis y Psicoterapia. Un estudio histórico* (Madrid: Espasa-Calpe, 1970)

30 For example, in his great compilation of eighteenth-century medical knowledge, James (1745) wrote: 'Hence it follows, that those very symptoms first mentioned, are really diseases in their turn, and very different in number, variety and effects. We may, however, in compliance with the sentiments of the ancients, conveniently enough reduce them, as they do, under three heads, and make them to be *either injuries of the natural functions. Defaults in retention and excretion, or alterations in the qualities of the body*' (italics in original). R James, *A Medicinal Dictionary*, Vol 3 (London: T Osborne, 1745), 697. This eighteenth-century lack of differentiation between symptom and disease is also reflected in the manner in which 'psychiatric' disorders were treated and classified.

31 In this regard, Boissier de Sauvages wrote: 'The Systematic method groups together the diseases that resemble each other, and separates them from those that do not have a resemblance; it reduces all the individual diseases to their species, these species to their genera, the genera to orders, and these to a small number of classes.' SE Starkstein and GE Berrios, 'The Preliminary Discourse to *Methodical Nosology* by François Boissier de Sauvages (1772),' *History of Psychiatry* 26 (2015): 489.

32 Larson, *Reason.*

33 M Adanson, *Familles des Plantes*, Parts I & II (Paris: Chez Vicent, 1763).

34 PHA Sneath and RR Sokal, *Numerical Taxonomy. The Principles and Practice of Numerical Classification* (San Francisco: W H Freeman, 1973); AR Webb, *Statistical Pattern Recognition* (London: John Wiley, 2002).

35 He defined them as '*sensus et motus læsi, sine pyrexia idiopathica, et sine morbi locali*' ('Sense and motion injured, without idiopathic pyrexia, and without local disease'.) W Cullen, *Synopsis Nosologiæ Methodicæ*, Vol. 1, 4th edn (Edinburgh: W Creech, 1785), 182. Cullen tried to see a continuity between his neurosis and the concept of nervous disease in Thomas Willis but this link is probably no more than a historical affectation. Cullen adhered to a version of the 'neuralpathology' theory according to which the aetiology for many diseases could be traced back to (a *sui generis* conception of) the nervous system: 'Cullen's system can be considered as a version of vitalism, a doctrine developed during the Enlightenment as an offshoot of the Hallerian concept of 'irritability'. He was the best representative of the school of so-called "neuropathology" (or neuralpathology) whose main postulate was the identification of the vital principle with the activity of the nervous system.' JM López Piñero, *Historical Origins of the Concept of Neurosis* (Cambridge: Cambridge University Press, 1983), 12.

36 Boissier de Sauvages attacked this classificatory tendency: 'Therefore, we have to consider as false the definitions of diseases which are based on the *disposition* of components that often elude the senses, and which are often hypothetical, or at least obscure: a *seat* is often presumed, set free into components which cannot be perceived, either because they are internal, or because they are too small to be perceived . . .' Starkstein and Berrios, 'Preliminary Discourse,' 490.

37 C Linné, *Genera Morborum* (Upsala: CE Steinert, 1763), 12–13.

38 F Boissier de Sauvages, *Nosologie Méthodique*, Vol. 7 (Lyon: J M Bruyset, 1772), 1–44.

39 GE Berrios, 'David Hartley's views on Madness,' *History of Psychiatry* 26 (2015): 105–116.

40 GE Berrios, 'The Role of Cultural Configurators.'

41 J Haslam, *Observations on Madness and Melancholy* (London: J Callow, 1809), 46.

42 R de Villargues, *Jurisprudence du Notariat* (Paris: Bureau de la Jurisprudence du Notariat, Decourchant, 1829), 48.

43 Cullen, *Synopsis Nosologiæ Methodicæ.*

44 Berrios, 'The Nineteenth-Century Nosology of Alienism.'

45 J Roubinovitch, *Des Variétés Cliniques de la Folie en France et en Allemagne* (Paris: Doin, 1896).

46 GE Berrios, 'Geschichte psychiatrischer Begriffe' in *Allgemeine Psychiatrie*, ed. H Helchen, F Henn, H Lauter and N Sartorius, (Heidelberg: Springer, 1999), 3–59.

47 This does not mean to say that mental symptoms did not exist; what it means is that complaints expressing mental distress started to be conceptualized as the (ontologically autonomous) units of analysis of madness. In other words, it was believed after that period that mental symptoms could perfectly exist either on their own or in clusters (in which case they constituted diseases). Diseases were characterized by the particular combination of symptoms that constituted them, not by anything special hovering over and above them. It was only later in the nineteenth century that the additional concept of 'pathognomonic' symptoms was introduced (i.e. symptoms which either on account of their form or content could only characterize one disease).

48 W Griesinger, *Pathologie und Therapie der psychischen Krankheiten*, 3rd edn (Braunschweig: F Wreden, 1871).

49 FJ Double, *Sémeïologie générale ou traité des signes et de leur valeur dans les maladies*, 2 Vol. (Paris: Croullebois, 1811).

50 AJ Landré-Beauvais, *Séméiotique ou traité des signes des maladies*, 3rd edn (Paris: Brosson, 1818).

51 For example, at the beginning of the nineteenth-century Pinel (1809) was still complaining about the limitations of the Condillacean method: 'I have seen at *Bicêtre* a manic patient whose symptoms would remain an enigma if Locke's and Condillac's views on insanity were to be followed.' P Pinel, *Traité médico-philosophique sur l'aliénation mentale*, Second edn (Paris: Brosson, 1809), 102. Indeed, by this time Pinel was coming increasingly under the influence of the Scottish philosophy of common sense. GE Berrios, *The History of Mental Symptoms. Psychopathology Since the Nineteenth Century* (Cambridge: Cambridge University Press, 1996).

52 An old word, 'Pathognomonic' has since its inception been used to refer to: 'a sign or symptom by which a disease may be known or distinguished; specifically characteristic or indicative of a particular disease.' *Oxford English Dictionary*, 2nd edn (Oxford: Oxford University Press, 1992). The French Encyclopaedia defines it as '*c'est un signe essentiel & caractéristique, ou un symptome particulier à quelque maladie, & qui en est inséparable, & même qui en est le siege. Mais la vérité est qu'il n'y a rien dans toute la médecine qui réponde à l'idée d'un pathognomonique ; la maladie & les symptomes sont trop compliqués ; nous ne pouvons juger de la premiere par quelque signe particulier, mais seulement par le concours de plusieurs*' Diderot and D'Alambert, ed., *Encyclopédie ou Dictionnaire Raisonné des Sciences, des Arts, et de Métières*, Vol. 12 (Paris : Briasson, David, Le Breton, Duran, 1754), 170. This sceptical view reflects the influence of Condillac's analytical method on the authors of the French Encyclopaedia.

53 K Jones, *Lunacy, Law, and Conscience* (London: Routledge and Keegan Paul, 1955).

54 W Parry-Jones, *The Trade in Lunacy: A Study of Private Madhouses in England in the Eighteenth and Nineteenth Centuries* (London: Routledge & Kegan Paul, 1972).

55 E von Feuchtersleben, *Lehrbuch der ärztlichen Seelenkunde* (Vienna: Carl Gerold, 1845).

56 E von Feuchtersleben, *The Principles of Medical Psychology*, translated by HE Evans and BG Babington (London: Printed for the Sydenham Society, 1847).

57 H Emminghaus, *Allgemeine Psychopathologie* (Leipzig: FCW Vogel, 1878); G Störring, *Vorlesungen über Psychopathologie* (Leipzig: W Engelmann, 1900).

58 K Jaspers, *Allgemeine Psychopathologie* (Heidelberg: Springer, 1913).

59 G Lanteri Laura, 'La Chronicité dans la Psychiatrie Moderne Française,' *Annales* 3 (1972): 548–568.

60 K Kahlbaum, *Die Gruppirung der psychischen Krankheiten und die Eintheilung der Seelenstörungen* (Danzig: AW Kafemann, 1863), translation by GE Berrios in *History of Psychiatry* 7 (1996): 167–181.

61 On the issue of the essential conceptual hybridity of psychiatry, see GE Berrios, 'Defining and Classifying Mental Illness,' in *Psychiatry: Past, Present and Prospect*, ed. S Bloch, SA Green, and J Holmes, (Oxford: Oxford University Press, 2014), 180–195; GE Berrios and IS Marková, 'Towards a New Epistemology of Psychiatry' in *Re-Visioning Psychiatry*, ed. LJ Kirmayer, R Lemelson, and CA Cummings (Cambridge: Cambridge University Press, 2015), 41–64.

62 P Engel, 'Psychology and Metaphysics from Maine de Biran to Bergson' *in Psychology and Philosophy. Inquiries into the Soul from Late Scholasticism to Contemporary Thought*, ed. S Heinämaa and M Reuter, (Berlin: Springer, 2009), 235–246.

63 Danziger has suggested that in other countries the reception of introspection was determined by whether they accepted that mind and consciousness were coterminous. They did in England but not fully in Germany. Further research is needed to confirm whether Danziger's account is sufficient to explain the differential way in which subjective data were used in the psychopathology of France, England and Germany, respectively. K Danziger, 'The History of Introspection Reconsidered,' *Journal of the History of the Behavioural Sciences*, 16 (1980): 241–262.

64 P Chaslin, *Eléments de Sémiologie et de Clinique Mentale* (Paris: Asselin et Houzeau, 1912); Emminghaus, Allgemeine Psychopathologie; A Marie, ed. *Traité International de Psychologie Pathologique*. 4 vols (Paris: Alcan, 1911–1912); E Morselli, *Manuale di Semeiotica delle Malattie Mentali*, 2 vols. (Milan: F Vallardi, 1885); Störring, *Vorlesungen über Psychopathologie*.

65 GE Berrios, 'Jaspers and the first Edition of Allgemeine Psychopathologie,' *British Journal of Psychiatry* 202 (2013): 433.

66 GE Berrios, 'Phenomenology, psychopathology and Jaspers: a conceptual history,' History *of Psychiatry* 3 (1992): 303–327.

67 LD Smith, *Cure, Comfort, and Safe Custody. Public Lunatic Asylums in Early Nineteenth-Century England* (Leicester: Leicester University Press, 1999).

68 S Piddock, *A Space of Their Own. The Archaeology of Nineteenth-Century Lunatic Asylums in Britain, South Australia, and Tasmania* (Heidelberg: Springer, 2007).

69 GE Berrios and H Freeman, *150 years of British Psychiatry 1841–1991* (London: Gaskell, 1991).

70 N Walker, *Crime and Insanity in England. Vol 1: Historical Perspective* (Edinburgh: Edinburgh University Press, 1968).

71 R Smith, *Trial by Medicine. Insanity and Responsibility in Victorian Trials* (Edinburgh: Edinburgh University Press, 1984).

72 Via parallel translations of the work of Cullen into French by Pinel and by Bousquillon.

73 JM López Piñero, *Historical Origins of the Concept of Neurosis* (Cambridge: Cambridge University Press, 1983).

74 CF Flemming, *Pathologie und Therapie der Psychosen* (Berlin: A Hirschwald, 1859).

75 A Axenfeld, *Traité des Névroses* (Paris: Baillière, 1883); M Leven, *La Névrose. Étude Clinique et Thérapeutique* (Paris: Masson, 1887). The old concept of irritation or irritability was taken up during the nineteenth century to explain certain motor disorders of the nervous system, for example, 'spinal irritation'. L Corning, 'Spinal Irritation,' *Boston Medical and Surgical Journal* 115 (1886): 541–543; E Shorter, *From Paralysis to Fatigue* (New York: Free Press, 1993).

76 López Piñero and Morales Meseguer, *Neurosis y Psicoterapia*.

77 GE Berrios, 'Historical Aspects of the Psychoses: Nineteenth-Century Issues,' *British Medical Bulletin* 43 (1987): 484–498.

78 Flemming, *Pathologie und Therapie*.

79 'On the other hand, there is a great difference of opinion amongst authors as to how to divide those mental diseases in which no anatomical changes have hitherto been met and which do not belong under any of the forms named. These are designated as functional psychoses, by which it is not said that anatomical changes do not exist, but only that we have so far been unable to verify them.' E Mendel, *Leitfaden der Psychiatrie* (Stuttgart: Ferdinand Enke, 1902), 121.

80 '. . . and are disposed in a way in which the older [layers] are at the centre and the younger ones at the circumference; from which it results that the plant hardens from inside out; I call these [vegetables] *Exogenes* (*exo* = outside; *genos* = to engender) . . . others organise themselves in a way in which the old, i.e. the harder [layers] are outside and growth occurs towards the centre; I call these the *Endogenes* (*endos* = inside; *genos* = to engender). (our translation). AP de Candolle, *Théorie élémentaire de la Botanique* (Paris: Deterville, 1819), 240.

81 MD Beer, 'The endogenous psychoses: a conceptual history,' *History of Psychiatry* 7 (1996): 1–29.; R Degkwitz, 'Entwicklung und Verfälschung des Begriffes 'endogen' in der Psychiatrie' in *Psychiatrie auf dem Wege zur Wissenschaft*, ed. G Nissen and G Keil, (Stuttgart, Thieme, 1985), 6–11; A Lewis, 'Endogenous and Exogenous: A Useful Dichotomy?' *Psychological Medicine* 1 (1971): 191–196.

82 PJ Möbius, *Abriss der Lehre von den Nervenkrankheiten* (Leipzig: Ambrosius Abel, 1893), 71ff.

83 Möbius, *Abriss*, 140. Much has been written on all aspects of the nineteenth-century theory of degeneration. G Genil-Perrin, *Histoire des origines et de l'évolution de l'idée de dégénérescence en médicine mentale* (Paris: A Leclerc, 1913); A Zaloszyc, *Elemens d'une histoire de la theorie des dégénérescences dans la psychiatrie française* (PhD Diss, Faculté de Médecine de Strasbourg, 1975). Started by Morel as a clinical allegory of the original sin, it was used during the second half of the century as a stopgap for concepts such as predisposition, inheritance, atavism, tainted ancestors, genetics, etc. L Hermie, 'Die Degenerationslehre in der Psychiatrie,' *Fortschritte Neurologie Psychiatrie* 54 (1986): 69–79; A Liégeois, 'Hidden

Philosophy and Theology in Morel's Theory of Degeneration and Nosology,' *History of Psychiatry* 2 (1991): 419–428; B Morel, *Traité des Dégénérescences Physiques Intellectuelles et Morales de l'Espèce Humaine* (Paris: Baillière, 1857).

84 GE Berrios, 'Baillarger's "Essay on a Classification of Different Genera of Insanity,"' *History of Psychiatry* 19 (2008): 358–373.

85 GE Berrios, 'Historical Development of Ideas about Psychiatric Aetiology' *in New Oxford textbook of Psychiatry*, ed. MG Gelder, JJ López-Ibor, and N Andreasen, (Oxford: Oxford University Press, 2000), 147–153.

86 GE Berrios and R Hauser, 'The Early Development of Kraepelin's Ideas on Classification: A Conceptual History,' *Psychological Medicine* 18 (1988): 813–821.

87 GE Berrios, 'Historiography of Mental Symptoms and Diseases,' *History of Psychiatry* 5 (1994): 175–190; M Lanczik, *Der Breslauer Psychiater Carl Wernicke* (Sigmaringen: Thorbecke, 1988).

88 K Leonhard, *Aufteilung der endogenen Psychosen* (Stuttgart: Thieme, 1995).

89 GE Berrios, 'Jackson's' "The Factors of Insanities,"' *History of Psychiatry* 12 (2001): 353–373.

90 GE Berrios, 'Historical Background to Abnormal Psychology' in *Adult Abnormal Psychology*, ed. E Miller and PJ Cooper, (Edinburgh: Churchill and Livingstone, 1988), 26–51.

91 S Halling and JD Nill, 'A Brief History of Existential-Phenomenological Psychiatry and Psychotherapy,' *Journal of Phenomenological Psychology* 26 (1995): 1–45.

92 S Halling and JD Nill, 'A Brief History of Existential-Phenomenological Psychiatry and Psychotherapy,' *Journal of Phenomenological Psychology* 26 (1995): 1–45.

93 Berrios, 'Phenomenology, Psychopathology and Jaspers.'

94 AH Caparrós, *Ebbinghaus. Un funcionalista investigador tipo dominio* (Barcelona: Publicacions Universitat de Barcelona, 1986); W Dilthey, *Descriptive Psychology and Historical Understanding* (The Hague: Nijhoff, 1977).

95 RA Makkreel and J Scanlon, *Dilthey and Phenomenology* (Washington: University Press of America, 1987).

96 T Fuchs, 'Phenomenology and Psychopathology' in *Handbook of Phenomenology and Cognitive Science*, ed. S Gallagher and D Schmicking (Berlin: Springer, 2010), 547–573.

97 The English term is a translation of *anti-psychiatrie*, coined in 1909 by Bernhard Bayer, a psychiatrist and freemason, from Bayreuth. T Szasz, *Antipsychiatry. Quackery Squared* (New York: Syracuse University Press, 2009), 4.

98 GE Berrios, 'Psychiatry and its Objects,' *Revista de Psiquiatria y Salud Mental* 4 (2011): 179–182.

99 GE Berrios, 'The History of Psychiatric Therapies' in *Cambridge Textbook of Effective Treatments in Psychiatry*, ed. P Tyrer and R Silk, (Cambridge: Cambridge University Press, 2008), 16–43.

100 Conventional histories of psychiatry do not cease to tell psychiatrists that their discipline is the result of a heroic march from darkness to light; and that the medicalization of madness must be considered as the achievement of a hidden truth.

101 GE Berrios and IS Marková, 'Towards a New Epistemology of Psychiatry' in *Re-Visioning Psychiatry*, ed. LJ Kirmayer, R Lemelson, and CA Cummings (Cambridge: Cambridge University Press, 2015), 41–64.

102 MB First, 'Harmonisation of ICD-11 and DSM-5,' *British Journal of Psychiatry* 195 (2009): 382–390; A Jablensky, 'Towards ICD 11 and DSM 5: Issues Beyond Harmonisation,' *British Journal of Psychiatry* 195 (2009): 379–381.

103 This type of work is of course not new only that now it is being called the 'philosophy of psychiatry'. GE Berrios, '"Body and Mind" by CK Clifford,' *History of Psychiatry* 11 (2000): 311–338; '"Mind in General" by Sir Alexander Crichton,' History of Psychiatry 17 (2006): 469–497; '"De la Folie" by P Despine (1875),' *History of Psychiatry* 20 (2009): 393–400.

104 GE Berrios '"Mind in General" by Sir Alexander Crichton,' *History of Psychiatry* 17 (2006): 469–497.

105 KWM Fulford, T Thornton, and G Graham, *Oxford Textbook of Philosophy and Psychiatry* (Oxford: Oxford University Press, 2006).

106 M Beane, *The Oxford Handbook of the History of Analytic Philosophy* (Oxford: Oxford University Press, 2013); M Bennett, D Dennett, P Hacker, and J Searle, *Neuroscience and Philosophy* (New York: Columbia University Press, 2003); R Rorty, JB Schneewind, and Q Skinner, eds., *Philosophy in History* (Cambridge: Cambridge University Press, 1984).

107 See, for example, CJ Blanc, *Psychiatrie et Penseé Philosophique* (Paris: L'Harmattan, 1988); GE Berrios and IS Marková, 'Biological Psychiatry: Conceptual Issues' *in Biological Psychiatry*, ed. H D'Haenen, JA den Boer and P Willner (New York: John Willey, 2002), 3–24; EM Hundert, *Philosophy, Psychiatry and Neuroscience* (Oxford; Clarendon Press, 1989); M Natanson, ed., *Psychiatry and Philosophy* (Berlin: Springer, 1969); RM Palem, *Henri Ey: Psychiatrie et Philosophie* (Paris: Rive Droite, 1997).

Part III

BEYOND MEDICINE

7

PSYCHIATRY AND RELIGION

Rhodri Hayward

In 1904, on a ship sailing from Ceylon to Egypt, the occultist and magician, Aleister Crowley first met the English alienist, Henry Maudsley. It was an unlikely meeting. Crowley, having abandoned his undergraduate studies at Cambridge and his occult training with the Hermetic Order of the Golden Dawn, was just beginning a quest to develop his own magical system. Maudsley, nearing the end of his life, had for a brief time been the leading figure within British psychological medicine before estranging many of his gentler and more optimistic colleagues through his bitter assessment of their discipline, his bleak materialism, his disdain of religion and his scorn of contemporary social mores.[1] Maudsley seemed to epitomise the secularising imperative we now commonly associate with nineteenth-century psychiatry. Yet as Crowley later recorded upon meeting, they discovered that their views 'fitted in exactly. He was', the magician reminisced, 'the very man I wanted'. Together they discussed Tantra and yogic meditation, looking to the possibility that new meditative practices might allow practitioners to "remove the inhibitions which repress the manifestations of genius or . . . enable one to tap the energy of the universe."[2] Two months later, Crowley claimed to have succeeded in his quest. Working with his wife, Rose, in their honeymoon flat in Cairo, he was able to invoke Aiwass, a spiritual emissary of the ancient Egyptian god, Horus. This demonic entity dictated a series of scripts to Crowley that would become the cornerstone of his system of Thelemic Magick and herald the beginning of a new magical age.

Maudsley and Crowley's encounter is unsettling, not simply because it led (apparently) to the successful invocation of demons and the inauguration of a new magical aeon, but because it disrupts our long-established preconceptions of the relationship between psychiatry and the supernatural. Traditionally, the rise of psychiatry is seen as overturning the claims of magic and religion. Visions, voices, ecstasies, conversions and possessions that had once demonstrated the fragility of our systems of knowledge and our sense of self were transformed, it was claimed, through the birth of psychiatry into unwitting demonstrations of human ignorance. Psychiatry naturalised miraculous phenomena, revealing the need for new forms of scientific expertise to sort the pathological chaff from the wheat of spiritual experience.

Of course naturalistic interpretations of religious claims predate the birth of psychiatry. In the Christian West they formed a central part of the Protestant and Catholic critiques that emerged during the Reformation and Counter-Reformation.[3] And before this time, across the world's religions the discrimination of inspired, magical or spiritual experiences from bodily appetites, pathological episodes or knowing dissimulation was a standard problem for religious authorities, given the social and political disruption that such claims often engendered. Partly because of this and partly because in many cultures the role of priest and physician was combined, the care of those we now term the mentally ill often fell upon religious communities or spiritual healers.[4] Such tasks were made more urgent as illness was often seen in moral terms. In Christianity, madness could be seen as a divine affliction, demonic possession, physical disruption or mystical grace.[5] Similarly within Islam, episodes of madness can be seen as demonstrations of divine presence or intervention by benign or malicious djinns, while Ayurvedic and Buddhist medical systems both uphold models of madness rooted in bodily imbalance while attributing certain cases to either possession (under Hinduism) or spiritual failure (under Buddhism).[6] As we shall see, religion, and Christianity in particular, has created a dual legacy for the modern discipline of psychiatry. Christianity has provided the vocabulary and framework for thinking through the boundaries of selfhood and the meaning of human action and created a programme of work for the new profession as it sought to discriminate the meaning and significance of individual and collective behaviour.

For many early practitioners of psychiatry, this Christian legacy was an embarrassment. A vocal coterie of alienists, physiologists, mesmerists, and physicians in the nineteenth century set out to establish the remit of their expertise, engaging in detailed and often vitriolic criticisms of both organised religion and informal spirituality. It was an exercise in professional imperialism and in disciplinary self-critique, as modernising practitioners sought to purge the nascent science of inherited assumptions. Maudsley himself was a leading exponent of this position. In his *Natural Causes and Supernatural Seemings* (1886), he complained that the miraculous phenomena that provided the foundations of different faiths were simply 'fables of the imagination'.[7] The ascetic practices adopted by the visionary leaders of new religions were, he argued, shortcuts to epilepsy and consumption: diseases which returned the brain to a more barbarous state in which sense and reason lost their hold over experience and the imagination.[8] His position would be embraced by other leading commentators: Charcot in Paris and Freud in Vienna, although they used it to advance very different understandings of psychiatry.

Maudsley's stance was never mainstream, yet the idea of a conflict between religious belief and psychiatric expertise remains with us today. In part this is simply due to the stentorian volume at which these particular claims have been repeated. The rhetoric, which was elaborated by the cheerleaders of psychiatry, is now rehearsed by its most vocal critics. It has become a commonplace to hold up psychiatrists, in Maurice North's phrase, as a caste of 'secular priests'.[9] The 'psy-professions', it is argued, have taken over the role of ministering to the community. It is they who now relieve the mental suffering of individuals, interpret inner experience and define the shape of our contemporary morality.[10] Psychiatrists and psychologists are seen as being at the frontline of an imagined battle between clerical and pastoral authority: a battle in which the retreat of religion is seen as inevitable.[11]

This rhetoric, of course, draws upon a larger sociological narrative that describes the disenchantment of the West. In his essay 'Science as a Vocation', Max Weber claimed that the social disruption wrought by industrialisation and the rise of the capitalism brought with it the imposition of an instrumental rationality in which sacred custom and folk tradition were broken down before the logic of calculation.[12] Yet in recent years, this idea of disenchantment or Entzauberung has been contested by historians and sociologists who have drawn attention to the rise of new religious movements and heterodox worship in the modern West.[13] The twentieth century, according to Michael Saler and his colleagues, has been characterised by moments of 're-enchantment' as conventional notions of time, place and identity are disrupted.[14] The process of secularisation, as Charles Taylor has stated, should not simply be seen in terms of a loss of faith. It involves the creation of new kinds of faith and new religious institutions.[15]

Certainly any process of disenchantment has been uneven, both within and between different communities and between different nations. There are now striking differences in patterns of religious affiliation between the United States, where religious affiliation is high although there is a formal separation between church and state, and European countries such as the United Kingdom where the separation of church and state is incomplete yet religious affiliation appears to be in long-term decline. These patterns are further complicated by the organisation of healthcare, where the rise of state welfare schemes including the delivery of mental health services has often moved in tandem with the decline of formal worship, even though religious organisations may remain part of the landscape of care.

The narratives of conflict between psychiatry and religion, whether empire building or critical, serve many different purposes. On the one hand, they promote a particular vision of psychiatry, its field of work and its social relations. At the same time, they advance a very particular reconstruction of the past. These reconstructions, as we shall see in the paragraphs that follow, serve very different agendas, but they share two common effects. First, they work to universalise the claims of psychiatry, showing that classifications, techniques, and theories developed in western asylums, laboratories, and mental hospitals in the nineteenth and twentieth centuries are applicable to phenomena experienced across global space and historical time.[16] Second, they work to mask the mutual entanglement of psychiatry with Christianity and other world religions. They obscure the intellectual and practical debt that psychiatry owes to Christianity and other world religions for many of its guiding assumptions and working approaches.

On first encounter, Maudsley's meeting with Crowley seems to share many of the characteristics we now associate with the disenchantment narrative. Both men had abandoned the communities of their childhood and through that separation developed a sceptical or anthropological perspective on the religions of their youth. Moreover, both men appeared to have adopted an instrumental approach to the world's faiths, treating the doctrines of Hindu Tantra and Theravada Buddhism as repositories of psychological techniques open to colonial exploitation. Yet we can also see, from Crowley's subsequent adventures, how this encounter engendered a process of re-enchantment: making possible new forms of faith and introducing new magical objects into the world. It was a process of re-enchantment that would unsettle everyday assumptions and perhaps only encourage both men in their contempt for conventional values enshrined in contemporary science and religion. In this, at least, they may have been correct. The encounter between psychiatry and religion has never been a simple process of conflict or dialogue in which faith was usurped by medicine.[17] Rather it should be seen as a productive, experimental entanglement through which religion and psychiatry were able to constitute new objects in the world, develop new techniques and perspectives, and both create and critique new values.[18] It has been a mutually constitutive process: a process so entangled that it is surprising that we ever believed the two discourses could ever be picked apart.[19]

Psychiatry and the policing of spiritual experience

The eighteenth-century separation of psychiatric expertise from mainstream medical practice was driven largely by jurisprudential concerns. A small number of physicians found themselves increasingly called on to give evidence on the limits of personal capacity and forensic responsibility. Such evidence, while framed through the concepts of medicine, was underwritten by a Christian understanding of human nature and driven by religious concerns. Although the Old Testament idea of madness as a divine or supernatural affliction had declined among educated classes in the wake of the Enlightenment, secular understandings of insanity were still largely conceived through the New Testament opposition of the divine spirit and the carnal self. Drawing upon Hellenic philosophy, St Paul in his letters to Romans and Galatians drew a strong contrast between the 'flesh', which is seen as part of the earthly or Adamic rebellion against God, and the immortal soul, a divine attribute sustained through the relationship with the Godhead. From this perspective, struggles over the governance of physical desires and episodes of madness in which divine reason was defeated by carnal desire took on a new significance as challenges to the divine order.[20] This moral understanding persisted in the dualist philosophy of Rene Descartes. In early modern medicine, the dethronement of reason could be attributed to physiological causes, such as excesses of bile or phlegm, or spiritual travails, making possible a mixed physic which combined physical and religious interventions.[21]

The analogy between social and spiritual disorder fostered in the New Testament was reinforced in the religious and political upheavals that wracked early modern Europe. These upheavals, which were in part sustained by the growth of millenarian belief and popular prophecy, were understood as demonstrations of the close connection between political stability and inner experience. The early enlightenment philosophies that emerged in the wake of these struggles emphasised the need to reconcile private belief and public consensus. In the writings of John Locke, whose *Essay Concerning Human Understanding* (1690) would provide the foundation for eighteenth-century experiments in asylum care, the authority of personal experience was consistently denigrated in favour of group agreement. Locke rejected the doctrine of innate ideas, arguing that human knowledge and indeed human identity were founded upon the accumulation of experience. The inner world was founded upon the outer senses. It was a model that was paralleled, as Steven Shapin and Simon Schaffer have shown, in the emergence of the experimental method in the natural sciences: a method embodied in the work of new scientific academies such as the Royal Society.[22] Collective agreement and public evidence now held dominion over the assurance of personal conviction.

By the end of the eighteenth century, the new models of mind and opinion developed in early modern philosophy had inspired a series of experiments in lunacy care. In Turin, Paris, Manchester, and York, asylum keepers developed new therapeutic regimes focused less on the breaking of the rebellious flesh than the cultivation of feeling and understanding. The mind was now seen as a project that could be transformed through example and encouragement. This standpoint, termed 'the moral treatment' by contemporaries, was sustained by a number of overlapping convictions. In France and Italy, Philippe Pinel and Vincenzo Chiarugi shared an enlightenment faith in the universality of human nature – a universality that was demonstrated in the persistence of basic passions and affections beneath the derangement of the intellect. In England, the Quaker proprietors of the York Retreat based their experiments in benevolent therapy upon the doctrine of inextinguishable inner light: a divine flame that could be rekindled through Christian kindness.[23]

The early development of psychiatry was thus underpinned by a Christian vocabulary and equipped with methods and approaches that had emerged in part in theological disputation and in part in response to the dangers of religious sectarianism. And in some ways it offered a new framework for addressing the task that had motivated its early modern forebears: that of policing spiritual experience. Questions about the veracity and interpretation of spiritual experience persisted into the nineteenth century and were reanimated by the wave of new religious movements that swept across Protestant Europe and North America. The experiential turn in Protestant religion, epitomised by the rise of Evangelical Movements, Methodism, and other forms of nonconformity, was soon followed by the rise of charismatic Catholicism and a host of unorthodox movements, such as Mormonism and Spiritualism, which raised new questions about the basis of religious authority and the policing of spiritual testimony.[24]

These new religious movements created a domestic parallel to the colonial project of policing other cultures. Visionary experience, demonic possession, witchcraft accusations, and prophetic movements remained a persistent challenge for colonial administrators and for Protestant and Catholic missionaries.[25] The refusal of mundane identity and the assumption of supernatural authority in popular prophecy opened up struggles against colonial government that often ended in violent confrontation. Similarly, within the space of the Victorian house, domestic experiments in clairvoyance or spirit communication challenged the familiar authority of household patriarchs as wives, servants, and children were enfranchised through spirit inspiration. Such scenes led to the development of new psychiatric concepts – 'automatism', the 'subliminal', 'regression' – as physicians and psychical researchers sought to explain away miraculous productions and restore the established natural order.[26] At the same time, such struggles worked to delimit the boundaries of psychiatric authority. High-profile cases of spiritualists committed to the asylum for the heterodox beliefs resulted in adherents of the new religions organising against the threat to personal liberty and freedom of conscience contained within the nascent sciences.[27]

Psychiatry, psychology, and the reconstitution of spirituality

Through the policing of the miraculous, spirituality itself was transformed. In the writings of early investigators, the sacred became bound up with the materials of personal and racial identity. It was imagined as a great storehouse of memory: subliminal memories that stretched far beyond the waking consciousness of the individual into our forgotten childhoods and the prehistory of the race. For English and German psychic investigators, experiments in mediumship, hypnotism, and telepathy demonstrated the persistence of memory beyond the bounds of the individual and thus provided the grounds for religious claims of immorality.[28] At the same time, this idea of an extended consciousness suggested the existence of personal capacities and human potentials that still awaited their proper exploitation. Drawing upon the recent reports of the healing miracles at Lourdes and Marpingen as well as the claims of Christian Science, the English psychical researcher Frederic Myers argued that such episodes revealed the existence of primitive capacities for self-repair and distant communication (i.e. telepathy) that could be recovered through expert psychological guidance.[29]

For William James, this conflation of the sacred with the subliminal provided the basis for a new kind of religion. James was a close colleague of Myers and shared his commitment to the investigation of mystical phenomena through psychical research. Like Myers, he became convinced that such phenomena served as demonstrations of the breadth of memory and personality beyond waking consciousness. From this perspective, the encounter with the divine took on a slightly solipsistic aspect as it simply involved the revelation of unrecognised aspects of our selves, albeit aspects that demonstrated our connection to and dependence upon others. Miraculous phenomena that had once marked the limits of human personality and heralded the entry of the divine now pointed toward the uncharted capacities and connections that lay beneath the skin. As James wrote:

> our lives are like islands in the sea, or like trees in the forest. The maple and the pine may whisper to each other with their leaves, and Conanicut and Newport hear each other's fog-horns. But the trees also commingle their roots in the darkness underground, and the islands also hang together on the ocean's bottom. Just as there is a continuum of consciousness, against which our individuality builds but accidental fence.[30]

Psychological and psychiatric investigations of the miraculous had produced a new kind of subject. In the newly founded university psychological laboratories at Clark University, Leipzig, and Harvard, investigators set out to chart this subject through statistical investigations of the religious life. Using large-scale questionnaires distributed to teachers, college students and trainee ministers they sought to map out the normal patterns of religious development tracking the age of conversion, spiritual baptism, and declining feelings of faith.[31] They found a close correlation with the pattern of sexual awakening. The Clark psychologist, G. Stanley Hall (who had mentored many of these early investigators) argued that this confluence of religious and sexual impulses demonstrated that the sense of spiritual connection which James had described, was, in reality, the awakening of racial consciousness within the life of the individual. Religious conversion, which regularly occurred in adolescence, should be seen, Hall insisted, as a developmental stage in which the individual and racial lives were fused. It was, he argued, a kind of psychic fall in which the 'old unity and harmony with nature is broken up; the child is driven from his paradise and must enter upon a long viaticum of ascent and conquer a higher kingdom of man for himself, break out a new sphere and evolve a more modern story to his psycho-physical nature'.[32]

Perhaps this is true. For our purposes it is worth noting here that the tools of investigation brought to bear against religious phenomena changed the way that it was understood. Statistics, a science that had developed in governmental and eugenic investigations of the population, now helped sustain a viewpoint in which the spiritual life took on the characteristics and history that had been associated with the race. Religious experiences – epiphanies, conversions, ecstasies and possessions were not supernatural moments of divine grace; they were manifestations of racial life playing itself out in the body of the individual.

This anthropological conflation of the racial and the spiritual was taken up in the psychoanalytic doctrines of Sigmund Freud. Freud, like many of his radical contemporaries, regarded religion with contempt. It was, he argued, an infantile delusion: a protective belief that worked to shield individuals from their true desires. The fact that religion was a collective achievement, unlike the idiosyncratic neuroses that Freud's patients developed to protect themselves, was an indication of its roots in the deep history of the race. In a series of speculative works, beginning with *Totem and Taboo* (1913), Freud sought to trace the emergence of religion back to a primitive drama in which the tribal horde of brothers overthrew and consumed their 'violent and jealous father', only to raise a totem in his place to assuage their collective guilt.[33] This was the Oedipal story he had recovered from his bourgeois Viennese patients, projected backwards onto the prehistory of mankind. It assumed that the memory of this primal parricide (or many parricides) persisted in modern populations through some mechanism of Lamarckian inheritance. It was this inheritance that gave religion its collective power: a power that Freud recognised. Although he had understood his patients' incest claims as mere fantasies, he insisted upon the reality of the prehistoric primal crime. As he wrote to Andreas Salome: "Religions owe their compulsive power to the return of the repressed; they are reawakened memories of very ancient, forgotten highly emotional episodes of human history . . . the strength of religion lies not in its material, but in its historical truth."[34]

Although psychoanalysis won a surprisingly large audience among European churchmen, few adopted Freud's speculative anthropology.[35] In its place, less violent and less sexualised origins for religious feeling were suggested. Oskar Pfister, a Swiss Lutheran pastor, lay analyst and close confidante of Freud, argued that only Christianity provided the means for the successful sublimation of the Id.[36] Ian Suttie, a heterodox Scottish psychoanalyst, argued that the real taboo which underlay modern social structures and, indeed, the discipline of psychoanalysis itself, was tenderness. For Suttie the real truth that we failed to confront was our primal state of maternal dependence.[37] Suttie's insight informed a generation of object relations analysts who rose to prominence in the United Kingdom after the Second World War. In the writings of D. W. Winnicott and John Bowlby, the mother–child bond was held up as the primary system, a system that was replicated in our imagined relationship with a loving God.[38]

New therapies for a new spirituality

Early investigations into the psychology of religion opened up the spiritual life to the possibility of a new kind of government. Although there was, of course, an age-old literature on the role of spiritual discipline in overcoming the fallen self and achieving salvation, the new psychology generated a more mundane project, in which the work of grace in bringing about conversion and sanctification could be measured and transformed into an object for targeted interventions. At the same time, in the rhetoric of the subliminal developed in the early investigations in psychical research and psychopathology, spiritual gifts, and the sense of the sacred were transformed into personal capacities that could be exploited through expert knowledge and practice. In combination, these developments would transform the basis of clerical pastoral work. It shifted, as the sociologist Andrew Abbott has noted, from an evangelistic concern with individual salvation to a psychological ministry directed at the care of the individual's inner life.[39] The psychotherapeutic translation of life's challenges, such as domestic difficulties or financial concerns, into psychological objects such as anxieties and obsessions revealed a new territory for pastoral intervention.[40]

The clearest manifestation of this new concern occurred in the work of the Emmanuel Church in Boston. Boston had for the latter part of the nineteenth century been caught up in successive waves of psychotherapeutic excitement, as the claims of Christian Science and New Thought circulated in the city. In 1906, Elwood Worcester, an Episcopalian minister with an academic training in psychology, set out to capitalise on this excitement by establishing a free clinic for the treatment of nervous disorders. His project helped to promote a new understanding of faith. It no longer simply reflected the achievement of a correct relationship with God and the acceptance of salvation; rather, it became a kind of psychological resource that would be drawn on and fielded to meet the new stresses attendant upon modern life. It was an understanding indebted to Boston neurologist G. M. Beard, who in developing his ideas of neurasthenia had held up established religion as a bulwark against the worry and anxiety that beset the modern citizen. Worcester pushed this argument further. Like James and the psychical researchers he saw faith making possible the achievement of new personal capacities.

In the work of the Emmanuel Movement, Christian faith was thus transformed into a strategic resource, a kind of psychological arsenal that could be drawn upon in confronting the signal stresses of twentieth century modernity. It was a vision that would have a far-reaching legacy. It helped to contribute to the Americanization of psychosomatic medicine pioneered by Helen Flanders Dunbar, a polymathic scholar who was closely involved with the successor organisations to the Emmanuel Church.[41] In her encyclopaedic writings, she held up the promise that faith did not simply safeguard our psychological health, but could also bring about our physical restoration.

This instrumental approach to religion, however, was never wholly accepted. In 1920 Anton Boisen, a Presbyterian Minister who, like Dunbar, had trained in sociology and psychology and was closely associated with the Emmanuel Movement, suffered an extended psychotic breakdown. Even in the depths of his illness he saw the crisis not as a simple problem to be resolved, but as a numinous experience which precipitated a new hunger for meaning.[42] This, he claimed, was a true spiritual hunger which men sought to escape through the artificial distractions of modern life but could never be satisfied until the real questions of existence were confronted. From this perspective, illness could not threaten man's essential existence. It was a reminder of the fragility of our systems and a call for spiritual growth.

Boisen's insight was shared by early psychoanalytic heretics, including Herbert Silberer and Carl Jung, who insisted on the insufficiency of conventional psychotherapeutic explanations.[43] As Jung wrote:

But what will the doctor do when he sees only too clearly why his patient is ill, when he sees that it arises from having no love, but only sexuality; no faith, because he is afraid to grope in the dark; no hope, because he is disillusioned by the world and by life; and no understanding, because he has failed to read the meaning of his own existence?[44]

This insight was echoed in the post-war development of existential analysis. In the writings of Rollo May and Victor Frankl, as with Boisen, the Freudian approach was reversed. Religion was no longer seen as an illusion or mask through which we could avoid confronting the base truth of our animal desires; rather, our carnal desires and the artificial systems of psychology that ministered to them, distracted us from confronting the emptiness of the absurd and our true relationship with the divine.[45] It was a perspective drawn from the Christian existentialism of Soren Kierkegaard, but recast in therapeutic terms. From this perspective, as the radical psychiatrist R. D. Laing would argue, illness could be seen as the first step in a meta-noic journey that would allow us to cast off our workaday identities and recover our ecstatic authenticity.[46]

Psychiatric knowledge and the making of new religions

The technical promise of psychological and psychiatric knowledge that had been explored in the work of interwar faith groups such as the Emmanuel Movement was taken up by a number of more unorthodox new religious movements in the wake of the Second World War. In 1950, L. Ron Hubbard, a science fiction writer outlined a new philosophy of self-transformation that he termed Dianetics.[47] Dianetics drew upon contemporary neuropsychiatry, suggesting that traumas experienced in one's present and past lives created a series of engrams or blocked circuits, that could be detected or 'audited' through structured interviews and resolved through group psychological training and therapeutic exercises.[48] By the 1970s the armamentarium had been expanded to include electrophysiological technologies ('the E-meter' or electropsy-chometer – a form of polygraph) and standardised treatment procedures.[49] The goal of Dianetic therapy was to achieve a 'clear' state, or the realisation of an immortal Thetan consciousness that remained clouded behind the accumulated traumas and anxieties of contemporary life. Despite establishment scepticism, the book was an immediate success, with over 800 Dianetics Clubs being set up by early readers. Hubbard capitalised on this achievement by organising the Church of Scientology to cultivate the spiritual potential unleashed by the new therapy.

The success of the Church of Scientology spurred many imitators. In the United Kingdom, Robert and Mary de Grimston drew upon its techniques in the establishment of the Process Church. Like Scientology, the Process offered a technological fix for the problems of existence, combining Adlerian Individual Psychology with a countercultural emphasis on the equal position of Satan and Lucifer alongside Jehovah and Christ.[50] Other groups, such as Erhard Training Seminars or EST, avoided such strong theological claims, but maintained the central Scientological innovation of using psychotherapeutic techniques to build new collective and quasi-religious institutions.[51] Alongside these spiritualised psychiatries, the resurgence of

145

the New Age movement in the 1960s and 1970s witnessed the wholesale incorporation of an armamentarium of psychiatric concepts and diagnostic categories into
a new programme of work – a programme that held up the promise of personal
and collective redemption through the recovery and revitalisation of lost traditions
of oriental and pagan wisdom.[52] The development of transpersonal psychology,
inspired to a large extent by Abraham Maslow's research into peak experience and
Roberto Assagioli's work on psychosynthesis, helped to turn the human potentials,
sketched out in late Victorian investigations into the miraculous, into a new framework for living.[53]

As well as offering a series of frameworks and technologies and that could be
exploited as spiritual exercises by new religious movements, post-war psychiatry also
made possible a reimagining of the transcendental. In the 1960s, a number of psychiatric researchers who were engaged in experimental investigations of altered states
claimed to have achieved a new level of insight into a transcendent reality.[54] John
C. Lilly at the National Institute of Mental Health in Bethesda engaged in a series of
experiments with LSD, sensory deprivation (using flotation tanks), and later ketamine. Lilly came to believe that his psychonautical adventures had revealed a complex
ontology populated by previously unrecognised entities including the Solid State
Intelligence – a malevolent self-organising machine – and the Earth Coincidence
Control Office, which oversaw terrestrial consciousness.[55] Similarly, the ecologist and
ethnobotanist Terence McKenna argued for the potential of psilocybin and ayahuasca
(and its derivative DMT) as pharmacological tools for psychological reconditioning,
before discovering in his self-experiments a pantheon of extra dimensional beings,
'machine elves', which were supervising the evolution of human consciousness.[56]
What was perhaps most remarkable about McKenna's claims was that machine elves
were soon a widely reported feature of the ketamine experience. Their disturbing
presence helped to demonstrate that psychiatry did not simply fabricate new linguistic categories, but went beneath the skin, creating new patterns of embodiment and
new forms of altered state.

Religious knowledge and the making
of new psychiatries

The emergence of psychiatrically-inspired new religious movements opened up
a series of challenges for mental health professionals. Sometimes these challenges
were overt. In the early 1970s, the Church of Scientology engaged in a number of
high-profile campaigns and lawsuits against psychiatrists arguing that modern medicine was engaged in coercive practices and forms of brainwashing. This led to the
Scientologists' formation of the Citizen's Commission on Human Rights, a front
organisation for the movement, which organised campaigns against perceived psychiatric abuses and the deployment of new pharmaceutical treatments such as Prozac
and Ritalin.[57] Yet this was only a dramatic example of a more subtle problem facing
practitioners: the growing complexity of belief in the landscape of care. The growth
of migration in the twentieth century and the emergence of new media created populations that embraced a variety of faiths and a variety of attitudes to medical intervention, which were often at odds with those of practitioners.[58] Although this had in some
ways been anticipated in the struggles over heterodox belief that formed a staple of

nineteenth-century medical debates, the scale and variety of beliefs became much greater in the post-war period.

The fragmentation of belief after the Second World War has led to a critical revival and domestication of the old project of colonial psychiatry, as attempts are made to assess the impact of specific faiths on the epidemiology and outcome of different illnesses. The results of these assessments are often highly favourable, with religion being held up as having a prophylactic effect against the onset of anxiety and depression, and forms of private and communal worship as reducing the need and call for hospitalisation. At the same time, psychiatrists face the professional threat of psychiatric care being organised through informal faith groups and around very different values systems from those encoded in the discipline. From its establishment in 1999, the American Association of Christian Counsellors now enjoys a membership of 50,000 and large-scale training programmes in Biblical counselling offering therapies based on a fundamentalist reading of the canon are now commonplace across Africa and the United States.[59] In the rhetoric of the AACC, the traditional narrative of psychiatric secularisation is reversed. They propose a five-wave model of development in psychiatry: psychodynamic; behavioural; humanistic; multicultural; and now spiritual psychology – the last wave bringing in a new dispensation initiated by the patients themselves.[60]

The resurgence of faith-based counselling programmes, alongside the growth of new age and spiritual psychotherapies, has helped to revive and transform old idioms of mental distress. In the 1980s, the discourse on trauma, which had largely worked through the idea that psychological harm creates gaps in consciousness and memory, was modified through the work of Christian counsellors. In its new iteration, absences in patient narratives were read as indications of the presence of alternate personalities. These personalities, interrogated in therapeutic work, often confessed to their demonic origin although others were more protective in nature, revealing their work as 'inner self helpers' protecting and guiding their proteges throughout a long history of abuse.[61] William James's prediction that 'The demon theory will have its innings again," has been borne out in late twentieth-century psychiatry.[62] The growth of spiritualised psychotherapies, such as Christian counselling, and psychiatric spiritualities, as in McKenna's visionary experience, has led to the creation of a new phenomenological landscape for psychiatric work.

Religion and the remaking of modern psychiatry

In *Moses and Monotheism* (1939), Freud engaged in an imaginative reconstruction of the origins of Judaism, arguing the emergence of the monotheistic religions could be seen as an example of the 'return of the repressed'. Describing the travails of the tribe of Moses following their murder of their leader, Freud argued that

> The religion of Moses, however, had not disappeared without leaving a trace. A kind of memory of it had survived, obscured and distorted, supported, perhaps, among individual members of the priestly caste by ancient records. And it was this tradition of a great past which continued to work in the background, as it were, which gradually gained more and more power over men's minds."[63]

It was, Freud insisted, enduring guilt over the murder of their patriarchal leader that led to the reinstatement of their lost monotheistic religion with its consolatory promise of the leader's Messianic return.

If one were to accept Freud's anthropological and metapsychological framework, and I accept that this is a big if, then it would not be too fanciful to imagine some similar process taking place in contemporary psychiatry. Since the start of the new millennium, the discipline has been animated by two developments that, in many ways, bear out the technological promise anticipated in the dialogue between Crowley and Maudsley. On the one hand, there has been a growing interest in the therapeutic potential of spritual philosophies (particularly those drawn from non-Western traditions such as the Buddhist practice of vipassana meditation) for managing states of consciousness and mood disorders. On the other hand, and partly because of these cultural encounters, there has been a renewed awareness of the specific values encoded in the Western psychiatric project and a growing reflexive interrogation of its ontological assumptions and its ethical basis.[64]

Neither of these developments is straightforward and neither can be seen as a wholesale importation of spiritual understandings into psychiatric practice. The development of the mindfulness agenda in contemporary psychiatry, which is understood by many as the incorporation of a mixture of Hindu and Buddhist insights and techniques into therapeutic practice, upholds a model of mind that very few practising Buddhists would share.[65] Driven largely by John Benson's investigations into transcendental meditation in the 1970s and, more recently, Jon Kabat-Zinn's research into strategies of attention management and self-examination drawn from vipassana yoga, mindfulness techniques hold out the promise of a form of secular spiritual exercise in which an escape from the pull of earthly care and feeling is achieved.[66]

It is tempting to see the promotion of secularised spiritual exercises as a side issue in the history of psychiatry: a kind of heterodox diversion, akin to the mid-twentieth-century excitement over faith healing, which distracts a few individuals while the real business of mental health care continues to be delivered through psychopharmaceutical interventions. Such a division would be a false one. The problematisations of belief and attitude raised in mindfulness work, persist in psychopharmacology. Over the last two decades, companies involved in the organisation of large-scale randomised control trials of new generation anti-depressants have faced growing claims that their drugs are becoming weaker or that placebo effects are becoming stronger.[67] Faith in psychiatry is now generating the same kind of disruptive effects that once bedevilled the excess of faith in religion.

The disruptive effects of psychiatric faith, alongside the often stark disparities of belief and value that can exist between patients and doctors has led to a new reflexive concern with the implicit goals and assumptions of modern medical practice. In the liberal democracies of the global north, governments have sought to redress this disparity, by encouraging practitioners to develop a deeper awareness of their clients' spiritual needs and world views.[68] At the same time, new efforts have been made to suspend judgement over previously pathologised spiritual phenomena such as visions or voice hearing, and incorporate them as active elements in therapeutic work.[69]

It is becoming more and more clear that psychiatry has not overcome religion and indeed it is difficult to imagine how it could ever do so. The cultures of both are so enmeshed that they cannot be disentangled. As we have seen, this entanglement, and ironically the promise of escaping this entanglement, has been productive of new objects and approaches that in turn have worked to create new forms of religious belief and psychiatric practice. The intellectual division between the fields of work of religion and psychiatry is a comparatively recent phenomenon. As the two fields continue to shape and inform each others' objects and horizons, and as new philosophies such as transhumanism hold up the promise of purely somatic pathways to salvation, it is clear that this separation may not last.[70]

Notes

1 For discussions see Marco Pasi, 'Varieties of Magical Experience: Aleister Crowley's Views on Occult Practice', *Magic, Ritual and Witchcraft* 6 (2011): 123–62 on 137–43; Egil Asprem, 'Magic Naturalized? Negotiating Science and Occult Experience in Crowley's Scientific Illuminism' *Aries* 8 (2008): 139–65 on 147–48.

2 Aleister Crowley, *The Confessions of Aleister Crowley*. [1929], ed. J. Symonds and K. Grant (London: Penguin Arkana, 1989), 386.

3 Stuart Clark, *Thinking with Demons: The Idea of Witchcraft in Early Modern Europe*, (Oxford: OUP, 1997), 526–60; Lorraine Daston and Katherine Park, *Wonders and the Order of Nature, 1150–1750* (New York: Zone Books, 1998), 187–201.

4 See for example the madness of Nebuchadnezzar 1 Samuel: 16–23, Daniel 4: 1–34; Christ's healing of the Gerasene Demoniac (Mark 5.1–20, Luke 8, 26–39) and the possession at Capernum (Mark 1.23–28; Luke 4,23–27) and the Pentecostal gifts (1 Corinthians 12; Romans 12). For an overview, Lesley Weatherhead, *Psychology, Religion and Healing*, (London: Hodder and Stoughton, 1959), ch. 2.

5 M. A. Screech, *Ecstasy and the Praise of Folly* (London: Duckworth, 1980); D. Lederer, *Madness, Religion and the State in Early Modern Europe* (Cambridge: Cambridge University Press, 2006); Michael MacDonald, *Mystical Bedlam: Madness, Anxiety and Healing in Seventeenth-Century England* (Cambridge: Cambridge University Press, 2008).

6 Michael Dols, 'Insanity and its Treatment in Islamic Society', *Medical History* 31 (1987): 1–14; idem., *Manjun: The Madman in Medieval Islamic Society* (Oxford: Clarendon Press, 1992).

7 H. Maudsley, *Natural Causes and Supernatural Seemings* (London: Kegan Paul, Trench & Co., 1886).

8 H. Maudsley, *Religion and Realities* (London: John Bale, 1918).

9 Maurice North, *The Secular Priests: Psychotherapists in Contemporary Society*, (London: George Allen and Unwin, 1972). For influential statements of this thesis, see: P. Rieff, *The Triumph of the Therapeutic* [1966] (London: Penguin University Paperbacks, 1969); C. Lasch, *The Culture of Narcisscism* (London: Picador, 1976); Eva Moskowitz, *In Therapy We Trust*, (Baltimore: Johns Hopkins, 2001). For a useful overview, see Katie Wright, 'Theorizing Therapeutic Culture: Past Influences, Future Directions', *Journal of Sociology* 44 (2008): 321–26.

10 Scott H. Nelson, and E. Fuller Torrey, 'The Religious Functions of Psychiatry', *American J. Orthopsychiatry* 43 (1973): 362–67.

11 J. C. Burnham, 'The Encounter of Christian Theology With Deterministic Psychology and Psychoanalysis', *Bull. Menninger Clinic* 49 (1985): 321–52.

12 M. Weber, 'Science as a Vocation' in *From Max Weber: Essays in Sociology*, eds H. H. Gerth and C. Wright Mills, (London: Oxford University Press, 1946), 129–56.

13 Dipesh Chakrabarty, *Provincializing Europe: Postcolonial Thought and Historical Difference* (Princeton, NJ: Princeton University Press, 2000), 89.

14 Michael Saler, 'Modernity and Enchantment', *American Historical Review* 111 (2006): 692–716; Joshua Landy and Michael Saler (eds.), *The Re-enchantment of the World: Secular Magic in a Rational Age* (Stanford, CA: Stanford University Press, 2009).

15 Charles Taylor, *A Secular Age* (Cambridge, MA: Harvard University Press, 2007), 621.

16 Nineteenth-century neurologists and alienists scoured the literature of medieval and early modern witchcraft and demonology for cases that could be retrospectively diagnosed through their schemes of abnormal psychology. See Rhodri Hayward, 'Demonology,

149

Neurology and Medicine in Edwardian Britain', *Bulletin of the History of Medicine* 78 (2004): 37–58.

17 On the limitations of such metaphors, see: Geoffrey Cantor, 'What shall we do with the 'Conflict Thesis'? in *Science and Religion: New Historical Perspectives*, ed. Thomas Dixon, Geoffrey Cantor, and Stephen Pumfrey (Cambridge: Cambridge University Press, 2010), ch. 16.

18 I borrow this concept of 'experimental entanglement' from recent work on interdisciplinarity in the neurosciences: Des Fitzgerald and Felicity Callard, 'Social Science and Neuroscience Beyond interdisciplinary: Experimental Entanglements', *Theory, Culture and Society,* 32 (2015): 3–32.

19 Bruno Latour, *On the Modern Cult of Factish Gods* (Durham, NC: Duke University Press, 2014).

20 Louis Dumont, 'A Modified View of our Origins: The Christian Beginnings of Modern Individualism' in *The Category of Person: Anthropology, Philosophy, History*, ed. Michael Carrithers, Steven Collins, Steven Lukes (Cambridge: Cambridge University Press, 1985), 93–122.

21 For its persistence into the nineteenth century, see Stephen. 'The Physiology of Mind, the Unity of Nature, and the Moral Order in Victorian Thought', *British Journal of the History of Science*, 14 (1981): 109–32.

22 Steven Shapin and Simon Schaffer, *Leviathan and the Air Pump* (Princeton: Princeton University Press, 1985): Daston and Park, *Wonders*, pp. 220–53.

23 L. C. Charland, 'Benevolent Theory: Moral Treatment at the Retreat', *History of Psychiatry* 18 (2007): 61–80

24 Ann Taves, *Fits, Trances and Visions: Experiencing Religion and Explaining Experience from Wesley to James* (Princeton, NJ: Princeton University Press, 1999), chs 1–5.

25 For an overview see Richard Keller, 'Madness and Colonization, Psychiatry in the British and French Empires', *Journal of Social History* 35 (2001): 295–326; Sloan Mahone and Magan Vaughan, eds, *Psychiatry and Empire* (Basingstoke: Palgrave, 2007); David Hardiman, *Healing Bodies, Saving Souls. Medical Missions in Asia and Africa* (Amsterdam: Rodopi, 2006).

26 Edward M. Brown, 'Neurology and Spiritualism in the 1870s', *Bulletin of the History of Medicine* 57 (1983): 562–77; S. E. D. Shortt, 'Physicians and Psychics: The Anglo-American Medical Response to Spiritualism', *Journal of the History of Medicine and Allied Sciences,* 39 (1984): 339–55; Ann Taves, *Fits, Trances and Visions*, 208–212.

27 Peter McCandless, '"Dangerous to Themselves and Others": The Victorian Debate over Wrongful Confinement", *Journal of British Studies*, 23 (1983): 84–10; J. J. Schwieso, 'Religious Fanaticism and Wrongful Confinement in Victorian England', *Social History of Medicine*, 9 (1996): 158–74.

28 On these investigations see Heather Wolfram, *Stepchildren of Science: Psychical Research and Parapsychology in Germany c. 1870–1939,* (Amsterdam: Rodopi, 2009); R. Plas, 'Psychical Research in France Around the End of the Nineteenth Century', *History of the Human Sciences*, 25 (2012): 91–107; Janet Oppenheim, *The Other World: Spiritualism and Psychical Research in England, 1850–1914* (Cambridge: Cambridge University Press, 1985).

29 A. T. Myers and F. W. H. Myers, 'Mind-cure, Faith-cure and the Miracles of Lourdes', *Proceedings of the Society for Psychical Research*, 9 (1893–94): 160–209; F. W. H. Myers, 'The Subliminal Consciousness VI: The Mechanism of Hysteria', *Proceedings of the Society for Psychical Research,* 9 (1893–94): 24–25.

30 William James, *Essays in Psychical Research*, (Cambridge, MA: Harvard University Press, 1986), 374.

31 E. D. Starbuck, *The Psychology of Religion: An Empirical Study of the Growth of Religious Consciousness* (London: Walter Scott, 1900).

32 G. Stanley Hall, *Adolescence: Its Psychology and its Relations to Physiology, Anthropology, Sociology, Sex, Crime, Religion, and Education.* 2 vols (London: Sidney Appleton, 1905), vol. 1, 242; G. Stanley Hall, 'The Moral and Religious Training of Children', *Princeton Review* 9 (1882): 26–48.

33 Sigmund Freud, 'Totem and Taboo' in *The Origins of Religion* [Pelican Freud Library no.13], (London: Penguin Books, 1990), 201–8.

34 Quoted in Eli Zaretsky, *The Secrets of the Soul: Social and Cultural History of Psychoanalysis* (New York: A. A. Knopf, 2004), 242.

35 Graham Richards, 'Psychology and the Churches in Britain 1919–39: Symptoms of Conversion', *History of the Human Sciences*, 13 (2000): 57–84.

36 H. N. Maloney and G. North, 'The Future of an Illusion: The Illusion of a Future', *Journal of the History of the Behavioral Sciences*, 15 (1979): 177–86.

37 Liz Bondi, 'Between Christianity and Secularity: Counselling and Psychotherapy Provision in Scotland', *Social and Cultural Geography*, 14 (2013): 668–88; D. Fergusson, 'Persons in Relation: The Interaction of Philosophy, Theology, and Psychotherapy in 20th Century Scotland', *Practical Theology*, 5 (2012): 287–306.

38 S. Akhtar and H. Parens, *Does God Help? Developmental and Clinical Aspects of Religious Belief* (Lanham MD: Aronson, 2001).

39 Andrew Abbott, 'Religion, Psychiatry and the Problems of Everyday Life', *Sociological Analysis*, 41 (1980): 164–71.

40 See Ibid. and also the general discussion in Richard Sennett, *The Fall of Public Man* (London: Faber & Faber, 1986).

41 Flanders Dunbar, *Emotions and Bodily Changes* (New York: Columbia University Press, 1935), 416–18.

42 Anton Boisen, 'Personality Changes and Upheaval Arising out of a Sense of Personal Failure', *American Journal of Psychiatry*, 5 (1926): 531–51; idem., *Out of the Depths*, (New York, Harper, 1960).

43 Sonu Shamdasani, *Jung and the Making of Modern Psychology* (Cambridge: Cambridge University Press, 2003), 137–57.

44 Carl Jung, *Modern Man in Search of a Soul* [1933] (London: Arkana, 1988), 226.

45 Rollo May, *Man's Search for Himself* (London: Allen and Unwin, 1953); Viktor Frankl, *The Doctor and the Soul: From Logotherapy to Psychotherapy* (London: Souvenir Press, 1969).

46 R. D. Laing, *The Politics of Experience* (Harmondsworth: Penguin Books, 1967). On the Christian roots of metanoia, see Gavin Miller, 'How Scottish was R. D. Laing', *History of Psychiatry*, 20 (2009): 226–32.

47 Roy Wallis 'Dianetics: A Marginal Psychotherapy' in *Marginal Medicine*, ed. R. Wallis and P. Morley, (London: Peter Owen, 1976), 77–109.

48 L. R. Hubbard, *Dianetics: The Modern Science of Mental Health: A Handbook of Dianetic Therapy* (East Grinstead, Sussex: Hubbard College of Scientology, 1958).

49 *Dianetics Today* (Los Angeles: Bridge Publications, 1975).

50 W. S. Bainbridge, *Satan's Power: A Deviant Psychotherapy Cult* (Berkeley: University of California Press, 1978). Bainbridge refers to the Process Church as the Power throughout the work.

51 W. W. Bratley, *Werner Erhard. The Transformation of a Man* (New York: Clarendon Press, 1978).

52 Wouter Hannegraff, *New Age Religion and Western Cutlure: Esotericism in the Mirror of Secular Thought* (Leiden: Brill, 1996); Pascal Eitler, 'Körper-Kosmos-Kybernetik. Transformationen der Religion im 'New Age' (Westdeutschland 1970–1990),' *Zeithistorische Forschungen*, 4 (2007): 116–36.

53 R. Assagioli, *Psychosynthesis* [1965], (London: Turnstone Press, 1975); A. Maslow, *Religions, Values and Peak Experiences*, [1964], (Harmondsworth: Penguin, 1970).

54 For an overview, see Stanley R. Dean, ed., *Psychiatry and Mysticism* (Chicago: Nelson Hall, 1975).

55 John C. Lilly, *The Centre of the Cyclone: An Autobiography of Inner Space* (London: Calder and Boyars, 1973).

56 Terence McKenna, *The Archaic Revival* (New York: HarperCollins, 1992); Rick Strassman, *Inner Paths to Outer Space: Journeys to Alien Worlds Through Psychedelics and Other Spiritual Technologies* (Rochester, VT: Inner Traditions, 2008).

57 Stephen A. Kent and Terra A. Manca, 'A War over Mental Health Professionalism: Scientology versus Psychiatry', *Mental Health, Religion & Culture*, 17 (2014): 1–23.

58 H. Koenig, E. G. Hooten, E. Lindsay Calkins, K. G. Meador, 'Spirituality in the Medical School Curricula: Findings From a National Survey', *International Journal of Psychiatry in Medicine*, 40 (2010): 391–98.

59 P. Cantz, 'Toward a Biblical Psychoanalysis: A Second Look at the First Book' *Mental Health Religion and Culture,* 15 (2011): 779–97.

60 Paul Cantz, 'Religiously Based Therapies' in *Cultural Sociology of Mental Illness,* vol. 2, ed. Andrew Scull (London: Sage, 2014), 752.

61 Mikkel Borch-Jacobsen, *Making Minds and Madness* (Cambridge: Cambridge University Press, 2009), ch. 3.

62 James, 'Report on Mrs Piper's Hodgson Control', [1909] repr. *Essays in Psychical Research,* ch. 37.

63 Sigmund Freud, 'Moses and Monotheism: Three Essays' in *The Origins of Religion,* 372. For clear critiques of Freud's thesis, see Michel de Certeau, 'The Fiction of History: The Writing of Moses and Monotheism' in *The Writing of History* (New York: Columbia University Press, 1988), 308–334.

64 K. W. M. Fulford, M. Broome, G. Stanghellini and T. Thornton, eds, 'Looking with Both Eyes Open: Fact and Value in Psychiatric Diagnosis', *World Psychiatry,* 4 (2005): 278–86.

65 Dinesh Bhugra, 'Hindu and Ayurvedic Understandings of the Person' in *Medicine of the Person,* ed. John Cox, Alastair V. Coleman, and Bill (K. W. M.) Fulford (London: Jessica Kingsley, 2007), ch. 9; Steven Stanley, '"Things Said or Done Long Ago Are Recalled and Remembered": The Ethics of Mindfulness in Early Buddhism, Psychotherapy, and Clinical Psychology', *European Journal of Psychotherapy and Counselling,* 15 (2013): 151–62.

66 Herbert Benson, *The Relaxation Response* (Bristol Avon Books, 1975); Jon Kabat-Zinn, *Full Catastrophe Living: Using the Wisdom of Your Body and Mind to Face Stress, Pain and Illness* [1990], (London: Piatkus, 2013). For discussion, see Anne Harrington, *The Cure Within: A History of Mind-Body Medicine* (New York: W. W. Norton, 2008), ch. 6.

67 Andrew Lakoff, 'The Right Patient for the Drug: Managing the Placebo Effect in Antidepressant Trials', *Biosocieties,* 2 (2007): 57–71; Gavin Andrews, 'Placebo Response in Depression: Bane of Research, Boon to Therapy', *British Journal of Psychiatry,* 178 (2001): 192–94.

68 Accreditation Council on Graduate Medical Education, *Special Requirements for Residency Training in Psychiatry* (1994); Department of Health, *Inspiring Hope: Recognising the Importance of Spirituality in a Whole Person: Approach to Mental Health* (London: NIMHE, 2003).

69 F. Larøi, T. M. Luhrmann, V. Bell, W. A. Christian, S. Deshpande, C. Fernyhough, J. Jenkins and A. Woods, 'Culture and Hallucinations: Overview and Future Directions', *Schizophrenia Bulletin* 40, Suppl 4 (2014): S213–S220.

70 On transhumanist approaches to salvation, see Brent Waters, 'Whose Salvation? Which Eschatology? Transhumanism and Christianity as Competing Salvific Religions' in *Transhumanism and Transcendence,* ed. Ronald Cole-Turner (Washington, DC: Georgetown University Press, 2012), ch. 11.

8

MADNESS IN WESTERN LITERATURE
AND THE ARTS

Ilya Vinitsky

MAD, adj. Affected with a high degree of intellectual independence; not conforming to standards of thought, speech and action derived by the conformants from study of themselves; at odds with the majority; in short, unusual. It is noteworthy that persons are pronounced mad by officials destitute of evidence that themselves are sane. For illustration, this present (and illustrious) lexicographer is no firmer in the faith of his own sanity than is any inmate of any madhouse in the land; yet for aught he knows to the contrary, instead of the lofty occupation that seems to him to be engaging his powers he may really be beating his hands against the window bars of an asylum and declaring himself Noah Webster, to the innocent delight of many thoughtless spectators.

Ambrose Bierce, *The Devil's Dictionary*

Clearly, the idea of narrating the Western history of madness in literature and the arts in 7,000-plus words is quite insane (in fact, it is easier and, perhaps, less pretentious to squeeze the project into one sentence: "The role of madness in Western literature and the arts has always been tremendous" – no one would argue with this statement). But this is also an intriguing and challenging task. There are many ways of dealing with it, and I considered some of them before making my final choice.

One can write a historical survey of treatments of madness and the mad in literature and the fine arts. However, this plan threatens to turn into an enormously long – much longer than Homer's list of ships – array of names, titles, and dates.

Another option is to present the cultural history of madness via its conventional periodization or a series of tectonic shifts in Western cultural perception of the mad (madness in ancient Greek and Roman culture; medieval madness; madness in the Age of Reason; Romantic madness, etc.).

One can also try to present a typology of mad heroes, elaborated in Western art since Plato: the mad poet, the mad lover, the mad philosopher, etc. Perhaps, it would be possible to create a kind of periodic table of the mad in culture and, if one is fortunate, to add a couple of new "elements" – the mad cultural historian, for instance.

Another option is to consider artistic representations of madness within a context of the history of science and medicine from Aristotle and Hippocrates to Dr. Freud (and beyond). But this plan is methodologically too complicated and could plunge anyone into depression.

Another option is to focus on a limited number of formative works in the cultural history of madness. My personal list would include Plato's *Phaedrus*, Euripides'

153

Heracles, Dürer's *Melencolia I*, Cervantes's *Don Quixote*, Hogarth's Bedlam scene (from *Rake's Progress*), Racine's *Andromache*, a couple of Romantic poems (Edgar Allan Poe's "Raven" would be a must), E.T.A. Hoffmann's "Sandman," a poem or two by Hölderlin, Coleridge's *Ancient Mariner*, Gogol's "Diary of a Madman," Dostoevsky's *Double* (and *Idiot*, of course), Chekhov's "Ward Number Six" or "Black Monk," Kafka's *Castle*, a Van Gogh painting, a couple of operas (like Berlioz's *Symphonie Fantastique*) and ballets (*Giselle!*), – but this "shortlist" has already turned into a program for an entire course of lectures, so I had better drop this option.

In what follows, I choose an unusual way to present the historical survey through a prism of a personal story (or, rather, a cultural myth) of one individual as it is revealed in a certain picture. This personal myth originates in the Age of Romanticism (a turning point in the history of madness in the West) and it is suitable for my purpose, since it condenses the major themes and concepts that have driven the history of madness in Western literature and arts into a single symbolic text, the one that triggers our intellectual search and imagination.[1]

Figure

Let us start with a psychological-artistic test. Please, take a quick look at the drawing below and summarize what you can detect in it:

Figure 8.1 Nikolai Berg, Poet *Konstantin Batiushkov in 1847*. Originally published in
S. P. Shevyrev, *Poezdka v Kirillo-Belozerskii monastyr': Vakatsionnye dni professora Shevyreva v 1847 godu*. Moscow: Universitetskaia tipografiia, 1850. Part 1. P.114.

We can see a little man standing in front of an open window, looking out. The windowpane is opened out, away from the building, like a door. A church with onion domes on the top of the hill is clearly seen through the window in front of him. The shape of the domes suggests that he is in Russia. The man's arms are apparently crossed on his chest. He is wearing a black hat (or a cap) and a coat that hangs past his knees. Although our sight moves through the window toward the church, the man is motionless. Moreover, he does not appear to be looking at the church; he seems to be looking straight ahead or even down, which suggests that maybe he is oblivious to all of this.

Just to the man's right, a large, heavy curtain is drawn aside and tied back. The light creates shadows beneath his legs and around the windowpane, and illuminates the bottom part of the drape and outlines his clothing. If one takes the trouble to notice, it is clear that the man is standing just behind the seam of the floorboards that delineates the space of the dormer from the room itself. One can say that he is probably about five feet away from the actual window, as if separated from the outside world by the solid windowsill and the heavy drape.[2]

The artist's device employed here is known in the Western history of art as a "principle of the window." It was discovered by German Romantic artists in the late eighteenth century in order to portray the duality of man's world, a split between material reality and fantasy, which causes a state of profound loneliness and striving towards the unknown.[3]

Compare this drawing with the famous portrait of young Goethe standing at the window of his lodgings in Rome by J. H. W. Tischbein (1787):

Figure 8.2 J. H. W. Tischbein, *Goethe am Fenster der römischen Wohnung am Corso.* © Freies Deutsches Hochstift/Frankfurter Goethe-Museum. Photo: David Hall.

As we can see, the artist uses the same device, but in a very different way and clearly for a different purpose. The window is opened inward, as if inviting the young man into the outer world. He is bending over a windowsill. He seems relaxed and even nonchalant. There is no invisible and wall-like boundary between him and the world outside, no sense of subtle sorrow, which characterizes the previous picture.

Indeed, unlike Goethe, the unknown man of the first picture looks lonely, alienated and unaware of a viewer's (our) presence. He is restrained, clenched. Perhaps, he is longing for and maybe afraid of the open view before him. In any case, he is mysterious, since we do not see his face, his eyes, and have no idea so far of what he is doing here, trapped in this dark room with a widely open window.

Face

Let us turn his figure toward us by means of the imagination and cultural commentary. The picture has a title, *Konstantin Batiushkov in 1847*. It was drawn by a young Russian poet and amateur artist, Nikolai Berg, and published in 1850.

Konstantin Batiushkov (1787–1855) was a major poet of Russia's Golden Age of poetry, one of the creators (along with Vassily Zhukovsky and Alexander Pushkin) of Russian Romanticism. Here is his portrait from his early years created by a famed Russian Romantic artist Orest Kiprensky:

Figure 8.3 Orest Kiprensky, *Konstantin Batiushkov*. © DeAgostini/Getty Images.

Batiushkov's poetic persona has been closely associated in the history of Russian literature with a newly discovered power of creative imagination. Fantasy was indeed one of his major themes. His first published poem was called *A Dream* and in his poetry he presented himself as a happy dreamer who lives mainly in his own enchanting world, populated by careless friends, pretty girls in transparent Greek garments, engaged in feasts and mirthful conversations, and seemingly unaware about the existence of the real world – the one he knew well. He had a reason to be oblivious: a participant of the bloody Napoleonic wars, he witnessed the destruction of Moscow by fire and the death of a close friend; he was unmarried, lonely, so that all erotic motifs of his poetry can be attributed to his pure imagination, rather than experience. A Russian poet, he was an ardent admirer of Italy and the Italian language. In his works, he even tried to beautify Russian phonetics (in reality, quite harsh with all these "y, shch, ch") and created a kind of imaginary Russian – melodic and mesmerizing. Consider the following lines from his "historical elegy" about the ruins of a medieval castle (no prior knowledge of Russian is required for this test):

V dolinakh Neistrii razdalsia branei grom,
Tumannyi Al'bion iz kraia v krai pylaet,
I Gela den' i noch' v Valkalu provozhdaet
Pogibshikh blednyi sonm.

[In the valleys of Neustria, the thunder of battle rings out,/Misty Albion is ablaze from end to end,/And, day and night, to Valhalla Hela escorts/The pale host of perished warriors.]

Yet, imagination in his writings is ambivalent: it is both rewarding and dangerous. His idol was Torquato Tasso, a sixteenth-century Italian poet, author of the celebrated *Jerusalem Delivered* (1580), who had been confined for several years in a cell of the mad asylum of St. Anna at Ferrara and was glorified in the poetry of the Romantic age as the embodiment of poetic genius.[4] In a poem portraying his death, young Batiushkov presented the tormented poet as a sufferer of fate, envy, and imagination. In his final monologue, he addresses his mourning admirers:

O brothers! Friends! Don't weep for me:
Your friend's attained his long-sought goal.
He will depart in peace and, strong of faith,
He will not heed the agonizing end:
There, there ... O joy! ... among the righteous wives,
Among the angels, Elenora waits!
(transl. by Ilya Kutik)

Batiushkov conceived of himself as a Russian Tasso, and so did his friends and admirers.

Story

In 1823, Batiushkov had a mental breakdown and was later pronounced insane. Madness was hereditary in his family, but his friends and fans interpreted his disease as a sign, a realization of his own Romantic premonition (the destiny of the Russian Tasso). In Romantic mythology, creative fantasy and dark madness go hand in hand, poets (and lovers) are the most vulnerable creatures, and, as one of his older friends and literary mentors wrote after a visit to the infamous Bedlam hospital in London, "a soul too sensitive to the pleasures of the passions also feels sharply the pain they cause . . . [i]n such a soul paradise and hell are neighbors. Ecstasy is followed by either despair or melancholy, each of which so often opens the door . . . to the madhouse."[5]

The doors were opened for Batiushkov indeed, but his madhouse was quite different from the proverbial nightmarish Bedlam – it was an institution of a new, humane, age in the history of psychiatry (see Andrew Scull's chapter in this volume): a sanatorium (the "Maison de santé") located in an old castle of Sonnenstein in Germany, built above the river Elbe. (Ironically, in the early 1940s, the sanatorium was converted by the Nazis into a killing laboratory: from June 1940 until September 1942 approximately 15,000 persons were murdered there in accordance with the Action T4 program for the "Elimination of life unworthy of life"[6] – the frightening extreme of the cold rationalism and fear of the mentally sick, originated, according to Michel Foucault, in the Age of Reason when madness "became the paradoxical manifestation of non-being" and was subjected to stigmatization and confinement[7]).

Many years later, Batiushkov's close friend and fellow poet Piotr Viazemsky would write a poem about this Romantic site and a man who suffered there:

Sonnenstein

The view of the majestic Elbe is splendid from here,
Its banks bloom with luxuriant life,
Forest after forest along the ridges of the mountains,
Villa after villa, havens of summer bliss.

All around, from stony frames,
Scenes shine with fresh beauty:
Straddling the cliff, the castle
Has gained a foothold at its summit.

Enchanting land, now bright, now gloomy!
Living album of all earth's charms!
But a meditation clouding my soul
You could not divert, or drive out of my soul.

I was devoted to a different impression –
A dear image appeared in my soul,
The image of a sufferer – and its sad shadow
Darkened the beauty of nature.

He suffered here, languished here once,
My soul mate, and Zhukovsky's,
He, with his sorrow and songs, our Torquato,
He, who saw his end while still alive.

Not for his eyes did nature bloom,
Her sacred word fell silent before him,
Here, for him, from the azure vault
The cheerful day did not blaze with joy.

In an inner world of night visions
He lived locked up, like a prisoner in a jail,
And he was dead to outer impressions,
For him God's world was an empire of darkness.

But he saw, but his mind troubled him –
What created the illness of his mind;
Thus, poor man, he lived through years of suffering,
And my hapless friend is still living like this now.
                    (1853; translated by Kirsten Lodge)

As we see, Batiushkov's madness is presented by Viazemsky both as a deep personal tragedy and mystery of life: it reveals the other – dark – side of the beautiful world. Tellingly,
he portrays his poor friend in this poetic requiem as a man buried alive in the prison
cell of his sick mind. However, Batiushkov is still alive in the memory of the author and
his intimate circle as an apparition haunting the dreamy Golden age of Russian poetry.

Doctor

At the turn of the eighteenth century, madness was reinterpreted in the West as a
disease, rather than a crime and became one of the core themes in western literature and the arts. The mad inspired physicians and artists alike, with medical cases
treated by doctors as literary and literary works about the mad as medical ones. In the
nineteenth century (and up until the age of Sigmund Freud and Carl Jung), German-
speaking countries were considered the motherland of a new science of psychiatry
and German mad-doctors were portrayed as a peculiar caste, knowledgeable in the
secrets of the dark side of the human soul.[8] In the Romantic period, the boundary
between science and literature was vague and many doctors appeared to be poets,
philosophers, or mystics as well. Thus, a prominent Romantic psychiatrist Dr. Justinus
Kerner created an entire mystical cult of one of his patients, known as a Seeress of
Prevorst. For him (and his colleagues and readers) her case was a source of both scientific insights and poetic and mystical inspiration.

Batiushkov was treated by a German physician Dr. Dietrich. As many other doctors of
this age, he was of a poetic nature. He liked Batiushkov a lot and described his case in the
minutest detail in his remarkable diary/anamnesis, called "On the Illness of the Russian
Nobleman and his Imperial Majesty's Court Councilor Sir Konstantin Batiushkov."

According to Dr. Dietrich, Batiushkov's abnormal behavior represented a *mania
religiosa* and was characterized by the following symptoms:

- fear of persecution (he believed that a host of his enemies led by the Devil wanted
  to destroy him);
- hatred of time (he believed that he lived in eternity and hated any signs of earthly
  time, both physical, like clocks, and natural, like the moon);

159

- complete separation from the world ("It was impossible to enter into a discussion with him, to start a conversation . . . The patient . . . had separated himself from the world, insofar as life in the world presupposes discourse");
- "clinical Italomania" (he "spoke in Italian and recalled in his imagination several lovely episodes of Tasso's 'Jerusalem Delivered,' which he discussed with himself aloud and loudly").[9]

The diary tells us about some "foolish" manifestations of Batiushkov's disease, which can be qualified by a reader as extremely eccentric and even comic. To be sure, stories about similar follies were typical for pre-Romantic treatises and articles on madness.[10] These texts often included tales of mental delusions – of people who thought they were God, or that they were made of glass or butter, or of the "Sienois gentleman" who was cured from his dread of flooding the whole world when he urinated by being told that the village was on fire, and that he would be a public benefactor. (I guess the village burned down.)[11] Characteristically, in some of these stories, mad fancies were treated as – in their specific way – logical and grand (compare the noble fear of the gentleman from Siena to flood the *whole world* with his urine). Sanity was considered to be the best remedy against these fantasies.

However, in Doctor Dietrich's interpretation, his patient's madness was not a mere delusion to be fixed by the intervention of reason, but rather a powerful force of the unknown origin, a spiritual enigma, the resolution of which could reveal some basic problems of the human spirit. Unlike eccentric delusions of the anonymous patients of the past, Batiushkov's illness was treated by the Romantic doctor as individual, rooted in his personal life and poetic worldview. Doctor Dietrich even learned Russian in order to comprehend Batiushkov's poetry – the window into his soul. The diagnosis he formulated can be considered as a sad parable of the poet's existence:

> The essence of Batiushkov's mental illness lies in the limitless dominance of the power of imagination (imaginatio) over the other powers of his mind. As a result they are all slowed and suppressed, so that the intellect is in no condition to recognize the absurdity and groundlessness of those thoughts and images which parade before him in an endless colorful sequence . . . He lives only through dreams, through daydreams.[12]

Ironically, Batiushkov, who was no longer able to compose poems (with a very few, yet notable, exceptions), turned into a tragic parody of the Romantic poet-dreamer: a poor madman unaware of his immensely pitiful state. The question posed by the doctor in his diary (where is the borderline between poetic and mad dreaming, art and disease?) was central to the age of Romanticism with its enormous interest in dreams, somnambulism and various kinds of visionary experiences, "located on the night-side of human nature."[13] As a contemporary scholar observes, a considerable number of Romantic texts deal with the problem whether "casting the light of reason upon the night-sides of nature necessarily means overcoming darkness, translating something incomprehensible into human terms and destroying its original quality."[14] One cannot get rid of a feeling that while treating Batiushkov for madness, the rational and compassionate doctor envies his patient's ability to observe the endless parade of dreams.

Fear

Dr. Dietrich didn't cure the poet. The latter was brought back to Russia where he spent the remaining half of his life (his violent fits left him with time; his main occupation was drawing pictures, mostly on the same obsessive subject – beautiful landscapes with horses and ancient castles; he also composed a couple of poems, including a magnificent version of Horace's "Exegi monumentum," in which he presented himself as a defiant emperor of poetry, brother of Venus and servant of sacred Death, and which, it seems, does not make any sense at all in its weird combination of images and random literary and political allusions). His contemporaries still enjoyed his early works, but believed that he was dead (again, the association between madness and death is prominent in the cultural history of madness). Thus, in 1830 a Russian Romantic historian Mikhail Pogodin visited Batiushkov and described his state as a tragic warning for every poet and intellectual: "He lies there virtually motionless. Wild glances. Sometimes he'll wave an arm or squeeze some wax. My Lord! Where are his intellect and sensibility? He's only a body, barely alive."[15]

In 1847 Batiushkov was visited by the young man who drew the picture that we discussed in the beginning of this chapter. Here is the background story that grasps one of the moments of the madman's pitiful existence and narrates the "idea" of the drawing:

> Having finished his coffee, he stood and resumed pacing the hall, pausing by the window and gazing out onto the street, occasionally shrugging his shoulders and muttering to himself. His indistinct whisper was akin to a hurried prayer – and perhaps he really was praying, since every so often he would throw his head back and, as it seemed to me, look skyward and whisper 'Lord!' In one such instance, as he was standing by the window with his back to me, it came into my head to sketch him. I thought to call it *the faceless Batiushkov*, with his back turned to the viewer, so I took out a pencil and paper and started to outline his figure as quickly as I could. However it did not take long for him to notice, leading him to cast a series of anxious and disapproving glares in my direction. His eyes lit up with madness once again, and I was forced to abandon my effort.[16]

This telling account reveals a characteristic fear of madness which often accompanies a paramount interest in it. It's safer to portray the faceless Batiushkov, rather than look into his eyes. "Tell me, what in a madman makes the most terrible impression of madness for you?" – asked the twentieth-century Russian poet Osip Mandelstam. "The widened pupils – because they are unseeing, not focused on anything in particular, empty. The mad speeches – because in addressing you, the madman does not take you into account, as if he does not wish to acknowledge your very existence, as if he's absolutely uninterested in you. Mainly, we fear in the madman that eerie absolute indifference which he displays to us."[17]

It won't be an exaggeration to say that literature and art turn the mad to us and force us to look into their eyes. In other words, writers and artists give voice and image to the ones who are silenced and invisible.

161

Prayer

An image of the poor mad poet has become haunting in the history of Russian culture. In 1833, Batiushkov's younger friend Alexander Pushkin wrote a poem which was very likely a poetic response to Batiushkov's tragedy (Pushkin visited him in 1830; Batiushkov didn't recognize him).[18]

The poem – one of the most paradoxical in Pushkin's poetry and, perhaps, in the history of Western poetry about madness – confronts and rejects both rationalist and romantic visions of insanity:

God grant that I not lose my mind.
No, easier were the staff and bag;
No, easier toil and want,
It is not my reason
I treasure; not that with it
I would not gladly part:

Were they to leave me
At liberty, how eagerly would I
Make for the darkling wood!
In flaming frenzy would I sing,
Forget myself within a haze
Of shapeless, wondrous dreams.

And I would hark my fill of waves,
And I would gaze, with gladness filled,
Into the empty skies;
And strong were I, and free were I
Like to the whirlwind gashing fields,
[And] breaking forests down.

But here's the rub: go off your mind,
And men will dread you like the plague,
[And] straightway lock you up,
Will put the madman on a chain
And through the screen like some small beast,
Will come to harass you.

And in the night I shall not hear
The nightingale's clear voice,
Nor oak groves' murmurous rustle –
But my companions' cries,
And the night warders' curses,
And shrieks, and clanging chains.
[Transl. by Walter Arndt]

The poem is written in the form of the poet's quiet prayer (recall Berg's account of Batiushkov whispering a kind of prayer and Pogodin's appellation to the Lord). In the first stanza, the poet expresses his fear of madness, yet – and this is the first paradox of the poem – he acknowledges that he doesn't value sanity for its own sake. In the following stanzas, he fantasizes himself mad and summarizes a romantic myth of madness as a natural state, leaning to a total liberation from all social restrains, bordering on a sense of absolute happiness. To be sure, the elemental happiness of a madman is an old theme. It was discussed (and questioned) in one of the formative texts of Western literature of the eighteenth century – Goethe's preromantic novel *Sorrows of Young Werther*. In the late nineteenth century, a Russian artist, Vassily Perov, portrayed the "Blessed One" (a wandering madman reminding us of Pushkin's imaginary refugee) as innately associated with the natural forces:

Yet, Pushkin poses that this myth of poetic madness is nothing but an illusion. The "rub" is in the fact that there is no room for beauty, happiness, and sense of freedom in madness in this world. The absolute freedom, glorified by radical romanticists, is senseless (the skies are empty for the madman) and momentous. It inevitably ends with a dismal incarceration in the hellish cell of a madhouse.

Let us pause here for a while. The association between mad asylum and prison goes back to the period when mental institutions were conceived as means of isolating the mentally sick from rational society (the Age of Great Confinement, as Foucault labeled this period).[19] In the seventeenth century, madness "ceased to be the sign of another world [as it was, to an extent, in the Middle Ages and especially during the Renaissance];

Figure 8.4 Vassily Perov, *The Blessed One.* © SuperStock/Alamy.

it became the paradoxical manifestation of non-being" (109). If reason is everything, then negativity of reason, i.e., insanity, is nothing. It is useless, dangerous, immoral, and ugly. However, the public interest into the mad hidden behind the walls of an asylum did not vanish even in this period. In the so-called Age of Reason (seventeenth to eighteenth centuries), sane people paid money to see the inhabitants of Bedlam as animals in a zoo, and artists portrayed asylums' cells as collections of human follies.

The new vision of the madhouse as a powerful metaphor for the human world originates in the second half of the eighteenth century. The symbol of the madhouse effectively replaced the one of the ship of fools, discussed in Foucault's *Madness and Civilization* as a manifestation of the medieval attitude towards the insane, entrusted to the care of boatmen.[20] Since the Romantic age, the madhouse has become the symbolic site of human delusions and spiritual suffering, which mirrors and exposes the passions and violence of the world outside of the asylum.

It has also become a testing ground of various artistic philosophies and social and political commentaries presented in different forms of art and different genres, from Hogarth's "Rake in Bedlam" and Goya's "Madhouse in Saragossa" to Dostoevsky's and Chekhov's stories and novels, to Maeterlinck's plays, to Philippe de Broca's witty *King of Hearts* ("Le roi de Coeur") or Forman's tragic *One Flew Over the Cuckoo's Nest*. In this context, Pushkin's poetic prayer is one of the first (and finest) works in the history of Russian literature which presents the cell of a mad asylum as a spiritual incarceration imposed by society: "The sounds of the madhouse and the prison replace the sounds of nightingales and oak groves. Nature and poetry are lost more irrevocably than before, replaced by even more oppressive social institutions for dealing with society's outcasts." There will be no poetry in insanity.[21]

It is noteworthy that the mode of prayer, favored by numerous Romantic poets, is deeply rooted in the Western history of insanity. The latter was originally interpreted as a divine punishment and the restoration of sanity was attributed to divine mercy (in the Middle Ages a prayer, along with holy water, was one of the common treatments for the

Figure 8.5 Francisco de Goya, *The Madhouse*. © Fine Art Images/Heritage Images/Getty Images.

mentally sick). As Sander Gilman summarizes this vision in his illuminating *Seeing the Insane: A Cultural History of Madness and Art in the Western World,* "the fool as madman is not merely ill, he is ill through denying God. His madness is thus a sign of this denial."[22] However, in Pushkin's poem the Lord is prayed to keep the poet sane not for the sake of reason as a divine gift but rather out of fear of losing freedom and dignity. (In this sense, one can call his poem a response to King Lear's fearful prayer: "O, let me not be mad, not mad, sweet heaven/Keep me in temper: I would not be mad!" [act 1, scene 5]).

The poem concludes with a sober and sorrowful vision of man's plight in the world. Yet, this sad revelation is crystallized in the form of a marvelous, sophisticatedly ordered (harmonious) poem. As a contemporary interpreter suggests, the poem represents the imaginary journey of a poet into the realm of madness, conducted under the control of his reason and mastery.[23] This is in fact what makes the best literary and artistic representations of insanity different from any clinical discussion of madness. One can say that in culture, madness is presented as an imaginary liminal state that is meaningful and controlled by aesthetic means (forms) of the respective art. Writing on or depicting madness is an attempt to find a creative balance between reason and unreason, art and nature, poetic imagination and the uncontrolled dreams of a madman.[24] It also teaches us to become slightly mad in order to remain human.

Tradition

Madness is an integral part of Batiushkov's legend in Russian poetry, which is, in turn, a part of the Romantic myth of the mad artist developed in Western art in the nineteenth century – Hölderlin, Edgar Allan Poe, Dante Gabriel Rossetti, Schumann – and canonized in the Age of Modernism, with its obsessive interest in mysticism and occultism, dreams, and paranormal states as conditions of supreme knowledge (van Gogh, Nijinsky, Klimt, Vrubel). These figures were interpreted by contemporaries as both enlightened geniuses and martyrs of their unbridled fantasy.

The tradition behind this myth is ancient and twofold. The "dark" part of it originates from a vision of madness as God's punishment and is closely associated with the themes of sin, rebellion against the patriarchal power, curse, and shame, as evidenced in the Bible or the ancient Greek tragedy. Yet, it is also rooted in the ancient debates on creative madness, which characterizes the chosen ones ("poetry," Aristotle asserted, "demands a man with special gift for it, or else one with a touch of madness in him"[25]). According to Plato, madness can be either base or divine. The philosopher distinguished four types of the divine insane: prophets, philosophers, poets, and lovers. Later on, other types have been added to the list, such as the revolutionary (Milton's Satan was one of the formative representative of this type in literature) and the scientist (how many contemporary books, movies, and cartoons deal with this type!).

Historians of art argue that the vision of madness as punishment prevailed in the Middle Ages. In turn, Plato's classification of the divinely mad was resurrected by the Italian humanists in the fifteenth century. Yet, even in the humanists' interpretation the state of divine madness, characteristic of the intellectuals and lovers, was portrayed as both dignified and terrifying. Consider Albrecht Dürer's artistic manifesto *Melencolia I* (the word "melancholy," originated from the ancient theory of four bodily humors [liquids], was used as a scientific name for insanity until the late nineteenth century):

Figure 8.6 Albrecht Dürer, *Melencolia I*. © Wellcome Library, London.

We see a winged figure, surrounded by numerous symbols of the arts and sciences and plunged into a state of deep depression. It is certainly not a representational kind of art, not a portrait, but rather a visualization of the inner processes occurring in the mind of an intellectual. It is psychological and symbolic, personal and universal, analytical and imaginary. In this engraving, man's mental state is reenacted as a spiritual drama: "with hair hanging down unkempt, and her gaze, thoughtful and sad, fixed on a point in the distance, she keeps watch, withdrawn from the world, under a darkening sky, while the bat begins its circling flight"[26]; "a genius with wings that she will not unfold, with a key that she will not use to unlock, with laurels on her brow, but with no smile of victory."[27]

This tragic vision of divine madness was absorbed by the Romantic poets who also inherited and developed the introspective method (an "inner portrait"), discovered by Humanist artists. There is a direct lineage between Dürer's allegorical "mental portrait" and Romantic and, later, Modernist artistic experiments in visualizing (or verbalizing) the inner workings of man's mind in different genres, ranging from Edgar Allan Poe's poems and tales to Faulkner's *Sound and Fury*, from Goya's *Dream of Reason* to Malevich's *Black Square* and Ron Howard's *Beautiful Mind*, etc.

Meaning

I chose Batiushkov's story not because (to paraphrase Pushkin's words) I treasure it so much, but rather for its almost parabolic implications within the cultural history of madness. It manifests a peculiar Romantic moment in the history of Western literature and the arts, characterized by the reinterpretation of madness as a disease, rather than a crime, the radical turn toward man's psyche, and individualization and aestheticization of the mad as modern-day heroes – radical dreamers, rebels, sufferers, and carriers of unique meaningful experience which sane people are unable to obtain. From the Romantic vantage point we can observe the multi-century tradition in its complex richness.

In conclusion, let me pose the question of what makes insanity so fascinating for Western writers and artists up until our days. There are certainly many reasons for this attraction (to be sure, writers and artists have always been interested in eccentrics and outcasts) but the main ones, in my opinion, include the following:

1   As a cultural trope, madness – in its numerous manifestations – has been a magisterial theme since the Romantic age (roughly, the 1790s) which reveals what Theodore Ziolkowski wisely calls "the natural rapport between literature and psychiatry."[28] However, doctors and writers have different (yet intersecting) agendas. Thus, Dostoevsky, famous for the depth of his psychological analysis (characteristically, Freud and Otto Rank illustrated their theories with Dostoevsky's literary cases), hated when he was referred to as a psychologist. Instead, he tellingly called himself "a realist in the higher sense," with a man's soul, rather than the workings of one's mind, as his major theme and hero.

2   In literary and artistic visions, madness is not literal, but metaphorical and meaningful, and a mad person is not a patient to be cured (or locked up in an asylum), but a living problem to be noticed and presented in the most effective (suggestive) way in order to explore the ethical, aesthetic, social, political, methodological, gender, linguistic, and metaphysical foundations (and limitations) of the man and society of a given period. What does a frightful delusion of Hoffmann's Nathaniel ("The Sandman") tell us about the existence of evil? Where does this evil come from? Why were his rationalistic, good-natured friends unable to save him? What are the connections between his "illness" and the supernatural, between madness and secret knowledge, imagination and terror? What is insanity? Is it a disease of the soul, the spirit, or the body? Is the madman a useless creature in a "normal" society or is he a genius who sees the mystery concealed from other people? Is there happiness in this knowledge? Where is the borderline between imagination and insanity? What is an insane asylum – a hospital or a prison? Who is really mad – those locked in a hospital, or those who seem "normal" but lead terrible and senseless lives? Is the mad asylum a collection of ravings and delusions that scare the reasonable man, or is it an awful mirror of the "normal" world, reflecting the furious passions, the morbid lust of pleasures, and the narcissism and ambitions of "normal" people? Can unruly madness be captured by means of language, music, or image? These or similar questions have constantly preoccupied writers and artists.

3 In cultural interpretation, madness is not a state but a story. It has its fictional prehistory (a hidden past) and inner plot driven by external and internal causes. The development of new narrative forms of the nineteenth century is closely connected to the rise of modern psychiatry. According to Ziolkowski, it was the genre of a novel that "provided an ideal opportunity not just to portray figures teetering on the edge of madness for the propagandistic purposes of education, but, more importantly, to explore the sources and causes of madness, to chart its growth, and to plot its function within the total context of a fully developed character."[29] How did it happen that Hermann, the paradoxical rationalistic gambler of Pushkin's "Queen of Spades," went mad? What is the secret of the mad woman in the attic? What are the sources and causes of Mr. Goliadkin's (the protagonist of Dostoevsky's *Double*) schizophrenia?

4 It is also a powerful visual image: every madman or madwoman has his or her own individual face which symbolically depicts a deep problem inherent in many "normal" people and society. Take, for example, Vassily Perov's image of the blessed one (a village idiot, filled with gladness, who is walking towards the viewer without "noticing" her) as a symbol of Russia's restless spirit of the troubled 1870s. It has its own musical rhythm and program. Consider Igor Stravinsky's "mad dances" in *The Rite of Spring* or the Dionysian "mad techniques" invented by the famous ballet dancer Nijinsky (who lost his mind at the peak of his career). It has its own (alternative or trans-rational) method, as evidenced by the works of such different authors as Lewis Carroll, Velimir Khlebnikov, or Samuel Beckett.[30]

5 Madness certainly attracts men of art due to its humanistic overtones (madmen are our suffering brothers and sisters; in the mad, Homo sapiens confronts her frightful reflection). Consider the following diary entry of Gogol's mad clerk (an innovative dark parody of a lofty Romantic madman), dated *34 March. February, 349.* "Why do they torture me? What do they want from one so wretched as myself? What can I give them? I possess nothing. I cannot bear all their tortures; my head aches as though everything were turning round in a circle. Save me! Carry me away! Give me three steeds swift as the wind! Mount your seat, coachman, ring bells, gallop horses, and carry me straight out of this world. Farther, ever farther, till nothing more is to be seen!"[31]

6 As Aristotle famously observed, there is a close link between madness and imagination and creativity (after all, these stories, paintings, and operas mirror the artists' defiant endeavors to undermine the universal claims of reason and established tradition and to explore new methods of creation, usually considered as crazy by contemporaries). In this context, Romantic madness (take Coleridge's visionary *Ancient Mariner* as an example) defies neo-classical treatments of insanity (all those mad tyrants and lovers who ruin themselves and their realms unable to restrain their passions by means of the sacred reason). In turn, the Realist Madness – mundane and caused by social and biological causes – debunks the Romantic one, and the Modernist Madness, with all its artistic experiments and glorification of the irrational, mysterious side of human life, effectively rejects the "scientific" Realist visions. Perhaps, portrayal of "madness" is one of the most powerful triggers and indicators of cultural development.

7 Last but not least, men of art have been obsessed with an unrealizable, powerful desire to grasp – at whatever cost – the elusive and dangerous matter that defies any rational approach, to reach the bottom line without crossing it, to take a look into the eyes of the Other-Inside-Of-Myself, to learn from it, and to hear and articulate "companions' cries, and the night warders' curses, and shrieks, and clanging chains." Yet, as a literary historian of madness justly observes, "artistic genius may cross over the borders of madness, but it remains productive only if it can return again," only if the artist, "gone forth on a mental journey of exploration, would come back and tell us what it was like in the realm beyond the borders of rationality."[32]

And it is in this hazardous quest ("for many there is no return") that writers and artists successfully compete with other experts in man's psyche, such as priests, mystics, doctors, philosophers, neuroscientists, and interrogators.

Notes

1 In this chapter, I focus on artistic usages of madness in the West, rather than works produced by patients in psychiatric clinics, the topic brilliantly presented and discussed in Lucienne Peiry's *Art Brut: The Origins of Outsider Art* (Paris: Flammarion, 2001).
2 This description is a summary of the observations made by my colleagues and students whom I asked to describe the picture without any knowledge of who was portrayed on it.
3 Norbert Wolf, *Caspar David Friedrich: 1774–1840: the Painter of Stillness* (Cologne: Taschen, 2003), 12.
4 Frederick Burwick, *Poetic Madness and the Romantic Imagination* (University Park: Pennsylvania State University Press, 1996), 112–125.
5 N.M. Karamzin, *Letters of a Russian Traveller, 1789–1790* (New York: Columbia University Press, 1957), 284–7.
6 On the Sonnenstein "euthanasia" facility, see Boris Böhm, *Geschichte des Sonnensteins und seiner Festung* (Dresden: Tierbs, 1994); Robert Jay Lifton, *The Nazi Doctors: Medical Killing and the Psychology of Genocide* (New York: Basic Books, 2000), 142–3, 278.
7 Michel Foucault, *Madness and Civilization: A History of Insanity in the Age of Reason* (Psychology Press, 2001), 109.
8 The term "night-side," originally used in astronomy to designate "those parts of a planet's surface which are turned away from the sun," was applied to psychology by a German author Gotthilf Schubert in his treatise *Aspects of the Night-Side of Science* (1808).
9 Anton Dietrich, "O bolezni russkogo imperatorskogo nadvornogo sovetnika i dvorianina gospodina Konstantina Batiushkova" (1829). L.N. Maikov, *Batiushkov, ego zhizn' i sochineniia* (St. Petersburg: A.F. Marks, 1896), 504. Quoted in Mikhail Epstein, "Methods of Madness and Madness as a Method" in *Madness and the Mad in Russian Culture*, ed. Angela Britlinger and Ilya Vinitsky, (Toronto, Buffalo, London: University of Toronto Press, 2007), 269–70.
10 Compare the following description of the crazy patients of Bedlam in a Russian account of the late eighteenth century: "Many of the men made us laugh. One imagines that he is a cannon and keeps firing charges through his mouth. Another grunts like a bear and walks on all fours. The maniacs are kept apart, some chained to the wall. One of them keeps laughing and calls people to him, saying, "I am happy. Draw near I shall breathe bliss into you." But he bites anyone who comes near him" [Karamzin, 284–7].
11 As I mentioned elsewhere, in many pre-nineteenth-century medical books and dictionaries this story (along with stories about men who thought they were urinals) was used as an exemplary case of the melancholy disorder. Ilya Vinitsky, "A Cheerful Empress and Her Gloomy Critics" in *Madness and the Mad in Russian Culture*, 28. To be sure, tests of

urine occupied an important place in medical treatments of the insane, with the case of King George III as one of the most striking. See, Lawrence Babb, *The Elizabethan Malady: A Study of Melancholia in English Literature from 1580 to 1642* (East Lansing, MI: Michigan State College Press, 1959), 43.

12 Quoted in Epstein, 269–70.

13 Consider in G. Schubert's *History of the Soul* (1830): "Dreams are a way of reckoning and combining that you and I do not understand; a higher kind of algebra, briefer and easier than ours, which only the hidden poet knows how to manipulate in his mind." See Monika Schmitz-Emans, "Night-sides of existence: Madness, dream, etc." in *Romantic Prose Fiction*, ed. Gerald Gillespie, Manfred Engel, Bernard Dietrerle, (Amsterdam: John Benjamins, 2008), 139.

14 Ibid.

15 Quoted in Epstein, p. 268.

16 S.P. Shevyrev, *Poezdka v Kirillo-Belozerskii monastyr'* (Moscow: Univ. tip., 1850), 114.

17 Quoted in Epstein, p. 268–9.

18 In the early 1830s, Pushkin, who was often seen by his contemporaries as the poet of supreme balance and harmony, was fascinated with the problem of mental illness. In 1833, he wrote three works in which madness plays an uncharacteristically central role, a fantastic tale about a gambler "The Queen of Spades," a historical epic poem *The Bronze Horseman*, and a poem "God grant that I not lose my mind . . ." In each of these works, madness is open to different, often equally valid interpretations and approaches. See Gary Rosenshield, *Pushkin and the Genres of Madness. The Masterpieces of 1833* (Madison, Wisconsin: University of Wisconsin Press, 2003).

19 According to Foucault, "Madness in the classical period ceased to be the sign of another world" and "became the paradoxical manifestation of non-being . . . by confinement, madness is acknowledged to be nothing" (Foucault, 109). As Paul Youngquist comments in *Madness and Blake's Myth* (University Park: Pennsylvania State University Press, 2010), "if the difference between the mad and the sane is in part an institutional one, then those possessing the keys to Bethlehem determine its population" (25). In this context, it is worthy to mention that madness has been used by the governmental "key-keepers" as an effective way to discredit and/or isolate their ideological and political opponents, from Marquis de Sade to Leo Tolstoy and Soviet dissidents of the 1960 to 1980s. Vinitsky, "A Cheerful Empress and Her Gloomy Critics," 37; Sidney Bloch and Peter Reddaway, *Psychiatric Terror: How Soviet Psychiatry Is Used to Suppress Dissent* (New York: Basic Books, 1977), 251–2.

20 "So the ship of fools was heavily loaded with meaning, and clearly carried a great social force . . . The madman on his crazy boat sets sail for the other world, and it is from the other world that he comes when he disembarks. This enforced navigation is both rigorous division and absolute Passage, serving to underline in real and imaginary terms the liminal situation of the mad in medieval society. It was a highly symbolic role, made clear by the mental geography involved, where the madman was confined at the gates of the cities. His expulsion was his confinement, and if he had no prison other than the threshold itself he was still detained at this place of passage. In a highly symbolic position he is placed on the inside of the outside, or vice versa . . . A prisoner in the midst of the ultimate freedom [the sea], on the most open road at all, chained solidly to the infinite crossroads. He is the Passenger par excellence, the prisoner of the passage. It is not known where he will land, and when he lands, he knows not whence he came. His truth and his home are the barren wasteland between two lands that can never be his own. Perhaps this ritual lies at the origins of the imaginary kinship common throughout the culture of the west . . . the link between water and madness is deeply rooted in the dream of the Western man" (Foucault, 10–11).

21 Gary Rosenshield, *Pushkin and the Genres of Madness*, 71.

22 Sander L. Gilman and Eric T. Carlson, *Seeing the Insane: A Cultural History of Madness and Art in the Western World* (Lincoln, NE: University of Nebraska Press, 1982), 8.

23 See Rosenschield, 81–82.
24 As Mikhail Epstein writes, "To part with one's reason, but not irredeemably, to lose one's mind within the limits of reason itself, to let it roam, but keep it on a leash: this is the salvatory outcome suggested by Pushkin's 'dialectic' of creative madness" (281).
25 Aristotle, *Poetics*, 1455a.
26 Raymond Klibansky, Erwin Panofsky, Fritz Saxl, *Saturn and Melancholy: Studies in the History of Natural Philosophy, Religion, and Art* (New York: Basic Books, 1964), 320.
27 Ibid., 312.
28 Theodore Ziolkowski, *German Romanticism and Its Institutions* (Princeton: Princeton University Press, 1992), 155.
29 Ibid., 156.
30 See Mikhail Epstein, "Methods of Madness and Madness as a Method," 263–82.
31 Nikolai Gogol (Translated by Claud Field), *The Mantle and Other Stories: Russian Literature* (The Floating Press, 2011), 108.
32 Burwick, 17.

9

PSYCHIATRY AND ITS VISUAL CULTURE IN THE MODERN ERA

Andreas Killen

The advent of the modern era in medicine brought with it new ways of observing, recording, and classifying. This was true in all fields and psychiatry was certainly no exception to this rule. One of the hallmarks of the history of psychiatry since the Enlightenment concerns the proliferation of images of madness and the deep faith that the profession placed in such images. This faith took many forms.

One expression of it may be seen on the occasion when, in the 1881 trial of Charles Guiteau for the assassination of President James Garfield, the psychiatrist Edward C. Spitzka took the stand to provide testimony concerning the defendant's mental state. Pronouncedly hereditarian in his views about the origins of mental illness, Spitzka had already made known the fact that he had diagnosed Guiteau as insane on the basis of a photograph that he had seen of the defendant. He later fleshed out this view following his actual examination of Guiteau, yet under cross-examination he repeatedly returned to this initial, hastily formed, yet utterly unshakeable conviction concerning the assassin's "moral monstrosity." The examination merely confirmed what, to his practised eye, had been obvious from glancing at the image reproduced in an illustrated weekly: namely, that the assassin's insanity was plainly visible in the numerous facial and cranial stigmata that bore witness to the hereditary condition that afflicted Guiteau and that were captured so faithfully by the photographer's camera.[1]

This vignette illustrates well the faith that psychiatrists in the modern era have placed in the power of visual images to help render judgment on matters of insanity. Yet this faith was not an untroubled one. If the Guiteau case famously became an important test for the insanity defense, it was also a test for a particular kind of knowledge claim anchored in the veracity of mechanically produced imagery. The authority based on such images was not uncontested: Spitzka's testimony proved, in the event, not decisive, for the court did not accept his opinion that Guiteau was not responsible for his actions. It may be speculated that his testimony was weakened by the fact that the image was not a scientific one; yet, as other practitioners would often discover, even the most rigorously controlled images did not always speak for themselves; nor did they always remain under the profession's control. The complex dynamic hinted at here raises many questions for the scholar: what was the basis for the psychiatric profession's deep investment in visual imagery? What kind of work were the psychiatric photograph and other forerunners of today's imaging methods expected to perform? How did the knowledge claims attached to such images function, both in a medical context and in the public realm? What sorts of wider social and cultural determinants mark this process?

Over the past several decades scholars seeking answers to such questions have paid increasing attention to the profusion of images that has accompanied the profession's development in the modern era. Long before today's fMRIs and other brain scanning techniques, whose recent rapid proliferation has no doubt played a role in stimulating this interest, the history of the profession was marked by an intense production of images of madness – whether painted or produced by means of lithography, photography, or the moving image. It should not surprise us that the profession invested so much in the power of images, for in the days prior to the advent of modern imaging techniques, they seemed to offer one of the most promising means of capturing and making real the elusive nature of mental illness. Nevertheless the nature of this promise and of the explanatory power that came to be attached to certain kinds of images requires consideration.

In the modern era, images of madness have been used to produce knowledge of disease pictures, to awaken understanding and sympathy for patients and for their physicians and caretakers, as well as to communicate knowledge of reforms and warnings about particular kinds of health risks. They have also figured prominently in the development of typological systems that identified classes of illness and in some cases entire categories of patients, categories whose hallmark (as Spitzka stressed in his testimony) was the physical stigmata they bore. Scholars have probed such images for insights into central aspects of the history of the field – in particular, what they reveal about the construction of disease pictures and the constitution of medical authority – and in doing so have shown that images of the mad occupy a central place in histories of psychiatric professionalization and knowledge formation.

At the same time, such images have also played a significant role in various counternarratives concerning the rise of the psychiatric profession in the modern era. Histories of psychoanalysis, for instance, have routinely taken one of their points of departure from Freud's famous account of Charcot as a "*visuel*," a "seer," in contrast to his own privileging of the dialogue between patient and doctor – an account that directly challenged the epistemological claims for the power of the image.[2] Similarly, feminist scholars have noted that in many images of madness, the subject is often a woman; and citing the role of such images in some of the key creation myths of the profession, they have seized on this fact to challenge central aspects of its history.[3]

The typological systems referred to above have also entered the historiography of the profession as a reflection of its darkest potentials – the role that such visual systems have often played in the stigmatization, marginalization, and persecution of the mad. Drawing attention to this fact, scholarly accounts influenced by the anti-psychiatric movement of the 1960s further called into question the professed naturalness of the profession's systems of classification and in so doing have turned the alliance forged between psychiatric medicine and modern visual media, so to speak, on its head. At the same time this scholarly trend has found numerous echoes in the cultural realm, where images of mad or transgressive science have long been a favorite motif. Such portrayals interrogate both the authority of the profession and the truth-claims attached to scientific image-making; in addition, they often explore the thinness of the line that separates patient from doctor.

173

Any attempt to come to grips with this complex and often contradictory history must thus begin by asking: what has been the purpose of all this image-making? At the same time, it must be asked: why has there been so much recent interest in this phenomenon? This latter development seems to reflect several distinct scholarly trends: 1) the so-called "visual turn" in the humanities; 2) growing interest in processes of scientific knowledge formation, in particular the role that images have played in the historical development of key concepts like objectivity, and in the way that visual technologies like photography have been bound up with the shifting epistemologies of modern science and medicine; and 3) lastly, interest in the broader social and cultural contexts in which modern psychiatry has operated.[4]

One of the assumptions that defines scholarship on the visual culture of modern psychiatry is that this culture represents a major departure in the field's larger history. To be sure, the pre-modern era had its own extensive visual tradition with regards to madness, a tradition that found iconic expression in an image like Albrecht Dürer's engraving *Melancholia* (1514), discussed earlier in this volume by Ilya Vinitsky. Yet the nineteenth-century proliferation of such imagery and the expectations attached to it were, in both quantitative and qualitative terms, a new phenomenon. Physicians of this era could not only call upon new techniques of image-making, but they also placed peculiar trust in the power of images to help them establish the truth of madness in all its manifold forms. From the 1820s onward lithography, photography, and eventually cinematography contributed to the production of a vast archive of images of the insane. The appearance of these techniques also gave rise to a community of experts, whose jurisdiction over madness rested in part on its claim to be able both to produce and to extract from such images reliable truths about the individuals or disease pictures captured in them.

Thus – to return to our earlier example – when the psychiatrist Spitzka was called upon to provide expert testimony in the Guiteau trial, it was only natural that he in turn called upon the authority of a photograph of the defendant as a key piece of evidence. The performative aspect of this claim to professional expertise should be noted here, for in entering the proceedings at this juncture, Spitzka was pitting his credentials against those of the more conservative alienists who still dominated the landscape of American mental medicine. So confident was Spitzka of the truths of physiognomy and of his own trained powers of observation that his lengthy examination of Guiteau (whose head, he opined, displayed "asymmetrical, rhombo-cephalic features") was only needed to confirm the snap judgment about Guiteau's hereditary insanity that he had earlier arrived at on the basis of a photograph.[5] Spitzka's claim speaks volumes for the consolidation of an emerging belief in the photographic medium's ability to capture objective and reliable signs of madness. The fact that he could assert his conclusions so forcefully also reflected his training in European centers of medical learning like Vienna, where he had been exposed to new hereditarian doctrines as well as to a increasingly widely circulated catalog of physiognomic imagery.[6] The role of such imagery in supporting professional claims to authority is illustrated in the following statement by Krafft-Ebing in 1879: "It may be stated that every psychopathic state, like the physiologic state of emotion, has its own peculiar facial expression and general manner of movement which, for the experienced, on superficial observation, make a probable diagnosis possible."[7]

Figure 9.1 The assassin Charles Guiteau. © Hulton Archive/Stringer/Getty Images.

By the 1880s this visual catalog had a well-established history behind it. As Sander Gilman has shown, the iconographic traditions of nineteenth-century psychiatry breathed the spirit of a new empiricism that emerged out of the Enlightenment. Phillipe Pinel's 1801 *Treatise on Insanity* signaled this new trend by including several plates illustrating the conditions of idiocy and mania. However it was with his student Jean-Etienne Dominique Esquirol that the visual representation of mental illness took on real significance, a development that directly reflected the impact of new techniques of mechanical reproduction. From the 1820s onwards Esquirol used visual documentation in his published papers, and his 1838 treatise *Mental Illness as Considered in Medical, Hygienic, and Medico-legal Reports*, which represented the first atlas of insanity, relied heavily on lithographs to represent the cases discussed in its pages. These works defined a new place for the visual representation of mental illness.

A further breakthrough occurred in the 1850s with the introduction of photography into psychiatry. Starting in 1852 the Englishman Hugh Diamond undertook the studies that would make his name as the "father of psychiatric photography."[8] Diamond articulated what can be taken as a central credo of the new faith: "The Photographer secures with unerring accuracy the external phenomena of each person as the really certain indication of internal derangement, and exhibits to the eye the well-known sympathy which exists between the diseased brain and the organs and features of

Figure 9.2 A manic patient (Esquirol). © Wellcome Library, London.

the body."[9] As formulated here, the new technology of photography and the nascent science of psychiatry came together to form a highly consequential partnership in the quest for reliable representations of disease states that were by their nature difficult to describe. It was in fact in the field of psychiatry, as Gilman stresses, that the first systematic use of clinical photography occurred. Diamond identified three principal uses of photography: 1) record-keeping; 2) archival (in case of later readmission or criminality); and 3) treatment. If the first two uses seem straightforward enough, the third requires explanation. It was Diamond's view that documenting the progression of an illness such as puerperal mania through its different phases represented not simply a significant gain in knowledge, but that this had therapeutic value: showing the patient images of herself taken during these phases could be used to enlist her own self-curative powers.

Diamond's photographs served as a direct inspiration to many leading physicians of his time. John Connolly's 1858 treatise "The Physiognomy of Insanity" stressed the particular advantages of the new medium over previous methods of reproducing the distinctive expressive features of madness. Within a year of the appearance of Diamond's book, Benedict Morel had published his own atlas of the physiognomy of the insane, using lithographic reproductions of photographs, in his landmark

Treatise on Degeneration. In the belief that the insane formed a separate category of beings, Morel claimed that these images demonstrated "the invariable, distinct, and immutable characteristics which distinguish the natural race from its degenerate variants."[10] Whereas Diamond claimed that his images could be used to help restore patients to themselves, and then to society, Morel's images contributed to the cultural construction of the mad as irredeemably other.

From this point onward, scientific endeavors to make madness knowable were increasingly bound up with producing images of it. Morel's *Treatise*, which we shall come back to later, formed simply one tributary to a tremendous flood of imagery that crested towards the end of the nineteenth century in what Georges Didi-Hubermann has called the "great optical machine" established at Jean-Martin Charcot's Salpetriere clinic.[11] That these images were increasingly produced through mechanical means identifies them as an expression of wider developments. On the one hand, this tendency corresponded to what Lisa Cartwright has called "the nineteenth-century sciences' fascination with visibility;" on the other, as Lorraine Daston and Peter Galison have shown in their history of the shifting epistemologies of modern science, the reliance on photography conformed to the emergence of a new ideal of "mechanical objectivity" that strove to standardize the object under observation through the use of purely mechanical means, ostensibly free of all traces of intervention on the part of the observer.[12]

Amidst this flood of mechanically produced imagery there was, to be sure, still space for older representational traditions. Just at the time Charcot was beginning to devote himself to his photographic studies, Tony Robert-Fleury produced in 1876 one of the iconic modern images of madness, his painting "Pinel Freeing the Insane;" a decade later André Brouillet followed suit with his painting of one of Charcot's famous Tuesday lectures, "A Clinical Lesson at the Salpetriere" (1887). But while these paintings took on the task of self-consciously capturing crucial moments in the profession's history – its foundation-myths – they also underscore the division of labor that had emerged within the field. It was the camera that assumed the crucial function of producing new knowledge in psychiatry, specifically knowledge of disease pictures such as hysteria. As one of Charcot's followers put it, "The camera was as crucial for the study of hysteria as the microscope was to histology."[13]

As this statement indicates, the turn to photography was patterned very much after the example of the life sciences, whose research agendas had been utterly transformed in previous decades under the impact of a host of new instruments and methods of observation. In similar fashion, reliance on photography became integral to research within the still nascent fields of psychiatry and neurology. At the most fundamental level it promised to answer the problem of knowledge confronting this field – its effort to acquire the status of a true science and distance itself from an earlier pre-scientific era, an effort so often frustrated by the object of its expertise: madness itself. What was it? How was it defined? How stable were these definitions? In the belief that photography might hold the answer to these fundamental questions, practitioners embraced it with a singular fervor. Visual media promised to help resolve what Alison Winter calls major "evidentiary problems in the sciences of mind" – to give these a sound epistemic basis in a context in which the mistrust of doctors towards patients' self-reporting was heightened by the inherently problematic nature of the mad-person's statements.[14]

Nowhere can this process be better observed than in the late nineenth-century medical encounter with hysteria; an encounter mediated in fundamental ways by photography. It was no accident that hysteria became a favorite subject of the psychiatric camera, for here the field was confronted by a disease defined by its theatricality – a disease often confused with other illnesses like epilepsy, on the one hand, but also one that routinely evoked the suspicion of simulation or hypochondria on the other. In the photographic studio created under the direction of Albert Londe, Charcot and his pupils produced thousands of images drawn from the Salpetriere's "great museum of hysteria." They then used these to draw conclusions about the course and nature of the hysteric attack. Distilling from the "super-abundance of hysterical symptoms" an "orderly sequence of photographs" enabled him to impose on hysteria a stable form.[15] Photographic studies thus naturalized the disease picture associated with this enigmatic syndrome and – at least in a provisional way – emancipated it from the shadow of malingering. This was a significant achievement: in doing so, as Freud would later write, Charcot made hysteria "real." Yet it came at a certain price, for Charcot was categorical in affirming that the will of the hysteric patient counted for nothing.[16] The photographic construction of hysteria as authentic malady could only occur at the cost of silencing the patient.

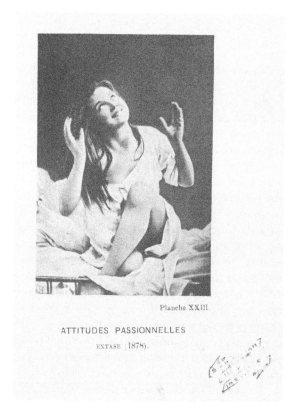

Planche XXIII

ATTITUDES PASSIONNELLES

EXTASE (1878).

Figure 9.3 Charcot's patient Albertine. © Wellcome Library, London.

The case of Charcot may seem to suggest that in certain respects to be a psychiatrist in the modern era meant to be a master of processes of image-making. Yet if the nineteenth-century culture of psychiatric image-making may be said to have reached its moment of triumph with Charcot and his students Richer and Londe, it also reached a moment of crisis. This crisis had already taken shape in other contexts – for instance, in the growing reservations expressed by Charles Darwin concerning the unreliability of photography in fixing human facial expression in a scientifically meaningful way. Charcot himself seems to have remained impervious to such doubts, yet by the 1890s the disease picture he had so laboriously constructed had come under sustained attack. However spectacular Charcot's demonstrations and the images that flowed from his clinic, it did not escape contemporaries' notice that the process of making hysterical symptoms visible often required manipulation on his part. Critics also voiced suspicions that these images had been produced in a hot-house of suggestion and were therefore unreliable. This critique, begun in the 1890s, was renewed much later in the 1980s by a generation of scholars informed by psychoanalytic, feminist, or other theoretical perspectives. Critics like Daphne de Marneffe and Elaine Showalter implicated the Charcotian photographic enterprise in a power dynamic that denied female patients agency or any real hope of treatment. They also challenged the camera's implicit claims to objectivity, showing how the somatic language of hysteria was one that patients became conditioned to speak, molding their symptoms to the needs of the camera in what became a kind of mutually staged spectacle or co-production.[17]

That this dynamic turns out to have been a far from stable one was something that, again, was not lost on contemporaries. Even in the face of mounting recognition of the medium's technical and other limitations, the photograph, as Alan Sekula writes, nevertheless continued to operate as "the image of scientific truth."[18] Yet persistent questions about the reliability of such images ensured that the twentieth century would be marked by a certain anxiety about the status of image making and its place in securing scientific knowledge and professional status. As Daston and Galison have argued, this heralded a wider shift in the status of mechanical objectivity as scientific ideal.[19]

The need to re-stabilize the culture of scientific image-making was further complicated by growing recognition of the way that, in escaping the confines of the clinic and entering into wider public circulation, medical imagery began to produce a variety of unanticipated effects. As Rae Beth Gordon has written, the fin-de-siècle cabaret and other popular performance venues offer much evidence of a convergence or inter-meshing of neurological and cultural languages of the body. At the same time the image of the doctor took on new and unintended associations and meanings; in many popular films around 1900, doctors are at work on their patients, hypnotizing, magnetizing, and performing experiments on them.[20] Many of these issues would resurface in the medical appropriation of the moving image.

As had earlier been the case with photography, psychiatrists and their neurological counterparts were quick to seize upon the potential of the cinematic medium. The first medical film in Germany was produced by the young neurologist Paul Schuster at Berlin's Charité hospital in 1897. The timing is significant, since it followed by one year the creation of the first German department of neurology under Hamburg's Max

Nonne, a figure who twenty years later would go on to produce an important example of wartime medical filmmaking. The turn to cinematography reflected neurology's status as a fledgling discipline that sought to position itself within a rapidly changing medical landscape in which technology was identified with scientific authority and progress. Schuster filmed several patients in the hospital's clinic, using the resulting footage to analyze the "movement-complexes" associated with disorders such as syphilis, multiple sclerosis, and epilepsy.[21] As Cartwright has written, cinematic frame analysis of patients' movements made it possible for clinicians to make differential diagnoses on the basis of differences in these movements that were undetectable to the naked eye.[22] Schuster later reported that he also adopted film to facilitate the demonstration and instruction of "theoretical questions" by means of moving images, independent of what he called the hospital's clinical "material" (i.e., patients). Such demonstrations would, he hoped, become the basis for creating a medical film archive encompassing most known diseases.

Many practitioners in the fields of neurology and psychiatry subsequently took up cinematographic studies in the conviction that that they opened up, as one put it, "a wealth of absolutely new facts."[23] Presentation of these facts in the form of motion picture screenings became a standard feature of medical congresses from the turn of the century on. This development really came into its own after the First World War, when neuropsychiatry became the medical specialty in which film production developed most extensively in Germany.[24] A key figure in this process was the Giessen psychiatrist Robert Sommer. In 1899 Sommer cited the enormous contribution made by Charcot's and Richer's *Nouvelle Icononographie de la Salpetriere* in establishing a new standard of objectivity in psychiatric observation. In Sommer's mind, photography had enabled the profession to move beyond the written case record and to largely free itself from "the interpretive problems inherent in language."[25] Yet Sommer saw that the ability of cinematography to capture motion gave it a distinct advantage over photography, and he soon integrated it into his techniques of psychiatric examination and diagnosis, using it to help analyze the movement disorders associated with epilepsy, hysteria, and related conditions. Sommer went on to found the German branch of the international mental hygiene movement and to become a leading theorist of racial hygiene, both fields in which visual evidence played a crucial role.

From the early twentieth century onwards, many significant figures in the field followed Sommer's lead. Emil Kraepelin created a film studio at his clinic in Munich in 1904 and continued to produce films of patients into the 1920s; like Nonne, he produced a wartime film (now lost) entitled *The Nervous System and the War*. In 1923 he reflected on the virtues of film as a means of capturing and studying disease pictures difficult to record by conventional means. Yet whereas in the early 1900s he had praised the medium's extraordinary "fidelity to life and uncanny speed," in this later article he tempered some of his earlier enthusiasm, acknowledging that the shutter speed of even the most advanced cameras of the day was not yet fast enough to register the rapid-fire twitching of, for instance, particularly agitated war neurotics. Moreover, he conceded that in some particularly obstinate cases, patients refused to show precisely the symptoms that he wished to capture on camera.[26]

Such caveats aside, practitioners remained deeply committed to investigating the medium's medical usages, and as Kraepelin's own work attests, one of the contexts in which this commitment found expression was in connection with the neuroses of war. In much the same way that the female hysteric had earlier been a favorite subject of still photography, during the Great War soldiers suffering from psychological disability were extensively filmed. Physicians in nearly all the major warring nations produced films documenting the phenomenon and treatment of war-related psychological trauma, and though most of these films are now lost, enough have survived to become the basis of a growing scholarly literature. Wartime psychiatric filmmaking, studies have shown, served numerous distinct purposes. Perhaps most importantly it demonstrated that physicians were able to resolve questions surrounding the deeply enigmatic disease picture associated with the neuroses of war. Indeed, as Julia Barbara Köhne has argued, these films did not merely represent war neurosis and its treatment; by actively producing the disease picture surrounding this disorder, they contributed to the production of new psychiatric knowledge.[27] They did so in two major respects: diagnostically, by capturing and fixing the often bewildering play of symptoms – paralyses, trembling, movement disorders – into a legible picture; and therapeutically, by asserting that the disorder was treatable, thus placing it within a clear prognostic and temporal (before and after) framework. In both respects, the films asserted a claim to medical knowledge of a disorder defined by its shape-shifting qualities, qualities that in the war's early stages had generated profound frustration on the part of military doctors and medical personnel.

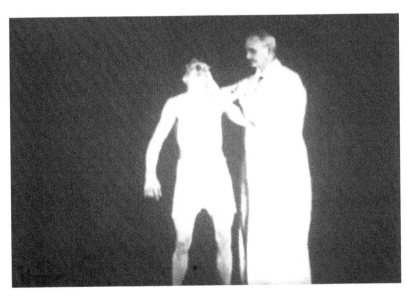

Figure 9.4 Hypnotic treatment of patient with "clown-like disturbances of movement caused by shock." Still from Max Nonne's *Funktionell-Motorische Reiz- und Lähmungszustand bei Kriegsteilnehmern und deren Heilung durch Suggestion in Hypnose* (1917).

Neuropsychiatry thus found in visual media a crucial aid in addressing the manifold issues surrounding war neurosis – its implications not just for morale and manpower, but for medical authority itself. For, as Doris Kaufmann has written, German military authorities broke with long-standing precedent in turning over to physicians the problem of war neurosis.[28] Standard practice treated soldiers claiming psychological disability as shirkers and punished them severely. Placing the problem of malingering in the hands of psychiatric experts turned it from a matter of military justice into a medical matter, but in doing so placed a high premium on the diagnostic methods used by those experts. Numerous practitioners embraced the medium on precisely these grounds, though – given the caveats of Kraepelin noted above – it remains an open question as to how real the benefits were.

Informed by the insights of media studies and science studies, the arguments of Köhne and others reflect the belief that scholars can no longer treat medical films as "positivist witnesses." Rather, scholars now push beyond the merely documentary function of such films to probe the way in which they contribute to the "cultural production of scientific representations of reality."[29] Yet stressing this aspect of medical filmmaking also entails recognition of the fact that such representations of reality are far from stable; indeed, that in at least some cases they may take on a life of their own. Beyond justifying the trust placed in the psychiatric community by the State, the wartime medical films also may have served another function, namely to reassure the public that psychiatric science could restore soldiers to health according to the principles of a humane form of treatment. Evidence suggests that at least some of these films were shown in public venues, as a way of responding to growing public unease. Yet, torn from its medical context, such imagery could take on what Ramon Reichert calls a "many-sided referentiality."[30] It was likely in recognition of this that one Austrian film on war neurosis was banned from public screenings – a ban reflecting mounting concern about the effect that widely circulated images of this malady could have on soldiers who, in an effort to escape the front or to claim disability benefits, might model their symptoms on those presented in such films.[31] At the same time, as we shall see later, the release into the public realm made medical imagery part of a wider cultural archive and as such may have contributed to a postwar genre of feature films that highlighted the ambiguous power dynamic between physician and patient.

The possibility that film might possess a more than simply documentary function also surfaced in claims, echoing Diamond's earlier assertions about photography, for the therapeutic properties of the moving image.[32] Such claims were voiced by numerous practitioners, and they also figure in the plot of several early feature films. In D.W. Griffith's *A Drunkard's Reformation* (1909), a film inspired by the mental hygiene movement founded by Clifford Beers, the drunkard is cured, according to an intertitle, by seeing "his own shortcomings mirrored in a stage-play."[33] The drama-within-a-drama became a common trope of films in mental hygiene.

The potential therapeutic properties of the medium were also thematized in a handful of early French feature films, among them *Amour et Science* (1912), which depicts a madman who is restored to himself by a screening of a film that documents the events that precipitated his psychological breakdown.[34] Similarly, the film *Le Mystère des Roches de Kador* (1912) includes a remarkable scene in which a young woman afflicted with hysteria is cured via a film screening.[35] This film includes images from a brochure written by the patient's doctor, which proclaims the following: "This remarkable discovery, which has so far been used by only a handful of doctors, will soon acquire a leading place in medicine. The vibrations of the cinematic beams of light, which are transmitted to the brain by means of the optical nerve, produce effects of hitherto undreamed of power." In a somewhat different and less extravagant vein, the innovative German clinician Ernst Simmel, who treated soldiers by means of hypnosis and psychoanalysis, explicitly compared the therapeutic recovery of memory via hypnosis to the unrolling of a film. Many psychoanalysts were similarly intrigued by the perceived affinity between film and their method, and sought to capitalize on this, most famously in G.W. Pabst's *Secrets of a Soul* (1925). This tendency, incidentally, calls into question the break with visuality alleged to have marked the advent of the talking cure.[36]

A somewhat more complex variant of the claim for the medium's therapeutic potential is demonstrated in the film *Anstaltsbehandlung in Eickelborn* (*Institutional Treatment in Eickelborn*, 1929). The film is now lost, but a lengthy account in the leading German journal of mental hygiene by a doctor involved in the film's making allows us to reconstruct its basic outlines.[37] According to this account, the film depicts the bucolic conditions that prevail at this provincial asylum: the peaceful, well-tended, almost park-like setting in which patients receive treatment, work, and mingle under the benevolent supervision of attendants; the well-appointed structures in which they are housed; the hygienic facilities where they receive treatment. Here, the audience is shown, the dark institutional past of the *Turm* (tower) or *Narrenhaus* (madhouse) has been left behind; the benefits of a reform-minded psychiatry find expression; patients are cared for according to the principles of a humane system of treatment.

Figure 9.5 Cinematic treatment of woman suffering hysterical amnesia. Still from Leonce Perret's *Le Mystere des roches de Kador* (1912).

Yet the film does not merely portray this new reality; as the review seems to suggest, it participates in the therapeutic process itself. The author links his account of the distance that psychiatry has traversed over the preceding century, and that now separates contemporary reformist initiatives in the field from the darker chapters of its earlier history, to an implicit appeal to the medium's "enlightening" properties. Darkness, enclosure, "prison-like conditions" are counter-posed by light, openness, tolerance, non-restraint – qualities embodied in the medium and integral to the modernization of psychiatric treatment. The moving image's capacity to dispel the mistrust and prejudice felt by much of the public towards such institutions and their personnel is defined here as a primary task of "psychiatric enlightenment" and this task is facilitated by the fact that psychiatry's sphere of influence now extends far beyond the walls of the institution, which makes the "work of enlightenment among the broad public possible."[38] Circling back, this then becomes analogized to the therapeutic process itself, by way of an argument that links the use of the most modern branch of treatment – psychotherapy – to a process of "psychic influence" or "enlightenment": many psychiatric patients can, it is implied, be positively enlisted in their own recovery through a combination of suggestive techniques and therapeutic pedagogy. That this form of psychotherapy is capable of accomplishing many things is clear, the author writes, and continues: "We have endeavored to show all this through filmic images and to show as well that even in those wings that formerly represented a chaos of disorder and agitation, calm and order now reign."[39]

This implicit self-reflexive element becomes clearest in the author's concluding remarks on the theatrical works staged by patients. The opportunity to perform roles in Schiller's "Wallenstein's Camp" on the open-air stage represents not merely a pleasant diversion but in itself a form of therapeutic education or enlightenment akin to that performed on a larger scale by the film. It is thus, according to this review, as though the medium itself, as symbol of modernity and rationality, has succeeded not just in bringing to light this normally sealed off world – breaking down the walls that separate the mad from society – but in imposing the sense of calm and order which is part of the new reality of the reformed institution. Enlightenment becomes synonymous with healing: of the patients themselves, but also of the wider public that is the intended audience.

If this film communicates a positive image of the effects achieved by a decade of reform, it is important to recognize that this portrayal is itself a response to a darker image whose provenance is, unlike that of the *Turm*, located in the more immediate past. This has several sources but reflects above all the wartime context in which psychiatry had been implicated in the abusive treatment of soldiers, and thousands of institutionalized patients had starved to death during the final years of extreme privation. Though it had emerged from the war with enhanced medical prestige, Germany's psychiatric community remained haunted by the public fallout from press accounts, trials, and Reichstag hearings. As earlier noted, evidence suggests that at least some of the wartime psychiatric films were screened in public, as part of an effort to combat what Julius Wagner-Jauregg, the eminent Austrian psychiatrist who became embroiled in one high-profile trial, the "lying propaganda" that circulated after the war concerning doctors' brutality. Films like *Anstaltsbehandlung* represented part of a continuing effort to combat the profession's low public standing by humanizing not just patients, but their institutions and doctors.

184

Yet even while this film strives to banish the dark chapters of the profession's history to its pre-scientific past, it points to the onset, only a few short years later, of a still darker chapter, one in which the images depicted in this film took on an entirely new meaning. Following the advent of the Third Reich, the resources devoted to the insane would become the focus of resentment of a population traumatized by the Depression and conditioned by the Third Reich's propaganda to accept the economic logic behind the persecution, sterilization, and ultimately murder of those identified as carriers of incurable diseases. Several hundred patients of the Eickelborn institution would be killed during the so-called Aktion T4 or euthanasia program that ultimately resulted in the killing of several hundred thousand victims. As scholars like Rost, Burleigh, and Schmidt have shown, this program fully mobilized all the resources of the cinematic medium, both to produce knowledge of the diseases that were targeted by the regime's racial policies and to enlighten the German populace about the need for radical measures of intervention.[40] Their work has shown in detail how an earlier faith in film's capacity to produce understanding and tolerance became transformed into a cinematic campaign that made use of images strategically chosen to elicit horror and fear in the audience. It is all too easy to find in accounts of this period distant echoes of the discourse on photography that had developed in the 1850s: echoing Hugh Diamond, the physician Ernst Herz stressed film's value in "fixing definitely the fleeting but characteristic movements, attitudes and gestures of an individual, so as to present them in the form of irrefutable evidence." Such "evidence" then became the basis for radical forms of intervention. Films of epileptic patients provided documentary support for sterilization legislation. During the Third Reich, film served, as Schmidt argues, as an "instrument of physiognomic diagnosis", in a way that had clear antecedents in Morel's *Treatise* of 1858.[41]

Figure 9.6 Still from the Nazi film *Erbkrank (Hereditarily Ill)* (1936).

Lest we ascribe to this history a too fatalistic dynamic, however, it is important to note countervailing examples. The films made by the Frankfurt neurologist Kurt Goldstein offer one such example. Following his exile from Germany in 1933, Goldstein authored his landmark book *The Organism*, whose argument for a phenomenological approach to medicine was anchored in a critique of the positivist and statistically-based conception of norm that dominated contemporary medicine. During his exile, Goldstein produced a number of films documenting tests performed by patients with motor and sensory disorders. As Stefanos Geroulanos and Todd Meyers have shown, Goldstein's films are marked by an unusual degree of intimacy that, in stressing the individual qualities of patients' performances, went against the grain of the tendency towards abstract or typological norms that featured so prominently in the bio-political discourse of the Third Reich.[42]

A similar concern for the specificities of individual patients' illness narratives informs John Huston's *Let There Be Light* (1946). This film was commissioned by the US Army to reassure an American public nervous at the prospect of the return of soldiers traumatized by war, and in its very title it signals the theme of enlightenment that marks earlier films of this genre. In preparation for the film Huston immersed himself in the details of soldiers' experiences and tracked their stories for over two months. The resulting film depicts several patients recovering traumatic memories under the influence of hypnosis, usually aided by pentothal. Ironically, Huston's depiction of soldiers' vulnerability to combat was ultimately deemed too disturbing by the Army, and the film's release was withheld for over three decades.

As Alison Winter has written, films like *Let There Be Light* underscore the way in which the use of film as a resource in psychiatry became constitutive of the twentieth-century re-conceptualization of essential features of selfhood. In this context, she highlights the cinematically-mediated construction within the sciences of mind of memory as both stable and unreliable. She cites Roy Grinker and John Spiegel, who echo the statement of Ernst Simmel cited earlier in writing of recovered memories that patients "produced like a vivid *recording* of the original experience." Yet as she also notes, in paranoid thrillers like *The Manchurian Candidate* (1962) cinematic techniques become wedded to the program of psychological manipulation and destabilization of identity popularly known as brainwashing.[43]

This mention of the role of popular cinema in constructing a portrait of the psychiatric profession deeply at odds with its own self-portrayal reminds us once again of the extent to which, despite the claims made for scientific cinema as a vehicle of truth, the medium remained caught up in "wider social and cultural determinants".[44] The modernization of psychiatry and of the gaze it directs at its patients was closely tied to the modern media. And yet if the camera represented a powerful expression of this gaze, it nevertheless could not escape the conditions of its own production and distribution. This is borne out by the ways in which postwar theatrical cinema so often thematized the doctor of the mind as a figure of anxiety and horror. For every positive representation – such as Hitchcock's *Spellbound* (1945) – there were many other exposés of the dark side of modern psychiatry and its institutions: *Shock Corridor*, *The Snake Pit*, *One Flew Over the Cuckoo's Nest*.

Such films tapped into a wider anti-psychiatric critique. Physicians were repeatedly confronted with the problem posed by the circulation of images of "mad science" in popular cinema. As we have already seen, this had an older history dating back to the

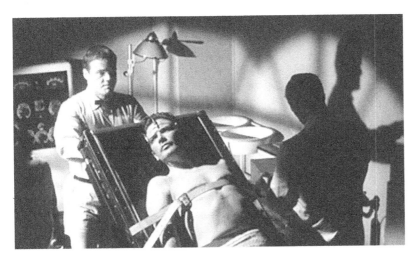

Figure 9.7 Still from Sam Fuller's *Shock Corridor* (1963).

turn of the century. From Charcot onwards the cultural trope of the doctor of the mind as master of a process of image-making had become so well-established that by the 1920s, fictional doctors like Caligari and Mabuse were depicted as exercising a kind of proprietary claim over the mass media. Insofar as this claim is revealed to be in the service of a charlatan or "mad doctor," the alliance between medicine and cinema is revealed to be a deeply ambivalent one. In such films we see played out on screen an instance of the performative contradiction that haunts the human sciences: the assumption that the psychiatrist stands apart or is of a fundamentally different kind from the patient under observation, is, so to speak, turned on its head. This further confirms the extent to which the history of the relation between psychiatry and the modern visual media remains deeply entangled in a wider culture and politics of image-making.

These tropes, which are so much a part of the history of the cultural representation of the mentally unwell and their doctors, remain alive and well today. Even as breakthroughs in brain imaging and pharmaceutical treatment drive the profession's prestige to new heights, its public image remains deeply conflicted, and this is reflected in the aura of simultaneous fascination and horror that surrounds the invasive practices that mark both the profession's history and its present. Organizations like the Church of Scientology devote considerable resources to publicizing these practices through travelling exhibitions and documentaries like *Psychiatry: An Industry of Death.*

However sensationalistic such efforts are, they nevertheless reflect deep popular uncertainty and anxiety about the profession's capacity for both good and ill. As the 2015 American Psychological Association report relating to psychologists' involvement in the Department of Defense's program of so-called "enhanced interrogation" warns, when the profession allows its members "to intentionally inflict pain on an individual with no ability to resist, regardless of the individual's background or motives, faith in the profession can diminish quickly."[45] Films like the Jason Bourne series, which update *The Manchurian Candidate* for the so-called "war on terror," show that this crisis of faith has found wide resonance in popular culture. Indeed, these films recuperate much of the history recounted in this chapter by demonstrating that "mind control" is both a clinical procedure and a modality deeply interwoven with the development of the mass media.

While television draws on these tropes as well, it is in this medium that we find clearest evidence of the emergence of other possibilities. The expanded, more episodic format seemingly allows greater latitude to explore the complexities of mental illness. In the show *Monk*, for instance, the OCD that plagues the eponymous detective is also a gift, producing insights into his cases that are denied to those not so afflicted. When in one episode he takes medication for his disorder it comes as no surprise that this robs him of those insights. A similar logic can be found in a series that offers yet another variant on the brainwashing scenario, *Homeland*. The show's protagonist, Carrie Mathison, suffers from bipolar disorder, and it is in the midst of one of her manic episodes that she finally pieces together the outlines of the terrorist plot that she has been tracking. However, this flash of illumination is then immediately erased from her memory when she is hospitalized and subjected to electroconvulsive treatment in the concluding scene of Season One. It remains in the end difficult to decide whether such a series reflects a wider understanding of and tolerance towards mental disability – the "enlightenment" sought by early nineteenth-century mental hygienists – or whether the protagonist's disability is merely a device intended to drive a plot that exploits public fascination with psychological torment.

Notes

1 See Henry Alexander, Report of Proceedings in US vs. Guiteau II (1882); Charles Rosenberg, *The Trial of the Assassin Guiteau* (Chicago: University of Chicago Press, 1968), 155–178; on the photographer Bell, idem, 43–4.
2 Sigmund Freud, "Charcot" (1893) in *The Standard Version of the Complete Psychological Works of Sigmund Freud*, ed. J. Strachey (London: Hogart, 1962) 3:9–23.
3 See for instance Elaine Showalter, *The Female Malady: Women, Madness, and English Culture, 1830–1980* (New York: Pantheon, 1985).
4 Christian Bonah and Anja Laukötter, "Moving Pictures and Medicine in the First Half of the 20th Century," *Gesnerus* 66 (2009): 135; Lisa Cartwright, *Screening the Body: Tracing Medicine's Visual Culture* (Minneapolis: University of Minnesota Press, 1995); Lorraine Daston and Peter Galison, *Objectivity* (New York: Zone, 2007).
5 Rosenberg, op cit, 207.
6 Sander Gilman, *Seeing the Insane* (New York: Wiley, 1982), Daniel Pick, *Faces of Degeneration: A European Disorder, c. 1848–1918* (Cambridge and New York: Cambridge University Press, 1989); Alan Sekula, "The Body and the Archive," *October*, 39 (1986): 3–64.
7 Cited in Gilman, *Seeing the Insane*, 187.
8 Gilman, *The Face of Madness: Hugh W. Diamond and the Origin of Psychiatric Photography* (New York: Brunner/Mazel, 1976), 5.
9 Hugh W. Diamond, "On the Application of Photography to the Physiognomic and Mental Phenomena of Insanity" (1856) in Gilman, *Face of Madness*, 20.
10 See Gilman, *Seeing the Insane*, 171.
11 Georges Didi-Huberman, *The Invention of Hysteria: Charcot and the Photographic Iconography of the Salpetriere* (Cambridge and London: MIT, 2003).
12 Cartwright, *Screening the Body;* Daston and Galison, *Objectivity.*
13 Showalter, *Female Malady*, 149.
14 Alison Winter, "Screening Selves: Sciences of Memory and Identity on Film, 1930–1960," *History of Psychology* 7 (2004): 367–401.

15 Daphne de Marneffe, "The Construction of Clinical Knowledge in Charcot and Freud," *Signs* 17 (1991): 80.

16 J.-M. Charcot, *Lectures on Diseases of the Nervous System, delivered at the Salpetriere* (London: [no press given], 1877).

17 Showalter, *Female Malady*; de Marneffe, op cit; Gilman, op cit.

18 Sekula, "The Body and the Archive."

19 Daston and Galison, op cit, ch. 6.

20 Rae Beth Gordon, "From Charcot to Charlot: Unconscious Imitation and Spectatorship in French Cabaret and Early Cinema," in *The Mind of Modernism: Medicine, Psychology, and the Cultural Arts in Europe and America, 1880–1940,* ed. Mark Micale (Stanford: Stanford University Press, 2004), 93–124; see especially 111–112.

21 Paul Schuster, "Vorführung pathologischer Bewegungscomplexe mittelst des Kinematographen und Erläuterung desselben," *Fortschritte der Neurologie und Psychiatrie* 66 (1898): 122–3; see also Klaus Podoll, "Geschichte des Wissenschaftlichen Films in der Nervenheilkunde in Deutschland 1895–1929," *Fortschritte der Neurologie und Psychiatrie* 66 (1998): 124.

22 Cartwright, op cit, 40.

23 Marinescu, cited in Adolf Nichtenhauser, *Films in Psychiatry, Psychology, and Mental Health* (New York: Health Educational Council,1953), 44.

24 Nichtenhauser, op cit.

25 Gilman, op cit, 189.

26 Emil Kraepelin, "Psychiatrische Bewegungsbilder," *Zeitschrift für die gesamte Neurologie und Psychiatrie* 85 (1923): 609–613.

27 Julia Barbara Köhne, *Kriegshysteriker. Strategische Bilder und mediale techniken* (Husum: Matthiesen, 2009).

28 Doris Kaufmann, "Science as Cultural Practice: Psychiatry in the First World War and Weimar Germany," *Journal of Contemporary History* 34, 1 (1999): 124–44; Paul Lerner, *Hysterical Men: War, Psychiatry, and the Politics of Trauma in Germany, 1890–1930* (Ithaca: Cornell University Press, 2003).

29 Bonah and Laukötter, op cit, 122, 134.

30 Ramon Reichert, "Kinematographie der Objektivität. Zur Medienästhetik des Wissens um 1900" in *Aisthesis: Wahrnehmungsprozesse und Visualisierungsformen in Kunst und Technik,* ed. Christoph Wagner, Mark Greenlee, and Christian Wolff (München: Schnell und Steiner, 2013), 93–105.

31 Hans-Georg Hofer, *Nervenschwäche und Krieg: Modernitätskritik und Krisenbewältigung in der österreichischen Psychiatrie (1880–1920)* (Vienna: Böhlau, 2004).

32 See Hermann Lemke, "Kino als Heilmittel," *Pädagogische-psychologische Studien* 10 (1910), cited in Julia Barbara Köhne, *Kriegshysteriker: Strategische Bilder und mediale Techniken militärpsychiatrischen Wissens* (Husum: Matthiesen, 2009), 186.

33 Anne Friedberg, "A Properly Adjusted Window: Vision and Sanity in D.W. Griffith's 1908–1909 Biograph Films," in *Early Cinema: Space, Frame, Narrative,* ed. Thomas Elsaesser (London: BFI, 1990), 326–335.

34 See Nichtenhauser, op cit; Paul Ries, "Popularise and/or Be Damned: Psychoanalysis and Film at the Crossroads in 1925," *International Journal of Psychoanalysis* 76 (1995): 762.

35 See Frank Kessler and Sabine Lenk, "Die Anwendung der Kinematographie auf Gemütskranke" in *Psyche im Kino: Sigmund Freud und der Film,* ed. Thomas Ballhausen, Günter Krenn, and Lydia Marinelli (Vienna: Filmarchiv Austria, 2006), 41–54.

36 Anton Kaes, *Shell Shock Cinema* (Princeton: Princeton University Press, 2009), 49–51, see also 8ff. for discussion of the film *Dem Licht Entgegen* (1918); Veronika Fuechtner, *Berlin Psychoanalytic: Psychoanalysis and Culture in Weimar Republic Germany and Beyond* (Berkeley: University of California Press, 2011); Ries, op cit.

37 Karl Hermkes, "Die neuzeitliche Anstaltsbehandlung der Geisteskranken, dargestellt in einem Film," *Zeitschrift für psychische Hygiene* 3 (1930): 78–84. The institution was the Provinzialheilanstalt Eickelborn i. W.

38 Ibid., 80.

39 Ibid., 82.

40 Karl Ludwig Rost, *Sterilisation und Euthanasie im Film des "Dritten Reiches"* (Husum: Matthiesen, 1987); Michael Burleigh, *Death and Deliverance: 'Euthanasia' in Germany*

1900–1945 (Cambridge: Cambridge University Press, 1994); Ulf Schmidt, *Medical Films, Ethics, and Euthanasia in Nazi Germany* (Husum: Matthiesen, 2002).
41 Schmidt, op cit, 185; idem, 87.
42 Stefanos Geroulanos and Todd Meyers, *Experimente im Individuum. Kurt Goldstein und die Frage des Organismus* (Cologne: August, 2014), 53–83.
43 Winter, "Screening Selves." See also Andreas Killen, "Homo Pavlovius: Cinema, Conditioning, and the Cold War Subject," *Grey Room* 45 (2011): 42–59
44 Bonah and Laukötter, op cit.
45 Report to the Special Committee of the Board of Directors of the American Psychological Association, July 2, 2015, p. 72.

Part IV

GLOBAL DIMENSIONS, COLONIAL, AND POST-COLONIAL SETTINGS

10

MADNESS AND PSYCHIATRY IN LATIN AMERICA'S LONG NINETEENTH CENTURY

Manuella Meyer

To understand madness in Latin America as a scholarly inquiry one must flesh out the ways that mental illness became a problem for both state and civil societies, and how many nations turned to psychiatry for solutions over the course of the long nineteenth century.[1] This essay takes the medicalization of madness within a context characterized by social secularization and public health modernization as its departure point. While the historiography of madness and psychiatry remains less well developed in Latin America than in the rest of the Atlantic world, interest in the subject is growing as more historians of the region turn their attention to how issues of public health, mental health, and professionalization intersect with nationalism and state formation. This chapter is by no means an exhaustive investigation of the insightful and important work on the history of madness and psychiatry on Latin America produced both inside and outside the region. It engages a modest sample of notable works published within the past twenty-five years to understand convergences and divergences between and among Latin American sites and to argue that the "domestication of madness," to borrow historian Andrew Scull's term,[2] was part of many modernization processes. Many national reform movements, of which psychiatrists often formed part of the vanguard, were committed to these sorts of modernization projects as they sought to revitalize both state and nation in the name of "order and progress." This essay is divided into four parts. Given that the work of theorist Michel Foucault casts a long shadow on the historiography of madness, most especially on the Anglophone scholarly literature, the first part provides a synopsis of Foucault's study and how it has influenced others. This work serves as an intellectual scaffolding from which to understand both how the Anglophone history of mental illness and psychiatry borrows and departs from the Foucauldian tradition. Part two explores how historians of Latin America have been influenced by these texts, and how they have specifically used the language of public health to understand madness and psychiatry. Part three examines scholarly works on the management of insanity in Latin America by first examining the literature related to the colonial and postcolonial periods. This part specifically looks at texts on Spanish America and then Brazil. While the scholarly literature on Brazil, the majority of which is produced in-country, shares many analytical commonalities with Spanish America, the socio-cultural, political, and economic particularities of Brazilian history reveal unique perspectives on the history of madness and its treatment that can be instructive for historians of Latin America and other regions. In part four, I suggest research areas for possible expansion that may generate discussion among historians of Latin America so that a more synthetic engagement with histories of madness and its treatment within a dynamic ecology of care and social assistance may be possible.

Foucault's long shadow

A foray into the Latin American historiography of madness and psychiatry requires some deep contextualization within the vastness of Anglophone literature. It has become an understatement to suggest that much of the rich historiography on the plight of the mentally ill can be traced to the generative work of theorist Michel Foucault.[3] One of his key insights, that to study the mentally ill is about far more than the study of mental illness, continues to inform historiography and has been taken up and complicated by detailed studies of madness, asylums and psychiatric thought in a variety of specific historical and cultural contexts, as scholars of Europe, Africa, Asia and Latin America continue to engage his work. By way of establishing an intellectual baseline on how his other insights have inflected Latin American historiography in particular, some review is necessary. Foucault's *Madness and Civilization* created a new paradigm for understanding the asylum and was immediately influential. The book elicited two main responses, which gradually and roughly fell into two separate schools of thought. Advocates of the "humanitarian school" continued to view asylums as an improvement over the combination of stigma and cruelty that they argued characterized the treatment of madness in an earlier era, despite the institutional emphasis on conformity and productivity. Those who advocated the "social control thesis" argued that an increasingly bureaucratic state suppressed dissidents and the working poor, too frequently and too casually classifying them as either criminal or insane in order to consolidate the power of the professional and elite classes. "Even though no epistemological consensus"[4] emerged, representative works of the social control thesis include David J. Rothman's *The Discovery of the Asylum: Social Order and Disorder in the New Republic* and Andrew T. Scull's *Museums of Madness: The Social Organization of Insanity in Nineteenth-Century England.* On the other side of the debate were Norman Dain's *Concepts of Insanity in the United States, 1789–1865*, and Gerald N. Grob's *The State and The Mentally Ill: A History of Worcester State Hospital in Massachusetts, 1830–1920* and *Mental Institutions in America: Social Policy to 1875.*[5] The social reform versus social control debates of the 1960s and 1970s reflect the spirit of the times – a period in which anti-colonialist movements called into question the beneficence of the European institutions that expanded as empires took root and grew in the seventeenth, eighteenth, and early nineteenth centuries.

Asylum scholars of the 1980s often expressed a desire to avoid reductive accounts in which administrators are villains and patients are victims. The problem with their approach, according to historian Thomas E. Brown, is that they turned away from theorizing the asylum and neglected to genuinely consider issues of power. Brown argues that by focusing on particularities and minutiae, counter-revisionist historians frequently retreated into "a mindless empiricism."[6] Moreover, Brown asserts that counter-revisionist accounts fail to account for the symbolic power of asylums on the public imagination – the way in which the institutions functioned as a reminder of state power and "of the potential dire consequences of any fall from grace from nineteenth-century society's creed of normative behavior."[7] There are, of course, notable exceptions. Martin Summers cites the works of Elizabeth Lunbeck and Joel Braslow as examples of scholarship that have "successfully blended the empirical specificity of the 'new consensus' methodology" with theoretical and practical exploration of the power dynamics of patient–staff interaction and the development of psychiatry as an influential field of knowledge."[8] But both these scholars address only the twentieth century, and neither deals extensively with the non-West.

In many of these works, historians of psychiatry and the mind sciences focused almost entirely on Western Europe and North America until the 1990s.[9] The notion that asylums and professional psychiatry were to be primarily understood as bastions of state power emerged from this Western bias. It was propagated by an entire generation of historians such as Scull, who reinforced the notion of the asylum as an impenetrable and imposing prison; and Rothman, who argued that the insane asylum was born in the same moment of institutional discipline as prisons and poorhouses in antebellum America.[10] Later scholars, such as Tomes, Grob, and Digby, criticized the analytical lens with which these historians had framed the asylum and interrogated a broader array of primary sources that painted a more nuanced history of mental illness's management; however, the historiographical preoccupation with the Eurocentric asylum and professional psychiatry remained until the late 1990s.[11] The literature on Latin America would then join other texts by historians whose focus on the non-West pushes for a nuanced reading of psychiatry and the asylum in their colonial and postcolonial contexts.[12] What these studies show is that madness is not peripheral to more "important" questions of politics, economics, society and culture, but can be embedded in them, since madness became a metaphor sometimes used to harness dimensions of experience, changes in cultural, political, and social responses to crises, which would otherwise be impossible to measure or document.

Mental illness as a threat to the public's health

Much of the Latin American historiography of the management of mental illness heavily focuses on the nineteenth and early twentieth centuries, given that this period correlates with the creation of public health bureaucracies and, within them, the construction of public state-funded asylums and the emergence of psychiatry as a profession. Since psychiatry came to form the vanguard of many national modernizing movements, the central role that psychiatrists came to play in newly created modernization schemes in post-independence Latin America warrants some consideration within the scholarship on public health. In order to investigate the history of psychiatry, historians of the region (myself included) have used the lens of public health as an entry point from which to examine psychiatric notions of madness and attempts to manage it. Public health served as one of the most agile and expansive regulatory mechanisms in nineteenth-century Latin American cities. Although municipal public health institutions often had small budgets and staffs, they had considerable legal authority to regulate property and personal conduct in order to remove threats to the general population's longevity, health, and wellbeing. The public health mandate linked the condition and conduct of individuals with the vitality, strength, and prosperity of society overall. Earlier histories of public health in Latin America lauded the "heroic" efforts of local and international physicians and medical institutions in trying to improve the health of Latin American populations, seen as inferior in race, body and cultural habits, from its supposed feeble constitutions. Yet by the mid-1990s, historian Marcos Cueto's contributions represented a fundamental shift in how scholars explored the relationship between medical science, public health, and nation-state building in the nineteenth and twentieth century. His work explored how disease, public health initiatives, and medical research intersected with the attempts of government officials to illustrate how important health and hygiene were to defining the modern nation and state. Cueto also demonstrated that public health policies and programs started by the government had ulterior motives regarding the health of lower-class citizens. Medical science, Cueto argued, allowed state officials and medical professionals to justify their characterizations of the lower class, by providing what was characterized as empirical proof of their innate inferiority. State officials used medical science to create a narrative that would require the segregation of lower class citizens from middle-class and upper-class citizens, often through measures such as prejudiced housing and employment opportunities.[13] Extending the work of Cueto, a more complex scholarship on the history of Latin American nation-state building through public health and medical science began to emerge in the late 1990s, and has continued to develop into a compelling area of research. In particular, this scholarship has developed unique and exciting ideas about how medical science was inextricably tied to nation-state building.

In their efforts to improve public health, the medical profession employed the language and methods of sanitarianism and hygienic improvement in which disease and poor health were attributed to a combination of environmental hazards, the population's ignorance of basic hygiene and unhealthy behaviors and practices. This basic framework for understanding disease prevailed until the early twentieth century, when health officials began to draw on microbiology, immunology, and germ theory in their response to public health crises. Thus, throughout much of the nineteenth century, physicians drew on the language and practices of sanitarianism to explain mental disorders. Everything from melancholy to epilepsy was attributed to a combination of environmental hazards, temperament and behavior. Mental illnesses, though to some extent recognized as distinct, became folded into the broader medical discourses concerned with public health.

By the early twentieth century, mental illness became a public health concern, albeit one that drew less attention than cholera, tuberculosis or a wide range of other infectious diseases that plagued the Latin America populations. The new framing of mental illness as a threat to the public should not lead to the conclusion that mental illnesses were on a meteoric rise. Instead, it reveals more about the mentalities and motivations of psychiatrists and state officials, who hoped to correct perceived mental defects and to instill proper mental habits among their fellow citizens. The majority of Latin American psychiatrists did not hope to orchestrate a "Great Confinement" of Foucauldian proportions, in part because many states did not have sufficient capital or organizational structures to make such a project possible, but primarily because their basic goals were more complex. As psychiatrists took over management of asylums, and by extension madness, they developed a basic therapeutic pessimism relative to their ability to cure madness. When asylums, like other organs of state care, became chronically overcrowded, many, while they did not abandon the asylum, directed their attention to the prevention of mental illness. In this manner, Latin American psychiatrists, like their counterparts in other national settings, left the asylum in order to facilitate the creation of mental hygiene leagues, out-reach clinics, and public campaigns that sought to educate the public about habits conducive to sound mental health. Given the racial, ethnic, gender, and class disparities of Latin America, many of these mental hygienic projects were fraught with tensions and disparities.

Historiography of madness in Latin America: the colonial preamble

The scholarly concentration of the historiography of madness and psychiatry in Latin America on the nineteenth and twentieth centuries should by no means suggest that mental illness did not affect individuals, their families, communities or even the state during the colonial period. Colonial Latin America saw an increased preoccupation with madness in almost every sector of society; for different reasons and in different ways, jurists, theologians, artists, advisors, and the royal court all found themselves debating, exploring, or dealing with madness and madmen. Yet the madnesses spoken of in elite literature, festivals, legal codes, and medical manuals were not always the same. In the cultural setting of colonial Latin America the question of meaning relative to madness was so deeply conflicted that it included a reluctance or inability to find any clear meaning at all. The historian who wishes to trace a constellation surrounding madness in any era has a multiplicity of ways to understand how it was managed and/or treated. The investigation of these issues for the colonial period, however, requires reading along and against the archival grain since source materials (often scarce) do not lead to facile analysis. Nonetheless, extensive mining of religious records by historians such as María Cristina Sacristán and Ronaldo Vainfas for colonial Mexico and colonial Brazil respectively yield fascinating insights on how madness was understood. For both religious and state officials in medieval and early modern Catholic theology, the issue of madness was of great significance given that, in many ways, more was at stake in the diagnosis of the mentally ill than the physically infirm, since mental illness was specifically attached to that which is divine in man. The words of Spanish playwright and satirist Alonso Jerónimo Salas de Barbadillo, though written of another context, can be applied to the colonial Americas: "[the insane were deprived of] the most noble action that a rational creature can perform, which is, to think well. [Madness] takes from his soul its most valued possession."[14] Thus, Christians in the Iberian peninsula and in the New World, were asked to provide charity for men and women with suffering bodies, but they had no greater obligation than to aid suffering souls.

Madness makes an entrance in Vainfas's work on the Inquisition during the latter half of the sixteenth century in Brazil when madness, constructed as a form of "un-reason," mitigated punishment for presumed acts of heresy.[15] Since madness served as an extenuating factor in heresy trials, inquisitors painstakingly interviewed not only the accused, but his/her family members, neighbors, employers, and associates, in order to ascertain the accused's "abnormal" mental state. If it was determined that the accused feigned madness, the punishment towards him/her would be particularly substantial given he attempt to use madness as a form of deception on top of the original alleged heresy.[16]

197

Both of Sacristán's important studies of madness that address its visibility in cases brought before the Inquisition in Mexico during the colonial era (1521–1810)[17] showcase a socio-cultural landscape in which multiple notions of madness operated. A central theme in Sacristán's *Locura y Inquisición en Nueva España* is the complex network of responsibility and care for those presumed to be insane. As she divides the mentally ill's interactions into three types: those with friends and family; those with officials and institutions; and finally, those with intermediary figures that included local priests, who often mediated between the first two groups, she illustrates that the problem of "madness," – that is, a state of subjective crisis – primarily fell upon friends, family, and community members. By way of anecdote, Sacristán presents the reader with Alonso Hernández Marín, a surgeon in Mexico, who was a popular and respected member of his community, prone to suffer from fits in which he was verbally incoherent and physically violent towards others. One neighbor noted that "he became enraged to the point that four or five were not enough to restrain him, to tie his hands and feet . . . and he broke the glasses in which they bring him food and drink . . . and he broke into pieces everything he could get his hands on."[18] Most of the witnesses who had seen Hernández Marín in such a state at some point or another restrained him, and in many cases, many neighbors helped his wife with the household while he was indisposed. After his fits, "he went back to being a 'good surgeon' and there were patients who came to him to be bled."[19] Sacristán succinctly notes "his case demonstrates . . . the integration of a madman into everyday life once he had recovered his sanity . . . at no point was he an outcast,"[20] thereby making apparent the relative ease with which neighbors seemed perfectly willing to integrate an individual who exhibited abnormal behavior into the folds of community life.

The moments in which adults wailed, fought, howled, blasphemed, and otherwise broke every rule of social decorum, followed by the immediate return to the social status quo, encapsulates the way that colonial Latin Americans understood madness. Similar to Rothman's colonial Americans, colonial Latin Americans would have found inconceivable the readiness to confine the insane, as a matter of course, for long periods of time. The pro-asylum impulse emerged during the late eighteenth-century Bourbon and Pombaline reforms in Spanish America and Brazil respectively, as the Spanish and Portuguese imperial states sought to not only streamline the political and economic affairs of their colonies, but to create a social engineering program that would produce productive rational subjects.

However, the pro-asylum tendency would become institutionalized as state-funded public asylums flourished in the post-independence era. They steadily outnumbered private asylums and general hospitals that housed people who suffered from all types of ailments (both physical and mental) created by colonial governments or religious orders. The independence movements in Spanish America that ushered in national governments hoping to make radical breaks from colonial traditions had large repercussions for the secularization of care and the practice of medicine in these new nations. No longer did men have to go to France or other European countries for medical training. The creation of medical schools in these newly created nations led to an increase in the number of doctors and, over time, the creation of home grown medico-intellectual infrastructures.

Historiography of madness and Latin America:
postcolonial malaise

Nineteenth-century Latin American republics faced the postcolonial dilemma of how to incorporate a diverse population, the majority of whom had been juridically unequal and culturally disparaged for centuries, into a national community. By century's end, many national leaderships' ambivalent, eclectic takes on liberalism, the uneasy coexistence of enduring colonial codes and practices alongside new, republican ones, and deep cultural anxieties about presumed barbarism, race and ethnicity, had left their imprint on the politics and culture of the region's cities. Doctors and political leaders in Latin America's pre-populist era still generally dismissed the so-called social question of how to address the plight of the working classes as a matter for the police. Scholarship on Porfirian Mexico (1876–1910),[21] for example, has demonstrated that the same subtext of moral panic that was behind urban modernizers' designs for orderly citizens and a disciplined citizenry underlay the obtrusive interference of the state, particularly the police, in the lives of the urban poor. Gambling, vagrancy, and prostitution were among the most prominent of practices marked by race and class that the state criminalized as part of the authoritarian politics that accompanied urban modernization in studies of the immediate aftermath of independence in Latin America. Central to modernization efforts was the creation of public health bureaucracies that, among other matters, sought to redeem the masses.

Investigating the patterns of disease and public health problems prevalent in Bolivia during the first half of the twentieth century, historian Ann Zulawski's *Unequal Cures* unearths the social and political conditions that facilitated their spread and obstructed the intervention of medical authorities. She explores why public health conditions improved very little between 1800 and the Revolution of 1952, and why changes in health infrastructure abounded after the revolution, joining universal suffrage, the nationalization of the tin mines (the main source of export revenues) and the onset of an agrarian reform designed to benefit the indigenous and mixed-race rural poor, in a wave of modernist reforms.[22] Zulawski's methodology weaves together intellectual and social history methodological practices to investigate how doctors and politicians thought about and explained the country's health problems. In doing so, she shows how the longer history of ethnic and cultural division in Bolivia shaped racialized and gendered ideas among doctors and government officials concerned both with disease as an obstacle to the nation's progress, and with the potential of indigenous populations for reform. By examining the influence of eugenics, indigenismo, populism, nationalism, international medical philanthropy, and other movements on these professionals' works, Zulawski also traces how existing racialized and gendered visions of Bolivia's health problems changed over time, giving rise to new health policies.

Zulawski's final chapter in *Unequal Cures* examines how notions about mental health changed in Bolivia's only mental hospital, the Manicomio Pacheco, during the 1940s. This was a period in which new treatments for psychiatric disease first became available and a new democratic and populist politics emerged in the country. More importantly, however, Zulawski studies how concepts of class, gender, and ethnicity influenced forms of diagnosis and treatment. She argues that this approach "reveals that contradictions evident in the elite's views about the correct social roles of Indians and women also influenced doctors' analysis of the causes of mental alienation."[23] She posits that indigenous men were considered mentally ill if they deviated too far from their expected behavior as "Indians" and, in fact, as "others," acting emotionally and intellectually too much like the normative creole male. Women could be pathologized and medicalized if they deviated too far from their expected role as well, either becoming overeducated, ignoring their duties as mothers, or attempting to assert the rights of full citizens. Zulawski argues that these racialized and gendered interpretations of mental illness endured despite the growing attraction of new democratic and socialist ideas in the 1940s. She also presents an on-the-ground, granular analysis of the patient–psychiatrist encounter at the Manicomio Pacheco by looking at how doctors' misdiagnoses of patients was often based on critical misunderstandings and racist scorn of patient behavior that corresponded to actual indigenous practices and beliefs.

Specifically, her discussion of the misdiagnosis of particular patients based on a close reading of their records insightfully showcases how the patient–psychiatric encounter yielded polyvalent layers of language and cultural meanings imbued with power dynamics. Another compelling element about the chapter on mental illness is the analysis of the failures and successes of the Manicomio Pacheco itself. When the asylum functioned as an institution open and free to the public, the very refusal of treatment for certain patients, the use of outdated and abusive treatment, and the failure to implement new forms of treatment appears to have aggravated patients' suffering as opposed to their reduction. Paradoxically, conditions within the asylum only began to improve gradually after the facility began charging patients and families for treatment, leading to a more hierarchical and differentiated set of treatment practices that left many without even the most minimal treatment offered.

The historian, fiction writer, and poet Cristina Rivera-Garza has also problematized the categories of the "normal," and the "abnormal" through the lens of modernization in early twentieth century Mexico, revealing the "march of progress" that began in earnest during the reign of Porfirio Díaz (1876–1911) as largely consistent of subtler and more insidious strategies of social regulation. Through a number of scholarly articles and a novella based on her dissertation-turned-book *La Castañeda: Narrativas dolientes desde el Manicomio General, México 1910–1930*, she explores how psychiatry was key among these strategies as a means of distinguishing those who would be allowed to participate as full citizens in the new, modern nation-state from those who would not.[24] In detailing the emergence of La Castañeda, Mexico's premier asylum, she also explores the formation of psychiatric discourse and critically undermines its apparent stability and naturalness by revealing it to have emerged through a highly contingent process. She posits that asylum doctors working with the destitute in Mexico City blamed "rapid modernization and social change" for the mentally ill, as much as they did heredity, despite their knowledge of European medical degeneration theories.[25] However, she asserts that by the end of the nineteenth century, doctors working for the Mexican government selectively highlighted heredity over modernization as the trigger for mental illness, as this minimized state responsibility for mental illness in an economically disparate society.[26] In her analysis of Mexican psychiatry's disciplinary development, she suggests that it fulfilled an important function in the process of nation-building in that it reasserted pre-established distinctions between those at the center and those on the periphery, adding a scientific means of classifying those who would be seen as legitimate members of the nation and citizens of the state, and those who would not. While both Zulawski and Rivera-Garza highlight psychiatrists' inability to deal with the racial, ethnic, gender, and class differences between themselves and the populations they served, both historians portray psychiatrists in slightly different ways. Bolivian psychiatrists come across as myopic and incompetent professionals who knew little, if anything, about their patients. Rivera-Garza portrays Mexican psychiatrists as similarly myopic, but in a more Foucauldian framework as modernizing agents primarily motivated by a functionary and self-interested desire for control, and whose primary method was confinement, both as control and as punishment of the generally poor masses. In "Becoming Mad," the Foucauldian frame is placed in sharp relief when Rivera-Garza observes:

> Dark-skinned and poor, immigrants [to Mexico City from the countryside] soon became a source of concern among city designers and social commentators for whom their ethnicity, class origins and lifestyles not only embodied the antithesis of modernization but also represented a social threat. Porfirian analysts thus unleashed an unprecedented effort to identify and control potentially dangerous members of society, especially targeting criminals, prostitutes, alcoholics and the insane. Committed to the protection of society, experts unabashedly supported the creation of institutions able to contain the pernicious influence of what they perceived as wayward men and women.[27]

The historiography of psychiatry as it relates to public health and modernization in Argentina, by far, however, proves to be the most expansive given the deep entrenchment of the psychiatric disciplines in Argentina. Indeed, it has become a truism that of all the societies of Latin America, Argentina is the one in which the "psy" disciplines, and Freudian psychoanalysis, in particular, came to carry the most weight, not just in the building of state institutions, but in broader cultural terms. Notably, the historian Mariano Ben Plotkin's publication of *Freud in the Pampas: The Emergence and Development of a Psychoanalytic Culture in Argentina* was one of the first key texts that introduced the Anglo-Atlantic scholarly community to the early growth of psychoanalytic ideas in Argentina, the relationship of the analysts to the local medical culture, and the critical role of psychoanalytical "diffusers."[28] Plotkin also explores the politicization of psychiatry itself through an analysis of the 1976 establishment of military dictatorship, and how Argentine society used psychoanalysis as a form of liberation in the face of a highly politically volatile and violent culture. By comprehensively showing the intricacies of how a psychoanalytic movement enveloped Argentine society, from the medical, psychological, and mental health communities, to education, institutional politics, and popular culture, Plotkin's work marries the innovative elements of medical and cultural histories. He singles out psychoanalysis as an exceptional and productive tool utilized in all sectors of society by providing accounts of how average citizens prioritized receiving formal psychoanalytic treatment to such a degree that they would budget their income, barter their services, and/or incur debt in order to lie on the couch. Apart from its insightful analysis of the workings of psychiatry within culture, the book undoubtedly illustrated how past scholars who focused on the international development of psychoanalysis missed Argentina as a critical site of psychoanalysis due to a series of disciplinary and cultural biases. By showcasing how specific cultural forces and movements radically shaped the receptivity and propagation of psychoanalytic ideas, institutional practices, and most importantly, social values, Plotkin portrays how both Argentina's psychiatrists and laypeople creatively used and interpreted psychoanalysis to their own ends.[29]

Contributing to a rich historiography that includes the work of Plotkin, Nancy Leys Stepan, among others, Julia Rodriguez's *Civilizing Argentina: Science, Medicine, and the Modern State* explores the connective tissue between Argentinian science, medicine, and state formation by arguing that emerging tensions, conflicts, and contradictions during the country's struggle for "civilization"-through-science laid the foundation for statehood during the so-called "golden era," which lasted from 1880 to 1914.[30] Furthermore, she posits that these struggles continued during the pre-World War I period and the rise of authoritarianism in the twentieth century. The book is organized into three sections: "Symptoms," "Diagnosis," and "Hygiene," where Rodriguez draws links between scientific discourses that were utilized to implement mechanisms of social control. First, the author analyzes how liberal intellectuals of the Generation of 1880 responded to a diverse and urban society by treating disorder as a social illness and embracing positivism to combat the threat of the urban masses. These intellectuals included physicians, public health experts and state officials such as José Ingenieros, Francisco de Veyga, José María Ramos Mejía, Emilio Coni, Eduardo Wilde, and Juan Vucetich. The "Diagnosis" section examines Argentinian criminologists' efforts to classify criminals and the mentally ill, showing how racial assumptions informed criminological ideas. *Civilizing Argentina* most succinctly shows how psychiatry cannot be disaggregated from politics. By exploring the relationship between social assistance and social control, Rodriguez demonstrates that liberal state formation in Argentina was not a process of equality, political participation, and universal notions of citizenship, but one in which government officials and psychiatrists, among others, produced and reproduced inequalities as they sought to exclude the majority of the population and establish rigid definitions of citizenship.

Jonathan Ablard's *Madness in Buenos Aires: Patients, Psychiatrists, and the Argentine State 1880–1983* is another important addition to the study of psychiatry and politics in Argentina.[31] By exploring government psychiatric hospitals (especially the two main institutions in Buenos Aires, one for men (Borda), and the one for women (Moyano)), Ablard manages to construct a political history of the Argentine state. As he succinctly asserts: "The experience of psychiatric patients serves as a useful case study of how Argentines interacted with it [the state]. Briefly this study argues that the capacity of the state to provide social services and also in different ways to control the populace was often circumscribed to an extent hitherto not recognized in the scholarly literature."[32] Going against claims about total social control that inform much of the literature about psychiatric institutions in Latin America, Ablard suggests instead that the capacity of the state was limited and that it was unable, in the end, to impose any kind of totalizing regime of surveillance and internalized discipline among its citizens.

The Brazilian counterpoint

The unique historical development of Brazil during the nineteenth century undoubtedly influenced both the state and civil society's responses to madness. Specifically, the transfer of the Portuguese Court to Rio de Janeiro in 1808 as a result of Napoleon's occupation of Lisbon generated a slate of urban reforms designed to remake Rio de Janeiro into an imperial city. Similar to post-independence Spanish America, the institutionalization of medical training compelled young doctors-to-be (all men) to stay in the country, as opposed to going to Europe, and in so doing they raised the profile and status of medicine as a respectable profession. The declaration of independence in 1822 by young Emperor Dom Pedro I galvanized a generation of doctors to launch an asylum-building campaign that featured the specter of the indigent mentally ill often seen roaming on city streets. Their activism led to the formal creation by imperial decree in 1841 of the Hospício Pedro I. Completed and inaugurated in 1851, it was the first asylum in Latin America, with a novel, and inter-estingly representational, joint management structure in which medical and religious influences and personnel shared power. The Santa Casa de Misericórdia Catholic lay brotherhood and prominent Brazilian doctors had joint management of the asy-lum and therefore, of mental illness. This hybrid model of institutional governance proved both managerially and therapeutically unproductive as doctors resented the lay brotherhood its religious workers, and their methods. It did, however, prove to be generative of a critical, activist and bureaucratic culture for psychiatry, as doctors gar-nered not only decades of experience working with the mentally ill, but also decades of experience defending the contours of their modernist superiority against deeply entrenched Catholic power. The declaration of the republic in 1889 would grant psychiatrists full control of the asylum, and with that, they dismissed the lay brother-hood's workers and replaced them with secular staff members. The "capturing of the asylum"[33] by psychiatrists represented a dramatic turning point for psychiatry, as the profession sought to gain professional and cultural legitimacy in the medical, politi-cal, and socio-cultural spheres.

As a number of historians have attempted to understand the role of madness in the colonial, imperial, and republican eras, it is no wonder that the Brazilian his-toriography of psychiatry is large and continues to grow. However, the exploration of the professionalization of psychiatry has traditionally characterized psychiatrists in Manichean terms.[34] While some historians present narratives that thoughtfully analyze psychiatrists, many have adhered to a Foucauldian framework by presenting psychiatrists as modernizing agents primarily motivated by a functionary and self-interested desire for control, and whose primary method was confinement, both as control and punishment of the marginalized masses. Nonetheless, there is a renais-sance underway in post-Foucauldian analysis of Brazilian psychiatry in upcoming books, articles and contemporaneous works that are currently in dissertation form in Brazil.[35] This body of work engages with psychiatrists as elite actors, as prejudiced men, as citizens of the Atlantic world, as tropical modernist urban reformers, and, in a departure from Foucault, as often well-meaning, and sometimes useful servants of the city's poor and disenfranchised.

A central theme in these works (whether the focus be on Spanish America or Brazil) is the frameshift in the understanding of social assistance from philanthropy to welfare under the banner of liberalism. In liberal democracies, the concept of citizenship, with the expectations and boundaries it entails, presumes a society that makes at least qualified claims of universal equality and access to political, economic, and social privilege, opportunity, and participation.[36] However, the Latin American emergence of iterations of the medical-legal state that sought to exercise control and authority over fragmented and regionalized populations is rife with instances of citizenship deprived and of liberties denied to individuals and groups on the basis of race, class, and gender. Any attempt to come to terms with how psychiatrists hoped to guide the modernization of the respective countries mentioned is confronted by this paradox of liberal professionals employing markedly illiberal means to carry out such programs.[37] At the core of this paradox is the notion that Latin American psychiatry was afflicted by a persistent gap between the universal liberal values that the profession purported to represent and the historical fact of difference that such universal claims failed to accommodate.[38] It was this gap that authorized and justified the exclusion, marginalization, and derision that psychiatrists visited upon those presumed mentally ill who were either indigent, indigenous, of African descent, and/ or non-conformist men/women. Thick hierarchies often lurked beneath the surface of social assistance programs' abstract language as liberalism's inclusive premises of moral equality often came riddled with perceptions of non-elites as fundamentally lacking the prerequisites for claiming the practical entailments of universal equality.

Paths ahead

Apart from the presentation of psychiatrists as multi-dimensional subjects, there is much work to be done in the historiography of psychiatry in Latin America.[39] One area in particular that deserves special consideration is how the presumed mentally ill, their families, and their communities consented to or rejected the meaning-making process of mental illness. Since historians such as Ablard, among others, note the critical absence of a strong functional state apparatus, how did a powerful pervasive discourse of madness and practice of relegating people to that category, and necessarily its attendant diagnostic sub-categories, emerge? It is not at all clear that psychiatrists achieved a great deal of success training individuals in self-governance as an aspect of moral treatment inside the asylum. Unlike other branches of medicine "psychiatric thought lacked a coherent intellectual paradigm and a generally agreed-upon body of etiological and therapeutic knowledge."[40] The effects of psychiatric thought are difficult to measure and assess, yet the view from the asylums and the ways in which psychiatrists in Mexico City, Sucre, Buenos Aires, or Rio de Janeiro wrote about mental illness and its causes strongly suggest that psychiatric ideas were not that generally influential in shaping specific public policies. The diffusion of psychoanalysis in Argentina, among other sites such as Brazil, illustrates how specific ideological currents gained cultural authority. However, the overcrowded asylum as a pan-Latin American reality raises a series of interesting analytical and archival questions about how social institutions developed and put into practice psychiatric thought and the extent to which they legitimized particular discourses and pathologized others. While such an inquiry would undoubtedly be best suited where a rich set of patient records and individual patient files are available, such an investigation could yield deeply nuanced understandings about the psychiatric perspective's diffusion through the public sphere and the extent to which individuals agreed or pretended to agree with such perspectives.

Another fruitful area of research concerns the kinds of diagnoses psychiatrists used and the extent to which they changed over time. More analysis of how particular ailments become psychiatric and political rallying points and in turn, how those mental illness categories (or archetypical psychiatric diagnoses) rose and fell in popularity, reflecting polymorphous anxieties at specific historical junctures can reveal not only medical preoccupations, but socio-cultural barometric pressures. Studies such as Gabriela Nouzeilles' article, "An Imaginary Plague in Turn-of-the-Century Buenos Aires: Hysteria, Discipline, and Languages of the Body," is among the few works that eloquently focuses entirely on how the discourse surrounding a hysteria epidemic, led by male psychiatrists and politicians alike, was primarily created as a response to new social phenomenona in late nineteenth century Buenos Aires – the entrance of women into the public sphere and the beginning of their struggle for universal suffrage, higher education, and economic independence.[11] These processes also operated alongside a more public expression of female sexuality, which became an alarming problem for men threatened by the erosion of their patriarchal and paternal authority. One of the most effective ways of dealing with these non-conformist women and their deviation from their previously normative social position was to classify them as suffering from hysteria, thus marginalizing their voices and giving them over to the strict supervision of psychiatrists, who did not conceal that their goals were subordination and re-education. The elusive epidemiology and pseudo-imaginary aspect of hysteria and certain other diseases by no means implies that they are irrelevant to the field of the history of psychiatry. Rather, these ailments suggest that scientific and socio-cultural conceptions surrounding a disease are as important as its psychological existence and consequences.

Lastly, historians of Latin American psychiatry need to embed psychiatry within a deeper context of healing and care so that psychiatric discourse represents one out of a spectrum of discourses, corresponding to different social groups and doctors. As a mainstay of the history of psychiatry, the asylum has been a useful and yet limiting point of focus with which to examine madness and psychiatry, since the institution has provided the greatest historical record with which to trace the treatment of insanity. However, inherent in conventional histories of the asylum is the notion that psychiatry was the only paradigm practiced inside. The construction of flagship asylums in Brazil, Argentina, and Mexico during the latter half of the nineteenth and early twentieth centuries did not lead to the de facto hegemony of psychiatric rule. When these institutions opened, Catholic nuns and priests, who had traditionally cared for the mentally ill, provided a steady pool of management and reliable labor. The religious palliative care-giving they espoused often clashed with psychiatrists' adherence to tenets of the moral treatment and their perhaps misguided and yet heroic quest to cure madness. Specifically, contestations between emergent psychiatrists and the Santa Casa de Misericórdia Catholic lay brotherhood and the Daughters of Charity order of French nuns over the governance of the Hospício Pedro II, Latin America's first public asylum, is a topic that has recently generated attention from scholars such as myself. In "Of Grand Intentions and Opaque Structures," I investigate how psychiatrists, as apostles of professional rationality, developed their ideology, strategy and tactics relative to reason and bureaucratic power in a contested site of religious charity during the latter half of the nineteenth century. While the aforementioned groups shared ideological ground about the need to seclude the insane in the asylum, their divergent and entangled epistemologies about the construction of madness, its treatment, and its bureaucratic governance shaped their conflicts.[12]

Discussions of boundary disputes have not only been confined to the domain of the asylum. Alexander Moreira-Almeida et al.'s "History of 'Spiritist Madness' in

Brazil"[43] explores how psychiatrists pathologized Kardecist spiritism. Spiritism's logics and logos fundamentally upset psychiatry's model of the self-possessed citizen and nation bound to the vicissitudes of time, materiality, and territoriality, and individuality. Indeed, psychiatrists' inability to curtail spiritism's popularity reflected a failure to articulate a compelling politics of persuasion to the very Brazilians they hoped to assist. Studies such as these deepen our understandings of competing models of care and the self-conscious ways that adversarial practitioners marketed themselves and their services. The public, that consisted of the presumed mentally ill and the sane for whom they performed their expertise and extolled their talents, thus becomes an important protagonist in historical analyses of mental illness and psychiatry. The history of contestation between psychiatry and Kardecist spiritism raises important research questions about the medical profession's relationship to Afro-Atlantic religions since spirit possession has long been applied as their defining and even constitutive feature. Whether it be candomblé in Brazil, vodoun in Haiti, santería in Cuba, Afro-Atlantic religions have also been historically denigrated as anti-modern and atavistic by Latin American elite reformers throughout the nineteenth and early twentieth centuries, even in cases where the religion in question was significantly more popular than psychiatry. More scholarly focus on why and how psychiatrists in particular denounced these religions would serve as a dynamic entrepôt for the history of madness and its management.

Notes

1 For Latin American historians, "the long nineteenth century" generally references the beginnings of the Bourbon and Pombaline reforms enacted in Spanish America and Brazil (respectively) primarily during the second half of the eighteenth century and ends with the Great Depression in 1930.
2 Andrew Scull, "Domestication of Madness," *Medical History* 27 (1983): 233–248.
3 Michel Foucault, *Madness and Civilization: A History of Insanity in the Age of Reason* (New York: Pantheon Books, 1965).
4 Martin Summers, "Suitable Care of the African When Afflicted With Insanity": Race, Madness, and Social Order in Comparative Perspective," *Bulletin of the History of Medicine* 84 (2010): 63. Foucault, Rothman and Scull approached the topic from different perspectives. Rothman argued that "social disorder" characterized Jacksonian America and led to the creation of asylums. Scull criticized Rothman for his vague, liberal analysis and promoted instead a structural Marxist interpretation that viewed the creation of asylums as an elite tool of repression in an emergent capitalist system. Foucault, on other hand, particularly as he developed his ideas in later works such as *Discipline and Punish: The Birth of the Prison* (New York: Vintage Books, 1979) and *The History of Sexuality, Vol. I: An Introduction* (New York: Vintage Books, 1980), rejected Marxist ideas of total state power. He argued instead that institutional power is reproduced or reified through education or disciplinary knowledge, especially through human sciences like medicine. However, despite these epistemological differences, the work of these three scholars was thought to epitomize the "social control thesis." See Thomas E. Brown, "Dance of the Dialectic? Some Reflections (Polemic and Otherwise) on the Present State of Nineteenth-Century Asylum Studies," *Canadian Bulletin of Medical History*, 11 (1994): 267–295.
5 For a more exhaustive list, see pp. 62–67 of Summers, "Suitable Care." Norman Dain, *Disordered Minds: The First Century of Eastern State Hospital in Williamsburg, Virginia, 1766–1866* (Williamsburg, VA: Colonial Williamsburg Foundation, 1971).
6 Brown quotes Gareth Stedman Jones, "History: The Poverty of Empiricism" in Robin Blackburn, ed., *Ideology in Social Science: Readings in Critical Social Theory* (London: Fontana, 1972).

7 Brown, "Dance of the Dialectic," 279.

8 Ibid.

9 Such canonical texts include: Erwin Ackerknecht, *A Short History of Psychiatry* (New York: Hafner, 1968); Gregory Zilboorg, *A History of Medical Psychology* (New York: W. W. Norton, 1967); Roy Porter, *A Social History of Madness: Stories of the Insane* (London: Phoenix Giants, 1996), among others.

10 Andrew Scull, *Museums of Madness: The Social Organization of Insanity in Nineteenth Century England* (London and New York: St. Martin's Press, 1979); David Rothman, *The Discovery of the Asylum: Social Order and Disorder in a new Republic* (Boston, MA: Little, Brown, 1971).

11 Representative works include Nancy Tomes, *A Generous Confidence: Thomas Story Kirkbride and the Art of Asylum-Keeping, 1840–1883* (Cambridge: Cambridge University Press, 1984); Gerald Grob, *The Mad Among Us: A History of the Care of America's Mentally Ill* (New York: Free Press, 1994); Anne Digby, *Madness, Morality and Medicine: A Study of the York Retreat, 1796–1914* (Cambridge: Cambridge University Press, 1985).

12 See Jonathan Sadowsky, *Imperial Bedlam: Institutions of Madness and Colonialism in Southwest Nigeria* (Berkeley: University of California Press, 1999); Richard Keller, *Colonial Madness: Psychiatry in French North Africa* (Chicago: University of Chicago Press, 2007); and Sloan Mahone and Megan Vaughan, eds, *Psychiatry and Empire* (Basingstoke and New York: Palgrave Macmillan 2008). These are some insightful studies along this line of work.

13 Marcos Cueto, *Missionaries of Science: The Rockefeller Foundation in Latin America* (Bloomington: Indiana University Press, 1994); *Saberes andinos: ciencia y tecnología en Bolivia, Ecuador, y Perú* (Lima: Instituto de Estudios Peruanos, 1995); *Salud, Cultura y sociedad en América Latina* (Lima: Instituto de Estudios Peruanos, 1996); and *El regreso de las epidemias: salud y sociedad en el Perú del siglo XX* (Lima: Instituto de Estudios Peruanos, 1997).

14 Alonso Jerónimo de Salas Barbadillo, *Corrección de vicios* (Madrid: s.n., 1615), 3.

15 See Ronaldo Vainfas, *Trópico dos Pecados: Moral, Sexualidade e Inquisição no Brasil* (*Rio de Janeiro: Nova Fronteira*, 1997) among his other works.

16 Ronaldo Vainfas, "Heréticos e Lunáticos," *Revista de História da Biblioteca Nacional* (São Paulo) Ano 1: No. 2 (2005): 24–26.

17 Maria Cristina Sacristán's two studies of madness in colonial Mexico are *Locura e Inquisición en Nueva España, 1571–1760* (Zamora: Colegio de Michoacán, 1992) and *Locura y Disidencia en el Mexico Ilustrado, 1760–1810* (Zamora: El Colegio de Michoacán and Mexico, D.F.: Instituto Mora, 1994). Both studies are based on her extensive work with Inquisition cases in which the possibility that the accused were insane has to be considered as a reason for their aberrant behavior and speech. As with Sara Nalle's study of Bartolomé Sánchez (*Mad for God: Bartolomé Sánchez, the Secret Messiah of Cardenete* (Charlottesville: University of Virginia Press, 2001)), Sacristán finds that Inquisitorial judges were genuinely concerned with the issue of whether or not a suspect was mad, and thus not responsible for their actions. In *Locura y Disidencia*, she argues that, partly in response to the diffusion of ideas associated with the enlightenment, madness acquired an explicitly political dimension, as judges (Inquisitorial and criminal) began to define expressions of social and political dissidence as a form of madness.

18 Maria Cristina Sacristán, *Locura e Inquisición en Nueva España, 1571–1760* (Zamora: Colegio de Michoacán, 1992), 39–40.

19 Ibid., 76.

20 Ibid., 75.

21 The era of Mexican president Porfirio Díaz's government from 1876–1911 is known as the *Porfiriato* and its motto was "Order and Progress."

22 Ann Zulawski, *Unequal Cures: Public Health and Political Change in Bolivia, 1900–1950* (Durham, NC: Duke University Press, 2007).

23 Ibid., 159.

24 See the following articles (among others) by Cristina Rivera-Garza: "'She Neither Respected nor Obeyed Anyone': Inmates and Psychiatrists Debate Gender and Class at the General Insane Asylum La Castañeda, Mexico, 1910–1930," *Hispanic American Historical Review*, 81 (2001): 653–688; "Dangerous Minds: Changing Psychiatric Views of the Mentally Ill in Porfirian Mexico, 1876–1911," *Journal of the History of Medicine and Allied Sciences*, 56 (2001):

36–67. See also the novella *Nadie Me Verá Llorar* (Mexico: Tusquets Editores, 2003) and her book *La Castañeda: Narrativas dolientes desde el Manicomio General, México 1910–1930* (Mexico: Tusquests, 2010).

25 Rivera-Garza, "Dangerous Minds," 43–54.

26 Ibid., 66.

27 Cristina Rivera-Garza, "Becoming Mad in Revolutionary Mexico: Mentally Ill Patients at the General Insane Asylum, Mexico, 1910–1930" in *The Confinement of the Insane: International Perspectives 1800–1965*, eds Roy Porter and David Wright (New York: Cambridge University Press, 2003), 254.

28 Mariano Ben Plotkin, *Freud in the Pampas: The Emergence and Development of a Psychoanalytic Culture in Argentina* (Stanford, CA: Stanford University Press, 2002).

29 Mariano Ben Plotkin's edited volume *Argentina on the Couch: Psychiatry, State, and Society, 1880 to the Present* (Albuquerque: University of New Mexico Press (Diálogos), 2003) brings together a variety of essays that reflect new trends in the history of the behavioral sciences. All of them share a critical approach that transcends Whiggish or celebratory points of view. The book primarily provides new sources and archival documents supporting the thesis that psychoanalysis has permeated Argentine culture. It also highlights the role of the state, of professional groups, and of cultural values in twentieth-century Argentina, and the remarkable gaps between some psychoanalytic conceptualizations and their effective applications in psychiatry and criminology.

30 See for example, Hugo Vezzeti, *La Locura en Argentina* (Buenos Aires: Folios, 1981) and Nancy Leys Stepan's classic *The Hour of Eugenics: Race, Gender, and Nation in Latin America* (Ithaca, NY: Cornell University Press, 1991) for their scholarly influence on Julia Rodriguez's, *Civilizing Argentina: Science, Medicine, and the Modern State* (Chapel Hill, NC: University of North Carolina Press, 2006).

31 Jonathan Ablard, *Madness in Buenos Aires: Patients, Psychiatrists, and the Argentine State 1880–1983* (Athens, OH: Ohio University Press/Calgary, Alberta: University of Calgary Press, 2008).

32 Ibid., 5.

33 Andrew Scull, *Social Order/Mental Disorder: Anglo-American Psychiatry in Historical Perspective* (California: University of California Press, 1989), 328.

34 See for example, the classic works by Jurandir Freire Costa, *História da Psiquiatria no Brasil: Um Corte Ideológico* (Rio de Janeiro: Venou, 1974) and Roberto Machado, Ângela Loureiro, Rogério Luz, and Kátia Muricy, *Danação da Norma: A Medicina Social e Constituição da Psiquiatria no Brasil* (Rio de Janeiro: Edições Graal, 1978). See also Maria Clementina Pereira Cunha, *O Espelho do Mundo Juquery a Historia de um Asilo* (São Paulo: Paz e Terra, 1986) and Magali Gouveia Engel, *Os Delírios da Razão: Médicos, Loucos e Hospício, Rio de Janeiro 1830–1930* (Rio de Janeiro: Ed. Fiocruz, 2001).

35 See for example, Richard Negreiros de Paula's "Um Doutor contra Doutos Leigos: Teixeira Brandão e suas Opiniões quanto ao Poder de Decisão sobre a Custódia Médica," *Revista de História (USP)*, 1 (2009): 169–194; Ana Teresa Venancio, "Da Colônia Agrícola ao Hospital-Colônia: Configurações para a Assistência Psiquiátrica no Brasil na Primeira Metade do Século XX," *História, Ciências, Saúde-Manguinhos*, 18, Suppl. 1 (2011): 35–52; Cristina Facchinetti edited a special issue of *História, Ciências, Saúde-Manguinhos* 17:2 (2012), with novel studies on psychiatry in Brazil during the early twentieth century. She also wrote with Pedro Felipe Neves de Muñoz, "Emil Kraepelin na Ciência Psiquiátrica do Rio de Janeiro, 1903–1933," *História, Ciências, Saúde-Manguinhos* 20 (2013): 239–262. See also William Vaz de Oliveira's dissertation *A Assistência a Alienados na Capital Federal da Primeira República: Discursos e Práticas entre Rupturas e Continuidades* (Rio de Janeiro: Universidade Federal Fluminense (Niterói), 2012).

36 Uday Sigh Mehta, *Liberalism and Empire: A Study in Nineteenth-Century British Liberal Thought* (Chicago: University of Chicago Press, 1999).

37 Uday Mehta, "Liberal Strategies of Exclusion," *Politics and Society*, 18 (December 1990): 427–454.

38 On the intersection of medical discourses and exclusionary policies in other contexts, see Ann Laura Stoler, *Carnal Knowledge: Race and the Intimate in Colonial Rule* (Berkeley: University of California Press, 2002) and Aihwa Ong, "Making the Biopolitical Subject: Cambodian Immigrants, Refugee Medicine, and Cultural Citizenship in California," *Social Science and Medicine*, 40 (1995): 1243–1257.

39 Nonetheless, recent dissertation works that prove to be promising include: Jennifer Lambe, *Baptism by Fire: The Making and Remaking of Madness in Cuba, 1857–1980* (Yale, New Haven, CT: PhD Dissertation (History), 2014), and Stephanie Ballenger, *Modernizing Madness: Doctors, Patients and Asylums in Nineteenth-Century Mexico City* (University of California, Berkeley: PhD Dissertation (History), 2009).

40 Charles Rosenberg, "The Crisis in Psychiatric Legitimacy: Reflections on Psychiatry, Medicine and Public Policy," in *Explaining Epidemics and Other Studies in the History of Medicine*, Charles Rosenberg, (New York: Cambridge University Press, 1992), 249–250.

41 Gabriela Nouzeilles, "An Imaginary Plague in turn-of-the-century Buenos Aires: Hysteria, Discipline, and Languages of the Body," in Diego Armus, ed., *Disease in the History of Modern Latin America: From Malaria to AIDS* (Durham, NC: Duke University Press, 2003), 51–75.

42 Manuella Meyer, "Of Grand Intentions and Opaque Structures: Managing the Hospício Dom Pedro II during Brazil's Second Empire (1852–1890)," *Bulletin of the History of Medicine*, 89 (2015): 733–760.

43 Alexander Moreira-Almeida et al., "History of 'Spiritist Madness' in Brazil," *History of Psychiatry* 16 (2005): 5–25.

11

HISTORIES OF MADNESS IN SOUTH ASIA

Waltraud Ernst

Diversity is a central feature of the Indian Subcontinent's economic, socio-political and cultural life, acknowledged if not venerated by historians and anthropologists alike. A succession of rulers and invaders of different stripes were well aware of it and at times accommodated and even encouraged it, while the British doctrine of divide and rule exploited it. Since the publication of Edward Said's *Orientalism*, South Asia's diversity has even been identified as one of the narrative tropes that the West employed in its hegemonic view of the East, coexisting alongside essentialist attributions such as 'unchanging', 'backward', and 'irrational'. During the period of British colonial rule and the postcolonial era, the Western 'gaze' engendered, in a Lacanian reading, different kinds of psychological responses on the part of those aware of being viewed and judged. This chapter focuses on the various gazes and responses to them: the historiographic perspectives and theories employed, the historical themes highlighted and 'the archive' investigated, and, last but not least, the locale-specific gazes of scholars seeking their professional niche and career path on the globalised map of waxing and waning academic fashions, temporarily quasi-hegemonic academic networks, research funding priorities and the more or less nationalist politics of the powers that be.

Historiographic approaches, methodologies, and theories

The period prior to British rule has mainly been assessed by Sanskritists in relation to Ayurvedic approaches as revealed in Indian medical compendia, such as *Carakasaṃhitā* (first century CE), Suśrutasaṃhitā (third century CE), and *Aṣṭāṅgahṛdayasaṃhitā* (seventh century CE; a synthesis of earlier texts).[1] Buddhist approaches, Siddha, the tradition mainly practised in South India, and Unani, which shares its Graeco-Roman origins with pre-modern Western medicine and was introduced to South Asia from Islamic countries, have been less focused on by Western scholars.[2] An exception is continued interest in the role of dervishes and of Sufism in regard to mental healing.[3] This can partly be explained by a longstanding fascination among Western-based authors with occidental as well as oriental mysticism, which gained particular momentum during the Romantic movement in the West and, more recently, by continued 'New Age' interest in holistic healing.[4]

Zimmermann and others have shown that in Ayurveda an individual's condition is seen to be intrinsically connected with the outer world.[5] A person's mental state therefore reflects circumstances in society at large, requiring treatment to consider environmental and, in some instances, supernatural factors. Ayurveda recognises states of endogenous and exogenous mental illness, *unmada*, as well as those due to possession by supernatural beings, *bhutanmada*. The three main South Asian traditions – Ayurveda, Unani, and Siddha – consider health as a state of complete well-being, both physical and mental, rather than as an absence of a particular illness. Their approaches therefore engage particularly well with the concerns of those suffering from mental imbalance.

Important themes that have emerged in philological debates on ancient Indian medical ideas and practices are relevant also for historians working on the development of non-Western modes of mental healing alongside Western-style approaches introduced by European colonisers from the seventeenth century onwards. Foremost amongst these are the extent to which different medical practices are subject to change over time and cross-fertilization between traditions; the latter has been variously conceptualised as hybridization, creolization, circulation, or entanglement of knowledges and practices. Written dogma as expounded in the founding texts of Indian traditions does not tell us about the manifold ways in which these were practised by a multitude of learned and itinerant healers, in syncretic and flexible ways. Nor can we assume its unchanging nature; what is to be defined as the 'original', 'authoritative' source or dogma, and the 'correct' or 'authentic' practice is subject to interpretation and prevalent power dynamics in the plural field of medicine.[6]

The status of bifurcated categories such as tradition *versus* modernity and indigenous *versus* western has been widely debated as these are based on the essentialist premise of discrete categories that can be clearly delineated.[7] In current historical and anthropological writing, both Eastern and Western medical 'systems' and cultural 'traditions' are considered to be subject to syncretism and vernacularisation, necessitating the recognition of both globalising and localising trends and forces.[8] Even in regard to Western 'New Age' conceptions of wellbeing and their preference for Eastern holistic practices such as Ayurveda and Yoga, analytical emphasis has changed from considering them as part of the 'Orientalist gaze' to identifying the ways in which a collection of particular medical ideas and practices is re-imagined (rather than intentionally misconstrued) on the basis of the needs and circumstances of groups and individuals in different localities.[9] Modern yoga, for example, while being celebrated and marketed as an ancient tradition, is a largely Western product whose creation goes back to the turn of the nineteenth to the twentieth century. Yet, it has been 'repatriated' to India, where it now proliferates alongside many other approaches.[10] Current analyses of how local Asian practices become globalised and re-localised are also closely informed by attention to commercial interests and the politics of medical competition and national(ist) agendas that have driven the popularity of particular approaches.[11]

As philological analysis privileges written accounts, 'folk practices' have naturally been marginal to its concerns. This has been echoed in the politics of medical organisation in South Asia, where village healers have remained at the bottom of the professional hierarchy. Colonialism has fossilised the marginalisation of those who are not only most prominent in terms of numbers but have also been the main port of call for the majority of the population. The treatment of madness along Western lines, by university-trained psychiatrists, in specialist institutions, has been available to (or endured by, depending on our interpretation) only a very small percentage of the population. Historical sources on folk practices are restricted and many of those that are available are problematic, consisting of European observations that tend to either romanticise or condemn them as superstition and fraud, and of sceptical if not downright disparaging accounts by Indian elite practitioners from the three main traditions. Hence, historians of mental health and healing who draw on written sources have tended to examine the development of institution-based psychiatry that emerged from the late eighteenth century onwards rather than folk healing.

In contrast to the textual and elite-medicine focus on the part of philologists, folk practitioners and, to a lesser degree, patients have been at the centre of attention in the numerous studies by anthropologists.[12] Prior to the 1960s and 1970s, this field was dominated by researchers with a medical background. Morris Carstairs, who was trained in general medicine and as a psychiatrist, is a good example. In his village studies of the 1950s, he focused on demon possession and witchcraft as well as the prevalence of mental illness as identified on the basis of modern psychiatric classifications.[13] Subsequently, non-medically trained scholars dominated in the emerging specialist discipline of medical anthropology.[14] However, the trend towards 'public outreach' projects and government and WHO consultancy in anthropology has led to a renewal of the link between anthropology and medicine in the shape of health policy-focused anthropological research.[15] Emphasis is on how health programmes need to be modified in order to facilitate cultural acceptability to particular populations.

A discussion of anthropological research is highly relevant for historians of psychiatry in South Asia, not only because of the wider anthropological and cultural 'turn' in regard to methodological issues that has characterised some branches of historical writing, but also because it constitutes an important source base for well-informed analyses of the local cultures that framed both indigenous healing practices and the world views of patients in Western-style institutions. The connection between the medical and anthropological or cultural has been prevalent also in regard to reappraisals of an earlier trend: 'ethnomedicine'.[16] Ethnomedicine and ethnopsychiatry were prominent academic disciplines during the 1960s and 1970s, focusing in particular on African regions. Ethnopsychiatry and ethnopsychology were fuelled by the ambition to avoid the imposition of Eurocentric psychological and psychiatric categories on populations from the non-Western world. But, by attributing ethno-specific psychological features and mechanisms to particular communities and to 'the colonised' it ran the danger of essentialising and reifying earlier ideas of racial characteristics and 'character'.

In India, the psychoanalyst Girindrasekhar Bose (1887–1953) could be regarded as an early predecessor of the mission that was to become ethnopsychiatry and psychology.[17] He 'Indianised' Freudian ideas and his contention that the Oedipus complex did not apply to Indians was widely discussed and seen as indicative of the uniqueness of the Indian psyche and the need to modify Western approaches to treatment. Bose's work was part of the widespread reception of psychoanalytical thinking and of sexological research during the early twentieth century, particularly in Bengal. Flourishing private psychoanalytical practices were established by Indian and British medical doctors during this period in Indian capitals. Even in psychiatric institutions, medical superintendents dabbled in Rorschach diagnostics and psychoanalytical treatment sessions for some of the privately funded inmates. The fascination with psychoanalysis is shared by modern-day researchers who either focus more narrowly on the historical development of psychoanalysis in India or provide psychoanalytically and psychologically informed readings to particular individuals and to events and processes in history.[18] Like many leading representatives of 1960s and 1970s psychohistory, the latter group of scholars is mostly medically or psychologically trained.[19]

A psychiatric, albeit not narrowly psychoanalytical, approach to the history of mental illness has been prominent alongside histories written by professional historians.[20] Both groups share their main sources, namely government proceedings, mental hospital records and statistics, psychiatrists' correspondence and publications, and case studies of patients discussed in institutional and government files.[21] Historians tend to set these sources within the wider social and political arenas in particular regions that framed the more narrowly medical, institutional and policy-oriented material. The topic areas covered and methodologies employed by these two academic constituencies accordingly tend to differ in terms of their historiographic provenance, namely a more narrowly traditional medical history, on the one hand, and social history and postcolonial approaches, on the other. Intriguingly, researchers from both medical and historical backgrounds tend to take modern or Western medicine as the default setting for their analyses, while philologists and the majority of medical anthropologists privilege indigenous modes as pre-sets.

With few exceptions, the majority of publications by historians on madness in South Asia have been written since the 1990s. Partly because of the comparative scarcity of documentation in regard to indigenous practices of – in contrast to medical texts on – mental healing, the majority of currently available histories focus on the development of Western or modern medicine and its hegemonic encounter with the various modes of healing that were predominant in South Asia during and following the period of colonisation. Another reason for the predominant focus on Western psychiatry pertains to the wider popularity among academics across the globe, since the time of the anti-psychiatry movement in Western countries during the 1960s and 1970s in particular, of Foucaultian ideas on the spread of 'the great confinement', the 'discourse of medicine', 'biopower', and 'surveillance'. These gelled with prevalent postcolonial approaches that focus on resistance, subalternity, hegemony and hybridity, and provided the impetus for the emergence of the field of 'history of colonial medicine', with a predominant focus on Africa and South Asia.[22]

In contrast to other former colonies, especially those in Africa, the colonial encounter in South Asia has been particularly prolonged. At a time when other regions were just beginning to experience European invasion and control, South Asia was well on the path towards anti-colonial resistance, if not decolonisation. In contrast to the majority of work in the history of colonial medicine, historical analyses of Western psychiatry in South Asia have hitherto mainly focused on the nineteenth century. Insights derived from these studies on the relationship between early colonialism and Western medicine cannot be applied to the later period of British rule on account of the very different nature and structure of the colonial state and resistance to it. Nor are features identified for colonial psychiatry in, say, twentieth-century French or Portuguese African territories necessarily identical with those characteristic of nineteenth-century developments in South Asia. Consideration of their very different temporal and spatial contexts is vital. Yet, British and American-influenced scholarship on the South Asian context has tended to exert an almost hegemonic influence on research in other regions since the rise of postcolonial and subaltern paradigms.

The role of locality is relevant also in regard to researchers' academic affiliations. Existing work on the history of madness in India has been undertaken mainly by scholars from Britain and, more recently, North America, employing a social or postcolonial history approach, and by India-based academics who tend to be either medically trained or, in the case of historians, influenced in particular by Foucaultian ideas and postcolonial and feminist theory. Foucault's work was received at different periods in various European countries, in the United States and in South Asia, leading to asynchronous trajectories of the application of his conceptual categories in historical analyses. In contrast, India-based researchers, especially those located outside history departments, are cognisant of recent developments in and lack of adequate provision of mental health care facilities and therefore employ a less theory-guided approach that balances the identification of historical abuse of patients and mismanagement in institutions with presentist assumptions and the need to make modern care and treatment facilities available to Indians. At the same time, some of these histories glorify developments in particular mental hospitals in an uncritical, and overly descriptive, vein. Recent work by Pakistan-based historians on psychiatry in South Asia is sadly absent, mirroring the wider discontinuity of scholarly traditions following the partition of colonial India into Pakistan and the Indian Union.[23]

The history of psychiatry in South Asia is currently located within the wider field of studies on colonial medicine and shares with it a wide range of approaches and central concerns. Gender historians have contributed to the field more recently, drawing their impetus from Showalter's (now dated) work on madness as the 'female malady'; gendered health inequities in South Asia; and postcolonial approaches that focus on the denigration of particular social and political groups by means of their feminisation and on the socio-political and cultural phenomena that drive them. Socio-economically based analyses seem to have gone out of fashion since the rise of postmodernism, but may see a revival in the wake of economic recession in the main countries that tend to continue to drive the agenda of historiographic engagement, despite attempts to 'provincialise Europe'.[24] A methodological problem affecting all current writing relates to its source base. Institutional material and medical case notes as well as representational sources (such as fiction, biographies, songs, imagery) are used by most professional historians. The question is how 'the imaginary' or public representations were related to government policies towards and medical treatment of mental hospital patients. Hospital populations are not representative of the population at large, and any assumed link between popular images and imaginations of madness and gender, on the one hand, and the treatment and experiences of institutionalised people, on the other, cannot a priori be taken for granted.

A limitation of some of the literature, irrespective of its methodological and conceptual provenance, has been the lack of attention paid to how developments in the colony reflected measures adopted in Britain itself. This issue has been at the centre of debates in the wider field of colonial medicine, most prominently in relation to the now hackneyed question, 'what is colonial about colonial medicine?'[25] In regard to the history of colonial psychiatry in South Asia, this question has only recently been addressed by India-based authors. In Britain, the relationship between state policies and psychiatry was part of wider debates and struggles between *laissez-faire* and interventionist approaches. Although local government officials in British India had to follow guidance from the London-based parliamentary Board of Control during the East India Company's period in the early nineteenth century and, from 1858 onwards, directly from British government, different policy emphases in regard to local colonial governance prevailed in the various provinces. Colonial psychiatry and its institutions were therefore framed by a variety of local administrative contexts, institutional preferences, and social cultures. Nonetheless, legal provision established uniformity in all provinces under British rule with the passing of the Criminal Lunatics Act of 1849 and largely followed the blueprints established in England and Wales. The Criminal Lunatics Act of 1851 was explicitly intended to integrate English and Indian Law, and the Indian Lunatics and Lunatic Asylums Act of 1858 adapted to local circumstances provision made earlier in the Lunatic Asylum Act of 1853 for England and Wales. Significant omissions, such as the clause that made the establishment of public lunatic asylums aimed at the poor compulsory in England and Wales, left the decision to provide public institutions for the insane in the colony to individual provincial governments. This clearly points at the intention to encourage the 'roll back' of the colonial state in regard to mental health, rather than to create a network of imposing (and costly to maintain) bricks and mortar manifestations of colonial surveillance – notwithstanding their ideological role in the legitimation of colonial rule.

Suggestions by various authors that the laws governing the detention of criminal and other lunatics were a specifically colonial intervention aimed at the repression and disciplining of colonial subjects and punishment of political dissidents may be in line with postcolonial analysis, but is ill-informed by the evidence we have on the wider legislative politics and public concerns pertaining to the mentally ill in Britain and British India. Legal provision for the care and custody of criminal and other lunatics had been hard fought for by humanitarian reformers in Britain during the late eighteenth and early nineteenth centuries in particular, as they considered it unacceptable for a modern, post-Enlightenment state to deprive those suffering from mental illness from expert treatment and management commensurate with their mental condition and to confine in prisons insane people who had been charged with a crime. Government protection, rather than punishment and neglect, was being campaigned for.[26]

In colonial India, in contrast, restricted measures were implemented that paid lip service to the colonial state's humanitarian and modernising agenda. This puts limitations on the suggestion of a 'great confinement of the insane' and of the pivotal role of biopower in the construction of colonial governmentality and in the minds of the majority of the population in South Asia. While the introduction of Western psychiatry and of institutional provision may be considered as an 'epistemological rupture' at the level of official discourse, the lack of access to and participation in this new worldview or cosmology by the majority of the population and its selective impact on urban elite communities cautions against an unqualified application of these concepts, at least for the nineteenth and most of the twentieth centuries. Psychiatry and its institutions, and the legal provision framing them, in colonial India need to be assessed in relation to local circumstances as well as developments in Britain, North America and other European countries and be focused on the complex inter-relationship between control and care, rather than be reduced to measures of discipline and punishment in congruence with Foucaultian and postcolonial theories or unquestionable signifiers of progress from the point of view of traditional medical history.

Historical themes

Madness, the colonial state and the colonisation of the mind

Following historiographic trends, analyses of the role of psychiatry in relation to the colonial state have predominated in the historical literature.[27] Early work on the late eighteenth and early nineteenth centuries showed the British focus on the confinement of Europeans and of a small number of Indians and Anglo-Indians (Eurasians, of mixed European-Indian parentage) who were closely connected with Europeans as staff or servants or picked up in a state of derangement in areas inhabited by Europeans.[28] Manderson has shown a similar focus on Europeans and indigenous people directly affiliated with them for British Malaya during the early decades of the colonial encounter.[29]

Europeans tended to be repatriated, but no uniform procedure was followed until the first decade of the nineteenth century, when an institution back in England was established by the East India Company dedicated to their reception.[30] However, given the restricted number of Europeans in the civil colonial service and discouragement of European settlement, the majority of Europeans afflicted with mental illness were dealt with by local military authorities through disciplinary procedures. Neither the Company nor the parliamentary Board of Control in London were in favour of an extension of public health services, mainly on cost grounds and a focus on trade. Still, the Company was obliged to make provision from the 1820s onwards for Indian lunatics picked up in urban centres in the steadily increasing number of provinces annexed by the British. This trend was due to the changing nature of Company rule in the East and the influence of humanitarian campaigners at a time when various reforms in regard to the treatment of the mentally ill were introduced in Britain. British parliamentary select committee hearings held every twenty years on the management of colonial affairs by the East India Company enabled reformers to press for changes that were modelled on what were considered as the most progressive and enlightened policies in the colonial motherland.

By the time the British Crown took over from the Company in 1858, in the wake of the Indian Revolt of 1857, a network of public institutions for Indians and of premises for Europeans and higher-class Anglo-Indians was under the control of colonial government. Following the demands of earlier reformers, lunacy policy in India remained closely modelled on the British blueprint, yet left it to local authorities to restrict its scope to urban areas and the confinement of those who were considered to constitute a threat to public safety. This approach continued until the provincialisation of public health services from 1919 onwards. The devolution of mental health to authorities in the provinces did not lead to any significant expansion of provision on account of austerity measures leading up to and in the wake of the two world wars and medical funding priorities that focused on general public health measures, such as vaccination, drainage, waste disposal and clean water supply in urban centres.

Existing writing has interpreted the repatriation of Europeans as a measure to maintain the prestige of the colonisers by means of moving out of sight those who might tarnish it.[31] The increased formalisation of provision for Indian lunatics from the 1920s onwards has been seen as a tool of empire, either in the sense of direct control and surveillance being imposed on Indians or as a way of legitimating and ennobling colonial rule. Within the context of aggressive military and political control exerted by the colonial state, the introduction of Western education and medicine were harnessed for purposes of balancing out the oppression and hardships occasioned by direct British rule. Towards the latter part of the nineteenth century, in the aftermath of the socio-political polarisation sharpened by debates on the Ilbert Bill of 1883 and the formation of the Indian Congress in 1885, public health measures and medical relief had become increasingly perceived by Indian reformers and political agitators as a tax-paying citizen's right. The bad conditions in some institutions became targets for concern and outrage, and better and more facilities were (largely unsuccessfully) mooted.

The process whereby asylums became seen as a public good alongside other medical and welfare measures, which gained momentum as the strength of the anti-colonial movement progressed, has been less well researched. Yet, once reformers' focus came to be on a citizen's right to care and the duty of the colonial state to provide it, the highly restricted scope of colonial psychiatry became even more evident than had been the case previously, when a single institution in each province was seen as a sufficient manifestation of enlightened governance and insurance of public safety from the antics and dangers posed by violent lunatics. This also brought into ever sharper relief the extent to which the colonial state relied on those indigenous ways of healing that it so condemned as mere superstition and proof of the ignorance of the populace. The devolution of services to provincial governments and indeed Indian Independence in 1947 did not change the situation, leading to woefully bad conditions for the mentally ill, as revealed in investigations instigated by campaigners from the 1980s to date.

The establishment of public mental institutions and the privileging of western mental science by the colonial state has been described as part of the 'colonisation of the mind'.[32] The limitations of this process on the ground, in particular in relation to rural populations, have been researched less. For example, in the late 1930s, the one and only public institution for the 105 million people of Bengal, Bihar, and Orissa received about 1300 inpatients per year. Existing work on the early twentieth century indicates that proponents of Western psychiatry in India drew on a multitude of ideas in the Western world rather than following British blueprints only.[33] Parts of the urban Indian elite had begun to see themselves as citizens of a globalising, modern world rather than merely British colonial subjects. Indian psychiatrists and government officials, even if trained by the British, supported connections with prominent people and organisations all over the world, in particular Northern America and Europe. 'Colonial psychiatry', if ever there was such a putatively discrete entity, became a cosmopolitan approach, practised by well-educated Indians who saw their work anchored in allegedly universal, capital-letter-science.

Madness in British India and in Princely India

To complete the picture of the history of psychiatry in South Asia during the modern period, assessment of how Western psychiatry and its institutions developed in the two-fifths of South Asian territories that were ruled by Indian 'princes', is needed.[34] These substantial areas were subject to indirect British governance. They were located as much at the periphery of British colonial rule as they have remained at the margins of research on the status of psychiatry within the wider context of empire. Scholarship to date has been focused on select north-Indian provinces of the British *Raj* and on the princely state of Mysore.[35] This has skewed existing historiography not least because of the danger of undue generalisations regarding other regions in South Asia.

Institutions

The development of the bricks and mortar manifestations of colonial or Western psychiatry has been a main focus of attention. The basic grid for the web of institutional provision in British-ruled India was fixed by the late 1840s, with lunatic asylums of sorts numbering around 15 to 20 throughout the nineteenth century. Some of the Indian states under princely rule that considered themselves as modern and enlightened rather than as backward and despotic established their own institutions in the second half of the nineteenth century. While all asylums intended for the reception of 'Natives only' were public institutions, those dedicated to the reception of Europeans and of the 'better classes' of the Anglo-Indian community were privately run until the 1850s.[36] The East India Company and the War Office reimbursed the private madhouse owners for expenses incurred for the treatment of civil and military Company personnel and officers of HMR forces respectively. The division between privately-run institutions for those perceived to be superior members of the wider community and public institutions for the rest of the populace was in line with developments in Britain and other Western countries. However, within the colonial setting class and gender as well as race, religion, and caste were inexorably the main criteria for institutional segregation. Racial segregation was mostly enforced by means of separate places of confinement for Europeans and Indians; division along the lines of gender, social class and caste was implemented within each single Indian institution.[37] The principle of racial segregation remained in place until Indian Independence in 1947. It was most acutely represented during the early twentieth century by the two public institutions at Ranchi, in the north east of the subcontinent: one, for Europeans and Anglo-Indians, was placed under the control of central government as the devolution of public services to local governments progressed, while the other, just a couple of miles along the road, received Indian lunatics only and was run by local government.[38]

An analytical focus on institutions is limited in scope as it fails to capture the plight of the majority of the mentally ill, both European and Indian. During the Company's period most Europeans afflicted by mental conditions did not pass through the asylum wards set up in Madras (Chennai), Calcutta (Kolkata), and Bombay (Mumbai), but were dealt with locally in regimental hospitals and jails or eventually died from some physical condition during a period when mortality rates among soldiers were extremely high on account of a range of endemic and epidemic disease and unhealthy living conditions. During the later period, those Europeans who could afford it preferred private treatment rather than reception into a public institution that catered for Europeans of all social backgrounds as well as Anglo-Indians. Social distance was maintained by higher-class Europeans towards the lower orders of their own race as well as in regard to Anglo-Indians and Indians. Anglo-Indians and Indians on their part were no less sensitive to issues of social position.

Eventually, provision for paying, first-class Indian and Anglo-Indian patients was made in superior lodgings within the public mental hospital compounds. Sentiments of caste and gender prohibitions still prevented those of elevated Hindu and women of both Muslim and Hindu background from entering a public institution on a voluntary basis. Hence, Indian asylums tended to be avoided by private patients, retaining their character as receptacles for violent and dangerous lunatics even once voluntary boarders were more widely admitted from the 1930s onwards, mirroring provision made for them and for outpatients in the Mental Treatment Act in 1930 in Britain. The establishment of outpatient departments connected with mental hospitals and adjacent to general hospitals at that time enabled a greater number of mentally ill people who were averse to inpatient treatment to be seen by specialist staff. However, the majority of the mentally ill did not present themselves at psychiatric institutions. It is therefore important to keep in mind the difference between a history of mental illness and a history of psychiatry and its institutions in South Asia. Current publications, except those dealing with popular images and public representations, invariably focus on the latter, not least for reasons of the greater ease of access to institutional and official sources.

Beyond the walls of the asylum

Attempts have been made to assess the role of families prior to and during admission to mental institutions, following the example of historians of psychiatry concerned with what was happening 'outside the walls' of the institutions.[39] The doctor-centred approach, too, has been complemented with discussions of the important part played by subordinate or subaltern Indian staff in the day-to-day running of institutions and their impact on the experience of inmates.[40] Lack of sources on this aspect, however, tend to hamper fuller investigations. Alongside race, gender, class and caste, patients' religious needs were addressed by asylum superintendents, by means of shrines and prayer facilities within the compound and observance of major festivals. Preachers and priests of various Christian, Muslim and Hindu denominations were allowed to visit at special occasions and a small number of patients were occasionally allowed parole to visit temples and mosques. Entertainment was provided in the form of singing, theatre performances, games, reading, pet corners, and the like. However, no generalisation can be made in regard to the availability of these facilities as conditions differed considerably in the various institutions and some superintendents favoured them more than others. Patient work figured highly in institutions apart from those short of space for workshops and agricultural pursuits.[41] The role of patient work has been interpreted by historians in both positive and negative terms, as empowerment of patients and an alternative to around-the-clock confinement in cells and wards on the one hand, and as exploitation of free labour on the other.[42] Setting lunatics to work was not a particularly 'colonial' practice; it was well in line with what was happening at public – and some private – institutions in the West. From the early twentieth century onwards, work became increasingly framed as occupational therapy. As in earlier decades, it was a core measure of institutional management at a time when effective medication was restricted and sedation made inmates compliant but unproductive and costly to support.

219

Criminal insanity and intellectual disability

The fact that the majority of admissions to public institutions remained restricted to the violent and dangerous indicates a certain deviation from the British blueprint. The colonial state did not encourage costly provision for 'harmless' lunatics. Public order and safety were main considerations for admission and superintends were empowered to discharge docile, chronically ill inmates periodically in order to free up space on overcrowded wards. It was however considered inadmissible to discharge patients unless their families could be traced and were willing and able to take charge of them. Criminal lunatics had to be restrained in separate cells and, as in Britain, their confinement was ruled by the terms of their sentence. An investigation into the offences and background of criminal lunatics is still needed, not least in order to settle the contested point whether at least some among them were engaged in anti-colonial initiatives.

Throughout most of the period, people with intellectual and developmental disabilities, or 'idiots' and the 'mentally deficient' as they were referred to, were confined alongside the mentally ill if their families could not be traced or when they had committed some crime, pilfering and stealing of food included. The need for separate facilities for the mentally deficient was frequently commented on in official correspondence, but it seems that apart from special wards in some mental hospitals, no measures were taken on an all-India basis until long after Indian Independence. The fate and needs of this group and its history inside and outside institutions during the colonial period has not yet been investigated. Only in relation to 'Shah Daulah's mice', namely children with microcephaly, who were sent by their families to a shrine in current-day Pakistan, has historical research been done more recently.[43] In Britain, the Idiots Act of 1886 allowed for the establishment of voluntary idiot asylums and in 1913 the Mental Deficiency Act empowered local authorities to build their own establishments. The colonial state preferred community provision in its *laissez-faire* approach to public health and welfare; devolution of public services to the provinces did not lead to concerted action by authorities on behalf of children and adults with intellectual and developmental disabilities until well after Independence.

Diagnoses and treatments

As is the case in the history of psychiatry more generally, comprehensive and locality-specific historical assessments of diagnostic and therapeutic *practices* (in contrast to ideas, nosologies as revealed in classification schemes and reports on treatments) are still relatively rare. Currently fashionable conditions such as depression, and hence melancholia and circular insanity, have been focused on mainly in relation to their conceptual developments over time. In regard to British India, too, details on diagnostic and treatment data have been mainly assessed via medical textbooks and journal articles and the forms and reports that had to be produced on an annual basis by asylum superintendents.[44] These sources do not tell us much about what was happening in practice, during the patient–doctor encounter. Nor do we learn about how different kinds of diagnoses and the therapeutic regimes based on them affected particular patient groups' experiences. Nosologies and the explication of therapeutic approaches merely indicate how staff preferred to re-present their role as clinicians to their peers and the medical authorities.

The classification schemes used in British India were prescribed by the central medical authorities and closely followed those extant in Britain, with but minor modifications to allow for locale-specific phenomena that captured European doctors' attention, such as Cannabis Insanity. In relation to therapies, too, approaches prevalent in Britain were followed, ranging from paraldehyde in the late nineteenth to Cardiazol and electroshock therapy in the twentieth centuries, alongside work and water therapy, and some exceptional trials such as mesmerism in the early period, and snake venom, sweet basil, and Indian snakeroot in the later periods.[45] Only few treatments were considered unsuitable and contra-indicated, such as malaria therapy in a region where malaria was endemic. Crucially, individual doctors did not derive their knowledge solely from British-bred ideas and practices. By the early twentieth century at the latest, different styles of nosology and therapy prevalent in Britain, Germany, and North America had become reference points for Indian practitioners who were invariably familiar with wider scientific debates and developments in their expert field through regular overseas research trips to Europe and North America and subscription to a range of relevant journals. We therefore have ample evidence of plurality in regard to the use of diagnostic categories and of treatments as revealed in the official annual reports on the twenty or so mental hospitals in British India as well as in those of some of the princely states.[46]

A noteworthy phenomenon is the presentation of melancholia in a number of institutions as a 'male malady', which disappears in the statistics only slowly towards the eve of Independence. The rise of schizophrenia and of circular insanity/manic depressive psychosis during the same period runs parallel to the steep decline of the use of mania in the aggregate statistics. Institutional variation in these trends is however considerable if the statistics are disaggregated. Further research is needed on the ways in which diagnostic and therapeutic trends varied, both in regard to actual practices and in relation to how these were notated in the prescribed classification schemes and reports.

Patients and families – gender and social background

In addition to institutional analyses, most research produced since the 1990s focuses on case studies of patients and their families. Some attempts have been made to recover the voices of the insane.[47] This tends to put some flesh on the dry bones of official declarations and asylum statistics. However, the question remains of how representative these select studies are of the wider asylum population and, indeed, of the wider population affected by mental conditions. Although a sufferer-focused 'history from below' that goes beyond Whig accounts of big ideas, eminent doctors, and institutions is vital for a 'thick description' and rich histories of mental illness and healing in India, some theory-guided postcolonial or feminist histories and health policy relevant research has, arguably, been guided by the dictates and current popularity of particular concepts and political causes rather than being concerned with what was important to particular individuals and their families at a particular period. Some analyses of gender, for example, have been based on Showalter's doctrine of the 'female malady' and on postcolonial precepts about the feminisation of the Orient and its peoples. These concepts are not easily reconciled with reported gender trends among institutionalised patient populations. Women from all but Christian communities were less likely than men to be confined in the few Western-style institutions that existed during the colonial period; albeit Indian men were for a while reported to have suffered more frequently than women from depression.

The analysis of patients' social background, too, requires more careful assessment than has hitherto been the case. Suggestions that the majority of asylum patients were drawn from the lowest castes and classes are largely un-evidenced. The debate about whether it was mainly the dregs of society and criminal elements who were incarcerated, which raged for a while among historians of psychiatry focusing on developments in Britain, France, and America during the 1980s and 1990s, seems to have bypassed researchers on Indian psychiatry, most of whom began their work only in the last couple of decades. There are two main problems with the assumption of down-and-outs and social rejects forming the majority of asylum inmates. One concerns the doubtful reliability of assessments by institutional staff of patients' caste and social background on admission. The second relates to the restrictive admission policies that privileged the reception of those who had committed crimes, ranging from murder to pilfering and disturbance of the peace in public places. The families of private patients or voluntary boarders for whom a small and invariably insufficient number of hospital beds were reserved in some public institutions had to pay for their upkeep and hence would not have come from deprived backgrounds. Nothing is as yet known about the social standing of the considerable number of outpatients who received treatment at some institutions from the early twentieth century onwards, nor about the clientele of private clinics dedicated to the treatment of mental conditions that emerged in major towns.

Available evidence from one public institution in northeast India points to the preponderance of inmates from what could be referred to as lower and lower-middle-class and caste communities rather than from outcaste groups and the bottom layer of Indian society.[48] Unfortunately, the institutional case books that contain information on individual patients tend to be increasingly silent on their family background from the middle to the late nineteenth century onwards, when restrictions were imposed on the length of official reports and the increased medicalisation of case notes led to a narrative disjuncture between patients' former lives and their institutionalised personae. The joy experienced by researchers who are lucky enough to find a rare comment on patients' families or even letters or diaries among the dull statistics and the professional 'doctorese' prevalent in medical case notes may be understandable and enviable, but it needs to be complemented by a soberly cautious approach as to what exactly this exceptional material is supposed to represent.

Conclusion

Despite certain scholarly lacunae, the history of madness in South Asia in its manifold guises seems to be in good health. Alongside its African twin, it occupies a prominent niche in the wider field of history of psychiatry, no doubt partly driven by current scholarly interests in globalisation and the prioritising by national and international funding agencies of potentially policy-relevant historical research and 'impact' studies. Despite fecundity within the field, there remains a lack of engagement with and crossovers between histories of different regions (and its historians). Diverse histori-ographic traditions of research on Western psychiatry and on the varied colonial and indigenous medicines that were situated within different kinds of colonialism (such as settler, imperial, indirect, French, British, American, Spanish, and so on) have emerged quite independently.[49] This attests to the diversity of Western and colonial experiences and indigenous actions as well as the need to disaggregate or decon-struct the meanings of 'colonial psychiatry', 'medical globalisation', and 'traditional healing' in contextually focused and localised ways.

Some conceptual and methodological challenges remain. One concerns a criti-cal conceptual approach that acknowledges connections and crossovers rather than merely dissemination and transfer, without losing sight of issues of power, resistance, and hegemony. Another relates to the woefully marginal position to which histories of madness in non-European/North American are relegated by 'mainstream' histo-ries of psychiatry, which on their part remain uninformed by the manifold insights they could garner from its subalternised 'others'. The onus is on historians of psychi-atry in Western countries to engage seriously with non-Western-focused scholarship, in its own right and in terms of what it has to contribute to putative mainstream paradigms and narratives, rather than viewing it as a fascinating, exotic extra on the conference circuit (that usually remains conveniently compartmentalised in its own panel labelled 'colonial/indigenous/other/etc.') and as a necessary addition to edited volumes that merely pay lip service to the requirements of academic inclusivity. Globalising and localising the history of madness is not enough; it also needs to be self-reflective and beware of historiographic hegemony.

Notes

1 For an introduction to the Āyurvedic tradition see Dagmar Benner, 'Healing and Medicine in Āyurveda and South Asia.' In Lindsay Jones (ed.), *Encyclopedia of Religion* (New York: Macmillan, 2005, 2nd edn), 3852–8. See also: Julius Jolly, *Indian Medicine*, Translated from German by C.G. Kashikar (New Delhi: Munshiram Manoharlal, 1994 [1951], 3rd edn). Horacio Fabrega Jr, *History of Mental Illness in India: A cultural Psychiatry Retrospective* (Delhi: Motilal Banarsidass Publishers, 2009). A.L. Basham, 'The Practice of Medicine in Ancient and Medieval India'. In C. Leslie (ed.), *Asian Medical Systems: A Comparative Study* (New Delhi: Motilal Banarsidass, 1998 [1976]), 18–43. M.V. Govindswamy, 'Need for research in systems of Indian Philosophy and Ayurveda with special reference to Psychological Medicine. *Journal of the Indian Medical Association* 18, 8 (1949), 283–6. Wilhelm Halbfass, 'The Therapeutic Paradigm and the Search for Identity in Indian Philosophy'. In W. Halbfass, *Tradition and Reflection: Explorations in Indian Thought* (Albany: SUNY Press, 1991). Dominik Wujastyk, *The Roots of Āyurveda: Selections from Sanskrit Medical Writings* (London and New York: Penguin Group, 2003, 3rd edn). Mitchell Weiss, 'History of Psychiatry in India: Toward a Culturally and Historiographically Informed Study of Indigenous Traditions', *Samiksa* 40, 2 (1986), 31–45.
2 On Siddha, see: T.N. Ganapathy, 'The Siddha Conception of the Human Body,' In T. N. Ganapathy, *The Philosophy of the Tamil Siddhas* (New Delhi: Indian Council of Philosophical Research, 1993), 115–140. David Gordon White, *The Alchemical Body: Siddha Traditions in Medieval India* (Chicago: University of Chicago Press, 1996). On Buddhism, see: Kenneth G. Zysk, *Asceticism and Healing in Ancient India: Medicine in the Buddhist Monastery* (Delhi: Motilal Banarsidass, 1998, 2nd edn). On Unani, see Hakim Syed Zillur Rahman, 'Unani Medicine in India: Its Origin and Fundamental Concepts'. In B. V. Subbarayappa (ed.) *History of Science, Philosophy and Culture in Indian Civilization* (New Delhi: Centre for Studies in Civilizations, 2001, Vol. IV Part 2), 298–325. Guy Attewell, 'Islamic Medicines'. In Helaine

Selin (ed.) *Medicine Across Cultures* (Boston: Kluwer, 2003). J.C. Buerger, 'The Practice of Medicine in Ancient and Medieval India'. In C. Leslie (ed.), *Asian Medical Systems: A Comparative Study* (New Delhi: Motilal Banarsidass, 1998 [1976]). Michael W. Dols, *Majnun: The madman in medieval Islamic society*, (Oxford: Clarendon, 1992; Oxford Scholarship Online: October 2011). Claudia Liebeskind, 'Unani Medicine of the Subcontinent'. In Jan van Alpen and Anthony Aris (eds), *Oriental Medicine* (Chicago: Serindia, 1995), 39–63.

3 The founding of the *Journal of Sufi Studies* in 2012, for example, is indicative of the popularity of the subject. Nile Green, *Sufism: A Global History* (Chichester: Wiley-Blackwell, 2012). Nile Green, 'Jack Sepoys and the Dervishes; Islam and the Indian Soldier in Princely India', *Journal of Royal Asiatic Society* 18 (2008), 31–46. Hakim G.M Chisti, A.A.G. Mainuddin and N.D. Chisti, *The Book of Sufi Healing* (Rochester, 1991). Thomas Daehnhardt, *Change and Continuity in Indian Sufism* (New Delhi: Printworld, 2002). Sudhir Kakar, *Shamans, Mystics, and Doctors: A Psychological Inquiry into India and its Healing Traditions* (New York: Knopf, 1982). Fabrizio Speziale, 'The relation between Galenic medicine and Sufism in India during the Delhi and Deccan Sultanates', *East and West* 53, 1–4 (2003), 149–178.

4 Francis Zimmermann, 'Gentle Purge. The flower power of Ayurveda'. In: Charles Leslie and Allan Young (eds), *Paths to Asian Medical Knowledge* (Berkeley: University of California Press, 1992). Elizabeth de Michelis, *A History of Modern Yoga, Patanjali and Western Exotericism* (New York: Continuum International, 2004).

5 Francis Zimmermann, *The Jungle and the Aroma of Meats. An ecological theme in Hindu Medicine* (Berkeley: University of California Press, 1987 [French: 1982]). Waltraud Ernst, review of *Francis Zimmermann, The Jungle and the Aroma of Meats.* (Delhi: Motilal Banarsidass, 1999), *Asian Medicine Newsletter* (September 2000): 14–16.

6 Waltraud Ernst (ed.), *Plural Medicine, Tradition and Modernity* (London: Routledge, 2002); Guy Attewell: Refiguring unani tibb: Plural healing in late colonial India (Hyderabad: Orient Longman, 2007). Dagmar Wujastyk and Frederick Smith (eds), *Modern and Global Ayurveda: Pluralism and Paradigms* (New York: Suny Press, 2008). V. Sujatha, 'Pluralism in Indian medicine: Medical lore as a genre of medical knowledge', *Contributions to Indian Sociology* 41, 2, 2007, 169–202.

7 For early literature on this issue see Charles Leslie (ed.), *Asian Medical Systems* (Berkeley: University of California Press, 1976; reprinted Delhi: Motilal, 1998).

8 Projit Mukharji, *Nationalizing the Body: The Medical Market, Print and Daktari Medicine* (London: Anthem Press 2009). Rachel Berger, *Ayurveda Made Modern: Political Histories of Indigenous Medicine in North India, 1900–1955* (Houndmills: Palgrave Macmillan, 2013). J.S. Alter (ed.), *Asian Medicine and Globalization* (Philadelphia: University of Pennsylvania Press, 2005).

9 See, for example, David Arnold and Sumit Sarkar, 'In Search of Rational Remedies: Homoeopathy in Nineteenth-Century Bengal'. In Waltraud Ernst (ed.), *Plural Medicine, Tradition and Modernity* (London: Routledge, 2002). H. Naraindas and C. Bastos, *Healing Holidays* (London: Routledge, 2015).

10 Elizabeth de Michelis, *A History of Modern Yoga, Patanjali and Western Exotericism* (New York: Continuum International, 2004). Waltraud Ernst, 'Cultural Import – Yoga, Plural Medicine and East-West Exchanges'. In K. Arnold and T. Boon (eds), *Treat Yourself* (London, Science Museum/Wellcome Publications, 2003), 12–4.

11 Maarten Bode, 'Taking Traditional Knowledge to the Market: The Commoditization of Indian Medicine', *Anthropology and Medicine* 13, 3 (2006) 225–36. Madhulika Banerjee, *Power, Knowledge, Medicine: Ayurvedic pharmaceuticals at home and in the world* (Hyderabad: Orient Blackswan, 2009). Rachel Berger, *Ayurveda Made Modern. Political Histories of Indigenous Medicine in North India, 1900–1955*, (Cambridge: University Press, 2013).

12 For example, see Maarten Bode and G. Hariramamurthi, 'Integrating folk healers in India's public health: acceptance, legitimacy and emancipation', *eJournal of Indian Medicine* 7 (2014): 1–20. V. Sujatha, 'Innovation within and between traditions: Dilemma of traditional medicine in contemporary India', *Science, Technology and Society* 16, 2 (2011), 191–213. Johannes Quack, 'Ignorance and utilization: mental health care outside the purview of the Indian state.' *Anthropology and Medicine* 19, 3 (2012), 277–90. Johannes Quack, '"What do I know?" Scholastic fallacies and pragmatic religiosity in mental health-seeking behaviour in India.' *Mental Health, Religion and Culture* 16, 4 (2013), 403–18. Darshan Shankar,

'Indigenous health services. The state of the art.' In Alok Mukhopadhyay (ed.), *State of India's Health* (New Delhi: Voluntary Health Association of India, 1992), 129–161. Darshan Shankar, 'Community-Based Oral Health Traditions in Rural India'. In D. Shankar and P.M. Unnikrishnan (eds), *Challenging the Indian Medical Heritage* (New Delhi: Foundation Books, 2004), 19–26. Kabir Sheikh and Asha George (eds), *Health Providers in India. On the Frontlines of Change* (London: Routledge, 2010). V. Sujatha and Leena Abraham (eds), *Indigenous Medicine, State and Society: Medical Pluralism in Contemporary India* (New Delhi: Orient Blackswan, 2012). For a sociological historical analysis, see Roger Jeffery, 'Policies towards Indigenous Healers in Independent India', *Social Science and Medicine* 16 (1982), 1835–41.

13 G.M. Carstairs, *Death of a Witch: A Village in North India, 1950–1981* (London: Hutchinson, 1983); G.M. Carstairs, *The Twice-Born: A Study of a Community of High-Caste Hindus* (Bloomington: Indiana University Press, 1958).

14 Gananath Obeyesekere, 'The Theory and Practice of Psychological Medicine in the Ayurvedic Tradition', *Culture, Medicine and Psychiatry* 1 (1977): 151–81.
Beatrix Pfleiderer, 'The semiotics of ritual healing in a North Indian Muslim shrine', *Social Science and Medicine* 27, 5 (1988), 417–24. Mark Nichter, 'Idioms of distress: alternatives in the expression of psychosocial distress: a case study from South India', *Culture Medicine, and Psychiatry*, 5 (1981), 379–408. Mark Nichter, 'Negotiation of the illness experience: the influence of ayurvedic therapy on the psychosocial dimensions of illness', *Culture, Medicine, and Psychiatry* 5 (1981), 5–24. There continued to exist an overlap between medically and anthropologically trained authors, as in the case of Arthur Kleinman, *Patients and Healers in the Context of Culture* (1980); *Social Origins of Distress and Disease* (1986); *Rethinking Psychiatry* (1988); and *Illness Narratives* (1988).

15 For example, Nichter's recent work is almost exclusively focused on policy-relevant research. *Global Health: Why Cultural Perceptions, Social Representations, and Biopolitics Matter* (Tucson: University of Arizona Press, 2008). Mark Nichter, Cecilia S. Acuin, and Alberta Vargas, *Introducing Zinc in a Diarrhoeal Disease Control Programme: Guide to Conducting Formative Research* (Geneva: World Health Organization, 2008). Mark Nichter and Margaret Lock (eds), *New Horizons in Medical Anthropology* (New York: Routledge, 2002). Mark Nichter and Mimi Nichter, *Anthropology and International Health: Asian Case Studies* (New York: Routledge, 1996).

16 Mark Nichter (ed.), *Anthropological Approaches to the Study of Ethnomedicine* (Amsterdam: Gordon and Breach Publishers, 1992). Different approaches to ethno-medicine and psychiatry were preferred by authors based in various European countries; for Germany, see Paul Parin, Fritz Morgenthaler and Goldy Parin-Matthèy: *Die Weißen denken zuviel. Psychoanalytische Untersuchungen bei den Dogon in Westafrika* (Europäische Verlags-Anstalt, Hamburg 1993 [1963]). Waltraud Ernst, *Land-Stadt Migration in Kenia. Handlungstheorie und ethno-psychoanalytische Fallstudien von Frauen* (Konstanz/Saarbruecken: Dipl-Psych Dissertation, 1982).

17 On Bose and psychoanalysis, see: Christiane Hartnack, *Psychoanalysis in Colonial India* (Oxford: University Press, 2001). Amit Ranjan Basu, 'Girindrasekhar Basu and the coming of psychology in colonial India,' *Theoretical Perspective* 6 (1999), 26–55. Christopher Harding, 'The Freud Franchise: Independence of Mind in India and Japan.' In R. Clarke (ed.), *Celebrity and Colonialism: Fame, Power and Representation in (Post) Colonial Cultures* (Newcastle: Cambridge Scholars Press, 2009). A.K. Ramanujan, 'The Indian Oedipus.' In Lowell Edmunds and Alan Dundas (eds), *Oedipus: A Folklore Casebook* (New York: Garland, 1983), 234–66. Tarun Chandra Sinha, 'Development of Psychoanalysis in India', *International Journal of Psychoanalysis* 47 (1966), 427–39. Shruti Kapila, 'Freud and His Indian Friends'. In Sloane Mahone and Megan Vaughan (eds) *Psychiatry and Empire* (Basingstoke: Palgrave Macmillan, 2007), 124–52.

18 Christiane Hartnack, *Psychoanalysis in Colonial* India (Oxford: University Press, 2001). A.R. Basu, 'The Coming of Psychoanalysis in Colonial India', *Centre for Studies in Social Sciences Occasional Paper* 5 (1999), 36–54. Ashis Nandy, *The Savage Freud and other essays on possible and retrievable selves* (Delhi: Oxford University Press, 1995). Ashis Nandy, 'History's forgotten doubles', *History and Theory* 34 (1995), 44–66. Ashis Nandy, *The Intimate Enemy: Loss and Recovery of Self under Colonialism* (Delhi and Oxford: Oxford University Press, 1983). Sudhir Kakar, *Culture and Psyche: Selected essays* (Delhi: Oxford University Press, 1997).

19 For example: Erik H. Erikson, *Gandhi's Truth: On the Origins of Militant Nonviolence* (New York: W.W. Norton and Co, *1969*). Sudhir Kakar, *The Inner World: A Psychoanalytic Study of Childhood and Society in India* (New Delhi: Oxford University Press, 2012 [1978]). Sudhir Kakar, *Shamans, Mystics and Doctors: a psychological inquiry into India and its healing traditions* (New Delhi: Oxford, 1982). Sudhir Kakar, 'Western Science, Eastern Minds', *The Wilson Quarterly* 15, 1 (1991 [1976]), 109–116.

20 James H. Mills and Sanjeev Jain, 'Mapother of the Maudsley and Psychiatry at the End of the Raj', in Sloan Mahone and Megan Vaughan (eds), *Psychiatry and Empire* (Basingstoke: Palgrave Macmillan, 2007). Sanjeev Jain, 'Psychiatry and confinement in India.' In Roy Porter and David Wright (eds), *The Confinement of the Insane. International Perspectives, 1800–1965* (Cambridge: University Press, 2003), 273–98. Sanjeev Jain and Alok Sarin, 'Some reflections on the development of psychiatry in India', *National Medical Journal of India* 13, 6 (2000), 329–30. Khin-Maung-Zaw, 'Psychiatric services in Myanmar. A historical perspective', *Psychiatric Bulletin* 21 (1997), 506–9. J. S. Neki, 'Psychotherapy in India', *Indian Journal of Psychiatry* 19, 2 (1977), 1–10. Sanjeev Jain and Pratima Murthy, 'The other Bose: an account of missed opportunities in the history of neurobiology in India', *Current Science* 97, 2 (2009), 266–9.

21 James Mills, 'The Mad and the Past: retrospective diagnosis, post-coloniality, discourse analysis and the asylum archive', *Journal of Medical Humanities* 3 (2000), 141–58. Alok Sarin and Sanjeev Jain, 'The census of India and the mentally ill', *Indian Journal of Psychiatry* 54, 1 (2012), 32–6. On the mismanagement of patient records in archives: Shilpi Rajpal, 'Experiencing the Indian Archives,' *Economic and Political Weekly* XLVII, no. 16 (April 2012): 19–21.

22 For an early assessment of the field see: Richard Keller, 'Madness and Colonization: Psychiatry in the British and French Empires, 1800–1962', *Journal of Social History* 35, 2 (2001), 269–94.

23 L.P. Verma, 'History of Psychiatry in India and Pakistan', *Indian Journal of Neurology and Psychiatry* 4 (1953), 138–64. On the experience of Partition, see Alok Sarin, Sarah Ghani and Sanjeev Jain, 'Bad Times and Sad Moods'. In: Urvashi Butalia (ed.), *Partition, The Long Shadow* (New Delhi: Penguin, 2015), 249–264. Sanjeev Jain and Alok Sarin, 'Partition and the Mentally Ill', *Economic and Political Weekly*, XLVII, 29 (2012), 4–5.

24 Dipesh Chakrabarty, *Provincializing Europe. Postcolonial Though and Historical Difference* (Princeton: University Press, 2000).

25 Waltraud Ernst, 'Beyond East and West: From the History of Colonial Medicine to a Social History of Medicine(s) in South Asia', *Social History of Medicine* 20 (2007), 505–24.

26 For a focus on the 'criminalisation of the insane', see Shilpi Rajpal, 'Colonial Psychiatry in Mid-Nineteenth Century: The James Clark Enquiry', *South Asia Research*, 35, 1 (2015), 61–80.

27 Jonathan Saha, 'Madness and the Making of a Colonial Order in Burma', *Modern Asian Studies* 47, 2 (2013), 406–35.

28 Waltraud Ernst, *Mad Tales from the Raj* (London: Routledge, 1991; new Introduction: London: Anthem, 2010). Waltraud Ernst, 'The Establishment of 'Native Lunatic Asylums' in Early Nineteenth-Century British India'. In Jan G. Meulenbeld and Dominik Wujastyk (eds), *Studies on Indian Medical Traditions* (Groningen: Egbert Forsten, 1987; Delhi: Motilal, 2001), 169–204.

29 Lenore Manderson, 'Health Services and the Legitimation of the Colonial State: British Malaya 1786–1941', *International Journal of Health Services* 17, 1 (1987), 91–112.

30 Waltraud Ernst, 'Asylum Provision and the East India Company in the Nineteenth Century', *Medical History* 42 (1998), 476–502.

31 Waltraud Ernst, *Mad Tales from the Raj*; Harald Fischer-Tiné, *Low and Licentious Europeans': Race, Class and White Subalternity in Colonial India* (New Delhi: Orient BlackSwan, 2009).

32 Dinesh Bhugra, 'The Colonized Psyche: British Influence on Indian Psychiatry'. In Dinesh Bhugra and Ronals Littlewood (eds), *Colonialism and Psychiatry* (New Delhi: Oxford University Press, 2001); 46–76. Shruti Kapila, 'Masculinity and Madness; Princely Personhood and Colonial Sciences of Mind in Western India, 1871–1940', *Past and Present*, 187 (2005), 121–56.

33 Waltraud Ernst, 'Practising "Colonial" or "Modern" Psychiatry in British India? Treatments at the Indian Mental Hospital at Ranchi, 1925–1940', in W. Ernst and T. Mueller (eds), *Transnational Psychiatries. Social and Cultural Histories of Psychiatry in Comparative Perspective* (Newcastle: Cambridge Scholars, 2010).

34 Waltraud Ernst, Biswamoy Pati and T. V. Sekher, *Health and Medicine in Indian Princely States, c. 1850–1950* (London and New York: Routledge, 2016).

35 Waltraud Ernst, 'Centres and Peripheries in the Periphery. Medicine and Psychiatry in British India, *c.* 1920–1940', in T. Mueller (ed.) Zentrum und Peripherie in der Geschichte der Medizin (Stuttgart: Franz Steiner, 2016). On Mysore, see Purushottama Bilimoria, S. Jain, J.H. Mills, P. Murthy, S. P. Wood, 'Lost souls, Troubled minds: The medicalization of madness in Mysore State during the British Raj.' In Purushottama Bilimoria and K. Sridhar Melukote (eds), *Traditions of Science: Cross-Cultural Perspectives* (Delhi: Munshiram Manoharial, 2007). Sanjeev Jain and P. Murthy, 'Madmen and specialists: the clientele and the staff of the Lunatic Asylum, Bangalore', *International Review of Psychiatry* 18, 4 (2006), 345–54. On Indian Princes and madness: Fiona Groenhout, 'Loyal Feudatories or Depraved Despots? The deposition of princes in the Central India Agency, c. 1880–1947.' In Waltrud Ernst and Biswampoy Pati (eds), *India's Princely States. People, Princes and Colonialism* (London: Routledge, 2007), 99–117. Shruti Kapila, 'Masculinity and Madness. Princely Personhood and Colonial Sciences of Mind in Western India, 1871–1940', *Past and Present* 187 (2005), 121–56.

36 On Indian mental hospitals in the late nineteenth century, see James H. Mills, *Madness, Cannabis and Colonialism: The 'Native-Only' Lunatic Asylums of British India, 1857–1900* (Great Britain: Macmillan, 2000). James Mills, 'The history of modern psychiatry in India, 1858–1947', *History of Psychiatry 12, 48 (2001), 431–58.* Debjani Das, *Houses of Madness: Insanity and Asylums of Bengal in Nineteenth-Century India* (New Delhi: Oxford University Press, 2015). Shilpi Rajpal, 'Colonial Psychiatry in Mid-Nineteenth Century: The James Clark Enquiry', *South Asia Research* 35, 1 (2015), 61–80. Waltraud Ernst, 'Institutions, People and Power'. In B. Pati and M. Harrison (eds), *The Social History of Health and Medicine in Colonial India* (London and New York, Routledge, 2009), 129–150. Waltraud Ernst, 'Madness and Colonial Spaces. British India, 1800–1947'. In Leslie Topp, James Moran and Jonathan Andrews (eds), *Madness, Architecture and the Built Environment* (London and New York: Routledge, 2007).

37 Waltraud Ernst, 'Idioms of madness and colonial boundaries', *Comparative Studies in Society and History* 39, 1 (1997), 153–81. Waltraud Ernst, 'Racial, social and cultural factors in the development of a colonial institution: The Bombay Lunatic Asylum, 1670–1858', *International Quarterly for Asian Studies* 1/2 (1992), 61–80. 'Colonial policies and the Madras Lunatic Asylum in the early nineteenth century', in M. Harrison and B. Pati (eds), *Medicine and Empire* (Hyderabad: Orient Longman, 2001), pp. 137–65. 'The establishment of "Native Lunatic Asylums" in early nineteenth-century British India', in Jan G. Meulenbeld and Dominik Wujastyk (eds), *Studies in Indian Medical History* (Delhi: Motilal Banarsidass, 2001) Revised edition, pp. 169–204.

38 On the former European Mental Hospital, Ranchi, see S. Haque *Nizamie, Nishant Goyal, Mohammad Ziaul Haq*, and *Sayeed Akhtar*, 'Central Institute of Psychiatry: a tradition in excellence', *Indian Journal of Psychiatry* 50, 2 (2008), 144–48. On the Indian Mental Hospital, Ranchi, see Waltraud Ernst, Colonialism *and Transnational Psychiatry. The Case of an Indian Mental Hospital in British India, c. 1920–1940* (London: Anthem, 2013).

39 Akihito Suzuki, *Madness at Home. The Psychiatrist, the Patient, and the Family in England, 1820–1860* (Berkeley: University of California Press, 2006). Lisa Smith, 'Reassessing the Role of the Family: Women's Medical Care in Eighteenth-Century England', *Social History of Medicine* 16, 3 (2003), 327–42. Peter Bartlett and David Wright (eds), *Outside the Walls of the Asylum: The History of Care in the Community 1750–2000* (London: Athlone Press, 1999).

40 H. Mills, *Madness, Cannabis and Colonialism: The 'Native-Only' Lunatic Asylums of British India, 1857–1900* (Great Britain: Macmillan, 2000). Debjani Das, *Houses of Madness: Insanity and Asylums of Bengal in Nineteenth-Century India* (New Delhi: Oxford University Press, 2015).

41 Waltraud Ernst, '"Useful both to the patients as well as to the State." Patient work in colonial mental hospitals in South Asia, *c.* 1818–1948', in W. Ernst (ed.), *Work, Psychiatry and Society,*

c. 1750–2010 (Manchester: University Press, 2016). Shilpi Rajpal, Quotidian Madness: 'Time, Management and Asylums in Colonial North India, *c.* 1850–1947', *Studies in History* 31, 2 (2015), 206–34. James H. Mills, '"More Important to Civilize Than Subdue"? Lunatic Asylums, Psychiatric Practice and Fantasies of "the Civilizing Mission" in British India, 1858–1900.' In Harald Fischer-Tine and Michael Mann (eds), *Colonialism as a Civilizing Mission: Cultural Ideology in British India* (London: Anthem, 2004), 186–87.

42 'Therapy and empowerment, coercion and punishment: historical and contemporary perspectives on work, psychiatry and society.' In W. Ernst (ed.), *Work, Psychiatry and Society, c. 1750–2010* (Manchester: University Press, 2016).

43 M. Miles, 'Pakistan's microcephalic chuas of Shah Daulah: Cursed, clamped or cherished?, *History of Psychiatry* 7 (1996), 571–89.

44 P. Radhika, Pratima Murthy, Alok Sarin, Sanjeev Jain, 'Psychological symptoms and medical responses in nineteenth-century India', *History of Psychiatry* 26, 1 (2015), 88–97. James H. Mills, 'Re-forming the Indian: Treatment Regimes in the Lunatic Asylums of British India, 1857–1880', *The Indian Economic and Social History Review* 36, 4 (1999), 431–59. For the twentieth century, see chapter 4 on 'Classifications, Types of Disorder and Aetiology' and chapter 5 on 'Treatments', in Waltraud Ernst, *Colonialism and Transnational Psychiatry. The Case of an Indian Mental Hospital in British India, c. 1920–1940* (London: Anthem, 2013).

45 Waltraud Ernst, 'Colonial psychiatry, magic and religion', *History of Psychiatry* 15, 1 (2004), 57–71. Waltraud Ernst, 'Under the influence in British India: Esdaile and the critics of his 'Mesmeric Hospital' in Calcutta', *Psychological Medicine* 25 (1995), 1113–23.

46 Waltraud Ernst, '"Colonial" and "Modern" Psychiatry in British India. Treatments at the Indian Mental Hospital at Ranchi, 1925–1940.' In W. Ernst and T. Mueller (eds), *Transnational Psychiatries* (Newcastle: Cambridge Scholars, 2010). Waltraud Ernst, 'The Indianization of Colonial Medicine', *NTM – Journal for the History of Science, Technology and Medicine* 20, 4 (2012), 61–89.

47 H. Mills, *Madness, Cannabis and Colonialism: The 'Native-Only' Lunatic Asylums of British India, 1857–1900* (Great Britain: Macmillan, 2000). Waltraud Ernst, 'Mad, Bad and/or Subaltern?', Paper presented at the Situating the Subaltern in South Asian Medical History Workshop, University of Warwick, 2009. Waltraud Ernst, 'Doctor-patient interaction in British India: A case of "intellectual insanity"', *History of Psychiatry* 1, 1 (1990), 207–22. Waltraud Ernst, 'European madness and gender in nineteenth-century British India', *Social History of Medicine* 9 (1996), 357–82. Waltraud Ernst, 'On being insane in alien places. Case-Histories from British India, c. 1800–1930.' In M. Harper (ed.) *Migration and Mental Health* (London: Palgrave Macmillan, 2016).

48 Waltraud Ernst, *Colonialism and Transnational Psychiatry. The Case of an Indian Mental Hospital in British India, c. 1920–1940* (London: Anthem, 2013).

49 Anne Digby, Waltraud Ernst and Projit B. Mukharji (eds), *Crossing Colonial Historiographies. Histories of Colonial and Indigenous Medicines in Transnational Perspective* (Newcastle: Cambridge Scholars, 2010).

12

MAD AFRICA

Sally Swartz

Opening questions: imagining Africa and encounters with the "other"

To write a brief history of the scholarship surrounding "madness" in Africa produces a series of problems, none of them solvable within the limits of a single book chapter. They must be entertained therefore as opening caveats, to be stitched into corners of a narrative that will inevitably be slimmer and less nuanced than the history itself deserves.

Africa is a continent. While there may be common themes with regard to the identification and treatment of madness across the stretch of the continent, the similarity to themes from other times and continents has a strong ring of the universal about it. Perhaps where there are common themes, this points simply to a universalizing lens, a phenomenology that reduces the particular to uniform sets of understandings, shaped by a long history of a certain kind of narrative encounter. The first caveat however is this: from its tip to its tail, "Africa" embraces extraordinary variation, the complexity of which is too often put aside. There is a sense in which the "dark continent" of the northern hemisphere imaginings, invoked as "primitive" or dangerous, and the site of corrupt governments, genocides and starvation, has worked to preclude careful regional explorations and comparisons of different trajectories in east and west Africa, south and north. It is heartening to see the emergence of properly localized studies in recent years, a body of scholarship that gives back to "Africa" cultural variation, nationhood, and unique identity.[1]

Africa's history is also a history of colonization. Histories of madness in Africa are frequently histories of colonizer encounters with mentally suffering colonial subjects, already deemed "other" by virtue of their racial, social and cultural difference to the ruling classes. Slippages between meanings of "otherness" in colonized Africa have affected and infected scholarship in several ways. In the late nineteenth and first half of the twentieth centuries, there was a history of descriptions of African "mind" or "mentality," as well as "personality," all fed directly by colonial psychiatric writing, and assuming a level of the primitive or childish, the impulsive and happy-go-lucky. "Otherness" of this kind assumed to exist in the general population of Africa was used to describe the mentality of psychiatric patients; and in an unremarked but nonetheless remarkable slide, the ways in which psychiatric patients were described were used as generalisations of "African" and assumed the possibility of aggregating all indigenous African populations under a single identity. Attempts to undo this version of scientific racism included inscription of insanity in colonized African regions as something other than individual mental suffering: as a form of rebellion, or symptomatic of a colonized self, or a political ploy through which colonizers were able to silence awkward challenges to their power. While some of these re-readings have local merit in specific instances, they also entail a set of generalizations about mental illness and disease that comes alarmingly close to the very theories they debunk, partly by making unwarranted generalizations across large groups of people and partly by giving a social and political reading of mental illness that helps to downplay a desperate need in those populations for basic psychiatric services. So this brings me to caveat number two. Histories of colonial encounters in Africa rehearse racial difference while often obscuring cultural variation; and the "otherness" of encounters across racial difference is too easily mapped onto meanings of "otherness" signified by states of insanity. To avoid a chapter that once again conflates "Africa" and "madness" with racial difference requires vigilance about the effects of context on diagnosis and treatment of mental illness and the relationship of both to developments in psychiatry as a discipline worldwide.

Histories of "madness" in Africa can be divided into disciplinary strands, and this further complicates the terrain. Social anthropologists have produced a rich seam of ethnographies that describe ways in which particular communities understand and treat states of mind that might seem "mad" to outsiders. When appropriated and used beyond the web of site-specific meanings, these have been transformed into narratives of spirituality, indigenous healing, ancestor communication, and clashes between good and evil. The pluralism of many communities' understandings of insanity during and after colonialism is sometimes obscured by these ethnographies, in a discipline with an early history of reifying difference in encounters with the exotic other.[2] A second strand involves histories of psychiatry and psychiatric institutions. In Africa these are embedded in colonial governments' ambivalent provision for psychiatric care in colonies, the differences between regimes of care for indigenous and settler communities, and changes in diagnosis and treatment during the nineteenth and twentieth centuries. Such histories draw on psychiatric writing, archives of lunatic asylums and mental hospitals, and state archives; they seldom address indigenous understandings of mental health and illness. Finally, an eclectic strand of postcolonial writing with a wide reach into art, literature, history, psychoanalysis, psychology and biography recreates "Africa" as both forever changed by the colonial encounter, but also as one in which interdisciplinary spaces might tilt the axis of received meanings away from those prescribed by northern hemisphere influence. So here is the third caveat. The diversity of material generated across these disciplinary spaces obviates against easy incorporation into a single coherent whole.

With these caveats in mind, this chapter will address itself to the Africa in which "madness," as it is described in the discipline of psychiatry, comes slowly into focus firstly as a social, and later as a medical, problem, requiring sustained attention at different levels of government. It will therefore largely be a history that describes colonial Africa and extends into the beginnings of decolonization. It will avoid assuming "Africa" as an entity and will instead suggest that colonialism, rather than Africa, is the common thread. It references, but does not describe separate and specialized scholarship surrounding indigenous communities' understanding of mind, spirituality, health and illness, except where these intersected directly with colonial psychiatric provision. In keeping with this psychiatric focus, the chapter is underpinned by histories of psychiatric institutions and the ways in which local practices were shaped by scientific knowledge on the one hand, and local contexts on the other. These local contexts include medical and legal regulation, tensions between settler colonies and "home," and the struggles within communities and families to cope with individuals who were a danger to themselves or others.

Just as there is not one "Africa," there is not one form taken by "insanity" experienced in African countries. The chapter will be working with a definition of "madness" that includes states of mind requiring some form of intervention, usually from family, the medical profession, and various branches of government, in terms of nursing, custody, or legal restraint. The mental states that are the focus of this chapter are a variety of psychotic states, serious addictions, severe responses to traumatic events, and insanity precipitated by underlying physical illness, such as dementia, syphilitic infection or head injury. These are states that form the common ground of patients referred to in histories of psychiatry, and are frequently characterized by behavioural disturbance severe enough to cause rupture with family, social group, or community.

This chapter will not attempt to tease out the intricacies of what might have been experienced as "mad" (possessed, affected by witchcraft, called by ancestors) when seen through the eyes of white settler communities. It will assume instead that all communities have definitions of what is "normal" and differentiate this from "mad." In terms of treatment, colonial psychiatry across Africa was poorly resourced and dealt only with individuals unassimilable into ordinary society regardless of how madness was locally perceived and described. This too involves a caveat. Psychiatric interventions in Africa were too small scale to constitute any form of social engineering or interference in locally constructed sets of cultural practices. Nonetheless, psychiatric knowledge imported from Western settings was deeply complicit in reproducing whiteness as both normative and "civilized," with deviations from this as abnormal, "primitive" and always close to the threat of breakdown, incapacity, irrationality, savagery, or violence.[3]

There is one further historiographic concern, which is directly connected to the opening caveats. The archives available to African historians working in either French or English represent a colonial apparatus and largely reflect its operational priorities. Hospital records are shaped both by reporting lines to colonial governments and by the strictures of medical discourse and knowledge. Doctors working in mental institutions across Africa regularly published their observations in medical journals, and this suggests that their work was of interest to an international audience and was widely read. That it had an audience is probably a result of its focus on a location, patients, and sometimes disorders, perceived to be fundamentally different to those encountered at "home."[4] While there are many alternative sources of information about states of insanity in African societies, these are still being curated and made accessible to historians.[5] For all of these reasons, the brief account that follows is of necessity in dialogue with the colonial archive, and while it might argue with its assumptions, it has limited parameters.

Institutional care for the insane in colonial Africa

Throughout the nineteenth century, provision of care for those afflicted with mental illness in colonized Africa was piecemeal and responsive primarily to the needs of colonizer populations. Custom-built mental hospitals were largely a twentieth-century phenomenon and responsive to the needs of settler populations, rather than any intervention in indigenous health systems, which had their own forms of care.[6] A cumbersome system of sending the insane to "home" facilities in France or Britain, for example, was used when needed, and temporary care was provided in hospitals and jails.[7] There also seems to have been deep ambivalence about accepting insanity as a substantial problem in the brave new worlds of settler colonies. After all, these conquering heroes were celebrated at "home" as hard-living survivors, a spin that jostled uneasily with the spectre of mental collapse in "untamed" lands.

Attempts of colonial governments to grapple with states of insanity in indigenous populations was compromised in several ways. While colonial regimes operated under an ideological banner that proclaimed its project as humanitarian and civilizing, it has been well established that there was ambivalence about spending substantial sums of money on building a system to care for patients likely to become a long-term drain on the coffers. Indigenous populations had their own systems for understanding mental affliction and managing insane members in their communities, and colonial governments seem to have been content to leave this in place. Deeply segregative colonial societies separating communities on the basis of race minimized social contact and almost entirely precluded opportunities in which a compassionate understanding of mental suffering and its causes could be built. This alienation was deepened by the lack of shared linguistic communities and entrenched by thin provision of frontier institutions such as schools and hospitals. For the most part, during the nineteenth century the "ordinary" mental illnesses in indigenous communities, some no doubt a result of the disruptions, losses and violence of the colonizing project, simply never reached the agenda of projects demanding a systematic institutional response.[8] Finally, where it was encountered, insanity in indigenous populations was characterized in two ways, both of which reinforced negligent provision of institutional care. On the one hand, white colonizer encounters with "African" mental states exoticized them, making them anthropologically "strange" and therefore not susceptible to care through the institutional machinery of European psychiatry. On the other, "the insane native" was frequently described as becoming ill as a result of contact with civilization and subsequent loss of stable traditional lifestyle. This way of framing increasing visibility of mental illness in colonized populations prompted debate about whether indigenous subjects had nervous systems able to withstand contact with rapidly changing Westernized society. It did not translate into any concerted attempt to mitigate the effects of this apparently damaging contact. Instead it fed into further entrenchment of segregation and differential systems of care that privileged white patients and serviced only basic needs in black ones. This was the beginning of fissure between provision for colonizer communities, some of which became permanent settler populations and attempts to deal with manifestations of insanity in indigenous populations.

However, as the colonial enterprise brought indigenous and colonizer communities increasingly into contact, the need for local forms of institutional care became urgent. As settler populations grew, so too did the numbers of insane among them. Sending the insane settler "home" was an inefficient system to administer. Visibly insane, suffering, or disruptive indigenous subjects could sometimes be banished from view through the simple expedient of ignoring their plight or sending them "home" to communities of kin, but as the demand for a black labour force grew, so too did the presence of mentally ill black subjects force itself into view. Some kind of institutional response was a necessity therefore for purely practical reasons, and building a network of asylums had the merit of bolstering the humanitarian and "civilizing" reputation of colonial regimes.

The makeshift provisions of the nineteenth century brought with them scandal and accusations of shamefully inhumane care. Reluctantly, colonial governments in Africa began to take on the business of building mental hospitals and a medical and legal infrastructure to underpin a solid framework for care. Provision varied depending on three factors: the size of the settler population, the colonial period, and the extent to which local, social, and customary contexts shaped European systems of psychiatric care.

Cape Colony, one of Britain's possessions in Africa, had a substantial asylum network by 1900, and in this respect its psychiatric history is unusual, but also a rich resource to be used in understanding the evolution of psychiatric practice on the continent. Its evolution into a relatively mature system of care evolved earlier than many similar systems elsewhere in Africa, but it nonetheless rehearses familiar themes. Its reputation and the services it offered were such that it regularly provided care for settler subjects north of its borders.[9]

The earliest provision for the insane in Cape Colony was provided at the Somerset Hospital, which first opened in 1818. It was not purpose-built and housed lunatics, lepers, paupers, and the chronic sick.[10] In 1825, the Medical Committee noted the "indiscriminate communication" between various classes of patients.[11] Moreover, the arrangement allowed for contact between men and women, leading to unwanted pregnancies in patients from different racial communities.[12] A pattern emerged of scandals related to negligent care and unsatisfactory staffing, poor boundaries between staff and patients, and shabby, unsanitary cells in desperate need of basic maintenance.[13]

This modest provision for lunatics was a convenient resource for successive governments in the Cape, and despite regular condemnation of its buildings and regime of care, it remained open to patients throughout the nineteenth century, partly as a way station before more permanent accommodation could be found. It stands out as emblematic of the pre-history of psychiatric provision on the continent, one in which an undifferentiated population of chronically dependent or deranged patients were grouped together, housed, and fed with minimal expenditure on their comfort, simply as a form of disposal and to all intents and purposes, erasure from ordinary society.

Running in parallel to this unsatisfactory hospital, jails throughout the colony were forced to provide accommodation for men and women requiring some sort of enforced care. Long distances between communities and thin availability of medical care and general hospitals made this inevitable. Until the late nineteenth century, jails were the essential resort of district surgeons and magistrates certifying patients as a danger to themselves and others. This pattern was repeated throughout Africa and persisted into the first decades of the twentieth century. Apart from jails, there is evidence that families, in both indigenous and settler families, resorted to a variety of desperate measures to contain insane relatives, including imprisonment in bedrooms and the use of shackles or chains to prevent wandering.[14]

The differentiated care for the insane in Cape Colony came with the opening of the lunatic asylum on Robben Island, off the coast of Cape Town, in 1846. This new space used discarded military and convict barracks to house lepers, the insane, and the chronic sick in different quarters. Robben Island Lunatic Asylum and its early regimes of care marked the beginning of progress away from chaotic and under-regulated provision towards imposition of order, central to which was the inception of segregated care for men and women, black from white patients, and attempts to create routines that might lead to improvements in mental states. Deacon's history of the institutions of Robben Island maps a gradual process of segregating "better class," quieter patients from those who were violent, even before there was clear separation of patients according to racial classification. While the Robben Island asylum did constitute an improvement on the Old Somerset lunatic wards and signalled that lunatic patients were coming into view in a new way, its history is also marred by a series of scandals, corruption, and failures of gender segregation, leading to unwanted sexual encounters between inmates. Moreover, the difficulties of getting patients onto the island in bad weather and its inaccessibility to visitors made it physically unapproachable as well as psychologically stigmatizing. The desirability of building an asylum suited to the care of lunatics from the settler population in particular was regularly discussed, but was regularly delayed, and as discussions went on, few improvements were made to the Robben Island facilities. Removal of the asylum to the mainland met with little enthusiasm in settler-dominated public opinion.[15]

While moving the lunatics from Robben Island was still in prospect, an asylum network in Cape Colony was beginning to take shape. Grahamstown Asylum opened in 1875 in the eastern Cape in discarded barracks. Prior to that, there was negligible provision in the eastern territory, with four spaces for patients in the local hospital. From 1908, it became a strictly whites-only institution. This and the vigilant work of Dr. T. Duncan Greenlees, superintendent from 1890 to 1907, led to Grahamstown Asylum gaining a reputation as an orderly institution, offering humane care equivalent to private nursing homes and county asylum at "home" in Britain.[16]

Port Alfred Asylum was the next institution to be opened, this one in an empty convict barracks. It opened in 1889 and housed an initial intake of 52 patients. Little money was spent on it, and although it grew in size over the years, as it took over other abandoned buildings, it was never regarded as a curative institution and was used largely to accommodate the chronic insane, particularly those who were accommodated at public expense and were not visited regularly by friends or relatives.

In 1890, the appointment of Dr. William Dodds as Inspector of Asylums consolidated the colony's efforts to create and maintain institutional provision for the insane. A growing settler population, the impossibility of continuing to house lunatics in jails and overcrowded, scandal-ridden asylums, increasing contact with the indigenous population through farming and industry, and a need to service the liberal humanitarian agenda under the aegis of which colonial expansion took place, all gave impetus to this, and the government set in place a thorough updated legal framework for the certification of lunatics, a system of reporting and inspections, as well as money to build an asylum in Cape Town on the mainland. This asylum,

Valkenberg, was at first a whites-only facility, purpose-built, with careful segregation and classification of patients in mind. It was on a property that included a working farm, facilities for gardening, croquet and cricket, dances, and theatre. It offered comfortable and comforting surroundings for patients, as well as some hope for cure, especially for cases brought for treatment in the early stages of illness.[17]

Valkenberg made clear that the Cape Colony's intention was to provide a high standard of care for the settler population. Black patients in and around Cape Town continued to be sent to the barren and desolate Robben Island facility. Racial segregation was further entrenched in 1894, when Fort Beaufort was opened in yet another discarded barracks building for 87 male black patients. The provision for black patients was modest in comparison to the relatively luxurious buildings of Valkenberg, a distinction strikingly underscored by the erection of "Conry's annexe," a series of daub-and-wattle huts erected in 1908 and named after the superintendent of the time. These huts were cheap and easy to build and were passed off as appropriate to the "quieter" patients housed in them by being replicas of indigenous dwellings, and therefore comfortingly familiar.[18]

Enforced racial segregation in the asylums of Cape Colony conformed to a pattern of social and political segregation, in both institutional and living spaces. It created one practical problem. Manual labour, during the time that the Cape asylum network was being established, was increasingly regarded as demeaning; this meant that white patients were reluctant to do the sorts of manual labour that outside the asylum were carried out by black men and women.[19] While light housework, sewing or gardening were regarded as remedial for white patients, black patients were routinely occupied with the kinds of labour essential to asylums' functioning – road-building, farming, laundry, running kitchens, and servicing boilers.[20]

During the period 1890–1910 therefore, the Cape Colony established a lunatic asylum network unparalleled in other British African colonies. The accommodation available was soon filled to capacity, and gradually buildings were added to existing establishments. By 1897, Cape Colony Asylums housed 1296 patients. Racial segregation was strictly enforced, although after 1916 there were no longer whole asylums reserved for one race or another, with the exception of Fort Beaufort, which remained a hospital for black patients only. The Cape network regularly received patients from surrounding territories, including German South West Africa, Bechuanaland, and Rhodesia.[21]

In the southern regions of Africa, later to become the Union of South Africa, development of facilities for the insane grew steadily in the period 1890–1920. The Natal Government Asylum opened to 68 patients in 1880, and Natal Colony passed lunacy legislation before the Cape, in 1868.[22] There was a very small asylum in Orange River colony at Bloemfontein. It had opened between 1883 and 1884 and had accommodation for only 10 patients, although by 1894 this had expanded to 50 beds. By the end of 1892 there were 29 inmates in the Pretoria Lunatic Asylum, which opened in that year in the Transvaal. In 1897, there were 90 beds available for lunatics.[23]

Elsewhere in Africa, provision for insane patients began slowly in the nineteenth and twentieth centuries and corresponded to growing maturity of settler colony populations and the practical need to find means of confinement for those urgently in need of care. Public alarm centred around the perceived dangerousness of lunatics wandering at large, on the one hand, and the need to provide a measure of humane care for those visibly suffering mental anguish, on the other. Where mental hospitals were established, they were designed to accommodate patients with illness sufficiently severe to warrant enforced periods of care. Kissy Asylum in Freetown, Sierra Leone opened in 1847. This replaced a facility much like Old Somerset in Cape Town, which gave shelter to an undifferentiated group of men and women unable to care for themselves because of chronic illnesses of all kinds.[24] On the Gold Coast, an asylum opened in Victoriaborg in1888, and by 1904 housed just over 100 patients. The Accra Asylum was built as a response to the need for additional accommodation in 1906.[25] Yaba Asylum in Nigeria opened in 1906, and by 1907 had 14 patients.[26] Calabar Asylum opened in 1904, with a similarly small intake. Both were quickly overcrowded and repeated the pattern that had played out in nineteenth-century Cape Colony of being forced to use jails as auxillary accommodation for those needing committal.[27] Ingutsheni in Rhodesia was opened in 1908 with a mere 20 beds.[28] Mathari Asylum in Kenya was opened in 1910 for 10 patients.[29] The Zomba facility in Zambia was established in 1910 as an annex to the central prison and housed 18 patients by 1912.[30] Numbers grew over the next decades, but the facilities remained under-resourced and over-crowded. In 1936, Dr. Cunyngham Browne undertook a tour of inspection, visiting the Gold Coast, Sierra Leone, Nigeria and the Gambia on behalf of the British government to report on the care and treatment of the insane. At that time Kissy Asylum in Sierra Leone had 98 inmates, and there were 145 in the Gold Coast's Accra Asylum. He found that the burden of care for the insane, and those with intellectual deficit or epilepsy fell on families and communities, with very little institutional support.[31]

In French North Africa – Algeria, Tunisia, and Morocco – the story of the colonial encounter with mental illness has some striking similarities to the British colonial experience. Serious attempts to provide accommodation were an early twentieth-century phenomenon. Prior to that, transportation to France and confinement in French institutions was the common route, especially for Algerians who held French citizenship. When institutions began to be built, they were partly in reaction to a growing need in settler communities and alarm at inhumane and neglectful provisions to be found in the Islamic maristans of the Maghreb. These were little more than places of temporary imprisonment, with little therapeutic care being offered.

However, as Keller's history of colonial madness in the Maghreb demonstrates, there were very important differences between British and French colonial experiences in institutional care for the insane. Keller convincingly argues that French psychiatrists in the Maghreb used their experience – and the relative freedom from the centre – to revitalise what they saw as the moribund state of French psychiatric knowledge. Experiments with asylum design and early intervention were intended as a vanguard response to an ossified knowledge system. There seems to have been no equivalent to this amongst the medical staff attending to the insane in British colonies. The British psychiatric establishment was assumed to be if not perfect, then certainly robust enough to be reproduced in less costly, miniature form across large swathes of territory. British psychiatric knowledge was in itself never questioned; it simply accrued more content by turning its gaze on colonized subjects.[32]

Diagnosing mental illness in Africa

The psychiatric profile of illness in the white populations in various African colonies suggests that it did not differ to any significant degree from those of "home" countries. Psychoses, addictions, and mental illnesses of organic origin all frequently produced symptoms of sufficient severity to demand confinement and care. Although there were popular fears that climate and contact with an unforgiving and unfamiliar environment might cause mental illness in colonizing subjects, systematic review of records from nineteenth-century Cape asylums suggests this never translated into doctors' diagnostic judgements in any significant way.

In the indigenous insane population, on the other hand, popular prejudice did for many years affect diagnostic practice. There is a long history of colonial psychiatrists in Africa, beginning with those working in Cape Colony towards the end of the nineteenth century, of assuming that the nervous systems of black Africans was too primitive to experience depressive disorders; rather they were assumed to suffer from "simpler forms of mania."[33] Partly responsible for this assumption was ignorance: there is substantial evidence that colonial doctors knew little about their black patients' histories, social contexts, and cultural beliefs. Moreover, they were linguistically challenged; having no skill in indigenous languages made any serious exploration of their patients' symptoms almost impossible. They were in effect reliant on behavioural observation and reports put together by those involved in the certification process. In British colonies, it seems that there was no systematic provision made for interpreters to be used in diagnostic interviews.[34] As differentiating between a wide variety of psychotic states depends on exploring both the content and form of thought, as well as its affective colouring, it is little wonder that many black patients entering colonial asylums or mental hospitals cannot be said to have had their acute functional illnesses diagnosed with any degree of accuracy.

Cape asylums in the nineteenth century were seldom used as a sanctuary for patients suffering from non-psychotic mental illnesses resulting from the ordinary stresses of living. For example, admissions following depressive crises caused by trauma or loss would have been unusual, unless the patient concerned had no friends or family in the colony, abused alcohol, or made a serious attempt at suicide. In this respect, the nineteenth-century asylums of the British colonies were no different from those in Britain: accommodation tended to be reserved for those most urgently in need of care and a danger to themselves or others. By the second decade of the twentieth century, this pattern had begun to shift. Understandings of psychiatric syndromes became more complex and susceptible to careful gradation; judgements about aetiology and prognosis were progressively rooted in a scientific literature based on systematic observation, detailed patient histories, and study of long-term outcome. The elaboration and complexity of psychiatry as a medical discipline was driven by a number of factors, some internal to medicine; but the drain on governments of large numbers of chronic patients in asylums would have been an added incentive for diagnostic exploration.

New diagnostic tables brought new patient populations into view, and in the 1920s South African mental institutions were beginning to admit a small, but growing, number of patients diagnosed with personality disorders or neurotic disorders, with anxiety and depression as symptoms. Some patients discovered to be pursuing homosexual liaisons or having sexual relationships across racial barriers, or both, were also caught in the net. The vast majority of these patients were drawn from the white settler population. Three factors appear to have driven this difference in diagnostic pattern across the black and white populations. First, colonial doctors were not in a position to make fine diagnostic judgements about many of their black patients, for the reasons described above. Moreover, black subjects with non-psychotic disorders would not have been brought to the attention of authorities, unless their behaviour was criminal or disruptive to their home or employment community. Second, this was the beginning of a period during which "African personality" was being stereotyped in a variety of ways. Such generalisations precluded any clear-sighted assessment of individual personality traits. Finally, given that their mental institutions had little spare accommodation, and also that there was little in the way of treatment for the personality and neurotic spectrum of the patient population, admissions were apparently directed at paying patients, on the one hand, and preserving the respectability of settler society, on the other.[35]

Assumptions were also made about the inferior intelligence of indigenous subjects, which was used to warrant under-resourced educational systems and the justification of subjugation as unenfranchised labouring classes. Assumptions about levels of "normal" African intelligence were such that those patients willing to share their astute judgements about the discriminatory institutional regime in which they were being offered care were in danger of being labelled as sly or disrespectful. Just as significantly, it is likely that prejudice about African intelligence deeply affected doctors' capacity to discriminate between intellectual deficit, effects of mental illness, and the impact of physical illnesses, such as malnutrition, fever, and dementia, on thinking.

In contrast to this, in South Africa immediately post-Union, concern about feeblemindedness in the white population became a focus for the newly appointed commissioner of mental hygiene. As with the mental hygiene movements in Britain and the United States, one motive was to prevent spread of feeblemindedness in the population by enforced sterilization or incarceration of sexually active young adults, mainly women. Deeply implicated in this was the wish to prevent miscegenation, by preventing feebleminded men and women, who were thought to lack sufficient judgement, from having sexual contact across race and reproducing. The racial/mental hygiene movement in South Africa had little flavour of protective care for the individuals so described: the tone of the Commissioner's appeals for government support for institutions dedicated to the care of the feebleminded in the Union of South Africa all emphasized the need for social control of an apparently morally vulnerable population, and there is evidence of similar concerns in relation to white settlers elsewhere in Africa.[36] Moreover, the need to help indigenous communities with care for intellectually disabled kin was never tabled as an urgent matter and was to remain an under-resourced sector of mental health provision throughout the twentieth century.

Treatments

The remaining archives from mental institutions in Africa paint a picture familiar to the great hospital networks of Europe and the United States. Until the appearance on the psychiatric scene of somatic treatments for mental illness, including hydrotherapy, malarial treatment for neurosyphilis, camphor, insulin, and electric shock treatments for psychotic states, all of which were regularly used from early in the third decade of the twentieth century, treatment possibilities were limited. Where there were mental hospitals in sub-Saharan Africa, they quickly filled up with chronically ill patients, and available accommodation was always outstripped by demand. Confinement to the hospital grounds – and in violent or suicidal cases, confinement to single rooms – remedial activity, occasional entertainments to break the monotony of hospital routines, and use of sedatives to reduce agitation and induce sleep formed the spine of treatment.

For the white patients in the Cape asylum network, and in the absence of effective medical treatments, attempts to create a homely environment for those suffering from mental disturbance became a central theme. This had two aims. Need for comfort, a serene environment, regular activity, routine, and entertainment were long established as a philosophy of treatment, and this the accepted regime. Secondly, the colony wanted to demonstrate that it was providing its settler population with care that would be at least equivalent to the better asylums at "home" in Britain. This was a flag of both good governance and settler respectability.[37] Both Valkenberg and Grahamstown Asylums prided themselves on the high standards of the facilities they offered white patients.

For the indigenous population in Cape Colony, the regime of care was altogether more spartan. In their case, remedial activity translated into labour; patients were deployed to build roads, tend farm animals, maintain laundries, cook, and sew hospital clothing. Superintendents were quite open about the difficulty of keeping whites-only asylums functioning without black patient labour; it seemed that white patients could be induced to undertake hard labour only with the greatest difficulty. Moreover, the facilities and provision on black and white wards differed in quality. For example, white patients' diet throughout this period was considerably more liberal than that given to black inmates. Again this was justified on the grounds that indigenous populations were used to certain kinds of food and would not flourish if exposed to the diet given to white patients.

In this regime of routine care, a significant proportion of the hospital population recovered sufficiently to be discharged, although white patients fared better than black ones.[38] Regular turnover of patients was the result of a number of factors. Some families chose to care for chronically ill family members whenever possible, and it is clear that ties of love and duty influenced this decision. There were also instances in which families seem to have opted for home care because payment to institutions for ongoing custody had become difficult.[39] Some illnesses required custodial care in acute phases that then were quickly resolved: into this category, behavioural and physical disturbance caused by substance abuse would have fallen. States of mania or melancholia also often took on a cyclical form, with periods of calm in between; these patients were discharged to families, or given a leave of absence until symptoms reoccurred.

Patient populations in mental asylums were also vulnerable to epidemics of influenza and enteritis. Tuberculosis was an ongoing problem, especially as patients shared crowded and poorly ventilated dormitories. Thus, a substantial and steady death rate contributed to turnover in the patient population, with the elderly or physically weak particularly susceptible to poor outcomes after periods of very serious illness.

Once somatic treatments for mental illness were an established part of the psychiatric armoury, the hospital networks in the Cape quickly took them on. From the 1930s, somatic therapies were regularly in use in South African mental hospitals. Trials of various treatments and apparently dramatic improvements in symptoms of psychotic patients infused a generation of doctors with new hope and energy. The flow of information between the South African medical profession and their colleagues particularly in Britain ensured that the lag between centre and periphery was negligible. The difference lay in two aspects: there was never enough money to give expensive treatments to a sizeable proportion of the hospital population, a fact that paradoxically spared patients from permanent deleterious effects that quickly became evident in British and US patient populations. So for example, frontal leucotomies were conducted only on a small scale; when chlorpromazine was beginning to be used, sustained high doses seem not to have been used, thus sparing patients long term side effects. Also, it seems that more expensive treatments were likely to be offered to white patients before black ones. In this, the South African regime perpetuated the racial discrimination of earlier generations of medical care.[40]

Twentieth-century developments: ethnopsychiatry and transcultural psychiatry

A survey of the ways in which psychiatry dealt its hand in Africa would be incomplete without some consideration of the transformation of ethnopsychiatry into its later, more complex and nuanced forms. From its earliest foothold in Africa, psychiatry used its contacts with indigenous subjects to provide "scientific" evidence for apparent differences between races. For example, in Cape Colony, both Dr. T Duncan Greenlees and Dr. Conry used their asylum experience to comment on what they saw as the intrinsic intellectual and personality differences between black and white patients. Such work was undoubtedly reflective of popular belief, but also was the beginning of a substantial body of work that stretched well into the twentieth century and reified differences between races.[41] The full implications of this scientific literature are hard to quantify with any certainty. It set in place a system that justified differential diagnostic practice and treatment for black patients certainly; but beyond that, it gave credence to colonialism itself, with all its erasures, exploitations, and refusals of full personhood. Frantz Fanon's body of work continues to be fundamental to attempts to describe and come to terms with the effects of colonialism not only on psychiatric practice, but also on mental well-being as the painful process of decolonization is undertaken.

There were counterweights to ethnopsychiatry, and chronologically the first of these was nested in the cultural relativism of anthropological studies that sought to understand the embeddedness and meaning of a variety of mental and behavioural states within particular social contexts. As a discipline, however, anthropology was not free from perspectives and judgements shaped by British and US intellectual traditions. Anthropological studies contributed significantly to a mapping of the differences between psychiatric disorder as it was represented in universally applied diagnostic manuals and culturally specific disturbances, often transient, and often related to social or spiritual problems or callings. They also at times re-inscribed and

240

exoticized African "madness" as essentially "other," perhaps not inferior to white and Western norms, but nonetheless distinctive and separate.

A second counterweight came in the form of international survey studies of psychiatric syndromes, mapping incidence and presentation of major psychiatric illness across continents. While there were some differences found between racial groups, such as the outcome of schizophrenic illness in some African societies, this body of work largely put to rest ethnopsychiatry's insistence on fundamental differences in mentality and personality based on racial identity. The problems inherent in finding universal patterns in psychiatric disorders by application of universalizing diagnostic tools are clear and have been subject to rigorous critique, not only in relation to these large-scale surveys, but also in the work of antipsychiatry scholars, arguing against diagnosis from a social constructionist perspective.[42] What is of significance in the context of studies of serious mental illness in Africa is the production of fully documented and systematic case studies, which challenge strongly the earlier, largely theoretical, work of ethnopsychiatrists, whose scholarship is strikingly thin on raw data about the populations they claimed to know.

Recent additions to scholarship are beginning to break the stranglehold that racial difference has had as the overriding focus for the history of psychiatry in Africa. While colonialism remains the defining political landscape and necessarily entails oppressive and racialized psychiatric practice as a significant theme, new work is beginning to describe the complexity of a variety of African colonial societies in the nineteenth and twentieth centuries, to unpack the web of relationships between class, race and gender, to look at the interface between Western and indigenous healing practices, and to map the ways in which systems of knowledge and experience travelled constantly between centre and periphery, "home" and colony, with challenges and contestations in both directions.[43]

A survey history of phenomena surrounding mental illness in Africa reads as a long and deeply disturbing narrative of physical neglect, racist prejudice, erasure of the trauma inflicted by colonialism, and the systematic attempts to erase or ignore the plight of individuals and their families simply by classifying Africans as incapable of certain kinds of suffering. While most histories of madness in Africa make the problems with colonial psychiatry painfully clear, they also rehearse at least one aspect of it in their focus on race and otherness. It is difficult to imagine another path, but histories of colonial Africa, often written from outside Africa, about mad black people is uncomfortable reading matter.

Notes

1 In this respect, the following monographs stand out: R. Keller, *Colonial Madness: Psychiatry in French North Africa* (London: University of Chicago Press, 2007); J. Sadowsky, *Imperial Bedlam: Institutions of Madness in Colonlial Southwest Nigeria* (Berkeley: University of California Press, 1999); M. Heaton, *Black Skin, White Coats: Nigerian Psychiatrists, Decolonization, and the Globalization of Psychiatry* (Athens, OH: Ohio University Press, 2013); J. Parle, *States of Mind: Mental Illness and the Quest for Mental Health in Natal and Zululand, 1868–1918* (Pietermaritzburg: University of KwaZulu-Natal, 2007); L. Jackson, *Surfacing Up: Psychiatry and Social Order in Colonial Zimbabwe, 1908–1968* (Ithaca: Cornell University Press, 2005); W. Jackson, *Madness and Marginality: the Lives of Kenya's White Insane* (Manchester: Manchester University Press, 2013).

2 For a discussion of the intersection between anthropological accounts and psychiatric practice, see L. Swartz, *Culture and Mental Health: A Southern African View* (Cape Town: Oxford University Press, 1998); J. McCulloch, *Colonial Psychiatry and "the African Mind"* (Cambridge: Cambridge University Press, 1995).

3 The psychological effects of assumptions of inferiority in colonized populations by colonizing regimes in Africa are searingly described in Frantz Fanon's *Black Skin, White Masks*, translation by Charles Lam Markmann (New York: Grove Press, 1952/1967). See also *The Wretched of the Earth*, translation by Constance Farrington (New York: Grove Weidenfeld, 1964/1969).

4 See T. D. Greenlees, "Statistics of Insanity in Grahamstown Asylum," *South African Medical Record*, 3 (1905): 217–24 (220); J. Conry, "Insanity Among Natives of Cape Colony," *South African Medical Record*, 5 (1907): 33–6.

5 See for example S. Jeppie and S. Bachir Diagne, eds, *The Meanings of Timbuktu* (Cape Town: HSRC Press, 2008).

6 This point is made repeatedly by scholars in the field. See S. Mahone and M. Vaughan, eds, *Psychiatry and Empire* (New York: Palgrave Macmillan, 2007).

7 On the tenuous provision for the insane in British colonies in the mid- to late nineteenth century, see S. Swartz, *Homeless Wanderers: Movement and Mental Illness in the Cape Colony in the Nineteenth Century* (Cape Town: University of Cape Town Press, 2015). On the Dutch East Indies, see H. Pols, "The Development of Psychiatry in Indonesia: From Colonial to Modern Times," *International Review of Psychiatry*, 18 (2006): 363–70. On the French colonies in Africa, see Keller, *Colonial Madness*.

8 Frontier institutions such as hospitals and schools, both of which were ideologically positioned as intrinsic to the civilizing and humanitarian colonial project, were for the most part seen by Britain as the responsibility of settler governments to sustain economically, and the resulting conflict over funding led to numbers of faltering attempts to build sturdy systems of education and medical care for indigenous subjects. See R. Swartz, "Educability and Civilization in British Imperial Contexts: Natal, Western Australia and Metropolitan Britain, 1830–1880," International Standing Conference on History of Education, Cape Town, July, 2013.

9 The Cape asylum network contrasts with surrounding territories: in Natal, one asylum was opened in 1880, and by 1887, housed only 112 patients. There was a very small asylum in Orange River colony at Bloemfontein. It had opened between 1883 and 1884 and had accommodation for only 10 patients, although by 1894, this had expanded to 50 beds. In Transvaal, by the end of 1892, there were 29 inmates in the Pretoria Lunatic Asylum, which opened in that year. In 1897, there were 90 beds available for lunatics. In the same year, Cape Colony Asylums housed 1296 patients. Report of the Inspector of Asylums for 1898, G.21-'99, 123. See E. Burrows, *A History of Medicine in South Africa* (Cape Town: A. A. Balkema, 1958), 293.

10 CA, CCP, G.12-1856, p.160.

11 CA, CO 226, February 24 1825.

12 CA, CO 226, February 24 1825.

13 CA, CO 1251, December 1883. For a discussion of the slow process of creating differentiated asylum facilities, see S. Swartz, "The Great Asylum Laundry: Space, Cassification, and Imperialism in Cape Town" in *Madness, Architecture and the Built Environment: Psychiatric Spaces in Historical Context*, ed. L. Topp, J. Moran, and J. Andrews (London: Routledge, 2007), 193–214.

14 See S. Swartz, *Homeless Wanderers*, Chs 3 & 4, and R. Cunyngham Browne, *Report III on the Care and Treatment of Lunatics in British West African Colonies* (Nigeria and London: Crown Agents, 1938).

15 A summary of the debate about the location of new asylum accommodation for the insane in the Western region of the Cape can be found in Dodds's Inspector of Asylums report for 1892, G. 17-1893:137–140. See also the brief history of Robben Island Asylum included in the Report of the Commissioner in Mental Disorders for the years 1916–1918, House of Assembly, U.G. 31-1920:17–19.

16 For a full description, see F. Swanson, "'Of unsound mind'": A history of Three Eastern Cape Mental Institutions, 1875–1910," M.A (History) thesis, University of Cape Town, 2001.

17 See S. Swartz, "The Black Insane in the Cape, 1891–1920," *Journal of Southern African Studies,* 21 (1995): 399–415.

18 U.G.31- '20, p. 23.

19 The preferences of black families, both Coloured and Native, are hard to discern in the remaining archive; it was white and literate settler communities who expressed strong views on the segregation issue.

20 Swartz, "The Black Insane in the Cape, 1891–1920."

21 For a full discussion of the movement of patients between territories and the practical difficulties this caused, see Swartz, *Homeless Wanderers,* ch. 5.

22 The Natal legislation was in fact used as a model for what followed in the Cape in 1879. See J. Parle's path-breaking account of mental health history in Natal and Zululand, *States of Mind: Searching for Mental Health in Natal and Zululand, 1868–1918* (Scottsville: UKZN Press, 2007).

23 Report of the Inspector of Asylums for 1898, G.21-'99, 123. See E. Burrows, *A History of Medicine in South Africa* (Cape Town: A. A. Balkema, 1958), 293.

24 Leland Bell, *Mental and Social Disorder in Sub-Saharan Africa: the Case of Sierra Leone, 1787–1990* (Westport, CT: Greenwood Publishing Group, 1991).

25 McCulloch, *Colonial Psychiatry.*

26 Sadowsky, *Imperial Bedlam.*

27 Sadowsky, *Imperial Bedlam.*

28 Jackson, *Surfacing Up.*

29 McCulloch, *Colonial Psychiatry,* 20.

30 M. Vaughan, *Curing Their Ills: Colonial Power and African Illness* (Oxford: Polity Press, 1991), ch. 5.

31 R. Cunyngham Browne, *Report III on the Care and Treatment of Lunatics in British West African Colonies.*

32 Keller, *Colonial Madness.*

33 T. D. Greenlees, "Insanity Among the Natives of South Africa", *The Journal of Mental Science,* 41 (1895): 71–8; J. Carothers, *The African Mind in Health and Disease: A Study in Ethnopsychiatry* (Geneva: World Health Organization, 1953). For discussion, see M. Vaughan, "Suicide in Late Colonial Africa: The Evidence of Inquests From Nyasaland," *The American Historical Review* 115 (2010): 385–404; and L. Swartz *Culture and Mental Health.*

34 Histories of black patients in Cape asylums were frequently recorded simply as "unknown." See S. Swartz, "The black insane," and "Colonizing the Insane: Causes of Insanity in the Cape, 1891–1920," *History of the Human Sciences,* 8 (1995): 39–57. Problems with language and the use of interpreters have persisted, see L. Swartz, and G. Drennan, "Beyond Words: Notes on the "Irrelevance" of Language to Mental Health Services in South Africa," *Transcultural Psychiatry,* 37 (2000): 185–201.

35 S. Swartz and F. Ismael, "A Motley Crowd: The Emergence of Personality Disorder as a Diagnostic Category in Early Twentieth Tentury Psychiatry," *History of Psychiatry* 12 (2001): 157–76; H. Laurenson and S. Swartz, "The Professionalization of Psychology Within the Apartheid State 1948–1978," *History of Psychology* 14 (2011): 249–63.

36 S. Klausen, "'For the Sake of the Race': Eugenic Discourses of Feeblemindedness and Motherhood in the South African Medical Record, 1903–1926," *Journal of Southern African Studies,* 23 (1997): 27–50. For an analysis of attempts at social control over poor whites in Kenya, see W. Jackson's incisive analysis, *Madness and Marginality.*

37 For an analysis of the multiple meanings of mental hospital facilities that were reminders of "home," see S. Swartz, *Homeless Wanderers,* ch. 7.

38 S. Swartz, "The Black Insane."

39 S. Swartz, *Homeless Wanderers,* ch. 4.

40 M. Carver, "Racial Discrimination in the Treatment of Psychosis in Cape Mental Hospitals, 1933–1956" (Unpublished Honours dissertation, Department of Psychology, 2001).

41 For a detailed account of this strand of historical research on mental illness in Africa, see M. Vaughan, *Curing Their Ills*; J. McCulloch, *Colonial Psychiatry and "the African Mind."*

42 L. Swartz gives a very clear summary of the differences between various approaches to the thorny issue of psychiatry and culture in *Culture and Mental Health*. For an excellent discussion of psychiatric diagnosis and the social construction of categories, see I. Parker, E. Georgaca, D. Harper, T. McLaughlin, and M. Stowell-Smith (1995), *Deconstructing Psychopathology* (London: Sage, 1995).

43 The contributions of Jackson's *Madness and Marginality* and Heaton's *Black Skin, White Coats* are exemplary.

13

VOICES OF MADNESS IN JAPAN

Narrative devices at the psychiatric bedside and in modern literature

Akihito Suzuki

This chapter will argue that there was a parallel development of writing about mental illness and/or madness in both psychiatry and literature in Japan in the early twentieth century. Early modern Japan did not record the voices of madness. Although it had sophisticated medicine based on Chinese medical systems, a highly developed medical market, and even a couple of private madhouses in large cities, there was no culture of recording the voices of madness; for example, writing about the ideas, delusional world, and the expressions of mental patients. In the late nineteenth and early twentieth centuries, with the introduction of German academic psychiatry, Japanese medicine acquired the device of recording the voices of madness. In published works of psychiatry, one encounters statements of patients, reproductions of literary and visual works of the patients. If one turns to the manuscript case-notes of psychiatric hospitals, one finds that the patients actively participated in this culture: they wrote letters to their doctor, to their family, to politicians, and to gods, and they described the actions of other patients, the doctors, and the nurses. These materials were kept in the archives of the case file of the patient, forming a material culture of the voices of madness. Close parallels can be found in literary works around the same time. The theme of madness, psychiatry, and mental illness was the subject of many works, including some canonical works of modern Japanese literature. Many of these works were connected with psychiatry and mental illness: the authors or their families were mentally ill and hospitalized, and the authors had close connection with psychiatrists of elite academic institutions. Modern Japanese literature thus created a world for the representation of madness and psychiatry and expressed the voices of madness through this device, parallel with the psychiatric bedside.

Histories of psychiatry in the West and East Asia present different features, both in terms of the structure of psychiatric provision and that of the representation of madness.[1] In the West, psychiatric institutions or hospitals for the cure, care, and confinement of those mentally ill loomed large in the representation of madness. Institutions provided a nodal point for the depiction of madness and many literary and visual representations of psychiatric patients had been set in the institutions. The situation had been very different in countries in East Asia before the introduction of the Western system. Institutionalization of the mentally ill had not developed in China, Korea, and Japan until the introduction of the Western model, which started in the late nineteenth and early twentieth centuries. Representations of madness in those countries before the modern period followed different styles and strategies. With the introduction of the system of Western psychiatry and its institutions, the representations of madness were quickly transformed and dominated by the images of the closed world of psychiatric hospitals. This paper will examine the historical connection between the practices of modern psychiatry and the representation of madness in modern literature in Japan.

Madness had been closely associated with the institution in Europe and the Islamic world since the medieval period. Driven by the ideas of charity in Christianity and Islam, hospitals and charitable institutions developed from the late antiquity and early medieval period, housing the poor, the old, the disabled, and the seriously sick.[2] These institutions often included a small section for those who were insane. This style of mixed institutionalization was followed by institutions specializing in the care and confinement of the mad. From the medieval period, specialist institutions started to appear in Europe, the Middle East, and the Mediterranean world and cities like Saragossa, London, Constantinople, Cairo and Damascus provided early models of the hospital for the insane.[3] These institutions had a profound impact upon the representation of madness in those countries, through making madness visible in the institution. In England, Bethlem Hospital, which had been established in London as a charitable institution and developed into a specialist institution for the mentally ill around the fifteenth century, provided powerful inspirations for many dramas around the time of Shakespeare. The image of Bethlem Hospital or "Bedlam" expanded into those who were not confined, and wandering lunatics were named after the institution as Tom o'Bedlam.[4] In the early eighteenth century, William Hogarth (1697–1764) concluded a moral tale of *Rake's Progress* with a scene of the major character confined in the ward of Bethlem.[5] Similar situations are found in other countries in early modern Europe and the Islamic world. In Italy, Torquato Tasso (1544–1595) was confined in a madhouse at Ferrara in his late years.[6] In Egypt in the seventeenth century, patients were depicted in their cells and behind the bars.[7] Interestingly, those literary, visual, or artistic representations of the confinement of the insane started when a relatively small number of institutional beds for lunatics existed. In the imaginary and discursive landscape, an institution played a much larger role than in the actual provision of care. When the major reform of the provision for the insane took place in European and North American countries in the late eighteenth and the early nineteenth century, madness in asylums or mentally ill patients in the closed space of confinement dominated the world of representation as well as that of psychiatric treatment and care. Illustrations in medical works provided patients confined in institutions often with restraints. Novels of Émile Zola and other authors described scenes within psychiatric institutions. Asylums and institutionalized patients dominated paintings of Goya and Van Gogh, photographs taken at Salpetriere, and many other fictional and non-fictional materials.[8]

In Japan, the situation had been very different. Hospitals or charitable institutions for the poor or the sick had not developed there. Around 1800, Edo (now Tokyo) had a population of about one million, but only one hospital whose number of beds was about one hundred. Likewise, provision for the mentally ill was not made at institutions but in their own homes.[9] Families were major providers of the care and treatment of the insane and local government encouraged the family to take care of such family members and to practice Confucian virtues within their family. Japanese domains in the early modern period praised children for taking care of their old parents and the seriously ill and disabled, including those mentally ill.[10] In the landscape of European and Islamic worlds, the mentally ill had long been in public spaces, while in Japan and other countries in East Asia, the private space of the family assumed the role of care, control, and confinement, that was often encouraged and promoted by public authorities through various practical and ideological means.

The actual lack of such institutional care in early modern Japan gave a different structure to the representation of madness. Natually, madness was neither depicted within the walls of a hospital nor behind iron bars, although fragmentary evidences and surveys in the modern period suggest that during the early modern period, a sizable number of patients were kept behind bars or with restraint in their own homes. Histories of madness in early modern Japan have uncovered several interesting sources about mental diseases, and by reflecting on the development of local administration and medical markets in early modern Japan, we are able to examine both in more detail. Although both produced practical materials, neither provided individual material about the behaviour and the statements of the patients. From local administration, Genshirō Hiruta, who has both psychiatric and historical backgrounds, has found about sixty cases of mental diseases from a small domain in Fukushima between c. 1700–c. 1860.[11] These documents present particularly rich materials on the viewpoints of the families and neighbours of the village, corresponding to the parish records of European and American countries. The Japanese accounts given by families and neighbours in the documents are about the practical problems and threats of the troublesome lunatics, particularly his or her violence against others or himself/herself, and abnormal attitudes. The accounts should be put in the context of petitions, which asked for the use of restraint or confinement in a cage. Hiruta comments on these cases that the villagers said they regarded the person as difficult to understand and their behaviors and statements did not make any sense and were incomprehensible. Again, we need to consider that these were statements made in the context of petition.

Likewise, religion and medicine responded to the problem of madness or mental illness. Some Buddhist temples provided medical-religious sites of treatment and care of patients. One of them, Daiunji Temple in the suburb of Kyoto developed a satellite system of organizing the local villagers into caretaking roles, with Daiunji Temple as the centre of spiritual treatment and local households as sites of care. This system was thought by the foreign and Japanese doctors there to resemble the system adopted at Gheel in Belgium.[12] From around the early nineteenth century, Japanese medicine started to respond to the problems of mental illness with specific establishments. Likewise, a few private madhouses appeared in large cities such as Edo and Osaka, clearly as a product of dynamic medical market in early modern Japan. Ken Tsuchida was one of those doctors who was based at such an institution and he published a monograph on the treatment of the insane entitled *Empirical Works on Epileptic Insanity* (1819).[13] The work argued that epileptic insanity had rapidly increased due to the life of luxury and ease accompanying the long age of peace and stability. Tsuchida narrated sixty case histories to show the efficacy of the drug he had invented. The cases, however, did not deliver individualized stories, but related brief and somewhat stereotypical symptoms and features and the drug that never failed to cure.[14] Local administrative materials gave practical descriptions of the problems caused by lunatics, and medical books authored by doctors who held positions at private hospitals did not write much about the behaviours and statements of the patients.

On the other hand, religious writings and literary fictions (some of which were based upon "real" events) gave much richer and more vivid narratives of madness and mental illnesses. In religion, a Zen priest, Hakuin (1686–1769), wrote a story that he had a critical experience of severe agony, mental pain, and disturbance in his youth, and the mental trouble was overcome through religious practice at a temple under the guidance of a specific religious priest. In 1757, Hakuin published *Yasen Kanwa*, in which the episode of his youthful mental agony and its cure through religious practice was told with personal details.[15] Its style resembles that of religious autobiographies of early modern Europe, which often included an episode of mental illness.[16]

In literary and performative works, the most important theme is possession. Possession was particularly important both in the high culture and popular worldviews of early modern Japan. It was a subject of most dramatic representations in the Tale of Genji, a work that was written by a female courtier in the eleventh century and elevated to the status of a canonical literary masterpiece of Japan. In the novel, one of the lovers of Genji became a possessive spirit through jealousy of other lovers and drove her rivals into fits of madness and strange psychosomatic symptoms. Inspired by classical female possession, the theme of female possession was employed in dozens of literary or performative works in popular culture in the early modern period. A popular story of the possessions of the spirits of two women was published in 1690 and influenced many subsequent publications. Many genres of art, such as dramas (kabuki), songs (jōruri) and comic storytelling (*rakugo*), repeated the theme of female possession during the early modern period, and it still continues today.[17] The fascination with the world of possessive spirits existed in the background of an interesting publication of another world by the scholar Atsutane Hirata (1776–1843). Atsutane tried to pursue the world of the Japanese gods and spirits and their interaction with this world, and when he heard of a boy who claimed a visit and stay in the world of spirits, Atsutane and other scholars conducted a series of detailed interviews that were published in 1822.[18] Although Atsutane did not suspect mental illness in the boy, the publication is somewhat similar to the narratives of the detailed stories of patients suffering from mental illnesses in modern Europe.[19]

Narrative devices at the psychiatric bedside

From the late nineteenth century, Japan started to modernize its state, society, and culture and to introduce the Western systems, as well as keep and develop what the Japanese regarded as their unique traditions. Historians naturally wonder whether this was a modernization of Japan or a Japanization of modernity. This paradoxical and binary development of the Western and the Japanese elements applies also to the history of madness and psychiatry in Japan.

Modern psychiatry and the asylum in Europe were closely connected with the political, ideological, and social changes accompanying the Enlightenment, industrialization, and revolutions of the nineteenth century. Imperialism from the late nineteenth century encouraged the spread of medicine, and the institutions of modern European and colonial psychiatry and asylums – as Ernst and Swartz show in this volume – started to appear in non-European regions like the Middle East, Africa, and the Indian subcontinent. Some aspects of this history of psychiatry fit nicely with the story of a Westernizing and globalizing system of psychiatry. The modernization of Japan did start after Meiji Restoration, a historical event that comes closest to the "revolution" in modern Europe. Early visitors to Europe and North America wrote excitedly about the asylum as a sign of advanced civilization,[20] and public and private psychiatric institutions started to be built in the 1870s in major cities such as Kyoto (1875) and Tokyo (1879). From the 1880s, government started to send young and bright students to universities in Germany and Austria to study medicine under famous professors, which became a crucial part in the modern development of academic psychiatry in Japan.[21] Western psychiatry and its institutions were a vital part of *Bunmei kaika*, a slogan of modernization meaning civilization and enlightenment.

We need to note, however, that the Japanese psychiatric system followed different paths in its academic and institutional aspects. On the academic side, the importation was quick and effective. An educational system was immediately established at the University of Tokyo and its teaching hospital was set up as a public asylum of the Prefecture of Tokyo. Lectures and clinical instructions were given by professors who had studied and completed medical theses in Germany and Austria under leading psychiatrists, such as Emil Kraepelin. At this level, psychiatry in Japan quickly assumed a structure that was closely modelled after the German system.

The story was entirely different when it comes to institutions, however. The system of sending mentally ill patients to a psychiatric hospital for a relatively long-term stay progressed very slowly through the first half of the twentieth century.[22] In the 1950s, the number of psychiatric beds was still astonishingly small, about one-twentieth of that found in countries in Europe. Japanese society long continued to rely on the early modern system of care at home for a few generations after it modernized the academic system of training professional doctors. In fact, the first national law on psychiatry actually legalized the system of confinement at home. The proponents of Western-style asylums were small in number, and they criticised the home confinement.[23] Shūzō Kure published an extensive and severe criticism against the system of home confinement in 1918.[24] His investigations, however, actually revealed that there were many good or tolerable cases of home confinement, and even his students were not entirely sure whether they should agree with their professor. Indeed, Kure's book was almost forgotten and only remembered and republished in the 1960s, when the astronomical growth in psychiatric beds began. Ironically, this was the period when Western countries started to depart from the asylum system and turned to community psychiatry. Unlike academic psychiatry, the Japanese societal system based on psychiatric institutions took a long time – nearly a century – to "catch up" with the European model. In other words, Japanese academic psychiatry, whose European prototype developed within the framework of the asylum, operated within the Japanese indigenous system that centered on the home as the place of care and confinement.

Under such historical circumstances, social and cultural historians of medicine tend to disregard academic medicine as doing nothing for society. This chapter, however, seeks to show that this was not the case. Actually, academic psychiatry established new socio-cultural elements involving the close observation of mental illness, the recording of patients' statements, and the archiving of patients' writings and other works. The introduction of German academic psychiatry and its system of recording case histories transformed the Japanese discourse on the features of mental illness; due to the German emphasis on close observation of the patient and the detailed recording of statements, Japanese doctors started a practice of detailed transcription of patients' statements, as well as other somatic symptoms, physical deformities, and chemical and physiological indices, and in doing so, it became clear that German academic psychiatry introduced a narrative device at the Japanese psychiatric bedside.

The new practice represented an opening of a genre of writing about madness. Modern medical writings on mental illness quickly introduced the detailed representation of the abnormal behaviour and strange statements of the patients.[25] Academic psychiatric writings and publications included the literary and visual reproduction of the patients' "works." Letters, poetry, drawings, graffiti, sculptures, and other works were presented and commented upon in academic psychiatric works. The drawings of patients were presented, often in specially prepared, high-quality pages. Works in forensic psychiatry, with detailed reports on patients, were regularly published by leading psychiatrists. They narrated the criminal acts, delusional ideas, and strange behaviours of the patients who committed crimes. When the crime attracted attention, their forensic psychiatric reports became hugely popular. The psychiatric report of "Abe Sada" (b. 1905) was a case in point. Her case records became a bestseller in the underground world and were hand-copied by those who were interested in her action of cutting off the penis of her lover. [26]

The new technique of recording gave new voice to psychiatric symptoms embedded in the traditional and indigenous culture of spirits and demons. The delusions of traditional spirits certainly had existed during the early modern period, when doctors or medical practitioners did not have the technique of recording them. With the introduction of German psychiatry, new observational and narrative devices appeared in Japanese medicine. Works based on the German psychiatric system and looking at traditional belief systems turned out to be particularly rich and unique resources of about folklore. *A New Treatise on Fox Possession* (1902) by a professionally-trained psychiatrist by the name of Masae Kadowaki (1872–1925) introduced a genre of recording patients' stories about the possessive power of the fox.[27] Some were the product of long interviews, including the patient's long responses. In fact, one woman requested that a nurse transcribe the narrative of her entire life: she insisted she was a fox and the spiritual queen of a new religion, and she treated her husband as a servant, drinking good wine, eating delicious foods, wearing beautiful clothes, and singing songs, while foregoing sleep. These detailed narratives from early psychiatric cases were unique sources for people's ideas about life under fox possession. Psychiatric books provided visual representations as well, photographically reproducing many writings, paintings, and drawings. One particularly interesting and high-quality set of drawings is that of so-called monstrous spirits and their families, with accounts provided by the patients.[28]

If we turn our eyes from psychiatric publications to manuscript case-notes of a psychiatric hospital, we are able to reconstruct the writing and recording practices found at the bedside.[29] Archives of psychiatric hospitals in Japan thus hold an enormous number of the products of the new narrative devices present in modern psychiatry. In other words, psychiatric hospitals opened up a discursive space for mental illness.[30] The case-notes I will rely on come from Ohji Brain Hospital, a flourishing private psychiatric hospital in Tokyo.

In its system of keeping patient's case records, Ohji Brain Hospital followed the practice adopted by the Department of Psychiatry of University of Tokyo, at which the medical superintendent Komine Shigeyuki studied. It had four sets of documents in each patient's case history: a bedside log, nurse log, weight table, and log of prescriptions. The first three types of documents contained everyday changes, and the last included new prescriptions. These case histories recorded the actions and the statements of every patient in detail. The records allow historians to analyse the encounter between psychiatry and individual patients and explore the medical, social, and cultural history of psychiatry in modern Japan.[31] Take, for instance, the case of a private male patient who stayed at the hospital for about six weeks in 1940 due to his addiction to a drug. At the moment of his hospitalization he was asked why he had started to take drugs, and his answer was recorded. In his statement, he explained that a friend of his had told him that they were going out to watch baseball, but instead the friend took him to a mental hospital. There, a nurse discovered that he secretly carried a syringe and injected it in his arm soon after admission. Likewise, a woman who stayed in the hospital for about two months in 1933 due to schizophrenia told doctors and nurses about her thoughts of being a child or infant, and even acting as if she were a baby. The bedside and nurses' logs recorded her behaviour and statements and include direct quotes. The basic format of the case history thus structured the encounter: psychiatrists or nurses observed, examined, and listened to the patients and recorded their observations.

We need to emphasize that patients were incorporated into this format not simply as objects of the discourses, but also as authors of statements. The materials authored by the patients were often preserved in their case files. Writing was not a case of one-way traffic; the patients also wrote about themselves, other patients, doctors, and nurses. The psychiatric hospital thus had a function of drawing out patients' ideas, writings, illustrations, and other products, and of keeping them in the archive. A piece of graffiti drawn by a patient, a letter written to the doctor, a petition to politicians, protests against the police about illegal confinement (some of which were actually true) were carefully inserted into the bedside log of the patient. A collection of more than twenty letters by a patient was kept in a separate file. As if to imitate the record-keeping activities of the doctors and nurses, some patients wrote their own case histories, reporting about other patients' activities and the management of the hospital. Case histories were thus both the repositories of the writings of the medical staff and the patients, and a device that encouraged some patients to speak and write about themselves, other patients, and medical staff, as well as many other things. Doctors and nurses were keen to hold the material, although we do not know how systematic and complete their preservation of occasional materials was.

One particularly noteworthy artifact is a manuscript autobiography and the record of delusions and fantasies of one patient. The patient was a taxi driver in Tokyo and suffered from general paresis. He stayed first in another private hospital for a few days and then moved to Ohji Brain Hospital as a patient whose expenses were paid from the public budget. He stayed in Ohji Brain Hospital for about 10 months. During his stay, he left a handwritten manuscript of about 120 pages, with numerous illustrations drawn by him. The title of the manuscript was "a story of dreams of an insane person," and contained a mixture of religious beliefs, space travel, and the war with the United States, as well as memories of his hometown fishing village. More important in the context of this chapter is that the author perhaps thought of publishing the work, or at least regarded the manuscript as a completed work. Indeed, a plan to publish a similar work was expressed by another patient. In that case, he had left a memorandum about publishing a collection of short stories, and whie he actually finished one novel, doctors found it incomprehensible.

Modern psychiatry thus started an expansive archive about mental illness and mental patients. The patients' symptoms, somatic indices, and personal histories were all recorded. More importantly for the argument of this chapter, the patients were also the authors of documents filed in the archive. Mental illnesses started to have their voices documented through mechanisms at the psychiatric bedside and participated in by doctors, nurses, and patients. My argument, still tentative, is that this creation of the archive or repository of the patients was relatively abrupt, and was imported from European and German psychiatry in the late nineteenth century.

Literature, madness, and psychiatric hospital

Voices of mental patients were listened to and recorded not only in clinical settings, but they were also resonant within society at large through literature. Following the description of clinical experiences during the first half of the twentieth century, this section considers literature and madness at that time. Especially remarkable was the burgeoning of literature that focused on mental diseases: narratives with mad protagonists and stories that take place in mental hospitals. Parallel to the establishment of the archive at the bedside, Japanese literature also started to talk about mental illness in detail.

Table 13.1 lists Japanese literary works published during the first half of the twentieth century that included madness and psychiatry as their subject. This is not a comprehensive list, but it demonstrates that important writers were engaged in writing about madness and mental diseases before the Second World War. There are four types of works, categorized in terms of how the authors were related to the theme: ones in which the authors themselves suffered from a mental disease; ones in which the authors had a family member or friend who fell ill; ones in which the authors were psychiatrists or had some connection with psychiatrists; and ones in which there was no direct association between the authors and mental illness or psychiatry.

Table 13.1 Japanese literary works about madness and psychiatry published during the first half of the twentieth century.

Author	Title	Year
Kokyo Nakamura	Shell	1913
Hiroshi Kikuhi	A Mad Person on the Roof	1916
Kazuo Hirotsu	An Age of Neurosis	1917
Seijiro Shimada	Essays and Mss. Works	1924–1930
Toson Shimazaki	Life of a Woman	1921
Motojiro Kajii	Lemon	1925
Ryunosuke Akutagawa	Kappa	1927
Takako Nakamoto	A Battle	1930
Hyakuzo Kurata	An Absolute Life	1930

Jun Tsuji	Essays and Mss. Works	1932
Toson Shimazaki	Before the Dawn	1935
Yumeno Kyusaku	Dogra Magra	1935
Shinkichi Takahashi	A Madman	1936
Osamu Dazai	Human Lost	1937
Masuji Ibuse	Tajiko Village	1939
Takamura Kotaro	Life of Chieko	1941
Ishigami Gen'ichiro	School of Psychiatry	1942
Ango Sakaguchi	An Idiot	1946
Sakunosuke Oda	Nostalgia	1946
Akatsuki Kambayashi	At St. John Hospital	1946
Fumio Niwa	The Age of Nuissance	1947
Masuji Ibuse	A Bowing Captain	1950

The first category includes the works of Seijiro Shimada (1899–1930), Kōji Uno (1891–1961), Jun Tsuji (1884–1944), Osamu Dazai (1909–1948), and Shinkichi Takahashi (1901–1987). Apart from Uno, these authors wrote about their own mental illnesses in their literary works, some of which were written during periods of illness and hospitalization.[32]

Shimada made a sensational debut, publishing a bestseller *Above Ground* (1919), followed by sequels that also sold well. He quickly became a young celebrity writer and a charismatic figure among young people, but his pretension to genius status and libertine freedom caused problems. In 1923 he tried to hold a woman aficionado as captive in an inn – an immense scandal that completely destroyed his reputation. Meanwhile, his schizophrenia deteriorated. In late July 1924, he was arrested after troubles with police. Following an examination of his mental condition, he was declared insane and detained as a publicly funded patient in Hoyōin, a private psychiatric hospital in Sugamo in Tokyo. Some men of letters who had found him unpleasant resorted to the bad joke of actually writing funeral addresses for him. Shimada, however, continued to write literary works in the hospital. Some of these works were published, as visiting journalists took the opportunity to publish his talks and essays.[33] In 1928 and 1929, some short poems supposedly written by the confined Shimada were published in Dadaist magazines. Although others remained unpublished, Shimada wrote numerous manuscripts in the hospital, many of which are now housed at the Shimada Museum.[34]

Shimada was confined in a hospital until his death, but that was not the case for Tsuji, Dazai, and Takahashi. Tsuji was featured in a newspaper article in 1932 as he "finally became a Tengu," flying in the air from the window in the upper storey (another instance of the traditional theme of spirits). He was committed to a psychiatric hospital, one that was originally established by a Buddhist monk. Like Shimada, Tsuji had visits from journalists, who published his pieces. After his first episode of hospitalization, he was in and out of mental hospitals and wandered around the country for the rest of his life. During this long period of intermittent hospitalization and wandering, he continued to write and publish many works. In Dazai's case, we have an almost complete set of writings by the doctor, the nurse, and the patient himself. He eventually became addicted to narcotics and was confined to a private hospital of Musashino Hospital for a month in 1936. The collected works of Dazai include hospital notes taken by the doctors and nurses as well as the temperature charts. These records show Dazai as the object of great attention for hospital staff. In the nurses' journals, for instance, Dazai is cited as having "read a book" and "read a magazine." He himself in fact wrote notes in the same style as the nurses' journal, notes that were turned into *Human Lost* and published the following year, immediately after he was discharged. In Dazai's case, clinical records, the patient's own notes, and literary works were all closely associated with one another.[35]

In the second type, involving the mental illness of a loved one, there are two canonical works in modern Japanese literature, namely *Before the Dawn* (1929–1935) by Tōson Shimazaki (1872–1943) and *Portrait of Chieko* (1941) by Kōtarō Takamura (1883–1956). The former is about the life of a squire, closely modelled after the author's father. Toward the end of the story, the major character sets fire to his own home after going mad, something linked to his disappointment with modern Japan. In the case of the latter, the author provides a poetic description of the last years of his wife, Chieko. She died in James Hill Hospital after three years of treatment there. In the supplementary piece called "Life of Chieko," Takamura looks back at her life, attributing her breakdown to her artistic orientation and their conjugal life.

Among less famous writers, Kokyō Nakamura (1881–1952) is worth noting. He first studied English literature at the University of Tokyo. While undertaking his studies, his younger brother was struck by a psychiatric disorder and subsequently died. Nakamura wrote about him in an installment novel published in the *Asahi* newspaper.[36] Afterwards, he continued to be engaged in thinking about psychiatry. Indeed he attempted to contexualize mental diseases and psychiatry in culture and society as an editor of the magazine *Perversion and Psychology* between 1917 and 1926. Later Nakamura studied psychiatry at a medical school and opened a psychiatric hospital on the outskirts of Tokyo. There he collected observations and wrote medical books for a general readership that provided detailed narratives of patients.[37]

Another novelist, Akatsuki Kambayashi (1902–1980), a popular writer and former journalist, wrote about his mad wife, Shigeko, in a few novels. Shigeko was in and out of hospital between the late 1930s and 1946, the year she died, and Kambayashi had the experience of accompanying her to the hospital. His works proved to be so popular that in 1956 they were turned into a film, *A Story of an Invalid Wife.*[38] These major and popular literary works suggest that the mental illness of the author's family member was frequently depicted in Japan in the earlier half of the twentieth century.

The third category concerns works written by psychiatrists and literary authors who worked closely with psychiatrists. Kokyō Nakamura falls under this category, as well as Mokichi Saito (1882–1953), the latter being a leading poet and an eminent practitioner of psychiatry in the Tokyo area. However, its most distinguishing examples are *Dogra Magra* (1935) by Kyūsaku Yumeno (1889–1936) and *School of Psychiatry* (1942) by Gen'ichiro Ishigami (1910–2009). *Dogra Magra* by Yumeno is now a hugely popular work and perhaps the most enigmatic piece in modern Japanese detective story genre, though many readers consider the plot too complicated and the solution – if it has any – too difficult to understand.[39] The inspiration for this work came directly from the psychiatry taught and practised at Kyushu Imperial University and its hospital. The author Yumeno was inspired by Yasusaburo Sakaki (1870–1929), professor at Kyushu Imperial University, and Tamotsu Moro'oka (1879–1946), an associate professor there.[40] These medical men were closely connected with Yumeno, who lived near the university and whose diaries recorded visits to Sakaki at the Department of Psychiatry. After ten years rewriting and revising, the author finally published *Dogra Magra* in 1935. The description in the novel centres around the psychiatric hospital of the University of Kyushu. Major characters are patients residing in the hospital as well as attending professors of psychiatry and medical jurisprudence. The patients present delusional fantasies, strange memories of events that took place centuries ago, while professors advocate curious psychiatric theories. Through working closely with actual psychiatrists, Yumeno produced a nightmarish masterpiece of strangely connected delusional worlds and psychiatric theories.

School of Psychiatry by Ishigami moved the scene from Kyushu to Tokyo and its psychiatric hospital.[41] Ishigami was expelled from Hirosaki High School for his proletarian activities and moved to Tokyo to become a communist activist and dissident author. In 1942 he published *School of Psychiatry* in a leading magazine, establishing himself as a young novelist with strong social concerns. The novel is about the dangers of eugenics, with the National Eugenics Law of 1940 in the foreground. Following the German example of eugenic euthanasia in 1920, a professor suggests to a young doctor to attempt a possibly fatal treatment on a patient who had been severely afflicted with an incurable mental illness. The highly technical information concerning the mental disease and its pathological appearance was taken from Takeichi Tsugawa (1910–1988), an assistant psychiatrist at University of Tokyo at the time. In fact, the head professor of psychiatry at the university thought Tsugawa wrote the novel, and he tried to expel Tsugawa from the Department.[42] Ishigami and Tsugawa were alumni of Hirosaki High School, and they knew each other through their political sympathies with communism. The fiction promoted a critical attitude toward eugenics, a view held by the majority of psychiatrists at Tokyo University at that time. Both *Dogra Magra* and *School of Psychiatry* were thus products of literary authors and psychiatrists based at elite universities and their hospitals.

The works in the final category do not suggest any direct source for their narratives, but nevertheless focus on mental illness. Among them, *Kappa* by Ryūnosuke Akutagawa (1892–1927) is a masterpiece usually taken as an incisive critique of human society through the views of Kappa, legendary magical creatures.[43] In this work, the story is told by a patient in a psychiatric hospital, who believes he wandered into the world of Kappa as he was climbing mountains. It is not known if Akugatawa learned the device of the frame of mental illness from works of literature such as Nikolai Gogol's *Diary of a Madman* (1835), Lu Xun's work of the same title published in 1918, or Jonathan Swift's *Gulliver's Travels*. Another possibility, however, is that he created the world through the experience of mental illness of one of his acquaintances, perhaps Kōji Uno, or even himself. A less renowned work, *Dream-Eaters* (1922) by Enzō Matsunaga (1895–1938), features patients suffering from mental disorders in a psychiatric ward of a public hospital in Yokohama.[44]

In the preface, the assistant in the ward works as a kind of window through which the lives of the patients are seen. The "honest and poor" assistant is thankful for "the mad patients' kindness to offer him lessons and life itself though in somewhat anti-physiological and irregular ways." This fiction refers to Freud as well as the film *The Cabinet of Dr. Caligari* (1920), an expressionist masterpiece based on a patient/doctor in a mental hospital. It is not certain if the author got inspiration from other works of art, or if his disability from spinal caries he suffered in his childhood had any effect. Significantly, this work relies on the same narrative structure as the clinical documents, told in the form of the journals and autobiographical records set down by the patients and doctors.

This very brief survey shows that many literary works took up the subject of mental illness and psychiatry in Japan during the first half of the twentieth century. Indeed, these works include such famous works as *Before the Dawn*, *Portrait of Chieko*, *Kappa*, and *Dogra Magra*. The publication of these stories coincided with the same time frame as the introduction and establishment in urban areas of the systematic recordkeeping involving the voices of patients. Early twentieth-century Japan thus witnessed the parallel development of new forms of representing the voices of the mental disorders both at the clinical bedside and within modern literary works. I have also tried to show that psychiatry, mental diseases, and mentally ill patients exercised a strong influence on the actual production of those works. The trends in clinical encounters and in literature operated *side by side*, and in some cases, there were influences and resonances *between* the two realms. In hospitals, patients wrote things that can be considered literary works, literary authors or their families were hospitalized and received forms of psychiatric care, which were then incorporated into literary works, and literary authors consulted psychiatrists as sources for their works. This chapter has analysed the triangular relationship of which academic psychiatry was at the core.

Conclusion

I have argued that a parallel development in psychiatry and literature took place in Japan during the first half of the twentieth century. Both realms started to incorporate voices of madness, engaged in observing, listening to, recording, and representing the subjectivities of psychiatric patients. Voices of madness as the expressions of individual patients started to be integrated into the medical, cultural, and social landscape of modern Japan. This is exactly counter to the conventional anti-psychiatric criticism of modern psychiatry as a power that silenced its patients. Actually, one can argue that Western-style psychiatry started to infiltrate the subjective voices of madness in culture and society at large via published psychiatric works and the archives of patients' records, both of which were based in the psychiatric hospital. Clearly, modernity in Japan gave voice to madness in the psychiatric hospital and the representational world of literature.

More difficult to explain is *why* this parallel occurrence took place. One reason may be the influence of the West. As for psychiatry, the Western influence is clear and evident: the entire academic system of psychiatry in Japan was imported from Germany and developed in elite institutions in Japan for further distribution. As for literature and art, there is some strong evidence to suggest that the influence of the West was crucial. Modernism in Europe narrowed the gap between the world of mental illness and that of literary and artistic works and created new concepts of art, denying pre-scribed artistic expressions.[45] It made art closer to the mental illness in principle and in practice. The leading artists, especially a surrealist like Andre Breton, saw the con-structive effects of mental illness on art. Psychiatrists collected paintings and works by patients. One of the wide-ranging collections was that of Hans Prinzhorn and his collection at Heidelberg University.

This trend, as well as the actual works themselves, exerted considerable influ-ence on the authors and doctors of Japan. Film director Kinugasa Teinosuke (1896–1982) directed *A Page of Madness* (1926), for instance, which was set in a psychiatric hospital, his source of inspiration being *The Cabinet of Dr. Caligari*. Significantly, the medical duty to write down case circumstances had already been introduced in Japan, making the visits meaningful.[46] Likewise, psychiatrist Shikiba Ryusaburō (1898–1965) learned from the Western world an interest in the artwork of mental patients and began his work of finding Japanese counterparts. Shikiba's thesis was about the works of Van Gogh, he surveyed a strange piece of architec-ture built by a mental patient and published articles on the subject, and after the war he was famous for his promotion of the paintings of Yamashita Kiyosi.[47] Westernization in this context meant fascination with the world and expressions of insanity, and literary and artistic developments of similar concerns in Japan were clearly due to influence from Europe.

Westernization in the realm of literary and artistic works was obviously not the only source of change, however. What should be noted is that diseases other than mental illness present somewhat similar phenomena around the same time period: the clinical and literary correspondence was seen not only in the realm of madness, but also in those attending tuberculosis and leprosy. In these diseases, the intro-duction of a new medical system in isolated facilities came almost simultaneously with the burgeoning of literary works by patients and the people close to them. In tuberculosis, the trend was referred to by Fukuda as the "Romanticization of tuberculosis."[48] Industrialization and labour mobility brought about an increase in the number of infected, causing severe medical and social problems. The develop-ment of the sanatorium to treat the patients and prevent infection went hand in hand with the mushrooming of consumption narratives. It included high quality and popular literature as well as in-house publication within the sanatoriums. In the case of Hansen's disease, detention in institutions was going on at the same time that the voices of the afflicted began to be heard in patients' works and films featuring doctors.[49] Moreover, if you think about Hansen's disease, this was not due to imitating the West, for the voices of Hansen's disease in Europe at the time were relatively quiet.

Notes

1 See Andrew Scull, *Madness in Civilization: A Cultural History of Insanity, From the Bible to Freud, From the Madhouse to Modern Medicine* (Princeton: Princeton University Press, 2015); Roy Porter and David Wright, eds, *The Confinement of the Insane: International Perspectives, 1800–1965* (Cambridge: Cambridge University Press, 2003).

2 Guenter Risse, *Mending Bodies, Saving Souls: A History of Hospitals* (Oxford: Oxford University Press, 1999).

3 See the chapter by Trenery and Horden in this volume. Also, see Scull, *Madness and Civilization*, pp. 48–85; Jonathan Andrews et al., *The History of Bethlem* (London: Routledge, 1997); Michael Dols, *Majnun: The Madman in Medieval Islamic Society* (Oxford: Clarendon Press, 1992). For the representations of madness in medieval Europe, see Penelope Doob, *Nebuchadnezzar's Children: Conventions of Madness in Middle English literature* (New Haven, CT: Yale University Press, 1974).

4 See Scull's chapter in this volume. See also Michael MacDonald, *Mystical Bedlam: Madness, Anxiety and Healing in Seventeenth-Century England* (Cambridge: Cambridge University Press, 1981); Natsu Hattori, *Performing Cures: Practice and Interplay in Theatre and Medicine of the English Renaissance* (D. Phil Thesis, University of Oxford, 1995).

5 Roy Porter, *Mind-Forg'd Manacles: A History of Madness in England from the Restoration to the Regency* (London: Athlone, 1987).

6 For Tasso, see Sander Gilman, *Seeing the Insane: A Cultural History of Madness and Art in the Western World* (New York and Chichester: Wiley in association with Brunner-Mazel, 1982), 130–1. An operatic work of the seventeenth century, with the title of l'Ospedale, sets the scenes in a psychiatric hospital and has been discovered by Dr. Naomi Matsumoto at Goldsmiths, University of London and was performed in 2015. See http://culturevulture. net/music/lospedale/, accessed May 15 2016.

7 Dols, *Majnun*, 273.

8 Roy Porter, ed., *The Faber Book of Madness* (London: Faber and Faber, 1993). Gilman, *Seeing the Insane*.

9 Akihito Suzuki, "Family, the State and the Insane in Japan 1900–1945" in *Psychiatric Confinement in International Perspective*, ed. Roy Porter and David Wright (Cambridge: Cambridge University Press, 2003), 193–225. See also Theodore Jun Yoo, *It's Madness: The Politics of Mental Health in Colonial Korea* (Berkeley: University of California Press, 2016).

10 Keio Yanagiya, "Kinsei Kazoku ni okeru Fuyō to Kaigo" [Provision and Care in Early Modern Families] in [*Popular Culture and Policies in Early Modern Japan*], ed. Nobuo Watanabe (Tokyo: Kawade Shobō Shinsha, 1992), 119–40.

11 Genshirō Hiruta, *Hayari Yamai to Kitsune Tsuki* [Epidemics and fox possessions] (Tokyo: Misuzu Shobō, 1985).

12 See Akira Hashimoto, "Work and Activity in Mental Hospitals in Modern Japan, c. 1868–2000" in *Work, Psychiatry, and Society, c. 1750–2015*, ed. Waltraud Ernst, (Manchester: Manchester University Press, 2016); idem., "Psychiatry and Religion in Modern Japan: Traditional Temple and Shrine Therapies" in *Religion and Psychotherapy in Modern Japan*, ed. Christopher Harding et al. (London: Routledge, 2015); idem., "Work and Activity in Mental Hospitals in Modern Japan, c. 1868–2000" in *Transnational Psychiatries: Social and Cultural Histories of Psychiatry in Comparative Perspective*, ed. Waltraud Ernst and Thomas Mueller (Cambridge: Cambridge Scholars Publishing, 2010). See also Osamu Nakamura, "Patient Work and Family Care."

13 Tsuchida's work was discovered by Shūzō Kure (1865–1932), professor of psychiatry at University of Tokyo, who collected and commented on many works and references on madness in Japan. Kure's writings were published as a separate book in 1923 and a series of articles between 1916 and 1925. They are now both available in modern reprints in the format of books and provide invaluable help in finding and reading early psychiatric works. Shūzō Kure, *Iseidō Sōsho* [Anthology from Great Doctors] (Kyoto: Shibunkaku, 1970) and *idem, Isobe Gūshō* [Selection from Early Materials on Mental Illnesses], 2 vols. (Tokyo: Sōzō Shuppan, 2004). Ken Tsuchida's *Empirical Works on Epileptic Insanity* and its translation into modern Japanese are attached at the end of the second volume of *Isobe Gūshō*.

14 An interesting counterpart in the West is George Cheyne (1671–1743), who recounted highly individualized case histories, including his own. See George Cheyne, *English Malady* (1733), edited with an introduction by Roy Porter (London: Routledge, 1990).

15 The work was discovered in the mid-twentieth century as a major Japanese work on the experience and psychological treatment of neurasthenia. Ekaku, *Hakuin Zenshi Yasen Kanwa* [The Story of Master Hakuin], ed. Takayama Shun (Tokyo: Daihorinkaku, 1975).

16 See, for example, the autobiography of George Trosse, which was published in the early eighteenth century. George Trosse, *The Life of the Reverend Mr. George Trosse. Written by Himself, and Published Posthumously According to his Order in 1714*, ed. A. W. Brink (Montreal: London, McGill-Queen's University Press, 1974).

17 Zanju, *Shiryō Gedatsu Monogatari Kikigaki* [A Real Tale of the Salvation of the Spirits of the Dead Women], ed. Seiji Konita, (Tokyo: Hakutakusha, 2012).

18 Atsutane Hirata, *Senkyo Ibun* [Interesting Tales from a Different World], ed. Nobukuni Koyasu, (Tokyo: Iwanami Shoten, 2000).

19 Daniel Paul Schreber, *Memoirs of My Nervous Illness*, ed. Ida Macalpine and Richard Hunter (New York: New York Review Books, 2000); Theodore Flournoy, *From India to the Planet Mars: A Case of Multiple Personality With Imaginary Languages*, ed. Sonu Shamdasani (Princeton, NJ: Princeton University Press, 1994).

20 Kunitake Kume, *Ōbei Kairan Jikki* [A tour through American and European Countries], 5 vols, translated into modern Japanese by Akira Tanaka (Tokyo: Iwanami Shoten, 1985). A partial English translation by Marius B. Jansen is available.

21 Akira Hashimoto, "A 'German world' Shared Among Doctors: A History of the Relationship Between Japanese and German psychiatry Before World War II," *History of Psychiatry*, 24 (2013): 180–95. See also Wenjing Li and Heinz-Peter Schmiedebach, "German Wine in an American Bottle: The Spread of Modern Psychiatry in China, 1898–1949," *History of Psychiatry*, 26 (2015): 348–58.

22 Suzuki, "Family, the State and the Insane in Japan."

23 An interesting point is that in Europe nineteenth-century reformers of psychiatry criticized old institutions, while Japanese reformers criticized home confinement.

24 Shūzō Kure, *Seishin-byōsha Shitaku Kanchi no Jikkyō* [The Observation and Statistical Analysis of the Cases of Home Confinement], introduction and modern Japanese translation by Kanekawa Hideo (Tokyo: Igaku Shoin, 2012).

25 Shūzō Kure, *Seishin Byōgaku Shūyō* [An Essence of Psychiatry] 3 vols., ed. Haruo Akiyama (Tokyo: Sōzōshuppan, 2002); Noboru Ishihara, *Shinsen Seishin Byōgaku* [New Psychiatry] (Tokyo: Sōzōshuppan, 2003).

26 On "Abe Sada," see William Johnston, *Geisha, Harlot, Strangler, Star: A Woman, Sex, and Morality in Modern Japan* (New York: Columbia University Press, 2005). More generally about forensic reports, see Akiko Hyōdō, *Seishinbyō no Nihon Kindai* [Mental Illness and Modern Japan] (Tokyo: Seikyūsha, 2008).

27 Masae Kadowaki, *Kohyōbyō Shinron* [A New Treatise on Fox Possession] (Tokyo: Sōzōshuppan, 2001).

28 Kure, *Seishin Byōgaku Shūyō*, vol.1, a sheet inserted between page 26 and page 27.

29 Established in 1902 in Takinogawa, situated in northeast suburb of Tokyo, Ohji Brain Hospital was one of the first private psychiatric hospitals in Tokyo. Its extremely detailed, voluminous, and uncatalogued case records from around 1920 to 1945 have survived intact – along with other archival materials – and are held by Komine Research Institute for History of Psychiatry run by Dr Kazushige Komine, a practising psychiatrist and historian of psychiatry based in Tokyo and kept in the author's office at Keio University.

30 Archives of psychiatric hospitals in Japan have just started to be accessible to historians, and scholars have started to publish their findings based on the analysis of case histories and other materials. See the studies of Eri Nakamura, Motoyuki Goto, and Yuki Mitsuhira on war neurosis, welfare policy, and music therapies respectively.

31 See, for example, Akihito Suzuki, "Between Two Psychiatric Regimes: Migration and Psychiatry in Early Twentieth-Century Japan" in *Migration, Ethnicity, and Mental Health: Historical Perspectives, 1840–2010*, ed. Angela McCarthy and Catharine Coleborne, (London: Routledge, 2012), 141–51.

32 Uno behaved in an eccentric way in 1927, resulting from some very complex relationships with women and the progression of his syphilis. He ordered expensive luxuries, such as a bulldog that was delivered from a department store to his bewildered family, he enjoyed shooting at sparrows sitting atop electric wires with his air gun, and he pressed the dean of Waseda University to accept him as a lecturer in English literature.

These eccentricities worried his friends, leading to his hospitalization at Ohji Brain Hospital. He stayed there for two months from June 1927 and recovered after undergoing malaria fever therapy. See Tsutomu Minakami, *Uno Kōji Den* [Uno Kōji: a Biography] (Tokyo: Chūō Kōronsha, 1979).

33 Visits to a psychiatric hospital by journalists and literary critics seem to have been fairly common around that time. They visited not only celebrities and literary figures, but also turned commoners into prominent figures themselves. Rokoh Hirayama wrote a series of articles in *Miyako Newspaper* in which he reported on conversations with deluded patients who talked about their fantastic lives being "Shakyamuni," a "petition-addict," a "granny-poetess," and a "mistress of Tokugawa shogun." See Hirayama's section in *Byōin to Byōki*, ed. Mahito Fukuda (Tokyo: Yumani Shobō, 2009).

34 For Shimada's life and works, see a wonderful biography written by the psychiatrist Haruki Kazano, *Shimada Seijirō* (Tokyo: Hon no Zasshi sha, 2013).

35 Osamu Dazai, *Dazai Osamu Zenshū* [Complete Works of Osamu Dazai] (Tokyo: Chikuma Shobō, 1989–1992), vol.10. Yamano'uchi Shōshi, "Tsusima Shūji Dono Kango Nisshi to Human Lost" [The Nurse's Case of Tsushima Shūji and Human Lost], *Kokubungaku*, 27 (1982): 100–6.

36 Kokyō Nakamura, *Kara* [Shell] (Tokyo: Shun'yōdō, 1913).

37 Kokyō Nakamura, *Hisuteri no Ryōhō* [Treatment of Hysteria] (Tokyo: Shufu no Tomo sha, 1932).

38 Akatsuki Kambayashi, *Kambayashi Akatsuki Zenshū* [Collected Works of Akatsuki Kambayashi] (Tokyo: Chikuma Shobō, 2000).

39 There are several versions of *Dogra Maga*, as well as French and Chinese translations and the transcript of the entire text can be found in Aozora Bunko. See Kyūsaku Yumeno, *Yumeno Kyūsaku Chosakushū* [Complete Works of Kyūsaku Yumeno] (Tokyo: Chikuma Shobō, 1992).

40 When *Dogra Magra* was published and the launch party was held in 1935, Sakaki was already dead, and Moro'oka, who moved to Tokyo to work at James Hill Hospital as well as to be a critic, delivered a speech for the work. For the record of Yumeno's visits to the Department of Psychiatry, see Kyūsaku Yumeno, *Yumeno Kyūsaku no Nikki* [Diaries of Yumeno Kyūsaku], ed. Ryūmaru Sugiyama (Fukuoka: Ashi Shobō, 1976).

41 Gen'ichiro Ishigami, *Ishigami Gen'ichiro Sakuhinshū* [Collected Works of Gen'ichirō Ishigami] (Tokyo: Nihon Tosho Senta, 2004).

42 Haru'o Akimoto, "Tsugawa Takeichi to Today Seisin Igaku Kyōshitsu" [Tugawa Takeichi and the Department of Psychiatry at the University of Tokyo], *Inochi to Kurashi*, 5 (2003): 38–45.

43 Ryūnosuke Akutagawa, *Kappa* (Tokyo: Iwanami Shoten, 2013).

44 Enzō Matsunaga, *Yume wo Ku'u Hito* [A Dream-Eater] (Tokyo: Tōgensha, 1973).

45 Louis Saas, *Madness and Modernism: Insanity in the Life of Modern Art, Literature, and Thought* (New York: Basic Books, 1992).

46 Teinosuke Kinugasa, *Waga Eiga no Seishun* [My Films and the Youth] (Tokyo: Chūōkōronsha, 1977).

47 Ryūzaburō Shikiba, *Teihon Nishōtei Kitan* [A Strange Story of Nishōtei] (Tokyo: Chikuma Shobō, 1993).

48 Mahito Fukuda, *Kekkaku no Bunkashi* [A Cultural History of Tuberculosis] (Nagoya: University of Nagoya Press, 1995).

49 See works in *Hansenbyō Bungaku Zenshū* [A Collection of Hansen's Disease and Literature], ten volumes, ed. Makoto Ōno et. al (Tokyo: Kōseisha, 2000).

Part V

PERSPECTIVES AND EXPERIENCES

14

THE STRAITJACKET, THE BED, AND THE PILL

Material culture and madness

Benoît Majerus

The seat [. . .] consists of a sinkhole (a), a pot (b), discharge pipes (c) ventilation tubes (d). The whole device is covered up to the mouth of the sinkhole and the pot with wood; the pot is closed with a screwable tight lid. Sinkhole and pot are constructed like faïence tubes and have a wall thickness of 0.1'. [. . .] The inside diameter of the upper sinkhole measures 1.0', the lower only 0.27'.[1]

The proliferation of asylums in the nineteenth century[2] resulted in an exhaustive and prescriptive literature, which went beyond discussion on the cardinal architectural principles to elaborate upon spaces for the insane. Any self-respecting psychiatrist had to take into account the materiality of these new places. If this aspect was gradually abandoned during the second half of the nineteenth century – Emile Kraepelin and George Beard, for instance, were more interested in nosological issues – the first half of the nineteenth century saw many psychiatrists, such as the likes of Joseph Guislain[3] or Etienne Esquirol,[4] debating the (future) materiality of institutions for the insane. These treatises offer easy access for anyone interested in the material culture of asylums.[5] The excerpt quoted above is taken from this corpus. In 1869, the German physician Emil Fries published a booklet devoted to the construction of toilets in asylums. Without wishing to declare a toilet an *objet social total* that might unravel the entire history of psychiatry, the object such as imagined by Fries nevertheless allows us to address several facets of psychiatric history and to uncover the potential of a narrative that is mindful of material culture: the importance attached to drilling patients through hygiene education, a history of odours inside asylums, the difficulty in managing persons suspected of misusing even such mundane objects as toilets.

Yet, until recently, historians of psychiatry have shown only scant interest in the material culture of asylums. While the narratives are full of evocative objects – the bed, the wall, the pill – our knowledge of the material culture surrounding madness remains rudimentary, especially when it comes to overcoming the imagined materiality and focus more specifically on the practices associated with objects.[6]

Who conceived of these objects? Who created and manufactured them? Who used them in the asylum and how? Objects, similar to images in other historiographical contexts, are often only treated as having illustrative purposes and are not taken into account as a specific source. Historians have relinquished the psychiatric object to art historians and museum curators. Art historians have been working for some years on the architectural aspects and also attach relevance to the material culture of these spaces.[7] And as a collection of objects often defines museums, curators have attached particular importance to their materiality.[8]

Lives of objects

The purpose of this chapter is not to present a comprehensive history of all objects in psychiatry. By concentrating on the nineteenth and twentieth centuries and by limiting itself to Western Europe, it attempts to show through three case studies not only the potential of such an analysis, but also the lacunas in current historiography. The three chosen objects – the straitjacket, the bed and the pill – offer diverse approaches and illustrate different master narratives of the historiography of psychiatry: the straitjacket represents confinement, the bed hospital culture, while the pill epitomises the so-called chemical revolution of the 1950s.

The straitjacket

In the introduction to his book *Understanding Material Culture*, the sociologist Ian Woodward argues that 'objects have symbolic potency because they have a place. They therefore also have a non-place: a place where they are out of context.'[9] Undoubtedly, the straitjacket possesses an intensely potent symbolic value, because its place seems naturally within the psychiatric world – even if the narrative is more complicated today.

Along with walls and railings, the straitjacket – originally referred to as the 'Spanish straitjacket', by German commentators in the nineteenth century – unquestionably represents the most paradigmatic image of confinement.[10] In popular culture, its mere mention suffices to evoke madness, be it in the Belgian comic *Tintin – Cigars of the Pharaoh* or in the American animated comedy *Who Framed Roger Rabbit*. In most museums dedicated to the history of medicine in general and to the history of psychiatry in particular, the story of madness is told to visitors through the straitjacket, which is presented as the natural 'witness-object'[11] to speak about psychiatry.

The origins of the straitjacket are usually dated back to the second half of the eighteenth century, at a time when the Western world was broadly transforming its mode of punishment in order to humanise it (the guillotine, too, emerged from a similar impulse at the same time). If the story of the invention of the straitjacket by the upholsterer Guilleret for the Bicêtre Hospital (Paris), as narrated by, among others, Michel Foucault, has proven to be a myth similar to the story of the liberation of the insane by Pinel, ample evidence exists of its use throughout Europe in the second half of the nineteenth century.[12] Unlike ropes or chains, the straitjacket allowed the patient to walk about and was considered more humane and progressive than traditional restraints: patients could stroll about and yet not pose risks to others. In 1789, the Scottish doctor William Cullen was full of its praise:

> Restraining the anger and violence of madmen is always necessary for preventing their hurting themselves or others: But this restraint is also to be considered as a remedy. [. . .] Restraint, therefore, is useful, and ought to be complete;

but it should be executed in the easiest manner possible for the patient, and the strait waistcoat answers every purpose better than any other that has yet been thought of.[13]

From the very outset the straitjacket was entangled in a history of therapeutic purpose and disciplinary function.

Frequently made of canvas, sometimes of leather, the straitjacket was initially designed to replace metal restraints. This apparent 'softness' explains why, at least until the middle of the nineteenth century, its use was also differentiated on the basis of gender. A French parliamentary report, for example, emphasised that the strait-jacket was more often used on women than on men.[14]

One may assume that from the second half of the nineteenth century onwards, most asylums had straitjackets at their disposal. Given their relatively high price, it is, however, highly unlikely that the ratio proposed by the French physician Bouchardat – 10 straitjackets per 100 patients – was respected.[15]

As an object, it was characterised by its great heterogeneity. Typically, it was a closed jacket, equipped with buttons or strings at the back and with long sleeves whose ends are tied to the back of the wearer. Some straitjackets also covered the head, while others immobilised the legs. Over time, smaller straitjackets materialised, such as leather gloves to restrict hand movements in order to avoid scratching, or underwear designed to prevent masturbation. Some straitjackets came with a device that secured the wearer directly to his or her bed.[16]

Yet, the straitjacket was a disputed object virtually from its implementation. Indeed, among psychiatrists, who were concurrently starting to advocate the use of the moral treatment, its use was immediately contested. The Italian physician Vincenzo Chiarugi spoke out against it in 1794.[17] Its very materiality, initially con-sidered advantageous, swiftly became problematic. Moisture made the jacket heavy and cumbersome. Friction, due among other things to sweat, engendered skin prob-lems and caused abrasions. Immobilising the hands caused hygiene complications: patients could neither blow their noses nor go to the toilet alone. Such criticism, particularly articulated by those involved in the non-restraint movement in England, provoked staunch responses from French and German psychiatrists who defended its use. Yet even in France, opinion changed rapidly. In 1871, Eugene Rouhier wrote in his dissertation at the Medicine Faculty in Paris, 'The straitjacket has introduced real progress, because it caused iron chains, rings attached to the walls, etc. to little by little disappear from asylums.'[18] However, thirty years later, in a similar exercise, Girard concluded that the 'mechanical containment [straitjacket] in asylums is the shame of the twentieth century; it must be banished'.[19] By the end of the nineteenth century, the straitjacket had already turned into the motif for a dehumanising psychi-atry. In travel reports by psychiatrists published at that time, the unrestrained use of the straitjacket became the symbol of an antiquated system of care.[20] And in the first anti-psychiatric wave of the second half of the nineteenth century, denouncing the straitjacket was to become a recurring leitmotif.[21]

As for its use, in the absence of historical literature on the matter, we can only make assumptions. The decision to deploy a straitjacket belonged mainly to the caretakers and keepers despite numerous recommendations, including those from Pinel, that its use should only be practised under a physician's direct supervision.[22] It is evident that it was handled by hospital staff and nurses without any involvement by psychiatrists. Putting a patient into a straitjacket required specific know-how and training in order to force the patient into the garment; the action was not without risk to the immobilised person's breathing:

> The best procedure consists of oneself moving both arms backwards into the straitjacket, and in this way to go through the opening in the shoulders in front of the patient's hands; then lead the patient into the straitjacket by leading him through the same path, while an assistant standing behind the patient, draws the body of the straitjacket towards himself and then laces it at the back, taking care not to tighten the neck nor to compress the chest so as not to interfere with the [patient's] breathing.[23]

This vivid description reveals little of the actual violence involved in putting someone into a straitjacket. While wearing the straitjacket in itself was a source of multiple injuries, putting someone into the straitjacket was an extremely violent moment during which numerous fractures could and did occur.[24] Psychiatric textbooks and

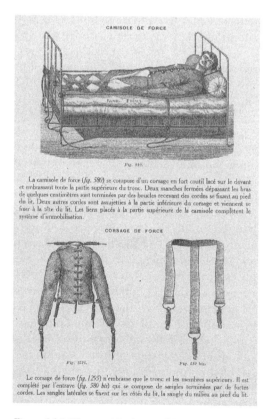

Figure 14.1 The straitjacket and its accessories. Extract from the Rainal Brothers' catalogue, suppliers of the military and civilian hospitals and the Faculty of Medicine in Paris.[25]

historians' written accounts, however, remain largely silent on practices – duration of confinement, patient's personal experiences, therapeutic goals – involving the straitjacket.

The object gradually disappeared from psychiatric textbooks over the course of the twentieth century.[26] In a profession that longed to be 'modern' and that relied on its first biological therapies (insulin shock, Cardiazol [PZT], etc.), the straitjacket became a proscribed object, at least in academic discourse. In his illustrious handbook on psychiatry, Emmanuel Régis used the word 'straitjacket' some twenty times in the first edition of 1885, but not at all in the sixth and final one in 1923.[27] Within the asylum, however, it did not disappear as quickly from practice. Again, in the absence of detailed studies, it is difficult to propose an exact chronology of its use. It would appear that since the 1960s, its usage has decreased. Nevertheless, in many psychiatric hospitals, the object remains on hand nowadays for particularly agitated patients, even if the object's materiality has changed fundamentally in order that it appears less enveloping. The Canadian company Segufix dominates today's market, priding itself on having invented 'human immobilisation'.[28]

Besides a bed for agitated patients (see below), the straitjacket was for a protracted period the only psychiatric object to be found in general medical catalogues. While other medical disciplines such as surgery, gastroenterology, ophthalmology, dermatology, and gynaecology were characterised by an ever-growing arsenal of instruments, psychiatry lagged relatively far behind in this respect.

Even if the straitjacket appears as the psychiatric object *par excellence*, its use nonetheless rapidly extended beyond the asylum's walls – and not only figuratively speaking.[29] It was already being used from the nineteenth century onwards on the outside; for example, by families who had custody of insane dependants.

Moreover, it was a commonplace device in general hospitals for patients with diseases that caused agitation such as smallpox; in prisons and institutions for children and difficult teenagers (hence its application was similar to that in psychiatry) from the nineteenth century on;[30] as well as in the entertainment world (escape artists and contortionists); and it remains an aid in sexual practises to this very day.

The bed

During the eighteenth century, the bed had become a central feature of the hospital, and to this day 'the hospital comprises hundreds of beds'.[31] In the second half of the nineteenth century, psychiatrists, in their efforts to integrate the medical field, organised wards around beds. The bed also served as the standard quantitative unit in hospitals. Thus, when discussing the capacity of asylums, policy makers and physicians spoke of 'x number of beds' and not 'x number of patients'. A bed needed a certain amount of cubic meters and had a 'daily price' and an 'annual price' that facilitated cost comparisons for various services and the calculation of over- and under-population. The psychiatric upheaval of the 1960s mobilised under the slogan of the 'reduction of psychiatric beds'. Moreover, the bed was an object that had to be adapted to the internal uses and needs of insane asylums. A peculiar material grammar emerges, but it was seldomly made explicit.

In the early nineteenth century, beds were made of wood, while mattresses were often filled with straw that required regular replacement. Many asylums had their own carpentry units where beds were built, while those facilities in the countryside also furnished their own straw. During the first half of the nineteenth century, medical institutions replaced their wooden beds with lacquered iron bedsteads, which, while certainly being more expensive, were considered more hygienic and less prone to infestation by vermin. Constructing these beds was no longer possible inside the asylum, but remained operative at a local or regional level and were not specific to individual asylums, even if some manufacturers specialised in what Erving Goffman termed 'total institutions'. (The Bouvier Company in Lyon, for instance, offered 'production of iron beds and patented mesh bases. Specialised items for colleges, seminaries, communities, asylums, orphanages, factories, etc.')[32] The hospital in general, and the asylum in particular, became an attractive market, and the burgeoning medical press of the nineteenth century partially lived off advertising revenues from these objects. Most hospital furniture manufacturers offered – besides the conventional hospital bed – a bed for agitated and/or senile patients equipped with bars making it difficult to get out of; they also proposed a solution to dispose of excrement without the patient having to leave the bed to go to the toilet.

In contrast to general hospital wards, where screens often separated beds in large dormitories, beds in psychiatric units remained visible to the scrutiny of psychiatrists, staff-members, nurses, as well as other patients.

Prior to the 1960s, patients were routinely put to bed upon being admitted. This procedure served several functions. The bed was primarily a symbol of the general hospital: a person confined to bed during the day was associated with being sick. The bed became a symbol for disease. Its use inside an asylum, therefore, meant that insanity should likewise be considered a disease. Confining someone to bed was a technique designed to discipline not only the body, but also the ward activity. The spatial organisation of each ward was dictated by the bed arrangement, an arrangement that was supposed to indicate order and cleanliness. This was true for medicine in general – just look at the numerous photos of medical services in which one sees beds carefully lined up – but even more so in psychiatry, where the bed was the crucial tool for controlling the patient. In their widely read textbook of psychiatry, Mignot and Marchand emphasised that:

> Beds should be wide enough apart so that patients cannot reach the neighbouring bed by hand and they must be at a distance from the walls; it is necessary that nurses can do their rounds effortlessly so as to take care of those agitated in their moments of excitement.[34]

Figure 14.2 Bed for senile and mentally ill patients[33]

The bed was also a potent indicator of social distinctions within the asylum system. Psychiatric spaces – asylums in the nineteenth century as well as psychiatric wards inside a general hospital in the early twenty-first century – remained places where class issues were deeply significant. In 1831, the German psychiatrist Christian Friedrich Wilhelm Roller proposed different categories of wood for different classes of patients.[35] Fifty years later, in 1885, the regulations in Stephansfeld, an asylum near Strasbourg, stipulated that patients from the first, second, and third classes were entitled to six bed sheets, while those from the fourth and fifth classes merely four.[36] Finally, there were also important distinctions between the standard hospital bed that structured the space in large dormitories and the bed of the wealthy bourgeois asylum. Such asylums strove to differentiate their space as much as possible from a standard asylum by replicating a typically bourgeois interior by means of a different material culture. John Perceval, a patient in Ticehurst – 'psychiatry for the rich' – made a list of the contents of his two-roomed apartment: 'the walls papered, the floor carpeted, a sofa in it, a small bookcase, mahogany table and chairs, a marble chimney-piece, a large sash-window; a cheerful fire in the grate.'[37]

The psychiatric bed was mostly a modified hospital bed. At the Institute of Psychiatry in Brussels,[38] the bed, built of iron with rounded corners, contained numerous details that revealed its psychiatric specificity. Admittedly, the beds were not fixed to the ground, as advocated in many psychiatric manuals, in order to ensure some flexibility in case of overcrowding, and to facilitate cleaning the floors. To ensure stability, the architect constructed beds 'with round wooden legs instead of casters.' Furthermore, and in contrast to beds in other medical departments inside the same hospital, those at the Institute of Psychiatry did not have bars at the head and foot of the bed, but instead full panels so as to prevent any suicide attempts were the patient to attach sheets to the bars. Psychiatric beds were not equipped with a small light as in other wards, in order to avoid burns, cuts, and electrocution. Until the 1950s, the bed was the place where medical records were written up and hence where a person was transformed into a 'patient'.[39] These records, however, were not attached to the patient's bed as in other medical departments. In psychiatry, they were often kept in the nurses' station.

For many psychiatrists, the bed had a therapeutic value. It was thought that resting the elongated human body was conducive to relaxing the nervous system.[40] The excitement aroused by modern urban life, inter alia, was considered one of the primary factors in the apparent increasing number of alienated. From the nurses' and attendants' perspective, to accept being put to bed during daylight hours was an indicator of the degree of the newcomer's obedience. This was often the moment the patient was initially confronted with the practical constraints of institutional life. Yet reforms and (apparent) therapeutic ruptures affecting psychiatry in the 1950s and 1960s also transformed the bed's role. Henceforth the psychiatric hospital began promoting the reintegration of patients into society as one of its primary functions, and it tried to simulate life and work conditions in the outside world. Lying in bed all day was no longer desirable. Admittedly, beds continued to organise the available space on the wards, but the nursing and medical staff no longer systematically forced patients to stay in bed for protracted periods. Resting in bed – an 'activity' considered as unproblematic during the interwar period – was to become a worrisome symptom from the 1960s onwards, as activities such as occupational therapy entered the asylum.

It was only at that juncture that another reality became apparent in doctors' and nurses' notes: the bed as the primary private space available to the recluse. The bed was often the only space that was specifically devoted to the individual. Unquestionably, all beds were alike and it was strictly forbidden to customise them, at least until the 1950s. Each patient was nonetheless given a specific bed upon being admitted to a ward, and they rarely switched beds during their stay, which at times could even last several months. The patient could withdraw to their beds where they had sheets under which to 'hide'. Curiously, it was through the resistance of those who did not want to quit their beds, despite the therapeutic changes introduced in the 1960s, that this appropriation of the bed became visible to historians.

The pill

The pill often only first appears in historical narratives of psychiatry with the discovery of neuroleptics in the 1950s. Yet it was a commonplace object inside many asylums at the latest from the latter half of the nineteenth century.[41] For many psychiatrists, these medications decisively excluded continued use of an item discussed above, namely, the straitjacket. Already in 1894, Paul Lefert wrote, 'Since 1873, I have always used this medication, with or without morphine, and success has been consistent each time patients have been spared the straitjacket.'[42]

If some authors deemed that a pharmacy was not really necessary inside an asylum,[43] others like Scipio Pinel in his manual on building institutions for the insane stressed its significance. 'The pharmacy,' he stated, 'is, after the kitchen, the most important room within a hospital.'[44] And when in 1862 the French psychiatrist Pierre Berthier published his travel notes on French asylums, he noted that several institutions had a room specifically set aside for drugs.[45] Yet, the object did not only determine the space, but also the professions working within the institution, as the position of the pharmacist became more common within asylums.[46]

If the straitjacket and the bed were both based on artisanal know-how, the pill was inscribed in other frameworks from the early nineteenth century on. Initially, drugs were fabricated in the pharmacy in diverse forms: pill, injection, medicinal-syrup.[47] Given that psychiatric patients proved especially reluctant to take drugs, psychiatrists began experimenting from the nineteenth century onwards with making medication more palatable. Thus paraldehyde, a sedative used in psychiatry since the 1880s, was administered with rum or lemon to camouflage its unpleasant taste,[48] but it did not succeed in removing the disagreeable odour characterising psychiatric wards till the 1950s when the use of paraldehyde fell into decline.[49]

From the second half of the nineteenth century, drugs were increasingly manufactured outside the asylums. Initially, they were handmade, but their production became increasingly industrial by the end of the nineteenth century. They were no longer produced by regional manufacturers who often worked in cooperation with renowned physicians, but instead by pharmaceutical companies operating at a national or international level and mobilising chemical knowledge that no longer had any direct link with psychiatry. Despite the fact that the drugs are often considered to have integrated psychiatry into the capitalistic system from the 1960s onwards, advertisement for medical drugs of all sorts were already filling pages of psychiatric journals in the late nineteenth century, thus ensuring continual funding.

Drug distribution also entailed the construction of a specific piece of furniture. In 1836, Scipion Pinel recommended making small boxes, a 'square containing drugs, with a number on it corresponding to the bed number'.[50] These pillboxes were present in non-psychiatric settings from the early nineteenth century on and experienced a new relevance with the release of psychiatric drugs outside asylums walls in the second half of the twentieth century. Psychiatric therapy became increasingly mobile with the consumption of pills and found its place in life beyond the walls.

Moreover, the issue of compliance in psychiatry arose at the same point as a new contingency. Although some of these substances came in liquid form that was to be injected, most antipsychotics were taken in tablet form. Due to their materiality, however, the administration of pills required some cooperation on the part of the patients. Compared with other prevalent psychiatric therapies, such as ECT, taking medication was an act that paradoxically served to weaken the medical grip. Not only did its materiality afford the patients some command over compliance or non-compliance, but it also enabled therapy outside the hospital walls.

To solve the problem of medical compliance outside an institutionalised setting, the pharmaceutical industry developed from the mid-1960s the so-called long-acting (depot) neuroleptics. Based on a similar process to that invented years earlier for insulin, the patient received a slow-release depot injection with a drug that would be effective not just for several hours, but for several weeks (usually one month). This transformative change in the function of medical drugs spread increasingly after the 1970s and was considered by certain researchers as the basis for a sustainable development of social psychiatry.[51] This produced paradoxical effects. While ex-patients could treat themselves at a remove from medical scrutiny, this innovative procedure nonetheless enabled psychiatrists to strengthen their grip on formerly institutionalised patients now outside the walls of the asylum.

While the question of whether a rupture was introduced by neuroleptics continues to occupy historians,[52] drugs in tablet form admittedly led to changes on many levels. Within a decade, pills achieved a therapeutic domination that no other form of treatment had hitherto accomplished. Considering neuroleptics through their chemical materiality induced a break in the design of pathological forms of the psychic. By analysing how Chlorpromazine (CPZ) – the first antipsychotic medication – worked, the dopamine hypothesis was developed. The neuroleptic blocks D2 dopamine receptors, and its antipsychotic effect was attributed by researchers to this blocking action. Consequently, a surplus of dopamine was considered responsible for fostering symptoms of schizophrenia.[53]

Of the three commonplace medical objects presented in this essay, the pill is undoubtedly the one that has been the most anthropomorphised. That it had its own agency was rarely contested. Many drugs had emotionally evocative names, and in popular culture, songs about particular neuroleptics are numerous: probably the best known are 'Purple Hearts', the name given to Drinamyl, a popular stimulant made from dexamphetamine and barbiturates, and 'Mother's Little Helper', the nickname given to Valium by the Rolling Stones.[54]

The consumption of neuroleptics also became a highly visible marker of differences in class, gender, and age. Consumption within the asylum remained strongly determined by non-negotiated prescriptions from the physician. Outside of the hospital, psychiatric medication became a distinguishing element just like other consumer goods. Thus Miltown (Mepromate) was first found in the mouths of Hollywood stars before becoming a mass-consumed commodity. If no antipsychotic attained the iconic character of the blue diamond of Viagra, the trade dress (i.e. the visual appearance of the drug and its packaging) played a key role.[55]

Psychiatric drugs also profoundly changed the relationship between patient and psychiatrist. Drug therapy – unlike nineteenth-century therapies such as the straitjacket – was no longer a measure always prescribed by the doctor, but was sometimes requested by the patients themselves. While initial attempts at biological therapies in the interwar period had already given rise to requests by patients, these were rare in psychiatry, owing to the fact that the side-effects of treatments like insulin and ECT were relatively disagreeable. Psychotropic drugs transformed that situation. In psychiatric hospitals, patients regularly demanded pills.[56] Some historians argue that outside of psychiatric institutions, demand was essentially driven by patients and ex-patients.[57] Drugs introduced, at least partially, 'consumer sovereignty within psychiatry'. The flagship of material cultural studies, the history of consumption, shatters the history of psychiatry focused exclusively on confinement. Psychiatric drugs deinstitutionalised the history of psychiatry and illustrates the ubiquitous presence of psychiatry in everyday life in Western society. Yet, they escaped not only from the asylum, but also from the grip of psychiatrists as well. In 1975 in the United States, 75 percent of minor tranquilizers were prescribed by general practitioners and only 25 percent by psychiatrists.[58]

If the first two objects examined clearly determined the psychiatric identities of their users – a person bound in a straitjacket was 'crazy' and the one lying in bed was sick – the pill, thanks to its ubiquitous use, did not perform a similarly total identification. Unlike the effects produced by the two other objects, a person taking psychiatric medication was not reduced to a psychiatric identity. Of the three objects selected to illustrate a material history of psychiatry, it is indisputably the last one for which the critical theory inspired by the Marxist idea of material culture was most often used: a pill as a commodity, as a product of capitalist society with a strong capacity to alienate.

The trajectory of objects

Studying material culture enables access to the history of people living and working inside the walls of an insane asylum. One could multiply the examples here, but I hope that this chapter provides sufficient material to open up four potentially fertile research fields.

The first and most obvious one is the interdependence between objects, which determine daily psychiatric practice and the psychiatry that transforms those objects. Thus, the bed changes its function when transposed from a standard room to an asylum. On a symbolic level, the bed that provides rest is transformed into a tool for classification and confinement. On a material level, this change results in slight, but significant modifications. And the bed structures psychiatric space, as it organises the layout of the hospital interior.

Second, the daily experience of psychiatry for doctors, nurses, and inmates has rarely been studied through the prism of its material culture. The history of asylums has for a long time been dominated by the history of psychiatrists. Over the last fifteen years, the voice of the inmate has become more audible, yet one set of actors remains largely unknown: nurses. This third party was particularly key in the daily running of the institution and in determining the use of many objects. When examining work-books, diaries, and memoirs, the materiality of these objects is always central in the writing of the attending nurses.

Third, when evaluating these objects in terms of their 'biography', one overcomes a static description and instead one sees how they often led a triple life. At first, they are conceived objects. In the case of the aforementioned bed at the Institute of Psychiatry, there was an engineer-architect and a psychiatrist, with manifold frames of references. The architect had already participated in the construction of several hospitals, and from the late 1920s the two men were visiting other asylums in Belgium and abroad as well as prisons. At that time, an asylum was still conceived as a confined space, a space in which to literally confine. Gradually, however, the anti-psychiatric wave that had been shaking Europe and northern America since the late nineteenth century left its mark on both movable and immovable objects that populated the asylums. The negative effects giving the impression of confinement were taken into account. This impulse expressed itself in the creation of a feeling of an architectural opening up: the garden fence disappeared behind the hedges or the steel window frame hidden behind a veneer. In a second step, these imaginary objects had to be transformed into lifelike objects. This transformation confronted numerous obstacles, such as technical impossibilities or manufacturing faults. Yet, discussions between architects, contractors, and psychiatrists were ultimately productive because they also involved new areas of experience. The craftsman, in response to specifications, often proposed alternative solutions which neither the engineer nor the psychiatrist had envisaged. It was only during a third stage that these objects became 'acted objects', objects that are incorporated by actors. Each of these lives and their interactions demand our attention. What is particularly interesting is the gap that may exist between the object as initially conceived and the 'acted object'. Particularly given that besides the function of the 'acted object', the straitjacket, the bed, and the pill also become 'acting objects' that ultimately shape and transform psychiatric space, practice, and experience. Based on the material culture of the asylums, the Australian historian Catherine Coleborne speaks of the psychiatric hospital as a 'myth' because it has only rarely been as people imagined it.[59] In exploring the three lives of objects and their interactions, we can try to alter this discrepancy to which researchers in the social sciences may equally fall victim to as 'ordinary people'. Material culture shows the heterogeneity of possible fields of action for all the actors in the history of psychiatry.

On a final note, scholarly interest in the material culture of the object always interrogated the means of production, a process that took place mainly on the hospital grounds during the nineteenth century, but went on elsewhere over the course of the twentieth century. Marketing was also another source of interest. Conceiving of and producing a straitjacket, a bed, or a psychiatric drug was increasingly undertaken outside of the psychiatric space during the twentieth century. The history of psychiatry must exit the institution – and that well before the deinstitutionalisation of the 1960s[60] – to write an economic history of psychiatry: a history of material culture which draws attention to the story of the marketplace and marketing of these psychiatric objects.

Notes

1 'Der Sitz (. . .) besteht aus dem Trichter (a), dem Topfe (b), dem Abführrohre (c) und dem Ventilationsrohre (d). Die ganze Vorrichtung ist bis auf die Mündungen von Trichter und Topf mit Holz verkleidet, der Topf durch einen dichtanliegenden Deckel verschlossen, der abgeschraubt werden kann. Trichter und Topf sind wie die Röhrenleitung von Steingut angefertigt, haben eine Wandstärke von 0.1'. (. . .) Die lichte Weite der oberen Trichtermündung beträgt 1,0', die der unteren nur 0.27'.' Emil Fries, *Das Latrinen-System der Kreis-Irrenanstalt Werneck* (Würzburg, A. Stuber, 1869), 8.

2 Cf. Andrew Scull's chapter in this volume.

3 Joseph Guislain, *Traité sur l'aliénation mentale et sur les hospices des aliénés* (Amsterdam: Van der Hey, 1826).

4 Etienne Esquirol, *Des établissements des aliénés en France et des moyens d'améliorer le sort de ces infortunés* (Paris: Huzard, 1819).

5 Given the significant digitalisation of nineteenth-century books, most of this literature is now accessible online. The school, another place of standardisation, was also a topic of intense discussion. These two institutions were sometimes addressed in a single book: Félix Narjoux, *Les écoles publiques en France et en Angleterre: construction et installation, documents officiels, services extérieurs, services intérieurs, salles d'asile, mobilier scolaire, services annexes* (Paris: Morel, 1877).

6 Jennifer L. Bazar's recent dissertation offers a powerful case advocating integrating the history of material culture into the historiography of psychiatry. Jennifer L. Bazar, *Objects of Daily Life: Materiality in North American Institutions for the Insane* (Ph.D. Diss., York University, 2013).

7 Leslie Topp, James E. Moran, and Jonathan Andrews, eds, *Madness, Architecture and the Built Environment: Psychiatric Spaces in Historical Context* (London: Routledge, 2007).

8 Catharine Coleborne and Dolly MacKinnon, *Exhibiting Madness in Museums: Remembering Psychiatry through Collections and Display* (New York: Routledge, 2011) and also the excellent blog 'Bethlem Museum of the Mind'. (http://museumofthemind.org.uk) that contains a section 'Object Lesson'.

9 Ian Woodward, *Understanding Material Culture* (Los Angeles: Sage, 2007), 66.

10 Will Wiles, 'Straitjacket: A Confined History' in *Insanity and the Lunatic Asylum in the Nineteenth Century*, ed. Thomas Knowles and Serena Trowbridge (London: Pickering & Chatto, 2014), 167–181.

11 Marie-Pierre Julien and Céline Rossenlin, *La culture matérielle* (Paris: La Découverte, 2005), 34.

12 Wiles, "Straitjacket: A Confined History," *op. cit.*

13 William Cullen, *First Lines of the Practice of Physic, Vol. 4* (Edinburgh: C. Elliot, 1789), 151–155; Wiles, "Straitjacket: A Confined History," *op. cit.*, 172.

14 France Commission d'enquête parlementaire sur le régime des établissements pénitentiaires, *Enquête parlementaire sur le régime des établissements pénitentiaires* (Paris: Cerf et fils, 1873), 41.

15 A. Bouchardat, "Mémoire sur l'hygiène des hôpitaux et hospices civils de Paris," *Annales d'hygiène publique et de médecine légale*, 17 (1837): 37–73, 71.

16 The manufacture of the straitjacket could not be elucidated in detail. In *La Lancette française, gazette des hôpitaux civils et militaires*, Dr. Nicole regularly published between 1837 and 1843 advertisements for iron beds, crutches and straitjackets. At the end of the nineteenth century, several patents were filed in relation to 'insane costumes', particularly by the Matray, Schmittbuhl & Company, suggesting that a craft around this product existed. The Drapier House in Paris, specialising in the manufacture of bandages and belts, featured a straitjacket in its catalogue in the early twentieth century: *Catalogue de la maison Drapier: bandages herniaires, ceintures – bas pour varices, accessoires* (Paris: Drapier et Fils, 1911).

17 Ian Robert Dowbiggin, *The Quest for Mental Health; A Tale of Science, Medicine, Scandal, Sorrow, and Mass Society* (New York: Cambridge University Press, 2011), 40.

18 "La camisole fut un progrès réel, car elle fit disparaître peu à peu des asiles, les chaînes en fer, les anneaux fixés aux murs, etc." Eugéne Rouhier, *De la camisole ou gilet de force* (Université de Paris, Faculté de médecine, 1871) 11.

19 "La contrainte mécanique dans les asiles d'aliénés est la honte du XXe siècle; il faut qu'elle disparaisse." P. Girard, *De la suppression de la camisole de force dans les asiles d'aliénés* (Impr. G. Firmin, Montane et Sicardi, 1904), 32.

20 Rudolf Arndt, *Lehrbuch der Psychiatrie für Ärzte und Studierende* (Vienna: Urban & Schwarzenberg, 1883), 325.

21 Aude Fauvel, 'La voix des fous. Hector Malot et les "romans d'asile,' *Romantisme*, n° 3 (2008): 51–64.

22 See, for example, Sophie Richelle, *Les 'folles' de Bailleul. Expériences et conditions d'internement dans un asile français (1880–1914)* (Brussels: Université des femmes, 2014), 110–111.

23 "Le meilleur procédé consiste à passer soi-même les deux bras au rebours dans les manches de la camisole, et d'aller ainsi, par l'ouverture des épaules, au devant des mains du malade, qu'on entraîne dans les siennes en sortant par la même voie, pendant qu'un aide, placé derrière le malade, tire à soi le corps de la camisole qu'il lui lace sur le dos, en ayant soin de ne pas serrer le cou ni de comprimer le thorax au point de gêner la respiration." Emmanuel Régis, *Manuel pratique de médecine mentale*, 1ʳᵉ éd. (Paris: Octave Doin, 1885), 486. In numerous nursing textbooks, there was a detailed description of how to set the straitjacket.

24 E. Rouhier, *De la camisole ou gilet de force, op. cit.*

25 Rainal Fréres, *Catalogue général* (Paris: Maréchal, 1925), 313. In the Rainal Brothers catalogue of 1934, the straitjacket no longer features.

26 In the Drapier catalogue (1929), the straitjacket is available in 1911, but no longer features in 1929.

27 Emmanuel Régis, *Manuel pratique de médecine mentale*, 1ʳᵉ éd. (Paris: Octave Doin, 1885) and *Précis de psychiatrie*, 6ᵉ éd. (Paris: Octave Doin, 1923).

28 www.segufix.com, accessed 2 April 2015.

29 From the nineteenth century onwards, the term *camisole de force* is used to figuratively express 'ce qui contraint' [that which constrains]: www.cnrtl.fr/definition/camisole, accessed 2 April 2015.

30 In Belgium, the female minor inmates at the *asile-clinique* in Bruges even manufactured straitjackets for other similar institutions. See Veerle Massin, *Protéger ou exclure? L'enfermement des 'filles perdues' de la Protection de l'enfance à Bruges (1922–1965)* (Thèse de doctorat, Université catholique de Louvain, 2011), 328.

31 Jean-François Laé, "Le lit, dispositif de l'institution totale" in *L'asile aux fous. Photographies de Roger Camar*, ed. Philippe Artières and Jean-François Laé, (Paris: Presses Universitaires de Vincennes, 2009), 99–117.

32 *Annuaire de l'Union fraternelle du commerce et de l'industrie* (Paris, 1892), 187.

33 Vve Dupont and André Dupont, *Lits, fauteuils, voitures et appareils mécaniques pour malades et blessés* (Paris: Farcy, 1914), 13.

34 'Les lits doivent être très écartés les uns des autres afin que les malades ne puissent atteindre avec la main les sujets des lits voisins; ils doivent être éloignés des murs; il faut que les infirmiers puissent en faire facilement le tour pour maintenir les agités dans les moments d'excitation.' Roger Mignot and Ludovic Marchand, *Manuel technique de l'infirmier des établissements d'aliénés* (Paris: Gaston Doin, 1931), 307.

35 Christian Friedrich Wilhelm Roller, *Die Irrenanstalt nach allen ihren Beziehungen* (Karlsruhe: Chr. Fr. Müller'schen Hofbuchhandlung, 1831), 133.

36 Asile de Stéphansfeld, 'Maison de Santé pour le traitement des malades mentales – Renseignements pour les familles.'

37 Charlotte MacKenzie, *Psychiatry for the Rich: A History of Ticehurst Private Asylum, 1792–1917* (London, Routledge, 1992), 70.

38 This paragraph is based on Benoît Majerus, 'La baignoire, le lit et la porte. La vie sociale des objets de la psychiatrie,' *Genèses*, 82 (2011): 95–119.

39 Karen Nolte, 'Vom Verschwinden der Laienperspektive aus der Krankengeschichte: Medizinische Fallberichte im 19. Jahrhundert' in *Zum Fall machen, zum Fall werden. Wissensproduktion und Patientenerfahrung in Medizin und Psychiatrie des 19. und 20. Jahrhunderts*, ed. Sibylle Brändli, Barbara Lüthi and Gregor Spuhler (Frankfurt a. M.: Campus, 2009), 33–61, 35.

40 S. Weir Mitchell proposed a particularly extreme form of rest cure whereby patients should stay in bed for up to six weeks without being allowed to sit, read, or even get up to go to the toilet. See S. Poirier, 'The Weir Mitchell Rest Cure: Doctor and Patients', *Women's Studies: An Interdisciplinary Journal*, 10 (1983): 15–40.

41 See Toine Pieters's chapter in this book as well as Sara Black's forthcoming dissertation entitled 'Psychotropic Society: The Medical and Cultural History of Drugs in France, 1840–1920.'

42 'Depuis 1873, j'ai toujours eu recours à ce médicament, avec ou sans morphine, et le succès a été constant, toutes les fois que les malades ont été préservés de la camisole de force.' Paul Lefert, *Manuel du médecin praticien. La pratique des maladies du système nerveux dans les hôpitaux de Paris, etc.* (Paris: Baillière, 1894), 13.

43 See, for example, Roller, *Die Irrenanstalt nach allen ihren Beziehungen, op. cit.*

44 'La pharmacie est, après la cuisine, la pièce la plus importante de l'hôpital.' Scipion Pinel, *Traité complet du régime sanitaire des aliénés, ou Manuel des établissemens qui leur sont consacrés* (Paris: Mauprivez, 1836), 37.

45 Pierre Berthier, *Excursions scientifiques dans les asiles d'aliénés* (Paris: Bourg-en-Bressr, 1862).

46 See, for example, a job advertisement for two pharmacists, published by the public asylums of the Seine Department in 1904. 'Chronique', *L'Union pharmaceutique: journal de la Pharmacie centrale de France: organe des intérêts scientifiques, pratiques et moraux de la profession* (1904), 592.

47 At the museum of Sainte-Anne (Paris), several devices have been preserved showing how such local production took place.

48 'Editorial', *The Alienist and Neurologist*, 5 (1884), 547–560, 554.

49 E. M. Tansey and D. A. Christie, "Drugs in Psychiatric Practice" in *Wellcome Witnesses in Twentieth-Century Medicine*, ed. E. M. Tansey and D. A. Christie (London: Wellcome Trust Centre for the History of Medicine at UCL, 1997), 131–205, 157.

50 S. Pinel, *Traité complet du régime sanitaire des aliénés, ou Manuel des établissemens qui leur sont consacrés., op. cit.*, p. 37.

51 Emile Meurice, *Psychiatrie et vie sociale* (Brussels: Editions Mardaga, 1977).

52 N. Henckes, "Magic Bullet in the Head? Psychiatric Revolutions and their Aftermath" in *The End of the Therapeutic Revolution?*, ed. J. Greene, F. Condrau, and E. S. Watkins (Chicago: University of Chicago Press, 2016), 65–96.

53 Alan A. Baumeister and Jennifer L. Francis, 'Historical Development of the Dopamine Hypothesis of Schizophrenia', *Journal of the History of Neurosciences*, 11 (2002): 265–277.

54 Andrea Tone, *The Age of Anxiety: A History of America's Turbulent Affair with Tranquilizers* (New York: Basic Books, 2009), IX.

55 Jeremy Greene and Aaron S. Kesselheim, 'Why Do the Same Drugs Look Different. Pills, Trade Dress and Public Health,' *The New England Journal of Medicine*, 365 (2011): 83–89.

56 Benoît Majerus, 'Making Sense of the "Chemical Revolution". Patients' Voices on the Introduction of Neuroleptics in the 1950s,' *Medical History*, 60 (2016): 54–66.

57 Tone, *The Age of Anxiety, op. cit.*, p. 95.

58 Andrea Tone, 'Tranquilizers on Trial: Psychopharmacology in the Age of Anxiety' in *Medicating Modern America: Prescription Drugs in History*, ed. Andrea Tone and Elizabeth Siegel Watkins (New York: New York University Press, 2007), 156–182, 164.

59 Catharine Coleborne, '"Madness": Material Culture and the Asylum', *Health and History*, 3 (2001): 104–117, 99.

60 Greg Eghigian, 'Deinstitutionalizing the History of Contemporary Psychiatry', *History of Psychiatry*, 22 (2011): 201–214.

15

FROM THE PERSPECTIVES
OF MAD PEOPLE

Geoffrey Reaume

The varied and diverse perspectives of mad people have existed since ancient times when the first concepts around mental difference began to be described, such as in regard to Nebuchadnezzar in the Book of Daniel in the Jewish Bible and the Christian Old Testament.[1] Though sources which uncover this history are difficult to locate the further back in time we go, the writing of mad people's history has emerged as a more widely accepted topic during the past thirty years. This chapter will examine key secondary literature and international trends on the historiography of mad people's perspectives and experiences. The writing of this history has evolved since the 1980s from interpreting previously published sources in anthologies to integrating unpublished first-person accounts in institutional histories, biographies, and accounts of advocacy efforts. In so doing, there has developed an effort to include a wider variety of mad people's perspectives, beyond the original group of privileged writers who left publicly available accounts in order to provide a more representative historical record of people who did not have the resources or education to publish anything in their own lifetimes. This effort for broader historiographical inclusivity is the most consistent theme here – from inclusion of mad voices in the first place, to inclusion of more diverse perspectives of people based on their gender, race, class, and ability.

It is worth noting at the outset of this chapter that even among the most influential writers on the history of madness, the perspectives of the mad were not given prominence. In Michel Foucault's immensely influential study on the history of madness, there is no serious attention devoted to mad people's experiences. His chapters on "Experiences of Madness" and "The Insane," focuses on secondary accounts of madness recounted by people who were not mad, and his final chapter "The Anthropological Circle," while containing references to famous mad people such as Vincent Van Gogh and Atonin Artaud, does so briefly and at the end of a massive study that does not integrate mad people's views elsewhere.[2] Thus, Foucault, like so many other scholars, did not include the voices of mad people. As will become evident, more researchers have been arguing for "another history for another psychiatry," in the words of Rafael Huertas, one which includes "the patient's view."[3] The broadening of these perspectives and experiences have enriched the history of madness in ways that have changed the field for the better, both in regard to representation and understanding of what this history is about for those who lived it.

Mad people's historical anthologies and republished writings

Mad people's histories began being analyzed long before there was such a thing as a discipline which focused on this, or any other, aspect of psychiatric history. Indeed, one of the earliest published "collections," of sorts, consisting of "Illustrations of Insanity Furnished by the Letters and Writings of the Insane" was published in 1848 in the *American Journal of Insanity* by editor and Utica Asylum superintendent, Amariah Brigham.[4] In this instance, the publication was not intended to validate the writings of mad people. It was instead meant to show how these writings were of clinical interest in proving their authors' pathological state and thus served as a justification for the work alienists like Brigham were doing at places like Utica. Printing such letters – presumably stolen from patients and printed without their consent – was as far removed from respecting the voices of mad people as one could get. Yet, it deserves to be included in this chapter by the very dint of whose perspectives are included in these writings and why, to remind ourselves that the publication of writings of the mad is not new in itself, though the justification for doing so has changed significantly over time.

By the mid-nineteenth century, mad people had already self-published accounts of their experiences in Europe and North America. While this paper will not be providing a discussion of the worthy topic of memoir writing by mad people, this important source of first-person accounts by individuals who were deemed mad, insane, mentally ill, and a host of related labels, provides an essential resource for uncovering history from mad people's perspectives. Writing styles ranged from religious confessionals expressing self-hatred for having fallen away from divine devotion, only to return and find redemption, dating from the earliest (in this case transcribed) memoir by Margery Kempe in 1436 to protest literature demanding justice for wrongful confinement exemplified by Alexander Cruden in 1739, a form of writing that was particularly notable by upper-class male writers of the eighteenth and ninteenth centuries, such as can also be seen in the writings of John Perceval from 1838 and 1840 and Isaac Hunt published in 1851.[5] There are also writing styles that crisscross from protest to advocacy, such as that by Elizabeth Packard, whose writings in the 1860s were intended to change policies around admission and treatment for women in particular.[6] Mad diary or journal writing is also a sub-genre of the preceding category, as is evident in the 1885 publication by Mary Heustis Pengilly, though diaries could also be published with no clear intention by the author to advocate for societal changes towards mad people, as is evident in Vaslav Nijinsky's 1918–19 diary entries, published long after he had written them, first issued in 1936 and reissued in a more complete, "unexpurgated" form in 1999.[7] Protest and advocacy memoirs continued throughout the latter part of the twentieth century, some of which were particularly influential as can be seen in the 1978 part-memoir, part-mad activist advocacy book by Judi Chamberlin which remains one of the best-known memoirs of its kind.[8] The past thirty years has also witnessed the increase of memoirs that accept the medical model of mental illness with a theme of "overcoming" madness, as for example in Carol North's 1987 account; this genre is also reflected in some celebrity memoirs, as with the accounts by Brooke Shields in 2006 and Margaret Trudeau in 2010.[9] Also, the impact of immigration and racism on an individual's mental state is reflected in recent memoirs, such as Fu Su's.[10] Creative works of fiction based on authors' lived experiences are another mad-memoir writing style, whether in the form of a short story, such as by Charlotte Perkins Gilman in 1892 and Margaret Gibson in 1976, or in a novel such as by Mary Jane Ward in 1946, or in collections of poetry, such as those composed by Antonin Artaud between 1924–48 and by novelist and poet Sylvia Plath.[11] This is but a miniscule sample of the immense bibliography of published mad memoirs that have contributed enormously to our historical understandings of perspectives from mad people.

Of course, it is one thing to compile a list of first-person accounts, and another to analyze them in a way that places these sources in a cohesive historical context. There exist a number of edited anthologies published over a fifty-year period including *The Inner World of Mental Illness* published in 1964, followed a decade later by *Voices From the Asylum*, as well as *Shrink Resistant* in 1988, *Cry of Invisible* in 1991 and *First Person Accounts of Mental Illness and Recovery* in 2012.[12] As these publications indicate, what was a radical approach in the latter part of the twentieth century became mainstream by the early twenty-first century.

While this publishing trajectory would be interesting to follow, it is the historical use of such sources that is the focus of this article. The above sources do not generally provide a historical context within which the sources are described, partly due to the lack of historical background of the editors and the contemporary nature of these publications (though the Kaplan and Glenn edited collections, published in 1964 and 1974 respectively, have short sections on historical first-person accounts, with very brief contextual editorial remarks). The first serious efforts to provide historical context to an edited collection of sources in mad people's history were published in the 1980s, first by Dale Peterson in 1982 and then by Roy Porter, who published two books on this topic in 1987.[13] Peterson's work is the first academically published book to take seriously the historical writings by mad people and is significant for this fact above all else. Beginning with *The Book of Margery Kempe* (written by scribes in 1436 since she was illiterate) and ending more than 500 years later with an excerpt from Kenneth Donaldson's 1976 memoir, *Insanity Inside Out*, Peterson provides a brief introduction to each of twenty-six authors, all but five of which are from the nineteenth and twentieth centuries. A professor of literature, Peterson's work was inspired by some of the patients he met while working as an attendant on a large psychiatric ward over a decade before. After asking questions about what is meant by madness, Peterson writes: "Experts and authorities have addressed these questions for centuries, with confused results. It is time to hear from those, who by experience, are more closely connected to the issues – mad people, mental patients, themselves. Perhaps they are less confused."[14] It is this attempt to understand mad people's writing on their own terms that marks Peterson's work as particularly significant given the paucity of such historically-oriented approaches during this period.

His book, with its editorial introduction at the beginning of each chapter followed by the writing of a person deemed mad, while well known, only gradually had an impact on the field since there was no significant rush by historians to revise the record and start searching for first-person accounts of mad people to include in histories related to this topic. Not all of the authors included by Peterson considered themselves mad, either at the time of confinement or later, though all were judged and treated as such by some of their contemporaries which therefore justified their inclusion in such a collection. This raises the methodological issue of how a historian determines whether or not someone belongs in a study of mad people's history. For example, British biblical scholar Alexander Cruden (1701–70), who is included in Peterson's anthology, and Leonard Roy Frank (1932–2015), a well known anti-psychiatry activist in the United States, both rejected the external definitions of madness that others placed on them, Cruden denying that he should have been sent to a madhouse and Frank denouncing schizophrenia as fraudulent and electroshock treatment as harmful.[15] The key methodological factor should be, in the case in which someone was locked up or treated as a mad person, whether or not the individual in question saw themselves as mad, then this person deserves to be included as part of mad people's history based on their experiences as being considered as such by their contemporaries.

The line does need to be carefully drawn, however, as retrospective diagnosis of someone as mad who was never treated as such and, so far as is known, did not consider themselves to be mad, underscores the point that such persons should not be included as mad. Otherwise, it becomes a catch-all label for anyone whom later generations decide to make an "honorary" mad person regardless of whether they actually were deemed as such in their own life by themselves or others. In Peterson's anthology, it is clear that each person included was deemed mad at some point in his or her life, whether or not the author agreed with this definition, and as such their perspectives have much to contribute, given their own lived experiences as being placed in this category of mental otherness. Peterson's work is less a narrative and more an episodic snapshot of particular mad people's experiences and the social and medical context of the period under consideration. Given the immense timeframe which this work covers and the lack of primary source material available for earlier periods, it is not surprising that the majority of writings are from the 1800s and 1900s. But this also means that the writings from previous centuries appear less connected to later writings, other than by dint of their varied experiences of madness. What Peterson's work lacks in narrative cohesiveness it gains in highlighting the importance of the authors' words as being an integral part of a history that had previously ignored, indeed, derided their thoughts. In his own work five years later, Roy Porter wrote that Peterson's book "constitutes the first proper scholarly account and anthology of mad people's writings over a long historical span. Peterson was the first to show that a history of the consciousness of the mad was feasible. I hope that this book proves a worthy complement to his."[16]

Porter's contributions to taking the "Stories of the Insane" seriously has been particularly significant and, indeed, complementary to that which his predecessor edited. In his two books published in 1987, *A Social History of Madness* (with the subtitle indicated in the previous sentence) and *Mind Forg'd Manacles*, Porter picked up where Peterson left off by writing a seamless narrative about and by mad people.[17] This is particularly so in *A Social History of Madness*, which focuses on the writings of mad people throughout while grounding his interpretation in the social and medical milieu of the periods under consideration. Porter noted how there was no one "single chronological line" to these histories since every "narrative is unique." At the same time he wrote that the most marked theme is that "down the centuries is a growing rapport, even convergence, between the consciousness of the mad as expressed in their own writings and the lore and language of psychiatry," notably beginning in the nineteenth century and crystallizing in the twentieth century.[18] This is in large part because Porter, like Peterson, focused on the writings of published authors, who thus sought to obtain some validation from their writings as serious-minded individuals rather than as people who made no sense. In making their experiences public, some of these published authors sought approval from psychiatrists, as Porter notes, and hence approval from the wider public who read their work. This, in itself, is very different from unpublished writers used by later historians, as will be seen. In a series of thematically arranged chapters, Porter considered the writings of mad people in relation to power, genius, religion, sex, and gender. A criticism that can be made is that some of these categories are not so categorical; for example, Margery Kempe is placed in the chapter on "Mad Women," though she could just as easily be included in the preceding chapter on "Religious Madness." Nevertheless, Porter's work here and elsewhere, including *Mind Forg'd Manacles* which has one chapter on mad voices as well as *Madness: A Brief History* published in the year of his death, brought to the fore, as did no historian before him, the need to take seriously the views of mad people when writing this history.[19] In doing so he demonstrated the richness of their perspectives and the immense historiographical gap of trying to understand this history without them.[20]

The path-breaking works by Peterson and Porter in the 1980s helped to develop a trend in which writings by mad people were published or republished in edited collections during the 1990s. This includes the collection, *Women of the Asylum: Voices from Behind the Walls, 1840–1945*, edited by two mental health professionals, psychiatrist Jeffrey Geller and psychologist Maxine Harris. In style and substance, this book indicates an affinity with Peterson's work in that a brief introduction is offered to each of the four chronological time periods in which six to eight women's "firsthand accounts" are excerpted, though Peterson introduced each author individually rather than collectively. Echoing the sentiments of both Peterson and Porter, Geller and Harris wrote: "To fully know what it was like to be a woman and a mental patient in the century between 1840 and 1945, we must listen to the women themselves."[21]

Allan Ingram's edited collection, *Voices of Madness,* also followed in the footsteps of Peterson and Porter by reprinting accounts of mad people who had been long forgotten, in this case one woman and three men who were published in the seventeenth and eighteenth centuries. In his introduction, Ingram, a professor of English, focuses on text and the way in which mad authors used words to validate themselves and their experiences with the "resistless urge for self-expression."[22]

Undoubtedly influenced by the increasing interest in first-hand historical accounts of mad people, there were several more publications during the 1990s and early 2000s in which the writings of individual mad people were published with editorial interpretations, similar to the above-mentioned studies. *The Letters of a Victorian Madwoman,* edited by John Hughes, is in some ways the most unique of these late twentieth century publications given that these letters were unpublished primary sources composed over thirty years beginning in 1890 by Andrew M. Sheffield, a woman given a man's name by her father who confined her in an asylum in Alabama where she remained until her death thirty years later.[23] An historian, Hughes provides an overall editorial introduction to Sheffield's life and letters as well as a short introduction to each chapter that contains letters in chronological order. Unlike all of the other authors whose words were republished in these various collections of mad people's writings,

Sheffield, so far as is known, had no intention of making a case for herself with the wider public as did authors William Belcher, Elizabeth Stone and others whose previously published works can be found in anthologies issued during the 1980s and 1990s.[24] Sheffield thus was published for the first time a century after her confinement, an unintended result of her private efforts to be heard, not by wider society, but by those people in her immediate vicinity from whom she most wanted a response. Her writings carry a resonance with many previously published mad writers in other collections in that, particularly during the early years of letter writing, she protests her confinement in an insane asylum instead of prison for trying to burn down the house of a nearby resident who was fighting with her lover. Given that she was trying to influence other family members and local politicians with her private writings, it is nevertheless clear that both published and unpublished mad authors had certain things in common – grievance at the reasons for their confinement and the way in which they were treated by asylum staff. This is a point which brings together all of these mad anthologies published during the late twentieth century.

It also connects more recent mad authors' works from recent decades with those of writers in eighteenth and nineteenth centuries, who wrote what amounted to protest literature about the unjust and arbitrary nature of their confinement and the brutal way in which they and their peers were treated whilst confined. Mad writers wanted to be heard on their own terms, and the above-cited editors and authors respected their words in this regard. By the end of the twentieth century the trend of older published works being revisited and republished is also reflected with the reissue sixty years after the original publication of Marle Woodson's 1932 book *Behind the Door of Delusion*, edited and introduced by William Savage and James Lazalier; it chronicles Woodson's time inside an Oklahoma insane asylum during the Great Depression.[25] Curiously, the publication of mad people's historical writings did not carry over into the early twenty-first century to a significant extent. Katharine Hodgkin's book, *Women, Madness and Sin in Early Modern England*, a detailed study of manuscripts written by Dionys Fitzherbert, who lived from approximately 1580 to 1640, is an exception in this regard.[26] This decline in further publications may be due to the lack of publicly available primary sources written by mad people, especially prior to the 1800s, with the limit on such material perhaps being reached with the above-noted sources (though there may be further previously forgotten published mad writings from this early period waiting to be rediscovered). Other avenues, however, for locating mad people's perspectives were being pursued by researchers. As will be discussed in the following section, mad voices were starting to be included in a more integrated way in historical studies during the same period when anthologies were being produced.

Mad people's perspectives in institutional histories

A significant trend growing out of this interest in the perspectives of mad people was an effort to include at least some of their views in historical studies on mental institutions. In her 1984 book, *A Generous Confidence*, on the Pennsylvania Hospital for the Insane and its superintendent T. S. Kirkbride, Nancy Tomes included a chapter on the patient population with sub-themes in the chapter devoted to patients' experiences and profiles. In doing so, Tomes used themes that sought to categorize patients as "compliant" and "non-compliant" ranging from individuals who expressed admiration for the superintendent to others who criticized the abusive and coercive nature of their confinement.[27] In recounting the perspectives of mad people in nineteenth-century asylums, Tomes argues that a "balance must be struck between the spheres of compliance and rebellion among the patients and the ideal and reality of asylum life."[28] This approach includes both supportive and critical perspectives about the operators of the institution from the perspectives of mad people confined therein. It is an approach that is also adopted in Ellen Dwyer's book, *Homes for the Mad*, where perspectives of patients confined in institutions in Utica and Willard, New York during the nineteenth century are included in a study that provides an overview of asylums from both the staff and inmates' points of view.[29] Like Tomes, in Dwyer's work patients' perspectives tend to be less obvious than staff's views, though unlike Tomes, Dwyer integrates mad people's perspectives throughout her book rather than concentrating them in one chapter. Taken together, these two books were significant in that, during the same decade that Peterson and Porter issued their path-breaking books giving serious attention to the published memoirs of mad people in history, Tomes and Dwyer published works which gave serious attention to mad people's experiences within the historical context of specific institutions.

Other historians who incorporated patients' perspectives in their books on institutional histories during this period, include Diana Gittins in her study of Severalls Hospital in England, my book on patient life at the Toronto, Canada asylum, and James Mills' study of "native-only" asylums in nineteenth-century British India.[30] While the extent of mad perspectives varies in each of these books, by the beginning of the twenty-first century there was a serious effort among more historians to include first-person accounts of madness in book-length institutional histories. An important part of the challenge in uncovering this history is what Mills refers to as "fragments" of voices in records about mad people authored by medical officials.[31] This difficulty in locating primary sources that include the perspectives of mad people has remained one of the primary challenges facing historians in this regard and undoubtedly has limited the ability of researchers to tell history from the perspectives of the mad. Oral history interviews, which Gittins includes in her study, is one way of trying to provide such perspectives, at least for more recent periods for which it is possible to have recorded interviews with former patients. For earlier periods in all histories prior to the second half of the twentieth century, oral history is obviously not an option when people from earlier times are long since dead. Given the class issues involved, where only well-to-do mad people had the resources, time and literacy to leave first-person accounts up to the latter part of the nineteenth century when more people could read and write, most of the historical perspectives prior to 1900 are from upper- and middle-class patients, and not from the vast majority of mad people who were confined in public institutions – poor people.

In a crucial historiographical development, the period since the early 2000s has seen historical publications that have included mad people's perspectives from a more diverse demographic than was published in preceding decades. Peter Barham's 2004 study, *Forgotten Lunatics of the Great War,* is perhaps one of the most effective of the twenty-first century books produced thus far which integrates first-person perspectives of madness within institutional settings. His book recounts the perspectives and experiences of British servicemen who experienced "shell shock" during the First World War and ended up being confined in mental hospitals, and in some cases, were later discharged into the community where they became activists advocating for fellow mad veterans.[32] Using a large cache of unpublished primary sources, Barham succeeds in bringing to life the experiences of generally unknown mad servicemen. His study is significant for helping to advance from a few individual case studies to a wider representation of mad people's experiences inside and outside asylums.

In contrast, Benjamin Reiss, in his study of cultural expressions found within mid-nineteenth-century American asylums, primarily used an administration-sanctioned publication, *The Opal*, edited by patients at Utica Asylum, New York to obtain the views of a small sample of elite, white patients. While his book, like most studies considered here, makes no claim to representativeness, it is in some ways even less so than other institutional histories which have included mad people's voices, given the high status of the patients who had access to publishing in this journal and the lack of serious criticism of the asylum that was not allowed by *The Opal's* official medical sponsors.[33]

Catherine Coleborne addresses the issue of representation, in her 2010 study on European family experiences of madness in colonial Australian and New Zealand institutions. In this study, she includes patient letters that reveal the interaction between officials, relatives, and mad people. In doing so she also queries how difficult it is to find representative accounts of ordinary families – and by extension mad people – given the unpredictability of what is, and is not, recorded and preserved in the archives: "past institutional and archival practices can also obscure these histories."[34] Indeed, the absence of first-person accounts not only from poor white people, but from racially marginalized and culturally oppressed people throughout this history, especially prior to the twentieth century, shows how little historians will ever know about the perspectives of large segments of populations who were institutionalized.

This point is further evidenced in Waltraud Ernst's work on asylums in British India, particularly her work on Ranchi Indian Mental Hospital where the perspectives of mad people are not included in what is an otherwise path-breaking book on the treatment of the local Indian population during the 1920s and 1930s.[35] Silence in histories around patients' perspectives is not always due to neglect of this experience by a researcher, but rather due to the absence of primary sources which could uncover mad voices. Given the already marginalized status of mad people in society, issues around race, class, and gender add further dimensions to this silence where people furthest from positions of power due to their social location had far fewer opportunities to have their views recorded to begin with, even before ending up in an insane asylum. Institutional studies have had a significant focus on the gendered and class experience of asylum confinement, which included attention devoted to the unpaid labour of asylum inmates, such as in the books by Dwyer and Ernst, cited above.

Race was also discussed by Ernst in the context of the confinement of British mad people in India during the first half of the nineteenth century.[36] Generally, however, the experiences and perspectives of mad people in regard to race were not as seriously studied by most scholars in the field as were class and gender until the early twenty-first century. Important articles which have brought to light mad perspectives of racially marginalized people who were institutionalized during the late nineteenth and early twentieth centuries include studies on experiences of indigenous people confined in the Canadian province of British Columbia by Robert Menzies and Ted Palys; Pemina Yellow Bird's study of "Wild Indians" confined in the Hiawatha Asylum for Insane Indians in Canton, South Dakota, a topic about which Susan Burch published an article a decade afterwards focusing specifically on the life and death after thirteen years' confinement of Elizabeth Alexis Fairbault along with the impact of dislocation on individuals, families and the historical record; and Lorelle Barry and Catharine Coleborne's article on the experiences of Maoris in the Auckland, New Zealand Mental Hospital.[37] Thus, the early twenty-first century has seen an increasing trend internationally to examine issues of madness based on the experiences and perspectives of indigenous people under colonial domination, long among the most neglected group in the history of psychiatry more generally. As will be seen in the next section, broadening this range of experience has much to do with focusing on individual mad people's biographies as it does on institutions in which mad people were confined.

At this point, it is important to note the use of primary sources created by operators of institutions where mad people were confined to try to read against the grain of a clinical chart or a doctor's letter to understand the experiences of mad people who were described therein. However difficult it is to determine the first-person perspectives of someone written by a third party, a critically engaged researcher who looks for references to a mad person's views when such views are directly quoted or inferred by staff members who interact with them, can glean otherwise lost perspectives that the subject themselves did not record. This is a difficult process that poses challenges for the historian. For example, should the records of a physician who records flattering references to themselves by a mad person be trusted as much as when criticisms of staff by mad people are also recorded? Given the less likely conflict in self-interest in the latter instance – unless the criticism is recorded to "confirm" a mad person's supposed unreliability – a researcher could be inclined to rely more on the critical reference than the flattering reference, but this too is a methodological problem given that it supposes such flattering references are less likely than criticisms by mad people of their treatment. There is also the possibility that the clinical records are less accurate about an individual's views than is supposed. Yet, for all of these hesitations, there can be no doubt that, short of first-person accounts written directly by an individual, third-party accounts in medical administrative records include mad people's perspectives that are recorded nowhere else. How to use such sources is as much a challenge for a writer of collective community histories in an institution as it is for a biographer of one person.

Mad people's historical biographies

Biographies provide perhaps the most tangible and detailed examples of historians' efforts to include the perspectives of individual mad people, with varying degrees of success. This trend, when examined over several decades, perhaps has had the least historiographical impact of all the approaches indicated here. This may be due to the exclusive focus on particular individuals who, in most cases, were unrepresentative of the mass of unknown mad (given that a book-length biography is usually only possible when a large collection of primary sources exists to document the views of a few upper- and middle-class mad people). It may also have to do with the low opinion academic historians have often had for biographies due to their focus on one person.

A good example of this is Norman Dain's biography of American Clifford Beers, founder of the National Committee for Mental Hygiene. Beers' bestselling 1908 memoir and his status as an "advocate for the insane," in Dain's words, made him into one of the most well-known figures in the mental health field in the early-1900s United States.[38] Beers, reflecting his high social status and access to resources, left a wealth of material enabling his first person perspectives to be easily accessible to researchers, in contrast to most mad people from this time period. Dain uses this material to produce a sympathetic portrait of a man whose views reflected his privileged socio-economic position. This and other biographies recounted here raise issues around how close the author is to his subject to the point of writing romanticized, even hagiographical, accounts of individuals. The opposite could also happen with an entirely negative portrayal, however in mad people's history the tendency has been towards the former rather than the latter.

A decade after Dain's book on Beers came out, Barbara Sapinsley published a book about a far different activist, Elizabeth Packard. Though not as wealthy as Beers, Packard was a renowned advocate in her day for the rights of asylum inmates, particularly female patients, after being released in 1863 following three years of confinement in Illinois. Reflecting her middle-class background and access to resources, Packard too left a good deal of primary source material, including published accounts of her confinement. Sapinsley, a journalist rather than an academic – unlike the vast majority of authors cited here – had the additional challenge of being outside the academic world with less access to getting published on a topic that was viewed as marginal; this may be why it took over twenty years for this biography to be published from the time research began.[39] Sapinsley's work succeeded in recording the life of a major figure in nineteenth-century American mad people's history who had been largely forgotten by the time her book appeared, and she did so using Packard's own words located in various private and public holdings. As such, her work constituted a major development in breaking through the historiographical haze behind which Packard's important advocacy work had been hidden for so long.

In contrast to Sapinsley's portrait of Packard who is largely taken at her own word, Linda Carlisle's biography of Packard takes a more critical approach. From the outset, Carlisle takes a more sympathetic view toward the nineteenth-century doctors whom Packard critiqued. Moreover, just as these doctors argued, Packard cannot be trusted to tell her own history. While claiming that Packard was "at times vengeful," Carlisle goes easier on those whom Packard said persecuted her:

> Certainly, the pioneers of American psychiatry were not the autocratic villains that Packard portrayed them as. They were, almost to a man, deeply concerned for the welfare of the insane and devoted to the profession they believed offered the most hope for those afflicted with mental illness.[40]

While Carlisle is anxious to reassure her readers that she does not share her historical subject's strong dislike of psychiatrists, she also makes sure readers know that dialogue Packard paraphrased and re-wrote in her writings "of course, cannot be accepted as accurate or truthful."[41] Such criticisms, however, are not expressed about the accuracy or truthfulness of the writings of her protagonists. Thus Packard's most trenchant critiques of the oppressive power dynamics involved in the patient-doctor relationship, particularly as it concerned women, are toned down in Carlisle's book. The result is that this second biography of Packard is mad people's history from a medical model perspective, devoid of any serious critical analysis of the institution of psychiatry and the way it mistreated people, issues which Packard engaged in while she was alive. It seeks to diminish her critiques throughout, even whilst offering praise for her efforts. In contrast, Sapinsley's 1991 biography on Packard – the first serious study of this pioneering activist – which is respectfully credited in Carlisle's book, while less scholarly than the latter study is nevertheless more respectful of Packard's words and lived experiences. The difference in approaches to Packard's words – and by extension, the words of those whom she criticized – in both biographies raises issues around trust in a subject's first-hand account. If biographies are tricky topics for a historian to tackle, given the specter of hagiography lingering over sympathetic portrayals, discounting the views of a subject on the other hand becomes embroiled in further historiographical snares when considering how mad people's views have historically been discounted, as described herein. If there is such a thing as balance in writing a biography, it would need to include avoiding universal statements about the truthfulness, or lack thereof, of any particular individual or group of people when interpretations, past and present, are open to such wide interpretations, particularly in regard to such a contentious topic as the views of a person deemed mad and those who confined them.

Packard, it needs to be emphasized, never considered herself mad, but rather as unjustly confined; however, she also supported other mad persons for whom she had an affinity based on her own experiences. Both Sapinsley and Carlisle, discuss this aspect of Packard's biography while being careful not to make her appear more respectable by *not* being mad. The same cannot be said for Julia Keay's work on Alexander Cruden, the eighteenth-century biblical scholar whose confinements in British madhouses led him to write scathing denunciations of his ill-treatment (which Peterson, Porter and Ingram, cited above, include in their works) and to proclaim that he was sane. This perspective is, of course, essential to interpret, but in doing so Keay, unlike the other authors noted in this chapter, seeks to present him as more respectable as a sane person than as a mad person. The biographer does this in a way that suggests Cruden needs to be cleared of the madness charge: ". . . he had never done anything that could possibly be construed as mad. Yet the label, once applied, was indelible. To those who knew him only by later repute, Alexander Cruden *was* mad" (author's emphasis).[42] In making this argument, the question arises: would readers today be more inclined to take Cruden's writings seriously if he was not thought to be mad? If so, what does this say about how far society has advanced in our respect for mad people's perspectives, past and present?

A similar, though not quite so categorical, approach is taken by Bethany Aram in her study, *Juana the Mad,* Queen of Castille during the first half of the sixteenth century, most of which she spent confined in a nunnery. The abuse of patriarchal authority in confining Juana is obvious from the complicity of her family, including her father and husband. Yet, Aram also writes that she is not certain "whether or not Juana was *really* mad."[43] This is partly due to absence of reliable sources on her mental state and partly due to the malleable nature of what madness meant at the time Juana was alive and how we view madness and gender five hundred years later. In this sense, Aram's study is more nuanced than Keay's work in that she does not rule out Juana as being mad, but also is not sure, a careful conclusion that respects the Queen of Castille as deserving of historical respect regardless of her label, even without knowing much about her own perspectives on this topic.

Biographies of immensely prominent figures can offer reams of evidence to researchers, particularly when it concerns a husband and wife who were at the apex of society during the most convulsive period in American history and whose mental state has been a subject of long-term interest. Joshua Wolf Shenk's book on *Lincoln's Melancholy* and Jason Emerson's analysis of *The Madness of Mary Lincoln* brings forward how scholars interpret the mental health of one of the most revered figures in a country's history, along with that of his wife.[44] Using Abraham Lincoln's own words and the memories of those who knew and quoted him, Shenk provides a detailed examination of how America's sixteenth president was affected by depression from his twenties, how he applied his own forms of therapy – such as reading favourite poets – and how his mental health struggles provided him with a degree of resilience and insight that was essential to his historic accomplishments. In doing so, Lincoln's perspectives provide food for thought about how one of the most famous figures of nineteenth-century American history survived depression over a protracted period of time: "'A good story', he said, 'has the same effect on me that I think a good square drink of whisky has to an old roper. It puts new life into me . . . good for both the mental and physical digestion.' And he often said, 'If it were not for these stories – jokes – jests I should die; they give vent – and the vents of my moods and gloom.'"[45] Of course, the question of whether Lincoln's well-known bouts of depression qualify him as mad – certainly he was never confined in a mental institution – also raise questions about what is meant by this term. If, however, it is accepted that prolonged despair, which Lincoln did have, places a person in the category of experiencing madness at times, even if the individual was not confined, then Lincoln belongs here.

In regard to his wife, Mary Todd Lincoln, she was certified as insane in 1875 and confined against her will for several months in an Illinois rest home for women at the instigation of her son, Robert. In his book, *The Madness of Mary Lincoln*, James Emerson uses previously lost letters by Mary Lincoln written while she was confined to argue that she experienced bipolar psychiatric disorder. Emerson's references to "Mary's lost insanity letters," which he was able to use and are republished in the book's appendix, are cited along with other existing evidence to argue that she indeed had experienced madness.[46] Her writings make it clear that, like her contemporary Elizabeth Packard, Mary Lincoln disagreed with her confinement, stating, "I cannot understand why I should have been brought out here."[47] Their inclusion in this book, while supporting the mad hypothesis that she herself refuted, nevertheless helps to restore her perspective. Like Carlisle on Packard, Emerson approaches his analysis of Mary Lincoln through a medical model perspective that privileges the views of twenty-first century psychiatric diagnoses over the first-person account of a nineteenth-century widow and embattled mother, thus raising issues of whose views are ultimately being respected.

In the case of Abraham and Mary Lincoln, researchers are fortunate in having access to records on figures of great public prominence who also left their own first-person views. For the vast majority of common mad people who did not have much, if any, access to writing material, let alone literacy skills prior to the twentieth century, it is rare for researchers to find such records, outside of previously noted published accounts by the well-to-do. So where does this leave a more representative account of mad people? While it is beneficial and an advance to the overall field to have biographies of mad people who were relatively privileged, it also serves to underline how much we do not know about common mad people who were of no interest to anyone, except, perhaps, to a few scattered people in their own lifetime. Even well into the twentieth century, with the spread of mass literacy and greater access to writing material, assembling biographies of mad people continues to be hampered by the absence of primary sources that can reveal first-person accounts.

A good example of this is the biography of Junius Wilson. In their book on Wilson, *Unspeakable*, Susan Burch and Hannah Joyner describe the racism and isolation of an African-American deaf man who was confined beginning in 1925 for seventy-six years, most of it on locked wards in a North Carolina mental institution.[48] The co-authors recount the circumstances of Wilson's confinement and the intersection of madness – though he was never certified as insane – with being a deaf black person in the segregated southern United States. Accused of a rape for which he was never convicted, castrated and locked away in an institution where, for most of his adult life, he was unable to communicate in his own language, Wilson's story raises a host of issues around race, class, deafness, madness, and what was perceived at times as what is now called intellectual disability by being labeled "feeble-minded." Yet, what is recorded about his experiences are gleaned from second-hand sources. While we learn much about his life, Junius Wilson's perspectives are absent.

The problem regarding the lack of voice in some biographies, including two very different people separated by hundreds of years and at complete opposite ends of the social scale in their respective societies – Queen Juana in 1500s Castile and Junius Wilson in 1900s United States – underlines how difficult the perspectives of mad people are to uncover across all historical time periods (though the further back historians reach, it is far more unlikely that such evidence will be available). This absence means that when material is found for a mad person who is more representative of the mass of ordinary people from lower class backgrounds it is likely to only be enough to present a brief biographical sketch, as is evident in some of the institutional histories cited earlier or in short essay articles. Examples of these latter secondary sources reveal an increasing international trend since the late twentieth century toward providing first-person accounts of madness through existing letters and artifacts, such as artwork, that mad people produced and often had confiscated in mental institutions around the world.

Art created by mad people has been amongst the most controversial topics in mad people's history, given the appropriating – indeed stealing – of this work by some academics who were not mad to build their own careers by interpreting the "artistry of the mentally ill," the English name given to the 1972 publication of Hans Prinzhorn's book originally published in Germany in 1922.[49] There have been subsequent book-length studies, such as by Sander M. Gilman on "seeing the insane," which includes both art by and about mad people, and John M. MacGregor's book on the "discovery" of mad people's visual art, which ostensibly is about taking such art seriously in refutation of the notion that such work has no merit beyond a psychopathic interpretation.[50] There are also book-length studies of individual artists who were confined in asylums. This includes Gail Hornstein's book on "Anges's Jacket," which seeks to understand the meaning behind the "mysterious biographical text" that Agnes Richter wove into her jacket while confined in a late nineteenth-century German asylum, while Nicholas Tromans explores the life and art of Richard Dadd, confined as criminally insane for killing his father in Victorian Britain.[51] Together these sources claim to be appreciating mad people's creativity in a way that few before them had done, aside from mad people themselves. Kay Redfield Jamison makes a similar claim to be providing a link between madness and "the artistic temperament" in her study of people labeled with manic-depression, which she herself identifies as having experienced.[52] A primary theme included in these studies is debate over the existence of a connection between madness and creativity and the related issue of romanticizing a person's mental anguish in producing art. What is left largely unaddressed is the extent to which visual art of mad people in asylums in particular was stolen from them and put on display without evidence that there was any reference back to the creator about what happened to their work. It was, in effect, recycled for observers to interpret and not mad people themselves. Unlike published sources where mad people had some control over what happened to their written work, the same cannot be said of the artwork created by mad people in asylums. The issue of provenance is one which researchers need to explore in greater depth when it comes to understanding this history, not only for what artistic creation says about mad people, but about how the uses of this same art has been used to impose interpretations that we cannot know to be the views of the creators themselves.

This, ironically, takes us back to the letters produced by Amariah Brigham, referred to at the start of this article. These more recent publications using this material, however, are more respectful, if only due to the passage of time and awareness of the injustice of objectifying people in the manner originally shown in Brigham's 1848 article. Again, as he did with manuscript-length studies on mad people's experiences, Roy Porter was one of the first to write articles based on such documents in the latter half of the 1980s and early 1990s, focusing in particular on historical writings of seventeenth- and eighteenth-century mad people in England.[53] Other examples since the late 1990s include primarily narrative accounts of asylum patients in Edinburgh, Scotland published by Alan Beveridge; Lykke de la Cour's work on women confined in the Cobourg, Ontario mental hospital; Matthew Gambino's article on black Americans at St. Elizabeths Hospital in Washington, DC; Gemma Blackshaw's essay on an early twentieth-century mad Viennese author, Peter Altenberg; Mab Segrest's article on "Mary Roberts," who was confined under the racially segregated hospital system in early twentieth-century Georgia; and a multi-authored article on Portuguese sculptor Herculano Sa de Figueiredo.[54] That there now exists an international trend to historically contextualize mad people's perspectives and experiences is well established, while at the same time the diversity of approaches reflect the varied orientations of the researchers involved – mainly historians, but also some mental health professionals. As the next section will show, some of the most important works are those that have been published about advocacy by mad people in works sometimes authored by mad activists themselves.

Mad people's activist histories

The history of mad activism has been expressed in a variety of forms, from individuals writing about and publicizing their usually negative experiences in madhouses and asylums to a wider public in the hope that there would be some kind of justice for themselves and others who were similarly treated. It also took on the form of efforts by groups of mad people who organized to advocate for changes in government policies, medical treatment, and societal attitudes that allowed the abuses they were criticizing to take place. Such efforts can be traced back to the eighteenth century with the works of individuals like Alexander Cruden in Britain and Elizabeth Packard in nineteenth-century United States, as has been previously noted. There have also been studies looking at organizational efforts of mad activists.

Nicholas Hervey published perhaps the most important article on this topic with his 1986 study on the Alleged Lunatics' Friend Society (ALFS) which operated in mid-nine-teenth-century Britain, the first known group of its kind organized by ex-inmates of mad houses.[55] In his study, Hervey recounts the significant contributions of the ALFS to advancing the rights of people confined in mad houses and asylums between 1845–63, while he also notes the internal problems encountered with infighting that led to the group's demise. As such, this article is the first essay published in an academic history journal that takes seriously the work and advocacy of mad people as worthy of serious consideration by later researchers. Ann Goldberg's article on middle class "'lunatics' rights" activists in late nineteenth- and early twentieth-century Germany takes a similar approach, though with more criticism of this group of male activists whose advocacy efforts were more mixed in impact and influence.[56] In both of these academic articles it becomes clear that the activists who were public as mad were privileged due to their gender and class, as well as their race and religion, reflecting the position of those who could engage in this sort of campaign at the time. As would be seen in publications about the history of later twentieth-century mad activists, the broadening of the circle of those who could take part in this form of public advocacy changed considerably in more recent times.

During the latter part of the twentieth century, mad activists themselves began to publish work about aspects of their own histories. This includes a 1986 book by Lenny Lapon that has a chapter on activist history in the United States.[57] Just over a decade later, Irit Shimrat published a book on the history of mad activists in Canada, based largely on interviews and her own experiences.[58] By the early 2000s, academically produced books appeared on the history and current status of the mad movement in Canada by Barbara Everett, and in the United States by Linda Morrison.[59] Three of these four books are by people who identify in some way as having experienced madness – Lapon, Shimrat, and Morrison. Academic articles on this topic also started to appear in recent years including Nick Crossley on British activism, as well as on the United States by Nancy Tomes and Heather Murray.[60] Increasingly during the late twentieth century, studies have reflected an activist consciousness, or at least an awareness of activism within the community of people these studies are about, unlike most of the aforementioned sources prior to 2000, which tend to be from a medical history perspective with no clearly mentioned influence from the activist community of mad people (except, of course, from the writings of activists themselves).

With the increasing publication of historical writing from a more activist orienta-tion, there is also the risk of writing celebratory accounts which are devoid of criticism of the internal dynamics of the community from which mad people come where all forms of prejudices have been, and are, part of this history. There is also the risk of simplifying this history as psychiatry versus anti-psychiatry, as does Murray, when recent activist history is far more complex than this either/or definition. As Duncan Scott Campbell has shown in his doctoral dissertation on the history of mad activism in the United States between 1970–99, there have always been a significant variety of perspectives among people involved in advocacy efforts, ranging from people who choose to work within the mental health system as current or former patients, to individuals who reject any involvement with psychiatric professionals, to still others who are somewhere in between, strongly critiquing the medical model, while also not choosing to identify with anti-psychiatry.[61] Furthermore, individuals can also change perspectives over time, so that a fluidity of views exists not only within the modern history of mad activism that go beyond any simple binary category, but often within specific individuals who have been engaged in this work. Given the generally recent interest in this topic, this area is one of the least developed fields of research within mad people's history overall, along with research about racially marginalized and colonized mad people, though this is likely to change as the above examples suggest.

Conclusion

Whatever the varied interpretations of researchers writing in this field, the fact that there has been increasingly more studies done from the perspectives of mad people over the past several decades is an enormously positive development. The broadening of historical perspectives by and about people who experienced madness has provided a fuller and more authentic understanding of meanings and experiences of mental disturbance as understood by people who lived this history beyond the views of observers. This history is fuller because such views significantly enhance and widen our understanding of what madness meant to people who lived it at different times – or what it did not mean, as the case may be for those who denied any such association. The horizons of the historical record are thus broadened by ensuring that the experiences and perspectives, where possible, of the people who are the primary reason for this history existing are taken into account as of essential importance for understanding the variety of experiences and expressions of those deemed mad, depending on the socio-economic status of those involved. This history is more authentic by including such perspectives to ensure that it is not only "about," but also "by," mad people. Such an approach therefore includes a wider array of historical participants – in this case, the people who are the central focus of attention – and thus avoids an exclusively top-down approach that would make accounts far too narrow and far less trustworthy due to neglect of the perspectives of those who have lived this history.

At the same time, to be mad and to write about it also means that the chronicler is observing other people around her or him, including other mad people, even if from a different perspective than a person who is not mad. Though it should be obvious that everyone experiences madness in their own unique way, it can be expected that an "insider's" account will have greater insights into this history than an outside observer. To understand a process, whether it is psychic, physical, or of some other form, people who undergo such an experience are best able to describe what is happening to their interior feelings than someone who is observing, but not undergoing this process. At the same time, interior processes of the mind are significantly influenced by the surrounding world, and to ignore external influences, as expressed and described by a mad person, is to risk ignoring what brought a person to be described as mad, either by themselves or others. It avoids the pitfall of reducing madness to an individual-biological-genetic entity. By trying to understand what a person deemed mad thinks of why they have been described as such, historical researchers fortunate enough to locate such evidence can hope to obtain a greater understanding about why a person has been so described from the individual who is the focus of this term within the context of the society in which they live.

One of the more recent publications that seeks to combine historical analysis within a personal account is by historian Barbara Taylor. She published a part-memoir and part-history of the Friern Hospital in England where Taylor was a patient in 1988–9, a few years before it closed. Her book considers the impact of moving mad people out of large-scale institutions and into the community by placing her personal experiences within this wider context. In so doing, she meditates on her place in possible future histories of *The Last Asylum*: "When the hospital closed in 1993, my patient records travelled to the London Metropolitan Archives along with the rest of the hospital's files . . . Perhaps one day some future chronicler of Friern will take my records down from the shelf and peruse them alongside those of my fellow Friernites, and so see for herself something of the story I am about to tell here, about the world in which I found myself in the twilight days of this famous old asylum."[62] Where mad people once struggled to get their voices heard, and still do in most of the world, historians who once ignored such perspectives are now part of the chronicle itself, through personal accounts of madness and exploring how individual experiences fit within this wider history. As historiographical developments recounted here indicate, the perspectives of mad people have made, and continue to make, an immense difference in interpretations of the history of madness.[63] The field can only advance by making such views central to the overall historical narrative. From anthologies to more detailed integrated, biographical and activist studies, writing on perspectives of mad people has advanced significantly from the 1980s, though it is also clear that more representation of the most marginalized needs to be a greater focus for researchers in the field. Ultimately, who is remembered in the history of madness is as important as whether or not primary sources exist to tell history from the perspectives of mad people

Notes

1 Book of Daniel, 4:25–34, *New American Bible* (New York: Catholic Book Publishing Company, 1992), 1028–9. See also Madalina Vartejanu-Joubert's chapter in this volume.
2 Michel Foucault, *Madness and Civilization: A History of Insanity in the Age of Reason* (New York: Vintage Books, 1965), 65–158; Foucault, *History of Madness* (London: Routledge, 2006), 108–59, 512–38.
3 Rafael Huertas, "Another History for Another Psychiatry: The Patient's View," *Culture & History Digital Journal*, 2 (June 2013): 1. Online at: http://cultureandhistory.revistas.csic.es/index.php/cultureandhistory/article/view/18/81, accessed December 6 2016.
4 Amariah Brigham, ed., "Illustrations of Insanity Furnished by the Letters and Writings of the Insane," *American Journal of Insanity*, 4 (1848): 290–303.
5 Excerpts from the writings of Kempe, Cruden and Perceval can be found in Dale Peterson, ed., *A Mad People's History of Madness* (Pittsburgh: University of Pittsburgh Press, 1982), 3–18, 39–56, 92–107 and summarized by Roy Porter, *A Social History of Madness: Stories of the Insane* (London: Weidenfeld and Nicolson, 1987), 105–12, 126–35, 169–88; the account by Isaac Hunt can be found online at the Disability History Museum web site: www.disabilitymuseum.org/dhm/lib/detail.html?id=736, accessed December 6 2016.
6 Excerpts from Packard's writings can be found in Peterson, *A Mad People's History of Madness*, 123–9, and more complete versions on the Disability History Museum web site at www.disabilitymuseum.org/dhm/lib/detail.html?id=1662 and www.disabilitymuseum.org/dhm/lib/detail.html?id=1663, both accessed December 6 2016.

7 Mary Huestis Pengilly, *Diary written in the Provincial Lunatic Asylum: The prison doors are open – I am free; Be this my messenger o'er land and sea* (Self published, St. John, New Brunswick, 1885). Download online at: www.canadiana.org/ECO/PageView/11978/0004?id=e5859fe9fe814777, accessed December 2016; Joan Acocella, ed., *The Diary of Vaslav Nijinsky: Unexpurgated Edition*, Kyril FitzLyon (translator) (New York: Farrar, Straus & Giroux, 1999). Excerpts from the earlier, 1936 edition, can be found in Peterson, *A Mad People's History of Madness*, 194–202 and summarized by Porter, *A Social History of Madness*, 71–6.
8 Judi Chamberlin, *On Our Own: Patient Controlled Alternatives to the Mental Health System* (New York: Hawthorn, 1978).
9 Carol North, *Welcome Silence: My Triumph Over Schizophrenia* (New York: Simon and Schuster, 1987); Brooke Shields, *Down Came the Rain: My Journey Through Postpartum Depression* (New York: Hyperion, 2006); Margaret Trudeau, *Changing my Mind* (Toronto: HarperCollins, 2010).
10 Fu Su, *I Once Was Lost: The Immigrant Experience and the Recovering Schizophrenic* (Toronto: Parkminister Publishing, 1997).
11 Charlotte Perkins Gilman, *The Yellow Wallpaper* (Old Westbury and New York: The Feminist Press, 1973 [first published in 1892]); Margaret Gibson, *The Butterfly Ward.* (Toronto: HarperCollins, 1976, 1994); Mary Jane Ward, *The Snake Pit* (New York: Random House, 1946); Antonin Artaud, *Artaud Anthology*, Jack Hirschman (translator) (San Francisco: City Light Books, 1965); Sylvia Plath, *The Bell Jar* (London: Faber, 1963) and *Ariel* (London: Faber, 1965).
12 Bert Kaplan, ed., *The Inner World of Mental Illness: A Series of First-Person Accounts of What It Was Like* (New York: Harper and Row, 1964); Michael Glenn, ed., *Voices from the Asylum* (New York: Harper Colophon Books, 1974); Bonnie Burstow and Don Weitz, eds., *Shrink Resistant: The Struggle Against Psychiatry in Canada* (Vancouver: New Star Books, 1988); Michael Susko, ed., *Cry of the Invisible: Writings from the Homeless and Survivors of Psychiatric Hospitals* (Baltimore: Conservatory Press, 1991); Craig Lecroy and Jane Holschuh, ed., *First Person Accounts of Mental Illness and Recovery* (New York: John Wiley and Sons, 2012).
13 Dale Peterson, ed., *A Mad People's History of Madness* (Pittsburgh: University of Pittsburgh Press, 1982); Roy Porter, *A Social History of Madness: Stories of the Insane* (London: Weidenfeld and Nicolson, 1987); Porter, *Mind-Forg'd Manacles: A History of Madness in England from the Restoration to the Regency* (London: Athlone, 1987).
14 Peterson, ed., *A Mad People's History of Madness*, xiv.
15 Alexander Cruden, "The London-Citizen Exceedingly Injured . . . , 1739" in *A Mad People's History of Madness*, ed. Peterson, 39–56; Leonard Roy Frank, *The History of Shock Treatment* (San Francisco: Frank, 1978).
16 Porter, *A Social History of Madness*, 7.
17 Porter, *A Social History of Madness*; Porter, *Mind-Forg'd Manacles*.
18 Porter, *A Social History of Madness*, 37.
19 Roy Porter, *Madness: A Brief History* (Oxford: Oxford University Press, 2002).
20 See *Medical History* 60 (2016) for six thematic articles on the influence of Roy Porter's work in the history of mad people's perspectives, particularly the lead article: Alexandra Bacopoulos-Viau and Aude Fauvel, "The Patient's Turn: Roy Porter and Psychiatry's Tales, Thirty Years On," *Medical History* 60 (2016), 1–18.
21 Jeffrey Geller and Maxine Harris, ed., *Women of the Asylum: Voices from Behind the Walls, 1840–1945* (New York: Anchor Books, 1994), xii.
22 Allan Ingram, ed., *Voices of Madness: Four Pamphlets, 1683–1796* (Gloucestershire: Sutton Publishing, 1997), xvii.
23 John S. Hughes, ed., *The Letters of a Victorian Madwomen* (Columbia, SC: University of South Carolina Press, 1993).
24 Belcher can be found in Ingram, *Voices of Madness* and Stone can be found in Geller and Harris, *Women of the Asylum.*
25 Marle Woodson, AKA "Inmate, Ward 8" in *Behind the Door of Delusion*, ed. William Savage and James Lazalier, (Niwot, CO: University Press of Colorado, 1994), originally published in 1932 by MacMillan Co.
26 Katharine Hodgkin, ed., *Women, Madness and Sin in Early Modern England: The Autobiographical Writings of Dionys Fitzherbert* (Surrey: Ashgate, 2010).

27 Nancy Tomes, *A Generous Confidence: Thomas Story Kirkbride and the Art of Asylum-Keeping, 1840–1883* (Cambridge: Cambridge University Press, 1984), 222–63.

28 Ibid., 263.

29 Ellen Dwyer, *Homes for the Mad: Life Inside Two Nineteenth-Century Asylums* (New Brunswick, NJ: Rutgers University Press, 1987).

30 Diana Gittins, *Madness in Its Place: Narratives of Severalls Hospital, 1913–1997* (London: Routledge, 1998); Geoffrey Reaume, *Remembrance of Patients Past: Patient Life at the Toronto Hospital for the Insane, 1870–1940* (Toronto: Oxford University Press Canada, 2000); James Mills, *Madness, Cannabis and Colonialism: The 'Native-Only' Lunatic Asylums of British India, 1857–1900* (London: Macmillan, 2000).

31 Mills, *Madness, Cannabis and Colonialism*, 166.

32 Peter Barham, *Forgotten Lunatics of the Great War* (New Haven: Yale University Press, 2004).

33 Benjamin Reiss, *Theaters of Madness: Insane Asylums and Nineteenth-Century American Culture* (Chicago: University of Chicago Press, 2008).

34 Catherine Coleborne *Madness in the Family: Insanity and Institutions in the Australasian Colonial World, 1860–1914* (London: Palgrave Macmillan, 2010), 151.

35 Waltraud Ernst, *Colonialism and Transnational Psychiatry: The Development of an Indian Mental Hospital in British India, c. 1925–1940* (London: Anthem Press, 2013).

36 Waltraud Ernst, *Mad Tales from the Raj: The European Insane in British India, 1800–1858* (London: Routledge, 1991).

37 Robert Menzies and Ted Palys, "Turbulent Spirits: Aboriginal Patients in the British Columbia Psychiatric System, 1879–1950" in *Mental Health and Canadian Society: Historical Perspectives*, ed. James Moran and David Wright, (Montreal and Kingston: McGill-Queen's University Press, 2006), 149–75; Pemina Yellow Bird, "Wild Indians: Native Perspectives on the Hiawatha Asylum for Insane Indians," Download at: dsmc.info/pdf/canton.pdf, accessed December 6 2016; Susan Burch, "'Dislocated Histories': The Canton Asylum for Insane Indians," *Women, Gender, and Families of Color,* 2 (Fall 2014): 141–62; Lorelle Barry and Catharine Coleborne, "Insanity and Ethnicity in New Zealand: Maori Encounters with the Auckland Mental Hospital, 1860–1900," *History of Psychiatry,* 22 (2011): 285–301.

38 Clifford Beers, *A Mind That Found Itself: An Autobiography* (New York: Longmans, Green, 1908); Norman Dain, *Clifford W. Beers: Advocate for the Insane* (Pittsburgh: University of Pittsburgh Press, 1980).

39 Barbara Sapinsley, *The Private War of Mrs. Packard* (New York: Paragon House, 1991), xv–xvii.

40 Linda Carlisle, *Elizabeth Packard: A Noble Fight* (Urbana: University of Illinois Press, 2010), 7.

41 Ibid., 9.

42 Julia Keay, *Alexander the Corrector: The Tormented Genius Who Unwrote the Bible* (London: Harper Collins, 2004), 172.

43 Bethany Aram, *Juana the Mad: Sovereignty and Dynasty in Renaissance Europe* (Baltimore: The Johns Hopkins University Press, 2005), 167–8.

44 Joshua Wolf Shenk, *Lincoln's Melancholy: How Depression Challenged a President and Fuelled His Greatness* (New York: Houghton Mifflin, 2005); Jason Emerson, *The Madness of Mary Lincoln* (Carbondale: Southern Illinois University Press, 2007).

45 Shenk, *Lincoln's Melancholy*, 116.

46 Emerson, *The Madness of Mary Lincoln*, 121–2.

47 Ibid., 165.

48 Susan Burch and Hannah Joyner, *Unspeakable: The Story of Junius Wilson* (Chapel Hill: University of North Carolina Press, 2007).

49 Hans Prinzhorn, *Artistry of the Mentally Ill*, translator E. von Brockdorff (New York, Heidelberg: Springer-Verlag, 1972), first published in Germany in 1922.

50 Sander L. Gilman, *Seeing the Insane* (Lincoln: University of Nebraska Press, 1982, 1996); John M. MacGregor, *The Discovery of the Art of the Insane* (Princeton: Princeton University Press, 1989).

51 Gail A. Hornstein, *Agnes's Jacket: A Psychologist's Search for the Meaning of Madness* (New York: Rodale, 2009). Quote is from inside dust jacket. Also, Nicholas Tromans, *Richard Dadd: The Artist and the Asylum* (London: Tate Publishing, 2011).

52 Kay Redfield Jamison, *Touched with Fire: Manic-Depressive Illness and the Artistic Temperament* (New York: Free Press, 1994).

53 Roy Porter, "The Patient's View: Doing Medical History from Below," *Theory and Society,* 14 (1985): 175–98; Porter, "Bedlam and Parnassus: Mad People's Writing in Georgian England" in *One Culture: Essays in Science and Literature,* ed. G. Levine, (Madison: University of Wisconsin Press, 1987), 258–84; Roy Porter, "The Diary of a Madman. 17th Century Style: Goodwin Wharton, MP, and Communer with the Fairy World," in *Lectures in the History of Psychiatry: The Squibb Series,* ed. R. Murray and T. Turner, (London: Royal College of Psychiatrists, 1990), 128–43.

54 Alan Beveridge, "Life in the Asylum: Patients' Letters from Morningside, 1873–1908," *History of Psychiatry,* 9 (December 1998): 431–69; Lykke de la Cour, "'She thinks this is the Queen's castle': Women Patients' Perceptions of an Ontario Psychiatric Hospital," *Health & Place,* 3 (June 1997): 131–41; Matthew Gambino, "'These Strangers Within Our Gates': Race, Psychiatry, and Mental Illness Among Black Americans at St. Elizabeths Hospital in Washington, DC, 1900–1940," *History of Psychiatry,* 19 (December 2008): 387–408; Gemma Blackshaw, "Peter Altenberg: Authoring Madness in Vienna circa 1900" in *Journeys into Madness: Mapping Mental Illness in the Austro-Hungarian Empire,* ed. G. Blackshaw, and S. Wieber (New York: Berghahn Books, 2012), 109–29; Mab Segrest, "Exalted on the Ward: 'Mary Roberts,' the Georgia State Sanitarium and the Psychiatric 'Specialty' of Race," *American Quarterly,* 66 (March 2014): 69–94; Adrián Gramary, Cláudia Lopes, and João Pedro Ribeiro, "Herculano Sá de Figueiredo (1911–74): A Sculptor in the Conde de Ferreira Hospital, Portugal," *History of Psychiatry,* 26 (June 2015): 200–213.

55 Nicholas Hervey, "Advocacy or Folly: The Alleged Lunatics' Friends Society, 1845–1863," *Medical History,* 30 (July 1986): 245–75.

56 Ann Goldberg, "A Reinvented Public: 'Lunatics' Rights' and Bourgeois Populism in the Kaiserreich," *German History,* 21 (May 2003): 159–82.

57 Lenny Lapon, *Mass Murderers in White Coats: Psychiatric Genocide in Nazi Germany and the United States* (Springfield, MA: Psychiatric Genocide Research Institute, 1986), 159–216.

58 Irit Shimrat, *Call Me Crazy: Stories from the Mad Movement* (Vancouver: Press Gang Publishers, 1997).

59 Barbara Everett, *A Fragile Revolution: Consumers and Psychiatric Survivors Confront the Power of the Mental Health System* (Waterloo: Wilfrid Laurier University Press, 2000); Linda Morrison, *Talking Back to Psychiatry: The Psychiatric Consumer/Survivor/Ex-Patient Movement* (New York: Routledge, 2005).

60 Nick Crossley, "The field of psychiatric contention in the UK, 1960–2000," *Social Science and Medicine,* 62 (2006): 552–63; Nancy Tomes, "The Patient as a Policy Factor: A Historical Case Study of the Consumer/Survivor Movement in Mental Health," *Health Affairs,* 25 (2006): 720–29; Heather Murray, "'My Place Was Set At the Terrible Feast': The Meanings of the 'Anti-Psychiatry' Movement and Responses in the United States, 1970s–1990s," *Journal of American Culture,* 37 (2014): 37–51.

61 Duncan Scott Campbell, *Unsettled: Discourse, Practice, Context and Collective Identity Among Mad People in the United States, 1970–1999* (Doctoral dissertation, Faculty of Environmental Studies, York University, 2011).

62 Barbara Taylor, *The Last Asylum: A Memoir of Madness in Our Times* (London: Hamish Hamilton, 2014), 103.

63 Two recent prominent examples of survey histories which include the perspectives of mad people are Petteri Pietikainen, *Madness: A History* (London: Routledge, 2015) and Andrew Scull, *Madness in Civilization: A Cultural History of Insanity from the Bible to Freud, from the Madhouse to Modern Medicine* (Princeton: Princeton University Press, 2015).

16

DEMENTIA

Confusion at the borderlands of aging
and madness

Jesse Ballenger

Of all the major categories of mental illness, indeed of illness of any kind, dementia may best illustrate the famous dictum of historian Charles Rosenberg that "In some ways disease does not exist until we have agreed that it does, by perceiving, naming, and responding to it."[1] Everything we know about the natural history of age-associated progressive dementia suggests that it has always been part of human experience, yet only in the modern era has it been regarded as a disease, and only in the last half of the twentieth century as a major public health issue. These dramatic changes in how dementia has been conceptualized by medicine were driven by a broader transformation in the social and cultural history of aging.

In part, the transformation of old age has been a simple matter of demography. In the late twentieth century, people over the age of 65 made up a much larger, growing, and visible part of the population in modern, developed societies than in earlier eras. But a popular misconception holds that because the average life expectancy at birth before the twentieth century was in the forties, very few people lived into old age and afflictions of old age such as senile dementia were thus scarcely noticed. In fact, low life expectancy at birth in the pre-modern era was largely the result of very high rates of infant and child mortality; so while it is certainly the case that increased longevity and the aging of the baby boom generation has given aging an unprecedented prominence since the latter half of the twentieth century, thus greatly increasing the prevalence of dementia, the elderly and their medical problems were far from unknown in societies of the distant past.

Whatever the historical prevalence of dementia, its rising prevalence in the modern era tells only part of the story. Increasing prevalence might explain *that* senile dementia attracted more attention, but it does not explain the *particular forms* that attention took. Why, for example, should dementia be regarded by modern medicine in some periods as a part of the aging process and in other periods as a disease? What explains the intensity of the fear and anxiety that dementia has aroused in recent decades?

This chapter will address questions about the growing salience of dementia by describing the different ways dementia has historically been framed by attitudes toward aging. It begins with a discussion of dementia in antiquity through the early modern period, then describes the three major ways that dementia has been framed by changing attitudes about aging since the nineteenth century, culminating in its emergence in the late twentieth century as one of the most prominent and feared medical conditions, even though its continued entanglement with aging leaves its status as a mental illness somewhat confused.

Dementia in the distant past

The loss of cognitive ability in old age had been recognized and described in literary, legal, and medical texts since antiquity, but no effort was made in these texts to disentangle it from the broad range of debilitating physical and mental losses associated with aging.[2] Classical, medieval, and early modern authors differed on the question of when the loss of intellectual ability associated with aging would occur and whether it could be delayed. A few authors described notable individuals who seemed to retain their full mental abilities deep into old age. But on the whole poets, philosophers, and physicians in the West tended to agree with Shakespeare's maxim that "when age is in, the wit is out."[3] This longstanding pessimism about dementia and aging is perhaps best embodied by Jonathan Swift's description of the senile Struldbrugs in *Gulliver's Travels*, unfortunate beings who are immortal, but suffer all the debilities of aging: "In talking, they forget the common appellation of things, and the names of persons, eve of those who are their nearest and dearest relations. For the same reason they can never amuse themselves with reading, because their memory will not serve to carry them from the beginning of a sentence to the end; and by this defect they are deprived of the only entertainment whereof they might otherwise be capable."[4] Swift's description is particularly poignant as he himself would suffer mental impairment beginning in middle age and die with dementia at age 77. A few years after *Gulliver* was published, Swift imagined in verse how his friends gloated over his intellectual deterioration:

> Yet thus, methinks, I hear 'em speak:
> "See, how the Dean begins to break!
> Poor gentleman, he droops apace!
> You plainly find it in his face.
> That old vertigo in his head
> Will never leave him till he's dead.
> Besides, his memory decays:
> He recollects not what he says;
> He cannot call his friends to mind:
> Forgets the place where last he din'd;
> Plies you with stories o'er and o'er;
> He told them fifty times before.
> How does he fancy we can sit
> To hear his out-of-fashion'd wit?"[5]

Framing dementia as a brain disease in modern German psychiatry

The modern concept of dementia begins with the effort of French alienist Philippe Pinel to rationalize the classification of mental disorders. In a widely influential book on nosography published in 1798, Pinel listed dementia as one of the four basic types of mental disorder, describing a broad range of symptoms and behaviors that all related to the loss of psychosocial competence. Throughout the nineteenth century, European psychiatrists further narrowed down the concept of dementia to include only the impairment of intellectual abilities; non-cognitive symptoms were moved into separate disease categories or regarded as mere epiphenomena of the primary dementia. At the same time, the growing influence of clinical-pathological correlation in medicine led psychiatrists to link dementia to a number of generalized pathological changes in the brain such as cortical atrophy and vascular deterioration, which increasingly associated dementia with aging.

By the end of the nineteenth century, clinical-pathological correlation took on greater urgency because of the fear that scientific medicine's ability to define the pathogenesis and etiology of discrete disease entities through bacteriological and pathological research was leaving clinical psychiatry behind.[6] Psychiatry's only triumph along these lines was the discovery by German psychiatrists in 1857 that general paresis, one of the most common forms of insanity, was caused by syphilitic infection. The example of general paresis raised new hope that clinical-pathological correlations for other forms of mental illness would be found, leading to etiological theories and ultimately therapeutic interventions.[7] In the first decade of the twentieth century, German researchers led by Emil Kraepelin and his protégés Alois Alzheimer and Franz Nissl were interested in senile dementia, hoping perhaps to establish it as the second major mental disorder for which a clear pathological basis had been established. The effort failed because the group could not resolve the fundamental issue of whether the clinical symptoms and pathological structures they described constituted a disease entity or a part of the normal processes of aging.

Historian Eric Engstrom has shown that the institutional structure of psychiatric care in Germany during this period presented serious challenges to Kraepelin and Alzheimer's work on dementia. Two types of institutions existed in Germany after 1860 – large, state-run asylums providing custodial care to patients deemed to be chronic and incurable, and smaller urban university hospitals that were created as centers for teaching and research. Working at a university clinic in Munich, Alzheimer and Kraepelin struggled to conduct their research because cases of senile dementia were admitted directly or quickly transferred to the asylums, making it difficult to obtain histopathological specimens or make clinical observations. Kraepelin in fact had begun a broad study of the psychosis in older patients with an aim of classifying all disorders arising in patients after the age of 45 in order to more precisely demarcate the full range of psychiatric disorders, but quickly abandoned the project because of a lack of patients in this age group at the university clinic.[8]

Before joining Kraepelin at a university clinic (first in Heidelberg, and then Munich), Alzheimer worked at an asylum in Frankfurt, and it was there in 1901 that he admitted Auguste Deter, the 51-year-old woman whose case would be the basis for establishing Alzheimer's disease as a distinct entity. After leaving the asylum in 1903 to join Kraepelin, Alzheimer continued to follow the case. In fact, Alzheimer twice blocked attempts by Deter's husband to have her transferred to a cheaper but more distant asylum, presumably so he would eventually be able to obtain post-mortem specimens. After she died in 1906, Alzheimer had her preserved brain sent to him at Munich where he conducted his histological examination.[9] Shortly after this,

Alzheimer first described the case at a meeting of the South West German Psychiatrists in Tübingen in 1906. It was a brief report, describing progressive dementia accompanied by focal signs (symptoms such as aphasia or apraxia that suggest damage to specific, localized areas of the brain), hallucinations and delusions, correlated with a distinct brain pathology: general cortical atrophy, histological findings of numerous senile plaques, and neurofibrillary tangles.[10] Alzheimer concluded the report by suggesting that "on the whole, it is evident that we are dealing with a peculiar, little-known disease process . . . We must not be satisfied to force it into the existing group of well-known disease patterns."[11]

On the basis of this description and a few additional cases, Kraepelin coined the term Alzheimer's disease in a short passage on senile dementia in the eighth edition of his massive and influential *Ein Lehrbuch der Psychiatrie* published in 1910.[12] In his schema, Alzheimer's disease distinguished the relatively rare cases in which dementia developed before the age of 65 (pre-senile dementia) from the common occurrence of dementia in more advanced ages (senile dementia). Kraepelin made this distinction despite the fact that the pathological hallmarks, clinical symptoms, and natural history of both pre-senile and senile dementia were virtually identical. Age of onset appeared to be the only criteria on which the distinction was made. In grappling with Kraepelin's classification of the dementias, subsequent researchers had to puzzle not only about the relationship of Alzheimer's disease to senile dementia, but about whether both of them were related to aging in the same way or at all.[13] In 1911, a year after Kraepelin's textbook declared that Alzheimer's disease existed, Alzheimer himself seemed to argue that it did not. In a lengthy paper that included a more thorough report of the first case as well as a second case and discussion of a handful of similar cases of pre-senile dementia reported by others, he wrote:

> As similar cases of disease obviously occur in the late old age, it is therefore not exclusively a presenile disease, and there are cases of senile dementia which do not differ from these presenile cases with respect to the severity of the disease process. There is then no tenable reason to consider these cases as caused by a specific disease process. *They are senile psychoses, atypical forms of senile dementia.* Nevertheless, they do assume a certain separate position, so that one has to know of their existence . . . in order to avoid misdiagnosis.[14]

As German Berrios concludes, it seems that all Alzheimer meant to emphasize in describing these cases in both the 1907 and 1911 publications was that senile dementia could occasionally occur in a relatively young person.[15]

So why then did Kraepelin assert the existence of Alzheimer's disease as a new entity? It has been theorized that he did so as part of a struggle against the inroads being made by Freud and psychoanalysis, hoping to create in Alzheimer's disease a second example (general paresis being the first) of a mental illness with a clearly defined pathological substrate;[16] that he did so in order to garner prestige for his department, which was in a rivalry with that of Arnold Pick in Prague;[17] that he did so in order to justify the creation of Alzheimer's expensive pathology lab in Munich;[18] or finally, that he did so with full intellectual honesty out of the assumption that differences in age of onset was a sufficient reason to make the distinction, and that in any case, he was reserving final judgment for more decisive evidence.[19] All of these explanations may be true, but further historical research on Kraepelin and Alzheimer's work on dementia is much needed. Until then, all explanations must remain speculative.

What does seem clear is that for Kraepelin it made no sense to call senile dementia a disease for the pathological processes of old age (which were understood to be "normal"), while dementia occurring at earlier ages, even though associated with the same brain pathology, seemed to suggest a disease. But this left Alzheimer's disease in a marginal nosological position and seems to explain why Alzheimer and Kraepelin showed little interest in pursuing research on it or the dementias following the flurry of publications around 1910. If thought of as a disease because of its seemingly clear pathological basis (though as described below, that basis would soon be called into question by a subsequent group of psychiatrists), it was a very rare one, and so of only limited interest. But if connected to the much more common occurrence of senile dementia, it seemed less like a disease than an exaggerated form of early aging – and so, much less interesting to those who were interested in finding examples of mental disorders grounded in brain pathology.

As many historians have pointed out, the assumption that mental and physical deterioration were normal in old age was deeply embedded in medicine and Western culture more broadly and remains powerful today.[20] This assumption seems sufficient to explain why the distinction between Alzheimer's as a rare disorder distinct from senile dementia persisted in the psychiatric literature through the 1970s, despite the fact that researchers were well aware of, and puzzled by, their similarity.[21]

Framing dementia as a problem in the adjustment to aging in mid-century American psychodynamic psychiatry

Beginning in the 1930s, a different orientation towards dementia in American psychiatry and the emergence of the field of social gerontology would challenge long-held assumptions about the relationship between dementia and aging, setting the context in the late 1970s for the emergence of the current understanding of Alzheimer's disease.

In the 1930s, age-associated dementia posed two kinds of problems for psychiatrists. It continued to present the vexing nosological puzzles described above, and a new question was raised about the role of the brain pathology associated with it, when a large autopsy series published in 1933 by Swedish pathologist Nils Gellerstedt reported that the correlation between the clinical symptoms of dementia and the presence of brain pathology post-mortem was surprisingly loose. In some cases, the senile plaques and neurofibrillary tangles that were found in the brains of patients suffering from dementia were also found in the brains of patients who had shown no sign of dementia in life. In other cases, the brains of patients who died severely demented were found at autopsy to be relatively intact.[22]

But the age-associated dementias posed a second, more practical sort of problem as well, at least for psychiatrists in the United States. In the late nineteenth century, reforms in public policy made care of the mentally ill the responsibility of state rather than local governments. An unintended result of this was that local welfare officials were given a strong financial incentive to regard the old people who could no longer live independently in the community as insane so that they would be institutionalized in the state mental hospitals at the expense of state governments. As a result, both the absolute and proportional number of aged patients admitted to the state hospitals increased dramatically, and the mental hospitals remained the institutional center of psychiatry in the United States during this period.[23] Because psychiatry regarded senile dementia as incurable, its rising prevalence in the state mental hospital patient population undermined the therapeutic environment that the state hospitals were supposed to provide. Because the overall population was aging, the problem was regarded by many as an impending crisis – a demographic avalanche that would bury the state hospital as a viable institution, and the professional legitimacy of psychiatry along with it.[24] This remained a concern for psychiatry through the mid-1950s, when American psychiatrists began to increasingly move toward office-based practice in the community. In 1965, provisions in the Medicare and Medicaid legislation made the federal government responsible for funding nursing-home care of the elderly, resulting in the shift of many thousands of elderly patients out of the mental hospitals and into nursing homes and various community care arrangements.[25]

In the mid-1930s, American psychiatrists, led by David Rothschild of the Worcester State Hospital, developed a new theory of dementia that seemed to answer both sorts of problems. The new concept of dementia emphasized psychosocial factors over brain pathology in the etiology of dementia – thus bringing the age-associated dementias into mainstream American psychiatry. The basis of this re-conceptualization was the finding described above that the correlation between clinical dementia and brain pathology at autopsy was surprisingly loose. Rothschild and his followers argued that the lack of correlation between clinical and pathological data could best be accounted for by a differing ability among individuals to compensate for organic lesions. Seen this way, age-associated dementia was more than the simple and inevitable outcome of a brain that was deteriorating due to disease and/or aging. Rather, dementia was a dialectical process between the brain and the psychosocial context in which the aging person was situated. Factors such as personality type, emotional trauma, disruptions of family support, and social isolation were regarded by this group as at least as important in explaining dementia as the biological processes within the brain that produced plaques and tangles.[26]

In psycho-dynamically oriented mid-twentieth-century American psychiatry at least, this psychosocial approach was a more satisfying theory of dementia and provided a logical basis for making meaningful therapeutic interventions. There was a surge of interest in age-associated dementias within American psychiatry during this period. In the ten years 1926–35, there had only been nine articles concerning senile dementia and/or Alzheimer's disease published in the *American Journal of Psychiatry* and the *Archives of Neurology and Psychiatry*, the two leading professional journals; in the following decade, thirty-six articles appeared. Much of this literature concerned the use of therapies that had previously been considered inappropriate for aged patients – including psychotherapy, ECT, hormones, vitamins, and other drug treatments. These reports were generally enthusiastic about the results, but this probably said as much about how badly clinicians wanted meaningful treatments for dementia as about the efficacy of these approaches. In any case, these initial studies were generally neither extensive nor rigorous, and positive results were usually not replicated when more careful studies began to be conducted in the 1970s.[27]

But the psychodynamic model offered more than a way around the nosological puzzles of dementia and a rationale for the therapeutic efforts of desperate psychiatrists in the state hospitals. It also seemed to provide insight into the entire experience of aging in post-Second World War America. In the 1940s and 1950s, virtually all American psychiatrists working on senile dementia, including Rothschild himself, who had developed his model on extensive post-mortem evidence, stopped investigating brain pathology. Nor did they attempt to delineate various disease entities based on pathological lesions, but folded Alzheimer-type dementia, cerebral arteriosclerosis, and functional mental disorders into a broad concept of senile mental deterioration, whose pathology was now understood in psychosocial terms. The locus of senile mental deterioration was no longer the aging brain, but a society that, through mandatory retirement, social isolation and the disintegration of traditional family ties, stripped the elderly of their role in life. Increasingly isolated, lacking any meaningful social role, and suffering the effects of intense stigma, it was not surprisingly that the elderly began to deteriorate mentally. "In our present social set-up, with its loosening of family ties, unsettled living conditions and fast economic pace, there are many hazards for individuals who are growing old," Rothschild argued. "Many of these persons have not had adequate psychological preparation for their inevitable loss of flexibility, restriction of outlets, and loss of friends or relatives; they are individuals who are facing the prospect of retirement from their life-long activities with few mental assets and perhaps meagre material resources."[28]

Other psychiatrists in the 1950s pushed the turn to the social much further than Rothschild, going so far as to argue that that social pathology should in fact be regarded as the *cause* of brain pathology. Maurice Linden and Douglas Courtney argued that "senility as an isolable state is largely a cultural artifact and . . . senile organic deterioration may be consequent on attitudinal alterations," though they acknowledged that their hypothesis was difficult to prove.[29] David C. Wilson was less circumspect, arguing that the link between social pathology and brain deterioration was simply a matter of waiting for "laboratory proof" to support what was adequately demonstrated by clinical experience – that the "pathology of senility is found not only in the tissues of the body but also in the concepts of the individual and in the attitude of society." Wilson cited the usual evidence of pathological social relations in old age: the break-up of the traditional family, mandatory retirement, and social isolation. "Factors that narrow the individual's life also influence the occurrence of senility," he asserted. "Lonesomeness, lack of responsibility, and a feeling of not being wanted all increase the restricted view of life which in turn leads to restricted blood flow."[30] Social pathology could even be discerned, it seemed, within the constricted blood vessels of the aging brain.

Because it brought together cultural anxieties about the isolation, emptiness, and stigma of aging in modern society with the frightening symptoms of dementia, the broad concept of senile mental deterioration gained currency far beyond professional psychiatry. It figured especially in popular and professional discourse that sought to make retirement a meaningful and desirable stage of life by making it financially secure and emotionally satisfying. To the emerging field of social gerontology, the high prevalence of senile mental deterioration, as construed by psychiatrists like Rothschild, was an indictment of society's failure to meet the needs of the elderly. The "adjustment" of the individual to aging was the key concept for social gerontologists in the 1940s and 1950s. This adjustment could be negative, resulting in senile mental deterioration, or it could be positive, resulting not only in the preservation of mental health, but the discovery of new and satisfying interests and activities to replace those that had been lost with age.[31]

Though adjustment to old age was ultimately a personal matter, prominent social scientists in the emerging field of social gerontology argued that "in modern America the community must carry the responsibility of creating conditions that make it possible for the great majority of older people to lead the independent and emotionally satisfying lives of which they are capable."[32] The community's responsibility went beyond altruism, for if their needs were not met, the burgeoning aging population would result in a catastrophic increase in senility. As Jerome Kaplan, an advocate for recreation programs argued, "with the number of people who are over 65 increasing significantly each year, our society is today finding itself faced with the problem of keeping a large share of its population from joining the living dead – those whose minds are allowed to die before their bodies do."[33] The solution was a program to provide older people with meaningful activities to fill the remainder of their lives.

Broadly construed, this was the program of social gerontology for reconstructing old age. And whatever the scientific merits of this model of the social production of "senility" as an account of the pathogenesis of dementia, those who embraced it were generally successful in winning a series of significant policy changes that helped to transform the experience of aging in America. By the 1970s, much of this program had in fact been accomplished. The material circumstances of old age had been markedly improved, though not to an equal extent for all older people; significant legal protections had been won against age discrimination; negative stereotypes in popular and professional discourse were increasingly challenged, and, perhaps most importantly, the elderly themselves organized for effective political advocacy and action on their own behalf.[34] In this context of heightened social and cultural expectations in old age, along with the increased burden that dementia posed for individual families following the deinstitutionalization of the elderly that followed the Medicare Act of 1965, the problem of age-associated dementia became more visible and tragic.

Framing dementia as dread disease and major public health crisis in an aging world

In the new era of aging that was taking shape in the 1970s, the expansive concept of senility that had been current in psychodynamic psychiatry and gerontology in the 1940s and 1950s no longer seemed appropriate. "Ageism" replaced "adjustment" as the key term in social gerontology for a more aggressive and politicized generation of American gerontologists. The term ageism was coined by psychiatrist and gerontologist Robert Butler in 1968 to describe the "process of systematic stereotyping of and discrimination against people because they are old, just as racism and sexism accomplish this with skin color and gender."[35] One of the worst aspects of the stereotypical view of aging, in Butler's view, was the belief that it entailed inevitable physical and mental decline. Butler and other gerontologist argued that virtually all of the physical and mental deterioration commonly attributed to old age was more properly understood as the product of disease processes distinct from aging. "Senility" in this view was not a medical diagnosis, but a "wastebasket term" applied to any person over 60 with a problem. Worse, it rationalized the neglect of those problems by assuming that they were inevitable and irreversible. As Butler argued:

"Senility" is a popularized layman's term used by doctors and the public alike to categorize the behavior of the old. Some of what is called senile is the result of brain damage. But anxiety and depression are also frequently lumped within the same category of senility, even though they are treatable and often reversible.

Because both doctors and the public found it so "convenient to dismiss all these manifestations by lumping them together under an improper and inaccurate diagnostic label, the elderly often did not receive the benefits of decent diagnosis and treatment."[36] Butler did not discount the reality of irreversible brain damage, as had some earlier psychiatrists. Rather, he argued that the refusal to systematically distinguish the various physical and mental disease processes from each other and from the process of aging itself was a manifestation of the ageism that kept society from taking seriously the problems of older people. In this context, Butler would be among a group of clinical neurologists and psychiatrists, neuropathologists and biochemists who entered the field in the 1960s and 1970s and worked to recast age-associated dementia as a number of disease entities distinct from aging.[37]

The first step in this was to put the connection between pathology and the clinical manifestation of dementia on a firmer foundation. The British research group of Martin Roth, Bernard Tomlinson, and Gary Blessed accomplished this by developing procedures for quantifying both the clinical manifestation of dementia and number of plaques and tangles found in the brain, enabling them to calculate the degree of correlation between them. In a series of heavily cited articles, the group provided statistically significant correlations between plaques and scores on a number of dementia scales and claimed that fully 90 percent of the cases in their demented group could be satisfactorily accounted for by pathological changes that distinguished them from the control group. Though it was true that to some degree the brains of all older people contained the pathological hallmarks of dementia, and some anomalies occurred where brains with heavy pathological loads did not appear to produce dementia, they argued that the strong correlation between pathology and dementia that their studies yielded definitively refuted the psychodynamic model of dementia.[38] Although the study did not completely resolve all issues regarding the relative importance of pathology, from the time in which it was published it was widely regarded as providing authoritative evidence for a strong and probably causal relationship between brain pathology and dementia.[39]

The second step was to clarify the nosological position of Alzheimer's. One aspect of this was distinguishing between irreversible age-associated progressive dementias and reversible dementias produced by treatable conditions. More importantly, it involved recasting irreversible progressive dementia in old age as a number of disease entities distinct from aging, the most important of them being Alzheimer's disease. In a 1976 editorial in the *Archives of Neurology*, neurologist Robert Katzman argued that distinction between Alzheimer's disease and senile dementia should be dropped because at both the clinical and pathological level they were identical. This dramatically increased the number of cases of Alzheimer's disease. Extrapolating from a number of small community studies that had been done in the 1950s and 1960s, Katzman estimated that there were as many as 1.2 million cases of Alzheimer's disease in the United States in 1976, and 60,000–90,000 deaths a year from it – putting it in the top five causes of death in the United States.[40]

This reformation of Alzheimer's disease was politically powerful, allowing researchers, aging advocates, and policymakers committed to Alzheimer's disease research to make a convincing case that public resources should be allocated for research into Alzheimer's disease. Perhaps the most prominent advocate for Alzheimer's disease research was Robert Butler, who became the founding director of the fledgling National Institute on Aging (NIA) in 1974. The NIA faced early opposition from other officials in the National Institutes of Health (NIH) on the grounds that it would create administrative duplication because an adequate amount of aging research was already being conducted within other institutes of the NIH. Moreover, the wider biomedical research community remained skeptical that significant breakthroughs in understanding the complex processes of aging were likely, and worried that a new institute focusing on aging would divert money from more worthwhile research. Following the successful strategy of other institutes (most obviously the National Cancer Institute), Butler determined that focusing on a specific disease would allow the NIA to overcome this resistance, and he decided that the NIA would take the lead on Alzheimer's disease research.[41]

In 1977, Butler joined Katzman and other researchers and leaders within the NIA, including the directors of the National Institute of Neurological Disorders and Stroke and the National Institute of Mental Health, to convene a major workshop conference on Alzheimer's disease to address nosological issues and encouraging talented researchers from a variety of fields to begin working on the disease. An essential outcome of this conference was consensus around Katzman's editorial that Alzheimer's disease and senile dementia should be regarded as a unified entity – Senile Dementia of the Alzheimer Type – and that this entity was not part of the normal aging process, but a disease whose mechanisms could be unraveled through basic research leading eventually to effective treatments and ultimately cure or prevention. And in 1979, Butler along with the director of the NINCDS, persuaded leaders from seven local support groups for family caregivers of people with dementia and similar conditions to form what would eventually become the national Alzheimer's Association to work for public awareness and support for research.[42] In 1988 the communicative disorders program was moved out of the institute to become the nucleus of a new institute – the National Institute of Deafness and Other Communication Disorders.

The disease-specific lobbying campaigns led by researchers like Katzman and NIH officials like Butler, and reinforced powerfully by the Alzheimer's Association, were highly successful. By the end of the 1980s, the unlikely eponym Alzheimer's disease had become a household word and one of the most feared medical conditions. The NIA budget for Alzheimer's disease research had increased by more than 800 percent, and federal funding for Alzheimer's disease research continued to grow even in an era characterized by budgetary constraints, reaching a level of around a half a billion dollars a year by the mid-1990s.

But these campaigns were also fraught with tensions that undermined two important additional goals of the Alzheimer's movement – to generate support and resources for caregivers and to lessen the anxiety and stigma suffered by those who have dementia. To make a compelling case for funding biomedical research aimed at treatment and prevention, advocates always implicitly and sometimes explicitly trafficked in what critics called "apocalyptic demography," arguing that massive investment in biomedical research was the only way to avoid an avalanche of dementia in the twenty-first century associated with the aging of the baby boom generation that would overwhelm the health care system. Public policy in the United States largely followed this logic, with the result being that while money for research dramatically increased, very little investment was made in providing specific supports for caregivers or research and developing creative approaches to improving the quality of care for people with dementia or in prevention through nonpharmacological means. Similarly, in order to make the case that Alzheimer's disease causes great suffering, advocates represented the losses associated with dementia as so total and irrevocable as to call into question whether people suffering from it could still properly be regarded as people at all, thus greatly deepening the stigmatization of those diagnosed with it and intensifying the anxiety people felt about aging itself.[43]

So far at least, the reformation of dementia in the 1970s has produced little in the way of therapeutic benefit. Beginning in the mid-1980s, a number of drugs targeting neurotransmitter deficits associated with Alzheimer's disease have been approved by the US Food and Drug Administration for symptomatic treatment. Although some of them were widely prescribed, these drugs quickly became mired in controversy, as they appeared to provide, at most, modest benefit for a small subset of patients. Many dementia experts questioned whether they were worth the cost, and critics argued that they were an example of the undue influence of Big Pharma in modern medicine.[44] By the late 1990s, enthusiasm (and funding) grew even higher for a new strategy targeting the accumulation of excess amyloid protein that manifested in the brain as plaques. Though breakthroughs were repeatedly reported in treatment of Alzheimer's transgenic mice models, and some drugs could even be shown to clear amyloid in the human brain, amyloid drugs have so far repeatedly failed decisively in clinical trials, leading some in the field to question the direction of Alzheimer's research.[45]

Conclusion: the ongoing entanglement of dementia and aging

Early in the new millennium, the diverse research initiatives organized around the unified Alzheimer's disease concept exerted a centrifugal force that seemed continually poised to pull it apart. For example, genetic research has identified several autosomal dominant gene mutations for the rare, highly heritable early onset form of Alzheimer's disease. But for the much more common late onset form of Alzheimer's disease, probabilistic genetic variants has been identified that are only marginally predictive, conferring a somewhat higher or lower risk for developing dementia.[46] These findings would seem to support the distinction originally made by Kraepelin between pre-senile dementia occurring before the age of 65 and senile dementia occurring at later ages. The search for more useful biomarkers has further splintered Alzheimer's disease into a number of distinct subtypes.[47]

At the same time, the repeated failure to find effective treatments for people with dementia has led to an emphasis on early detection and prevention. The creation of the category of Mild Cognitive Impairment (MCI) to describe measurable cognitive deterioration that does not impair sufficiently to warrant a diagnosis of dementia suggests that it is a prodromal form of Alzheimer's disease, but as many critics have pointed out, the relationship between them is far from clear. Researchers cannot consistently predict which people labeled with MCI will develop dementia and which will not, let alone explain why.[48] Despite these shortcomings, MCI remains widely accepted in the field because the identification of a population of people more likely to develop dementia has great potential for studying the pathogenesis of dementia and offers the possibility that the drugs that have proved so disappointing in treating dementia might prove to be effective in preventing patients from progressing beyond MCI. But the implicit connection between the serious cognitive losses associated with dementia and more nebulous age-associated cognitive decline associated with MCI seems to herald a return to the broad concept of senility that was replaced by disease entities like Alzheimer's disease.

Despite its limitations, MCI and its putative relationship to Alzheimer's disease is being incorporated into the fifth version of the *Diagnostic and Statistical Manual of Mental Disorders* under the category of "Minor Neurocognitive Disorder," while Alzheimer's disease will be brought under the category of "Major Neurocognitive Disorder," on the rationale that MCI "may be a focus of early intervention. Early intervention efforts may enable the use of treatments that are not effective at more severe levels of impairment and/or neuronal damage, and, in the case of neurodegenerative disease, may enable a clinical trial to prevent or slow progression."[49] This is a fairly transparent statement of the hope that the drugs found to be of dubious value to patients diagnosed with Alzheimer's disease might be found to offer greater benefit to patients in putative prodromal stages. Whether these drugs prove to be of any benefit, their use in MCI will certainly create a lucrative new market for drug companies to exploit.[50]

From within the field, critics have seized on such uncertainties to challenge the legitimacy of the unified concept of Alzheimer's disease. Peter J. Whitehouse, a neurologist at the forefront of the development and clinical testing of drug treatments in the 1980s and 1990s, was arguing by the early twenty-first century that the concept of Alzheimer's disease ought to be abandoned in favor of a broader concept of brain aging, with a shift in emphasis toward promoting brain health across the life span.[51]

Medical anthropologist Margaret Lock has documented the challenges dementia continued to pose to researchers, clinicians, caregivers and patients. While biomedicine has produced powerful technologies that have increasingly revealed some of the basic mechanisms involved in age-associated, progressive cognitive decline, they seem to have produced ever greater uncertainties about both the nature of dementia and its relationship to aging, as well as what people experiencing or at risk for dementia can do about it. Though genetic tests have been developed that could provide everyone with information about their odds of developing dementia, individuals who have undergone such tests have had difficulty in assimilating this knowledge, falling back on common sense or cultural frameworks to make sense of it and have typically become more, not less, anxious about their futures.[52]

Given the risks and uncertainties associated with aging and dementia, it is not surprising that, despite the tone of optimism among researchers and activists, Alzheimer's disease, as more carefully and rigorously defined and described by contemporary biomedicine, continues to generate anxiety about the prospect of aging.

Notes

1 Charles E. Rosenberg, "Framing Disease: Illness, Society and History" in *Framing Disease: Studies in Cultural History,* ed. Charles E. Rosenberg and Janet Lynne Golden (New Brunswick, NJ: Rutgers University Press, 1992), xiii.
2 The most comprehensive scholarly account of old age in antiquity through the Middle Ages remains George Minois, *History of Old Age: From Antiquity to the Renaissance* (Chicago: University of Chicago Press, 1989).
3 Shakespeare, *As You Like It,* Act 3, Scene 5.
4 Jonathan Swift, *Gulliver's Travels* (Signet Classic, 1960 [1735]), 230–31.
5 Swift, "Verses on the Death of Dr. Swift, D.S.P.D," http://andromeda.rutgers.edu/~jlynch/ Texts/verses.html, accessed December 6 2016. On Swift's likely inspiration for the Struldbrugs in early modern medical discourse, see Daniel Schäfer, "Gulliver Meets Descartes: Early Modern Concepts of Age-Related Memory Loss," *Journal of the History of the Neurosciences,* 12 (2003): 1–11. On Swift's mental impairment and pessimistic ideas about old age and dementia in the West, see Roy Porter "Dementia: Social Section I" in *A History of Clinical Psychiatry: The Origin and History of Psychiatric Disorders,* ed. German Berrios and Roy Porter (London: Athlone Press, 1995), 52–62.
6 Charles Rosenberg, "The Crisis in Psychiatric Legitimacy: Reflections on Psychiatry, Medicine, and Public Policy," in *Explaining Epidemics and Other Essays, in the History of Medicine,* Charles Rosenberg, (New York: Cambridge University Press, 1992), 245–57.
7 Erwin H. Ackerknecht, *A Short History of Psychiatry* (New York: Hafner, 1959), 66. The development of psychiatric knowledge about the cause and eventual treatment of general paresis took decades however. In 1822, Antoine Bayle first linked the clinical symptoms of what he called paralysie générale to inflammation of the meninges and cerebral atrophy, but made no suggestion about the cause. Andrew Scull, *Madness in Civilization: A Cultural History of Insanity from the Bible to Freud, From the Madhouse to the Modern Era* (Princeton: Princeton University Press, 2015), 217–18. And the claim by German psychiatrists that general paralysis was caused by syphilitic infection remained controversial until 1913, when researchers in the United States identified syphilis spirochetes in the brains of paretics. Ibid, 263. In 1917, Austrian Julius Wagner-Jauregg developed an effective though dangerous treatment for general paresis that involved infecting patients with malaria to induce high fever, for which he won a Nobel Prize in 1927. Ibid, 300–1.
8 Eric J. Engstrom, "Researching Dementia in Imperial Germany: Alois Alzheimer and the Economies of Psychiatric Practice," *Culture, Medicine and Psychiatry,* 31 (2007): 405–13.
9 Ibid.
10 Though this is a fair summary of the conventional account of Alzheimer's report, the case has many complexities. For an interesting discussion of the epistemological conundrums entailed in Alzheimer's description of this case and Kraepelin's decision to declare it a distinct disease entity, see Rob Dillman "Alzheimer Disease: Epistemological Lessons from History?" in *Concepts of Alzheimer Disease: Biological, Clinical and Cultural Perspectives,* ed. Peter J. Whitehouse, Konrad Maurer and Jesse F. Ballenger, (Baltimore, MD: Johns Hopkins University Press, 2000), 129–57.
11 "Über eine eigenartige Erkrankung der Hirnrinde," translated by Katherine Bick as "A Characteristic Disease of the Neocortex" in *The Early Story of Alzheimer's Disease: Translation of the Historical Papers by Alois Alzheimer, Oskar Fischer, Emil Kraepelin, Gaetano Perusini,* ed. Luigi Amaducci Bick and Giancarlo Pepeu, (Padova, Italy: Liviana Press, 1987), 1–3.
12 On Kraepelin's importance to the subsequent history of psychiatry of Kraepelin and his textbook, see Shorter, *A History of Psychiatry,* 99–109. For a translation into English of the passage by Kraepelin, as well as key papers by Alzheimer and others, see Katherine L. Bick, Luigi Amaducci, and Giancarlo Pepeu, *The Early Story of Alzheimer's Disease: Translation of the Historical Papers by Alois Alzheimer, Oskar Fischer, Francesco Bonfiglio, Emil Kraepelin, Gaetano Perusini* (Padova, Italy: Liviana Press, 1987).
13 Thomas Beach, "The History of Alzheimer's Disease: Three Debates," *Journal of the History of Medicine and Allied Sciences,* 42 (1987): 327–49.

14 Alois Alzheimer, "Über eigenartige Krankheitsfälle des späteren Alters." Translated by Hans Förstl and Raymond Levy as "On Certain Peculiar Diseases of Old Age." *History of Psychiatry*, 2 (1991): 71–101.

15 Berrios, "Alzheimer's Disease," 360.

16 R.M. Torack, "Adult Dementia: History, Biopsy, Pathology," *Neurosurgery* 4 (1979): 434–42.

17 Luigi A. Amaducci, W. A. Rocca, and B. S. Schoenberg, "Origin of the Distinction between Alzheimer's Disease and Senile Dementia: How History Can Clarify Nosology," *Neurology*, 36 (1986): 1497–9.

18 Thomas Myfanwy and Michael Isaac, "Alois Alzheimer: A Memoir," *Trends in Neuroscience*, 10 (1987): 306–7.

19 Beach, "History of Alzheimer's Disease."

20 For example, see Carole Haber, *Beyond Sixty-Five: The Dilemma of Old Age in America's Past* (Cambridge: Cambridge University Press, 1983); Stephen Katz, *Disciplining Old Age: The Formation of Gerontological Knowledge* (Charlottesville: University Press of Virginia, 1996).

21 Martha Holstein, "Aging, Culture, and the Framing of Alzheimer Disease" in *Concepts of Alzheimer Disease: Biological, Clinical and Cultural Perspectives*, ed. Peter J. Whitehouse, Konrad Maurer, and Jesse F. Ballenger, (Baltimore, MD: Johns Hopkins University Press, 2000), 158–80.

22 Jesse F. Ballenger, "Beyond the Characteristic Plaques and Tangles: Mid-Twentieth Century US Psychiatry and the Fight against Senility" in *Concepts of Alzheimer Disease*, 83–103.

23 Gerald N. Grob, *Mental Illness and American Society, 1875–1940* (Princeton, NJ: Princeton University Press, 1983) and "Explaining Old Age History: The Need for Empiricism" in *Old Age in a Bureaucratic Society*, ed. David D. Van Tassel and Peter N. Stearns, (New York: Greenwood Press, 1986), 30–45.

24 Ballenger, "Beyond the Characteristic Plaques and Tangles."

25 Gerald N. Grob, *From Asylum to Community: Mental Health Policy in Modern America* (Princeton, NJ: Princeton University Press, 1991).

26 Ballenger, "Beyond the Characteristic Plaques and Tangles."

27 Ibid.

28 David Rothschild, "The Practical Value of Research in the Psychoses of Later Life," *Diseases of the Nervous System*, 8 (1947): 125.

29 Maurice Linden and Douglas Courtney, "The Human Life Cycle and its Interruptions: A Psychologic Hypothesis," *American Journal of Psychiatry*, 109 (1953): 912.

30 David C. Wilson, "The Pathology of Senility," *American Journal of Psychiatry*, 111 (1955): 905.

31 For a fuller version of the argument in this section, see Chapter 3 of Jesse F. Ballenger, *Self, Senility and Alzheimer's Disease in Modern America* (Baltimore, MD: Johns Hopkins University Press, 2006), 56–80.

32 Robert J Havighurst, "Social and Psychological Needs of the Aging," *Annals of the American Academy of Political and Social Science*, 279 (1952): 17.

33 Jerome Kaplan, *A Social Program for Older People* (Minneapolis: University of Minnesota Press, 1953), 3.

34 Richard B. Calhoun, *In Search of the New Old; Redefining Old Age in America, 1945–1970* (New York: Elsevier, 1978); Carole Haber and Brian Gratton, *Old Age and the Search for Security: An American Social History* (Bloomington: Indiana University Press, 1994).

35 Robert N. Butler, *Why Survive? Being Old in America*, 1st edition (New York: Harper & Row, 1975), 12.

36 Ibid., 9–10.

37 For a fuller version of the argument in this section, see Chapters 4 and 5 of Ballenger, *Self, Senility and Alzheimer's Disease in Modern America*, 81–151.

38 Gary Blessed, Bernard E. Tomlinson, and Martub Roth, "The Association Between Quantitative Measures of Dementia and of Senile Change in the Cerebral Grey Matter of Elderly Subjects." *British Journal of Psychiatry*, 114 (1968): 797–811 and "Observations on the Brains of Non-Demented Old People," *Journal of Neurological Science*, 7 (1968): 331–56.

39 Robert Katzman and Katherine L. Bick, "The Rediscovery of Alzheimer Disease during the 1960s and 1970s" in *Concepts of Alzheimer Disease*, 104–14.

40 Robert Katzman, "Editorial: The Prevalence and Malignancy of Alzheimer Disease. A Major Killer," *Archives of Neurology,* 33 (1976): 217–18.
41 Patrick Fox, "From Senility to Alzheimer's Disease: The Rise of the Alzheimer's Disease Movement," *Milbank Quarterly,* 67 (1989): 58–102.
42 Ibid. For an account of the reconceptualization of Alzheimer's and its emergence as a major public issue from the perspective of Katzman, Butler and others involved in the events described in this paragraph, see Robert Katzman and Katherine L. Bick, eds, *Alzheimer Disease: The Changing View* (San Diego, CA: Academic, 2000).
43 Ballenger, *Self, Senility and Alzheimer's Disease,* chapter 5, 113–51.
44 Jesse F. Ballenger, Peter J. Whitehouse, Constantine Lyketsos, Peter Rabins and Jason Karlawish, eds, *Treating Dementia: Do We Have a Pill for It?* (Baltimore, MD: Johns Hopkins University Press, 2009).
45 K. Mullane, and M. Williams, "Alzheimer's Therapeutics: Continued Clinical Failures Question the Validity of the Amyloid Hypothesis – But What Lies Beyond?" *Biochemical Pharmacology,* 85 (2013): 289–305.
46 E. Rogaeva, T. Kawarai, et al., "Genetic Complexity of Alzheimer's Disease: Successes and Challenges," *Journal of Alzheimer's Disease,* 9, Suppl (2006): 381–87.
47 J. L. Whitwell, D. W. Dickson, M. E. Murray, S. D. Weigand, N. Tosakulwong, M. L. Senjem, D. S. Knopman, et al., "Neuroimaging Correlates of Pathologically Defined Subtypes of Alzheimer's Disease: A Case-Control Study" *Lancet Neurology* 11 (2012): 868–77.
48 Atwood Gaines and Peter Whitehouse, "Building a Mystery: Alzheimer's Disease, Mild Cognitive Impairment, and Beyond," *Philosophy, Psychiatry & Psychology,* 13 (2006): 61–74.
49 American Psychiatric Association, DSM-V Development, "S 12 Mild Cognitive Disorder," www.dsm5.org/ProposedRevision/Pages/proposedrevision.aspx?rid=420#, accessed December 1 2011.
50 Daniel R. George, Peter J. Whitehouse, and Jesse F. Ballenger, "The Evolving Classification of Dementia: Placing the DSM-V in a Meaningful Historical and Cultural Context and Pondering the Future of 'Alzheimer's,'" *Culture, Medicine and Psychiatry,* 35 (2011): 417–35.
51 Peter J. Whitehouse and Daniel George, *The Myth of Alzheimer's: What You Aren't Being Told About Today's Most Dreaded Diagnosis* (New York: St. Martin's Press, 2008).
52 Margaret M. Lock, *The Alzheimer Conundrum: Entanglements of Dementia and Aging,* (Princeton, NJ: Princeton University Press, 2013).

Part VI

MALADIES, DISORDERS, AND TREATMENTS

17

PASSIONS AND MOODS

Laura Hirshbein

Passions and moods are diffuse concepts that have been defined and interpreted in many different ways over the centuries. A passion might be an intense feeling about something, a characteristic of an approach to a situation, or a sign of a loss of control. A mood could be an internal state (happy, sad, angry, anxious), but could also be part of a disease (too high as in mania or too low as in depression or melancholia). To define them requires choosing a historical or psychological framework – frameworks that have themselves changed over time. Though descriptions of passions and moods have been ubiquitous throughout written texts over the millennia, several groups of scholars have been specifically active in describing their characteristics and parameters: historians, mental health professionals, and critics of mental health professionals. These are not necessarily mutually exclusive groups, nor have they taken characteristic stands about descriptions of passions and moods or how to address issues that accompany them.

One place to find discussions of passions and moods is within the growing literature on emotions in history. Although there are methodological challenges in locating and understanding emotions, scholars are increasingly asking questions about how emotions on individual, social, and conceptual levels played roles in societies over time. In addition, emotions are being used to help illuminate historical themes. Much of the literature on mood in particular is located within scholarly examination of mental disorders over time. Some authors take a broad view of historical change and describe mood problems over multiple centuries and continents. Others have more specifically inquired about local conditions and circumstances that shaped both professionals and potential or actual patients in changing healthcare dynamics. The historiography of mood, like the concept itself, is diffuse and expansive, and there is no way to capture all writings in a single essay. The following discussion touches on the work of a number of authors, but cannot do justice to all of the scholarship in this area.

Emotions in history

Emotions have not always been a topic for historians to question or engage (though philosophers – and later psychologists – certainly described them over time). In the late nineteenth and early twentieth centuries within the historical profession, scholars viewed rationality as the highest ideal. At a time when historians typically used an intellectual approach, scholars were certain that there was a clear distinction between the cool logic of statesmen (in a lineage from Greek philosophers to Western political men) and the passionate excesses in mob actions or in peoples from countries they deemed uncivilized. Further, scholars embraced science in their own work and idealized rationality – which they explicitly saw as an absence of passion – in the past.[1] When historians focused on the political realm, their interpretation of historical actors' words and deeds reinforced the idea of an evolution in politics and society from a primitive, irrational, and passionate state to a rational ideal. This assumption persisted in some areas of history, and also functioned in law to explain certain kinds of crimes.[2]

Later generations of historians began to break down assumptions about rationality and the exclusive focus on Western men and to examine the value judgments inherent in projecting unrestrained emotion onto groups such as women and non-Western people of color. And contributions by feminist scholars inside and outside the discipline of history helped to break down the characterization of rationality as the epitome of human and social development. Psychologist Carol Gilligan pointed out in 1982 that girls and boys approached ethical problem-solving from different perspectives and concluded that defining ethics in terms of male behavior privileged rationality over relationships.[3] It became possible to see passion as an aspect of personality rather than something foreign, other, or to be overcome by rational thought or action.[4]

The older scholarly work in history and political theory had focused on abstract ideas within the work of elite philosophers and scientists and celebrated the role of reason in individuals and institutions.[5] Historians with more of an interest in the social phenomena in everyday people, though, began to look at how emotion was described and functioned within different elements of society.[6] American historian Peter Stearns has been a frequent contributor to the literature on the history of emotion. Stearns argued not only that emotional expression depends on historical context, but also that history is a valuable tool in understanding emotions.[7] Stearns and others in the emerging field of family history addressed emotional themes such as attachments to children and relationships between husbands and wives.[8] Stearns and like-minded scholars also pointed out the extent to which gender norms shaped emotional expression.[9]

Although a family history perspective helped to include emotion in history, many scholars in the field made value judgments about a progression from presumed extremes of emotion in the medieval and early modern periods to greater restraint and rationality by the nineteenth and twentieth centuries. Medieval historian Barbara Rosenwein, though, noted that it was not accurate nor fair to characterize the Middle Ages as unrestrained in its passions, with the implication that the modern state represented a more evolved state of existence. She called for attention to emotion in historically specific times and places.[10] Nicole Eustace utilized this approach to emotion in history in her examination of eighteenth-century American politics and the ways in which the language of passion permeated Revolutionary-era culture. She examined not only elite writings, but also diaries and letters from the time period.[11] Instead of a hierarchy from passionate to rational, scholars such as Rosenwein and Eustace demonstrated that emotions are part of the rich context of historical change. And as William Reddy pointed out, emotions are entwined with political events and their study helps to illuminate all aspects of history, even traditional descriptions of governmental regime change.[12] Beyond Western traditions, historian of Africa Nancy Rose Hunt has shown that historical analysis through the lens of gender (not just women and emotions) brings affective elements of history into clearer focus.[13]

Within the expanding area of emotions in history, medical historians contributed by tying theories about the body and the mind to social and cultural context. Though traditional views of philosophy and political history assumed a connection between political theories and the absence of passion, historians of medicine explored in more detail how political ideas over time related to theories about the body and reflected and reinforced the roles of reason and passion. Harold Cook, for example, explored the perspective of seventeenth-century Dutch philosophers, including Rene Descartes, and found they viewed passions as something positive to be understood, rather than subjugated to reason. Bodily health was affected by the passions for good and for ill, and the goal was to avoid excess, not eliminate the passions. As Cook further argued, this framework of thinking about the balance of passions was echoed in political theory of the time. Thus medicine and philosophy were not isolated realms, but affected society as a whole.[14]

The attention to context has expanded the understanding of classic writers. For example, Louis Charland has reexamined the work of seventeenth-century English philosopher John Locke and the extent to which his theories on madness incorporated observations about passion and other feeling states, not just the departure from reason.[15] But the language of passion and the language of emotion were not necessarily the same. Some scholars have pointed out that scientific frameworks shifted discussions from passions (with religious overtones) to emotions (presumably entities that could be studied by scientists).[16] Historians have looked more specifically at the context of the scientific study of emotions, particularly the work of German physiologist Wilhelm Wundt whose theories informed debates about the nature of emotion in early psychology research in the late nineteenth and early twentieth centuries.[17]

Within these historical works, there are two basic approaches to the nature of emotion. One is to use the insights of psychology and psychiatry to interpret human action over time with the assumption that emotions are universal phenomena and can be understood by modern scientific discoveries. There has been a tradition since the days of Sigmund Freud to use psychoanalytic insights, for example, to understand historical actors in the past. Contributors to journals such as *Psychoanalysis in History* interpreted the past as they would patients in the present.[18] Cultural historian Peter Gay was one of the best-known scholars to incorporate this kind of approach in history and explored emotions such as what he identified as the "tender passion of love" over time.[19]

The other approach is to view emotions and their expression as specific to times and places and to examine their meanings in context. Part of that specificity involves a recognition that the concept of selfhood is itself constructed and that the modern view of the self as an autonomous individual is a product of history. Psychotherapist Philip Cushman pointed out that European and American understandings of the psychological self have had very different relationships to the broader society in the last two centuries.[20] Professions such as psychology and psychiatry have not been innocent bystanders to shifts in popular views of the self. As historian Ellen Herman has explained, the professional work of psychologists in America in the twentieth century helped to engineer a popular view of the self that focused on internal experiences.[21]

As these examples make clear, there is not a clear divide between mental health professionals and historians or critics in terms of approach toward passions or moods in history. Some scholars in history assume that modern science in psychology or psychiatry is truth that can be used to understand the past, while mental health professionals often critique the idea that there is universal emotion over time. But the difference between an approach to emotions as universal and one that identifies emotions within a historically specific context is also replicated among those who describe mental disease.

Grand narratives and overarching themes

One of the most common ways that passions and moods have been described in history has been in discussions of their disorders. Medical historians such as Roy Porter explained transitions of views of madness away from religious interpretations of possession or witchcraft to philosophical ideas based in reason. Key thinkers from the ancient Greeks to Descartes postulated that the presence of passions or extremes in mood were abnormal for otherwise rational Man. Treatment over time involved a range of activities from spiritual interventions to balancing humors through bleeding or purging.[22] By the eighteenth century, physicians such as French luminary Phillipe Pinel introduced scientific treatment and articulated the idea that excessive passion needed to be handled through housing in an asylum.[23] By the late nineteenth and early twentieth centuries, Sigmund Freud and his international group of disciples explained that unconscious conflicts derived from frustrated drives in early life led to all mental and emotional problems.[24] Individuals with severe problems or those who were not able to participate in psychoanalysis were often housed in increasingly crowded mental institutions through the middle of the twentieth century.[25] After the Second World War, the evolution of medications to treat mental distress gradually became the most common form of intervention.[26]

Many scholars in different disciplines have approached these disorders in passions and moods through work that covers broad expanses of time and geography. Some used the big picture to gain perspective on differences in descriptions and treatments of mental diseases over time. Others have been interested in continuities over time, often with a goal of validating present-day views or as evidence for the evolution of current theories. The scholarly writings that utilized grand narratives of change over time focused on two primary disorders of mood: melancholia (called depression in more recent time periods) and mania.

The late Yale psychiatrist Stanley Jackson wrote perhaps the most exhaustive work on melancholia. He argued that there had been remarkable persistence of the concept for millennia, and so he used its various descriptions as a way to understand changes in medical theories and practice over the whole expanse of human history (though with a predominant focus on Western traditions). Jackson's account followed Biblical descriptions of sadness or despair through Hippocratic discussions of black bile to Richard Burton's classic seventeenth-century literary text. Jackson tracked elite medical theory and practice as it transitioned from mid-nineteenth-century Germany to twentieth-century England and the United States.[27] Jackson's second major volume, on the history of healing over time, identified the issue of opposite passions to treat emotional disturbances.[28]

While Jackson's comprehensive volumes focused on clinical descriptions, other scholars examined the many literary and philosophical connections to the same texts on melancholia. Jennifer Radden collected a variety of medical and literary sources on the topic of melancholia over the centuries and noted the ways in which the sources referred back to common themes and to each other.[29] Literature professor Matthew Bell broadened the conversation about melancholia from the usual texts to explore the relationship between melancholia and culture, as well as gender implications over time.[30] Scholars who addressed the arc of history from classic Greek descriptions of mood problems through modern depression were necessarily limited to broad themes rather than specifics of how time and place might affect physician or patient ideas or experiences.[31]

Many scholars have noted the changes in interpretations of melancholia from ancient ideas about humors to older conceptions of the working of the mind to modern biochemistry. But some have assumed that the disease is fundamentally the same even though it might appear somewhat differently in disparate times and places. Within these works, scholars have often accepted a current truism of the modern diagnosis of depression, that it is more common in women than in men. As a result, work on the history of depression in women has become a feature in women's history and feminist scholarship.[32]

Historian Jill Oppenheim's work on "nervous breakdown" in Victorian England looked at a wide variety of symptoms and illness descriptions. Oppenheim argued that these were the Victorian expressions of depression, and explored how class, gender, and medical professional issues helped to shape the parameters of clinical interactions and life experiences. Oppenheim's study illustrated that growing medical expertise and shifts in professional structures helped to make mental maladies more accepted as ailments that required treatment. But though Oppenheim used a broader range of materials to explore Victorian experiences in Britain than some of the traditional histories, she still presumed that there was an illness that was continuous over time and that the only difference for the modern era was the significance with which contemporary actors viewed and explained the illness. Thus Oppenheim's study constantly used the word "depression," even though the term was not used during the time period of her study.[33]

While historians have used modern assumptions about disease to help shape their interpretations of the past, others with a more present focus have used history to validate their current ideas. Many noted what appears to be a continuity of description over time and some focused on similarities rather than differences. Modern clinicians have incorporated historical evidence to argue for the validity of the diagnosis of depression (though ancient melancholia is certainly not the same as the current diagnosis of depression).[34]

The use of history as validation has also been valuable for advocates and sufferers of mental illness. Some literature in this vein has highlighted the perception that melancholics or those with manic depression were geniuses or especially gifted – when they were not immediately prostrated by sadness or incapacitated because of mania. It has become common to identify who over time might have been melancholic or manic depressive – inevitably the list includes luminaries such as the biblical King David, Ludwig von Beethoven, Abraham Lincoln, and Winston Churchill. The theme of exceptionalism has especially been embraced by scholars who have looked to history to find inspiration for their own struggles with depression and manic depression. And those who have had experiences as patients have special authority, especially in their descriptions of mania.[35]

These approaches share a model of human mood that assumes it is intrinsic to the organism and can be traced through time. While older scholarly work such as that of psychoanalyst Henri Ellenberger presumed that inner emotional lives throughout history could be understood with the tools of psychoanalysis applied retrospectively, more modern scientists assert that discoveries since the nineteenth century helped to shed light on emotions as scientific phenomena.[36] For some historians and modern neuroscientists, British evolutionary biologist Charles Darwin's genius lay in his insistence that emotions were a part of biology and that there was some common element in passions in humans and strong emotions in animals.[37] Some scholars take Darwin's insights further to argue that evolution can help us understand the persistence of some problematic emotions over time. For those who believe that human biology is determinant, the question becomes why abnormally elevated or depressed moods survived natural selection.[38] From this perspective, evolution is not just a theory in history, but also a frame of reference to understand modern emotion.

Not all who assume continuity of human moods over time believe that the modern period is the best able to answer questions about its dysregulation, however. Scholars of moods have sometimes suggested that the past holds answers that are on occasion better than the present, and that the weight of history offers evidence that we should not ignore. German Berrios, for example, carefully analyzed the meanings of concepts in descriptive psychopathology over the past two centuries to make important historical ideas accessible, in part so that they could be used by clinicians looking for validity in the continuity of processes over time.[39]

And for historians of psychiatry, the past has the virtue of being untainted by commercial interests, such as the modern pharmaceutical industry. Psychiatrist and historian David Healy completed a biography of mania in which he traced some of the common features of elevated mood over time. In his work, Healy complained (as he expressed in many of his publications) that the modern pharmaceutical industry had highjacked the idea of a disease of changing moods in order to promote their products. Healy did not doubt that there was a mental disease that involved a problem with mood – it just needed better boundaries around it, and the past was the place to find genuine mental illness.[40] Edward Shorter took this argument further to claim that as a historian he had better answers than current clinicians because he could use history to see where modern psychiatrists went wrong with their distinctions between different kinds of mood problems.[41]

These scholarly works on emotions and disease assumed that as biological organisms we share a propensity to problems in mood that can be traced through time, even though past individuals – including providers and patients – might have used different language or frameworks to articulate it. For some, history is a source of authority. If melancholy, for example, has been fairly consistently described over time and space, it should theoretically be possible to capture the essential elements of the experience to describe the disease. And for those scholars who utilize grand themes over time, the particulars of time and place are less relevant.

The challenge with the assumption about the universality of emotions and mental problems is that it privileges a disease view that is often Western in orientation and presentist in its framework. The roles of physician (or healer) and patient are held fairly constant over time (even with changing types of interventions). And scholars with this approach presume that while social, cultural, and economic forces can affect disease and its treatment, they do not fundamentally shape the real disease that is at the root of the problem. But these assumptions are rejected by a number of historians and critics of mental health professions who have raised questions about the boundaries around mental illness, the roles of providers and society to determine them – and even the existence of mental illness itself.

Specific stories and critical contexts

While broad narratives about melancholia and mania focused on continuities over time or highlighted themes that could be traced over many time periods and locations, scholars with more of a focus on specific contingencies and settings have emphasized that mood disorders look very different if they are closely examined. German Berrios and Roy Porter, for example, edited a volume of essays that reviewed symptoms of disorders and social and cultural contexts of illnesses over time. Contributions that focused on a broad range of physician sources were paired with essays that addressed the social context for a variety of symptoms. The volume included essays on mood disorders in general, as well as some on older concepts such as hysteria and neurasthenia.[42] Efforts such as the one by Berrios and Porter illustrate that context is critical to understanding mental symptoms and experiences. Historian Angus Gowland stressed that scholars who get caught up in modern concerns miss critical understandings of mood in the past. In his analysis of melancholy in the sixteenth and seventeenth centuries, Gowland identified medical and theological relationships to social and political change that reflected and reinforced one another.[43] And Herman Westerink pointed out that assumptions that enlightenment science overcame religion are not supported by the evidence gained from a close reading of religious denominational struggles and their relationship to the emergence of psychiatry as a field.[44]

In the same way that scholars such as Gowland and Westerink tried to disrupt modern assumptions about illness, others examined disease entities that do not have modern equivalents to gain critical perspective on past understandings of mental phenomena. Several scholars examined nineteenth-century ideas about neurosis, which had a component of mood disturbance. Historian David Schuster analyzed the social contexts in nineteenth-century America that led to the diagnosis of neurasthenia, a disorder that could include depression and that seemed a quintessential American response to the rush of the modern world.[45] Involutional melancholia is another extinct diagnosis that represented a kind of depression defined primarily around aging women. Involutional melancholia was very popular among physicians in the late nineteenth and early twentieth centuries, but disappeared by the 1970s.[46] And treatments for these disorders and others have gone in and out of fashion, from attempts to balance humors prior to the eighteenth century to institutionalization in the nineteenth and twentieth centuries to somatic therapies such as fever therapy, metrazol treatment, electroconvulsive therapy (ECT), and medications from amphetamines to selective serotonin reuptake inhibitors.[47]

Scholars have used stories specific to a location or a time period in order to indicate the contingencies in psychiatric theories and practices, arguing against grand narratives or universal truths in emotions or illness. Some emphasized the professionalizing factors that motivated psychiatrists and others as they constructed their theories about illness.[48] Other authors more explicitly condemned contemporary mental health practices. In the area of criticism of psychiatric providers, there is a wider range of scholarship, from those influenced by the 1960s cultural critiques of psychiatry to activists who themselves experienced psychiatric power to critics who were concerned with the role of commercial influences on the theories and practices in mental health.

In the 1960s, British psychiatrist R. D. Laing questioned the wisdom of labeling people as being mentally ill, while American sociologist Erving Goffman observed that mental institutions took complete control over their inhabitants. And American psychiatrist Thomas Szasz argued that mental illness did not exist at all. These authors all protested against the prevailing psychoanalytic approach of the time period that had suggested that pathology lay inside the individual person and that treatment necessarily involved focus on that individual. Instead, as historian Michael Staub pointed out, these critics argued (in different ways) that the environment could create conditions of mental stress or instability and that the solution was not to treat (incarcerate) the individual.[49]

In their critiques of the psychiatric establishment, Laing, Goffman, and Szasz and others influenced by them did not differentiate among types of mental illness. Many used the term "mad" to describe all the individuals who were subjected to psychiatric control. Scholars, academics, and social activists in America and in Europe were highly critical of the work of psychiatrists.[50] And as anger at the psychiatric establishment spread out from academic concerns into popular culture, people who had experienced psychiatric power first hand also gathered together to protest against their treatment by psychiatrists. In the United States and the UK, individuals who identified themselves as "survivors" of psychiatrists – including those who had been treated by ECT (which was often used for depression) – created networks of consumers in what became a mental health consumer movement.[51]

As mental health consumers articulated their concerns with what they saw as abuses of power by psychiatric professionals, critics in academia also described the role of power in psychiatric institutions and their relationship to the State. In the 1960s, French philosopher Michel Foucault insisted that the modern State and an aggressive psychiatric profession had erected arbitrary boundaries around groups of people in the interests of State control.[52] In Foucault's analysis, the problem was not just that individual patients were incarcerated by individual providers – the problem was that the exercise of psychiatric power was in itself part of a larger and nefarious process by which social structures codified behavior and boundaries in order to control the subjects of the state. He argued that it did not matter what kinds of mental problems individuals displayed or how they might have experienced mental distress – the problem was that the State took control of people based on social imperatives rather than a desire to help.

Feminist critics in the 1970s also began to question the extent to which psychiatric power defined women as mentally ill based on their role in society.[53] American psychologist Phyllis Chesler argued in 1972 that male misogyny was the lens through which women had been declared mad over time, and that their moods and passions were interpreted as illness.[54] English professor Elaine Showalter extended Foucault's analysis to explore how much the category of women became the category of madness itself. She examined representations of women by both physicians and by women

322

themselves in England over a century and a half beginning in the early nineteenth century and analyzed the ways in which women's moods and passions were tied up in social and cultural judgments of women's roles in society. As a result, women's experiences were defined as madness – whether it be melancholy or an excess of passion.[55]

But while 1970s activism in both the mental health consumer and feminist movements protested against psychiatric authority as a whole, the tide began to shift toward more engagement with mental health by the 1980s. During that decade, scholars used a new focus on women's stories as a reason to explore what seemed to be the quintessential women's illness: depression.[56] Researchers within mental health circles and observers outside the professions began to focus significant attention on the apparent frequency of depression among women. Women's historians in the second wave – who were less preoccupied by the discouraging stories of limited numbers of pioneering women and more interested in looking at women's worlds – picked up the theme that it was a feminist project to explore diseases specific to women.[57]

As a result of identification of depression as a women's illness and lingering arguments that psychiatry was synonymous with social control, there is now a significant split in the scholarly literature between those who embrace the idea of psychiatric diagnosis as validation of suffering and those who view it as ongoing social control. Paula Caplan, a psychologist who was a consultant in the 1980s in the process of revising the landmark American Diagnostic and Statistical Manual, condemned the American Psychiatric Association (APA) for creating a diagnosis of Premenstrual Dysphoric Disorder (PMDD) for the 1987 revision of the manual (*DSM-III-R*). Caplan argued that PMDD, or mood disturbance the week before a woman's period, enshrined sexist determinism and created a category for which a substantial portion of the population could be diagnosed at any given time. But she was opposed by women on the committee who insisted that PMDD was a real diagnosis, and that it was not fair to women to eliminate it from the official diagnostic nomenclature.[58]

As the example of Caplan's activism makes clear, the compilers of the American DSM system have been the focus of a great deal of argument about mental disorders. Beginning with *DSM-III* in 1980, the APA's system of nomenclature has been seen as both the source of truth about mental illness (often referred to as the Bible of mental disorders) and as the source of the runaway rates of diagnoses of mental illness in the United States and around the world.[59] Passions are entirely absent from the volumes of specific diagnostic criteria for mental disorders, as formulated by the APA in what many critics complained was a grab for professional and economic turf against other professionals.[60] But two major groups of diagnoses in the DSM seem to many psychiatrists and observers to be robust – depression and bipolar disorder (manic depression). One of the reasons for this, of course, is the long history of similar-sounding diseases. But the current diagnosis of a mood disorder involves symptom criteria that were created by a consensus committee of psychiatrists during the 1970s. None of these symptoms is objective – or even consists of an objective measurement that could be interpreted. All symptoms for depression and bipolar disorder rely on patient reports and do not include a consideration of the context of the symptoms. Allan Horwitz and Jerome Wakefield pointed out that the diagnosis of major depressive disorder can pathologize normal sadness – a trend that became worse when the newest edition of the DSM (*DSM-5*) removed a natural exclusion from depression (acute bereavement).[61]

Gender expectations have been incorporated into mood categories of disease. Psychiatric researchers who gave medications to populations of patients – who were predominantly women – in mental hospitals from the 1960s through the 1980s used their patients' symptoms to construct a diagnosis of major depressive disorder. Perhaps not surprisingly, when those symptoms were translated to an epidemiological tool it diagnosed a higher proportion of women than men with depression. Was this biology or self-fulfilling prophecy?[62] Medical and popular understandings of femininity and masculinity affected how women and men engaged with psychiatry and with diagnosis and treatment.[63]

Much of the criticism centered on the American DSM system has emphasized the problematic role of psychiatrists who use their professional power to make judgments about people's lives. But that presumes that patients are passive recipients of diagnoses. Social and cultural constructs of health and disease, however, shape how experiences are perceived and interpreted. Anthropologist Emily Martin looked at the modern diagnosis of bipolar disorder in its social and cultural context, including the popularity of the diagnosis for the general public. Martin's work illustrated that the interplay between mental health professional and patient is more complex than just a dichotomy between powerful figure and disease victim.[64]

One of the issues in the apparent growth of public interest in psychiatric diagnosis is the ready availability of psychiatric medications. Advertising from pharmaceutical companies to patients and practitioners has increased not just the visibility of certain medicinal remedies, but also awareness of diagnoses themselves. The DSM is an American product, though the APA has attempted to export its diagnoses (with varying degrees of success) to other countries. Scholars in the UK have suggested that America is uniquely problematic in its wholesale embrace of the free market to sell pharmaceuticals.[65] Others have pointed out that the modern research enterprise – with large corporations that export clinical trials to third world nations (in order to evade the regulatory processes for research in the United States and the UK) – raises questions about the validity of pharmaceutical studies.[66] Even for psychiatric insiders such as Allen Frances, who was the editor of the *DSM-IV* (1994), whatever kernel of truth may be buried within current diagnostic categories has been undermined by the influence of the pharmaceutical industry on the process of defining psychiatric illness.[67]

By looking in detail at specific times and places where people have been diagnosed with mental illness, a number of scholars have argued that what we identify as mental illness is in essence a cultural construct. This way of framing understandings about mental illness affect not just diagnosis, but also treatment. As psychologist Robert Fancher pointed out, the psychotherapeutic systems of care that evolved over the last century were constructed by frameworks of health and disease. There is no absolute objective reality outside these frameworks (though Fancher explains that individual patients can derive benefit within the framework if they choose to accept it).[68]

While it may make sense from both a historical and therapeutic point of view to see that shared understandings in psychotherapy help shape both concepts of illness and health, it becomes a little more challenging to understand the meanings of somatic therapies over time. For therapies that were introduced in the late nineteenth and early twentieth centuries, some scholars become preoccupied with the question about whether a particular intervention worked. While few modern scholars (or practitioners) would stop to ask the question of whether bloodletting helped patients, it becomes more complicated around treatments such as ECT or medications that are still in use today. But a modern focus on efficacy in therapies in the past can shut down important areas of inquiry. As Jack Pressman pointed out in his critically important work on the history of frontal lobotomy (which was performed for some cases of agitated depression), it is essential to understand why a technique made sense at the time it was introduced rather than just judge it from the perspective of the present.[69] As Jonathan Sadowsky provocatively suggests in his chapter in this book, frameworks of meanings shape the function and practice of somatic treatments in the same way as talk therapies.

For example, electroconvulsive therapy (ECT) – also called shock therapy – was introduced in Italy in the 1930s and spread around the globe, despite the hardships of the Second World War.[70] The rationale behind the treatment was never very clear, and it has been interpreted and reinterpreted in hindsight. But practitioners in Europe and America utilized shock therapy throughout the middle of the twentieth century at fairly high rates for hospitalized patients and without necessarily seeing it as being opposed to psychotherapeutic interventions.[71] Initially the treatment was intended to remove harmful memories and help with agitation. By the 1960s it had been modified to reduce memory side effects (though this remained a source of controversy).[72] ECT became a well-respected intervention for involutional melancholia and was also the standard of efficacy by which medications were measured when drug treatments began to come into vogue in the 1960s and 1970s.[73] Its use waned in the 1980s with the rise of drug treatments (and with the criticism of the procedure by anti-psychiatry activists), but enjoyed somewhat of a resurgence in subsequent decades in the context of expanded attention to the problems of profound depression.[74]

The history of ECT is about much more than just the history of the procedure. Instead, the history itself has been a battleground for friends and foes of psychiatry. Early critical accounts of ECT took the point of view that electroshock was alarming and wrong, like something out of a horror movie.[75] ECT opponents argued that it was barbaric, and even now tell its history as a tale of systematic torture perpetuated on innocent victims by greedy or ambitious psychiatrists.[76] More recently, the narrative of ECT has become even more complex as self-identified patients such as American Kitty Dukakis, the wife of former Massachusetts governor Michael Dukakis, extolled the virtues of the treatment (even while acknowledging significant side effects).[77]

As the narrative by Dukakis suggests, the newest trend in the history of moods and their disorders is the engagement of patients as consumers in the mental health marketplace. Although the mental health consumer movement arose in opposition to psychiatric authority, the role of the mental health consumer has considerably expanded in the past few decades to include many enthusiasts about mental health interventions. Within that market, patients endorse products that promise optimal mental health – including freedom from mood disturbances. And the blame, as it were, for diagnosing and treating with pharmaceuticals also is directed to members of the consumer public who seek out happiness – not just the eradication of deep sadness – in pill form.[78] While the pharmaceutical companies may sell, consumers also seem to be buying the idea that they should expect perfect mood balance at all times, as well as cheerful engagement with all the challenges of life.[79]

Conclusion and areas for further scholarship

As Roy Porter and Mark Micale explained in the introduction to their valuable collection *Discovering the History of Psychiatry*, historical accounts of psychiatry – whether they are positive or highly critical – often share a preoccupation with concerns of the present day.[80] That in and of itself may not be an issue – to a certain extent all historians are necessarily contained within their own contexts and cannot achieve ultimate objectivity (any more than scientists or other seekers of truth).[81] And as contemporary issues rise to the fore, it is likely that they will become more interesting to historians. Suicide, for example, has had relatively little attention from historians of emotions, demographics, or psychiatric disorders, though recent increases in suicide in the aftermath of military service may generate new historical inquiry.[82]

One issue that often vexes scholars who approach mood over time is the question of boundaries. When does passion cross a line from enthusiasm to irrationality? When is a mood too high or too low? Who gets to decide? In what context? Does it matter whether something is normal or abnormal? What lessons can we learn from the boundaries? Boundaries change at different times and places based on many factors such as gender, class, race, and sexuality. They might not be the same for all people within a time period. And boundaries are not solely determined by mental health professionals or other authority figures.

There may also be a lingering fantasy that the universal will turn out to be true – maybe a biological marker will uncover the "real" depression or bipolar disorder. Maybe we'll find a spot in the brain that we can identify as the seat of mood disturbance. But what happens if we do identify something as a disease? Does a disease result in limitation of activity, or does it allow a person or group to be cared for by their families or institutions? Are disease labels used to control or to help? Is disease an essential biological process? To what extent is it socially or culturally constructed? How, when, and what treatment should be provided? By whom? What are the driving forces behind treatment? And is it ever justified to force treatment?

Historians who consider passions and moods in the future will need to decide whether they are going to rely on modern scientific understandings of emotion and disease or see ideas and events from the past in context. They will also need to look at their sources and the material available to contextualize them. One challenge relates to the source material for older time periods and non-Western countries – is there a way of breaking out of physician-authored texts? Are emotions expressed in other venues? How do we read enough in the time period to understand the context? Is there a way to approach emotions over time that avoids the binary of provider-patient? In the end, it may not be possible to overcome our own biases and projections onto the past, since we cannot achieve absolute truth about other people, especially through historical analysis. Still, passions and moods are part of the human experience and therefore appropriate subjects for historical inquiry.

Notes

1 Peter Novick, *That Noble Dream: The "Objectivity Question" and the American Historical Profession* (New York: Cambridge University Press, 1988).
2 See for example, Susan K. Besse, "Crimes of Passion: The Campaign Against Wife Killing in Brazil, 1910–1940," *Journal of Social History* 22 (1989): 653–666.

3 Carol Gilligan, *In a Different Voice: Psychological Theory and Women's Development* (Cambridge, MA: Harvard University Press, 1982).

4 For an example of the problems of passion in non-Western peoples, see for example Sloan Mahone and Megan Vaughan, eds, *Psychiatry and Empire* (New York: Palgrave, 2007).

5 For a classic complaint about social history and the loss of rational man, see for example Gertrude Himmelfarb, "Denigrating the Rule of Reason," *Harper's*, April 1984, 84–90.

6 Peter N. Stearns and Carol Z. Stearns, "Emotionology: Clarifying the History of Emotions and Emotional Standards," *American Historical Review* 90 (1985): 813–836.

7 P. N. Stearns, "History of Emotions: The Issue of Change," in *Handbook of Emotions*, ed. Michael Lewis and Jeannette M. Haviland (New York: Guilford Press, 1993), 17–28. See also C. Z. Stearns and P. N. Stearns, eds, *Emotion and Social Change: Toward a New Psychohistory* (New York: Holmes & Meier, 1988).

8 On the emerging history of the family, see for example Philippe Aries, *Centuries of Childhood: A Social History of Family Life*, trans. Robert Baldick (New York: Vintage Books, 1962); Mary Ryan, *Cradle of the Middle Class: The Family in Oneida County, New York 1790–1885* (New York: Cambridge University Press, 1981); Edward Shorter, *The Making of the Modern Family* (New York: Basic Books, 1975); Steven Mintz and Susan Kellogg, *Domestic Revolutions: A Social History of American Family Life* (New York: Free Press, 1988). The *Journal of Family History* has been published since 1976.

9 See for example, P. N. Stearns, "Girls, Boys, and Emotions: Redefinitions and Historical Change," *Journal of American History* 80 (1993): 36–74.

10 Barbara H. Rosenwein, "Worrying about Emotions in History," *American Historical Review* 107 (2002): 821–845.

11 Nicole Eustace, *Passion Is the Gale: Emotion, Power, and the Coming of the American Revolution* (Chapel Hill: University of North Carolina Press, 2008).

12 William M. Reddy, *The Navigation of Feeling: A Framework for the History of Emotions* (Cambridge: Cambridge University Press, 2001).

13 Nancy Rose Hunt, "The Affective, the Intellectual, and Gender History," *Journal of African History* 55 (2014): 331–345.

14 Harold J. Cook, "Body and Passions: Materialism and the Early Modern State," *Osiris* 17 (2002): 25–48.

15 Louis C. Charland, "John Locke on Madness: Redressing the Intellectualist Bias," *History of Psychiatry* 25 (2014): 137–153.

16 See for example, Thomas Dixon, "The Psychology of the Emotions in Britain and America in the Nineteenth Century: The Role of Religious and Antireligious Commitments," *Osiris* 16 (2001): 288–320; Charland, "The Distinction Between 'Passion' and 'Emotion.' Vincenzo Chiarugi: A Case Study," *History of Psychiatry* 25 (2014): 477–484.

17 Claudia Wassmann, "Physiological Optics, Cognition and Emotion: A Novel Look at the Early Work of Wilhelm Wundt," *Journal of the History of Medicine & Allied Sciences* 64 (2009): 213–249.

18 Peter Burke, "Freud and Cultural History," *Psychoanalysis and History* 9 (2007): 5–15. For a classic work in this genre, see for example, Erik Erikson, *Young Man Luther* (New York: Norton, 1958).

19 Peter Gay, *The Tender Passion: The Bourgeois Experience: Victoria to Freud, Volume 2* (Oxford: Oxford University Press, 1986).

20 Philip Cushman, *Constructing the Self, Constructing America: A Cultural History of Psychotherapy* (Boston: Addison-Wesley, 1995).

21 Ellen Herman, *The Romance of American Psychology: Political Culture in the Age of Experts* (Berkeley: University of California Press, 1995).

22 For an easily accessible version of this narrative, see Roy Porter, *Madness: A Brief History* (New York: Oxford University Press, 2002).

23 Charland, "Science and Morals in the Affective Psychopathology of Philippe Pinel," *History of Psychiatry* 21 (2010): 38–53. For more on Pinel, see D. B. Weiner, "'Le geste de Pinel': The History of a Psychiatric Myth," in *Discovering the History of Psychiatry*, ed. Mark S. Micale and Roy Porter (New York: Oxford University Press, 1994), 232–247.

24 George J. Makari, *Revolution in Mind: The Creation of Psychoanalysis* (New York: Harper, 2008).

25 Edward Shorter, *A History of Psychiatry: From the Era of the Asylum to the Age of Prozac* (New York: John Wiley & Sons, 1997).

26 David Healy, *The Creation of Psychopharmacology* (Cambridge, MA: Harvard University Press, 2002).

27 Stanley W. Jackson, *Melancholia and Depression: From Hippocratic Times to Modern Times* (New Haven, CT: Yale University Press, 1986).

28 Stanley W. Jackson, *Care of the Psyche: A History of Psychological Healing* (New Haven, CT: Yale University Press, 1999).

29 Jennifer Radden, ed. *The Nature of Melancholy: From Aristotle to Kristeva* (New York: Oxford University Press, 2000).

30 Matthew Bell, *Melancholia: The Western Malady* (Cambridge: Cambridge University Press, 2014). See also, Juliana Schiesari, *The Gendering of Melancholia: Feminism, Psychoanalysis, and the Symbolics of Loss in Renaissance Literature* (Ithaca, NY: Cornell University Press, 1992).

31 See for example, Clark Lawlor, *From Melancholy to Prozac: A History of Depression* (Oxford: Oxford University Press, 2012).

32 See for example, Nancy Tomes, "Devils in the Heart: Historical Perspectives on Women and Depression in Nineteenth-Century America," *Transactions and Studies of the College of Physicians of Philadelphia* 13 (1991): 363–386.

33 Janet Oppenheim, "*Shattered Nerves*": Doctors, Patients, and Depression in Victorian England (New York: Oxford University Press, 1991).

34 See for example, Michael Alan Taylor and Max Fink, *Melancholia: The Diagnosis, Pathophysiology, and Treatment of Depressive Illness* (New York: Cambridge University Press, 2006).

35 See Geoffrey Reaume's chapter in this book and, for example, Kay Redfield Jamison, *Touched with Fire: Manic-Depressive Illness and the Artistic Temperament* (New York: Free Press, 1996); Andrew Solomon, *The Noonday Demon: An Atlas of Depression* (New York: Scribner, 2001); Lisa M. Hermsen, *Manic Minds: Mania's Mad History and its Neuro-Future* (New Brunswick, NJ: Rutgers University Press, 2011).

36 Henri F. Ellenberger, *The Discovery of the Unconscious: The History and Evolution of Dynamic Psychiatry* (New York: Basic Books, 1970).

37 Peter J. Snyder et al., "Charles Darwin's Emotional Expression 'Experiment' and His Contribution to Modern Neuropharmacology," *Journal of the History of the Neurosciences* 19 (2010): 158–170. For a critical view of how his own emotional life affected his scientific work and the construction of scientific objective, see Paul White, "Darwin's Emotions: The Scientific Self and the Sentiment of Objectivity," *Isis* 100 (2009): 811–826.

38 Randolph M. Nesse and George C. Williams, *Why We Get Sick: The New Science of Darwinian Medicine* (New York: Vintage Books, 1994).

39 German E. Berrios, *The History of Mental Symptoms: Descriptive Psychopathology Since the Nineteenth Century* (New York: Cambridge University Press, 1996).

40 David Healy, *Mania: A Short History of Bipolar Disorder* (Baltimore: Johns Hopkins University Press, 2008). See also S. Nassir Ghaemi, *On Depression: Drugs, Diagnosis, and Despair in the Modern World* (Baltimore: Johns Hopkins University Press, 2013).

41 Edward Shorter, *How Everyone Became Depressed: The Rise and Fall of the Nervous Breakdown* (Oxford: Oxford University Press, 2013).

42 German E. Berrios and Roy Porter, eds, *A History of Clinical Psychiatry: The Origin and History of Psychiatric Disorders* (New York: New York University Press, 1995).

43 Angus Gowland, "The Problem of Early Modern Melancholy," *Past and Present* 191 (2006): 77–120.

44 Herman Westerink, "Demonic Possession and the Historical Construction of Melancholy and Hysteria," *History of Psychiatry* 25 (2014): 335–349.

45 David G. Schuster, *Neurasthenic Nation: America's Search for Health, Happiness, and Comfort, 1869–1920* (New Brunswick, NJ: Rutgers University Press, 2011). For some other histories of neurasthenia, see Charles E. Rosenberg, "George M. Beard and American Nervousness," in *No Other Gods: On Science and American Social Thought* (Baltimore: Johns Hopkins University Press, 1976), 98–108; Marijke Gijswijt-Hofstra and Roy Porter, eds, *Cultures of Neurasthenia From Beard to the First World War* (Amsterdam: Rodopi, 2001).

46 Laura D. Hirshbein, "Gender, Age, and Diagnosis: The Rise and Fall of Involutional Melancholia in American Psychiatry, 1900–1980," *Bulletin of the History of Medicine* 83 (2009): 710–745.

47 Joel T. Braslow, *Mental Ills and Bodily Cures: Psychiatric Treatment in the First Half of the Twentieth Century* (Berkeley: University of California Press, 1997); Niall McCrae, "'A Violent Thunderstorm': Cardiazol Treatment in British Mental Hospitals," *History of Psychiatry* 17 (2006): 67–90; Nicolas Rasmussen, *On Speed: The Many Lives of Amphetamine* (New York: New York University Press, 2008).

48 See for example, Judith Misbach and Henderikus J. Stam, "Medicalizing Melancholia: Exploring Profiles of Psychiatric Professionalization," *Journal of the History of the Behavioral Sciences* 42 (2006): 41–59.

49 Michael E. Staub, *Madness Is Civilization: When the Diagnosis Was Social, 1948–1980* (Chicago: University of Chicago Press, 2011).

50 On the broad context of anti-psychiatry in the United States, see Norman Dain, "Psychiatry and Anti-Psychiatry in the United States," in *Discovering the History of Psychiatry*, 415–444. For anti-psychiatry in some parts of Europe, see Marijke Gijswijt-Hofstra and Roy Porter, eds, *Cultures of Psychiatry and Mental Health Care in Postwar Britain and the Netherlands* (Amsterdam: Rodopi,1998); John Foot, "Photography and Radical Psychiatry in Italy in the 1960s: The Case of the Photobook Morire di Classe (1969)," *History of Psychiatry* 26 (2015): 19–35; Oisin Wall, "The Birth and Death of Villa 21," *History of Psychiatry* 24 (2013): 326–340.

51 See Nancy Tomes, "The Patient as a Policy Factor: A Historical Case Study of the Consumer/ Survivor Movement in Mental Health," *Health Affairs* 25 (2006): 720–729; Nancy Tomes, "From Outsiders to Insiders: The Consumer-Survivor Movement and Its Impact on US Mental Health Policy," in *Patients as Policy Actors*, ed. Beatrix Hoffman, et al. (New Brunswick, NJ: Rutgers University Press, 2011), 113–131; Philip R. Beard, "The Consumer Movement," in *American Psychiatry After World War II (1944–1994)*, ed. Roy W. Menninger and John C. Nemiah (Washington, DC: American Psychiatric Press, 2000), 299–320. On the legal transformations in the United States with regard to rights, see Paul S. Appelbaum, *Almost a Revolution: Mental Health Law and the Limits of Change* (New York: Oxford University Press, 1994). For the mental health consumer movement in the UK, see Nick Crossley, *Contesting Psychiatry: Social Movements in Mental Health* (New York: Routledge, 2006).

52 Michel Foucault, *Madness and Civilization: A History of Insanity in the Age of Reason*, trans. R. Howard (New York: Pantheon, 1967). Originally published in French in 1961. See also Gary Gutting, "Michel Foucault's *Phenomenologie des Krankengeistes*," in *Discovering the History of Psychiatry*, 331–347.

53 Betty Friedan named psychiatrists as particular offenders in her landmark work. Friedan, *The Feminine Mystique* (New York: Dell Publishing, 1963).

54 For the classic critique of this, see Phyllis Chesler, *Women & Madness* (New York: Avon Books, 1972).

55 Elaine Showalter, *The Female Malady: Women, Madness, and English Culture, 1830–1980* (New York: Penguin Books, 1985). See also, Lisa Appignanesi, *Mad, Bad and Sad: A History of Women and the Mind Doctors from 1800 to the Present* (London: Virago Press, 2008).

56 Nancy Tomes, "Historical Perspectives on Women and Mental Illness," in *Women, Health, and Medicine in America*, ed. Rima D. Apple (New York: Garland Publishing, Inc., 1990), 143–172.

57 See for example, David L. Eng, "Melancholia in the Late Twentieth Century," *Signs* 25 (2000): 1275–1281.

58 Paula J. Caplan, *They Say You're Crazy: How the World's Most Powerful Psychiatrists Decide Who's Normal* (Reading, MA: Addison-Wesley Publishing Company, 1995); Judith H. Gold, "Historical Perspective of Premenstrual Syndrome," in *Premenstrual Dysphorias: Myths and Realities*, ed. Judith H. Gold and Sally K. Severino (Washington, DC: American Psychiatric Press, 1994), 171–183.

59 Allan V. Horwitz, *Creating Mental Illness* (Chicago: University of Chicago Press, 2002).

60 Stuart A. Kirk and Herb Kutchins, *The Selling of DSM: The Rhetoric of Science in Psychiatry* (New York: Aldine de Gruyter, 1992); Herb Kutchins and Stuart A. Kirk, *Making Us Crazy: DSM, The Psychiatric Bible and the Creation of Mental Disorders* (New York: Free Press, 1997).

Even those with a more sympathetic view toward the framers of the DSM such as Hannah Decker have suggested that other factors – such as economic considerations around possible insurance reimbursement – affected the process of constructing psychiatric diagnoses. Hannah S. Decker, *The Making of DSM-III: A Diagnostic Manual's Conquest of American Psychiatry* (New York: Oxford University Press, 2013).

61 Allan V. Horwitz and Jerome C. Wakefield, *The Loss of Sadness: How Psychiatry Transformed Normal Sorrow Into Depressive Disorder* (New York: Oxford University Press, 2007).

62 Laura D. Hirshbein, *American Melancholy: Constructions of Depression in the Twentieth Century* (New Brunswick, NJ: Rutgers University Press, 2009).

63 For more on how men's distress was perceived in medical and popular American culture, see David Herzberg, *Happy Pills in America: From Miltown to Prozac* (Baltimore: Johns Hopkins University Press, 2009).

64 Emily Martin, *Bipolar Expeditions: Mania and Depression in American Culture* (Princeton, NJ: Princeton University Press, 2007).

65 See for example, David Healy, *Pharmageddon* (Berkeley: University of California Press, 2012).

66 Adriana Petryna, *When Experiments Travel: Clinical Trials and the Global Search for Human Subjects* (Princeton, NJ: Princeton University Press, 2009).

67 Allen Frances, *Saving Normal: An Insider's Revolt Against Out-of-Control Psychiatric Diagnosis, DSM-5, Big Pharma, and the Medicalization of Ordinary Life* (New York: HarperCollins, 2013).

68 Robert T. Fancher, *Cultures of Healing: Correcting the Image of American Mental Health Care* (New York: W. H. Freeman and Company, 1995).

69 Jack D. Pressman, *Last Resort: Psychosurgery and the Limits of Medicine* (New York: Cambridge University Press, 1998).

70 Roberta Passione, "Italian Psychiatry in an International Context: Ugo Cerletti and the Case of Electroshock," *History of Psychiatry* 15 (2004): 83–104.

71 Jonathan Sadowsky, "Beyond the Metaphor of the Pendulum: Electroconvulsive Therapy, Psychoanalysis, and the Styles of American Psychiatry," *Journal of the History of Medicine & Allied Sciences* 61 (2006): 1–25.

72 Laura D. Hirshbein, "Historical Essay: Electroconvulsive Therapy, Memory, and Self in America," *Journal of the History of the Neurosciences* 21 (2012): 147–169.

73 David Healy, *The Antidepressant Era* (Cambridge, MA: Harvard University Press, 1997).

74 Edward Shorter and David Healy, *Shock Therapy: A History of Electroconvulsive Treatment in Mental Illness* (New Brunswick, NJ: Rutgers University Press, 2007). See also, German E. Berrios, "The Scientific Origins of Electroconvulsive Therapy: A Conceptual History," *History of Psychiatry* 8 (1997): 105–119.

75 See for example, Timothy W. Kneeland and Carol A. B. Warren, *Pushbutton Psychiatry: A History of Electroshock in America* (Westport, CT: Praeger, 2002).

76 See for example, Linda Andre, *Doctors of Deception: What They Don't Want You to Know About Shock Treatment* (New Brunswick, NJ: Rutgers University Press, 2009). Andre's work does not represent scholarship in history, but she uses the history of psychiatry to make her arguments.

77 Kitty Dukakis and Larry Tye, *Shock: The Healing Power of Electroconvulsive Therapy* (New York: Avery, 2006).

78 Carl Elliott, *Better Than Well: American Medicine Meets the American Dream* (New York: W. W. Norton & Company, 2003).

79 For more discussion of the history of cheerfulness, see Christina Kotchemidova, "From Good Cheer to 'Drive-by-Smiling': A Social History of Cheerfulness," *Journal of Social History* 39 (2005): 5–37.

80 Roy Porter and Mark Micale, "Introduction: Reflections on Psychiatry and Its Historians," in *Discovering the History of Psychiatry*, 3–36.

81 On the inevitable biases in scientific work, see especially Stephen Jay Gould, *The Mismeasure of Man*, revised edn (New York: W. W. Norton & Company, 1996).

82 There have been a few works, especially Georges Minois, *History of Suicide: Voluntary Death in Western Culture*, trans. Lydia G. Cochrane (Baltimore, MD: Johns Hopkins University Press, 1999); Howard I. Kushner, "American Psychiatry and the Cause of Suicide, 1844–1917," *Bulletin of the History of Medicine* 60 (1986): 36–57.

18

PSYCHOSIS

Richard Noll

Madness

Let's begin with three melodies of madness:

(1) A man of approximately 30 years in age abruptly leaves his home without explanation. During his baptism in a river by a charismatic preacher, he has a vision and hears a message from God and then disappears into an isolated rural area for six weeks. During that time of complete social withdrawal, he continues to hear the voice of God, communicates with Satan, and has further visions. He is now convinced that he is of an ancient royal blood line, has special powers to heal the sick and raise the dead, and that God has chosen him to communicate an important message of redemption to prepare others for the end of the world. He wanders about and attracts a few illiterate friends who believe his stories about "the Way." At least three of them also see visions and hear voices, including the voice of God coming out of the sky. They join him in a life of chronic vagabondage. He is observed placing a magical curse on a fig tree, verbally scorning it because it has no fruit and he is hungry. His family is distraught, believing he is "beside himself" and worries about his safety. Since he is living in a Middle Eastern region under military occupation by a repressive Western power, his deviant activities soon come to the attention of the authorities, and he is arrested, imprisoned, tortured, and executed. Later, books are written about him in German, French, and English by physicians, who conclude that hereditary taint precipitated a "hebephrenic crisis" in a temple at the age of 12, leading to a course of chronic affliction by various forms of "paranoia."[1]

(2) A wealthy, prominent 38-year-old European physician and scientist withdraws from his family and friends as often as possible to read books on mythology, mysticism, Hellenistic mystery cults, Gnosticism, spiritualism, and parapsychology in his home library. Horrifying, repetitive, spontaneous visions of waves of blood flooding Europe begin to panic him. One night while alone in his study, like Faust, he decides to contact his "soul" and awaits a response. He soon hears the disembodied voice of a woman who encourages him to engage in an auditory dialogue with her. After a few weeks the sensory modality of these solitary sessions changes from auditory to visual mental imagery. He finds himself lost in intense, vivid visions of otherworldly journeys and auditory dialogues with the Dead that he consciously decides to accept as ontologically "real" events. But over a period of time the

RICHARD NOLL

intensity of these experiences increases, and at least twice he is transformed into a god: once, on Christmas Day 1913, a lion-headed deity who has the power to heal the blindness of a woman named Salome who tells him "You are Christ," as he sweats blood, arms outstretched as if impaled on a cross; and again when he is hanged upside down from a tree like the Norse god Odin in a wrenching cruci-fixion-like apotheosis. He eats the raw liver of a murdered child. He is told he is the prophet of a new age. He later tells close associates he received regular reve-latory instruction from the same "Master" who taught Buddha, Mani, Christ, and Mahomet. His mission, which he must communicate to others, is the redemption of God, not for our sake, but for the sake of God. Souls of dead Christians, find-ing no sign of God when they entered the afterlife in the Middle Ages, enter his home demanding redemption. Although he believes he can control the initiation and cessation of these experiments, in part by keeping diaries and illustrating the places he travels and entities he encounters, roiling emotional riptides spill out into his everyday life, and he begins to fear he is on the edge of a profound crisis. He decides to keep a loaded pistol next to his bed, vowing to blow his brains out if he is flooded with insanity. His wife and children see his instability and the gun and are afraid. His relationships with professional colleagues rupture, and one publishes a thinly disguised essay about him that slyly diagnoses him as having a "god-complex" with delusional fantasies of having special powers and insights and a special mission to redeem the world.[2]

(3) An unemployed 44-year-old ex-forester and self-styled "Presbygationalist" minis-ter from a well-educated American family begins to have unusual overpowering thoughts while writing a theological essay. Some of these concern the influence on all of our lives of the vitally important "Family of Four," the Strong and the Weak, the Perfect and the Imperfect. The day after informing his family at dinner that "the study of insanity is the most important problem in the world today" he finds himself involuntarily committed by them to the Boston Psychopathic Hospital. He proudly tells his doctors he has "broken down the wall between religion and medicine." A week later he is transferred to the Westboro State Hospital, where he resides for the next fifteen months. His diagnosis is catatonic schizophrenia. He will have three other such episodes in his life at ages 54, 59, and again just before his death at 89. During these hospitalizations he passes through all the stages of evolution of life on this planet, he climbs onto the sun and is repulsed by the inhabitants of the moon and their obsession with sex and reproduction, he becomes Mary Magdalene, insists he must "go insane in order to get married," and has a direct mystical encounter with God that convinces him for the rest of his life he is a prophet with a special mission. Witches are an annoyance in the hospital, and he stuffs a blanket in the ventilator shaft to block black cats. Often he is found naked on the hospital floor, refuses food, and is occasionally violent. After release from his first extended hospitalization, he earns a divinity degree from Harvard, begins a pastoral counseling training program for young divinity students at Worcester State Hospital, creates the first psychotic symptoms rat-ing scale for researchers, and writes a well-received book about his experiences with the help of psychoanalyst and psychiatrist Harry Stack Sullivan. Intellectually gifted but socially anxious and affectively flat, he is admired by many with whom he can never emotionally connect.[3]

As this volume attests, and as these stories indicate, madness is a moving target.

Historians of madness such as Roy Porter, Andrew Scull, Petteri Pietikainen, and now Greg Eghigian are our "resurrection men," snatching the corpse of an archaic term for new kinds of scholarly dissection.[1] For contemporary historians looking for a word that is wide enough to envelope new globalized histories that do not privilege European, British, or American master narratives of the history of psychiatry, madness has a seductive charm. Madness implies no necessary historical or geographical or epistemic center. New histories of madness, so it is hoped, are therefore less likely to perpetuate translations of past mentalities into modern medical language. But a stubborn presentist bias persists in the new historical literature: madness is deviance, disorder, and disease. Indeed, it persists in this chapter: madness as psychosis, madness as schizophrenia.

I chose the three madmen above, and skewed their vignettes, to highlight the limitations of our presentist framings of madness. Even if we stay within the historical flow of Western civilization, madness once meant much more than deviance, disorder, and disease.

For example, madness as *mania* could be insanity as well as divine inspiration or revelation to the ancient Greeks, both curse and blessing. Whether voluntary or involuntary, deliberately cultivated or the scourge of disease, madness was an undeniable and necessary fact of human experience.[5] But "divine madness" wasn't directly synonymous with mental illness or Unreason. It was a madness that breached the wall between medicine and religion, folly and genius, mundane, and sacred. Whatever happened to *this* madness?

The mad lives of Jesus of Nazareth (*c.* 7–2 BCE to 30–33 CE), Swiss psychiatrist and psychoanalyst Carl Gustav Jung (1875–1961) and Anton Boisen (1876–1965), the founder of the influential clinical pastoral education movement in the United States, are not easily problematized. These stories remind us that both spontaneous and cultivated experiences of an extraordinary nature may or may not translate well into medical discourse, but as creatures of our historical era we reflexively reach for the medical dictionary to find analogues – like psychosis or schizophrenia – that we can grasp. Early twentieth-century physicians did so to understand Jesus, and both intimates of Jung as well as later commentators who never knew him saw evidence of psychotic-like grandiosity in his behavior.[6] These three vignettes also remind us that madness, even when melodically manifest through the clear curse of illness (as in Boisen's story), can be integrated into a creative life of meaning.

Is there a space for madness without medicine? Discourses within the literatures of clinical and experimental psychiatry, psychoanalysis, and in their histories, do not know how to negotiate such boundary violations. They privilege post-1800 European medical references to insanity or psychosis or schizophrenia or their presumed prodromes. For a long time, this style of interpretation flooded other disciplines, especially anthropology during the reign of Freud. For example, in 1939 ethnologist (and later in his career, psychoanalyst) George Devereux (1908–1985) expressed a view that was taken quite seriously by intellectual elites for decades in the mid-twentieth century: "Primitive religion and in general 'quaint' primitive areas are organized schizophrenia."[7] In contemporary personality trait research we find equally absurd statements such as "psychotic traits constitute an essentially healthy dimension of personality." An un-understandable oxymoron – healthy psychosis – is posited as a generative source of creativity and religious beliefs and experiences.[8] Reversing the arrow of causality, we find others who share with us their eccentric reading of history and wield it as a blunt instrument to argue that Christianity is a transcultural risk factor for chronic psychosis (schizophrenia).[9]

Today it is not "primitives" but the "general population" who are scoured for "psychosis-like symptoms" or "psychotic experiences" without sensitivity to the individual personal context or sociocultural milieu in which such experiences might arise.[10] It is perhaps a mad fantasy of our age that the masses must be under surveillance for signs of psychotic qualities – psychosis is not Ebola, after all – but maybe we live in a postlapsarian nightmare landscape of our own creation where "God's earth was, and is, but a gigantic state hospital and pathography becomes the unique and universal science."[11] Biased toward the assumption of nascent illness, indeed openly apprehensive about endemic psychosis, medical researchers ignore the alternative: that human beings naturally, automatically, intuitively, non-reflectively, hyperactively attribute agency and minds to both visible and invisible entities and objects, and that transient sensory and perceptual anomalies – "sensory overrides," as anthropologist Tanya Luhrmann calls them – are the norm.[12] What researchers medicalize as "delusions" or fantasize as a Platonic "latent dimension of schizotypy" in the general population based on responses to rating scales for "psychosis-like symptoms" may sometimes simply be natural, normal attributional thought processes that all people engage in to self-explain their unusual sensory and perceptual experiences. Such may be the basis for claims of alien abductions – unless of course they are accurate reports of extraterrestrial contacts.[13]

Unsure of the boundaries between the territories of "truly psychotic" symptoms, "psychotic-like experiences," and "unusual subjective experiences," research on "psychosis proneness" in the general population nonetheless plunges blindly ahead. Conversion rates from "psychosis-proneness" to psychosis or schizophrenia are consistently found to be very low.[14] As you would expect, this surprises and disappoints medical researchers.

Historians of medicine and psychiatry have found themselves equally sight-blinded. They have offered few options for understanding such boundary violations other than romantic notions such as psychiatrist and historian Henri Ellenberger's (1905–1993) "creative illness," suffered by shamans and psychoanalysts alike.[15] But a creative illness is still an "illness." Perhaps as medical historian Erwin Ackerknecht (1906–1988) warned in a brilliant essay in 1943, "*Psychopathological labeling seems to be foremost an expression for helplessness, a specific attitude of our culture toward the unknown.*"[16] Madness as sought, madness as meaningful, madness as natural and universal is left for the musings of anthropologists, historians and cognitive scientists of religion, medical humanities researchers, and the "mad professors" of "mad studies" who are in open revolt against "sanism."[17]

Psychosis is a special thing

Psychosis is our era's medical term that comes closest to the ancient sense of madness as spectacular involuntary affliction, madness as curse. Psychosis is a breach, a state change, a special thing. One is no longer here, but *there*. One fails the tests of reality. It is a powerful judgment in our globalized medical culture. Psychosis is severe, severity itself.

Historians of psychiatry – beginning with British psychiatrists German E. Berrios (1940–) and Michael Dominic Beer (1956–2013) – have spent almost three decades documenting the story of psychosis.[18] At first the publications of Berrios and Beer on the history of concepts in descriptive psychopathology were outliers, out of place among historians of psychiatry still fixated on Freud, Foucault, antipsychiatry, and asylums.[19] By making Sigmund Freud's (1858–1939) obsessions their own and focusing on the rise of dynamic psychiatry or on hysteria or other psychoneuroses, previous generations of historians shared his distaste for psychosis. The rise of biological psychiatry and decline of psychoanalysis between the mid-1970s and the mid-1990s in the United States inspired scholars to explore the roots of the new orientation. Biological psychiatry's ascent was initially fueled after 1950 by pharmacological, genetic, and cognitive neuroscientific foci on severe mental disorders such as schizophrenia. The history of psychosis thus became a relevant topic for investigation.

Since the mid-1990s, a new cohort of scholars has approached the problem of psychosis in two ways. The first is to trace the word itself from "who said it first" through all subsequent mutations of definition as it passed through the thought collectives of European, British, and American physicians. Dominant themes in this literature are structured by the dynamics of binary oppositions such as psychosis vs. neurosis (starting in the 1840s), unitary psychosis vs. multiple psychoses, transient vs. chronic, continuous with normal mental states vs. discontinuous, functional vs. organic psychoses (1881), exogenous vs. endogenous (1886), and bounded "syndrome" or disease (beginning in the 1880s) vs. deconstructed "features" (since 1980). As the historical literature illustrates, the definition of the boundaries of each term within these binary oppositions underwent significant transformations over time, altering the meaning of psychosis accordingly.[20] It is a highly complex story. Readers of both the primary and secondary literatures on psychosis soon feel as if they have plummeted into a narrative maze with only an unreliable protagonist to follow as a guide. Psychosis is a mad traveler.

The second approach starts with the general (but by no means universally consensual) meanings of psychosis or psychotic qualities today, then searching past literatures for concepts or tropes that seem similar in meaning to ours but which may have had different names and bundles of their own distinctive, historically contingent resonances. This approach has followed two paths: (1) tracing past discourses regarding the degree of *severity* of mental disturbance; and (2) reconstructing the historical trajectories of *specific mental symptoms* such as delusions, disorders of perception (hallucinations and illusions), and formal thought disorder (disorganized thought/language). These are today's three "core" symptoms of psychosis, all cognitive, all failures of "reality testing," which cut across diagnostic categories and North American and European classification systems.[21]

German E. Berrios's book, *The History of Mental Symptoms: Descriptive Psychopathology Since the Nineteenth Century* (1996) remains the unsurpassed model for this sort of historical analysis of the psychosis concept. Carving core symptoms into clusters of "cognition and consciousness," "mood and emotions," and "volition and action," he deconstructs psychosis without any reference to it as a distinct syndrome. Single mental symptoms (e.g. "delusions") are historicized without any necessary embedding in particular clinical syndromes or specified disease concepts. To some degree, Berrios (a psychiatrist, after all) chose a historical method that was congruent with the *Zeitgeist* that emerged from North America in the 1970s: disarticulated diagnostic criteria. The publication of *DSM-III* in 1980 was the decisive turning point. As psychiatrist Martin Bürgy observed, "From this point onward, the noun *psychosis* was limited to its adjectival form *psychotic*."[22] In 1994 the World Health Organization followed the American Psychiatric Association and dumped "neurosis" and "psychosis" in favor of "neurotic" and "psychotic." The "Glossary of Technical Terms" in *DSM-III* (1980), *DSM-III-R* (1987), *DSM-IV* (1994), and *DSM-IV-TR* (2000) contain entries for "psychotic," not "psychosis." Even in today's *DSM-5* (2013) there are only entries for "psychotic features" and "psychoticism" (as a dimensional personality trait domain).[23]

If "psychotic" means "psychosis-like," then what, pray tell, is psychosis *like*?

Historical research can offer only limited answers. Although Berrios did not do so, such narratives could conceivably start from antiquity with all possible general cultural concepts of madness across the world. But historians of psychosis have not been able to easily penetrate a temporal wall of incomprehension. Most accounts limit themselves to the European medical literature that began *c.* 1800 with the discernible rise of a medical specialty for the treatment of madness/lunacy/insanity/*Wahnsinn*/*délire*/mental alienation/*pazzia*.[24] Alas, even the early nineteenth-century literature often seems indecipherable to us. Berrios argued in his magisterial history of the language of descriptive psychopathology that only the period from the mid-1800s to today constitutes an "episteme" underlying a commonality of concepts.[25] He argued that most concepts familiar to us were in place by the 1880s, but the process started in the second decade of the 1800s and ended just before the First World War. If he is correct, this may account for the seeming incommensurability of present conceptions of psychosis or schizophrenia with the madness of yesteryear.

Although "psychotic features" has officially usurped "psychosis" in today's psychiatric discourse, psychosis as a syndrome or symptom-complex, a recognizable altered state of consciousness, continues to be an unspoken assumption behind everyday clinical communication. Parts factored out from deconstructed wholes fascinate researchers but seem impractical to practicing clinicians. Psychosis as syndrome remains a resilient *Gestalt* that resists recentering.[26] When and where did this psychosis-as-syndrome development first take place? Berrios argued that it emerged from a conceptual splitting of the ancient clinical syndrome of *delirium* in the 1880s in French and German psychiatry:

> During the nineteenth century, from being a state of excited behavior accompanied by fever (*phrenitis*), delirium became a disorder of consciousness, attention, cognition, and orientation; in this process the transitional concept of *confusion* played a crucial role . . . it was delirium, and not progressive paralysis of the insane, that served as the clinical model for the *current notion of psychosis*.[27]

By also transferring the organic assumptions underlying acute delirium, psychosis carried with it a biological heritage that blurred the border between syndrome and disease. The more severe the symptoms, then the more deeply physical must be the origin, therefore the more disease-concept-like it would be: this was the simplistic assumption that drove the developing psychosis concept. This would be true for the disease concepts of Parisian *alieniste* Valentin Magnan (1835–1916) and his *délire chronique à evolution systématique* (chronic systematized delusional disorder) of 1886 with its strong hereditary influences; for Emil Kraepelin (1856–1926) and his systemic or "whole body" psychoses of dementia praecox and manic-depressive insanity of the late 1890s; for Eugen Bleuler (1857–1939) and his group of schizophrenias (1908, 1911) as systemic physical disease; and for the later "Heidelberg school" of German psychiatrist and philosopher Karl Jaspers (1883–1967) and those influenced by him such as Kurt Schneider (1887–1967), and so on.[28]

Rational treatments based on the assumption of psychosis as a specified biological disease concept routinely, and often tragically, failed. First surgery (starting in the 1880s) and then organotherapy (in the 1890s) persisted into the twentieth century, followed by many other somatic interventions. To cite one of hundreds of extreme examples: the noted German psychiatrist Karl Wilmanns (1873–1945) complained that "neither the administrations of all possible preparations of sexual glands, nor, after two years, the implantation . . . at our suggestion, of a sound testicle in the abdominal cavity of a katatonic, had any influence on the symptomatology of the disease."[29]

So who said it first? The current front-runner is German physician Carl Friedrich Canstatt (1807–1850), who introduced the term in his *Handbuch der Medizinische Klinik* of 1841.[30] Canstatt coined the term to mean a "psychic neurosis," or mental symptoms due to an underlying somatic illness. Decades of scholars have incorrectly cited Viennese physician Ernst von Feuchtersleben (1806–1849) as the originator of the term in his *Lehrbuch der ärztlichen Seelenkunde* (1845). However, the terms "neurosis" and "psychosis" were used by him in an exactly opposite fashion as they would be by the 1890s: for von Feuchtersleben, a psychosis was a disorder of the psyche and a neurosis was a disorder of the brain and nervous system (the classic definition of neurosis since the 1770s). The "psychoses" gained wide popularity in medicine after the appearance of a textbook by Carl Friedrich Flemming (1799–1880), *Pathologie und Therapie der Psychosen* (*Pathology and Therapy of the Psychoses*) in 1859. By 1875, in Germany, the "psychoses" (plural, not singular) was a widely accepted general term for abnormal mental conditions regardless of severity, but most often applied to the asylum conditions seen by the authors of textbooks who had little experience with what was called "nervousness" in the general population seen by general practitioners.[31] German neurologist Carl Wernicke (1848–1905) used "psychosis" in this manner throughout his brain-based, novel symptomatology that did not posit psychotic disease categories.[32] With decreasing frequency, this usage persisted until at least the First World War in some corners of the psychiatric literature.

But was there one general condition of mental disorder – a unitary psychosis – or were there discrete psychoses? Was insanity a hydra with many heads or separate creatures? The roots of this controversy in European medicine run deep and are complex.[33] The idea of what was later called an *Einheitspsychose* (unitary psychosis) found many adherents after its advocacy in an 1859 textbook of psychiatry by Heinrich Neumann (1814–1884). Neumann proposed an *Einheit der Psychosen* (unity of psychoses) into only one form (*Wahnsinn*) that followed an organic unfolding in stages (an echo of the *Stufenfolge* of the old German Romantic biology of *Naturphilosophie*) from health to sleeplessness to illusions to hypersensitivity to illness to mental illness to confusion to terminal dementia. Stage theories were a dominant part of nineteenth-century German psychiatry, particularly in the publications of Ernest Zeller (1804–1877) in 1844 and Wilhelm Griesinger (1817–1868) in 1845 and 1861. Most experts agreed that a stage of delusions, hallucinations and confusion immediately preceded the last stage, which was always severe and chronic (incurable, or "terminal dementia" as the alienists termed it).[34]

The nineteenth-century transformation of general medicine via the clinic-anatomical method and the laboratory revolution (experimental medicine), particularly in France and Germanophone areas since the 1830s, led to the general acceptance of the doctrine of disease specificity by 1860. Illnesses were no longer variables bound to the idiosyncracies of place and person ("childbed fever," and so on), but instead became manifestations of specific diseases that were identified by their unique biological mechanisms (etiology and pathophysiology) as well as their typical age of onsets, symptoms and signs, courses and outcomes. For alienists and neurologists (in the sense of "nerve doctors" treating "nervousness" or neurasthenia), it soon became clear that their professional status within the community of physicians was threatened by the laboratory turn in medicine unless they, too, adopted this doctrine. The hunt for biologically specifiable disease concepts became a professional necessity. Otherwise, alienists *everywhere* would be regarded as nothing more than the practitioners of a queer therapeutic sect outside the bounds of scientific medicine.

In history, timing is everything. Reception and reputation depend on it. After 1896, when German psychiatrist Emil Kraepelin (1856–1926) introduced a novel nosology based on course and outcome for provisional natural disease entities in the fifth edition of his *Psychiatrie,* his orientation began to exert an enormous dampening impact on the unitary psychosis idea. Others, such as the astute Thomas Clouston (1840–1915) of Edinburgh, retained clinically useful classifications of mental diseases based on the main presenting symptom approach (mania, melancholia, etc.) of traditional alienism.[35] Kraepelin was by no means the only player on the field but he was taken more seriously by many of his contemporaries for two reasons: because of his commitment to laboratory research (also shared by many others) and especially because of the claim that his new mental diseases were derived from multi-year longitudinal studies of hundreds of his patients – heretofore something no other researcher had attempted.[36] It was the *method* behind his madnesses that impressed.

Critics of Kraepelin and of natural disease entities in psychiatry abounded, with "symptom-complexes," "reaction types," Freudian mental mechanisms and other alternatives offered as serious challenges, particularly in German-speaking Europe, Britain and the United States. German psychiatrist Alfred Hoche (1865–1943) dismissed Kraepelin's assertion of natural disease entities underlying mental disorders as "a hunt after a phantom."[37] But discourses of disease concepts in psychiatry accelerated. Starting around 1910 medical journals in Europe, Britain and the United States contained more articles on specific mental diseases than on insanity as a general medical condition.[38]

Still, the unitary psychosis idea persisted in an implicit form throughout the twentieth century, primarily in the United States and Britain, where holistic elite discourses based on the "dynamic psychiatry" or "psychobiology" of Adolf Meyer (1866–1950) and (especially in the United States) on psychoanalysis remained deeply skeptical of natural disease concepts in psychiatry. Meyer, who introduced Kraepelinian mental diseases to the United States in late 1896, turned his back on both Kraepelin and the assumption of natural disease entities in psychiatry by late 1902. Beginning around this time Meyer became a dominating influence on the rising institutional structures of the nascent psychiatric profession in America. Elite Meyerians and Freudians merged into a syncretic blend by 1908 and promoted a notion of a continuum of general vulnerability in which everyone was potentially "at risk" for developing any mental disorder at any time in their lives, including psychosis. Freudians explained such severe conditions as a regression to a level of more primitive defense mechanisms and an infantile, psychotic core within each of us. Hallucinations and delusions were seen as feeble attempts by the ego to reconstitute itself by creating a false reality. There were no clear distinctions between "well" and "ill," no "courses" or rules of remission. By default, these American eclectics had kept alive a unitary psychosis idea by reframing the presumed biological mechanisms of European disease concepts such as dementia praecox and schizophrenia into the functionalized language of "reactions" and Freudian mental mechanisms.[39]

Salvation of the not-yet-psychotic through early detection, intervention, prevention, and mental hygiene has always been the dominant self-justification for the rise and continued existence of a profession of psychiatry as a legitimate medical specialty in American biomedicine. This path dependence in American psychiatry originated in 1889 with the work of Edward Cowles (1837–1919), superintendent of the McLean Asylum in Massachusetts, who set up the first American research laboratory to study neurasthenic exhaustion as the initial (but non-insane) stage of a unitary psychosis that progressed into the stages of melancholia, mania, a brief transitional period of confusion, then terminal dementia. It continues today through the "high-risk" studies that have been ongoing in various forms since the 1960s and in the research on "psychosis-proneness."[40]

Case histories, particularly the historical reconstruction of the lives of patients before they came to the attention of physicians, were the preferred evidence base of many in the American psychiatric elite until the 1970s.[41] In stark contrast to the long traditions of European psychopathology, until circa 1960, Americans maintained a curious lack of interest in detailing the variations of ongoing signs, symptoms, courses, and outcomes of psychosis *after people became ill*. Biological research in some form was acknowledged as necessary for professional survival, but for most of the twentieth century American psychiatric elites regarded it as secondary and perhaps futile. Elite discourse centered on "habit deterioration types" (1903), "reaction types" (1906), "shut-in personalities" (1908), "pre-dementia praecox" (1907) and, after 1911, a rampant misreading and reframing of Eugen Bleuler's "latent schizophrenia" (1911) as a general functional or psychoanalytic condition of vulnerability rather than as the onset of a physical disease process, as Bleuler actually meant.[42]

Degree of severity is what eventually distinguished psychosis from neurosis on the continuum of mental symptoms that did not have an identifiable physical cause. This development was already apparent in the German-language psychiatric literature by 1890, as was the widespread adoption of the principle that the psychoses could be grouped by causes, symptoms, course, and brain findings.[43] All of this was intensified by the push from the laboratory revolution in medicine to find specifiable disease concepts for psychiatry. To some degree, inspired by the international success of the "neurasthenia" concept of American electrotherapist George Beard (1839–1883) in the 1880s, the widespread assumption by physicians and the public alike was that there were basically three human conditions – sane, nervous, and insane. Hence the seeds of such a differentiation based on severity were already in place.

Prognosis had always been linked to severity at first contact in traditional medical practice, but modern medicine demanded more. Persons who were severely disordered upon first presentation sometimes followed quite different fates: the question now became "Why?" In a new era of scientific medicine, finer distinctions had to be agreed upon. After Emil Kraepelin introduced a dichotomy of two grand, multiform psychoses in 1899 in the sixth edition of his *Psychiatrie* – dementia praecox (poor prognosis, primary symptoms were cognitive) and manic-depressive insanity (better prognosis, primary symptoms were affective) – there was an increasing tendency in the early twentieth century to equate psychosis with *severity of primarily cognitive symptoms* (as in today's "core syndrome" of delusions, hallucinations and disorganized thought/language) and not define psychosis by primarily affective symptoms or behavioral signs. This was how dementia praecox, and then schizophrenia, became interchangeable synonyms for psychosis.

For persons so disordered that they required institutionalization, diagnoses that served as synonyms for severity (dementia praecox and schizophrenia, in particular) were widely (and wildly) dispensed. For persons who were more troubled than the typical "nervous" patient but, still might benefit from outpatient treatment, a diagnosis of one of the "minor psychoses" would do.

To cite one example: Charles Dana (1852–1935), a New York City neurologist and past president of the American Neurological Association, incorporated a section on "mental diseases" for the first time in the sixth edition of his influential textbook on nervous diseases. The various editions of Dana's book were the most widely assigned text on these subjects in American medical schools in the 1892 to 1920 period.[44] Dana's sixth edition of 1904 was the second American textbook to introduce Kraepelinian classification and nomenclature. Dana did not give Kraepelin an unqualified endorsement. In his vexed preface he wrote,

> I have thought it of especial importance to insist on a distinction between major and minor psychoses, and to emphasize the fact that one may have a psychosis and yet not be in any sense insane. In fact I am in sympathy with the view that makes as few people insane as possible, of narrowing the conception of the major psychoses and enlarging that of the minor.

These latter conditions to be broadened were the "borderland psychoses" and "psychoneuroses" which "really might have a psychical basis." Dana admitted that some might be "prodromes" (his exact word) for dementia praecox.[45] Dana's "minor psychoses" were actually bricks in a firewall, enclosing a larger space on the continuum of severity that would allow private practitioners such as himself to maintain jurisdictional control of difficult patients who might otherwise be lost to the asylums.

Dana's worry about the new import from German medical science, dementia praecox, reflected fulminant reality: within just a few years Kraepelin's incurable disease had entered the asylums of multiple countries, often characterizing a quarter to a half of all patients. It became the most feared and best known psychiatric diagnosis in medicine and culture until the 1920s, when it began to be replaced by schizophrenia.[46]

Schizophrenia

First dementia praecox, then schizophrenia, served as synonyms for psychosis in the twentieth century. This was true not only in elite literary discourse, but widespread in everyday practice. A person exhibiting psychotic symptoms (delusions, hallucinations, thought/language disorganization) was usually a "praecox" or a "schizophrenic" or "schizophrene" until proven otherwise. But, in truth, any person who seemed strange, enigmatic, alien, bizarre, disagreeable, remote, and beyond the physician's capacity to empathize with him or her might receive these diagnoses even in the absence of delusions, hallucinations and disorganized speech.[47]

Testimonials of elite physicians abound with such admissions. "I personally have not the time to work out any new schemes either as to classification or scientific research," said E.C. Runge, the superintendent of the City Asylum in St. Louis in 1900. "In going through the wards there are many cases which puzzle us, and we do not know how to classify them. I have found dementia praecox a very comfortable, I may say vulgarly, dumping ground."[48] William Alanson White, superintendent of the Government Hospital for the Insane in Washington, D.C., confessed in 1916 that, "Praecox is nothing more than a waste-basket into which we throw all the cases we know nothing about."[49] And perhaps most revealing are the comments made by Charles Macfie Campbell, the director of the Boston Psychiatric Hospital, in a personal letter from December 1934:

> I do not believe that there is such a thing as schizophrenia, and on the other hand I think it is the most important topic for investigation in our field. To put it another way, I do not think there is a *disease* schizophrenia, but, on the other hand, it is useful at this period to have some group term for an extremely large number of cases of mental disorder of the more serious type . . . From the point of view of one who is angling for money to support his work, it is a great advantage to believe in a specific disease . . . he can specify the general group of forces within which the real cause is to be found like the nigger in the woodpile, he can budget the funds necessary for the investigation and even suggest certain time limits within which the nigger will be discovered, the woodpile will be safe, schizophrenia will be eliminated, the taxpayers' burden will be alleviated.[50]

Determinations of psychosis were just as capricious later in the century. In 1970 one physician actually admitted in print, "It is well known that the more we like a patient, the less likely we are to place him on the psychotic end of the psychiatric spectrum."[51]

Historians of psychosis and schizophrenia tend to skip these messy realities of how diagnoses are actually made in the real world and focus on elite literary discourses about how determinations of psychosis or dementia praecox or schizophrenia *should be made* in practice. Their master narrative continues to be one of scientific progress and continuity: "The history of schizophrenia is actually the history of the psychoses in general," claimed German psychiatrist Hans W. Gruhle (1880–1958) in 1932, adding,

> out of the whole of what was called mental disease at the beginning of psychiatric science . . . insanity, mental derangement, madness, derangement of mind, alienation . . . the exogenous psychoses were increasingly split off, and schizophrenia remained the actual core of insanity."[52]

An identical historical narrative was offered in 2015 by William T. Carpenter, Jr., (1936–) a prominent schizophrenia researcher and current editor-in-chief of the journal *Schizophrenia Bulletin*: "Schizophrenia remains a diagnosis of exclusion where other causes of psychosis take precedent."[53]

However, this master narrative was challenged as an unsubstantiated "myth" by German Berrios, Rogelio Luque, and José M. Villagrán in a persuasive polemic in 2003. What they term the "continuity hypothesis" is regarded as a presentist assumption that schizophrenia is a *"real, recognizable, unitary and stable* object of inquiry" throughout history. They reject the narrative that "schizophrenia has always existed, and in the nineteenth and twentieth centuries, alienists have polished away its blemishes and impurities, culminating in the DSM-IV definition which can therefore be considered as a real, recognizable, unitary and stable object of inquiry." Instead, they offer their "discontinuity hypothesis": "The history of schizophrenia can best be described as the history of a set of research programmes running in parallel rather than serialism and each based on a different concept of disease, of mental symptoms and of mind."[54] Such discontinuity reigns today as psychosis and schizophrenia are defined and researched differently within parallel universes exploring biological hypotheses,[55] factor analytic studies of symptoms from rating scales,[56] and even philosophical expositions on the phenomenology of schizophrenia as an "ipseity" disorder (a disorder of the experience of the self) – just to name a few.[57]

The first decade of the twenty-first century has been marked by a tendency to employ the term "chronic psychosis" instead of schizophrenia. This is an acknowledgment that psychosis, transient or persistent, cuts across diagnostic categories. Schizophrenia, it seems, is finally on its way out as a category for researchers, but is still in *DSM-5* (as part of a "schizophrenia spectrum") to be used by clinicians. Schizophrenia has been factor-analyzed into five "domains" of psychopathology – hallucinations; delusions; disorganized thought/speech; disorganized or abnormal motor behavior; and negative symptoms), and it is suggested that a *DSM-5* diagnosis should be made by rating items from 0 (not present) to 4 (present and severe) along eight "dimensions of psychosis" (the five for schizophrenia in addition to those for cognitive impairment, mania and depression).[58] Rating scales are all the rage.[59]

Psychosis is severity. Severity is a score. Indeed, it must be, even though nothing is really *counted* by rating scales. Our "trust in numbers . . . is about the containment of subjectivity . . . the replacement of opinion by calculation," observed historian Theodore Porter.[60] Rating scales are affectations of objectivity, diversions from the professionally embarrassing language of "praecox feelings" reported by clinicians while in the presence of certain patients. They are instruments of liminality. It is often forgotten that rating scales are the reflections or *end-products* of subjective clinical experience and theory, not objective starting points for the generation and validation of truly countable claims. "Rating scales are not really suitable for exploring a new field of knowledge," cautioned Max Hamilton, the creator of two of the most widely used scales for depression and anxiety.[61] Will clinicians use these rating scales, or will they just roll their eyes and groan? And will dimensions of psychosis save science from the schizophrenia heuristic? Time will tell.

Since the turn of the current century a revolt against madness as deviance, disorder and disease has arisen in the mental health field, led mostly by British psychologists and members of the general population who are weary of their confinement in the discourses of the medical model. Madness is openly used as a term to bridge psychosis and human nature, and we are told that madness has now been explained.[62] Psychosis and schizophrenia are now understood as well. They are merely attributions that imply illness, and illness is only one way among many of interpreting the experience of hearing voices or feeling paranoid.[63]

Madness has returned.

Notes

1 Between 1905 and 1915 pathographies of Jesus were published by physicians Georg Lomer (1877–1957), a German occultist and Ariosophist who argued in 1905 (writing under the name George de Loosten) that Jesus was a degenerate *Mischling* (of mixed blood or race); William Hirsch, a German psychiatrist and eugenicist who argued in 1910 that "Christ was sexually impotent" in addition to being insane; and Charles Binet-Sanglé (1868–1941), a neo-Lamarckian eugenicist and author of a 1918 book entitled *Le haras humain* (*The Human Stud Farm*) that appeared after his four-volume *La folie de Jésus* (1908–1915). All agreed Jesus was a degenerate and exhibited paranoid delusions of grandeur, auditory and visual hallucinations, and bizarre behavior. Binet-Sanglé added the "hebephrenic crisis" due to "pubertal autointoxication" and referred to Jesus as a tubercular "theomegalomaniac." A rather unsophisticated refutation of these three authors can be found in the 1913 doctoral thesis of physician Albert Schweitzer (1875–1965), *The Psychiatric Study of Jesus: Exposition and Criticism*, trans. Charles R. Joy (Boston, MA: The Beacon Press, 1948). A more detailed summary of these and other pathographers can be found in Walter E. Bundy, *The Psychic Health of Jesus* (New York: Macmillan, 1922). See also "The Christomaniacs" chapter in Theodore Ziolkowski, *Fictional Transfigurations of Jesus* (Eugene, Oregon: Wipf and Stack, 2002), 98–141.

2 Richard Noll, "Jung the Leontocephalus [1992]," in *Jung in Contexts: A Reader*, ed. Paul Bishop (London and New York: Routledge, 1999), 51–91; Richard Noll, *The Jung Cult: Origins of a Charismatic Movement* (Princeton, NJ: Princeton University Press, 1994); Richard Noll, *The Aryan Christ: the Secret Life of Carl Jung* (New York: Random House, 1997); Wouter Hanegraaff, "The Great War of the Soul: Divine and Human Madness in Carl Gustav Jung's *Liber Novus*," in *Krise und religiöser Wahn-Sinn un 1900: Religiöse Devianz zwischen Psychopathologie und Befreiung/Crisis and Religious Madness around 1900: Religious Deviance between Abnormal Psychology and Liberation*, ed. Lutz Greisiger, Alexander van der Haven and Sebastian Schüler (Würzburg: Ergon Verlag, forthcoming); Carrie B. Dohe, *Jung's Wandering Archetype: Race and Religion in Analytical Psychology* (London: Routledge, 2016); Ernest Jones, "The God Complex: The Belief That One is God and the Resulting Character Traits [1913]," in Ernest Jones, *Essays in Applied Psychoanalysis, Volume II* (New York: International Universities Press, 1964), 247–261. Marked changes in Jung's mental state and behavior had been observed and discussed by those who knew him for at least a year prior to the repetitive visions of waves of blood flooding Europe in October 1913 that made him fear he was being menaced by a psychosis. Ten months before Jung's first unbidden blood vision and before he began his deliberately induced mental imagery/inner sense cultivation experiments on 12 November 1913, Jones wrote to Freud on 29 December 1912: "This week I hope to finish my paper on God-men, in which there is the opportunity of saying some sweet things, quite indirectly to Jung; it is very enjoyable." Sigmund Freud and Ernest Jones, *The Complete Correspondence of Sigmund Freud and Ernest Jones, 1908–1939*, ed. R. Andrew Paskauskas (Cambridge, MA: Harvard University Press, 1995), 189 (letter 112).

3 Anton Boisen, *Out of the Depths* (New York: Harper and Brothers, 1960); Anton Boisen, *Exploration of the Inner World: A Study of Mental Disorder and Religious Experiences* (New York: Willett Clark and Company, 1936); Susan E. Myers-Shirk, *Helping the Good Shepherd: Pastoral Counselors in a Psychotherapeutic Culture, 1925–1975* (Baltimore, MD: Johns Hopkins University Press, 2009), 16–39. Using his own psychotic episodes as a source of insight, in 1925 Boisen developed what is arguably the first structured interview instrument specifically

343

designed for rating the phenomenology of schizophrenic experiences and behavior, the Schizophrenic Thinking: Psychiatric Examination [Content of Thought] questionnaire. The presence or absence of phenomena such as "type of onset," "sense of mystery," or "sense of peril" were checked off on scoring forms, but there was no quantitative score. See R. C. Powell, "Anton T. Boisen's 'Psychiatric Examination: Content of Thought' (c. 1925–31): An Attempt to Grasp the Meaning of Mental Disorder," *Psychiatry* 40 (1977), 369–375. Boisen's autobiographical accounts of his own madness are included in the programmatic extension of his phenomenological "first-person account" approach to understanding psychosis in the posthumously published volume by the New York State Psychiatric Institute experimental psychologist Carney Landis (1897–1962), *Varieties of Psychopathological Experience* (New York: Holt, Rinehart and Winston, 1964). It is a compendium of published "descriptions of the nature of the 'inner' experience that went on during an episode that others have called a psychosis" (p. xvi).

4 Roy Porter, *Madness: A Brief History* (Oxford: Oxford University Press, 2002); Andrew Scull, *Madness: A Very Short Introduction* (Oxford: Oxford University Press, 2011); Andrew Scull, *Madness in Civilization: A Cultural History of Insanity from the Bible to Freud, From the Madhouse to Modern Medicine* (Princeton, NJ: Princeton University Press, 2015); Petteri Pietikainen, *Madness: A History* (London: Routledge, 2015). While most are critical of his theories, all tend to follow the usage of "madness" by Michel Foucault (1926–1984) since 1961 as Unreason and deviance. All acknowledge the medicalization of older religious or supernatural models of madness.

5 Yulia Ustinova, "Madness into Memory: *Mania* and *Mnēmē* in Greek Culture," *Scripta Classica Israelica* 31 (2002): 109–131; Ruth Padel, *Whom the Gods Destroy: Elements of Greek and Tragic Madness* (Princeton, NJ: Princeton University Press, 1995). The lineage of "divine madness" from Plato's *Phaedrus* to the Renaissance is traced in Wouter Hanegraaff, "The Platonic Frenzies in Marsilio Ficino," in *Myths, Martyrs and Modernity: Studies in the History of Religious in Honour of Jan N. Bremmer*, ed. Jitse Dijkstra, Justin Kroesen and Yme Kuiper (Leiden and Boston, MA: Brill, 2010), 553–567; for the survival of this ancient framing of madness into sixteenth-century Europe, see M. A. Screech, "Good Madness in Christendom," in *The Anatomy of Madness: Essays in the History of Psychiatry. Volume I. People and Ideas*, ed. W. F. Bynum, Roy Porter and Michael Shepherd (London and New York: Tavistock, 1981), 25–39; and especially H. C. Erik Midelfort, *A History of Madness in Sixteenth-Century Germany* (Stanford, CA: Stanford University Press, 1999).

6 Peter Homans, *Jung in Context: Modernity and the Making of a Psychology* (Chicago and London: University of Chicago Press, 1979), 87.

7 George Devereux, "A Sociological Theory of Schizophrenia," *Psychoanalytic Review* 26 (1939): 338.

8 D. Rawlings, B., Williams, N. Haslam, G. Claridge, "Taxometric Analysis Supports a Dimensional Latent Structure for Schizotypy," *Personality and Individual Differences* 44 (2008): 1670.

9 Roland Littlewood and Simon Dein, "Did Christianity Lead to Schizophrenia? Psychosis, Psychology and Self-Reference," *Transcultural Psychiatry* 50 (2013): 397–420.

10 John J. McGrath, et al., "Psychotic Experiences in the General Population: A Cross-National Analysis Based on 31 261 Respondents From 18 Countries," *JAMA Psychiatry* 72 (2015): 697–705; Daphne Kounali, et al., "Common *versus* Psychopathology-Specific Risk Factors for Psychotic Experiences and Depression During Adolescence," *Psychological Medicine* 44 (2014): 2557–2566; Frank Larøi, Andrea Raballo and Vaughan Bell, "Psychosis-like Experiences in Non-Clinical Populations," in *The Assessment of Psychosis: A Reference Book and Rating Scales for Research and Practice*, ed. Flavie Waters and Massoud Stephane (New York and London: Routledge, 2015), 92–111.

Psychosis-like experiences is a problematic term with conceptual overlaps with other phenomena that researchers look for, and find, in the undiagnosed general population: *schizotypal traits, attenuated psychotic symptoms, near-psychotic experience, subthreshold psychotic experiences, at-risk mental states, psychoticism, anomalous perceptual experiences, delusional ideation* and *magical thinking*. These conditions are found through the use of more than 120 different rating scales, each reflecting an implicit theory of their hypothetical construct via item selection and composition, and which by their subjective nature generate considerable error due to bias on the parts of both the observer/rater (no matter how well "trained") and the respondent, or the respondent as self-rater. *Rating scales are the fundamental weakness of almost all clinical research, including factor analytic studies that are used to deconstruct psychosis. Rating is not counting. It is not measurement. It is grading.* This "measurement problem" inherent in the use of rating scales is, understandably, rarely acknowledged in the publications of researchers who use them. A refreshing exception is the blunt admission that rating scales are an "ever-present nightmare for psychopathology" research by Mark Lenzenweger, *Schizotypy and Schizophrenia: The View From Experimental Psychopathology* (New York and London: The Guilford Press, 2010), 46–49. Additionally, ". . . psychiatric scales are no more than grading labels, and that the 'dimensions' they purport to 'measure' are no more than qualities stretched out along arbitrary ranges," note German E. Berrios and Ivana S. Marková, "Is the Concept of 'Dimension' Applicable to Psychiatric Objects?", *World Psychiatry* 12 (2013): 77. It is important to remember that, "Instruments cannot be understood as black boxes, meaning neutral tools that require no further discussion; understanding their varied roles, requires a grasp of the goals, methods, and beliefs within which they have been developed and used." Thomas Sturm and Mitchell G. Ash, "Roles of Instruments in Psychological Research," *History of Psychology* 8 (2005): 7. Also, "Scientists' tools are not neutral . . . the mind has been recreated in their image." Gerd Gigerenzer, "From Tools to Theories: A Heuristic of Discovery in Cognitive Psychology," *Psychological Review* 98 (1991): 264.

11 Erwin Ackerknecht, "The Shaman and Primitive Psychopathology in General [1943]," in Erwin Ackerknecht, *Medicine and Ethnology: Selected Essays*, ed. H. H. Walser and H. M. Koelbing (Baltimore, MD: Johns Hopkins University Press, 1971), 61.

12 Justin L. Barrett, *Cognitive Science, Religion and Theology: From Human Minds to Divine Minds* (West Conshohonken, PA: Templeton Press, 2011); Jesse M. Bering, "The Folk Psychology of Souls," *Behavioral and Brain Sciences* 29 (2006): 453–462; Scott Atran, *In Gods We Trust: The Evolutionary Landscape of Religion* (Oxford: Oxford University Press, 2002); T. M. Luhrmann, "Hallucinations and Sensory Overrides," *Annual Review of Anthropology* 40 (2011): 71–85.

13 Susan A. Clancy, *Abducted: How People Come to Believe They Were Kidnapped By Aliens* (Cambridge: Harvard University Press, 2005).

14 Paolo Fusar-Poli, S. Borgwardt, A. Bechdolf, et al., "The Psychosis High-Risk State: a Comprehensive State-of-the-Art Review," *JAMA Psychiatry* 70 (2013): 107–120; Nil Kaymaz, M. Drukker, R. Lieb, et al., "Do Subthreshold Psychotic Experiences Predict Clinical Outcomes in Unselected Non-Help-Seeking Population-Based Samples? A Systematic Review and Meta-Analysis, Enriched with New Results," *Psychological Medicine* 42 (2012): 2239–2253.

15 Henri Ellenberger, "The Concept of Maladie Créatrice" [1964]", in *Beyond the Unconscious: Essays of Henri Ellenberger in the History of Psychiatry*, ed. Mark Micale (Princeton: Princeton University Press, 1993), 328–340.

16 Ackerknecht, "The Shaman," 59–60.

17 Richard Noll, "Mental Imagery Cultivation as a Cultural Phenomenon: The Role of Visions in Shamanism," *Current Anthropology* 26, (1985): 443–461; Barbara Newman, "What Did It Mean to Say 'I Saw'? The Clash Between Theory and Practice in Medieval Visionary Culture," *Speculum* 80 (2005): 1–43; T. M. Luhrmann and Rachel Morgain, "Prayer as Inner Sense Cultivation: An Attentional Learning Theory of Spiritual Experience," *Ethos* 40, no. 4 (2012): 359–389; Frank Larøi, T. M. Luhrmann, Vaughan Bell et al., "Culture and Hallucinations: Overview and Future Directions," *Schizophrenia Bulletin* 40 (2014), S213–S220; William A. Christian, Jr. and Gabor Klaniczay (ed.), *The "Vision Thing:" Studying Divine Intervention* (Budapest: Collegium Budapest Institute for Advanced Study, Workshop Series No. 18, 2009); Ann Taves, *Religious Experience Reconsidered: A Building-Block Approach to the Study of Religion and Other Special Things* (Princeton: Princeton University Press, 1999); Ann Taves and Egil Asprem, "Experience as Event: Event Cognition and the Study of (Religious) Experience," *Religion, Brain and Behavior* (forthcoming); Robert N. McCauley, *Why Religion is Natural and Science Is Not* (Oxford: Oxford University Press, 2011); Marco Bernini and Angela Woods, "Interdisciplinarity of Cognitive Integration: Auditory Verbal Hallucinations as a Case Study," *Wiley Interdisciplinary Reviews: Cognitive Science* 5 (2014): 603–612; Jijian

Voronka, "Making Britney Bipolar: Proliferating Psychiatric Diagnosis Through Tabloid Media," *Radical Psychology* 7 (2008): 1–19; Brenda LeFrancois, Robert Menzies, Geoffrey Reaume, eds., *Mad Matters: A Critical Reader in Canadian Mad Studies* (Toronto: Canadian Scholars Press, 2013).

18 German E. Berrios, "Historical Aspects of the Psychoses: Nineteenth-Century Issues," *British Medical* Bulletin 43 (1987): 484–489; German E. Berrios and M. Dominic Beer, "The Notation of Unitary Psychosis: A Conceptual History," *History of Psychiatry* 5 (1994): 13–36; M. Dominic Beer, "Psychosis: From Mental Disorder to Disease Concept," *History of Psychiatry* 6 (1995): 177–200; M. Dominic Beer, "The Importance of the Social and the Intellectual Contexts in a Discussion of the History of the Concept of Psychosis," *Psychological Medicine* 25 (1995): 317–321; M. Dominic Beer, "Psychosis: A History of the Concept," *Comprehensive Psychiatry* 37 (1996): 273–291. Werner Janzarik, "Der Psychose-Begriff und die Qualität des Psychotischen," *Nervenarzt* 74 (2003): 3–11; German E. Berrios, Rogelio Luque, and José M. Villagrán, "Schizophrenia: A Conceptual History," *International Journal of Psychology and Psychological Therapy* 3 (2003): 111–140; Martin Bürgy, "The Concept of Psychosis: Historical and Phenomenological Aspects," *Schizophrenia Bulletin* 34 (2008): 1200–1210; Edward Shorter, *A Historical Dictionary of Psychiatry* (Oxford: Oxford University Press, 2005), 238–245; Simon McCarthy Jones, "History of Concepts about Psychosis: What Was It, What Is It?," in *The Assessment of Psychosis,* ed. Waters and Stephane, 3–16.

19 The end of an era that spanned decades is enshrined in Mark Micale and Roy Porter, eds., *Discovering the History of Psychiatry* (Oxford: Oxford University Press, 1994).

20 M. Dominic Beer, "The Dichotomies: Psychoses/Neuroses and Functional/Organic: A Historical Perspective," *History of Psychiatry* 7 (1996): 231–255; "The Endogenous Psychoses: A Conceptual History," *History of Psychiatry* 7 (1996) 1–29.

21 Wolfgang Gaebel and Jürgen Zielasek, "Focus on Psychosis," *Dialogues in Clinical Neuroscience* 17 (2015): 9–18.

22 Bürgy, "Concept of Psychosis," 1203.

23 Each *DSM* glossary entry since 1980 begins with a very revealing thesis statement that succinctly redefines "psychotic" according to changing fashions of medical certainty/humility: "A term indicating gross impairment in reality testing" (*DSM-III*, 1980, 367); "Gross impairment in reality testing and the creation of a new reality" (*DSM-III-R*, 1987, 404); "The term has historically received a number of different definitions, none of which has achieved universal acceptance" (*DSM-IV*, 1994, 770; *DSM-IV-TR*, 2000, 827); "Features characterized by delusions, hallucinations, and formal thought disorder" (*DSM-5*, 2013, 827). New in *DSM-5*, "psychoticism" is defined as "Exhibiting a wide range of culturally incongruent odd, eccentric or unusual behaviors and cognitions, including both process [e.g., perception and dissociation] and content [e.g., beliefs]" (2013, 827–828). Psychoticism is one of five personality trait domains offered as an alternative dimensional rating scale for personality disorders. In *ICD-10* (1994), "'Psychotic' has been retained as a convenient descriptive term . . . (Psychotic) simply indicates the presence of hallucinations, delusions, or a limited number of severe abnormalities of behavior, such as gross excitement and overactivity, marked psychomotor retardation, and catatonic behavior," World Health Organization, *The ICD-10 Classification of Mental and Behavioural Disorders: Classification and Diagnostic Guidelines* (Geneva: World Health Organization, 1994), 10.

24 Edward Shorter, *A History of Psychiatry: From the Era of the Asylum to the Age of Prozac* (New York: John Wiley and Sons, 1997.

25 German E. Berrios, *The History of Mental Symptoms: Descriptive Psychopathology Since the Nineteenth Century* (Cambridge: Cambridge University Press, 1996), 2.

26 Carol A. Tamminga, Paul J. Sirovatka, Darrel A. Regier, and Jim van Os, eds, *Deconstructing Psychosis: Refining the Research Agenda for DSM-5* (Washington, DC: American Psychiatric Press, 2010); Gaebel and Zielasek, "Focus on Psychosis."

27 German E. Berrios, "Delirium and Cognate States," in *A History of Clinical Psychiatry: The Origin and History of Psychiatric Disorders,* ed. German Berrios and Roy Porter (London and New Brunswick, NJ: The Athalone Press, 1995), 3.

28 Werner Janzarik, "Wandlungen des Schizophreniebegriffes," *Nervenarzt* 49 (1978): 133–139; Werner Janzarik, "Kurt Schneider and the Heidelberg School of Psychiatry," *History of*

Psychiatry 9 (1998): 241–252; Marc-Antoine Crocq, "French Perspectives on Psychiatric Classification," *Dialogues in Clinical Neuroscience* 17 (2015): 51–57. Kraepelin has been widely misunderstood as "brain-centric" when in fact his commitment to systemic or "whole body" disease processes for the psychoses makes him "body-centric." See Eric J. Engstrom and Kenneth S. Kendler, "Emil Kraepelin: Icon and Reality," *American Journal of Psychiatry* 172 (2015): 1190–1196.

29 For an excellent summary of such radically rational treatments, see Mary de Young, *Encyclopedia of Asylum Therapeutics, 1750–1950s* (Jefferson, North Carolina: McFarland and Company, 2015). The report of failed organotherapy is in Karl Willmans, "Schizophrenia," *Bulletin of the Massachusetts Department of Mental Diseases* 7 (August 1923): 22.

30 Carl Scharfetter, "Psychische Vulnerabilität—Canstatt 1841," *Nervenarzt* 58 (1987): 527; Martin Bürgy, "The Origin of the Concept of Psychosis: Canstatt 1841," *Psychopathology* 45 (2012): 133–134.

31 However, "Used very loosely for mental phenomena, states of consciousness, thoughts, ideas, &c, German alienists restrict the meaning of psychose (sing.) to healthy states of mind" Daniel Hack Tuke, *A Dictionary of Psychological Medicine, Vol II* (Philadelphia: P. Blakiston, Son & Co., 1892), 1025.

32 Carl Wernicke, *Grundriss der Psychiatrie in klinischen Vorlesungen. Zweite revidierte Auflage* (Leipzig: Verlag von George Thieme, 1906). The first complete English translation with extensive editorial commentary is Robert Miller and John Dennison, eds, *An Outline of Psychiatry in Clinical Lectures: The Lectures of Carl Wernicke* (Heidelberg and New York: Springer, 2015).

33 Different lineages are offered in the following: Christoph Mundt and Henning Sass, eds, *Für und Wieder die Einheitspsychose* (Stuttgart: Thieme, 1992); German E. Berrios and M. Dominic Beer, "Unitary Psychosis," in *A History of Clinical Psychiatry: The Origin and History of Psychiatric Disorders*, ed. Berrios and Porter, 313–335; Edward Shorter, *A Historical Dictionary of Psychiatry* (Oxford: Oxford University Press, 2005), 294–295.

34 Edward Shorter, *What Psychiatry Left Out of the DSM-5: Historical Mental Disorders Today* (New York and London: Routledge, 2015), 147–159.

35 Kenneth S. Kendler, "The Transformation of American Psychiatric Nosology at the Dawn of the Twentieth Century," *Molecular Psychiatry* 21 (2016): 152–158.

36 Richard Noll, *American Madness: The Rise and Fall of Dementia Praecox* (Cambridge: Harvard University Press, 2011), 49–73.

37 T. R. Denning and G. E. Berrios, "Introduction to 'The Significance of Symptom-Complexes in Psychiatry' by Alfred Hoche [1912]," (Classic Text No. 7), *History of Psychiatry* 2 (1991): 329–333; Noll, *American Madness*, 313.

38 Andrew Abbott, "The Emergence of American Psychiatry, 1880–1930" (PhD diss., University of Chicago, 1982), 328–329.

39 Noll, *American Madness*, 148–193. For a discussion of how the unitary psychosis idea was revived in postwar Germany see Yazan Abu Ghazal, "Perspectivity in Psychiatric Research: The Psychopathology of Schizophrenia in Postwar Germany (1955–1961)," *Medicine Studies* 4 (2014): 103–111.

40 A useful historical and clinical summary is threaded throughout Matthew M. Kurtz, *Schizophrenia and Its Treatment: Where Is the Progress?* (Oxford and New York: Oxford University Press, 2015).

41 See, for example, the co-winner of the 1975 National Book Award for Science, Silvano Arieti, *Interpretation of Schizophrenia*, 2nd edn (New York: Basic Books, 1974). Arieti argued that mothers were clearly the cause of schizophrenia in 25 percent of his case histories.

42 Noll, *American Madness*, 166–188.

43 Hans W. Gruhle, "Geschichtliches," in *Handbuch der Geisteskrankheiten, Band IX, Spezieller Teil V, Die Schizophrenie*, ed. Oswald Bumke (Berlin: Verlag von Julius Springer, 1932), 22.

44 Abbott, "The Emergence of American Psychiatry," 410.

45 Charles L. Dana, *Textbook of Nervous Diseases and Psychiatry: For the Use of Students and Practitioners of Medicine, 6th revised and enlarged edition* (New York: William Wood and Company, 1904), vii, 628. Kraepelinian classification and nomenclature first entered American medical textbooks the previous year via a special insert by Adolf Meyer, "A Review of Recent Problems

of Psychiatry," embedded in Archibald Church and Frederick Peterson, *Nervous and Mental Diseases, fourth edition, thoroughly revised* (Philadelphia, New York and London: W.B. Saunders & Co., 1903), 650–688.

46 Kraepelin and his colleagues at the University Clinic in Munich began dropping dementia praecox as a diagnosis in favor of schizophrenia as early as the last quarter of 1921. In the United States, at least in publications, schizophrenia became the preferred term starting in 1927. See Noll, *American Madness*, 261–264, 271. The year 1927 is also cited as the point at which published cases of multiple personality declined markedly, such persons now "seen" differently by clinicians as cases of schizophrenia as they followed Bleuler's emphasis on dissociation (*Spaltung*, or "splitting") as the core phenomenological feature of his disease concept. See Milton Rosenbaum, "The Role of the Term Schizophrenia in the Decline of Multiple Personality," *Archives of General Psychiatry* 37 (1980): 1383–1385. For a superb summary of viewpoints as this transition was in progress, see the useful English translations of primary German texts in James V. May, "The Dementia Praecox-Schizophrenia Problem," *Psychiatric Quarterly* 6 (1932): 40–88.

47 For a fascinating meditation on "the schizophrenic" as a liminal anomaly, see Robert J. Barrett, "The 'Schizophrenic' and the Liminal Persona in Modern Society," *Culture, Medicine and Psychiatry* 22 (1998), 465–494. This is a review of Louis A. Sass, *Madness and Modernism: Insanity in the Light of Modern Art, Literature and Thought* (New York: Basic Books, 1992). See also Angela Woods, *The Sublime Object of Psychiatry: Schizophrenia in Clinical and Cultural Theory* (Oxford: Oxford University Press, 2011).

48 Runge's comments follow Gershom H. Hill, "Dementia Praecox," *Proceedings of the Medico-Psychological Association* 7 (1900): 288.

49 White's comment follows L. Vernon Briggs, "Environmental Origin of Mental Disease in Certain Families," *American Journal of Insanity* 73 (October 1916): 240.

50 Excerpts from Campbell's letter are found in Gerald Grob, *The Inner World of American Psychiatry 1890–1940: Selected Correspondence* (New Brunswick, NJ: Rutgers University Press, 1985), 48–49.

51 Basil Jackson, "The Revised Diagnostic and Statistical Manual of the American Psychiatric Association," *American Journal of Psychiatry* 127 (1970): 67.

52 Gruhle, "Geschichtliches,"1.

53 William T. Carpenter, Jr., "Foreword," in Waters and Stephane, *The Assessment of Psychosis*, xviii. See also William T. Carpenter, Jr., "Schizophrenia: Disease, Syndrome or Dimensions?," *Family Process* 46 (2007): 199–206.

54 Berrios, Lugue and Villagrán, "Schizophrenia: A Conceptual History," 112, 111. This point is intelligently illustrated in Kieran McNally, *A Critical History of Schizophrenia* (London: Palgrave Macmillan, 2016).

55 Michael S. Ritsner and Irving I. Gottesman, "The Schizophrenia Construct After 100 Years of Challenges," in *Handbook of Schizophrenia Spectrum Disorders, Volume I*, ed. Michael S. Ritsner (Berlin: Springer, 2011), 1–44; Brett B. Clementz, et al., "Identification of Distinct Psychosis Biotypes Using Brain-Based Biomarkers," *American Journal of Psychiatry* 173 (2016): 373–384.

56 Richard P. Bentall, "The Search for Elusive Structure: A Promiscuous Realist Case for Researching Specific Psychotic Experiences Such as Hallucinations," *Schizophrenia Bulletin* 40 (Supplement no 4) (2014): S198–S204. Factor analytic studies of symptoms are touted as the dimensional path beyond categories of mental disorders. Bentall included a diagram of a "speculative hierarchical classification of psychopathology" based on the three best factor analytic models of symptoms. It is a wedding cake chart topped by a general psychopathology or "P factor" common to all psychopathology, which branches down into a layer of three clusters of dimensions of "psychosis," "internalizing" symptoms and "externalizing" symptoms, and then into the next level of a "five factor psychosis" model of positive symptoms, negative symptoms, disorganization, depression, mania. It bears a remarkable similarity to the pre-Kraepelinian consensus of 19th century alienists who classified insanity according to unitary psychosis (Bentall's P factor, to them, "insanity") and its three forms: dementia (primary and terminal, defined by cognitive symptoms); melancholia (a depression of activity); and mania (an excess of activity). So much for the triumph of statistical over clinical prediction . . . the old asylum doctors may have gotten it right the first time.

57 Josef Parnas, "Philosophical and Phenomenological Perspectives on Psychosis," in Waters and Stephane, *The Assessment of Psychosis,* 18–43.

58 Steven Heckers et al., "Structure of the Psychotic Disorders Classification in DSM-5," *Schizophrenia Research* 150 (2013): 11–14.

59 Thomas Verner Moore (1877–1969) of the Catholic University of America in Washington, D.C., was first psychiatric researcher to create quantitative symptom rating scales and use factor analysis to deconstruct psychosis. "Our method is without precedent in psychiatry," Moore correctly stated in his pioneering monograph, and its goal was "the dismemberment of the manifestations of insanity into a group of symptoms and the empirical synthesis of these symptoms by a mathematical technique." Thomas Verner Moore, *The Essential Psychoses and Their Fundamental Syndromes. Studies in Psychology and Psychiatry from the Catholic University of America. Volume III. Number 1* (Baltimore, MD: The Williams and Wilkins Company, 1933), ix, 30. No one used these methods again until the late 1940s. See Roger Blashfield, *The Classification of Psychopathology: Neo-Kraepelinian and Quantitative Approaches* (Berlin and New York: Springer, 1984, 186–205; and Maurice Lorr, C. James Klett and Douglas M. McNair, *Syndromes of Psychosis* (New York: The Macmillian Company, 1963). Moore was a polymath. He was a Roman Catholic priest, an experimental psychologist who had worked under Wilhelm Wundt (1832–1920) in Leipzig and Oswald Külpe (1862–1915) in Munich, a psychiatrist who had worked under Emil Kraepelin in Munich and Adolf Meyer in Baltimore, and (later) a hermetic Carthusian monk who spent his last years in total silence while tinkering with the application of factor analysis to the study of mystical experiences.

60 Theodore Porter, "Funny Numbers," *Culture Unbound* 4 (2012): 595.

61 Max Hamilton, "Editorial: The Role of Rating Scales in Psychiatry," *Psychological Medicine* 6 (1976): 347.

62 Richard Bentall, *Madness Explained: Psychosis and Human Nature* (London: Penguin, 2003).

63 British Psychological Society, *Understanding Psychosis and Schizophrenia: Why People Sometimes Hear Voices, Believe Things Others Find Strange, Or Appear Out of Touch With Reality, And What Can Help,* ed. Anne Cooke (Leicester, UK: British Psychological Society Division of Clinical Psychology, 2014).

19

SOMATIC TREATMENTS

Jonathan Sadowsky

The presence of this chapter is a philosophical mistake.[1] The principle that the history of psychiatric treatments can be divided between those that are "somatic" and those that are "talk" is deeply lodged in the history of psychiatry, but reflects a confusion. Advocates of "somatic" treatments, often also referred to as "biological" treatments, are often styled as realists or materialists, who have little patience for the healing of the mind, the soul, or other immaterial things of dubious, or at least epiphenomenal, existence. What is striking about this view—usually expressed implicitly—is how much it owes to, and reproduces, a dualism it seeks to overturn. In a truly materialist world-view, everything is physical, including talk and the mind. When a therapist makes an interpretation or offers advice, she is moving molecules to send sound waves through the air, where they are received and interpreted by the brain of her patient. The brain then changes, either modestly, or dramatically. To a true materialist, talk therapy is as physical or biological as any other. Having a separate chapter on "somatic" treatments, then, reproduces a cultural artifact embedded in psychiatry. I hope also to use the occasion to question it.

The confusion, of course, is rooted in the mind/body dualism that is so deeply ingrained in Western thought. It runs too deeply in Western "common sense" for historians to ignore it. The *perception* that talk therapies differ fundamentally from physical ones is of deep significance for the history of psychiatry. It is also possible for historians to treat the two streams separately, for although there is no question that they have influenced each other, the belief that they are different has meant that to a certain extent they have separate intellectual trajectories. But it remains important to keep in mind that the distinction is misleading, because it is linked to both scientific and moral evaluations that are prejudicial. For example, proponents of somatic treatments for mental illness have frequently assumed that those treatments are more scientific or more medical than talk therapies. But while any given somatic treatment might, in principle, be shown to be more clinically effective than a particular talk therapy, there is no reason to treat somatic treatments as inherently more scientific. Similarly, opponents of somatic treatments often work from the assumption that those treatments are less humane or more abusive than talk therapies. But while any given somatic treatment might be shown to be abusive, harmful, or dehumanizing, it is not so simply by virtue of being a somatic treatment. Particular "talk" interventions can be harmful and abusive as well.

The use of relatively direct interventions on the body to treat madness is both longstanding, and cross-culturally common. Modern psychiatry has expanded the purview of what counts as a mental illness, a process that has included both the proliferation of new diagnostic categories and the expansion of the boundaries of old ones, such as depression, to cover more situations.[2] This medicalization of life's distress has been driven not just by the psychiatric profession, but also by pharmaceutical companies, patients and their families, even if all actors in the process do not hold equal power.[3] It has occasioned much debate, as well as wry criticism of diagnostic manuals, which have been subject to significant critique and even satire, but are nevertheless extremely influential. But regardless of this debate, the treatment of madness in widely recognized forms, such as florid psychosis or extreme melancholia, are and have been considered part of medicine's mission, cross-culturally and since antiquity. They were, for example, addressed in the Hippocratic corpus. So the attempts by critics of psychiatry such as Thomas Szasz to sever psychiatry from medicine run against not only recent psychiatric entrepreneurship, but also long and widely held precedents.[4] And, as madness has been widely recognized as a medical problem, it has always been treated with both seemingly physical means as drugs and other bodily interventions, as well as spiritual, moral, behavioral, ritualistic—all the means we might now classify as "talk."

There have been periodic attempts to reduce mental illness to the somatic, or to the purely "mental" (whatever that may mean), or to the "social." In antiquity, for example, Scull observes that "Even physicians, wedded as they were to organic accounts of mental disturbance, could not at times escape recognizing that madness was defined socially, and was more than simply a bodily condition."[5] Conversely, and quite a bit more recently, some radical psychiatrists and critics of psychiatry of the middle twentieth century have sought to portray madness as a mainly social phenomenon.[6] This was a conceit that probably contributed, dialectically, to the new biological reductionism of the Age of Prozac. These attempts to locate madness solely in one realm or the other are likely to continue. They have little basis in either logic or evidence—which is why, in practice, most societies have treated madness eclectically.

The historiography of psychiatry has shown vividly how the present shapes the representation of the past. When the historiography was nascent, psychoanalytic approaches were popular among clinicians, and the radical psychiatry and antipsychiatry movements had broad cultural followings. These movements tended to be more skeptical of somatic treatments, when not outright hostile, and this was reflected in the rendering of the history.[7] With DSM-III—with its purging of psychoanalytic concepts—and the "Age of Prozac," somatic treatments came into both clinical and cultural vogue, though as famous Prozac commentator Peter Kramer noted at the time, the enthusiasm for brain-based approaches over mind-based approaches was a cultural phenomenon that outstripped the relevant scientific advances.[8] In an environment more sympathetic to brain-based approaches, historians began to ask why physicians used apparent barbarities such as lobotomy in the first place, what context they flourished in, and how they appeared to work.[9] There are signs now of attempts to bring back a critical edge to the subject, without sacrificing some of the gains made in the reconstruction of context.[10] I do not mean to suggest that historians have reflected their times in lockstep. During the heyday of the Age of Prozac, Andrew Scull published a blistering and thoughtful critical review of the somatic treatments.[11] And there have always been historians inclined to a balanced approach.[12] But to the

351

extent that the historiography has reflected changing times and cultural assumptions, it is a signal that historians should adopt the same humility we presume to teach others.

Eclecticism was evident in the humoral medicine practised in most of the Christian and Islamic worlds. Humoral treatments of madness were deeply somatic in their theory and interventions, the latter featuring purging medicines and bleedings, as well as preventive practices such as exercise and fresh air, for example.[13] These ideas received dizzying expression in Robert Burtons's *Anatomy of Melancholy* (1621).[14] Burton's work attempts such an exhaustive inventory of the dimensions of melancholy, it should embarrass the well-intentioned reductionisms of the twentieth century, however mystical portions of the text might seem from the perspective of modern science.

Benjamin Rush practiced bleeding to bring fluids into balance as a cure for madness (and virtually everything else) in early America. He also used "spinning," a therapy where the mad were spun around in a chair to induce vertigo and exhaustion.[15] More originally, Rush developed a form of sensory deprivation called the "tranquilizer chair," where the patient's limbs and head were confined and vision blocked.[16] Rush's etiological theories were thoroughly somatic. He located the source of madness in the brain.[17] His therapeutic regimens, though, were not entirely somatic. He strongly believed, for example, in the importance of establishing the physician's authority, and believed that terror could help to restore sanity.[18]

The moral treatment starting in the late eighteenth century was a hopeful nonsomatic approach that in some ways anticipated more contemporary practices, such as cognitive-behavioral therapy. Philippe Pinel, one of its most important proponents, may not have actually unchained the mad, as the legend has held, but he did attempt to liberate them from somatic treatments such as bloodletting and drugs, which he thought should be used only as a last resort.[19] Similar reforms were practised by Samuel and William Tuke at the famous York Retreat in Great Britain. The justified aura of enlightened reform that surrounded moral treatment probably helped contribute to the modern intuition among many people that talking treatments are more humane, and treat patients more like people. However, this posed a problem for the profession that would later be called psychiatry. If the patients were to be treated by talking to them and modifying their behavior, why exactly was this a job for physicians?[20] Thus was fractured a fault line that continues to cause tremors, and periodic earthquakes, in the field of mental health care.

This fracture in turn raises a question: for a historian, what exactly should count as a somatic treatment? The "animal magnetism" promoted by Anton Mesmer and his followers in the late eighteenth century might seem to belong not to the history of somatic treatments, but to the history of cures by suggestion. At least one book has considered Mesmer a "mental healer," and thus predecessor to Mary Baker Eddy and Sigmund Freud.[21] But to Mesmer, his followers, and his patients, Mesmerism was a physical intervention.[22] It worked by the manipulation of magnetic fluids that surrounded people. It also used massage, and patients sometimes had fits.[23] If it did indeed work simply by suggestion, it nevertheless presaged a new moment, one where prestige could accrue to a treatment by virtue of it being seen as scientific, and where being scientific meant manipulating the physical world.

The late nineteenth-century "rest cure" is another example. American neurologist Silas Weir Mitchell developed the rest cure as a treatment for the then-current and widely diagnosed illness "neurasthenia." As the name implies, enforced rest was central to the treatment, but it also involved a high-protein diet and other interventions. It became internationally famous and widely employed. Its application was notoriously gendered. This, and its emphasis on submission to male and medical authority, have been remembered through Charlotte Perkins Gilman's dark novella *The Yellow Wallpaper*, where it appears as a form of psychological manipulation with iatrogenic consequences.[24] But Mitchell and other purveyors understood the rest cure as a somatic treatment, a way of treating what was essentially a disease of exhaustion and depletion of nerves.[25]

The rest cure also included electrical stimulation, which became part of medicine's repertoire for an amazingly broad range of afflictions, including infectious diseases such as tuberculosis, chronic diseases such as gout, and madness, over the course of the nineteenth century.[26] George Beard, famous for the treatment of the nineteenth-century ailment neurasthenia, used mainly electrical treatments. Electrical stimulation in this period for the most part was not meant to induce convulsions, as it was in the treatment now known as electroconvulsive therapy, or ECT, which grew out of other convulsive therapies in the 1930s.

Electrical treatment in the First World War added layers of confusion to the contested borderland between the soma and psyche. European powers used one dramatically somatic intervention—electric shocks for war neurosis, hysteria, or suspected malingering—for blatantly psychological purposes. The shocks were designed to induce pain, in order to reduce the attractions of staying away from the front. Thus a starkly bodily treatment was intentionally employed for blatantly psychological purposes.[27]

The dramatic decreases in mortality and morbidity from infectious disease in the first half of the twentieth century form an important part of the backdrop to the flurry of somatic experimentation for mental illness in the same period.[28] The success of vaccines, and later antibiotics, led psychiatrists to increasingly seek similar specificity in both etiology and treatment, and the discovery of the linkage of syphilis and paresis offered the hope that all mental illnesses might be found to have straightforward organic etiologies and cures. Psychiatry was nevertheless seen, with reason, as lagging in its effectiveness. But it would be a mistake to see the early twentieth century as characterized by therapeutic pessimism in psychiatry. The late nineteenth century, with its fatalistic theories of degeneration, was far more pessimistic. In the early decades of the twentieth century there were several sources and manifestations of therapeutic optimism, from the hope placed in psychoanalysis and related dynamic treatments, to the mental hygiene movements.

Many of the new somatic treatments developed between about 1920 and 1950 were no doubt dangerous. And they were often tested on a captive asylum population in conditions very far from the informed consent we would like to see as standard today.[29] Some psychoanalysts went so far as to speculate that these treatments reflected unconscious sadism towards the mentally ill, though there were also psychoanalysts who found them to be helpful adjuncts. But we must also remember that the experimenters were doing their job—testing hypotheses, in order to try to find remedies for serious and often chronic distress. And while some treatments might seem in retrospect like extreme measures, their adoption cannot be seen as representing only the imperial ambitions of doctors. Chronic mental illness is trying for patients and their families, who could be supportive of physicians' efforts to do something, anything.[30]

The twentieth-century treatments come in a succession that has become canonical in overviews, many of them associated with a particular innovator. The major developments include hydrotherapy; the prolonged sleep therapy developed by Jakob Klaesi in Zurich from 1920; Julius Wagner-Jauregg's malaria fever therapy for neurosyphilis, developed in Vienna in the 1920s; insulin coma therapy, pioneered by Manfred Sakel in Berlin in 1930; chemical convulsive therapy, championed by Ladislas von Meduna in Budapest in 1934; lobotomy, developed by Egas Monizin Lisbon in 1935; and ECT, invented by Ugo Cerletti and Lucio Bini in Rome in 1938. All of these treatments were announced as clinical successes, though for the most part they were not subject to clinical trials, which would become the gold standard for efficacy research after the Second World War. This canon usually omits one of the most important developments, namely the use of amphetamine to treat depression. This was notably promoted by Boston psychiatrist Abraham Myerson in the 1930s. As Rasmussen has shown, amphetamine has a claim to be the first psychopharmaceutical. He also shows that clinical trials were used to establish its efficacy.[31]

The history of somatic treatments is replete with new therapies hailed as a departure from previous practices deemed inhumane or coercive, only to be regarded themselves as inhumane and coercive in retrospect. Hydrotherapy is an example. It refers to an array of uses for water that were widely used in the late nineteenth and early twentieth centuries, including the continuous bath and the wet sheet pack. For the wet sheet pack, patients were wrapped tightly in sheets, at gradually rising temperatures. For continuous baths, patients were fastened to a hammock and placed in a tub, which was then covered in canvas, leaving just a hole for the head.[32] These highly restraining procedures were praised for being departures from the use of restraints. As Braslow's account makes clear, physicians liked the hydrotherapies precisely because they allowed doctors to control the behavior of the patients. And patients resisted them, sometimes strenuously.

The more subtle point that emerges here is that the line between control and therapy is not a neat one. Sometimes therapies may appear to be more for the convenience of the doctors, or the patients' families, or the wider society, than for alleviating the suffering of the afflicted. And we can certainly identify different levels of coerciveness not only among treatments, but in the application of particular treatments. But to some extent treating madness was and remains a way of controlling people who were out of control. People who are suffering from morbid paranoid delusions that are disrupting family relations, or from catatonic depression that prevents any effective work or creative activity, may receive a treatment that increases their subjective sense of well-being, allows them to improve familial relations, and prosper in a fulfilling career. No doubt this can in some way accurately be called "social control," but is there much moral or analytic gain in doing so? There are always important questions to ask about the physical, psychic, or financial costs of the treatment. There are also undoubtedly instances where psychiatric interventions are used in troubling ways to silence dissent, sometimes intentionally, and sometimes not. And finally, there is no question that many treatments can be used in punishing and coercive ways. But these are issues that need to be weighed in specific instances. A psychiatric treatment is not coercive in a sinister way simply because it returns a person to their expected social role, any more than it is coercive simply because it is somatic.

Wagner-Jauregg, who had been among those administering shocks to soldiers during the First World War, had also been exploring the use of infectious agents that cause fevers for the use of psychiatric conditions since the 1880s. In 1917, he first treated a patient with neurosyphilis, and shortly thereafter reported success with nine patients.[33] Although unquestionably a scary, painful, and risky treatment, malaria fever therapy was considered efficacious, not just by physicians, but by patients.[34] Malaria fever therapy was the first treatment in psychiatry to garner the Nobel Prize for Medicine. It has become axiomatic in the history of psychiatry to note how important malaria fever therapy was for establishing the optimistic precedent that somatic interventions could actually work. But it also established another optimistic precedent, as the treatment was used for an extremely wide variety of mental illnesses.[35] This pattern would repeat with ECT, which in its early years was tried for nearly everything that was called mental illness, until its use was narrowed to the management of affective disorders—an indication for which it had not been originally developed. Lobotomy would also later be used for a wide variety of diagnoses.[36]

The shock therapies are conventionally grouped as insulin coma therapy, chemical convulsive therapy, and ECT. Historians have not imposed this grouping; the psychiatric profession used it when these therapies were developed.[37] How exactly they constitute a group is less obvious than one might think, but they were all initially motivated by a belief that severe mental illness required some kind of major shock to the physical and psychical entity, to break through the illness and to the person. Insulin coma therapy was the first, developed by Manfred Sakel in Berlin. Sakel was experimenting with the use of insulin to treat addicts, and sometimes inadvertently induced hypoglycemic coma. Sakel found that for many patients, desire for alcohol disappeared, as did symptoms of agitation, and he began to theorize that insulin coma might cure schizophrenia. When he tried it, he reported a success rate of 70 percent. Mental hospitals throughout the industrialized world adopted insulin coma therapy.[38] Its foundations were shaky, though. Doctors who used it often reported symptom remission, but if it was effective, its mechanism was unknown. Some of the patients experienced convulsions, and while Sakel himself believed the convulsions were the effective part of the process, there was no consensus about this among clinicians who employed it. What was clear was that the procedure was dangerous, with patients dying from it at a rate of 2 to 5 percent.[39]

Ladislas von Meduna, the Hungarian physician who developed chemical convulsive therapy, was looking specifically for a way to induce convulsions. He and some contemporaries believed that epilepsy and schizophrenia were inversely correlated, a now-discredited premise. Meduna reasoned that if the symptoms of epilepsy could be induced in psychotic patients, their psychosis would remit. He first used camphor oil, before adopting a chemical known as Metrazol. The psychiatric profession was generally enthusiastic about Metrazol, and it too was widely adopted in hospitals. But while there were many reports of patients whose symptoms remitted, patients hated Metrazol therapy, almost universally. Doctors and nurses had to go to great lengths to get patients to swallow the medicine. In particular, patients often reported feelings of intense terror during the short interlude between swallowing the medicine and the beginning of the convulsions.

Electroconvulsive therapy is conspicuous among the somatic treatments developed in the first half of the twentieth century, because it is still used. Its continued use is one of the many aspects of its history that are deployed in contrary ways by partisans and opponents. Supporters generally see its longevity as evidence of its clinical efficacy, detractors as showing the continuing barbarity of psychiatry. And, in one of the many other ironies in the history of ECT, the treatment became an icon for psychiatric terror in the popular imagination, but was originally developed in the search for a safer, more humane, and less terrifying, way to induce convulsions. Bini had, famously or infamously, noticed animals in a slaughterhouse convulsing after receiving electric shocks meant to stun them before they were killed. He and Cerletti thought that this might be a way to induce safe convulsions in people, and they did trials on dogs to ascertain this. In this sense, ECT was not a new therapy, but a technical modification to already existing chemical convulsive therapy. Since the efficacy of Metrazol was widely accepted, it is not surprising that ECT was quickly adopted in the world's mental hospitals. In its early years, it was painful and marred by serious physical complications, such as bone fractures caused by the convulsions. By the late 1950s, the use of anesthesia for the pain and muscle relaxants to prevent wild motions were becoming the standard of care.

One constant observed—by doctors, but also by patients and their families—throughout the history of ECT has been its remarkable power to cause remission of the symptoms of severe affective disorder.[40] But since its introduction, ECT has nevertheless been the subject of ongoing contested representations that can be reduced to one main question: is it therapy or control? This contest has been the main subject of its historiography as well. But the history of ECT is more aptly illustrative of how the coerciveness of a treatment varies by context, rather than being a property inherent in the treatment itself. In the first decades of its use, it was often involuntary. And while current proponents resent the image of abusive control fostered by movies like *One Flew Over the Cuckoo's Nest*, there is abundant evidence that mental hospitals did in fact use ECT to induce order on the wards and to discipline disobedient patients.[41] To equate these openly punitive uses with, say, repeated voluntary treatments by patients seeking to reduce the toll of serious affective disorder and name them both "social control" requires a pretty strained theory of false consciousness.

This does not mean contemporary ECT is necessarily without costs. All of the somatic treatments chronicled in this chapter have carried adverse effects. This is why there have been ongoing efforts to replace or refine them. For ECT, controversies continue concerning memory loss. All agree that some short-term memory loss of events immediately before and after the treatment is likely. The main contested issue is permanent long-term losses. Much clinical science and most clinical handbooks describe the risk of permanent long-term losses as very low.[42] But the patient narratives of ECT treatment describe it ubiquitously—even in accounts that are appreciative of the therapeutic effects of the ECT.[43]

The shock therapies have become, in retrospect, icons of the mid-twentieth-century somatic treatments, treatments that disregarded the patients' psychology in order to work directly on the body. As counter-intuitive as it may seem now, not all regarded them as purely somatic treatments at the time. Many clinicians, particularly psychoanalysts, regarded any efficacy they showed as being the result of psychological manipulations, much as we might see now regard the rest cure. There were many forms this reasoning took. Probably most common was the theory that the mentally ill suffered from overactive and highly punitive superegos. Their illnesses were thus self-inflicted, if unconsciously so. The punitive nature of the somatic treatment relieved the need for the masochistic impulse behind the illness.[44] This was a view, it seems, that could be internalized by some patients. In her journal, following her own (apparently effective) ECT, poet Sylvia Plath wrote, "Why, after the 'amazingly short' three or so shock treatments did I rocket uphill? Why did I feel I needed to be punished, to punish myself."[45] There were, of course, many doctors who regarded these psychological theories skeptically. Many of these positively favored somatic approaches, but even many who preferred talk therapy valued shock treatments for their power to minimize some of the most florid symptoms of madness, rendering the patient capable of the work insight-oriented therapy demanded. Psychological theories of the efficacy of shock therapies appear more rarely in medical literature after about 1960. There are two probable reasons for this. First, in the late 1950s, it was shown that convulsions were necessary for ECT to be effective—in other words, jolts of electricity at subconvulsive levels did not lead to the same symptom remission—and this may have spelled the end of the punitive superego theory.[46] It would have been hard to argue that jolts of electricity need to reach convulsive levels in order for the unconscious to deem them punitive. Second, the use of muscle relaxants and anesthesia were becoming standard of care for ECT, making it a less painful procedure.

The psychological theories were not confined to the shock therapies. It would be hard to imagine procedures that worked more directly on the body, and did so more invasively, than the psychosurgical interventions known as lobotomy. But there were those who believed that the means of efficacy even for lobotomy was psychological.[47]

A primary attraction of somatic treatments has often been the speed of efficacy, compared to talk therapies. Conversely, for the last 100 years or so, critics of somatic treatments have lamented them as "shortcuts" around the real work needed for mental wellness. This was one of the many arguments that surrounded the development of lobotomy. Lobotomy was first developed in Portugal by Egas Moniz, who then received the second, and so far the last, Nobel Prize in Medicine for a psychiatric intervention. Walter Freeman promoted it zealously in the United States. There were variations of the procedure, but all its forms consisted mainly of cutting connections between the pre-frontal cortex and other parts of the brain. Psychiatrists were enormously impressed by the power of lobotomy to provide a sense of calm relief to highly agitated patients. And it was valued by some families precisely because it was seen as less barbaric than ECT.[48]

Lobotomy has a slightly more developed historiography than most other somatic treatments in psychiatry. That historiography is an interesting study in how the present influences the representation of the past. The first book to provide a lengthy and well-researched history of psychosurgery was *Great and Desperate Cures*, by biological psychologist Elliot Valenstein, whose depiction was also filled with moral outrage.[49] In the 1990s, during the Age of Prozac, and the decade pronounced by George H. W. Bush to be the "decade of the brain," Pressman and Braslow produced accounts that were more balanced, and more sensitive to the context within which lobotomy was seen as cure.[50] More recently, as the excitement about antidepressants that characterized the 1990s has given way to mixed feelings following growing recognition of their limits and adverse effects, Raz has produced an account showing that while patients and doctors might value the therapeutic powers of lobotomy, it carried serious risks, and Freeman's zealous application was an example of well-intentioned medical overreach.[51] Jenell Johnson's recent study of lobotomy in America recognizes the enthusiasm over positive effects perceived by clinicians, as well as the very considerable public demand that has had no space in social memory.[52] Johnson also shows clearly, however, in ways that Pressman de-emphasized, that the categories of therapy and control were deeply intertwined in lobotomy's use. Freeman was quite open about wanting to promote docility in difficult people and openly made the case for sacrificing creativity and even dignity in exchange for social adaptability.[53]

Pressman showed that the adverse effects of lobotomy became more apparent over time. As they did, antipsychotic medications were simultaneously coming into use, and lobotomy came to be seen as obsolete, at best. The decline of lobotomy began earlier, however, and Johnson argues that it was its image as an authoritarian "mind control" in a Cold War culture represented in films like "Invasion of the Body Snatchers."[54]

It is a puzzle of the history of psychiatry that age of psychopharmaceuticals dawned in the 1950s, but the "Age of Prozac" did not. By this I do not refer to the fact that the specific drug fluoxetine (Prozac) was yet to be prescribed. Rather, when the new drug became available, its efficacy was widely seen as a refutation of psychological, especially psychoanalytic theories of and approaches to mental illness. In some media representations, both in popular media and clinical opinion, Prozac was announced as nothing less than a mortal threat to anything resembling Freudian theory. The same never applied to the same degree to any of the other somatic treatments, or to the use of lithium for mania first in the nineteenth century and again in the 1940s, or for the use of tranquilizers, or for the antidepressant or antipsychotic medications deployed in the 1950s. This was certainly not because those medications lacked impact. The antipsychotic medications are widely viewed as having led to the end of lobotomy, and the decline of ECT in the 1960s. They are regarded sometimes as having made de-institutionalization possible, and while de-institutionalization had many causes, the coming of antipsychotics undoubtedly helped. Nor was the new cultural disparagement of psychological views simply due to the cultural sensation of Prozac. Calming drugs such as Miltown had also been cultural sensations,[55] but their efficacy was never seen as proof that mental disorder was "just chemical."

Innovation in non-pharmaceutical somatic treatments has been modest since the 1950s. New therapies such as deep brain stimulation and transcranial magnetic stimulation are promising therapeutic effects at least comparable to ECT, with lower risk of adverse effects.[56] Some reins on enthusiasm may seem warranted, since the history of somatic treatments has shown that adverse effects are not always recognized early in a new treatment's use. But it would be equally uncritical to allow for no possibility of progress. Whatever flaws there may be in current treatments, from ECT to antidepressants and antipsychotic medications, they remain good reasons not to revive the use of insulin coma therapy.

Conclusion

I wish to emphasize four main conclusions that a historical study of somatic treatments for madness yields:

1) What counts as a somatic treatment is historically variable. The division between the physical and the psychological is, not surprisingly, as deeply lodged in psychiatry as it is more widely. But this is unfortunate, because psychiatry is distinctively suited to probe the weaknesses of that division. In practice, it often has done so, but in theory it has often offered explicit or implicit manifestos reifying the division, in the name of either science or humanism. As historians, we always like to be able to show that things are historically variable, but it matters here for at least two reasons beyond our professional self-importance. First, although they have been stigmatized as abusive and dehumanizing—in some cases, with good reason—somatic treatments have on the other hand often been granted the veneer of being more scientific, more medical, than competing therapies. But the real scientific measure of any medical treatment is its empirically demonstrated ability to relieve suffering or prolong life, with a minimum of adverse effects. This ability is not determined a priori by how directly it appears to treat the body – an appearance that is itself less self-evident than it appears. Second, the historical variability of the meaning of "somatic" matters because it has a powerful impact on patient experience of both illness and treatment. Plath's reflection on her ECT shows that she saw it as a psychological therapy, and this had consequences for her reflections on the aftermath. In his book on depression, Andrew Solomon notes that in the Age of Prozac, it has become common for sufferers to report that their affliction is "just chemical."[57] Solomon rightly questions how useful such a formulation is. At the same time, it is not useless because, given the cultural moment, it is perceived as de-stigmatizing, as well as "real." It is clear that in the treatment of madness, any somatic treatment is intended to influence the mind. What is less intuitive, but no less true, is that any treatment aimed at the mind should, from a materialist perspective, influence the body. To argue what is somatic or not based on current perceptions of such runs a high risk of anachronism.

2) Social control is best regarded as a spectrum, and the degree of coerciveness does not necessarily correlate with the degree of "bodiliness." In some accounts of psychiatry, somatic treatments are equated with coercive measures of discipline, and talk therapies idealized as humane and voluntary.[58] Any correlation demands demonstration in particular instances. A somatic treatment is not abusive simply by virtue of being a somatic treatment. One might imagine that talk therapies, because they are dedicated to the subjectivity of the patient, might be inherently less inclined to abusive, punitive, or coercive practices. Perhaps. But it is easy to find people who felt abused, punished, or coerced by their therapists. What is most important to remember is that the question is always empirical, with the answer to be sought in examination of the record, not in dogmatic presumptions of the essence of somatic, or talk, therapies.

3) The invention and dissemination of new somatic treatments has followed a predictable cycle. The new treatment is usually introduced as a safer, more effective, and more humane alternative to existing treatments. If it is judged to work, it becomes widely adopted, and often idealized in a kind of clinical euphoria. Adverse effects are noticed gradually, erode the effect of idealization, and a period of uneasy acceptance settles in. This has been as true of psychopharmaceutical as other somatic treatments.[59] We are currently in one of those periods

of uneasy acceptance with regard to antidepressants and antipsychotics. Whether they will be displaced by new treatments that generate clinical euphoria, justified or not, remains to be seen.

4) The historiography of somatic treatments has been influenced by prevailing conceptions of science, the body, and the person. These conceptions are often deeply implicit, and therefore have a self-evident quality that seems questionable in retrospect. While it is axiomatic that knowledge is embedded in culture, and that the present influences the representation of the past, it is not yet truism. Historians, we know, are not neutral. We make moral and political judgments. Historians should not refrain from criticizing abusive or dehumanizing practices when we see them, nor refrain from celebrating those that are liberatory and reduce suffering. To assume that either of these axes line up neatly with whether a psychiatric treatment is somatic or not is, however, not a properly historical judgment, but a reproduction of an ideology of our object of study.

Memoirs of madness have become a proliferating genre of literature. Elyn Saks has provided a vivid account of her struggle with schizophrenia that has received particular attention in recent years.[60] Saks's narrative fails to conform either to simple narratives of cure and redemption, or to antipsychiatric narratives of abuse, and this may be one reason it is so compelling. Saks suffered for years before she found herself able to say she in fact had an illness and believed at first that needing medications was a sign of failure. To her, taking medications at first meant something was wrong with her, in a way that psychoanalysis did not. By contrast, psychoanalytic interpretation of the meaning of her thoughts she always found valuable. For other psychiatric patients, something like the opposite could be true—they might feel that the usefulness of a somatic treatment showed, say, that they had a real disease, whereas plunging into memories of life events was the distasteful treatment. When Saks came to believe that she would need to be on medications for life, the new value she found in them did not lead her to discard psychoanalysis. Rather, she came to see the two modalities as working in concert. She in fact underwent psychoanalytic training herself, something she arguably would not have been able to do without the help of the medications.

One thing Saks's story shows is that people managing symptoms of madness are often less interested in a dogmatic conception of a certain kind of science or a certain conception of personhood than they are in relief of suffering. Having to choose between somatic and other modalities ultimately emerges as an impractical choice to make. It is a choice that historians of psychiatry have too often made themselves. The history of psychiatry is replete with clinicians claiming the complete and final victory of one modality over another. Historians should not repeat this mistake.

Notes

1 I would like to thank Jesse Ballenger, Jenell Johnson, Hans Pols, Alan Rocke, Elizabeth Salem, Katherine Schroeder, and Ted Steinberg for their comments on earlier versions.
2 The literature on the proliferation of psychiatric diagnostic categories, and the consequent medicalization of human experience, is extensive. Two good accounts include Christopher Lane, *Shyness: How Normal Behavior Became a Sickness* (New Haven, CT: Yale University Press, 2007) and Allan V. Horwitz and Jerome Wakefield, *The Loss of Sadness: How Psychiatry Transformed Normal Sorrow into Depressive Disorder* (Oxford: Oxford University Press, 2007).

3 See Peter Conrad, *The Medicalization of Society: On the Transformation of Human Conditions into Treatable Disorders* (Baltimore, MD: The Johns Hopkins University Press, 2007).

4 Thomas Szasz, *Coercion as Cure: A Critical History of Psychiatry* (New Brunswick, NJ: Transaction Publishers, 2009).

5 Andrew Scull, *Madness in Civilization: A Cultural History of Insanity from the Bible to Freud, From the Madhouse to Modern Medicine* (Princeton and Oxford: Princeton University Press, 2015), 43.

6 Michael E. Staub, *Madness is Civilization: When the Diagnosis Was Social, 1948–1980* (Chicago: University of Chicago Press, 2011).

7 See Gregory Zilboorg and George W. Henry, *A History of Medical Psychology* (New York: W. W. Norton and Company, 1941).

8 Peter Kramer, *Listening to Prozac* (New York: Penguin Books, 1993), 48–49.

9 See, for especially good examples, Edward Shorter, *A History of Psychiatry: From the Era of the Asylum to the Age of Prozac* (New York: John Wiley and Sons, 1997) and Jack Pressman, *Last Resort: Psychosurgery and the Limits of Medicine* (Cambridge: Cambridge University Press, 1998).

10 See, for example, Mical Raz's recent *The Lobotomy Letters: The Making of American Psychosurgery* (Rochester, NY: University of Rochester Press, 2013) and Jenell Johnson, *American Lobotomy: A Rhetorical History* (Ann Arbor, MI: University of Michigan Press, 2014).

11 Andrew Scull, "Somatic Treatments and the Historiography of Psychiatry," *History of Psychiatry* 5 (1994): 1–12; Joel Braslow, *Mental Ills and Bodily Cures: Psychiatric Treatment in the First Half of the Twentieth Century* (Berkeley: University of California, 1997.

12 Braslow, *Mental Ills and Bodily Cures* (Berkeley: University of California, 1997) is exemplary.

13 On humoral medicine, see Noga Arikha, *Passions and Tempers; A History of the Humours* (New York: Harper Perennial, 2008).

14 Scull, *Madness in Civilization*, 94.

15 Petteri Peitikainen, *Madness: A History* (New York: Routledge, 2015), 142–43.

16 Peitikainen, *Madness: A History*, 143.

17 Shorter, *A History of Psychiatry*, 15–16, 27–28.

18 Peitikainen, *Madness: A History*, 143.

19 Scull, *Madness in Civilization*, 208.

20 Scull, *Madness in Civilization*.

21 Anton Zweig, *Mental Healers: Mesmer, Eddy, Freud* (New York: F. Ungar, 1962, originally published 1932).

22 On mesmerism, see Robert Darnton *Mesmerism and the End of the Enlightenment in France* (Cambridge: Harvard University Press, 1986) and Alison Winter, *Mesmerized: Powers of Mind in Victorian Britain* (Chicago: University of Chicago Press, 1998).

23 Scull, *Madness in Civilization*, 182.

24 For a reappraisal of Mitchell, including his relationship with Gilman, see David G. Schuster, "Personalizing Illness and Modernity: S. Weir Mitchell, Literary Women, and Neurasthenia, 1870–1914," *Bulletin of the History of Medicine* 79 (Winter 2005): 695–722.

25 Eric Caplan, *Mind Games: American Culture and the Birth of Psychotherapy* (Berkeley: University of California Press, 2001).

26 See, for example, Alan Gauld, *Electrotherapy in the United States* (Minneapolis: The Company, 1977); Paola Bertucci and Giulano Pancaldi, *Electric Bodies: Episodes in the History of Medical Electricity* (Bologna: Universita di Bologna, 2001); Carolyn Thomas de la Pena, *The Body Electric: How Strange Machines Built the Modern American* (New York: New York University Press, 2003).

27 Scull, *Madness in Civilization*, 297–299.

28 As is well known to historians of medicine, the degree to which these declines should be attributed to nutritional and sanitary improvements, one the one hand, or new therapies on the other, can be hard to tease out. See the introduction to Nancy Tomes, *The Gospel of Germs: Men, Women, and the Microbe in American Life* (Cambridge: Harvard University Press: 1988) for an overview of the literature. There is no question that medicine played some role, though, particularly from the introduction of antibiotics.

29 Scull, *Madness in Civilization*, 508.

30 This point is effectively developed in Raz, *The Lobotomy Letters*.

31 Nicolas Rasmussen, *On Speed: The Many Lives of Amphetamine* ((New York: New York University Press, 2008).

32 On hydrotherapy, see Braslow, *Mental Ills and Bodily Cures*, 38–52.

33 Shorter, *A History of Psychiatry*, 194–94.

34 Scull, *Madness in Civilization*, 302.

35 Shorter, *A History of Psychiatry*, 194.

36 Jenell Johnson, *American Lobotomy: A Rhetorical History* (Ann Arbor, MI: University of Michigan Press, 2014), 29.

37 See, for example, Lothar B. Kalinowsky and Paul H. Hoch, *Shock Treatments and Other Somatic Procedures in Psychiatry* ((New York: Grune and Stratton, 1946), one of the most widely used textbooks of the era.

38 On insulin coma therapy in an American hospital, see D. B. Doroshow, "Performing a Cure for Schizophrenia: Insulin Coma Therapy on the Wards," *Journal of the History of Medicine and Allied Sciences* 62 (2007): 213–43.

39 Scull, *Madness in Civilization*, 502.

40 ECT also seemed in its early years to bring about remission of symptoms for schizophrenia, but since that has not been the main indication for decades, it has seen less investigation.

41 Braslow, *Mental Ills and Bodily Cures*, 105–106, Peter G. Cranford, *But for the Grace of God: The Inside Story of the World's Largest Insane Asylum* (Augusta, GA: Great Pyramid Press, 1981); Ivan Belknap, *Human Problems of a State Mental Hospital* (New York: McGraw-Hill Book Company, 1956).

42 See Richard Abrams, *Electroconvulsive Therapy*, fourth edition (Oxford: Oxford University Press, 2002) chapter 10, and Charles H. Kellner, John T. Pritchett, Mark D. Beale, C. Edward Coffey, *Handbook of ECT* (Washington, DC: American Psychiatric Press, 1997) 87–89.

43 See, for example, Anne B. Donahue, "Electroconvulsive Therapy and Memory Loss: A Personal Journey," *The Journal of ECT* 16 (2000): 133–143. The quotes reproduced here are on pages 134 and 138. Also see Kitty Dukakis and Larry Tye, *Shock: The Healing Power of Electroconvulsive Therapy* (New York: Penguin, 2006) and Martha Manning, *Undercurrents: A Life Beneath the Surface* (New York: HarperSanFrancisco, 1994).

44 See Braslow, *Mental Ills and Bodily Cures;* Jonathan Sadowsky, "Beyond the Metaphor of the Pendulum: Electroconvulsive Therapy, Psychoanalysis, and the Styles of American Psychiatry," *The Journal of the History of Medicine and Allied Sciences* 61 (2006): 1–25.

45 Karen V. Kukil, ed., *The Unabridged Journals of Sylvia Plath, 1950–1962* (New York: Anchor Books, 2000).

46 J. O. Ottoson, "Seizure Characteristics and Therapeutic Efficiency in Electroconvulsive Therapy: An Analysis of the Antidepressive Efficiency of Grand Mal and Lidocaine-Modified Seizures," *Journal of Nervous and Mental Diseases* 135 (1962): 239–251.

47 Raz, *The Lobotomy Letters*; Elliot S. Valenstein, *Great and Desperate Cures: The Rise and Decline of Psychosurgery and Other Radical Treatments for Mental Illness* (New York: Basic Books, 1986)

48 Braslow, *Mental Ills and Bodily Cures*, 137.

49 Valenstein, *Great and Desperate Cures*.

50 Pressman, *Last Resort;* Braslow, *Mental Ills and Bodily Cures*.

51 Raz, *The Lobotomy Letters*.

52 Johnson, *American Lobotomy*.

53 Johnson, *American Lobotomy*, 30.

54 Johnson, *American Lobotomy*, 74–105. See also Scull, *Madness in Civilization*, 318–319.

55 Andrea Tone, *The Age of Anxiety: A History of America's Turbulent Affair with Tranquilizers* (New York: Basic Books: 2009).

56 See Sarah Lisanby, ed., *Brian Stimulation in Psychiatric Treatment* (Washington, DC: American Psychiatric Publishing Inc., 2004).

57 Andrew Solomon, *The Noonday Demon: An Atlas of Depression* (New York: Scribner, 2001), 22.

58 See, for example, Thomas Szasz, *Coercion as Cure*.

59 On antipsychotics, see Sheldon Gelman, *Medicating Schizophrenia: A History* (New Brunswick, NJ: Rutgers University Press, 1999).

60 Elyn R. Saks, *The Center Cannot Hold: My Journey Through Madness* (New York: Hachette Books, 2007).

20

PSYCHOTHERAPY IN SOCIETY

Historical reflections

Sonu Shamdasani

What is psychotherapy? Any historical inquiry into the subject must begin by posing this question. One of the earliest definitions from 1892 by the Dutch psychiatrist Frederick van Eeden (1869–1932), ran as follows: 'I call psychotherapy all curative methods which use psychic agents to combat illness through the intervention of psychic functions.'[1] This was a wide, all-embracing definition, simply setting aside the body. Half a century later, Karl Jaspers (1883–1969) proposed the following: 'Psychotherapy is the name given to all those methods of treatment that affect both psyche and body by measures which proceed via the psyche. The co-operation of the patient is always required.'[2] Little had changed. In 1973, Thomas Szasz (1920–2012) attempted to gather together the plethora of definitions into one:

> We have come to accept as psychotherapy all conceivable situations in which the soul, spirit, mind, or personality of an individual who claims to be a healer is employed to bring about some sort of change called 'therapeutic' in the soul, spirit, mind or personality of another individual, called the 'patient'.[3]

Given the breadth and vagueness of what is covered by these definitions, it is fruitful to begin with consideration of the term itself.

In 1853, a surgeon to the royal infirmary for diseases of children in London and former president of the medical society, Walter Cooper Dendy (1794–1871), published a book entitled *Psyche: A Discourse on the Birth and Pilgrimage of Thought*, in which he described 'psychotherapeia' as the 'antidote of thought'.[4] For Dendy, psychotherapeia represented the use of the remedial influence of the mind: 'We know how instantaneously a thought will stimulate the salivary, the spermatic and other glands.'[5] As mental states induced disorder, prevention and cure could be brought about by inducing a contrary state of mind. Dendy was in effect referring to the long-standing medicine of the imagination. The following year, an anonymous reviewer of Forbes Winslow's *Lectures on Insanity* in the *Asylum Journal* referred to the moral and medical treatment of insanity as the 'the twin brothers of the psychotherapeutic art, the Castor and Pollux of mental medicine'.[6] The reference here was clearly to moral treatment.

The term was picked up two decades later by Daniel Hack Tuke (1827–1895) in 1872. A psychiatrist and the great-grandson of William Tuke, the founder of the York Retreat, he used the term 'psycho-therapeutics' in his *Illustrations of the Influence of the Mind Upon the Body in Health and Disease Designed to Elucidate the Action of the Imagination*.[7] He claimed that physicians had long known the healing power of the imagination, but that now it could be made rational. This would serve to distinguish them from quacks – the latter being individuals who healed without knowing how they did so. The spectre of quackery has haunted psychotherapy, and most schools have commenced by arguing why they (as opposed to their rivals) should not be regarded as quacks. The penultimate chapter of Tuke's book was titled 'Psycho-Therapeutics – Practical Applications of the Influence of the Mind on the Body to Medical Practice'. Whilst discussing animal magnetism, he argued that the 1784 French Commission on animal magnetism were correct in attributing the phenomena that they observed to the effect of the imagination and imitation, and that this could form the basis of a new science, 'that of the Moral over the Physical'.[8] For Tuke, mesmerism thus displayed how 'certain purely psychical agencies produce certain physical results'.[9] Whilst boldly proclaiming the new science of psycho-therapeutics, Tuke appears not to have made further use of the term.

It might well have ended there, had it not caught the attention of Hippolyte Bernheim (1840–1919). A professor of medicine at Nancy, he had become interested in the work of Auguste Ambroise Liébault (1823–1904), a country doctor who practised hypnosis. According to Bernheim, it was Liébault who established 'the doctrine of therapeutic suggestion'.[10] Bernheim claimed that suggestion was as 'old as the world'.[11] What was new was its systematic application to therapeutics. For Bernheim, the use of suggestion not only featured prominently in his practice, it formed the theoretical key to understanding hypnosis and a general psychology of the mind. Hypnosis was understood as a state of heightened suggestibility, akin to sleep. He defined suggestion widely, as the act by which an idea is accepted in the brain. For Bernheim and the Nancy school, suggestive therapeutics consisted in the deliberate manipulation of credence, belief, and expectation under the rubric of suggestion and autosuggestion in the treatment of a wide range of psychological and physical conditions. In addition to functional neuroses, Bernheim claimed that it was effective in cases of paralyses, contractures, insomnia, muscular pain, hemiplegia, paraplegia, rheumatism, anaesthesia, gastric disorders, neuralgia, and sciatica. The common factor active in religious healing as well as in many therapeutic practices, was held to be suggestion.[12] Thus 'suggestion' was presented as a modern rational scientific concept which both explained and unmasked prior and contemporary medical therapies and forms of religious healing. Individuals flocked to Nancy to visit Bernheim and Liébault and watch them at work and gain instruction in hypnosis. Nancy became a 'medical Mecca'.[13] A hypnotic movement spread rapidly through Europe. A controversy raged between the Nancy school and the Salpêtrière school, under the neurologist Jean-Martin Charcot (1825–1893). For Charcot and his followers, hypnosis was only found in cases of hysteria. What Charcot described as 'grand hypnotisme' followed three stages, each of which had distinct physiological characteristics: catalepsy, lethargy, and somnambulism. At the Salpêtrière, Charcot used hypnosis to study the underlying architecture of hysteria; because he claimed it was a pathological state, he was not interested in its therapeutic applications.[14]

Addressing the conflict that raged between the hypnotic schools, the Belgian philosopher and hypnotist Joseph Delboeuf (1831–1896) stated that in addition to the well-known influence of the hypnotiser on the hypnotised, the influence in the reciprocal direction was critical.[15] The subjects, generally the first or paradigm case, trained the experimenter and influenced his methods without his realising it.

This set up a template, as the experimenter reported his results to his disciples who 'replicated' them. It was this circuit of reciprocal influence which gave rise to the hypnotic schools, each monopolising special phenomena. Delboeuf claimed that it was impossible for the experimenter to situate himself outside of the field of effects of the suggestive influence they were attempting to objectively study. His critique suggested that the respective hypnotic schools had become veritable influencing machines for the generation of evidence. The fact that different traits could be paraded forth as constituting the essence of hypnosis and appear to gain confirmation from other practitioners indicated that the mode of institutionalisation was itself subject to the effects of hypnosis and suggestion, which could not be neutralised. The conflicts between the various schools were insolvable, for each of them could point to evidence that supported their particular theories.

In 1886, in the second expanded edition of his book, Bernheim took up the term from Tuke, whose book had just appeared in French.[16] Citing Tuke, Bernheim referred to the 'psycho-therapeutic action' of suggestion and the 'hypnotic psycho-therapeutic'.[17] As Tuke's term had been adopted as a synonym, there was no need for a separate definition of psycho-therapeutics. It was through the hypnotic movement that the term psychotherapy became rapidly disseminated in an open source manner and was widely adopted. Psychotherapy rode on the back of the burgeoning hypnotic movement; consequently there was no need for a separate definition of it. The genie quickly escaped from the bottle, and through the Nancy school discussion of suggestion rapidly entered popular culture, as questions concerning mental influence, the limits of free will, the hidden powers of the mind, the nature of the social bond, the basis of political organisation and religious authority. The theory of suggestion became the lynchpin of a new ontology.

This in turn set up a feedback loop that affected the very practice itself. As Delboeuf pointed out, it had become rare to encounter a naive subject, who has never heard discussion of magnetism or hypnotism. Subjects were already being schooled by society at large. Subjects had preconceived ideas, from conversations or lectures or public demonstrations, which influenced their conduct and set up expectations that in turn structured the therapeutic encounter – ruling out of question the possibility of a naive empiricism – and one which still forms the basis of outcome studies in psychotherapy today. Delboeuf drew the radical conclusion that hypnosis did not exist, or, in other words, that 'the power of hypnotism consists above all in the very word of hypnotism, because [the subject] does not understand it well'.[18] The term itself had a suggestive effect.

Critically, as hypnosis increasingly fell into disrepute, the term psychotherapy presented itself as a ready alternative for an eclectic mix of practices. The decline of hypnosis was accompanied by a revival of moral therapy. A prominent advocate of this was Paul Dubois (1884–1918), a Swiss physician and professor of neuropathology in Bern. In 1904, he published the extremely popular *Psychoneuroses and Their Moral Treatment*. Dubois launched a critique of suggestion, claiming that it only increased the state of servitude of patients. Psychoneurotics needed to be immunised from suggestion, so that they would accept 'nothing but the councils of reason'.[19] Patients needed to regain their self-mastery. In place of suggestion, he spoke of moral persuasion. Critically, Dubois took up the term psychotherapy, seeking to dissociate it from suggestive therapeutics.[20] For him, it was Pinel who 'first introduced psychotherapy in the treatment of mental diseases'.[21] Liébault and Bernheim, and the whole magnetic and hypnotic traditions, were displaced. The implications were clear: psychotherapy was simply the modern form of moral treatment.[22]

Whilst Bernheim had stressed the application of suggestion – and hence psychotherapy – to physical and what would today be classed as psychosomatic disorders, the purview of psychotherapy became increasingly restricted to the 'psychoneuroses'. Dubois argued that he commenced by eliminating the neuroses with a probable somatic origin, restricting himself to 'neurasthenia, hysteria, hystero-neurasthenia, the light forms of hypochondria and melancholy [and . . .] certain more serious states of disequilibrium, such as vesania'.[23] The conditions noted by Dubois do not feature in contemporary diagnostic manuals. Part of the longevity of psychotherapy as a profession has resided in its effectiveness in ever formulating and catering for new disorders.[24]

In 1904, Jean Camus and Philippe Pagniez presented a history of psychotherapy. They differentiated between the conscious manifestations of psychotherapy and its unconscious use. They argued that both modalities went back to antiquity and arranged their history thematically under four headings: psychotherapy by remedies, by which they meant 'suggestion by medicinal therapeutics'; psychotherapy by 'the marvellous' (understood as the intervention of supernatural beings); psychotherapy by hypnotism and suggestion; and psychotherapy by persuasion. If psychotherapy was nothing new, the value of the present was one of 'determining its mechanism of action, of making its usage precise and of grouping together all the scattered rules and indications'.[25]

By the beginning of the twentieth century, the word 'psychotherapy' had become firmly established, but it was not the exclusive preserve of any one figure or school. It was variously adopted to refer to a variety of procedures, ranging from mesmerism, hypnosis, suggestive therapy, moral therapy, Mind-Cure, mental healing, strengthening of the will, reeducation, the cathartic method, rational persuasion, to general medical practice or the 'art' of medicine. Histories had started to be written and contested. A heterogeneous cluster of therapeutic practices to be grouped together under the term, identified as a modern, rational, scientific discipline. This pre-staged its development in the twentieth century and the vast range of denotation that it acquired. The term was adopted by an array of divergent practices and disciplines, a development facilitated by the fact that it never was one thing.

Thus psychotherapy has no one origin, no one clear genealogy. One can begin a history of psychotherapy almost wherever one likes – which is reflected in the literature on the topic. We find no consensus regarding which millennia to commence with, let alone century. We are confronted then with a series of 'connected histories', to adopt Sanjay Subrahmanyan's term, which come together, intersect, and branch apart.[26] 'Psychotherapy' is a set of historically situated practices, which both embody and produce specific cultural values. Rather than presupposing an essence at the level of the referent, one needs to follow the circulation, exchange, and shifting modalities of a network of related practices in different domains. What follows then is simply an attempt to trace some of these routes, highlighting certain nodal points and intersections, while remaining mindful of the manner in which histories have been used to construct the very identity of the field.

In the twentieth century, psychotherapy was an ontology-making practice.[27] The therapeutic encounter became a site where individuals not only were cured, or not, as the case might be; but also learnt to articulate their suffering in new idioms, reconceive their lives according to particular narrative templates, and take on conceptions concerning the nature of the mind and reality. The consequence of this has been the generation of a plethora of optional ontologies. These have come to encompass world views, codes of conduct, and, at times, full-blown soteriologies or systems of salvation. A history of psychotherapies then, informs us not only about the history of discrete therapeutic practices, but also how psychotherapies have generated new conceptions of the mind, conduct, and behaviour that were, and continue to be, taken up by the public at large.

For Bernheim, the practice of psychotherapy was an outpatient medical procedure that used existing medical nosologies. From the 1890s onwards, there was a rapid expansion of the notion of functional nervous disorders, or the neuroses. From hereon, psychotherapy was to minister to its own set of proprietary ailments; furthermore, each school increasingly came to have its own set. The central figure in this regard was Pierre Janet. Janet (1857–1947) initially trained in philosophy. From 1883 to 1889, he taught at Le Havre and commenced studying hypnosis and suggestion. Janet's investigations resulted in a series of landmark articles, culminating in 1889 in *Psychological Automatism*.[28] He presented a position between that of the Nancy and Salpêtrière schools. He articulated his model of the dissociation of consciousness and the role of the subconscious. Whilst these terms were already in use, they became firmly associated with Janet. For Janet, hypnosis offered an experimental means to study the personality. It demonstrated the existence of separate memory chains, or 'automatisms', which could go as far as to form alternate or double personalities. For Janet, the dissociation of consciousness formed an explanation of suggestion, hypnotic and post-hypnotic states, as well as hysteria. Janet referred to the subconscious as opposed to the unconscious as the acts in question, whilst not 'conscious' to the primary consciousness, were 'conscious' to the secondary consciousness.

Continuing his research under Charcot at the Salpêtrière hospital in Paris, he completed his medical studies in 1893 with a dissertation, *The Mental States of Hysterics*.[29] That year, Charcot opened a psychological laboratory at the Salpêtrière, which he entrusted to Janet. Developing Charcot's research, Janet viewed hysteria as a psychogenic disorder, characterised by a narrowing of the field of personal consciousness and a tendency to the dissociation of sensations and memories. These dissociated memories and sensations continued to exist in the subconscious and have effects. He laid particular emphasis on the pathogenic effect of traumatic events in lives of patients and held that they could be led to recollect such events under hypnosis, automatic writing, and crystal gazing.

During this period, Janet paid attention to dreams and subconscious reveries. The therapeutic significance of the former was that they often revealed the pathogenic event, and brought to light subconscious fixed ideas that could subsequently be liquidated. With the sick, subconscious reveries became involuntary, and Janet characterised hysterics as individuals who, not content to dream at night, dreamt all day long. Neurotics had the need to be directed, and this role had to be assumed by the physician, in order for the patient to regain their self-mastery. Janet called his method 'psychological analysis'. In Vienna, Breuer and Freud drew upon Janet's work, and a priority dispute later broke out between them. Subsequent historical research has tended to support Janet's claims. In 1902, he succeeded Théodule Ribot in his post at the Collège de France. Though prominent in his lifetime, Janet never formed a school or movement and did not cultivate disciples. Janet's conception of the dissociation of consciousness was widely taken up. In many respects, the pathological psychology which he developed had its greatest impact on the burgeoning field of psychotherapy. Through the effects of the Freudian legend, much that should have been attributed to his work was instead ascribed to psychoanalysis.

In 1903, Janet reflected on the social historical significance of psychotherapy. He observed that when patients found a friend or someone whom they could obey, their problems ceased. He argued that priests had formerly fulfilled this function, and doctors could now do the same. Priests had done this in a haphazard manner, and no longer had the authority that they once had: 'It is a characteristic of our time that this work of moral direction has sometimes returned to the doctor, who is now often charged with this role of moral direction when the patient does not find enough support around him.'[30] This notion of psychotherapy as fulfilling a function previously served by the Church became increasingly signficant in the decades that followed, particularly in the work of Jung, alongside attempts to combine psychotherapy with pastoral care.[31]

In 1919, Janet published his *Psychological Medications*, which presented a seminally important account of the history of psychotherapy combined with a full articulation of his new system, recasting his earlier studies in the light of the latter.[32] It presented an elaborate new model of psychotherapy, underpinned by psychological energetics. It was never taken up in the manner in which his early studies of dissociation had and continue to be taken up. However, his account of the relations of magnetic tradition to the hypnotic tradition provided one of the main templates for how it has been subsequently viewed.[33] In a similar manner to Bernheim, he held to the negative model of the goal of psychotherapy, as the removal of pathology. For him, it constituted the totality of physical and mental procedures applied to mental and bodily disorders through consideration of psychological phenemona. It thus represented the application of psychological science to the treatment of disease.[34]

For decades, we have laboured under the spell of the Freud legend, which has led to the wholesale mystification of the history of psychotherapy.[35] Freud started as a neurologist in private practice, and, as was common, utilised electrotherapy and the Weir Mitchell rest cure. In 1885, he went to study with Charcot in Paris and became interested in hysteria. In 1893, Freud, published, together with his senior colleague and mentor, Josef Breuer, 'On the Psychical Mechanism of Hysteria: Preliminary Communication'.[36] At this time, a number of figures were interested in issues related to catharsis in psychotherapy. Breuer and Freud argued that the symptoms of hysteria were due to a precipitating trauma. They represented symbolic connections, for example, vomiting after experiencing feeling of mental disgust. In effect, they were expanding and generalising Charcot's concept of traumatic hysteria and notion of 'passionate attitudes'. They argued that in hysteria, the psychical trauma acted like a foreign body. Patients failed to fully react to a trauma. They claimed that the splitting of consciousness described in dual personality happened in every hysteria. However, hidden memories were retrievable under hypnosis. Each hysterical symptom disappeared when one succeeded in bringing to light the memory of the event which provoked it, and the patient had put the affect into words. The psychical processes had to be brought back 'in statu nascendi'. They famously concluded that, 'Hysterics suffer mainly from reminiscences.'[37] After the collapse of Freud's so-called seduction theory and his abandonment of hypnosis, the therapeutic emphasis no longer focussed on rememoration and catharsis, but on the interpretation of and working through of Oedipal fantasies by way of free association, dream analysis, and transference interpretation.

In the psychoanalytic and psychotherapeutic literature, 'interpretation' increasingly came to take the preeminent place previously occupied by 'suggestion'. Jacqueline Carroy has noted that in the hypnotic literature, suggestion functioned as a heterodox, umbrella term, which, as well as imperative suggestion, included paradoxical injunctions and interpretations.[38] In a similar manner, if one studies psychoanalytic and psychotherapeutic cases in the twentieth century, one finds that 'interpretation' functioned in a similar catch-all manner. Whilst the theoretical account of practices changed considerably, the same was not the case in the practices themselves, and under the rubric of interpretation in the psychoanalytic literature, it is not hard to find some of the best examples of authoritarian directives.

It was with the entrance of Bleuler (1857–1939), Jung (1875–1961), and the Zürich school that the psychoanalytic movement truly become international. It was Bleuler and Jung that put psychoanalysis on the map in the German-speaking psychiatric world. The ease with which individuals could gain instruction in psychoanalytic techniques in the Burghölzli was similar to Bernheim's clinic in Nancy, and led greatly to their dissemination. Indeed, for psychiatrists interested in psychoanalysis, Zürich, and not Vienna, was initially the instruction centre of choice. As Ernst Falzeder notes, a large proportion of significant figures in dynamic psychiatry and psychoanalysis either worked or visited the Burghölzli.[39] The open model of instruction practised there greatly contributed to the spread of psychoanalysis. However, it quickly came into collision with the closed feudal structure which Freud was establishing.

In 1909, August Forel (1848–1931), a major champion of hypnosis and suggestion, founded the International Society for Medical Psychology and Psychotherapy. In August, he sent circulars off to the principal representatives of European psychotherapy, including Freud and Jung, asking them to join. Forel felt that the lack of coordination between different orientations in psychotherapy was a critical problem. He wanted to create order in this 'Tower of Babel' by facilitating scientific exchanges and establishing 'a clear international terminology, capable of being accepted in a general manner by different people'[40] – in other words, to form one general science of psychotherapy. Shortly after, Freud proposed the idea of a rival association of psychoanalysis, firmly grouping together adherents to his doctrine. This timing was not accidental.[41]

Freud contended that psychoanalytic technique could as yet not be learnt from books, but only from someone already proficient in it. Due to the dangers of 'wild' psychoanalysis, he and his co-workers had founded the International Psycho-Analtyic Association.[42] Freud was militantly opposed to psychoanalysis freely entering general medical practice as an auxiliary psychotherapeutic procedure – not out of some concern with safeguarding the public, but with safeguarding psychoanalysis and the purity of the doctrine. Indeed, it was due to the increasing isolationist policy of psychoanalysis *vis-à-vis* medicine and psychiatry that Eugen Bleuler resigned from the

IPA in 1911.[43] It was Freud's institutional model rather than Forel's that came to predominate in the twentieth century.

In 1912, Jung put forward the recommendation that every prospective analyst had to undergo an analysis, arguing that success in analysis depended upon how far the analyst had been analysed himself.[44] Jung's suggestion was quickly seconded by Freud. It was insufficient simply to be a doctor or psychiatrist to practise psychoanalysis. Whilst claiming that psychoanalysis was a medical technique, further qualification was required. In terms of current practices in psychotherapy, this was a striking departure. It would have been unthinkable to have established the hypnotic treatment of the physician as an essential training requirement. Freud argued that the would-be analyst had to undergo a 'psycho-analytic purification'.[45] The training analysis was the means by which the faithful transmission of analytic knowledge was safeguarded.

Jung's suggestion has had an overpowering effect, not only on the subsequent organisation of psychoanalysis, but on modern psychotherapy. Until recently, this requirement has been one of the few common denominators in the plethora of psychotherapeutic schools. The institution of training analysis became critical in providing a financial base for private practice psychoanalysis and helped to make it a viable professional proposition.

After the hiatus of the Second World War, the institutionalisation of the psychoanalytic movement spread place rapidly.[46] The Berlin society, founded by Karl Abraham in 1920, began to formalise its training. It was here that the triad of personal analysis, supervised analysis, and seminars was established that became the basic template of all psychoanalytic institutes. In 1925, at the psychoanalytic congress in Bad Homburg, the stipulation the requirement that every prospective analyst had to be analysed was passed.

It was through the training enterprise that psychoanalysis prospered from the 1920s onwards. The formation of a psychoanalytic training system, detached from medicine and psychiatry was crucial in the survival of psychoanalysis, and greatly contributed to its success in comparison with other forms of psychotherapy, as no other school had established a comparable system. The public success of psychoanalysis was not due to any inherent therapeutic or theoretical superiority, but from the particular mode of institutional organisation that it adopted and the consequent suggestive effect on the wider populace. Without this, the Freudian legend would have been ineffective. It was the effectiveness of the institutional structures of psychoanalysis that gave it public visibility, such that cultural debates about the new psychology were nominally cast in the idiom of psychoanalysis.

If the establishment of the psychoanalytic training system played a crucial role in the establishment of psychoanalysis, it was also an unstable matrix, as it could easily become adapted to any theoretical model. This has indeed been the case, and a myriad of psychotherapeutic schools adopted the same institutional structure to propagate their therapies. The success of these rival schools, adopting the same institutional structures as psychoanalysis, contributed to the decline of psychoanalysis.

In addition to being a psychotherapeutic procedure, Freud extended the scope of psychoanalysis to the analysis and diagnosis of culture in general, in such works as *Civilisation and its Discontents* and *The Future of an Illusion*.[47] Freud's expansion of the neurosis concept in works such as *The Psychopathology of Everyday Life*,[48] and his pathologisation of culture, led to an implicit conception that the freedom from neurosis promised by psychoanalytic therapy constituted, if not a state of well-being, a lesser state of ill-being than of a large proportion of the population. The patient pool for psychoanalytic therapy had in effect been extended to everyone.

A similar expansion took place in the work of Jung, in a radically different and more melioristic manner. In 1913, Jung had a series of apocalyptic visions. Struck by the correspondence between these and the subsequent onset of the war, Jung engaged in a process of self-experimentation which he termed his 'confrontation with the unconscious'. At the heart of this project was Jung's attempt to get to know his own 'myth' as a solution to the mythless predicament of secular modernity. This took the form of provoking an extended series of waking fantasies in himself. Jung elaborated, illustrated, and commented on these fantasies in a work that he called *Liber Novus*, or *The Red Book*, which was at the centre of his later work.[49] This depicted the process through which Jung regained his soul and overcame the contemporary malaise of spiritual alienation, which was achieved through enabling the rebirth of a new image of God in his soul and developing a new world view in the form of a psychological and theological cosmology. *Liber Novus* presented the prototype of Jung's conception of the individuation process, which he held to be the universal form of individual psychological development.

In 1916, Jung wrote a paper on 'The Transcendent Function', developing a generalisable psychotherapeutic method from his self-experimentation. He later termed this 'active imagination'. One commenced by concentrating on a particular mood and attempting to become as conscious as possible of all fantasies and associations which came up in connection with it. The aim was to allow fantasy free play, but without departing from the initial affect in a free associative process. This led to a concrete or symbolic expression of the mood, which had the result of bringing the affect nearer to consciousness, hence making it more understandable. The mere process of doing this could have a vitalising effect. Individuals could write, draw, paint or sculpt, depending on their propensities.[50] Once these fantasies had been produced and embodied, two approaches were possible: creative formulation and understanding. Each needed the other, and both were necessary to produce the transcendent function, which arose out of the union of conscious and unconscious contents, and resulted in a widening of consciousness. In his practice at this time, Jung encouraged his patients to undertake similar forms of self-investigation. His use and advocacy of nonverbal techniques in psychotherapy was to play an important role in the rise of art therapies.[51]

Jung maintained that his fantasies and those of his patients stemmed from the mythopoetic imagination which was missing in the present rational age. Reconnecting with this could form the basis for cultural renewal. The task of moderns was one of establishing a dialogue with the contents of the collective unconscious and integrating them into consciousness. This was to play an important part in the popular 'mythic revival'. He maintained that cultural renewal could only come about through self-regeneration of the individual; in other words, through the individuation process. Consequently, for Jung psychotherapy was no longer a process solely preoccupied with the treatment of psychopathology. It became a practice to enable the higher development of the individual through fostering individuation. Jung noted that a third of his cases had no neurosis, and were highly functioning and well-adapted individuals, but who had an acute sense of aimlessness.[52] The task that they confronted

was that of a recovery of a sense of meaning in their life, made more pressing with
the secularisation and rationalisation of contemporary culture. Thus such individuals were suffering from a condition that afflicted the culture at large. Consequently,
individuals who managed to recover a sense of meaning in their lives were healing
not only themselves, but also the culture. This broadening of the aims of psychotherapy to encompass the higher, spiritual development of the individual played an
important role in the rise of humanistic and transpersonal psychologies and psychotherapies, and soul therapies.[53]

Shellshock during the First World War had led to an increasing recognition of
the prevalence of purely psychic disorders and legitimacy of psychic treatment.
Correspondingly, the expansion of the neurosis concept was linked with an increasing destigmatisation. During the 1920s and 1930s, psychotherapy was dominated, on
the one hand, by the still-widespread, eclectic use of hypnosis and suggestion, and
on the other, by the work of figures such as Janet, Freud, Jung, and Adler, in which
conceptions of psychotherapy were tighly linked to proprietary systems of dynamic
psychology. Bernheim's ontology of suggestion was a relatively sparse and simple
one. By contrast the ontologies of the unconscious on offer in Freudian and Jungian
therapies were vast baroque structures that generated some of the most complex hermeneutic systems of the twentieth century.[54] They took hold in the humanities and
social sciences and also had powerful effects on the wider populace, furnishing compelling forms of self-description and other-ascription.

After Freud, there was also a shift in psychoanalysis to more melioristic conceptions of the aims and possibilities of psychoanalytic therapy. For example, in her
work, *Neurosis and Human Growth: The Struggle Toward Self Realization* (1951), Karen
Horney (1885–1952) tried to shift psychoanalysis away from a medical model, arguing instead that it was a practice that fostered self-realisation. Its aim was one of
aiding an individual to outgrow difficulties so that their development 'may assume
a more constructive course' through releasing innate healing forces and mobilising
the real self.[55] As a consequence, analysis came to be seen to be following in the
footsteps of distinguished forebears: 'The road of analytic therapy is an old one, advocated time and again throughout human history. In the terms of Socrates and the
Hindu philosophy, among others, it is the *road to reorientation through self-knowledge.*'[56]
Self-realisation, in turn, was now depicted in a psychological idiom, consisting in a
deeper experiencing of one's feelings, wishes and beliefs, the ability to use one's
resources, a greater sense of responsibility, relating to others with genuine feelings,
respecting them as individuals in a spirit of mutuality, becoming more productive,
and valuing work intrinsically, rather than as a means to satisfy pride and vanity.
The result of this was facilitating the desire for and the possibility of happiness.[57]
Throughout Horney's work, there was a clear alignment of the goals of therapy with
dominant cultural norms.

The 1940s and 1950s saw the rise of systems of psychotherapy no longer tightly
linked with general systems of psychology, such as the humanistic psychotherapy, or the
'client-centered therapy', promulgated by Carl Rogers (1902–1987). In 1951, Rogers
argued that in client-centered therapy there was no need for theories without phenomena to explain in the form of observable changes.[58] In place of top-down theory
dominated psychotherapies, Rogers advocated what one could call 'theory-lite' psychotherapies, legitimated by the study of process notes and outcomes. Under Rogers'

ministrations, psychotherapy led to certain characteristic changes of behaviour: an increased discussion of plans and behavioral steps to be undertaken while in therapy; a change from relatively immature to mature behaviour; a decrease in psychological tension and defensive behaviours coupled with greater awareness of those defensive behaviours which are present; an increased tolerance for frustration as objectively measured in physiological terms; and improved functioning in life tasks and in adjustment to job training and job performance.[59] The successful clients of Rogers's therapy – a term popularised in his 1942 study[60] – were clearly intended to take up their role as good citizens in advanced liberal democratic societies. For Rogers, they would not necessarily be adjusted to the culture, nor be conformists, but would live constructively and be in sync with their culture to the extent required by a balanced satisfaction of needs. As a result, they would be vanguards of human evolution.[61] Rogers in turn attributed the rise of psychotherapy to societal transformations, and in particular, to the manner in which, as culture became less homogenous, it gave less support to individuals, who consequently could no longer rely on culture and tradition. Hence individuals needed to resolve in themselves issues previously determined by society. As it offered a means of resolving such conflicts, psychotherapy had increasingly become a public and professional focal point.[62]

Rogers's work is an example of the malleability of psychotherapy, with regard to determination of the changes deemed beneficial and held to be therapeutic in a particular social epoch, and one resting on a particular 'image of man', which it in turn helped to promote: 'The basic nature of the human being, when functioning freely, is constructive and trustworthy.'[63] This was presented as an alternative to Freud's mordant, tragic vision.

The rise of the psychotherapies also played a significant factor in the development of what cultural historians have called the 'therapeutic ethos'. Jackson Lears has argued that the first decades of the twentieth century in America were marked by a crucial moral change from 'a Protestant ethos of salvation through self-denial toward a therapeutic ethos stressing self-realization in this world'.[64] This therapeutic ethos was in turn taken up and reinforced by advertisers, who attempted to respond to and shape the emotional needs of consumers. This led to the presentation of products as embodiments of the therapeutic ethos. As Lears puts it, 'the promise was that the product would contribute to the buyer's physical, psychic, or social well-being; and the threat was that his well-being would be undermined if he failed to buy it.'[65] In this way the therapeutic ethos was a critical constituent of mass consumer culture. Consequently, psychotherapies were having far-ranging effects beyond therapists' consulting rooms.

The same period saw the rise of the existential psychotherapies, predicated on a different 'image of man'. Existential therapists articulated cultural critiques, coupled with critiques of the role of psychotherapies in contributing to the modern malaise of social alienation. In his contribution to the volume that did much to popularise existential therapies in the English-speaking world, *Existence*, Rollo May argued that 'the fundamental neurotic process in our day is the repression of the ontological sense.'[66] This resulted in a truncation of awareness and loss of innate potentialities. The diagnosis for the problems afflicting moderns was to be found in Heidegger's *Being and Time*. For May, practised in an unreflective manner, psychotherapy could simply serve to make matters worse by simply reflecting 'the fragmentation of the culture', and hence 'structuralizing neurosis rather than curing it'.[67] The fact that patients came to psychotherapy aiming to be cured from neurotic symptoms was itself the problem, which therapists should not collude in. The 'promise' that psychotherapies were offering of curing pathology – of conceiving the problems of existence in quasi-medical terms – was actually making things worse. By contrast, May argued that therapy should be concerned with enabling an individual to experience their existence. Any relief of symptoms which arose would be a by-product of this. The ideal of 'cure' conceived of as adjustment and fitting in with culture could be brought about through technically conceived therapies, as contemporary culture mandated living in a calculated well-managed manner. Such practices would lead to a lessening of anxiety, through a curtailment of the freedom which gave rise to anxiety, but this only resulted in a constriction of one's existence. Psychotherapists had become agents of the culture, and the practice of psychotherapy had become an expression of contemporary fragmentation, rather than a solution to it. Sartre, Heidegger, and Kierkegaard were now mobilised and operationalised into psychotherapeutic discourse.

Cultural critique took an explicit form in Gestalt therapy. In 1951, Frederick Perls (1893–1970), Ralph Hefferline (1910–1974), and Paul Goodman (1911–1972) argued that in contrast to other therapies, Gestalt therapy focussed on the actual situation, rather than viewing it as a symptom or as an expression of some unconscious content.[68] They were directly challenging prevailing value systems in psychotherapy, proposing a transvaluation of values, such as 'infantile' and 'mature'. The personalities of psychotherapists and their social role had led to the championing of the latter over the former: devaluing childhood traits and promoting adaptation to 'a standard of adult reality that is not worth adjusting to'.[69] In place of conformity to the so-called 'reality principle', they championed creative adjustment, arguing that the former consisted of social illusions that cast creative spontaneity as dangerous or psychotic.[70] Gestalt therapy aligned itself with the burgeoning counter-culture.

Meanwhile, other forms of psychotherapy arose which presented themselves as more culturally syntonic. In his landmark *Cognitive Therapy and the Emotional Disorders* of 1976, Aaron Beck (1921–), an American psychiatrist and psychoanalyst presented the following 'Formula for treatment': 'The therapist helps a patient to unravel his distortions in thinking and to learn alternative, more realistic ways to formulate his experiences.'[71] No reader of Paul Dubois can read this without a sense of déjà vu, nor fail to see cognitive therapy as a revival of a revival of moral treatment. Pinel is truly back. Beck quite consciously viewed cognitive therapy as the promotion of a new 'image of man':

> This new approach to emotional disorders changes man's perspective on himself and his problems. Rather than viewing himself as the helpless creature of his own biochemical reactions, or of blind impulses, or of automatic reflexes, he can regard himself as prone to learning erroneous, self-defeating notions and capable of *unlearning* or correcting them as well.[72]

What is on offer here is, in effect, a new optional ontology: one that can be characterised as 'therapeutic rationality'. In 'therapeutic rationality', disordered thought is the pathogen, and regulation of thought is the cure. Rachel Rosner has recently demonstrated that far from being an alternative to psychoanalysis, Beck conceived of cognitive therapy as a branch of neo-Freudianism.[73] For Beck, cognitive therapy had the advantages of psychoanalysis, without the drawbacks. Critically, it was readily amenable to experimental testing and easily accomodatable to the protocols of evidence-based medicine. Compared to psychoanalysis, the ontology on offer in cognitive therapy is a radically stripped down one – gone are all the denizens of the inner world and their metapsychological doubles. Cognitive therapy represents a new minimalism of the mind. Critically, gone too was the elaborate, lengthy, and costly apprenticeship system of psychoanalytic and psychotherapeutic training, and with it, the essential requirement that a would-be practitioner was required to undergo an initiatory treatment themselves, to experience the practice at first hand. This shift in mode of instruction has enabled the mass rollout of state-funded cognitive behaviour therapy in the UK, to take one example.[74]

As Delboeuf had pointed out with regard to hypnosis, the cultural dissemination of psychotherapeutic ideas in turn shaped the patients who came to psychotherapy, leading to a Moebius strip of circulating feedback loops. By the mid-twentieth century, the psychotherapeutic scene was a teeming marketplace, offering a plethora of competing optional ontologies: conceptions not only of the reasons for one's maladies and how to be cured of them, but of how to be well and take up one's place in society and the world. These were not only illness narratives in Arthur Kleinman's sense,[75] but also what one could call transformation narratives. Psychotherapy had become not only a palliative for psychological disorders, but a form of life enhancement. As such, it increasingly became a lifestyle choice. The varieties of psychotherapy on offer constituted choices of various regimens of well-being, of achieving, in the Aristotelian sense, the good life. The conceptions of well-being on offer were seen to be legitimated by, if not science, something close to it, with the same universalistic aspirations.

Thus, psychotherapies have played critical roles in fostering conceptions of psychological disorder as well as of psychological well-being and identity itself. Since psychotherapy began to gain increasing currency towards the end of the nineteenth century, it and its surrounding cultures have both undergone mutations and transformations, acting on and reacting to one another in a series of relations, at times in concert, at times antagonistically. We have yet to comprehend the full scale of its effects on contemporary societies which have, in part, become psychotherapeutic societies. It was not for nothing that that Marshall McLuhan stated in 1964, 'ours is the century of the psychiatrist's couch.'[76]

Notes

1 Frederick van Eeden, 'Les principes de la psychothérapie', *Revue de l'hypnotisme*, 7 (1893): 99. Van Eeden had founded a 'clinique de psycho-thérapeutique suggestive' in 1889 with Albert van Rentergehm.

2 Karl Jaspers, *General Psychopathology*, tr. J. Hoening and Marian Hamilton (Manchester: Manchester University Press, 1963), 834.

3 Thomas Szasz, 'The Myth of Psychotherapy', *Proceedings of the 9th International Congress of Psychotherapy, Oslo, 1973* (Basel: S. Karger, 1975), 220.

4 This was presented in a series of linked neologisms: 'Psychogenesis – the birth of thought/ psychophrenologia – the home of thought/psychopathia – the bane of thought/ psychotherapeia – the antidote of thought/psychonoesis – the force of thought.' See the table of contents in Walter Cooper Dendy, *Psyche: A Discourse on the Birth and Pilgrimage of Thought* (London: Longman, Brown, Green and Longmans, 1853).

5 Dendy, 'Psychotherapeia, or the Remedial Influence of Mind', *Journal of Psychological Medicine and Mental Pathology*, 6 (1853): 268.

6 *Asylum Journal*, 8 (1854): 127.

7 D. H. Tuke, *Illustrations of the Influence of the Mind Upon the Body in Health and Disease Designed to Elucidate the Action of the Imagination* (London: J. & A. Churchill, 1872). The next few pages draw from my '"Psychotherapy": The Invention of a Word', *History of the Human Sciences*, 18 (2005): 1–25, in a revised and modified form.

8 Ibid., 405. Tuke was referring to *Report of Dr. Benjamin Franklin and other commissioners charged by the King of France with the examination of the animal magnetism, as now practised at Paris*, tr. William Goodwin (London: J. Johnson, 1785).

9 Ibid., 5.

10 Hippolyte Bernheim, *Bernheim's New Studies in Hypnotism* [Hypnotisme, suggestion, psycho-thérapie: études nouvelles, 1891], tr. R. Sandor (New York: International Universities Press, 1980), 16.

11 Ibid., 18.

12 Bernheim, in Tuke ed., *A Dictionary of Psychological Medicine* (London: J. A. Churchill, 1892), 1214.

13 Henrik Petersen, 'Hypno-suggestion, etc., Medical letters' in Otto Wetterstrand, *Hypnotism and its Application to Practical Medicine*, tr. Petersen (New York: G. P. Putnam, 1897), 126.

14 Jean-Martin Charcot, *Clinical Lectures on the Diseases of the Nervous System*, ed. Ruth Harris (London: Routledge, 1991).

15 Joseph Delboeuf, 'De l'influence de l'education et de l'imitation dans le somnambulisme provoqué', *Revue Philosophique*, 22 (1886): 52–3.

16 Tuke, *Le corps et l'esprit. Action du moral et de l'imagination sur le physique*, tr. V. Parent (Paris: J.-B. Ballière, 1886).

17 Bernheim, *De la suggestion et de ses applications à la thérapeutique* (Paris: Doin, 1886), 218.

18 Delboeuf, 'Quelques considérations sur la psychologie de l'hypnotisme, à propos d'un cas de manie homicide guérie par suggestion', (1893), in *Le Sommeil et les rêves et autres textes* (Paris: Fayard, 1993), 421.

19 Paul Dubois, *Psychic Treatment of Nervous Disorders* [*Les Psychonévroses et leur traitement moral*] (1904), tr. S. E. Jeliffe and W. A. White (New York: Funk & Wagnalls, 1909), 221.

20 Ibid., xiii.

21 Ibid., 96.

22 A similar perspective was presented by Jules Déjerine and E. Glaucker, *The Psychoneuroses and their Treatment by Psychotherapy* (1911) [*Les manifestations fonctionnelles des psychonévroses: leur traitement par la psychothérapie*], tr. S. E. Jelliffe (Philadelphia, PA: J. B. Lippincott, 1918). On this question, see Marcel Gauchet and Gladys Swain, 'Du traitement moral aux psy-chothérapies: remarque sur la formation de l'idée contemporaine de psychothérapie', in Gladys Swain, *Dialogues avec l'insensé* (Paris: Gallimard, 1994), 237–262.

23 Dubois, *Les psychonévroses et leur traitement moral*, (Paris: Masson, 1905, 2nd edn), 19.

24 On this question, see Mikkel Borch-Jacobsen, *Making Minds and Madness: From Hysteria to Depression* (Cambridge: Cambridge University Press, 2009), and my 'Claire, Lise, Jean, Nadia, and Gisèle: Preliminary Notes towards a Characterisation of Pierre Janet's Psychasthenia' in *Cultures of Neurasthenia: From Beard to the First World War*, ed. Marijke Gijswijt-Hofstra and Roy Porter (Amsterdam: Rodopi, 2001), 362–385.

25 Jean Camus and Philippe Pagniez, *Isolement et psychothérapie: traitement de l'hystérie et de la neurasthénie, pratique de la rééducation morale et physique* (Paris: Alcan, 1904), 26.

26 See Sanjay Subrahmanyam, *Explorations in Connected History: From the Tagus to the Ganges* (Delhi: Oxford University Press, 2004).

27 On this issue, see my 'Psychologies as Ontology-Making Practices: William James and the Pluralities of Psychological Experience' in *William James and the Varieties of Religious Experience*, ed. Jeremy Carrette, (London: Routledge, 2004), 27–46.

28 Pierre Janet, *L'Automatisme psychologique: essais de psychologie expérimentale sur les formes inférieures de l'activité humaine*, 4th edition (Paris: Alcan, 1903).

29 Pierre Janet, *Mental State of Hystericals: A Study of Mental Stigmata and Mental Accidents*, tr. C. Corson (New York: G. P. Putnam's Sons, 1901).

30 Pierre Janet, *Les obsessions et la psychasthénie* I (Paris: Alcan, 1903), 727.
31 See for instance Elwood Worcester, Samuel McComb and Isador Coriat, *Religion and Medicine: The Moral Control of Nervous Disorders* (New York: Moffat Yard, 1908). See Eric Caplan, *Mind Games: American Culture and the Birth of Psychotherapy* (Berkeley, CA: University of California Press, 2001).
32 Pierre Janet, *Psychological Healing*, tr. E & C Paul, (London: Allen & Unwin, 1925).
33 See for example, Henri Ellenberger, *The Discovery of the Unconscious: The History and Evolution of Dynamic Psychiatry* (New York: Basic Books, 1970).
34 Ibid., 1208.
35 See Frank Sulloway, *Freud, Biologist of the Mind: Beyond the Psychoanalytic Legend*, (Cambridge, MA: Harvard University Press, 1992) and Mikkel Borch-Jacobsen and Sonu Shamdasani, *The Freud Files: An Inquiry into the History of Psychoanalysis*, (Cambridge: Cambridge University Press, 2012).
36 Josef Breuer and Sigmund Freud, 'On the Psychical Mechanism of Hysteria: Preliminary Communication,' *The Standard Edition of the Complete Psychological Works of Sigmund Freud*, ed. James Strachey, Anna Freud, Alix Strachey, Alan Tyson and Angela Richards (London: Hogarth Press and the Institute of Psycho-Analysis, 1953–1974). (Hereafter, SE), vol. 2.
37 Ibid., 10.
38 Jacqueline Carroy, *Hypnose, suggestion et psychologie: l'invention de sujets* (Paris: PUF, 1991), 179–200.
39 Ernst Falzeder, 'The Threads of Psychoanalytic Filiations or Psychoanalysis Taking Effect', in *100 Years of Psychoanalysis: Contributions to the History of Psychoanalysis*, ed. André Haynal and Ernst Falzeder, special issue of *Cahiers Psychiatriques Genevois* 1994, 172.
40 August Forel, 'La psychologie et la psychothérapie à l'université', *Journal für Psychologie und Neurologie*, 17 (1910): 315–316.
41 See Mikkel Borch-Jacobsen and Sonu Shamdasani, *The Freud Files: An Inquiry into the History of Psychoanalysis* (Cambridge: Cambridge University Press), 77f., and my '"Psychotherapy in 1909: Notes on a Vintage', in *After Freud Left: New Reflections on a Century of Psychoanalysis in America*, ed. John Burnham (Chicago: University of Chicago Press, 2012), 31–47.
42 Freud, '"Wild" Psycho-analysis', *SE* 11, 226–227.
43 Bleuler to Freud, in Eugen Bleuler and Sigmund Freud, *'Ich bin zuversichtlich, wir erorbern bald die Psychiatrie.' Briefwechsel 1904–1937*, ed, Michael Schröter (Basel: Schwabe, 2012), 153f. See Ernst Falzeder, 'The Story of an Ambivalent Relationship: Sigmund Freud and Eugen Bleuler', *Journal of Analytical Psychology*, 52 (2007): 343–368.
44 Jung, 'Attempt at a Portrayal of Psychoanalytic Theory', *Collected Works*, 4, ed. Gerhard Adler, Michael Fordham, Herbert Read, William McGuire, tr. R. F. C. Hull, (New York and Princeton: Bollingen Series and London, 1953–1983), (hereafter, *CW*) vol. 4, section 449.
45 Freud, 'Recommendations to Physicians Practising Psycho-analysis', (1912) *SE* 12, 116.
46 See Ernst Falzeder, *Psychoanalytic Filiations: Mapping the Psychoanalytic Movement* (London: Karnac, 2015) and George Makari, *Revolution in Mind: The Creation of Psychoanalysis* (New York: HarperCollins, 2008).
47 Freud, *SE* 21.
48 Freud, *SE* 6.
49 Jung, *The Red Book. Liber Novus*, ed. Sonu Shamdasani, trs. Mark Kyburz, John Peck and Sonu Shamdasani (New York: W. W. Norton, 2009).
50 Jung, *CW* 8, sections 170–171.
51 See Susan Hogan, *Healing Arts: The History of Art Therapy* (London: Jessica Kingsley, 2001).
52 'The Aims of Psychotherapy' (1929), *CW* 6, § 83.
53 See Eugene Taylor, *Shadow Culture: Psychology and Spirituality in America* (Washington, DC: Counterpoint, 1999).
54 See my 'The Optional Unconscious' in *Thinking the Unconscious: Nineteenth-Century German Thought*, ed. Martin Liebscher and Angus Nicholls (Cambridge: Cambridge University Press, 2010), 287–296.
55 Karen Horney, *Neurosis and Human Growth: the Struggle Toward Self Realization* (New York: W. W. Norton, 1951), 33.
56 Ibid., 341.

57 Karen Horney, *New Ways in Psychoanalysis* (London: Kegan Paul, Trench and Trubner, 1947), 290.

58 Carl Rogers, *Client-Centered Therapy: Its Current Practice, Implications and Theory* (Boston: Houghton Mifflin Co., 1951), 15.

59 Ibid., 179f.

60 Carl Rogers, *Counselling and Psychotherapy* (New York: Houghton, Mifflin & Co, 1942).

61 Carl Rogers, *On Becoming a Person: A Therapist's View of Psychotherapy* (London: John Constable, 1961), 191f.

62 Carl Rogers, *Client-Centered Therapy: Its Current Practice, Implications and Theory*, 4.

63 Carl Rogers, *On Becoming a Person: A Therapist's View of Psychotherapy*, 194.

64 T. J. Jackson Lears, "From Salvation to Self-Realization: Advertising and the Therapeutic Roots of the Consumer Culture, 1880–1930," *Advertising & Society Review*, 1 (2000), E-ISSSN, section 4.

65 Ibid., 50.

66 Rollo May, 'Contributions of Existential Psychotherapy' in *Existence: A New Dimension in Psychology and Psychiatry*, ed. Rollo May, Ernest Angel and Henri Ellenberger (New York: Basic Books, 1958), 86.

67 Ibid., 86–7.

68 Frederick Perls, Ralph Hefferline and Paul Goodman, et al., *Gestalt therapy: Excitement and Growth in the Human Personality* (New York: Julian Press, 1951), 237.

69 Ibid., 241.

70 Ibid., 394.

71 Aaoron Beck, *Cognitive Therapy and the Emotional Disorders* (New York: International Universities Press, 1976), 3.

72 Ibid., 4.

73 Rachel Rosner, 'The "Splendid Isolation" of Aaron T. Beck', *Isis* 105 (2014): 736.

74 See Richard Layard and David Clark, *Thrive: The Power of Evidence-Based Psychological Therapies* (London: Penguin, 2014). On the history of cognitive behaviour therapy, see Sarah Marks, 'Cognitive Behaviour Therapies in Britain: The Historical Context and Present Situation', in *Cognitive Behaviour Therapies*, ed. Windy Dryden, (London: Sage, 2012), 1–25.

75 Arthur Kleinman, *The Illness Narratives: Suffering Healing, and the Human Condition* (New York: Basic Books, 1988).

76 Marshall McLuhan, *Understanding Media: The Extensions of Man* (New York: McGraw Hill, 1964), 7.

21

THE ANTIDEPRESSANT
ERA REVISITED

Towards differentiation and patient-empowerment in diagnosis and treatment

Toine Pieters

In 1997, during the heyday of what has been labelled the 'business of selling mental disease and psychotropic drugs', David Healy published his book, *The Antidepressant Era*. In the postscript, Healy argued that the majority of people who meet diagnostic criteria for depression or anxiety seek treatment for a condition, which in principle cannot scientifically be shown to specifically benefit from available treatments.[1] Whether or not you agree with this statement, at least Healy has a point when saying that available psychotropic drugs do not have comparable specificity as antibiotics and other drug treatments do, such as insulin for diabetes or Viagra for erectile dysfunction. In this chapter, I will show that the addictive promise of the psychoactive magic bullet with a controllable and specific effect on the chemistry of the brain has not and will not materialize due to the complex and contextualized nature of mental disorders. Even molecular biologists have had to admit that they cannot find a single genetic cause for depression, anxiety or schizophrenia. The one-gene-one-disease ('O-GOD') champions of the 1990s met their Waterloo in mental illness and have turned to epigenetics to develop new forms of neurogenetic and neuropharmacological modelling.[2]

Despite the ever-growing demand for psychotropic drugs, patients have been the first to point to the remarkably non-specific, sometimes harmful and addictive nature of drug treatments by pioneering a new form of patient power through trial at the bar against drug icons like Halcion, Prozac, and Paxil.[3] However annoying, the reason for trial at the bar are the side effects which represent the price that many chronic sufferers living a pharmaceutical life have been willing to pay since the introduction of the first mood molecules in a frantic search for relief of their mental illness. At the same time, consumer demand for alternative psychotherapy packages has grown just as fast. Mental illness was, is, and will remain, a mind-blowing social and economic health problem that supersedes the demand and costs of all other major diseases like cancer, heart disease, or diabetes.[4] The historical lessons are challenging yet engaging. They teach us, as I will argue, that coping with mental illness requires a differentiated and personalized therapy package approach that includes pharmacotherapy, psychotherapy, and self-help programmes.

Psychopharmacology and historiography

There can be no history of psychiatry without a history of psychopharmacology. Whether by medical prescription or as self-medication, whether to sedate or cure, whether pushed by pharmaceutical companies or clamoured for by an anxious population, the consumption of psychoactive drugs has been an integral part of mental health care. Psychotropic drugs have been and still are important, although a recurrently controversial intervention tool in psychiatry. The administration of psychoactive substances has remained an underlying undulation in mental health care, regardless of changes in therapeutic fashion. Psychiatrists, as trained physicians, have continued to prescribe drug medication, while at the same time there has been steady consumer demand for both psychotropic drugs and alternative treatments, in the form of natural remedies, recreational drugs, psychotherapy, yoga, or mindfulness-training programmes. Even during the heyday of an anti-psychiatric revolt and critique of psychopharmacology, chemical liberation with the help of *other* drugs like LSD was regarded as an alternative for chemical 'strait-jackets'.[5]

The historiography of psychiatry has shown that relatively little attention has been given to the use of psychotropic drugs or other bodily cures in mental health care. Fortunately, in the past two decades, the specifics and contexts of psychotropic drug use have been studied more rigorously than ever before.[6] A basic problem with the integration of the history of psychopharmacology in the history of psychiatry is the tendency to use a perspective based on the dichotomy between a 'biological' and a 'psychosocial' psychiatry.[7] This perspective often hides the far more complex and versatile historical and current role of psychotropic drugs in treating mental illnesses. Developments and transformations do not necessarily align with the constructions of a biological and a psychosocial psychiatry or with theses of the 'first', 'second', or 'third' biological revolution in psychiatry. There has always been a gap in psychiatry between theoretical concepts and actual practice. Psychiatry has never been a 'royal' science with a practice symmetrically based on consistent theories.[8]

The uses and meanings of psychotropic drugs cannot be understood without taking into account the broader intellectual, social, economic, and political contexts that shape their historical trajectories.[9] Psychochemicals stand at the centre of complex networks binding a variety of actors and disciplinary fields. Investigating the specific realms in which a psychoactive drug's profile and identity is formed, involves the study of the historically situated process by which scientists, doctors, patients, drug company executives, and regulators (among others) handle psychochemicals in the laboratory, at the bedside, and in the household. This may include how laboratories develop drug tests, how doctors decide on prescribing psychotropic drugs in dialogue with their patients, how governments organize drug monitoring and regulation, how companies distribute and market drugs, how regulators set safety standards, how consumers choose to use these drugs (in a multitude of social settings), and how media report on these drugs.[10]

Imagery was and is as much a part of the fabric of psychotropic drugs as chemistry and pharmacology. Given psychotropic drugs' increasing visibility due to industry's persistent marketing efforts and their use in contexts of increasing media attention, psychotropic drugs have become important focal points of cultural mediation and imagination in the public sphere. They have taken on a special symbolic significance as icons of the increasing healing powers of modern medicine. From the early twentieth century onwards, the image makers of the drug industry and the media alike have succeeded in bringing immaterial qualities to psychotropic drugs: an aura of allure or fantasy; the mysterious fever of the benefit of the new that will wash away your blues, anxiety, or psychosis; the promise of doing good and no harm to body and mind.[11] This incorporeal nature of psychotropic drug images accounts for the many-sided connections these commodities have established in the various landscapes of our society as patent medicines, prescription medicines, natural remedies or recreational agents. In the next section, I will debunk the direct and indirect paths that shape the holy grail of neuro-psychopharmacology and biological psychiatry with 'happiness pills', 'emotional aspirins', 'mood' molecules, and 'mood' genes or biomarkers.

Towards a new chemistry of the mind

In the post-Second World War period, a new generation of chemists and psychopharmacologists worked hand in hand with the pharmaceutical industry to rejuvenate the 'materia medica' for the mind. They did so in a medical market that was saturated with the traditional and commercially squeezed-out psychoactive substances – hypnotics, sedatives, tonics, stimulants, and salts for treatment of overstrained nerves. The new generation of tranquilizers promised to do more than just stimulate or relax the nerves of businessmen, schoolteachers, and housewives. Technological optimism linked advances in neuropsychopharmacology to beliefs in scientific progress, freedom, democracy, and healthy bodies and minds. The popular media helped to spread belief in the treatable nature of mental illness and encouraged ideas about the healing potential of both psychopharmacology and Freudian psychoanalysis. Nowhere was the shift in the public perception of the diagnosis and therapy of mental illnesses more dramatic than in the United States. There was a growing belief that undesirable states of mind and forms of conduct could be changed into less undesirable or even desirable ones. Self-awareness was promoted as a means to the end of engendering a better and healthier self and a better society. With a kind of iatrogenic effect, the psychologization of health and illness resulted in the growth of a need for therapy and not only of the therapeutic talk variety. General practitioners began hearing from all sides that they needed to recognize concealed mental health problems and patients became much more willing to accept a diagnosis of a nervous illness and a matching prescription for psychotropic medication.[12]

Historians generally agree that the introduction of chlorpromazine, in 1952, marketed either as Thorazine®, Largactil® or Megaphen®, marked the start of a new era of drug treatment in psychiatry.[13] Chlorpromazine, together with the drug compound reserpine, transformed prospects for the treatment of mental illness. The concept of a therapeutic revolution, however, is a contested notion, since historical evidence points to continuity with earlier therapeutic developments in psychiatry. As far as the daily treatment practices are concerned, it is more appropriate to speak in terms of evolution.[14]

Chlorpromazine, marketed in Europe by the French chemical company, Rhône Poulenc, initially entered psychiatry as an *ad hoc* adjunct to existing psychotropic drug therapies and other bodily cures. Instead of promoting chlorpromazine as a revolutionary therapy, efforts to promote Largactil as a supplement to the existing armoury

381

of psychiatric treatments began in the early 1950s. These marketing efforts matched the idiosyncrasies of national and local styles and cultures for healing the mind. Gradually scientists, doctors, nurses, patients, and marketers attributed new features, meanings, and identities to chlorpromazine and reserpine. Depending on the local culture of treatment and rehabilitation, chlorpromazine or reserpine came to be regarded as either the most humane form of chemical restraint or as an important aid to existing social and psychotherapeutic treatment programs. In order to capture the new therapeutic profile and distinguish it from sedation proper, scientists began to label chlorpromazine and reserpine as major tranquilizers from the 1960s onwards. As a consequence, chlorpromazine and reserpine were instrumental in redrawing the map of diagnostic and therapeutic regimes in everyday psychiatric practice – and served as a prototype of a specific class of modern-day drugs, antipsychotics.[15]

The shifting routines, lexicons and logics surrounding the use of the major tranquilizers was given additional impetus by the observation that both chlorpromazine and reserpine counteracted the so-called psychosis induced by the hallucinogenic drug LSD. The suggestion of a relationship between chemical and clinical psychosis opened up a new scientific, medical, and public horizon of brain chemistry and statistics in mental health care.[16] The gradual acceptance of the 'chemistry of the brain' neurotransmitter paradigm paved the way for a productive alliance between psychopathology and clinical epidemiology. Over time this would turn the so-called 'neurotransmitter revolution in medicine' into an addictive form of neurological mythology – the chemically transformable mind.[17] Developments in the field of psychopharmacology had the breath of a scientific spring. The scientific claims of a chemically transformable mind were further popularized by the gurus of the 1960s counterculture who spoke of unlimited possibilities for the transformation of mind and body, psyche, and soma. The evolutionary jump towards a mental Superman seemed at hand with a revolutionary molecule like LSD.[18]

The pharmaceutical industry was quick to capitalize on the success of what became known as major tranquilizers. Like many other companies at the time, the Swiss-based pharmaceutical company Geigy started a search for chlorpromazine-like compounds. They asked the Swiss psychiatrist Roland Kuhn to test the various agents on patients with psychosis and schizophrenia. However, none of the tested substances appeared to be as effective as chlorpromazine. One compound, G22355 or imipramine, which was closest in molecular structure to chlorpromazine, even seemed to have an adverse effect. When imipramine was administered to formerly well-medicated patients with schizophrenia they became increasingly agitated and manic. Initially, Kuhn and Geigy were alarmed by the unexpected effect of imipramine and decided to halt the trial, but in the course of 1955 various parties decided to change the trial criteria and test the substance on patients who were suffering from depression. Once again, the trial results with imipramine turned out to be dramatic, but this time spectacularly successful, and all those involved spoke of a 'miracle cure'. Senior management did not know what to make of Kuhn's claim that imipramine lifted a patient's mood without being a stimulant and qualified the treatment of depression as a commercially less interesting niche market.[19]

Geigy management came round in the end and, in the spring of 1957, the company decided to market imipramine under the trade name of Tofranil. However, Tofranil sales did not take off until the early 1960s, when the pharmaceutical company Merck started marketing the concept of masked depression in primary care as part of their efforts to create a market for their own imipramine-like antidepressant amitryptiline under the trade name Tryptizol.[20]

With Merck's greater market sophistication, the antidepressant market received a boost, but depression as a psychiatric disorder was heavily stigmatized and therefore it was anxiety that turned the tide for minor tranquilizers and the so-called 'happiness pills'.[21]

Mother's little helpers

In 1960, the Swiss pharmaceutical company Hoffmann-La Roche launched a new psychotropic drug. The black-green capsules with the benzodiazepine compound chlordiazepoxyde became available as medication for anxiety and tension.[22] The drug had been synthesized in 1955 by the legendary company chemist Leo Sternbach (1908–2005) and received the trade name Librium. Librium was claimed to fill the 'gap' between the newly developed antipsychotics (e.g., chlorpromazine and reserpine and antidepressant medications imipramine and amitryptiline) on the one hand, and traditional sedatives and hypnotics on the other. Librium promised to be an anxiolytic without the problems of dependence and overdosing associated with the barbiturates.

The public presentation of Librium as the first representative of a new group of benzodiazepine drugs or 'benzos' and of a new therapeutic class of 'minor tranquilizers' suggested the arrival of a new era in psychotropic research and therapeutics. The term tranquilizer had already been coined in 1955 to try to distinguish the newly developed meprobamate (Miltown, Equanil) drug from the barbiturates. Whereas 'major tranquilizers' like chlorpromazine were claimed to have created a revolution in the doctoring of madness, minor tranquilizers promised to open up the field of the mass treatment of nervous problems in 'the age of anxiety'.[23]

Roche's extensive worldwide information campaign directed at specialists and general practitioners alike, and the inflationary spiral of media stories about a new medicinal drug with miraculous calming effects in small doses and no manifest side-effects, turned Librium into an overnight sensation. The 1960 phrase in *Life Magazine*: 'The drug that tames wild cats – What will it do for nervous women?' became a self-fulfilling prophecy.[24] Whereas the intense excitement about Miltown as the first tranquilizer was essentially an Anglo-American affair, Librium was world news. Roche set a new global marketing standard for blockbuster drugs. Not only did they decide in favour of a single brand name, but they also chose to market an all-embracing revolutionary treatment concept – a comprehensible and practical system of symptom identification, diagnostics, mode of action, and therapy. At the centre was the flexible, understandable (for both general practitioners and specialists), and manageable concept of chemically restoring the balance between body and mind through a specific switcher mechanism, the so-called 'limbic system'.[25] In print promotions, Librium was portrayed as an instant limbic stabilizer 'whatever the diagnosis'. But Librium was not presented as the one and only compound to make this new chemotherapeutic approach to nervous problems feasible. Librium cleared the way for the introduction of supplementary tranquilizers with various therapeutic profiles. Roche also led the way in 1963 by bringing out the more potent and anxiety-specific benzodiazepine analogue diazepam under the trade name Valium.[26]

Librium turned out to be only the prelude to the Valium frenzy or 'Valiummania'.[27] Marketed as the most potent, safe, and sane anxiolytic of the day, the pill with the tell-tale 'V', Valium rapidly surpassed Librium as the bestselling tranquilizer in Western countries. In 1965, Roche introduced yet another benzo, the sleeping pill Mogadon (nitrazepam).[28] This drug, in contrast to the 'traditional hypnotics' (i.e., the barbiturates), was claimed to be reliable and safe and did not lead to narcosis, coma, or death in case of an overdose.[29] The British and American Roche advertisements brought home the message of Mogadon's superiority in a rather candid way: 'Some patients stay on barbiturates until the day they die.'[30]

With the fast-growing popularity of the benzos, the therapeutic areas in which they were applied seemed to multiply unchecked.[31] Sleeplessness, nervousness, overexertion, stomach and back pains, hypertension and heart problems, and even psychotic disorders such as schizophrenia and manic depression became indications for the administration of members of the extended 'benzo-family'. These drugs were touted as the answer to everything, including the 'normal' emotional reactions to life's everyday challenges.[32] In Germany and the Netherlands, the following aphorism became popular among physicians: 'Wenn man nicht weiss, wie, was, warum, dann gibt man immer Valium' (when you don't know how, what, and why, then it is time for Valium).[33] Popular representations mirrored consumer statistics. From the early 1960s to the late 1970s, Librium, Valium, Mogadon, and other benzos led the drugs list in Western countries. This was in spite of the accumulation of reports on observed side-effects as early as 1961 by the American medical internist Leo Hollister, including: tolerance, dependence, drowsiness, reduced alertness, and other reactions leading to traffic accidents.[34]

The promise of a psychoactive magic bullet with a controllable and a specific effect on the chemistry of the brain was not fulfilled by benzodiazepines, LSD, or any other new synthetic compound. On the contrary, the chemical effects of the drugs on the mind turned out to be remarkably *non*-specific and addictive. Apart from medical side-effects, cultural and social 'side-effects' became manifest.

In 1966, when the psychologist Leslie Farber wrote his essay, 'Ours is the Addicted Society', the Rolling Stones produced their classic hit 'Mother's Little Helper', epitomizing the critique of middle-class tranquilizer addiction, alienation, and hypocrisy. Susan Speaker showed how the critique on the making and taking of benzos in the United States was tied up with their becoming a symbolic focal point for articulating and addressing social anxiety and tension as well as expectations regarding 'The Good Life'.[35]

Appetite for new chemical wonders for the mind

Regardless of the public portrayal of the benzodiazepines as addictive and dangerous medicines in the 1980s, the public desire for and expectations of new medications to restore one's brain chemistry to normal continued to grow as part of a process of individual empowerment.

This drive for self-development and self-expression resulted in a search for equality and appreciation of the 'other', the deviant. While mental disorders, including depression, were no longer taboo, there was a growing public interest in the pathological aspects of 'normal' people. Medical consumers began to consider everyday problems as inconvenient and undesirable sooner and more often and sought treatment. The growing popularity of biological theories of mental disorders and rising expectations surrounding the bio-revolution in medicine whetted the appetite for new wonders from the 'doctor's bag'. The introduction of operational diagnostic criteria for psychiatric disorders in a series of diagnostic manuals from the *DSM-III* in 1980 up to the *DSM-5* in the 2000s acted as an important catalyst. The steady growth in the number of independent and treatable categories of disorders (including broadening the definitions of depression and anxiety) – in what became widely regarded as the 'diagnostic bible' of mental disorders – stimulated the need and demand for medical treatments.[36]

The pharmaceutical industry was first to recognize the marketing potential of the DSM and the rising tide of bio-optimism. The US drug company Eli Lilly led the way with a new antidepressant Prozac (fluoxetine) launched at the end of the 1980s. Prozac was presented as a revolution in the psychopharmacology of depression. Based on the latest scientific evidence, depression had been shown to demonstrate a lowering of serotonin, a brain neurotransmitter. Fluoxetine was claimed to selectively restore the serotonin levels in the brain back to normal, a so-called selective serotonin reuptake inhibitor (SSRI). By prescribing a compound-like fluoxetine that lacked the nasty side effects of the older tricyclic antidepressants, doctors would be able to provide their patients with a safe and effective depression therapy.[37]

The message of a revolution in brain chemistry and a therapeutic breakthrough was picked up rather swiftly and turned into a self-fulfilling prophecy. The cycle of events following the introduction of Prozac even took Lilly's marketers by surprise. Peter Kramer's book *Listening to Prozac* celebrated the drug as a wonder drug effecting miraculous changes in personality and this helped to create a worldwide pill-taking hype that promoted Prozac and other SSRIs (e.g. Paxil and Zoloft) to the commercially attractive league of blockbusters. In 1994, Prozac was the second bestselling medication, just behind the ulcer drug Zantac, and Paxil would follow suit.[38]

In the meantime, prevalence rates of depression continued to rise significantly. Within three decades, the percentage of the population in the UK, the United States and European countries like the Netherlands with depression requiring treatment rose five-fold on average; it is now presumed to be more than five per cent. It is hard to believe that the Dutch or English population has grown five times as depressed in less than thirty years. What we do see in this period, however, is that medical journals and post-academic courses have paid increasing attention to the recognition, diagnosis, and treatment of mood and behaviour disorders. Furthermore, in daily practice, social and cultural factors, promise, hope, fashion, and taboo have been major influences. This holds for familiarity with mental disorders, recognition and acceptance, and ultimately the choice of treatment. What is recognized and accepted as depression, and what is not? Are consumers familiar with the possibilities of diagnosis and treatment? What expectations do they have for drug treatment? These aspects have been influenced significantly by mood drug publicity and media attention.

The above-mentioned process is dynamic. Pharmaceutical company advertisements and product information are important in this process. The companies have continuously looked for new markets by researching and influencing patient needs in the consulting room and translating them into treatment options. By supplying information to physicians and more and more to potential consumers, drug companies stimulate the tendency to increase drug prescriptions for mood and behaviour disorders. The drug company Pfizer once advertised that depression was the most democratic of all disorders. It could affect anyone at any moment, for a short or long duration, and without a recognizable course. However important the impact of this kind of disease-mongering may be, it still depends on physician and consumer cooperation. Therefore, it is important to assess the impact of the so-called SSRI suicide controversy on the prescription of SSRIs in the first decade of the twenty-first century, when the patents on most antidepressant blockbusters had expired and cheap generics flooded global medical markets alongside a steep decline in pharmaceutical marketing and prescriptions directly affecting profits.

In the period 2003–8, regulatory authorities like the Food and Drug Administration (FDA), Medicines and Healthcare products Regulatory Agency (MHRA), and European Medicines Agency (EMA), among others, issued several warnings restricting the use of SSRIs in paediatrics in reaction to safety concerns regarding suicidal ideation. While some scientists adulated the warnings, others expressed their concerns about the implied consequences. The safety issue arose following GlaxoSmithKline's (GSK) request for a six-month market exclusivity extension with the FDA for the use of paroxetine (an SSRI) to treat paediatric depression in response to the FDA Modernization Act. GSK submitted the results of unpublished paediatric clinical data to the FDA. Meanwhile, the BBC aired a documentary entitled 'The Secrets of Seroxat' on 13 October 2002 in which it was alleged that GSK internal documents showed that the dissemination of trial data on paroxetine in childhood depression was spun 'to minimise any negative commercial impact'.[39] GSK was accused of underplaying the association between SSRIs and suicidality. The ensuing worldwide media exposure played a role in driving the SSRI suicide controversy. In the process, confidence in the pharmaceutical industry and regulatory authorities decreased significantly.[40] However, the periods of intense media coverage of regulatory warnings did not have a significant impact on the overall upward trend of SSRI use as a drug class. In the UK and the Netherlands, there was a twofold increase in SSRI use over the period 2000–10.[41]

Doctors and patients, apparently, have not lost confidence in medication that promises to exploit brain chemistry to promote feelings of well-being and which is experienced as a helpful catalyst for lifting hopelessness, anxiety, and depression, regardless of the side-effects. To date, evidence suggests that SSRIs are still widely regarded as quite useful first-line treatments for depression and most anxiety disorders. Patients seeking relief for mental suffering do not care whether the ultimate catalyst for healing is a triumph of pharmacology, a compassionate therapist, or a placebo response. The Netherlands Study of Depression and Anxiety (NESDA) shows that what most patients want is a reasonable expectation of getting better and a better understanding of what makes them suffer and how to cope with recovery, relapse, and recurrence of depression and anxiety.[42] To achieve this goal, patients informally exchange and evaluate research results as well as treatment experiences on a regular basis. It is exemplary how concepts about the aetiology and treatment of mental disorders circulate between science and the public.[43] A case in point is the patient-oriented effort to conquer mental illness in the era of genomics.

Towards differentiation and patient empowerment in the era of genomics

The aforementioned NESDA study has provided important new insights and useful knowledge. There may be several genes and associated genetic risk areas that could be associated with depression, anxiety, and other mental disorders. All these genes contribute to the risk of having a psychiatric disorder. This is called the 'polygenetic' vulnerability to depression and anxiety. These risk genes have meaning only in mutual interaction with groups of individual carriers (risk groups) and in combination with environmental factors (among others, housing, food and traumatic events).[44] Integrating knowledge about biological and environmental factors has yielded key insights for the care of patients with mental illness. Polygenetic vulnerability combined with experiencing trauma, especially in childhood, has been shown to be a major risk factor for depression, anxiety disorder, or psychosis. What does this mean for mental healthcare? This knowledge emphasizes the importance of prevention and early detection that have been hidden by the biological and pharmacological turn in the treatment of mental illness the past fifty years.[45]

To whatever extent genes, proteins, neurotransmitters, or other elements in the human body have a role in the onset and course of mental disorders, the above findings show that environmental factors (youth, education, lifestyle) always come into play. The psychosocial factors prominently studied on research agendas are visible through the back door of neurobiological and genetic research. Ultimately, the biological twist in research has led to a re-evaluation of the biopsychosocial disease model.

For patients and those closely involved, it is reassuring to know that mental illness is associated with risk genes or traumatic events; this provides some support and hope that their condition can be influenced or fixed. Hope has proven to be a potent medicine. Prevention and early detection in combination with self-monitoring of psychiatric disorders are now increasingly seen as a priority within the mental health system. With a new self-monitoring instrument, the PsyMate, patients may be able to recognize and differentiate symptoms and relate to everyday events. Thus, patients seem far more able to act as active partners in the therapeutic process. This is also reflected in the recent revitalization of the Recovery Movement in psychiatry.[46] In the eyes of the Recovery Movement, patients are best empowered by teaching them to assess their own possibilities and limitations through self-help programs. Investing in these personal assessments is regarded as an important means to help stimulate one's own recovery.

One possible historically-informed problem is psychiatric patients' limited capacity for self-control and harm-control. The mantra of self-control can lead to further stigmatization of subgroups of psychiatric patients who are not able to individually work on their recovery. Active coaching and guidance in self-care and rehabilitation programs are not a luxury in this context. With hindsight, one might expect an easy return on investment by paying specific attention to patient participation in drug counselling and monitoring. The long-term effects of taking antidepressants can be quite profound. Cardiovascular disease and diabetes occur more frequently in those who depend on the long-term use of these drugs. The life expectancy of chronic psychiatric patients is on average more than five to ten years less than normal.[47]

At this time, prevention and early detection are the most promising interventions, in contrast to the historically more difficult trajectory of antidepressant treatments that may be effective to a greater or lesser degree. Therefore, it is important to create optimal social and living conditions and to ensure safety and security from the cradle to the grave for everyone. The path of prevention, however, is not without pitfalls. Collective interests (mental health and safety) may come to conflict with individual interests (privacy and autonomy). Furthermore, the historical promise that each individual can remake himself or herself in the pursuit of happiness by pharmacological and biomolecular means provides a persistent horizon of longing for gobbling pills to achieve a mind that provides instantaneous relief of mental suffering. The overall challenge will be to further capitalize on this alluring historical promise by stimulating productive alliances between scientists, doctors, and patients that aim at the development of innovative tailor-made coping strategies with mental illness encompassing pharmacotherapy, psychotherapy, self-help programmes, and community care.

Notes

1 D. Healy, *The Antidepressant Era* (Cambridge, MA: Harvard University Press, 1997), 257.
2 N. C. Andreasen, *Brave New Brain* (Oxford: Oxford University Press, 2001); A. C. Mitchell et al., 'The Genome in Three Dimensions: A New Frontier in Human Brain Research', *Biological Psychiatry*, 75 (2014): 961–69; D. F. Simola et al., 'Epigenetic (Re)programming of Caste-Specific Behavior in the Ant *Camponotus floridanus*', *Science*, 351 (2016): 6268; DOI: 10.1126/science.aac6633.
3 T. Pieters and S. Snelders, 'Managing Double Binds in the Pharmaceutical Prescription Market: The Case of Halcion' in *Ways of Regulating Drugs in the 19th and 20th Centuries*, ed. J. P. Gaudillière, V. Hess (London: Palgrave Macmillan, 2012), 270–286.
4 D. E. Bloom, et al., *The Global Economic Burden of Non-communicable Diseases* (Geneva: World Economic Forum, 2011). See www.weforum.org/EconomicsOfNCD (accessed 3 January 2016).
5 S. Snelders and Ch. Kaplan, "LSD Therapy in Dutch Psychiatry: Changing Socio-political Settings and Medical Sets," *Medical History* 46 (2002): 221–240; T. Pieters and S. Snelders, "Mental Ills and the 'Hidden History' of Drug Treatment Practices" in *Psychiatric Cultures Compared: Psychiatry and Mental Health Care in the Twentieth Century: Comparisons and Approaches*, ed. M. Gijswijt, et al., (Amsterdam: Amsterdam University Press, 2005), 381–401.
6 This is exemplified by the following series of publications, including Healy, *Antidepressant Era* and *The Creation of Psychopharmacology* (Cambridge, MA: Harvard University Press, 2002); F. W. Geels, T. Pieters, and S. Snelders, 'Cultural Enthusiasm, Resistance and the Societal Embedding of New (Medical) Technologies: Psychotropic Drugs in the Twentieth Century', *Technology Analysis & Strategic Management*, 19 (2007): 145–165; T. Pieters and S. Snelders, 'Psychotropic Drug Use: Between Healing and Enhancing the Mind', *Neuroethics*, 2 (2009): 63–73; E. Shorter, *Before Prozac* (Oxford: Oxford University Press, 2009); D. Herzberg, *Happy Pills in America* (Baltimore: The Johns Hopkins University Press, 2009); A. Tone, *The Age of Anxiety* (New York: Basic, 2009); V. Balz, *Zwischen Wirkung und Erfahrung – eine Geschichte der Psychopharmaka* (Bielefeld: Transcript, 2010); Pieters T. and Majerus B., 'The Introduction of Chlorpromazine in Belgium and the Netherlands (1951–1968): Tango Between Old and New Treatment Features', *Studies in the History and Philosophy of the Biological and Biomedical Sciences*, 42: (2011) 443–453; N. Henckes, 'Reshaping Chronicity: Neuroleptics and Changing Meanings of Therapy in French psychiatry, 1950–1975', *Studies in the History and Philosophy of the Biological and Biomedical Sciences*, 42 (2011): 434–43.
7 In the 1970s, Andrew Scull pointed out a similar problem in the conventional one-sided explanations for decarceration (the social versus the medical fix): A. T. Scull, *Decarceration* (Englewood Cliffs, NJ: Prentice Hall, 1977), 77–78.

8 For the difference between a 'royal' and a 'minor' science, see G. Deleuze and F. Guattari, *Nomadology: The War Machine* (New York: Semiotext(e), 1986).

9 I have elaborated the concept of trajectories and careers of psychotropic drugs together with Stephen Snelders in: S. Snelders, C. Kaplan, and T. Pieters, 'On Cannabis, Chloral Hydrate, and Career Cycles of Psychotropic Drugs in Medicine', *Bulletin of the History of Medicine*, 80 (2006): 95–114; Pieters and Snelders, 'Managing Double Binds'.

10 T. Pieters and S. Snelders, 'Standardizing Psychotropic Drugs and Drug Practices in the Twentieth Century: Paradox of Order and Disorder', *Studies in the History and Philosophy of the Biological and Biomedical Sciences*, 42 (2011): 412–415, 412.

11 A. Roersch van der Hoogte and T. Pieters, 'Advertenties voor hypnotica en sedativa in het Nederlands Tijdschrift voor Geneeskunde 1900–1940: Historische veranderingen in de vorm en inhoud van een informatiebron voor artsen', *Studium*, 4 (2010): 139–154; J. Greene and D. Herzberg, 'Hidden in Plain Sight: The Popular Promotion of Prescription Drugs in the 20th century', *American Journal of Public Health* 100 (2010): 793–803; http://prescription-drugs.procon.org/view.resource.php?resourceID=005586 (accessed 9 January 2016).

12 Pieters and Snelders, 'Psychotropic Drug Use', 66.

13 E. H. Ackerknecht, *A Short History of Psychiatry* (New York: Hafner, 1959), 8–11; J. P. Swazey, *Chlorpromazine in Psychiatry: A Study of Therapeutic Innovation* (Cambridge, MA: MIT Press, 1974), 7–9; A. Scull, 'Somatic Treatments and the Historiography of Psychiatry', *History of Psychiatry*, 5 (1994): 1–12; E. Shorter, *A History of Psychiatry* (New York: John Wiley, 1997), 255; M. Weber, *Die Entwicklung der Psychopharmakologie im Zeitalter der naturwissenschaftlichen Medizin. Ideeengeschichte eines psychiatrischen Therapiesystems* (Munich: Urban & Vogel, 1999); Healy, *Creation of Psychopharmacology*, 76–101; Pieters and Snelders, 'Mental Ills', 394; Balz, *Zwischen Wirkung und Erfahrung*, 29–33.

14 Pieters and Majerus, 'Introduction of Chlorpromazine.'

15 Ibid., 449–451.

16 Ibid.; R. Campbell, 'The Chemistry of Madness', *Life* (26 November 1971): 66–86.

17 Healy, *Creation of Psychopharmacology*, 106–109; C. Regan, *Intoxicating Minds* (London: Orion, 2000), 121–122; A. Solomon, *The Noonday Demon: An Atlas of Depression* (New York: Scribner, 2001), 22–26; J. Frantzen, *The Corrections* (London: Fourth Estate, 2001), 364–374; E. Wurtzel, *More, Now, Again* (New York: Simon & Schuster, 2002).

18 Pieters and Snelders, 'Psychotropic Drug Use', 67.

19 Healy, *The Antidepressant Era*, 48–52.

20 Ibid., 74–77.

21 D. Herzberg, "Blockbusters and Controlled Substances: Miltown, Quaalude, and Consumer Demand for Drugs in Postwar America," *Studies in the History and Philosophy of the Biological and Biomedical Sciences* 42(2011): 415–27, 419.

22 A. Baenninger, J. A. Costa e Silva, I. Hindmarch, H. Moeller, K. Rickels, *Good Chemistry: The Life and Legacy of Valium Inventor Leo Sternbach* (New York: McGraw Hill, 2004), 65–75.

23 See for an extensive account of the Miltown story, see Tone, *The Age of Anxiety*.

24 A. Baenninger, et al., *Good Chemistry*, 74; A. Tone, 'Listening to the Past: History, Psychiatry, and Anxiety', *Canadian Journal of Psychiatry* 50 (2005): 373–380, 378.

25 T. Pieters, S. Snelders, "Antidepressiva van 1950 tot heden; Een halve eeuw op chemisch wolken," *Maandblad Geestelijke volksgezondheid*, 60 (2005): 207–222, 212.

26 Baenninger et al., *Good Chemistry*, 103.

27 Shorter, *Before Prozac*, 98–100.

28 L. H. Sternbach, 'The Benzodiazepine Story' in *Benzodiazepines Today and Tomorrow*, ed. R.G. Priest, U. Viuanna Filho, R. Amrein, M. Skreta (Trowbridge: Redwood Burn, 1980), 5–19, 15.

29 Advertisements for Mogadon in 1967 in the *Nederlands Tijdschrift voor Geneeskunde* and in *Huisarts en Wetenschap*. F. Hoffmann – La Roche, Mogadon reclame, code 67573.

30 C. Medawar, *Power and Dependence* (London: Social Audit, 1992), 96.

31 S. L. Speaker, 'From "Happiness Pills" to "National Nightmare": Changing Cultural Assessment of Minor Tranquilizers in America, 1955–1980', *Journal of the History of Medicine* 52 (1997): 338–376, 350; H. M. van Praag, *Psychofarmaca. Een leidraad voor de praktiserend medicus* (Assen: Van Gorcum & Comp, 1966), 114.

32 Tone, *Age of Anxiety*, 78.
33 T. Pieters and S. Snelders, 'From King Kong pills to Mother's Little Helpers – Career Cycles of Two Families of Psychotropic Drugs: The Barbiturates and Benzodiazepines', *Canadian Bulletin of Medical History* 24 (2007): 93–112, 104.
34 Geels, Pieters, and Snelders, 'Cultural Enthusiasm157.
35 Speaker, "From 'Happiness Pills,'" 350.
36 R. Whitaker, *Anatomy of an Epidemic* (New York: Crown Publishers, 2010).
37 D. Healy, *Let Them Eat Prozac* (New York: New York University Press, 2004), 37–38.
38 E. S. Valenstein, *Blaming the Brain* (New York: Free Press, 1998), 174–182.
39 BBC, *Panorama: The Secrets of Seroxat* (London: BBC, 2002). http://news.bbc.co.uk/panorama/hi/front_page/newsid_8425000/8425414.stm (accessed 6 Feb 2016).
40 J. F. Hernandez, G. J. M. W. van Thiel, A. K. Mantel-Teeuwisse, J. A. M. Raaijmakers, and T. Pieters, 'Restoring Trust in the Pharmaceutical Sector on the Basis of the SSRI Case', *Drug Discovery Today* 19 (2014): 523–527. Available from: 10.1016/j.drudis.2013.11.019.
41 J. F. Hernandez, A. K. Mantel-Teeuwisse, G. J. M. W. van Thiel, S. V. Belitser, J. Warmerdam, V. de Valk, J. A. M. Raaijmakers, and T. Pieters, 'A 10-Year Analysis of the Effects of Media Coverage of Regulatory Warnings on Antidepressant Use in The Netherlands and UK', *PLOS-ONE* 7 (2012): e45515.
42 I. L. M. A. Baart and T. A. Abma, 'Patient Participation in Fundamental Psychiatric Genomics Research: A Dutch Case Study', *Health Expectations* 14 (2011): 240–249, www.nesda.nl/ (accessed 7 February 2016).
43 A. Horwitz and J. Wakefield, *The Loss of Sadness* (Oxford: Oxford University Press, 2007).
44 A. L. van Harmelen, P. J. de Jong, K. A. Glashouwer, P. Spinhoven, B. W. Penninx, and B. M. Elzinga, 'Child Abuse and Negative Explicit and Automatic Self-associations: The Cognitive Scars of Emotional Maltreatment', *Behavior Research and Therapy*, 48 (2010): 486–94; R. Van Winkel, 'Genome-wide Findings in Schizophrenics and the Role of Gene Environment Interplay', *CNS Neuroscience and Therapeutics* 16 (2010): 185–192.
45 T. Pieters and M. Bakker, *Genen, omgeving en psyche; Een nieuwe integrale kijk op psychische ziekten. E-boek: De meetbare mens. Digitaal meten van het zieke en gezonde lichaam* (Den Haag, Rathenau Instituut, 2016), 117–130. https://www.rathenau.nl/nl/publicatie/e-boek-de-meetbare-mens-digitaal-meten-van-het-zieke-en-gezonde-lichaam, (accessed 25 January 2017).
46 L. Davidson, J. Rakfeldt, and J. Strauss, *The Roots of the Recovery Movement in Psychiatry: Lessons Learned* (Hoboken: Wiley-Blackwell, 2010).
47 C. M. Licht, et al., 'Longitudinal Eidence for Unfavorable Effects of Antidepressants on Heart Rate Variability', *Biological Psychiatry* 68 (2010): 861–868; F. M. Van Hasselt, *Improving the Physical Health of People with Severe Mental Illness: The Need for Tailor Made Care and Uniform Evaluation of Interventions* (Ph.D. Diss., University Groningen, 2013).

INDEX

Made in the USA
Monee, IL
28 August 2021

76689586R00223